# FIRE IN FORESTRY

## Volume I

Photo by Bluford Muir

# FIRE IN FORESTRY

## Volume I
## Forest Fire Behavior and Effects

**CRAIG CHANDLER**   *Director, Forest Fire and Atmospheric Sciences Research, U.S. Forest Service, Washington, D.C.*

**PHILLIP CHENEY**   *Chief Fire Scientist, Commonwealth Scientific and Industrial Research Organization, Canberra, Australia*

**PHILIP THOMAS**   *Head of Special Projects, Fire Research Station, Borehamwood, Herts., England*

**LOUIS TRABAUD**   *Principal Ecologist, Centre National de la Recherche Scientifique, Montpellier, France*

**DAVE WILLIAMS**   *Program Manager, Fire and Remote Sensing, Petawawa National Forestry Institute, Chalk River, Ontario, Canada*

A Wiley-Interscience Publication

JOHN WILEY & SONS

New York   Chichester   Brisbane   Toronto   Singapore

**Library of Congress Cataloging in Publication Data:**

Main entry under title:

Forest fire behavior and effects.

(Fire in forestry ; v. 1)
"A Wiley-Interscience publication."
Includes indexes.
1. Forest fires. 2. Fire ecology. I. Chandler,
Craig C. II. Title. III. Series.

SD420.55.F57 1983 vol. 1 [SD421]    634.9′618s    83-5088
ISBN 0-471-87442-6            [634.9′618]

Printed in the United States of America

10 9 8 7 6 5 4 3 2 1

*To Charlie Buck, Alan McArthur and Jim Wright*
*for reasons that*
*only they would appreciate*

# PREFACE

Before the industrial revolution almost 50 percent of the world's land surface was covered with forest. By 1955 this area had been cut in half. In 1980 the forest area of the world was estimated at 2.5 billion hectares, or one-fifth of the land surface. By the year 2000 it is expected to shrink by another half-billion hectares. To supply an expanding world population with adequate fiber, forage, fuel, and oxygen from a steadily shrinking land base will require the utmost of the forester's skill.

Fire has been the primary agent of deforestation. Paradoxically, fire, when properly used, can be a most effective and least expensive tool in maintaining a healthy and productive forest economy. Excepting tropical rainforests, fire has played a natural and important role in the development of virtually all forest, woodland, and grassland ecosystems. If fire is excluded, other processes must be substituted to fill fire's role if the ecosystem is to be maintained. If fire is to be utilized in land management, its role in the dynamics of the ecosystem must be clearly understood and fire applied at the proper time and the proper intensity.

Like fire in the home, fire in the forest can bring comfort and benefit or threat and destruction depending on how wisely it is utilized and controlled. Proper fire management requires an understanding of how a forest fire burns, how it affects the ecosystem through which it burns, and how managers over the years have developed organizations, systems, and equipment to ensure that fire in forestry is a benefit rather than a liability. It is to these ends that we dedicate this book.

CRAIG CHANDLER
PHILLIP CHENEY
PHILIP THOMAS
LOUIS TRABAUD
DAVE WILLIAMS

*Arlington, Virginia*
*Canberra, Australia*
*Herts, England*
*Montpellier, France*
*Ontario, Canada*

*June 1983*

# ACKNOWLEDGMENTS

The authors particularly wish to acknowledge the cooperation of Nicolai Andreev, Chief of the Central Air Base, Pushkino, USSR and his Deputy, Evgenii Shchetinskii. Without their wholehearted assistance both in the office and in the field, this book would be much less comprehensive than it is. We only regret that it was not possible to make coauthorship arrangements.

We are also indebted to Fernando Maldonado, Corporacion Nacional Forestal de Chile, for insight into fire problems and practices in South America; P. J. Germishuizen, USUTU Pulp Co., Ltd. of Swaziland, for background information on fire management in southern Africa; Shan Chengyu, Chief of Forest Fire Control, Heilongjiang Province, People's Republic of China, for his frank and candid discussions of forest fire problems and practices in northern China; Captain Bernard of the Service d'Incendié et de Secours du Département de l'Herault for outlining the firefighting organization of France; and Vilhelm Sjolin of the Swedish Fire Research Board for his encouragement as well as for helping us gain access to the Swedish forest fire research literature.

Many colleagues have reviewed this book in whole or in part, but A. A. Brown, C. Bentley Lyon, Steve Pyne, and William T. Sommers provided perceptions and critiques that amounted to substantial contributions to the text.

We are grateful to Jane Conway for translating the French chapters into English and offer our respects to the senior author for his light touch in homogenizing the Canadian, Australian, British, and American versions of that mother tongue.

Special thanks are also due to Bill Hauser, Chief of the U.S. Forest Service Photo Library, who was always helpful in finding the right picture to illustrate a point.

Last, and most, we wish to thank Peggy Casey who was able to decipher the most inscrutable handwriting, spent untold hours over hot and cold typewriters, and added a bit of Irish charm to our commonwealth of firemen. Without her this book could never have been published.

THE AUTHORS

# CONTENTS

# CONTENTS OF VOLUME II

# FIRE IN FORESTRY

## Volume I

# CHAPTER ONE

# Chemistry and Physics of Ignition and Combustion

## CHEMISTRY OF FOREST FUELS

All vegetative materials found in the forest are composed of complicated arrangements of cellulose, hemicellulose, and lignin, incorporated with a wide range of extractives and mineral constituents.

Cellulose, $(C_6H_{10}O_5)n$, is the major constituent and most studied component of plant tissue. Cellulose is a carbohydrate and, like starch, a glucoside. The chain length of cellulose is of the order of 15,000 to 20,000 glucose units and the molecular weight varies from 300,000 to 500,000. The fibrous nature of cellulose indicates a long chain structure.

Hemicellulose or, more properly, hemicelluloses are those carbohydrate polysaccharides with shorter chain lengths than cellulose that are found in association with cellulose in the cell walls of plants. The distinction between cellulose and hemicellulose is an important one for the pulp and paper industry since the compounds have quite different extractive properties. The distinction is unimportant for combustion studies inasmuch as their thermal degradation pathways are very similar. The heat of combustion of cellulose and hemicelluloses is 3850 calories per gram, markedly lower than that of lignin or the plant extractives (Rothermel 1976). Fifty to seventy-five percent of most plant tissues consist of cellulose and hemicelluloses.

Lignin is the aromatic polymer of wood, consisting of four or more phenylpropane monomers per molecule. Various forms of lignin with molecular weights ranging from 400 to 960 have been obtained. Lignin is the material that gives wood its stiffness. Its heat of combustion is 5860 calories

1

per gram, half again as high as cellulose. However, lignin burns primarily by glowing combustion rather than flaming. Consequently, little of its heat of combustion contributes directly to fire spread although it provides its proportionate share in determining fire intensity. In living plant materials lignin comprises from 15 to 35 percent of the dry weight. Since cellulose is degraded more easily than lignin, dead fuels have progressively higher lignin contents as they weather. Punky wood may be 75 percent lignin.

Two classes of extractives have an important bearing on fire behavior. Terpenes are isoprene polymers of the elementary composition $(C_{10}H_{16})n$. The terpene content of leaves and twigs varies with species, generally from 0 to 2 percent preferentially in conifers, but reaching as much as 6 percent in some cedars and pines. Terpenes have low boiling points (it is terpenes that give the "piney woods" their characteristic smell on warm sunny days) and can form flammable volatile mixtures well in advance of the flame front in a forest fire. Resins are nonvolatile, ether-soluble chemicals consisting primarily of fats, fatty acids, fatty alcohols, resin acids, and phytosterols. The extractives, as a class, have a heat of combustion of 7720 calories per gram, more than twice that of cellulose. Moreover, the extractives are outgassed very early in the pyrolysis process and are burned in the flame zone. It has been shown that about three-fourths of the total flame height from burning dry aspen (*Populus tremuloides*) foliage is contributed by extractives (Philpot 1969) and it is doubtful that living fuels with moisture contents in excess of 100 percent dry weight could support combustion at all in the absence of extractives. Extractive content varies widely—from 0.2 percent to 15 percent—by species and may vary by more than a factor of 2 over a growing season within a single species. Much of the inherent differences in flammability between species is due to differences in extractive content.

Minerals play an important role in the combustion process even though they are a relatively minor constituent of forest fuels. Wood generally contains less than 2 percent ash content. Bark is higher in ash, and leaves and needles even more so. The average ash content for needles, grasses, and the leaves of most broadleaf trees and shrubs is in the 5 to 10 percent range except for certain arid shrubs such as Atriplex and Tamarix which may have ash contents as high as 40 percent of their dry weight. Minerals evidently affect combustion by catalyzing certain of the early pyrolytic reactions of cellulose, causing an increase in char production and a decrease in the formation of tars. Tar is the primary contributor of energy for flame formation and decreases in tar yield are accompanied by markedly lower flaming activity. Only certain minerals are active in the catalytic process, although it is by no means certain which minerals are important. Several studies have shown that the proportion of silica-free ash correlates (inversely) much better with flammability than does total ash content. There have been suggestions that phosphates are primarily responsible for suppressing flammability (Lindenmuth and Davis 1973). Phosphates are the active ingredients in several proprietary fire-retardant formulations.

## THERMAL DEGRADATION OF WOOD

When a forest fuel is exposed to an external source of heat, the surface temperature rises rapidly and, simultaneously, heat is conducted inward from the surface. Free moisture is vaporized as soon as the temperature of a layer reaches 100°C. Some of this moisture passes out of the wood as water vapor and some diffuses inward, away from the source of heat thus increasing the moisture content of interior layers. Lignins and hemicelluloses begin to degrade at temperatures ranging from 130 to 190°C depending on the amount of available moisture—the more available moisture, the lower the dissociation temperature. Although some carbon monoxide formation occurs with the breakdown of hemicellulose, the liberated gases are predominantly nonflammable water vapor and carbon dioxide. The reactions taking place at temperatures below 200°C are endothermic.

Decomposition of lignin and hemicelluloses becomes rapid at 200°C with the ratio of CO to $CO_2$ formation increasing linearly with temperature. Between 200 and 280°C, cellulose undergoes a chemical dehydration process in which molecular bonding occurs between adjacent cellulose chains (Kilzer and Broido 1964). It is this reaction that is catalyzed by trace elements, and the proportion of cellulose so dehydrated depends both on the amount of minerals present and the rate of heating—slow heating being more efficient in the dehydration process. The net effect of all reactions taking place below 280°C is weakly endothermic. About 35 percent of the total weight loss in the fuel occurs before the sample reaches 280°C (Figure 1.1).

Once the fuel temperature exceeds 280°C, exothermic reactions predominate and the fuel may be said to have achieved ignition if the fuel is insulated from external cooling since the reactions will proceed to completion even if the external heat source is removed. The exothermic peak is reached at 320° and most destructive distillation takes place at temperatures between 280 and 320°C. Two reactions predominate: the dehydrocellulose formed during earlier heating decomposes to form char plus $H_2O$, CO, $CO_2$, and low molecular weight gases such as methane and ethane; the cellulose remaining undehydrated decomposes to form levoglucosan which, in turn, forms a number of complex tars with molecular weights ranging from 130 to 250. The tars are expelled from the sample along with the other gases and provide about 70 percent of the caloric value of the resultant stream of volatiles. The proportion of tar to char is important to combustion not only because, in the absence of considerable tar production, the water vapor and carbon dioxide content of the pyrolysis products are sufficient to preclude flaming, but also because the greater the production of low density, low conductivity char, the slower the movement of heat into deeper layers of fuel. Consequently, the zones undergoing rapid pyrolysis are narrower and the rate of combustion is slower.

When surface temperatures reach 500 to 600°C glowing combustion commences if oxygen is not excluded from the char surface. In the glowing

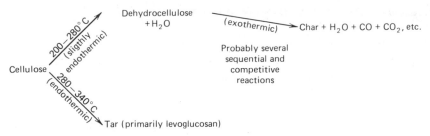

**Figure 1.1.**   General scheme for the pyrolysis of cellulose.

process the charcoal is converted directly to carbon monoxide at the charcoal surface and the monoxide oxidized to $CO_2$ immediately above the surface. At temperatures somewhat above 1000°C carbon is consumed at the surface as rapidly as char is produced.

## IGNITION

Although the rapid oxidation of wood will proceed to completion once the exothermic reaction temperature of 280°C is reached and maintained, we usually think of ignition as the appearance of flame or glow. In this sense, ignition is merely an instability in the transient process that leads to the steady state process called combustion, and has no uniquely defined temperature. Ignition can be characterized as flaming or glowing, depending on which combustion process it initiates; as sustained or transient, depending on whether combustion continues after the external source of heat has been removed; spontaneous or piloted, depending on whether it depends on the presence of a flame or spark from an already burning fuel.

Before examining the various theories of ignition, let us review the pyrolysis process to see what factors are likely to affect the manner and speed with which a forest fuel will commence to burn. Think of a twig exposed to radiant or convective heat from an approaching fire front. Heat is received by the surface of the twig that "sees" the fire, but not by the other surfaces. Therefore, the shape of the fuel, specifically the ratio of fuel surface to fuel volume, bears a direct relationship to how much heat can be absorbed per unit mass or volume per unit time. When radiation or hot gases strike the twig some heat will be absorbed and some will be reflected, thus thermal absorptance should be a factor in determining how fast the twig is heated. Actually, however, darkening of the surface due to charring takes place fairly rapidly and for most forest fuels thermal absorptance is not important except for very high irradiance levels over very short time periods such as those associated with nuclear weapons explosions. Once the heat is absorbed at the surface, part of it is conducted into the interior and part is used to raise the surface temperature of the twig. In forest fuels, thermal conductivity is overwhelmingly controlled by two variables: fuel density and moisture content. Working with wood samples, MacLean (1941) develops the empirical equations

$$K = [(4.78 + 0.97M)S + 0.568] \times 10^{-4} \qquad (0 < M < 40)$$

$$K = [(4.78 + 0.13M)S + 0.58] \times 10^{-4} \qquad (M > 40)$$

where   $K$ = thermal conductivity in cal/sec cm$^2$ (°C/cm)
   $M$ = moisture content in percent of oven dry weight
   $S$ = specific gravity based on oven dry weight and wet volume at $M$

Later investigations confirmed these results for a number of common forest fuels and suggested that the equations should be applicable to most fibrous vegetable materials (Byram et al. 1952). Table 1.1 lists the specific gravity and oven dry thermal conductivity of several forest fuels. The effect of moisture depends on the specific gravity as shown in Figure 1.2. The denser the fuel particle, the greater the effect of moisture content.

Once the rate of heat flow into the twig has been established by the rate of absorptance and the rate of conduction, then the temperature rise of any given layer is a function of the fuel density and specific heat. The specific heat of forest fuels depends on the temperature and moisture content of the material, but is practically independent of specific gravity or chemical composition. The specific heat of dry wood is approximately $H = 0.25 + .00013T$ where $T$ is the temperature in °C. Because of the wood–water bonding energies, the specific heat of moist wood is a complex function and not simply the sum of the specific heats of the water and the wood. A plot of specific heat vs. moisture content at 100°C is shown in Figure 1.3.

As soon as the temperature of the surface layer reaches 100°C the twig starts outgassing its water as steam. This process uses appreciable energy that would otherwise have been used to distill flammable gases from the surface layer of the twig and to raise the temperature of the interior layers. After the water has been evaporated from the surface layer its temperature rises rapidly and combustible volatiles are produced in quantity. However, at the same time the moisture in the underlying layer of wood is being vaporized and driven outward to mix with and dilute the volatiles being produced nearer the surface.

Soon a char layer is formed at the surface of the twig. Glowing combustion will take place at the surface as soon as it reaches 500 to 600°C unless the output of volatiles from the interior of the twig is sufficiently rapid to exclude oxygen from reaching the char surface.

By now the space immediately around the twig is occupied by a mixture of ambient air and the volatiles produced by pyrolysis of the fuel. If the volatile mixture is within its flammable range, and if a suitable heat source

*Table 1.1.  Specific Gravity and Thermal Conductivity of Forest Fuels (Oven Dry)*

| Specific Gravity | Thermal Conductivity, $10^{-4}$ cal/cm$^2$ sec (°C/cm) | Material |
|---|---|---|
| 0.10 | 1.05 | White fir punk, sapwood (*Abies concolor*) |
| 0.25 | 1.75 | Douglas fir punk (*Pseudotsuga taxifolia*) |
| 0.25 | 1.75 | White fir punk, heart wood (*Abies menziesii*) |
| 0.35 | 2.25 | Wheat straw (*Triticum* spp.) |
| 0.37 | 2.35 | Cheatgrass (*Bromus tectorum*) |
| 0.37 | 2.35 | Chestnut oak leaves (*Quercus montana*) |
| 0.39 | 2.45 | Beech leaves (*Fagus* spp.) |
| — | 2.45 | European beech leaves (*Fagus sylvatica*) |
| 0.39 | 2.45 | Harding grass (*Phalaris tuberosa* var. *stenoptera*) |
| 0.42 | 2.60 | Redwood leaves (*Sequoia sempervirens*) |
| 0.44 | 2.70 | Knobcone pine needles (*Pinus attenuata*) |
| 0.45 | 2.75 | Madrone leaves (*Arbutus menziesii*) |
| 0.46 | 2.80 | Coulter pine needles (*Pinus coulteri*) |
| 0.48 | 2.90 | Manzanita leaves, weathered (*Arctostaphylos patula*) |
| 0.50 | 2.95 | Rhododendron leaves (*Rhododendron catawbiense*) |
| 0.51 | 3.00 | Sedge (*Carex geyeri*) |
| 0.51 | 3.00 | Ponderosa pine needles(*Pinus ponderosa*) |
| 0.52 | 3.05 | Shortleaf pine needles (*Pinus echinata*) |
| — | 3.05 | Scotch pine needles (*Pinus sylvestris*) |
| — | 3.10 | White pine needles (*Pinus strobus*) |
| 0.53 | 3.15 | Desert stipa (*Stipa* spp.) |
| 0.54 | 3.15 | Chinquapin (*Castanopsis chrysophylla*) |
| 0.54 | 3.15 | Sugar pine needles (*Pinus lambertiana*) |
| 0.55 | 3.20 | White fir needles (*Abies concolor*) |
| — | 3.20 | Norway spruce needles (*Picea excelsa*) |
| 0.56 | — | White bursage twigs (*Franseria dumosa*) |
| 0.56 | — | Jointfir twigs (*Ephedra* spp.) |
| 0.57 | 3.30 | Snowbrush leaves (*Ceanothus velutinus*) |
| 0.57 | 3.30 | Lodgepole pine needles (*Pinus contorta*) |
| 0.59 | 3.40 | Scarlet oak leaves (*Quercus coccinea*) |
| 0.64 | 3.65 | Manzanita leaves, newly fallen (*Arctostaphylos patula*) |
| 0.65 | 3.70 | Horsehair lichen (*Alectoria jubata*) |
| 0.67 | — | Wiregrass (*Aristida striota*) |

exists, the gases will ignite and burn as a flame. Flammable range is the range of gas–air mixture within which combustion can take place. If the volatiles are above their upper flammable limit (i.e., too rich), they cannot burn until further diluted with air. This is often the case as the gases are being expelled from the wood and cause the base of the flame to lie some distance above the solid fuel surface. The mixture can also be too rich when

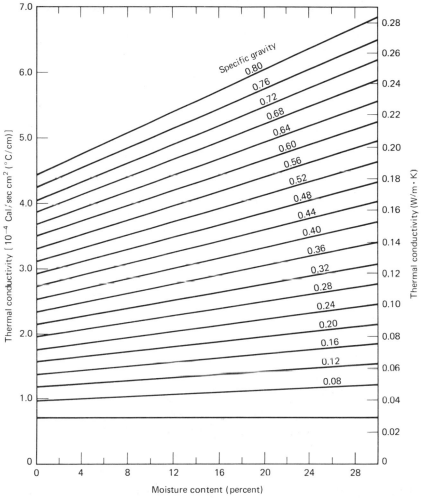

**Figure 1.2.** Thermal conductivity of wood perpendicular to the grain as related to moisture content and specific gravity.

excessive water vapor or $CO_2$ reduces the relative amount of air in the mixture of air and volatiles. If the mixture is below its lower flammable limit (i.e., too lean), combustion is also impossible. This occurs when the pyrolysis of flammable volatiles drops below some minimum level or when wind or other air movements cause too rapid dilution of the volatile pyrolysis products. Flammability limits in hydrocarbons are directly related to their heat of combustion; therefore, in forest fuels the flammability limit depends on the kind and amount of volatiles and extractives. These are species related and season dependent.

Looking back at ignition processes, we see that a twig may be ignited in

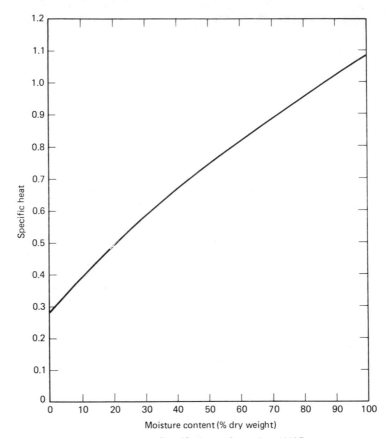

*Figure 1.3.*    Specific heat of wood at 100°C.

several different ways. When the surface char temperature reaches 500 to 600°C, spontaneous glowing ignition will occur if oxygen is available at the char surface. If oxygen is not available because of a high rate of production of pyrolytic volatiles, then the volatiles may undergo spontaneous flaming ignition as they are heated by the char layer. Or, if neither process occurs, which may be the case when the volatiles are too rich when passing through the char layer and cool below ignition temperature before they reach their upper flammable limit, they may be pilot flame ignited by contact with flames or embers from the approaching fire front.

Although there are several modes of ignition, the work on cellulosic fuels in the early 1960s in the United States by Martin and in the United Kingdom by Simms and their colleagues demonstrates that ignition time is largely controlled by heating the fuel surface to a particular temperature. The important fuel properties are therefore fuel density ($\rho$), specific heat ($c$), fuel thickness ($L$), thermal conductivity ($K$), irradiance ($Q$), and the ignition

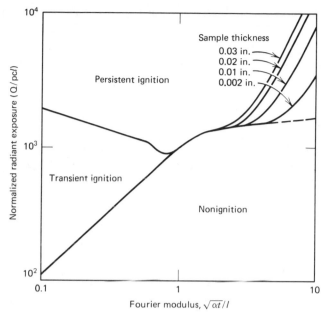

**Figure 1.4.**  Generalized ignition behavior of cellulose (after Martin 1956).

temperature itself. Because chemical reaction rates vary rapidly with temperature, one can treat ignition temperature as being effectively a constant property of the particular fuel surface: about 325°C for pilot flame ignition and about 600°C for spontaneous ignition.

This concept and the numerical values apply to the first ignition that may prove transient. For thick fuels undergoing rapid heating, ignition will not be sustained once the ignition source is removed and heat conduction to the interior fuel cools the surface. If the fuelbed consists of several individual pieces of fuel, mutual support between the pieces reduces radiation loss and helps to sustain burning. Figure 1.4 shows the conditions required for each of these types of ignition. If $Q$ is large compared with the rate of loss of heat from the surface at ignition, the cooling coefficient $H$ is not important, but for smaller $Q$ it is. This heat loss determines a minimum value of $Q$—that is, a "critical irradiance," 0.5 cal cm$^{-2}$ sec$^{-1}$ (2.1 W/cm$^2$) for spontaneous ignition and as low as 0.2 cal cm$^{-2}$ s$^{-1}$ (0.8 W/cm$^2$) for piloted ignition.

Except for calculating the width of fireline necessary to prevent radiative ignition across it, calculations of ignition times vs. irradiance are of limited value since in a forest fire the fire front is moving toward the fuel and the irradiance is constantly changing during the pyrolysis period. There have been some attempts to overcome this difficulty by calculating a fixed "heat of preignition" that eliminates the problem of fluctuating irradiance (Frandsen 1968), but since this requires that the mode of ignition be precisely specified, the results have not had much application in the field.

*Table 1.2.    Thickness and Surface/Volume Ratio of Some Common Forest Fuels*

| Material | Thickness (Cm) | Surface/Volume Ratio |
|---|---|---|
| Medusahead (*Taeniatherum asperum*) | 0.005 | 380 |
| Wiregrass (*Aristida stricta*) | 0.007 | 286 |
| Pinegrass (*Calamagrostis rubescens*) | 0.008 | 240 |
| Beech Leaves (*Fagus sylvatica*) | 0.009 | 222 |
| Cheatgrass (*Bromus tectorum*) | 0.011 | 189 |
| Maple Leaves (*Acer rubrum*) | 0.013 | 154 |
| Western Larch Needles (*Laris occidentalis*) | 0.014 | 184 |
| Hickory Leaves (*Carya* spp.) | 0.016 | 125 |
| Scarlet Oak Leaves (*Quercus coccinea*) | 0.018 | 111 |
| Western Hemlock Needles (*Tsuga heterophylla*) | 0.024 | 100 |
| Rhododendron Leaves (*Rhododendron catawbiense*) | 0.025 | 80 |
| Madrone Leaves (*Arbutus menziesii*) | 0.028 | 71 |
| White Pine Needles (*Pinus monticola*) | 0.034 | 91 |
| Douglas Fir Needles (*Pseudotsuga menziesii*) | 0.045 | 69 |
| Engelmann Spruce Needles (*Picea engelmannii*) | 0.067 | 54 |
| Norway Spruce Needles (*Picea excelsa*) | 0.084 | 43 |
| Twigs (cylinders) | 0.1 | 40 |
| Twigs (cylinders) | 0.5 | 8 |
| Twigs (cylinders) | 1.0 | 4 |
| Twigs (cylinders) | 2.0 | 2 |

For most practical applications it is sufficient to understand the primary factors that influence ignitibility and to learn to recognize them in forest situations. Thin fuels ignite more easily than thick fuels because they have less mass to be heated. Fuels with a large surface/volume ratio will ignite more easily than those of the same size with a smaller ratio because they will intercept more radiant heat (Table 1.2). Low density fuels ignite readily because their low thermal conductivity retains heat at their surface. And, of course, moisture in the fuel retards ignition in several different ways.

## COMBUSTION

Once the twig has become ignited, the rate and intensity with which it burns will be affected by many different factors. Since combustion in any but the thinnest fuels can be considered as a series of ignitions of progressively deeper layers, all the variables influencing ignition will also affect combustion. However, some variables that do not affect ignition have a marked effect on combustion, and some of the variables that do affect ignition affect combustion in a different way.

Take fuel moisture, for example. Moisture affects ignition primarily by increasing the specific heat and thermal conductivity of the fuel so that more heat must be absorbed in order for the surface layer to reach ignition temperature. Once ignition has occurred and active combustion is taking place, the primary effect of moisture is as a diluent to the combustible gases being pyrolyzed from the burning fuel. Steam has a very high specific volume (i.e., volume per unit of mass). At 100°C steam has a volume 1700 times that of water. Since the specific volume of the volatiles produced by the pyrolysis of dry wood is only 590 (which includes 64 percent by volume of dissociated water vapor), each volume of free water in the fuel will displace nearly three volumes of volatilized fuel gases (Browne 1958). The maximum moisture content that a fuel can have and still support flaming combustion is called the moisture of extinction. Because the moisture of extinction depends both on the chemistry of the fuel and the conditions under which it is heated, its value can only be determined empirically. Measured values for moisture of extinction range from 12 percent for some grasses to nearly 200 percent for some resinous conifer needles. For most dead forest fuels the moisture of extinction is between 25 and 40 percent, and for most living fuels between 120 and 160 percent. In general, the moisture of extinction is higher in living fuels, in thicker fuels, in fuel mixtures where oxygen supply is optimal, and in hotter fires.

Next to moisture content, the most important attribute of a forest fuel governing its combustion characteristics is its chemical composition. The role of volatiles, extractives, minerals, and intermediate tars has already been discussed in the section on fuel chemistry. It is worth repeating that the basic gaseous product of low temperature pyrolysis of cellulose (8 hr at 300°C) gives, by volume, 64 percent water vapor, 13 percent $CO_2$, 23 percent CO, methane, ethane, and other flammable lower hydrocarbons) is a nonflammable mixture (Martin 1956). The existence of flame is due entirely to the higher hydrocarbons already existing in the fuel or produced as intermediates by high heating rate pyrolysis.

The third most important characteristic of a fuel particle with respect to its combustion rate is its surface/volume ratio which, for a given particle density, is directly related to particle thickness. The combustible volatiles can mix with oxygen only after diffusing across the fuel surface boundary layer. For a fuel of a specific density, chemical composition, and moisture content, the residence time, or length of time that the particle will support flaming, is directly proportional to its thickness. For wood fuels with moisture contents in the 4 to 10 percent range, the residence time in minutes is approximately 3 times the fuel thickness in centimeters; for example, a stick 10 cm in diameter will continue to flame after ignition for about 30 minutes.

A more complete discussion of the role of fuel properties on the flaming combustion process can be found in Albini's (1980) excellent paper on flame thermodynamics.

Smoldering, or glowing combustion, is the dominant process (1) after the volatiles have been expelled from a cellulosic fuel leaving a shell of charcoal, (2) when ash contents are high and volatiles low (as in organic soils) so that combustible gas mixtures are not produced by heating, and (3) when the specific gravity of the fuel is too low to conduct heat rapidly enough to evolve a flammable gas mixture (as in punky logs). In glowing combustion oxygen diffusing to the fuel surface combines directly with carbon to form carbon monoxide. This reaction takes place at or slightly below 600°C and releases approximately one-third as much heat as the high temperature direct conversion of carbon to carbon dioxide that occurs in flames. If the surface temperature is raised to 650 to 700°C and sufficient oxygen is available, the carbon monoxide will undergo further oxidation to carbon dioxide. The C–CO reaction can take place in atmospheres with oxygen contents as low as 5 percent whereas flaming combustion and the $CO–CO_2$ reaction require oxygen levels of at least 15 percent (NFPA 1976). The $CO–CO_2$ reaction also releases about one-third the heat of the direct $C–CO_2$ reaction. As a result, smoldering compared to flaming is a relatively low temperature process with a low heat yield, often accompanied by the release of considerable carbon monoxide, and completely controlled by the diffusion of oxygen to the fuel surface. Because smoldering is characteristic of low density fuels, however, conduction losses are low and smoldering will continue under conditions of high moisture content and low oxygen supply where flaming combustion would be impossible.

The moisture of extinction for smoldering combustion is in the range of 110 percent (Sandberg 1980) to over 135 percent (McMahon et al. 1980), about the same as that of living fuels. Smoldering is self sustaining at very low rates—organic soils can burn for weeks at rates of less than 1.5 grams per square meter per hour or 0.025 centimeters depth reduction per hour. Since the reaction rates are entirely controlled by oxygen availability, high winds can quickly increase the temperatures in a smoldering fire sufficiently to ignite any unburned materials capable of flaming combustion. It is this property of retaining fire for long periods with the potential for rapidly igniting unburned fuels when conditions change that makes glowing combustion so dangerous and thorough mop-up of every fire so essential.

## HEAT TRANSFER

Although an individual fuel particle may become ignited and burn fiercely, unless its liberated heat can be effectively transferred to adjacent fuel particles the fire will not sustain itself. Perhaps the best way to illustrate this is with an ordinary wood splint match. Strike one and hold it vertically with the head on top. The flame will get progressively shorter and soon go out, thus implying that wood is noncombustible. Strike a second match and hold it horizontally. Flame progresses slowly but steadily down the match, thus implying that wood is combustible but easily controllable. Strike a third and hold it vertically with the head downward. The entire match and the fingers holding it are engulfed in flames in a few seconds, thus implying that wood presents a nearly explosive fire hazard!

Since in this experiment the fuel is identical, what explains the tremendous difference in the rate and intensity of combustion? The difference is explained by the differing modes and mechanisms of heat transfer in the three instances. When the match is held vertically with the head up, the unburned wood is shielded from most of the flame radiation by the charred residue of the match head material and small upward drafts are induced that tend to cool the unburned fuel. The main source of heat moving downward into the wood is that conducted through the match from the glowing char. As we already know, wood is a very poor conductor of heat (steel is 260 times as efficient), and the flow of heat is not sufficient to pyrolyze enough volatiles to sustain flaming.

When the match is held horizontally, one surface of the flame is directly visible to one surface of the matchstick. Radiation transfer is increased and heat may be conducted through the air more easily than when the flame must travel downward. This heat, as well as the heat from the glowing char, is conducted into the interior of the match. There is also a small amount of convective heat exchange at the 90-degree angle where the base of the flame intersects the unburned match.

When the match is held vertically with the head downward, all surfaces of the matchstick are exposed to the flame, and from a much closer distance. The hot gases distilled from the match rise along the sides of the unburned matchstick transferring heat by convection and all this absorbed heat moves into the matchstick by conduction.

Before looking at these three heat transfer mechanisms individually, we should precisely define them. *Conduction* is the transfer of heat from one part of a body to another part of the same body, or to another in direct physical contact with it, without appreciable displacement of the particles of the body. Conduction acts from molecule to adjacent molecule. *Convection* is the transfer of heat from one point to another within a fluid by the mixing of one portion of the fluid with another. *Radiation* is the transfer of heat from one body to another, not on contact with it, by electromagnetic wave motion. The relative importance of these processes differs according to circumstances.

As our experiment with the three matches showed, conduction is not a predominant mechanism of fire spread in forest fuels. However, conduction is important in a negative sense. Porous fuels of very low conductivity, primarily rotten wood, conduct heat so slowly that their surface temperature rises very rapidly when exposed to a radiant or convective heat source. Since very little volume is heated, there is insufficient volatile production to permit flaming, but these fuels can achieve glowing ignition from a relatively modest input of heat. Once ignited they will smolder for weeks until extinguished by rain or fanned into renewed activity by dry winds. This is why rotten logs and stumps are so conducive to spot fires ahead of the main blaze—embers that cannot ignite leaves or sound wood will readily ignite punk.

Heat transfer by convection is important in forest fire spread. In fact, in very small and very large forest fires, convection is usually the dominant mechanism of fire spread. *Free* convection is the process in which the motion of the fluid is entirely the result of differences in density resulting from temperature differences. The formation of a convection column above a forest fire and the heating of brush and tree crowns above a surface fire are examples of heat transfer by free convection. Free convection is covered in more detail in the sections on fire weather and fire behavior. In *forced* convection external mechanical forces alter the fluid flow from its natural "free" direction and velocity. The predominant example of forced convection in forest fires is the tilting of flames by wind. For small circular fires, the effect of wind on flame angle, at angles up to 60 degrees, is expressed by the equation

$$\frac{\tan \Theta}{\cos \Theta} = \frac{aV^2}{bR},$$

where $\Theta$ is the flame angle, $V$ is the wind velocity, $R$ is the burning rate of the entire fire (not the unit area burning rate), and $a$ and $b$ are constants depending on fuelbed properties (Huffman et al. 1967). For line fires at angles up to 60 degrees, $\tan \Theta$ is proportional to the cube of the wind speed and inversely proportional to flame depth (Albini 1981). At angles above 60 degrees, the flame no longer lifts from the fuelbed, but "trails" along the surface downwind for a distance equivalent to

$$\frac{D_1}{D_o} = K\left(\frac{V^2}{D_o g}\right)$$

where   $D_1$ = distance from the flame front to the trailing edge
   $D_o$ = original (no wind) flame depth
   $V$ = wind velocity
   $g$ = acceleration due to gravity
   $K$ = a constant

For the initial stages of grass and litter fires in high winds, flame trailing due to forced convection is the mechanism of fire spread.

In a forest fire most of the heat transfer from the burning fuels is by convection. In a small line fire in pine litter, the ratio of convective to radiant heat is 3 to 1 (Packham 1972) whereas in a large stationary fire in pine slash the ratio is nearly 9 to 1 (Kaysen and Muzaffar 1960). Conductive heat losses during forest fire are negligible except for fires in very heavy fuels with long smoldering times. However, for most forest fires, at least in their incipient stages, radiation is the major heat transfer mechanism. For this reason, and because most mathematical models of forest fire spread are based on the assumption of radiative heat transfer, we discuss the theory of thermal radiation in some detail.

Any substance will emit electromagnetic radiation at a rate

$$W = e\sigma T^4$$

where  $W$ = total emitted energy per unit time per unit surface area
$e$ = emissivity of the substance (ratio between the energy emitted by the substance and that which would be emitted by a "black body" or perfect radiator at the same temperature)
$\sigma$ = Stephan–Boltzman constant ($5.67 \times 10^{-8}$ W/m$^2$ °K$^4$)
$T$ = absolute temperature of the substance (°K)

The preceding equation allows calculation of the total energy emitted, but says nothing about the wavelengths at which it is emitted. This is described by Wien's displacement law which states that

$$\lambda_{max} = \frac{2855}{T}$$

where  $\lambda_{max}$ = wavelength of the maximum radiant output in microns
and $T$ = temperature in °K

This is important in forest fires for, as shown later, certain fire gases absorb radiation preferentially in certain wavelengths and the degree to which they will be heated depends on the temperature of the radiating source.

Since a radiating substance emits its heat uniformly in all directions, and since the surface area of a sphere varies as the square of its diameter, it is apparent that the heat received from a point source of radiation will vary inversely with the square of the distance from the source. That is, the heat received 20 m from a point radiator will be one-fourth that received at 10 m distant. For radiation sources that are not points (and few are), the relationship between radiation received and distance from the source is not so simple, but engineering tables and graphs are available for most common configurations.

Radiation calculations involving the fuelbed are relatively straightforward. Charcoal radiates as an ideal gray body and its emissivity may be taken as unity over all temperatures of interest. The surface temperature of glowing charcoal is independent of moisture content and varies with wind velocity according to the formula (Bhagat 1977):

$$T = 850 + 5.08V$$

where    $T$ is the surface temperature in °C
            $V$ is the wind velocity in m/sec

Therefore, for a fire burning in still air, the radiation emitted from the fuel-bed will be $1.0 \times 5.67 \times 10^{-8} \times (850 + 273)^4$ which equals 90 kW/sq m or 2.15 cal/cm$^2$ sec. By determining the appropriate view factor for a surface at any distance from the fire, one can calculate the rate of radiant heat received at the surface and the likelihood of the surface being ignited.

Unfortunately, calculations involving the flames above the fuelbed are not nearly so straightforward. Flame temperatures vary over a considerable range and fluctuate fairly rapidly (Figure 1.5). Since radiation depends on the fourth power of the temperature, any errors in flame temperature measurement result in vastly larger errors in calculated radiation output. Also, the mean radiation *cannot* be calculated from the mean flame temperature unless the statistical distribution of temperatures about the mean is precisely known, which is seldom the case. In addition, the flame from a forest fuel is not a single substance but a mixture of gases, liquids, and solids, each with

*Figure 1.5.*    Flames are complex and rapidly changing bodies. Photo by U.S. Forest Service.

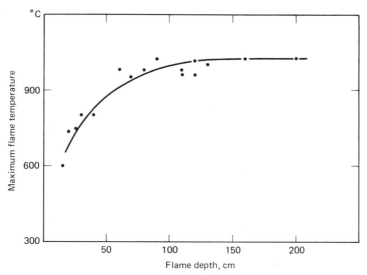

*Figure 1.6.* Flame temperature vs. flame depth.

its own emissivity and temperature. Virtually all of the visible portion of the spectrum in forest fires is emitted by incandescent solid carbon particles formed as soot by incomplete combustion of the higher hydrocarbons. However, an appreciable portion of the total energy is radiated by the fire gases, principally, water vapor and carbon dioxide. These gases are band emitters, with water vapor emitting strongly at 1.4 and 1.9 microns, $CO_2$ at 4.4 microns, and both water vapor and $CO_2$ at 2.7 microns. All these wavelengths are in the infrared region.

In a careful series of experiments at the Swedish Defense Research Institute, it was shown that the temperature, radiant intensity, emissivity, and ratio of gas radiation to soot radiation all varied markedly as flame depth increased in the flames above cribs of *Picea excelsa* (Hagglund and Persson 1974). Figures 1.6, 1.7, 1.8, and 1.9 illustrate these relationships for flame depths from 15 to 200 centimeters. Actually, the effect of flame depth on flame radiation is even more dramatic than the Swedish data indicate. Flame height is directly correlated with flame depth. Thomas (1963, 1967), combining theoretical considerations and experimental data, predicts flame height to vary as the $\frac{2}{3}$ power of the flame depth, whereas Byram (1966), using empirical observations of forest fires, scales flame height as the 0.46 power of the flame depth. Since the area of the radiating flame is directly proportional to the flame height, the total radiant output will be larger as flame depth increases than is suggested by Figures 1.6 through 1.9. Furthermore, the water vapor and carbon dioxide naturally present in the atmosphere preferentially absorb radiation in the same bandwidths that they radiate. In

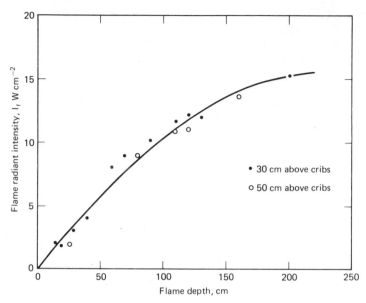

***Figure 1.7.*** Flame intensity vs. flame depth.

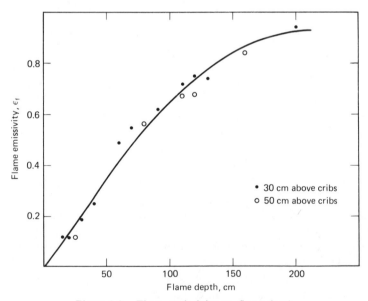

***Figure 1.8.*** Flame emissivity vs. flame depth.

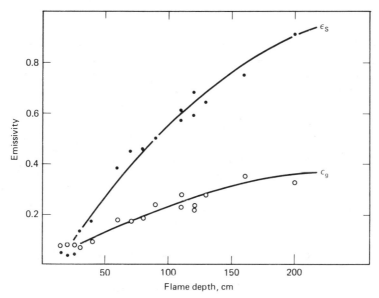

***Figure 1.9.*** Soot emissivity and gas emissivity vs. flame depth.

experiments with large pools of liquefied natural gas, it was shown that over 98 percent of the $H_2O$ and $CO_2$ emissions was absorbed within 200 m of the fire (Raj et al. 1979). Consequently, the effective radiation of the fire gases, as opposed to the soot radiation, is inversely related to the distance from the flames irrespective of view factor. Lastly, although there are little available data, one would expect the relative proportions of soot and gas radiation to vary markedly with fuel chemistry and fuel moisture since these factors strongly affect the pyrolysis and combustion process.

Therefore, it is virtually impossible to extrapolate flame radiation measurements from one fire to another, and flame radiation calculations have more value in post facto studies of fire behavior than they do as predictive tools. It is helpful, however, to remember that flame radiation is virtually negligible in very small fires, becomes increasingly dominant as flame depth and height increase, and becomes subservient to convection again as the fire becomes larger still as shown in the next section.

One often overlooked source of radiant energy that has a measurable effect on fire behavior is solar radiation. At midsummer in middle latitudes solar radiation levels reach 0.0064 cal/cm$^2$ sec, far below the 0.2 to 0.5 cal/cm$^2$ sec needed for ignition, but sufficient to raise the surface temperature of fuels in full sun 30 to 40°C above the ambient air temperature (Countryman 1955). This preheating is sufficient to make a noticeable difference in the rate of spread and flame height of light surface fires. The effect has been noted when moving clouds produce shadows over fires and also, in one Australian instance, when a fire occurred during a total eclipse (McArthur 1959).

## MASS TRANSPORT

A fourth method of heat transfer, and one not discussed in textbooks on thermodynamics, is *spotting*, that is, the physical removal of burning material and its deposition in unignited fuels meters or kilometers away. In many forest fires this is the predominant mechanism of fire spread. One of the authors still vividly recalls his consternation whiles flying at 1000 m above a forest fire in northern California when an entire flaming arctostaphylos bush at least 2 m tall passed by the cockpit window. The pilot was equally astonished and immediately headed for less turbulent surroundings.

Theoretically, it should be relatively simple to predict spotting distances. If one knows the aerodynamic properties of a piece of fuel and its burning time, then one should be able to predict how far it could float and still land with sufficient heat energy left to produce ignition in the fuels where it landed. In fact, such calculations and some experiments have been made with varying degrees of sophistication (Muraszew and Fedele 1976, Tarifa 1967). Thus far, both the theories and the experiments have been relatively successful in predicting the downward trajectories of burning objects, but singularly unsuccessful in postulating the objects off the ground and up to the top of their trajectory. When the fuels to be lofted are already above the ground surface (e.g., bark plates, leaves, or conifer cones), they can be lifted directly by the hot gases rising from fire in the ground litter below. However, when the fuels are lying on the ground surface it takes considerable turbulent energy to lift them into the convection column. In fires where the ambient windspeeds are less than 15 to 20 m/sec only organized vortices such as fire whirls can provide the required energy. As shown in Chapter 4, the exact mechanisms of fire whirl formation are not yet well understood. Similarly, the precise nature of air movement within the active convection column is virtually unknown. At present, our ability to predict spot fire distances is empirical and based largely on Austrailian experience, where the peculiarities of the eucalypt fuel type produce the nastiest spot fire problems in the world (Luke and McArthur 1978).

As with so many aspects of forest fire behavior, fuel moisture content is critical to spot fire formation. If fuel moisture is high, more energy is required for ignition than can be supplied by embers light enough to be windborne. On the other hand, if fuel moisture is very low, the embers tend to burn up completely before landing in fresh fuels. Australian experience, confirmed by American observations, shows that fine fuel moistures of 7 percent are about the upper limit where concentrations of spot fires can be anticipated, and that a fuel moisture of 4 percent is optimum for massive spotting.

The truly long distance spotting of 30 or more kilometers is a uniquely Australian phenomenon caused by the tendency of candle-bark species of eucalyptus to decorticate their bark in long streamers that dry and curl into hollow cylinders. These are readily ignited and torn off by convective currents. If the fire is sufficiently hot to lift them to a height of 3000 to 4000 m they can easily be carried for tens of kilometers with the fire in the center of the cylinder protected from the ambient wind.

Spotting distances for less exotic fuel types are normally limited to 10 km or less with massive spotting occurring less than 2 km from the flame front. The primary fire-carrying agents are bark plates, cone bracts, and leaf or needle clusters. Spotting also occurs in grass fires but is seldom noticeable because the spot fires are overrun by the main flame front before they can develop independently. However, spotting can be a major factor in causing grass fires to jump roads or other barriers.

## FIRE SPREAD

Even before the beginning of organized forest fire suppression, the ability to predict the rate of spread of a fire has been recognized as the most important single requirement for successful fire suppression (U.S. Army Signal Service 1881). This is scarcely surprising since the size of the fire and hence the amount of fireline that must be built to contain it depends on the rate of fire spread and the time required to get firefighters to the scene. Up until about the end of World War II it was common practice to consider fire spread vs. control action as a two-dimensional problem: the fire would increase its perimeter at a rate $X$, so sufficient forces should be mustered to build fireline at a rate greater than $X$. In publications prior to the 1950s, rate of spread is usually expressed in units of perimeter increase. After World War II, possibly as a result of being exposed to examples of more sophisticated strategy and tactics, foresters realized that fires were not actually fought by simply marching up to a random point on the perimeter and starting to dig line. Instead, fire commanders were taught to first attack the head, or fastest portion of the fire, if possible. If the fire was too intense for a frontal attack, then the rear was to be secured and line built along both flanks simultaneously until the head could be pinched off. If there were too few forces available for a flank attack, then the firefighters were to drop back some distance from the head of the fire and build sufficient fireline perpendicular to the head to stop it when the fire arrived at the line. In all three of these scenarios it is the rate of forward spread, not the rate of perimeter increase, that is the variable of interest. Consequently, virtually all recent fire spread prediction schemes have been aimed at predicting the rate of forward spread and it has become axiomatic that "rate of spread" means forward spread. However, it was not always so and one should be careful in reviewing literature to determine what spread rate is being referenced.

There are three general methods by which one can prepare prediction schemes for rate of spread. These are empirical, statistical, and theoretical. The empirical schemes are developed by collecting data on a large number of fires, either wildfires or prescribed fires, subdividing them into sets where all parameters except one are held constant, and determining the effect of that one variable on rate of spread. Examples of this approach can be found in the work of Jemison and Keetch (1942) and also McArthur and Luke (1963). The biggest practical difficulty with the empirical approach is the very large number of fires required to develop the necessary number of homogeneous sets. McArthur's database had to exceed 5000 wildfire documentaries and 500 intensively measured prescribed fires in order to arrive at meaningful relationships. The biggest difficulty with the approach is that any interaction effects among the variables (such as temperature effects on fuel moisture with humidity held constant) tend to be overlooked in the analysis. The overwhelming advantage of empirical rate of spread schemes is that they include the full range of variation in the geographical area from which the data was collected, and extrapolation of the data, which is always risky, is unnecessary.

The statistical method of developing rate of spread predictive schemes is similar to the empirical method in that relatively large quantities of data are required. It differs from the empirical approach in that the data are not stratified by single variables, but are manipulated by statistical techniques based on variants of classical multiple-regression methods. Examples of statistically derived schemes are those of McMasters (1973) as well as Lindenmuth and Davis (op. cit.). The advantages of statistical models are that intercorrelations between dependent variables can be expressed and displayed, and that the confidence limits of the predictions can be made known to the user. There are two major disadvantages to the statistical approach. The most serious is that the relationships among the variables are often highly nonlinear and much accuracy is lost in the linearization process that is a necessary step in multiple-regression analysis. The other major disadvantage is that new data cannot be added without having to repeat the entire computation process.

A purely theoretical predictive model of fire spread should be based strictly on first principles of physics and thermodynamics. There are not too many "first principles" models available, but Van Wagner's (1967) and Kurbatsky and Telitsin's (1977) are examples. The most obvious advantage of a "first principles" model is that it is based on known and tested relationships and expressed in physical units that can be formed into those dimensionless groups that permit unlimited scaling and delight the heart of every true engineer or physicist. And, because they can be scaled, theoretical models can be validated against a much more limited set of data than is true for empirical or statistical prediction schemes. However, theoretical models have major drawbacks as well. First, many of the fundamental variables such as flame emissivity, stack gas viscosity, or even the effective temperature of the radiating source are extremely difficult or even impossible to measure in the field. Consequently, these values are either assumed or measured under laboratory conditions and inferred to the real world. Second, a forest fire is an extremely complex phenomenon compared to a heated tungsten wire, or even to a gas jet in a furnace, and deciding which first principles to apply is not an easy process. Lastly, as we have seen in the preceding sections, the spread of a forest fire is dominated by various heat transfer processes at various stages in its life cycle. A model that predicts rate of spread by calculation of flame radiation can only give correct predictions when the fire is actually being driven by flame radiation. The relative importance of radiation and convection will vary from fire to fire and specifying an exact combination is difficult (Thomas 1971).

Because of these difficulties, most theoretical models are called *thermal models* and are actually based on what might be termed *second principles*. That is, heat fluxes and required heats of ignition are postulated without strict regard to the mode of heat transfer or the mechanism of heat absorptance by the fuel. An excellent example of this approach can be found in Pagni and Peterson (1973). The various constants governing the variation in the heat flux and absorption terms are then determined experimentally. One of the most fully developed models of this type and one being used operationally in the United States and some other countries is that of Rothermel (1972). Its general development is covered here, but for a step-by-step description the reader should obtain the original reference.

The fundamental equation of the Rothermel model assumes that rate of fire spread is a function of only certain variables: (1) the horizontal heat flux absorbed by a unit volume of fuel at the time of ignition, (2) the vertical heat flux, equal to the gradient of the vertical intensity evaluated at a plane at a constant depth of the fuelbed, (3) the heat required to bring a unit weight of fuel to ignition, and (4) an effective bulk density, or the amount of fuel that is heated to ignition at the edge of the fire front.

The following assumptions are then made: (1) all factors affecting the fire are in a steady state; (2) the horizontal heat flux is a function of the mass loss rate of the burning fuel; (3) the vertical heat flux is negligible in the absence of wind and slope; (4) ignition temperature is constant so that heat required for ignition is a function of fuel moisture; (5) since only a certain depth of each piece of fuel will be heated, effective bulk density is a function of the bulk density of the fuelbed and the size of the particles in the bed; (6) ignition is piloted and occurs at 320°C; (7) the effect of moisture on the energy release rate is the same for all woody fuels.

A very careful series of experiments was conducted measuring the rate of fire spread and rate of weight loss in arrays of excelsior, $\frac{1}{4}$ in. square wooden sticks and $\frac{1}{2}$ in. sticks, respectively. From these data the effects of particle surface/volume ratio and packing ratio (the fraction of the fuelbed occupied by fuel) on both rate of spread and the horizontal heat flux were determined and fitted to the theoretical equations. Next, the effects of wind and slope were determined by burning similar fuelbeds in a wind tunnel and on tilted tables. Finally, all the data were combined to produce equations that predict rate of spread and reaction intensity from measured values of fuel loading, fuel depth, fuel particle surface/volume ratio, particle density, moisture content, mineral content (both total and silica-free), wind velocity, slope, and moisture of extinction.

Since all of the input variables except mineral content and moisture of extinction can be measured in the field, these equations have had considerable acceptance worldwide. The equations have been programmed for a handheld calculator that can be taken to the fire scene, appropriate variables entered, and fire spread and intensity predictions calculated on the spot (Burgan 1979).

## FIRE INTENSITY

Fire intensity refers to the rate at which a fire is producing thermal energy and is always expressed in terms of heat (calories) or power (watts). However, there are several ways of expressing fire intensity and it is important not to get them confused.

Radiant intensity refers to the rate of thermal radiation emission, either across the entire radiomagnetic spectrum or within specified wavelengths (spectral intensity). In forest fire usage, radiant intensity almost invariably refers to the radiant energy intercepted at or near the ground surface at some specified distance ahead of the flame front. The units are usually expressed in $cal/cm^2$ sec.

Convective intensity is that portion of the total heat output that is used to lift the stack gases and entrained air above the flame zone. Convective energy is not measurable by present techniques but is calculated by subtracting conductive and radiant heat losses from the total energy release rate. Convective intensity calculations are used to predict convection column phenomena and are discussed further in Chapter 4. The units are usually expressed as $kcal/m^2$ min or as $kW/m^2$.

Total fire intensity refers to the rate of heat output (usually the maximum rate) of the fire as a whole. It, too, is a calculated, not a measured, value and is determined by multiplying the rate of area burned by the fuel loading by the estimated heat yield. Its only utility is in obtaining press coverage and the units are usually expressed in kilotons/min or megatons/hr (e.g., "The Malibu Fire raged with a force of 3.6 kilotons per minute or one Hiroshima type bomb every $5\frac{1}{2}$ minutes. Firefighters were helpless in the face of such a firestorm.").

Reaction intensity is the total heat release of a unit area of fuelbed divided by the burning time. This is equivalent to the time-averaged rate of heat release of the active fire front. Under laboratory conditions reaction intensity can be measured by recording weight loss and determining the heat release through calorimetry. In the field, reaction intensity is usually calculated from estimated amounts of fuel burned and assumed heat yields. Reaction intensity is used in several formulas for predicting various fire behavior parameters. It is usually expressed in $kcal/m^2$ sec.

Fireline intensity, sometimes called Byram's intensity, is the most common and most useful measure of fire intensity. Fireline intensity is the product of the available heat of combustion per unit area of ground and the rate of spread of the fire (Byram 1959).

$$I = 0.007 \; HWR$$

where     $I$ = fireline intensity in kW/m
            $H$ = heat yield in cal/g
            $W$ = fuel loading in tonnes/ha
            $R$ = rate of spread in m/min

Fireline intensity is equivalent to the heat output of a unit length of fire front per unit time and is equal to the reaction intensity multiplied by the depth of fire front.

The principle reason for the popularity of fireline intensity is that it has been shown to be directly related to flame length, and flame length is an easily observable phenomena (though much more easily observed than measured). The relationship, as determined empirically by Byram (op. cit.) is:

***Figure 1.10.*** With flames slightly over 1 m high and a fireline intensity of 400 to 425 kW/m, this fire is about at the limit for direct attack with hand tools. Photo by U.S. Forest Service.

*Figure 1.11.*    Flame heights of 2½ m and fireline intensities of 1700 to 1750 kW/m are marginal for control by mechanical equipment. Photo by U.S. Forest Service.

$$I = 273(h)^{2.17}$$

where    $I$ is fireline intensity in kW/m
        $h$ is flame height in meters

For field use, the formula $I = 3 (10h)^2$ comes within ±20 percent accuracy within the intensity range of interest. Since it is difficult to estimate flame length to better than 20 percent accuracy anyway, the simple formula is usually adequate.

Fireline intensity has been found to correlate well with several important wildfire characteristics. Direct attack with hand tools and assured control of prescribed fires is possible when fireline intensity is less than 400 to 425 kW/m (Figure 1.10; Hodgson 1968). Heavy mechanical equipment can usually control a fire if fireline intensity is below 1700 to 1750 kW/m (Figure 1.11; U.S. Forest Service 1978). Spot fires become serious at 2000 to 2100

*Figure 1.12.*    With flame heights of 20 meters and fireline intensities over 6000 kW/m, these fires are unstoppable until burning conditions ease. Photos by Craig Chandler and U.S. Forest Service.

*Figure 1.12*

27

kW/m (Hodgson op. cit.) and fires are completely uncontrollable with fireline intensities above 3500 to 3700 kW/m (Figure 1.12; U.S. Forest Service op. cit.). Fireline intensity has also been correlated with the lethal scorch height of conifer foliage (Van Wagner 1973) by the rather formidable formula:

$$S = \left( \frac{35}{60 - T} \right) \left[ \frac{I^{7/6}}{.79 \, (I + 47W^3)^{1/2}} \right]$$

where  $S$ = scorch height in meters
$T$ = air temperature in °C
$I$ = fireline intensity in kW/m
$W$ = windspeed in m/sec

As previously mentioned, fireline intensity is the most common and most useful measure of fire intensity. In this book, whenever the word *intensity* is used alone, it refers to fireline intensity. In early references concerned with fire and fire effects, the term has been applied to many diverse aspects of fire including, but not exclusive to, peak flame temperature, maximum convection column height, change in soil temperature, color of residual ash, and fraction of trees killed. The reader should always search for the context when encountering an unqualified *intensity*.

## BIBLIOGRAPHY

Albini, F. A. 1980. *Thermochemical properties of flame gases from fine wildland fuels.* U.S. For. Serv. Res. Paper INT-243, 42 pp.

Albini, F. A. 1981. A model for the wind-blown flame from a line fire. *Comb. and Flame* **43**:155–174.

Bhagat, P. M. 1977. *Effects of water on wood charcoal combustion.* Harvard Univ. Div. of Eng. and Appl. Physics, Home Fire Project Tech. Report No. 22, 104 pp., illus.

Browne, F. L. 1958. *Theories of the combustion of wood and its control.* U.S. For. Serv., For. Prod. Lab. Report No. 2136, 65 pp.

Burgan, R. E. 1979. *Fire danger/fire behavior computations with the Texas Instrument TI-59 calculator: users manual.* U.S. For. Serv. Gen. Tech. Report INT-61, 25 pp.

Byram, G. M. 1959. Combustion of forest fuels, in K. P. Davis, Ed., *Forest Fire Control and Use,* McGraw Hill, New York.

Byram, G. M. 1966. Scaling laws for modeling mass fires. *Pyrodynamics,* Vol. 4, pp. 271–284.

Byram, G. M., W. L. Fons, F. M. Sauer, and R. K. Arnold. 1952. *Thermal conductivity of some common forest fuels.* U.S. For. Serv. Div. Fire Res., 13 pp., processed.

Countryman, C. M. 1955. *Old-growth conversion also converts fireclimate.* Proc. Soc. Am. Foresters, pp. 158–160.

Frandsen, W. H. 1968. *A proposed measurement of the heat of preignition of fine forest fuels.* Western States Section, The Combustion Inst., 17 pp.

Hagglund, B. and L.-E. Persson. 1974. *An experimental study of the radiation from wood flames.* Forsvarets Forshningsanstalt. FAO 4 Rapport C4589-D6(A3), 26 pp.

Hodgson, A. 1968. Control burning in eucalypt forests in Victoria, Australia. *J. For.* 66(8):601–605.

Huffman, K. G., J. R. Welker, and C. M. Slipcevich. 1967. *Wind and interaction effects of free burning fires.* National Bureau of Standards Tech. Report 1441-3, 67 pp., illus.

Jemison, G. M. and J. J. Keetch. 1942. *Rate of spread of fire and its resistance to control in the fuel types of eastern mountain forests.* U.S. For. Serv., Appalachian For. Exp. Sta. Tech. Note No. 52, 15 pp.

Kaysen, H. M. and B. E. Muzaffar. 1960. *Transient convection and radiation heat flux of combustion of a wood fuel.* Univ. Calif., Los Angeles, Report No. 60–34. 36 pp.

Kilzer, F. J. and A. Broido. 1964. *Speculations on the nature of cellulose pyrolysis.* Western States Section, The Combustion Inst., 15 pp.

Kurbatsky, N. P. 1966. Some regularities in fire concentration and spread in the Taiga, in *Forestry and Industrial Utilization of Wood in the USSR,* Paper for the VI World Forestry Congress.

Kurbatsky, N. P. and G. P. Telitsin. 1977. *Theoretical and experimental analysis of radiation mechanisms for the spread of forest fires.* USSR Academy of Sciences, Siberian Branch, Krasnoyarsk. 33 pp.

Lindenmuth, A. W. Jr., and James B. Davis. 1973. *Predicting fire spread in Arizona's oak chaparral.* U.S. For. Serv. Res. Paper RM-101, 11 pp., illus.

Luke, R. H. and A. G. McArthur. 1978. *Bushfires in Australia.* CSIRO Div. of For. Res., Canberra, 359 pp., illus.

MacLean, J. D. 1941. Thermal conductivity of wood. *Heat., Piping and Air Cond.* XIII:380–391.

Martin, S. B. 1956. *The mechanisms of ignition of cellulosic materials by intense thermal radiation.* U.S. Naval Radiological Defense Lab. Report TR-102.

McArthur, A. G. 1959. The effects of solar radiation of fire behavior. *Inst. For. Australia Newsletter* 2(4):13–14.

McArthur, A. G. and R. H. Luke. 1963. Fire behavior studies in Australia. *Fire Control Notes* 24(4):87–92.

McMahon, C. K. and others. 1980. *Combustion characteristics and emissions from burning organic soils.* Proc. 73rd Annual Meeting, Air Pollution Control Assoc., 1016 pp.

McMasters, A. W. 1973. *A statistical fire spread model for forest fires.* Univ. of Calif. at Riverside, Dept. of Statistics, Tech. Report No. 13 under Nat. Sci. Found. Grant Gl-31891-X. 35 pp.

Muraszew, A. and J. B. Fedele. 1976. *Statistical model for spot fire hazard.* Aerospace Corp., Report No. ATR-77(7588)-1, 109 pp.

NFPA 1976. *Fire protection handbook,* 14th ed., Nat. Fire. Prot. Assoc., Boston, Mass.

Packham, D. R. 1972. Heat transfer above a small ground fire. *Aust. For. Res.* 5(1):19–24.

Pagni, P. J. and T. G. Peterson. 1973. *Flame spread through porous fuels.* Fourteenth Symp. (Intl.) on Combustion, The Combustion Inst., pp. 1099–1107.

Philpot, C. W. 1969. *The effects of reduced extractive content on the burning rate of aspen leaves.* U.S. For. Serv. Note INT-92, 6 pp., illus.

Raj, P. P. K., A. N. Moussa, and K. Aravasmudan. 1979. *Experiments involving pool and vapor fires from spills of liquefied natural gas on water.* U.S. Coast Guard Report No. CG-D-55-79, 185 pp., illus.

Rothermel, R. C. 1972. *A mathematical model for predicting fire spread in wildland fuels.* U.S. For. Serv. Res. Paper INT-115, 40 pp., illus.

Rothermel, R. C. 1976. *Thermal uses and properties of carbohydrates and lignins*. Academic, San Francisco, pp. 245–259.

Sandberg, D. 1980. *Duff reduction by prescribed underburning in Douglas-fir*. U.S. For. Serv. Res. Paper PNW-272, 18 pp., illus.

Simms, D. L. 1960. Ignition of cellulosic materials by radiation. *Comb. and Flame* **4**(4):293–300.

Tarifa, C. S. 1967. *Transport and combustion of firebrands*. Instituto Nacional de Technica Aeroespacial, Final Report of Grants FG-SP-114 and FG-SP-146 (Vol. II), 90 pp., illus.

Thomas, P. H. 1963. *The size of flames from natural fires*. Ninth Symp. (Intl.) on Combustion, The Combustion Inst., pp. 844–859.

Thomas, P. H. 1967. Some aspects of the growth and spread of fire in the open. *Forestry* **XL**(2):139–164.

Thomas, P. H. 1971. Rates of spread of some wind-driven fires. *Forestry* **XLIV**(2):155–175.

U.S. Army Signal Service. 1881. *Report on the Michigan forest fires of 1881*. Sig. Serv. Notes 1, 74 pp.

U.S. Forest Service. 1978. *FBO field reference*. Processed.

Van Wagner, C. E. 1967. *Calculations on forest fire spread by flame radiation*. Canada Dept. For. and Rural Dev., For. Branch, Dept. Pub. No. 1185, 14 pp.

Van Wagner, C. E. 1973. Height of crown scorch in forest fires. *Can. J. For. Res.* **3**(3):373–378.

# CHAPTER TWO

# *Forest Fuels*

In the preceding chapter we looked at some of the characteristics of fuel particles as they affect ignition and combustion. At the risk of some redundancy, we review these again from a slightly different perspective.

## FUEL CHEMISTRY

With respect to fuel chemistry, the two most important variables are the relative amounts of ether extractives and silica-free ash. Both of these constituents will vary markedly by species, geographic location, season (physiological growth stage), and degree of weathering. The greatest variations are found between species. Silica-free ash contents, for example, range from 2 percent for the leaves of chamise (*Adenostoma fasciculatum*) to 40 percent for Tamarix species. Extractives vary from 0.27 percent for some grasses to over 15 percent for some pine species. Many Mediterranean shrub species are also high in extractives. Considerable differences occur between samples collected in different locations even though analysis techniques are identical. Compare the values for *Tamarix, Atriplex,* and *Populus* samples collected in Queensland and California as shown in Table 2.1. Whether these differences are a result of soils, climate, or genetic factors is unknown.

Extractives and, to a lesser extent, ash content vary seasonally. Figure 2.1 shows the annual variation in ether extractives for *Adenostoma* from California and *Pinus clausa* from Georgia. Extractives accumulate during the dormant period and are drawn down during active growth phases. Ash contents follow a similar though less dramatic pattern. There is also some evidence that in perennial grasses and shrubs, both ash content and extractives increase with age of the plant (Van Dyne et al. 1965).

Because the mineral constituents of plant parts are selectively resistant to decay processes, ash content increases as fuels weather. In the southeastern

**Table 2.1. Ash Contents of Various Leaves**

| Species | Queensland[a] | | California[b] | |
|---|---|---|---|---|
| | CA[c] | SFA[d] | CA | SFA |
| *Tamarix* spp. | 39.5 | 26.4 | 16.6 | 14.5 |
| *Atriplex* spp. | — | 28.0 | 26.8 | 23.6 |
| *Phytolacca octandra* | 30.9 | 25.8 | — | — |
| *Ficus fraseri* | 20.2 | 14.3 | — | — |
| *Taeniatherum asperum* | — | — | 16.0 | 1.2 |
| *Acacia longifola* | 21.7 | 11.6 | — | — |
| *Acacia maidenii* | 10.2 | 6.9 | — | — |
| *Populus* spp. | — | 14.0 | 5.3 | 5.3 |
| *Eucalyptus acmenioides* | 10.0 | 5.8 | — | — |
| *Eucalyptus* spp. | 7.0 | 4.2 | — | — |
| *Pinus ponderosa* | — | — | 3.9 | 1.6 |
| *Adenostoma fasciculatum* | — | — | 3.6 | 3.3 |

[a] King and Vines 1969.
[b] Philpot 1970.
[c] Crude ash.
[d] Silica-free ash.

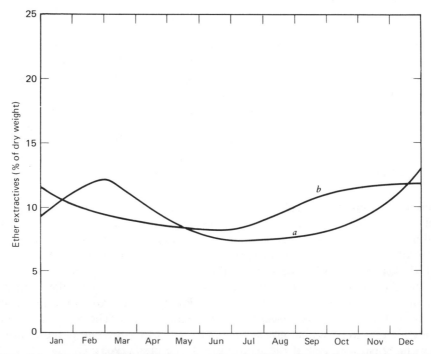

**Figure 2.1.** Seasonal variation in ether extractives. (*a*) *Pinus clausa* foliage (Hough 1973). (*b*) *Adenostoma fasciculatum* foliage (Philpot 1969).

United States, a region of relatively rapid decay, ash content of forest litter increased by one-third after one year of weathering, and the lowest litter layers had two to eight times the ash content of fresh litter (Hough 1969).


## FUEL MOISTURE

The physical attributes of fuel particles such as density, thickness, and surface/volume ratio have been adequately treated in Chapter 1 and are not discussed further here. However, fuel moisture content is so overwhelmingly crucial to forest fire behavior that it requires further elaboration.

Fuel moisture relationships are quite complex and the history of attempts to accurately predict the moisture contents of forest fuels have been an endless series of beautiful theories demolished by ugly facts. In living fuels, the moisture content of foliage and small twigs (the only living plant parts that play an important role in forest fire behavior) is governed by physiological processes. Internal water deficits in plants are controlled by the relative rates of water uptake through the roots and water loss by transpiration. These two processes, which are partly controlled by different sets of factors, usually are out of phase (Kozlowski 1968). Transpiration is controlled by the aerial environment (solar radiation, temperature, humidity, and wind) as well as by leaf structure and degree of stomatal opening. Absorption is controlled by soil factors such as aeration, soil temperature, moisture tension, and solute concentration as well as the size and distribution of the root system. On sunny days, even on well-watered sites, leaf moisture contents will decrease in the afternoon and recover rapidly after sunset. The amount of moisture change is most closely correlated with daily temperature changes rather than with fluctuations in humidity or soil moisture. Figure 2.2 shows diurnal moisture content changes for two species of shrubs and two species of conifers growing under markedly different site conditions. Note that the conifers have a second minimum during the early morning hours, whereas the shrubs continue to gain moisture throughout the night.

Figure 2.3 shows an idealized annual variation in foliage and twig moisture for conifers and broadleaf species assuming a climate where new growth is initiated on May 1. The reason for the dramatic rise in foliage moisture with the initiation of new growth is that current annual foliage makes up a much greater percentage of the total foliage weight in broadleaf species, even evergreens, than it does in conifers. Twig moisture in all species is about 20 percent below foliage moisture and increases much less than foliage when new growth is initiated.

During prolonged droughts, foliage moisture can drop to values markedly below those shown in Figure 2.3. Trees and mature shrubs can recover even when foliage moisture drops to 50 to 60 percent of their dry weight. There has been little formal research on the relationship between foliage moisture and fire behavior, primarily because such experiments involve the deliberate initiation of crown fires in living fuels. To explore the full range of variables

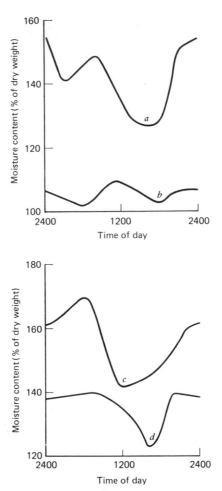

***Figure 2.2.*** Diurnal changes in leaf moisture. (*a*) *Pinus ponderosa*, dry site, summer (Philpot 1965). (*b*) *Pinus edulis*, moist site, winter (Jamison 1966). (*c*) *Ilex glabra*, moist site, summer (Blackmarr and Flanner 1968). (*d*) *Arctostaphylos viscida*, dry site, summer (Philpot 1965).

would be both expensive and dangerous. Van Wagner (1968) in Canada undertook two half-acre experimental crown fires in a *Pinus resinosa* plantation, both under similar weather conditions but with quite different foliar moisture with the following results:

|  | Foliar M.C.% | Rates of Spread | Flame Height |
|---|---|---|---|
| Fire A | 135 | 17m/min | 20 m |
| Fire B | 95 | 27m/min | 30 m |

With this and other data (Van Wagner 1974), he constructs an index of the relative rate of spread of crowning forest fires during spring and early sum-

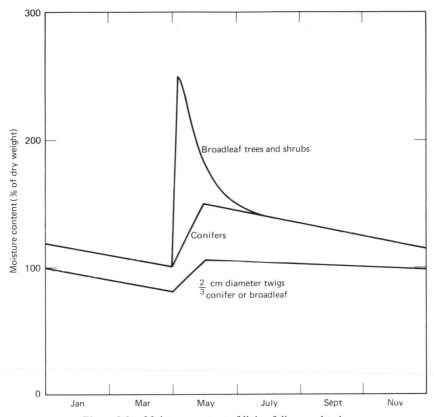

*Figure 2.3.*  Moisture content of living foliage and twigs.

mer based on his findings that the moisture content of foliage is appreciably lower at this period of the year.

Van Wagner also experimented with individual conifers that were cut and allowed to dry to specified moisture contents (Van Wagner 1961). However, his results are probably not applicable to field conditions since volatiles were undoubtedly lost from the needles during storage. Experiments in desiccating arctostaphylos with herbicides to assist in burning brush fields in California failed because, although foliage moisture was reduced from 114 percent to 8 percent, ether extractives were reduced from 16 percent to 3 percent and the treated dry brush was less flammable than the untreated controls.

A general rule of thumb with regard to living foliage moisture is that crown fire potential in conifers is high whenever needle moisture drops below 100 percent of dry weight. In Mediterranean shrub communities fires burn intensely when foliage moisture drops below 75 percent. In northern latitudes, in spring, it is not unusual to experience sudden changes in weather resulting from a warm dry flow of air from the south while the soil is still frozen. These conditions encourage rapid leaf development but, because of low humidities and frozen root systems, the foliage cannot sustain the required transpirational demands and becomes desiccated. The resulting very low foliage moistures can result in extreme fire behavior.

Such a sequence of conditions, augmented by a preceding period of drought, occurring in Alberta, Canada in 1968 is described by A. D. Kiil and J. E. Grigel (1969). During a 15-day period from May 16 to 31, extreme rates of spread were observed and the uniformity of crown fire spread in both conifer and mixedwood stands demonstrated the effect of relatively low foliage moisture in deciduous as well as coniferous species.

As opposed to living fuels that have received comparatively little attention, moisture relations in dead wood and litter have been studied intensively for over 50 years. Despite this effort, our ability to accurately predict the moisture content of forest fuels, either from measurements of antecedent weather or from measurements of analogue materials, is not very good for the following reasons.

1.   A forest fuel is not a homogeneous material like a bar of metal or a cube of plastic. Rather, forest fuels are the decomposing skeletons of complex organic members. In life they transport and expire water along intricate pathways and through special pores. Even after death moisture moves preferentially along these routes.

2.   Moisture is lost from woody materials by three different mechanisms that involve quite different physical processes. Moisture on the outer surface is removed by evaporation. Evaporation depends on the difference between the saturation vapor pressure at the temperature of the water surface and the actual vapor pressure of the air immediately above it. The first term is a function of air temperature and solar radiation; the second term is a function of relative humidity and wind velocity.

Inside the fuel particle, when the moisture content is above 30 to 35 percent, water moves to the surface by capillary diffusion resisted by surface tension forces only. The rate of diffusion is governed largely by the internal structure of the fuel.

Thirty percent or so of the dry weight of woody material represents "bound moisture"—so called because it is chemically attached to the wood substance by interlocked hydrogen bonds. Progressively more energy is required to remove this water as fuel moisture decreases.

For a thorough discussion of the physics involved in all three processes, the reader should review a series of papers by Simard (1968a,b,c).

3.   Forest fuels absorb water by various unrelated mechanisms. Rain, snowmelt, dew, fog drip, ground moisture, and direct atmosphere adsorption all contribute to the wetting of forest fuel, and only the first and last of these processes are well understood or even routinely measured. Precipitation in the open is measured routinely, but the amount reaching dead fuels on the ground is complicated by interception losses due to overstory canopies and stemflow. After many years of trying to devise methods for

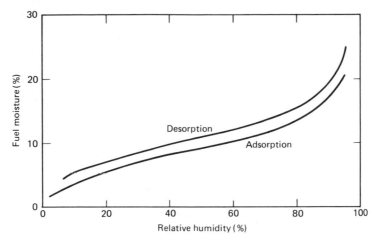

*Figure 2.4.* Equilibrium moisture content *Pinus ponderosa* needles 24°C.

estimating these losses, American researchers finally conclude that better correlations could be made if the amount of precipitation were disregarded completely and the duration of precipitation used instead to predict fuel moisture content (Fosberg 1977).

Dead forest fuels are hygroscopic; that is, they take on (or give off) moisture from the surrounding atmosphere until the amount of moisture in the fuel is in balance with that in the atmosphere. The moisture content of the fuel at this point of balance is called the equilibrium moisture content. It is controlled by atmospheric relative humidity and temperature, and by several poorly understood internal properties of the fuel itself. Because the forces acting to bind the moisture to the fuel substance operate differently when the water is being bound than when it is unbound, the equilibrium moisture content is different for adsorption (rising humidity) than for desorption (falling humidity). Figure 2.4 shows the equilibrium moisture content curves for *Pinus ponderosa* needles, a common North American fuel (Anderson et al. 1978). These curves illustrate one reason why fuel moistures do not react immediately to changes in humidity. If, for example, the air were at 20 percent relative humidity in the afternoon and pine needles had dried to equilibrium, the humidity would have to rise above 30 percent before any change in moisture content could be expected, simply because of the differences in the desorption and adsorption equilibrium moisture content values.

Both the absolute values and the shape of the curves vary by species. Figure 2.5 shows the desorption curves for several common forest fuels.

Equilibrium moisture content is also weakly affected by temperature. The effect is species dependent and also probably dependent on the degree of weathering of the fuel being sampled. Temperature dependence ranges from a decrease of 0.09 percent EMC per °C increase in temperature for freshly cut sound wood to 0.21 percent per °C for weathered fir litter.

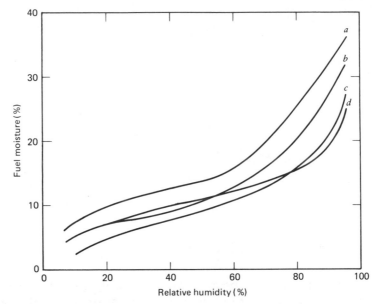

**Figure 2.5.** Desorption EMC curves for common forest fuels 27°C. (*a*) *Quercus stellata* leaves (Blackmarr 1971). (*b*) *Aristida stricta* clipped plant (Blackmarr 1971). (*c*) Wood (Smith 1956). (*d*) *P. ponderosa* needles (Anderson et al. 1978).

Inasmuch as moisture can evaporate from the fuel surface much more rapidly than it can diffuse through the solid fuel to reach the surface, it should be intuitively obvious that the rate at which a fuel will reach equilibrium will decrease as fuel thickness increases. In the early 1960s Byram developed the *time lag* concept based on the fact that any quantity that decreases at an exponential rate will lose approximately two-thirds of its value (precisely $1-1/e$ or 63.2 percent) in each unit time (Byram 1963). Consequently, if one measures the time required for a certain fuel to lose $\frac{2}{3}$ of the difference between its initial moisture content and its equilibrium moisture content under any given set of temperature and humidity conditions, then that fuel will come $\frac{2}{3}$ of the way to equilibrium in that time period under *all* sets of temperature and humidity changes. For example, in Figure 2.4 if the time lag constant for ponderosa pine needles is known to be 4 hr, a sample has a measured moisture content of 16 percent at noon, and the relative humidity is expected to be 20 percent at 4 PM, then the 4 PM moisture content will be 10 percent $\{16 - [\frac{2}{3}(16 - 7)]\} = 10$. The time lag concept has proven to be a very useful tool in fuel moisture prediction and in fuel classification since very diverse types of fuel can be aggregated into similar time lag regimes. Even though later research has shown that forest fuels do not, in fact, dry at an exponential rate and that the time lag concept is not reliable for more than the first drying period, its utility has led to widespread acceptance (Nelson 1969).

## FUELBEDS

Although the properties of the individual fuel particles have a direct influence on ignition and combustion, the behavior of an established fire depends principally on the characteristics of the fuelbed, that is, the association of living and dead plant materials of various sizes and shapes that extend from mineral soil to the top of the vegetation canopy. Unfortunately, natural fuelbeds are usually heterogeneous and discontinuous and thus extremely difficult to quantify or even characterize. This difficulty, however, in no way detracts from their importance. In the following sections we look at some of the properties of fuelbeds that influence fire behavior.

### Fuel Loading

The first difficulty in discussing fuelbeds arises in the very definition of the word *fuel*. In forestry terminology *fuel* is defined as "any substance or composite mixture susceptible to ignition and combustion" (Ford-Robertson 1971). Because all the fuel that is theoretically capable of burning never burns in any given forest fire, several different definitions have been coined. It is important to distinguish among them.

*Phytomass,* or total fuel loading, is the amount of plant material, both living and dead, to be found above mineral soil. This definition of phytomass differs from that of *biomass,* often found in the ecological literature, in that roots and animal matter are not included, whereas dead plant materials are included. This definition of phytomass comes closest to the FAO/IUFRO definition of fuel quoted in the previous paragraph since it includes large living stems that are never consumed in a single forest fire but may be killed by one fire and then consumed in subsequent fires. The total phytomass on any site has a physiological upper limit:

$$W = 26 \sqrt{A}$$

where   $W$ = total phytomass in tonnes per hectare
        $A$ = stand age in years

The degree to which a stand will approach this limit is a function of site quality, but is unrelated to vegetation type (Magorian 1967). Consequently, the projected phytomass at any future time when the present phytomass is known can be found by substituting $c$ for the constant 26 in the equation, solving for $c$, and computing $W$ for the desired future stand age.

Potential fuel loading is the amount of material that could be consumed in the most intense fire that could be expected to develop on the specific site. Potential fuel loading is a maximum value; virtually all forest fires will consume less. Available fuel loading is the amount of fuel that is expected to burn under specified fire weather conditions. It is a valuable and often-used

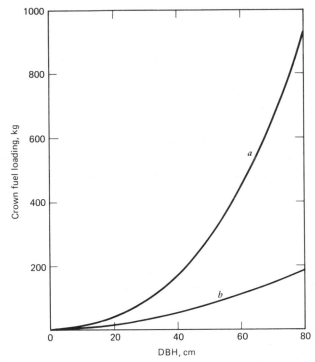

*Figure 2.6.*   Range of crown fuel loading in North American conifers (Brown 1976). (*a*) *Pinus ponderosa.* (*b*) *Tarif occidentalis.*

term for planning prescribed fires where the weather conditions are specified in advance. It is also useful in postfire analyses where the amount of material actually burned can be compared with the potential fuel load and the weather conditions at the time of the burn. The available fuel is always less than the potential fuel, sometimes much less, and in reviewing literature on forest fuels it is important to know which term is being used.

Fuel loading (other terms common in the literature are fuel weight and/or fuel volume) is expressed in terms of weight per unit area, usually kilograms per square meter or tonnes per hectare. In this book we shall use tonnes per hectare (t/ha) in all expressions of fuel loading because the units are more convenient over the range of fuel loadings commonly found in forests.

The fuel loading from commercial tree species has been intensively studied because of the need to predict the amount of residue to be expected following logging operations. A Canadian bibliography published in 1971 lists 193 references to fuel loadings of tree crowns, and the list has at least doubled since that time (Keays 1971). Virtually all tree crown loading tables correlate crown weight against species and diameter breast height (DBH), and many use multiple regressions including such other variables (in order of

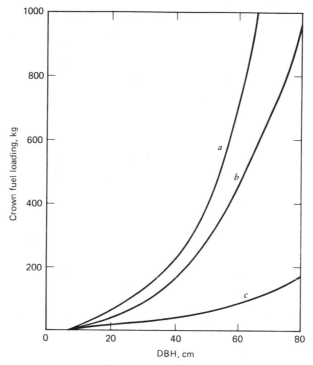

*Figure 2.7.* Range in crown fuel loading for *Pinus ponderosa*. (*a*) Crown length 80% of tree height (Chandler 1960). (*b*) Brown 1976. (*c*) Crown length 20% of tree height (Chandler 1960).

importance) as crown length, site index, stocking percent, and crown width. With the variance associated with the samples, most researchers have concluded that species and DBH (with a sizable minority insisting on adding crown length) are sufficient to produce useful predictions. Figure 2.6 shows the range in crown fuel loading for North American conifer species and Figure 2.7 shows the variation in a single species.

Considerable work has also been undertaken to evaluate the loading of forest residues in place. In contrast to the fuel loading prediction schemes for live trees which rely on multiple-regression equations developed from dissections of individual trees, determination of residue loadings relies on field sampling based on planar intersect techniques (Beaufait et al. 1974, Brown 1974) augmented with specially prepared graphic aids (Anderson 1978) or standardized photographic comparisons (Maxwell and Ward 1980).

These enable calculations of either potential or available fuel loading to be made rapidly on site. This site specificity is necessary in deciding whether hazard reduction measures should be required, and in planning for prescribed fires when they are needed.

Shrub and understory species have received less attention, but estimation guides are available for several species. Some require measurements of stem diameter, whereas others use height and crown area. All are species dependent.

Grass and litter are relatively easy to measure directly in the field and little effort has been made to develop prediction schemes.

## Size Distribution

Measurements of gross phytomass are sufficient when prediction of potential fuel loading is all that is desired. However, in order to estimate available fuel loading, something must be known about the size distribution of both the living and dead materials. Dead fuels larger than 1 to 2 cm in diameter have little influence on a fire's rate of spread, although they do contribute their proportionate share to both convective intensity and reaction intensity. Living fuels larger than 2 to 5 cm in diameter seldom burn at all but act as heat sinks, trapping energy that would otherwise be utilized to increase fire spread. Separation of fuel loading estimates into categories of foliage, material less than 0.5 cm in diameter, 0.5 to 1 cm, 1 to 2 cm, 2 to 5 cm, 5 to 10 cm, and over 10 cm is sufficient to permit reasonably accurate calculation of available fuel loading under any assumed set of burning conditions.

## Compactness

The other fuelbed variables known to influence forest fire behavior are either extremely difficult or extremely tedious to measure. Compactness refers to the tightness with which the individual particles are packed within the fuelbed. Compactness affects both the air supply to the individual burning particles and the ease of heat transfer to particles in the bed ahead of the flame front. For assessing air supply, bulk density (the mass of fuel per unit volume of fuelbed) is an adequate and relatively easily measured quantity. For heat transfer considerations it is the distribution of fuel surfaces, not fuel weights that is important, and for fuelbeds with mixed particles of different sizes, shapes, and densities, characterizing these surface distributions is difficult. Rothermel and Anderson (1966), working with fuelbeds of uniform particle sizes, find that rate of fire spread through the bed is directly related to the product of the surface volume ratio of the particles and the porosity of the fuelbed. They define porosity as the void volume of the bed divided by the total surface area of fuel in the bed. Table 2.2 gives some representative porosities for grass, brush, and timber fuelbeds.

Compactness has an even more marked effect on combustion rates and flame heights. Particle spacing affects both heat transfer between particles and air supply to the individual particles. For beds of any given size of particles there is an optimum compactness. The larger the particles, the greater the optimum compaction. Logs, for example, burn best when tightly packed and will cease to burn if separated by much more than one diameter

*Table 2.2.  Fuelbed Porosity by Fuel Type*

| Fuel Type | Porosity[a] | | |
|---|---|---|---|
| | Max | Mean | Min |
| *Pinus ponderosa* Litter[b] | 12 | 34 | 104 |
| *Pinus contorta* Midcrown[c] | 714 | 833 | 1690 |
| *Adenostoma fasciculatum* Whole plant[d] | 237 | 468 | 1470 |
| *Bromus tectorum*[b] | 809 | 1070 | 2740 |

[a] Bed volume/fuel volume.
[b] Brown 1970.
[c] Gary 1976.
[d] Countryman and Philpot 1970.

from each other. Fine grasses, on the other hand, burn best in loose arrays and combustion rates can be drastically reduced by compaction. In a field trial with tropical sorghum (Rowell and Cheney 1979), the bulk density of a 10 t/ha stand was increased from 1.3 kh/m$^3$ to 5.3 kg/m$^3$ by crushing with a grass roller. Although rates of spread were not perceptibly altered, flame heights were reduced by more than 75 percent, from 10 m to 2 m, whereas flame depths were increased in similar proportions.

## Continuity

Both horizontal and vertical continuity of fuelbeds are extremely important to fire behavior even though no way has yet been found to express them mathematically. Gaps in vertical continuity of about $1\frac{1}{2}$ flame heights will virtually preclude the fire from burning into the overhead stratum. The tendency of forest fuels to develop vertically stratified layers is so universal that fires are often classified by the fuel strata in which they burn.

Ground fuels are the duff and roots lying beneath the current year's accumulation of fallen material. Ground fuels are generally highly compacted and partially decomposed. Consequently, fires spread slowly with little or no flaming, but with a glowing combustion that is persistent and very difficult to extinguish. Failure to completely extinguish or isolate all burning ground fuels near the fireline has been the cause of many fires escaping days or weeks after being declared controlled. Ground fires in deep organic soils are nearly impossible to extinguish without vast supplies of water and specialized trenching and water dispersal equipment.

Surface fuels consist of the dead leaves, needles, twigs, and other litter that have fallen sufficiently recently as to be neither decomposed nor excessively compacted. Surface fuels are by far the most common carriers of forest fires. Because of differences in fuel particle properties and compactness, surface fires spread slowest in beds of single needle conifers such as fir and spruce whose shorter needles tend to form compact mats; fire spread is more rapid in newly fallen hardwood leaves, particularly oak leaves, which have a tendency to curl and present a maximum of aerated surface; surface fires spread most rapidly in pine litter where the long needles, bundled in fascicles of two to five, tend to develop a deep, well-aerated fuelbed.

Herbaceous fuels such as grasses and ferns are sometimes classed as surface fuels. They deserve special distinction though, because unlike the litter fuels, they originate as living plants in situ. Consequently, their compactness is determined biologically rather than mechanically. Herbaceous plants attempt to expose the maximum photosynthetic area to potential sunlight within the volume of space occupied by the plant. This results in a mass of finely divided particles of low bulk density that is as ideally suited to transmit a fire's radiant energy as it is to absorb solar energy. Grass fires spread more rapidly than fires in any other natural fuel.

Midlevel fuels are those shrubs and trees either less than two meters in total height or taller plants that have branches and/or foliage within one meter of the ground surface. These plants are primarily important as a means of transmitting fire to the crowns of larger forest trees. When they grow in continuous stands as in the chaparral of the western United States or the garrigue of the Mediterranean region, they burn fiercely on their own. Such *brush* fires have been the cause of much property destruction and loss of life.

Upper level or *crown* fuels consist of the foliage, twigs, and smaller branches of the overstory vegetation. Inasmuch as the majority of this material is living, except under exceptional circumstances such as follow insect epidemics, moisture contents are high and the fuels will not burn unless they are heated for long time periods or directly bathed in flames. Gaps of about $1\frac{1}{2}$ flame heights between crown bases and surface or midlevel fuels will virtually preclude the development of crown fires. In addition, fire cannot propagate from crown to crown unless there is sufficient wind or ground sufficiently steep to tilt the flames from one burning tree into the foliage of the next. Since crown fires only occur when conditions are dry (producing long flames) and windy, they are always intense, fast moving, and extremely dangerous. When the weather is dry enough for individual crowns to be easily ignited but there is not sufficient wind to sustain a crown fire, the resulting phenomenon is called *torching* (Figure 2.8). Torching is always a danger signal to firefighters as it means that any increase in wind may result in a crown fire and also because needle clusters, bark platelets, and other material may be lifted above the burning tree and cause spot fires some distance away.

Horizontal distribution or continuity of fuel is also an important determinant of fire behavior (Figures 2.9 and 2.10). A gap of 100 m or so is sufficient to bring a crown fire down to the ground where it must reestablish itself after crossing the opening as a surface fire. Even though a fire may burn around

**Figure 2.8.** Torching is a common phenomenon when fire reaches the top of a ridge. Photo by Bluford Muir.

barriers such as green meadows or rock outcroppings, its rate of spread is slowed because it must reundergo its initial acceleration stage before it can again establish a line front.

These fuelbed variables, compactness, vertical distribution, and continuity, because of the difficulty in measuring them and thus reproducing them, make it extremely difficult to conduct experimental fires in prepared fuelbeds. It is virtually impossible to, first, reproduce a *natural* fuelbed and, second, replicate the identical fuel conditions to repeat burns under varying fuel moisture and other conditions. This is one of the reasons why Canadian and Australian forest fire researchers have opted to obtain correlations between fuel moisture and fire behavior through the conduct of many small test fires in actual forest sites. This empirical approach, although time-consuming, requiring up to three fire seasons to obtain the needed data for any particular region, does give useful results and data that are of use in applications other than fire danger rating such as fire growth modeling.

### Changes Over Time

Although fuels are usually characterized as one of the "constant" factors of fire danger, they do change over time. Fuel moisture changes hour by hour,

**Figure 2.9.**    Continuous fuels both horizontally and vertically make this *Pinus* halipensis forest ripe for a conflagration. Photo by Louis Trabaud.

but most other fuel properties change at a much slower rate, seasonally or over years or even decades.

The accumulation of dead fuel on the forest floor depends not only on the obvious factors of plant species, age, and density, but is influenced to a much greater degree by the climatic factors of temperature and moisture that determine the rate of decay of the material after it reaches the ground. Annual litterfall can range from 1 to 8 t/ha, averaging about 2 t/ha in shrub stands and 3.5 t/ha in forests, but decay rates can range from 20 t/h/y in the tropics to virtually nil in arctic or desert climates. Consequently, the floor in a scrubby boreal forest may contain 300 t/ha, whereas the floor under a rainforest with many times the total phytomass may be totally bare.

Decay rates cannot be predicted from a knowledge of mean annual temperature and precipitation alone. Moisture must be available at the time temperatures are high enough for active fungal and bacterial activity. In Mediterranean climates where rainfall is largely confined to the winter months, decay can be extraordinarily slow. The *decay constant*, or period of time from the initiation of a stand until the rate of decay equals the annual accumulation of litter, is between 50 and 70 years in Mediterranean shrub fields, approximately that of beech forests (45 years) and spruce forests (70

*Figure 2.10.* Discontinuous fuels like this Mediterranean garrigue make sustained fire runs unlikely unless surface winds are strong. Photo by Louis Trabaud.

years) in northern Germany. In the southeastern United States where summer rainfall is abundant the decay constant is 17 to 20 years. The amount of living understory material (grass and shrubs) is a function of climate, soil, and the species and density of the overstory. The variation in understory fuel loading with overstory density can be expressed by the equation (Jamison 1967):

$$V = X - [(X - Y)(1 - e^{ac})^b]$$

where   $V$ = understory fuel loading, t/ha
$X$ = understory fuel loading with no overstory
$Y$ = understory fuel loading with completely closed crown canopy
$c$ = crown canopy density, percent closure
$a$ = constant dependent on overstory species
$b$ = constant dependent on overstory species
$e$ = base of Naperian logarithms (~2.71828)

Figure 2.11 shows the variation in understory beneath two dissimilar types of overstory.

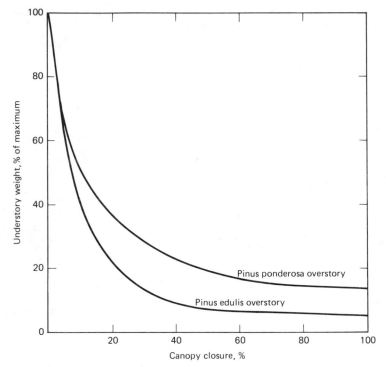

*Figure 2.11.*   Understory weight vs. crown canopy density.

## FUEL CLASSIFICATION

The purpose of classifying forest fuels is to enable the fire planning specialist or the land management planning specialist to identify the inherent potential for fire problems on the lands under his jurisdiction. What is needed then is a system to link the vegetative or ecological aspects of the cover with the fire behavior determinants of fuel and weather. Because this linkage can be accomplished starting at either end, there are several, quite different, systems in use throughout the world for fuel type classification.

### Classification by Direct Estimation

The most obvious and direct method of rating the fire behavior of a parcel of land is to obtain the subjective opinion of trained fire specialists who have experience with fires on similar parcels. This procedure was formalized and codified by the U.S. Forest Service prior to World War II (Hornby 1936). Fuels were rated into one of four categories (low, medium, high, or extreme) for both rate of spread and, separately, resistance to control. The weather was specified to be that "normal for the area after one month of continuous midsummer drought" and control action was specified to be a small crew of men with hand tools. The most serious difficulty with this system of classification was not its subjectivity, but the fact that fuels were rated for a single set of weather conditions. Fuels that have a given relative ranking under one set of weather conditions may behave quite differently when conditions are more or less severe. Comparing scrub oak (*Quercus dumosa*) to chamise (*Adenostoma fasciculatum*), for example, results in a "medium" vs. "high" rating for rate of spread under the normal midsummer conditions specified by Hornby, but under severe conditions in late summer the oak becomes nearly explosive, whereas fire behavior in chamise is little changed. Despite this handicap, fuel classification by "rate of spread–resistance to control" remained the official fuel classification system in the United States for nearly 40 years. It was not until fire planning began to integrate with land management planning that a system had to be adopted that was less dependent on fire behavior expertise.

**Classification by Plant Communities**

Because ecologists are more numerous than fire scientists and preceded them by at least a century, the most common method of classifying forest fuels, as well as the forests themselves, is to use the locally accepted silvicultural or ecological nomenclature and characterize the fire behavior in each type through a combination of historical fire records and expert opinion. This method of classification has the advantage of being readily understandable to the land manager who may not be a fire specialist since it uses type classifications with which the manager is already familiar. It has the additional advantage of being extremely flexible. Type classification can range from the all-inclusive trio of grass, brush, and timber, used in the earliest fire planning studies, to such sophisticated classification systems as the 64 forest habitat types used to classify the forests of Montana (Pfister et al. 1980). One method used in southern France (Trabaud 1974, 1978) is to consider both the floristic and the physical features of each plant community. First, the relative proportion of trees, shrubs, and herbs is calculated together with the percentage of woody species greater or less than two meters in height. This serves to generalize the vertical and horizontal continuity of the stand. Next, the volume occupied by each class is estimated to characterize the phytomass. Finally, since several stands may be physically similar but have different combustion characteristics, they are typed by two or three dominant species. However, there are also disadvantages to ecological classifications. There is no firm agreement among ecologists on how vegetation maps should be constructed (Kuchler 1967 gives a fascinating history of the vicissitudes in this field since 1447), and various land managers may use different classification schemes for the same general area. If the type classifications are too narrow, gathering the necessary fire behavior information may be inordinately time-consuming and expensive (Arno and

Sneck 1977), and there may be more variation in fire behavior characteristics within a class than between classes. This latter difficulty can be overcome by the third method of fuel classification.

## Classification by Fuel Models

A fuel model is a mathematical representation of a fuelbed with all variables included necessary to compute the selected fire behavior characteristics, usually spread rate and fireline intensity (Deeming 1975). Thus a fuel model will represent all cover types whose fuel characteristics, such as loading, packing ratio, and surface/volume ratio are equivalent to those of the model. There are certain distinct advantages to fuel models as opposed to plant communities for classifying forest fuels. First, because fuel models are based on the physical rather than the floristic parameters of the fuelbed, a single model can represent a wide variety of cover types. Second, and an advantage that is unique to fuel models among all classification methods, fire behavior characteristics of the model can be calculated over the full range of slope and weather variables. The principal disadvantage to fuel models is that their validation in the field is difficult and tedious (Bevins and Martin 1978) and they must generally be taken on faith by the land manager who neither understands nor particularly cares about fuel physics. This can be partially obviated by a fourth method of fuel classification.

## Classification by Photo Series

The photo series represents a combination of the plant community and the fuel model approach to forest fuel classification. Small representative plots of selected fuel types are photographed and described in terms familiar to the land manager. Then the plots are dissected and measured for the fuelbed properties needed to develop a fuel model. Thus both the land manager and the fuels specialist are provided with information in a standardized format usable by either (Maxwell and Ward 1979, 1980). Photo series have been adopted by the U.S. Forest Service and several other agencies as the national system for classifying forest fuels in the United States. The main disadvantage of the system is its cost. It takes approximately six man-hours for a well-trained crew to measure and photograph a single plot. An additional disadvantage is that the method is too complex and time-consuming to be used on a routine basis—when evaluating the potential of a wildfire or prescribed burn, for example. Other methods of classifying fuels must be used for these purposes.

## Classification by Dichotomous Keys

Keys are widely used in the natural sciences for classification and identification. Several keys have been developed for ready use in the field

**Table 2.3. Crowning Potential Key**[a]

|  | Rating[b] |
|---|---|
| A. Foliage present, trees living or dead—B | |
|    B. Foliage living—C | |
|       C. Leaves deciduous or, if evergreen, usually soft, pliant, and moist; never oily, waxy, or resinous | 0 |
|      CC. Leaves evergreen, not as preceding—D | |
|         D. Foliage resinous, waxy or oily—E | |
|           E. Crowns dense—F | |
|             F. Ladder fuels plentiful—G | |
|               G. Canopy closure 75 percent | 9 |
|              GG. Canopy closure less than 75 percent | 7 |
|            FF. Ladder fuels sparse or absent—H | |
|               H. Canopy closure 75 percent | 7 |
|              HH. Canopy closure less than 75 percent | 5 |
|         EE. Crowns open—I | |
|              I. Ladder fuels plentiful | 4 |
|             II. Ladder fuels sparse or absent | 2 |
|       DD. Foliage not resinous, waxy or oily—J | |
|         J. Crowns dense—K | |
|           K. Ladder fuels plentiful—L | |
|              L. Canopy closure 75 percent | 7 |
|              LL. Canopy closure less than 75 percent | 7 |
|           KK. Ladder fuels sparse or absent—M | |
|               M. Canopy closure 75 percent | 5 |
|              MM. Canopy closure less than 75 percent | 3 |
|         JJ. Crowns open—N | |
|              N. Ladder fuels plentiful | 3 |
|             NN. Ladder fuels sparse or absent | 1 |
|   BB. Foliage dead—O | |
|      O. Crowns dense—P | |
|         P. Ladder fuels plentiful—Q | |
|           Q. Canopy closure 75 percent | 10 |
|          QQ. Canopy closure less than 75 percent | 9 |
|        PP. Ladder fuels sparse or absent—R | |
|           R. Canopy closure 75 percent | 8 |
|          RR. Canopy closure less than 75 percent | 4 |
|     OO. Crowns open—S | |
|        S. Ladder fuels plentiful | 6 |
|       SS. Ladder fuels sparse or absent | 2 |
| AA. Foliage absent, trees dead—T | |
|   T. Average distance between trees 33 feet or less—U | |
|     U. Ladder fuels plentiful—V | |
|       V. Trees with shaggy bark and/or abundant tinder | 10 |
|      VV. Trees without shaggy bark and/or abundant tinder | 8 |
|     UU. Ladder fuels sparse or absent—W | |
|       W. Trees with shaggy bark and/or abundant tinder | 10 |
|      WW. Trees without shaggy bark and/or abundant tinder | 5 |
|  TT. Average distance between trees 33 feet | 2 |

[a] From Fahnestock 1970.
[b] Arbitrary rating on a scale of 0 to 10.

for evaluating specific fire behavior characteristics such as blowup potential (Wendel et al. 1962), rate of spread, or crowning potential (Fahnestock 1970). Table 2.3 shows Fahnestock's key for crowning potential and illustrates the strengths and weaknesses of this method of fuel classification. Its strength is simplicity. A maximum of seven choices is required to achieve a rating. The choices are plain, involving only ocular estimation and requiring at the most a few minutes of time. However, the weaknesses of the method derive directly from its strengths. The choices are subjective, and personnel with no fire behavior experience have difficulty distinguishing among plentiful, abundant, and sparse. On the other hand, experienced fire people can easily judge relative crowning potential from the overall appearance of the stand without breaking down their impressions to the seven separate steps. Dichotomous keys have found their greatest use as training devices. They are seldom used in field practice.

## BIBLIOGRAPHY

Anderson, H. E. 1978. *Graphic aids for field calculations of dead, down forest fuels.* U.S. For. Serv. Gen. Tech. Report INT-45, 21 pp.

Anderson, H. E., R. D. Schuette, and R. W. Mutch. 1978. *Timelag and equilibrium moisture content of ponderosa pine needles.* U.S. For. Serv. Res. Paper INT-202, 28 pp., illus.

Arno, S. F. and K. M. Sneck. 1977. *A method for determining fire history in coniferous forests of the mountain west.* U.S. For. Serv. Gen. Tech. Report INT-42, 28 pp., illus.

Beaufait, W. R., M. A. Marsden, and R. A. Norum. 1974. *Inventory of slash fuels using 3P subsampling.* U.S. For. Serv. Gen. Tech. Report INT-13, 17 pp., illus.

Bevins, C. D. and R. E. Martin. 1978. *An evaluation of the slash (I) fuel model of the 1972 national fire danger rating system.* U.S. For. Serv. Res. Paper PNW-247, 17 pp.

Blackmarr, W. H. 1971. *Equilibrium moisture content of common fire fuels in southeastern forests.* U.S. For. Serv. Res. Paper SE-74, 8 pp.

Blackmarr, W. H. and W. B. Flanner. 1968. *Seasonal and diurnal variation in moisture content of six species of pocosin shrubs.* U.S. For. Serv. Res. Paper SE-33, 11 pp.

Brown, J. K. 1970. *Physical fuel properties of ponderosa pine forest floors and cheatgrass.* U.S. For. Serv. Res. Paper INT-74, 16 pp., illus.

Brown, J. K. 1974. *Handbook for inventorying down woody material.* U.S. For. Serv. Gen. Tech. Report INT-16, 24 pp., illus.

Brown, J. K. 1976. *Predicting crown weights for 11 Rocky Mountain conifers.* Proc. Oslo Biomass Studies, IUFRO Congress, pp. 103–115.

Byram, G. M. 1963. *An analysis of the drying process in forest fuel material.* Int. Symp. on Humidity and Moisture, Washington, D.C., 38 pp.

Chandler, C. C. 1960. *Slash weight tables for westside mixed conifers.* U.S. For. Serv. Tech. Paper No. 48, 21 pp.

Countryman, C. M. and C. W. Philpot. 1970. *Physical characteristics of chamise as a wildland fuel.* U.S. For. Serv. Res. Paper PSW-66, 16 pp., illus.

Deeming, J. E. 1975. Fuel models in the national fire danger rating system. *J. For.* 73(6):347–350.

Fahnestock, G. R. 1970. *Two keys for appraising forest fire fuels.* U.S. For. Serv. Res. Paper PNW-99, 26 pp.

Ford-Robertson, F. C. 1971. *Terminology of forest science, technology, practice and products (English language version).* Soc. Am. For., Washington, D.C., 349 pp.

Fosberg, M. A. 1977. *Forecasting the 10-hour timelag fuel moisture.* U.S. For. Serv. Res. Paper RM-187, 10 pp.

Gary, L. 1976. *Crown structure and distributions of biomass in a lodgepole pine stand.* U.S. For. Serv. Res. Paper RM-165, 179 pp., illus.

Hornby, G. L. 1936. *Fire control planning in the Northern Rocky Mountain region.* U.S. For. Serv. Prog. Report No. 1. 179 pp., illus.

Hough, W. A. 1969. *Caloric value of some forest fuels of the southern United States.* U.S. For. Serv. Res. Note SE-120, 6 pp.

Hough, W. A. 1973. *Fuel and weather influence wildfires in sand pine forests.* U.S. For. Serv. Res. Paper SE-106, 11 pp.

Jamison, D. A. 1966. *Diurnal and seasonal fluctuations in moisture content of pinyon pine and juniper.* U.S. For. Serv. Res. Note RM-67, 7 pp.

Jamison, D. A. 1967. The relationship of tree overstory and herbaceous understory vegetation. *J. Range Mgt.* **20**(4):247–249.

Keays, J. L. 1971. *Complete tree utilization: an analysis of the literature. Part IV. crown and slash.* Canadian Forestry Service, For. Prod. Lab. Info. Report WX77, 79 pp.

Kiil, A. D. and J. E. Grigel. 1969. *The May 1968 forest conflagration in central Alberta.* Canada, Forestry Branch Info. Report A-X-24.

King, N. K. and R. G. Vines. 1969. *Variation in the flammability of the leaves of some Australian forest species.* CSIRO Div. of Appl. Chem., 14 pp.

Kozlowski, T. T. 1968. *Water deficits and plant growth,* Vol. 1, Academic, New York and London.

Kuchler, A. W. 1967. *Vegetation mapping.* Ronald Press, New York.

Magorian, T. R. 1967. *Characteristics of vegetation at field test sites and various geographic areas.* Army Mat. Syst. Anal. Agency Report GM-2338-G-1.

Maxwell, W. G. and F. R. Ward. 1979. *Photo series for quantifying forest residues in common vegetation types of the Pacific Northwest.* U.S. For. Serv. Gen. Tech. Report PNW-105, 229 pp.

Maxwell, W. G. and F. R. Ward. 1980. *Guidelines for developing or supplementing natural photo series.* U.S. For. Serv. Res. Note PNW-358, 16 pp.

Nelson, R. M., Jr. 1969. *Some factors affecting the timelags of woody materials.* U.S. For. Serv. Res. Paper SE-44, 16 pp.

Pfister, R. D., B. L. Kovalchik, S. F. Arno, and R. C. Presby. 1980. *Forest habitat types of Montana.* U.S. For. Serv. Gen. Tech. Report INT-34, 174 pp., illus.

Philpot, C. W. 1965. *Diurnal fluctuation in moisture content of ponderosa pine and whiteleaf manzanita leaves.* U.S. For. Serv. Res. Note PSW-67, 7 pp.

Philpot, C. W. 1969. *Seasonal changes in heat content and ether extractive content of chamise.* U.S. For. Serv. Res. Paper INT-61, 10 pp., illus.

Philpot, C. W. 1970. Influence of minerals on the pyrolysis of plant materials. *For. Sci.* **16**(4):461–471.

Rothermel, R. C. and H. E. Anderson. 1966. *Fire spread characteristics determined in the laboratory.* U.S. For. Serv. Res. Paper INT-30, 34 pp., illus.

Rowell, M. N. and N. P. Cheney. 1979. Firebreak preparation in tropical areas by rolling and burning. *Aust. For.* **42**(1):8–12.

Simard, A. J. 1968a. *The moisture content of forest fuels—I. a review of the basic concepts.* Canada For. Fire Res. Inst., Info. Report FF-X-14, 47 pp.

Simard, A. J. 1968b. *The moisture content of forest fuels—II. comparison of moisture content variations above the fibre saturation point between a number of fuel types.* Canada For. Fire Res. Inst., Info. Report FF-X-15, 68 pp.

Simard, A. J. 1968c. *The moisture content of forest fuels—III. moisture content variations below the fibre saturation content.* Canada For. Fire Res. Inst., Info. Report FF-X-16, 62 pp.

Smith, H. H. 1956. *Relative humidity and equilibrium moisture content graphs and tables for use in kiln drying lumber.* U.S. For. Serv. For. Prod. Lab. Report No. 1651, 9 pp.

Trabaud, L. 1974. Apport des études ecologiques dans la lutte contre feu. *Rev. For. Francaise* No. Special 1974.

Trabaud, L. 1978. Fuel mapping helps forest firefighting in southern France. *Fire Mgt. Notes* **39**(1):14–17.

Van Dyne, G. M., G. F. Payne, and O. O. Thomas. 1965. *Chemical composition of individual range plants from the U.S. range station, Miles City, Montana, from 1955–1960.* U.S. Atomic Energy Comm., ORNL-TM-1279, 24 pp.

Van Wagner, C. E. 1961. *Moisture content and inflammability in spruce, fir, and scots pine Christmas trees.* Canada Dept. For., For. Res. Branch, Tech. Note No. 109, 16 pp., illus.

Van Wagner, C. E. 1968. *Season variation in moisture content of eastern Canadian tree foliage and the possible effect on crown fires.* Canada For. Branch, Dept. Pub. No. 1204, 15 pp.

Van Wagner, C. E. 1974. *A spread index for crown fires in spring.* Canada, For. Serv., Info. Report PS-X-55.

Wendel, G. W., T. G. Storey and G. M. Byram. 1962. *Forest fuels on organic and associated soils on the coastal plain of North Carolina.* U.S. For. Serv. Sta. Paper SE-144, 46 pp.

# CHAPTER THREE

# *Forest Fire Weather*

As has been mentioned earlier, for many parts of the world's forests, particularly those in the temperate zones, fire has always been one means to restore an old decadent forest with new healthy growth, and many temperate zone forest species have adapted very well to this fire role. In the tropical zone fire has not had such a predominant role in forest development although, with human intervention, the picture has changed somewhat. Plantations of pines or eucalypts, for example, pose a serious fire problem whenever they are established. However, because of the higher level of importance of fire weather in the temperate zones this chapter refers mainly to these forests with reference at the end of the chapter to the tropics.

In the beginning of temperate zone forestry, fire was a constant threat to forest workers as it had been for many years to farmers and settlers who were surrounded by forests that, during the summer months, could become a flaming threat to their livelihood and to their very lives. Fire was another enemy that had to be fought whenever it was encountered with everyone helping with whatever tools were at hand. To early settlers the main objective was to keep the fire out of the settlements and in the forest where it belonged. To early foresters, of course, this was not good enough. Fires in the forest threatened their livelihood and had, somehow, to be kept under control. To some of these foresters, the wisdom of establishing some type of organization and planning for forest fire control became evident, and in most such forested areas, some type of forest fire control organization was established with the simple goals of finding forest fires and putting them out before they became serious threats. In most countries these organizations were under government control although in some instances large forestry companies set up fire control organizations of their own.

Many of the first foresters and forest rangers responsible for forest fire control noticed that the moisture content of the dead material on the forest floor changed appreciably from day to day and, more importantly, that the behavior of a fire once ignited was closely related to this moisture content. Many of these pioneer forest fire specialists became expert at predicting how intense fires might be simply by feeling the moisture of a handful of forest litter or by noting how brittle pine needles had become. Some of these men came to the conclusion that if they could measure daily fuel moisture with a little more accuracy and somehow keep an account of how it changed from one day to the next, they would have a form of warning of how serious the fire potential had become: some relative measure of how many fires to expect, how quickly they might spread, and how difficult they might be to control.

Early attempts at measuring fuel moisture included such crude devices as a hemp sack filled with moss suspended on a simple balance: the heavier the bag of moss, the higher the moisture content and hence the easier the fire day and vice versa. With experience, a fire ranger could become expert at judging the level of fire danger by observing the changing weight of the moss bag or other simple device. One of the problems, however, with such a device was that there was no way of knowing if the basic or dry weight of the indicator had changed. The moss, for example, would deteriorate over time, become infested with insects, mice, and other small creatures and, as a result, would give inconsistent results.

In North America in the late 1920s fledgling forest fire researchers took note of these early attempts at measuring forest fire potential, later to be known as "forest fire danger," and recognized the advantages to be gained by putting such measurements on a scientific basis. They recognized, as had many of the early rangers, that fluctuations in fuel moisture were controlled by weather elements. Obviously, rainfall would increase the moisture content of the fuels and dry weather would decrease it. Less obvious were the effects of other weather elements such as temperature, humidity, wind, solar radiation, or other factors such as latitude and season as reflected in day length. More or less independently, researchers in both the United States and Canada in the mid1920s began decade-long studies of these intriguing fuel moisture–weather–fire relationships, with the aim of developing comprehensive systems for estimating tables or meters that could be used by the forest ranger (Beal 1939, Gisborne 1933, Hornby 1936, Wright 1932).

These early systems met with varying degrees of skepticism by forest fire control personnel but, in general, were gradually accepted and, as the validity of their ratings were proven, increasing use was made of them in almost all aspects of forest fire control. These applications are discussed later in this chapter.

It had become apparent to researchers looking into weather–fuel–fire behavior relationships that whereas the basic relationships are relatively simple—the fuel takes on moisture from precipitation and loses it during "dry" weather—there are many complex interrelationships and other influences that have a bearing on fuel moisture, hence flammability. Wind, for example, has distinct effects. First, it plays an important role in drying rates of most forest fuels, and second, it has a very strong influence on the spread of fire once it has been ignited. In the drying influence of wind we find that there are complex interrelationships with such other factors as the relative humidity of the air surrounding the fuel, air and fuel temperatures, and the physical condition of the fuel (arrangement, density, etc.) to name a few.

Realization of these complexities coupled with a desire to make fire danger rating as accurate as possible yet simple enough to be calculated and understood by the field person led many researchers to develop a wide variety of danger rating schemes for various parts of the world, principally, North America and Australia. These schemes took various forms. Tables, meters, graphs, and alignment charts were developed as a number of researchers attempted to design the perfect fire danger rating system.

The most notable early developments in the United States were those of Gisborne (op. cit.) and Hornby (op. cit.) working in the northern Rocky Mountain region where Hornby's practical application of a fire danger rating system provided inspiration to many other investigators. In Canada, similar studies into the relationship between weather and fuel moisture aimed at the development of a systematic method of measuring fire danger was begun in 1929 at the Petawawa Forest Experiment Station in the Ottawa valley by J. G. Wright (op. cit.). He published the first forest fire hazard tables for Canada in 1933.

In Australia measurements of rates of spread of fires were made and correlated with weather data taken at the same time. Tables indicating the expected fire behavior for various sets of weather data were published by A. McArthur (1976).

From these early beginnings a continuing effort has been made to further refine and improve fire danger rating systems in many countries. Many such systems have now been reduced to formulas and written in the form of computer programs that enable the fire officer to quickly obtain a measure of fire danger by computer. Examples of modern systems are described in a later chapter.

## WEATHER AND FOREST FIRE

Forests exist within the earth's atmosphere and are greatly influenced by changes in this atmosphere, both long and short-term change. In general, these changing conditions of the atmosphere are known as weather and the terms used to describe it, temperature, wind, humidity, and so on, are familiar to all. Much has been written about weather and its effect on forests. It is not the intention here to duplicate these excellent references, but to discuss the influence of weather on forest fires.

As was noted in the previous section, early foresters interested in fire behavior became aware of the importance of the amount of fuel available to burn and the level of moisture within these fuels. The atmosphere in which forests exist has an influence on both these aspects. In the long run, climate controls the establishment and growth of forests, hence the amount of fuel and, in the short run, weather controls the amount of moisture in the fuel, hence its ability to ignite and sustain combustion.

It was obvious too to these early foresters that, once ignited, certain weather elements also control the behavior of the fire apart from its influence on fuel moisture. The two most obvious factors are precipitation and wind.

Weather and climate then affects forest fires in different but related ways: (1) climate determines the total amount of fuel available for combustion; (2) climate determines the length and severity of the fire season; (3) weather regulates the moisture content, and hence flammability, of dead forest fuels; (4) weather has an independent influence on the ignition and spread of forest fires.

## FIRE CLIMATE

It has been noted earlier that climate is related to forest fires in two ways. It determines the length and severity of fire seasons and it determines the amount of forest fuel on an area. Climate is an expression of the weather experienced at a place over the long run. It is expressed usually as averages of the various weather elements and their reduced extremes and is useful in giving a general picture of what might be expected in weather. For example, if one is planning a visit to a different part of the world, it is very useful to know how hot or how cold it might be, how much precipitation to expect, and whether it will be likely dry or damp in order to plan a wardrobe to take. Similarly, a fire management organization can make good use of climatic data for their area to determine average fire occurrence over time on which to base action plans and to obtain a warning on what extremes they should anticipate.

This is usually done with statistical analysis of numbers of fires and areas burned by month. An example of the results of one such analysis is given in Table 3.1. Another approach is to produce a map of the forest fire weather zones such as those of Canada (Figure 3.1), the United States (Figure 3.2), and Australia (Figure 3.3).

Because of differing latitudes, topography, and position relative to large bodies of water, fire climates differ in their severity and occurrence throughout the year. In high latitudes the fire season is usually quite severe, relatively short, and peaks during the summer. As one moves closer to the equator, the fire season tends to be longer in duration until in the general area of the equator it may extend all through the year with, of course, variations as noted resulting from differences in topography and the influence of large bodies of water. As discussed earlier, the various fire climate regions may be delineated on a map as was done by Schroeder and Buck (1970) in Figure 3.2, where they divide the North American continent into 15

Table 3.1. *Fire Distribution by Month, Canada*

| | 1978 | | | | Annual Average 1968–1977 | | | |
|---|---|---|---|---|---|---|---|---|
| Month | Number of Fires | % | Area Burned in Hectares | % | Number of Fires | % | Area Burned in Hectares | % |
| January | 5 | — | 59 | — | 13 | — | 30 | — |
| February | 1 | — | 1 | — | 6 | — | 7 | — |
| March | 66 | 1 | 227 | — | 43 | — | 541 | — |
| April | 461 | 6 | 5,330 | 2 | 651 | 7 | 20,895 | 2 |
| May | 1,555 | 19 | 24,793 | 9 | 2,012 | 23 | 166,202 | 14 |
| June | 1,438 | 18 | 169,025 | 58 | 1,493 | 17 | 438,563 | 38 |
| July | 1,639 | 20 | 70,390 | 24 | 1,906 | 22 | 370,915 | 32 |
| August | 2,173 | 27 | 11,729 | 4 | 1,781 | 21 | 151,172 | 13 |
| September | 398 | 5 | 4,830 | 2 | 507 | 6 | 14,517 | 1 |
| October | 215 | 3 | 1,843 | 1 | 222 | 3 | 4,420 | — |
| November | 97 | 1 | 1,186 | — | 44 | 1 | 1,714 | — |
| December | 1 | — | — | — | 6 | — | 10 | — |
| Total | 8,049 | 100 | 289,413 | 100 | 8,684 | 100 | 1,168,986 | 100 |

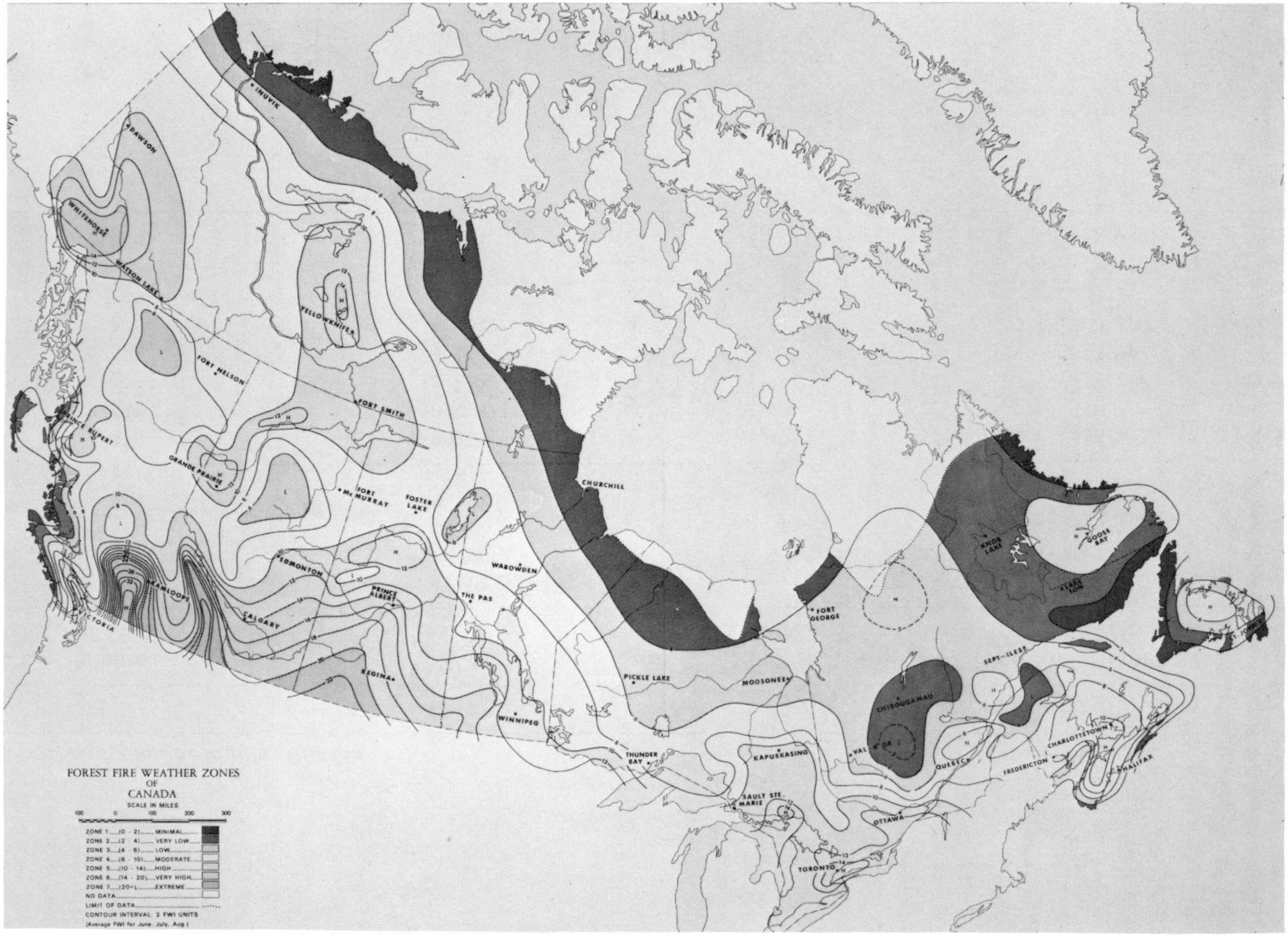

*Figure 3.1.* Forest fire weather zones of Canada.

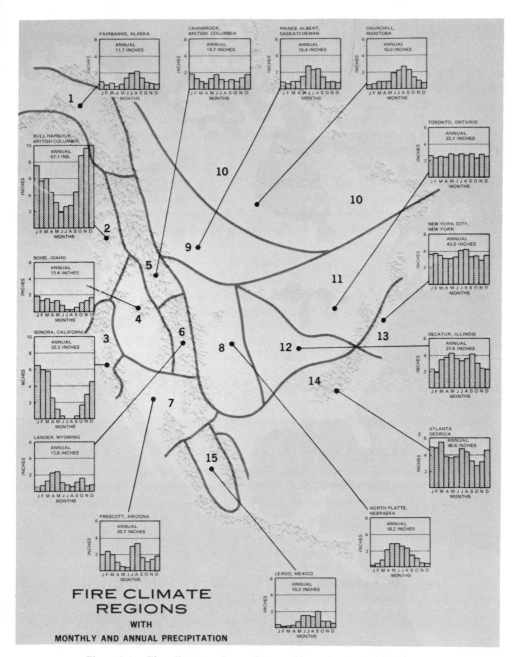

**Figure 3.2.** Fire climate regions with monthly and annual precipitation.

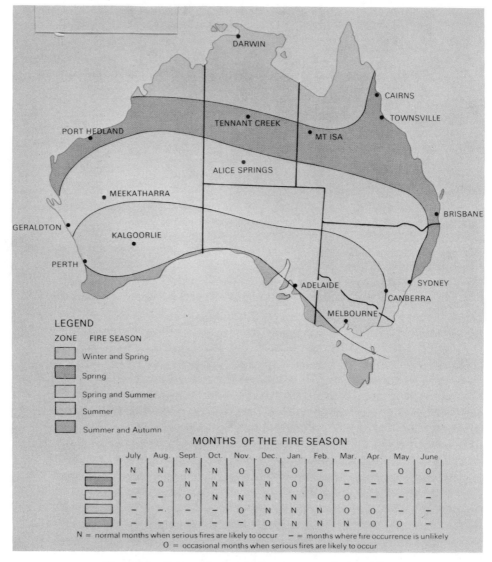

*Figure 3.3.*   Pattern of seasonal fire occurrence in Australia.

fire climate regions based on geographic and climatic factors. In the figure they also show, graphically, monthly and annual precipitation for centers within each region. This, of course, is very useful information since it is important to know not only how much precipitation normally falls in a region but also how it is distributed throughout the year. The authors also give in the handbook a complete description of each region, its general climate and unusual features, as well as the timing of the average fire season. This type of information points out, graphically, the differences between fire climate that can exist from one region to another. For example, the difference between the fire climate of the east and of the west coast of North America is well depicted, particularly with reference to precipitation distribution.

## THE ATMOSPHERE

Before individually considering the various factors of weather that affect forest fires, it would be helpful to take a brief look at the earth's atmosphere—that envelope of air surrounding the earth consisting mainly of nitrogen (78%) and oxygen (21%), and within which a constant energy exchange takes place. The atmosphere is a relatively thin envelope approximately 80 km in depth but, because of the compaction of air (Figure 3.4), the lower layer, called the troposphere, contains 75 percent of the air in the atmosphere and almost all of its moisture. It is within this layer, averaging about 18 km in depth (thinner at the poles and thicker at the equator), that most of the weather activity as we know it takes place. Tremendous amounts of energy are required to generate this activity and it all reaches the troposphere either directly or indirectly from the sun. That portion of the incoming energy absorbed directly by the atmosphere, about 20 percent, is simply taken in mainly by the water vapor in the air, and is utilized in raising the temperature of the gas that absorbed it. Of the remaining incoming solar energy, about 45 percent is reflected back into space and the remaining 55 percent is absorbed by the surface of the earth. These are average figures. Actual values will vary with the amount of cloud in the atmosphere. However, the overall energy exchange is much more complicated than might be assumed from the simple figures given. Part of the complication is introduced because of a well-known phenomenon referred to as the *greenhouse effect* which has a strong influence on the distribution of solar energy in the troposphere. Simply, the greenhouse effect traps solar energy within the troposphere as a result of the air's variability in transmitting energy of different wavelengths. It takes effect in the following way. The sun emits its radiation at very high temperatures (6000°C). Radiation at such temperatures is transmitted through space to the earth's atmosphere mainly in the short wavelength (0.15 to 4 micron) portion of the spectrum. The earth's atmosphere is highly transparent to energy at these wavelengths and it can pass readily (in the absence of clouds, of course) through to the earth's surface. The earth and the objects on its surface, including forest fuels, reradiate energy back through the atmosphere into space. However, they do so at their own temperature which is, of course, much lower than that of the sun and hence at much longer wavelengths (4 to 120 microns). The atmosphere is not very transparent to energy at these longer wavelengths and thus much of it is absorbed and trapped in the atmosphere, mainly in the troposphere

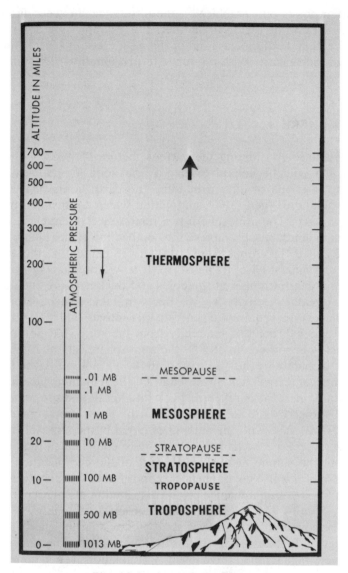

*Figure 3.4.* Atmosphere of the earth.

where most of the air and water vapor is. Therefore, like a greenhouse, the troposphere becomes warmed.

Another complication that enters into the greenhouse picture is introduced by the relationship between energy and water vapor. As was mentioned earlier, the component of the air that absorbs most of this radiated energy is the water vapor and, as a result, the greenhouse effect is more pronounced in moist air than in dry air. This results in the hot day–cold night situation common to deserts and the much less pronounced diurnal variation in regions of high humidity such as the tropics. The relationship between heat energy and moisture is an important one and is discussed again in later sections of this chapter.

## AIR MASSES AND FRONTS

Air masses are bodies of air, usually 1500 km or more across, that have developed uniform characteristics of temperature and moisture because they have remained stationary over part of the earth long enough to have reached equilibrium. Air masses originating over the oceans are designated as (m) for maritime and those over land as (c) for continental. Air masses formed over the cold regions of high latitudes are called (P) for polar and those of the warmer lower latitudes (T) for tropical. Thus we find four basic types of air masses, each with its own characteristics and each with its own associated fire weather. The cP air mass is cold and dry. If it migrates southward, it becomes warmed from below by contact with the land and becomes more unstable with strong daytime convective activity. Continental polar air masses are associated more often with major forest fires than any other type. The cT air mass is hot and dry. Continental tropical air is associated with heat waves, droughts, and low fuel moistures. However, because of its higher temperatures aloft, cT air is more stable than cP and less subject to the gustiness and strong convection that can raise havoc with a firefighter's best laid plans. The mP air mass is cooled from below by contact with the water and, consequently, very stable. There is little convection and thus little moisture exchange between the saturated surface layers and the upper air which may be quite dry. When mP air moves on to a coast, fogs and low stratus clouds develop, but mountainous elevations above the marine inversion may remain dry. Maritime tropical air masses are highly unstable as well as moist and are associated with towering cumulus clouds and thunderstorms.

Because air masses are large and migratory, it is inevitable that they will sometimes meet and interact. Since air masses have different temperatures and moisture contents, they also have different densities and tend not to mix but rather to slide under or over each other. The central portions of air masses tend to have the highest pressures, with pressures falling off toward the edges. Therefore, it follows that the zone where the edges of two air masses meet, called the front or frontal zone, has the lowest pressure with rising pressures on both sides of the front. Inasmuch as the wind blows nearly parallel to the isobars with high pressure on the left (in the northern hemisphere, right in the southern) as one stands facing into the wind, the wind blows from one direction on one side of the front and from a different direction on the other. Frontal wind shifts are of supreme importance to fire behavior because they can quickly turn the long quiet flank of a fire into a raging head.

Fronts are designated by the relative temperature of the air moving into the area. In a cold front, cooler air slides under the warm air mass and the wind shifts sharply—clockwise in the northern hemisphere, counterclockwise in the southern—90 to 135° with strong gusts accompanying the frontal passage. If the warm air being displaced is moist, showers and thunderstorms or even steady rain will precede and accompany the passage of the front, though skies will clear and the air will be drier behind the front. However, if the warm air is dry, the wind shift, gustiness, and reduced humidity that follow the front will be unalleviated by precipitation. The passage of a strong, dry cold front across an uncontrolled forest fire is every firefighter's nightmare.

The leading edge of an advancing warm air mass produces a warm front. Because it is warmer and less dense, the warm air slides over the top of the cold air mass and, cooling as it rises, forms a broad band of cloudiness and, possibly, precipitation ahead of the frontal passage on the ground. The approach of warm fronts is slower than that of cold fronts; the winds accompanying them are not as strong and the wind shift is gradual and only 45 to 90° (in the same direction as that of a cold front). The air behind the warm front is often more moist and always more stable than that it displaces. The warm front is usually the firefighter's friend.

With this general picture of the large scale mechanics of weather and climate we will proceed to examine the individual aspects of weather that most influence fire in the forest.


## TEMPERATURE

As shown in the previous section, the heat energy absorbed by the troposphere, hence its temperature, comes partly by direct short-wave solar radiation but mainly from the heated surface of the earth and objects on it. This heating is extremely important in determining the weather activity taking place within the troposphere—in the development and movement of patterns that result in what we call weather. These large-scale effects are examined in a later section. What we want to look at here are the effects of temperature on a smaller scale, mainly its effect on forest fuels and forest fires. To meteorologists, studies of weather on this scale are termed *micrometeorology*.

The temperature of forest fuels is one of the important factors controlling their susceptibility to ignition and the rate at which they burn. Their temperature is attained by absorption of direct solar radiation and conduction from their surroundings including the air enveloping them. There are a number of different factors that control the amount of solar radiation reaching these fuels. Shielding, either from a cloud cover or from a forest canopy, is one example. Another is the angle at which the radiation strikes the fuel which, in turn, is dependent on the elevation of the sun above the horizon. The nearer to perpendicular the sun's rays, the greater the heating effect; thus the heating is greater at midday than in the morning or evening, and greater in summer than winter. The atmosphere, as mentioned earlier, gains much of its heat from radiation from the earth's surface and, since the air is constantly in motion, there is a continuous exchange of heat between the lower part of the troposphere and the earth's surface. In general, the earth's surface and objects on it have a greater temperature range than the air in contact with them. Consequently, the surface and the layer of air immediately above it are warmer than the upper air layers in the daytime, and cooler than the upper air at night.

Air temperature, then, is one indicator of forest fuel condition and its measurement is included in inputs required for most fire danger rating systems.

Temperature is most conveniently measured by a mercury or alcohol thermometer kept in a standard shelter under standard conditions as described in manuals pertaining to the particular fire danger rating systems in use (e.g., Fischer and Hardy 1976, Williams 1963). It is important to adhere to these standards and avoid as much as possible the variations in air temperature that are caused by bodies of water, different ground surfaces, proximity to buildings or forests, and the like.

In summary, air temperature is a constantly changing factor influencing not only fuel temperature and hence flammability but also other important weather factors as well. One of these is the humidity of the air or the amount of water vapor it contains.

## ATMOSPHERE HUMIDITY

The earth's atmosphere, and particularly the troposphere, always contains a variable amount of water. Even though water vapor represents a maximum of five percent of the earth's atmosphere, it still represents an enormous volume of matter. For example, it has been stated that "the total amount of water vapor that flows across the land in air currents originating over water is estimated to be more than six times the water carried by all our rivers" (Schroeder and Buck op. cit.). This component of the air is very important in many aspects of life on earth. Clouds and precipitation result from the condensation of water vapor in the atmosphere. This water exists in three forms; as water vapor which is an invisible gas and which reacts in the same way as any other gas; as liquid where it takes the form of drops of varying sizes; as a solid in the form of ice crystals which can precipitate as snow, hail, or sleet.

In changing from one form to another, atmospheric moisture either absorbs or releases energy and these changes in energy have a profound effect on weather. For example, in a rainstorm millions of tons of water fall. In condensing from water vapor each of these tons releases close to a half-million kilocalories of energy back into the atmosphere. This energy is then available to heat the air and to produce clouds and thunderstorms with the sometimes violent air movements associated with them.

As we have seen in the chapter on forest fuels, the amount of moisture in any forest fuel is critical in determining the flammability of that fuel. In turn, the amount of moisture in dead forest fuel is highly dependent on the moisture in the atmosphere.

The moisture reaches the fuel either in the form of liquid moisture from precipitation or in the form of water vapor in the air that may condense on the fuel and be absorbed by it. This second action is reversible. That is, moisture may move from the fuel into the air through the process of evaporation. There is, in fact, a continuing exchange of moisture between forest fuels and the air that surrounds them. The direction of the net exchange is dependent on a rather complex set of circumstances of temperature and moisture that exist in the atmosphere and in the fuel.

Temperature is, in effect, a measure of the velocity of molecules within a substance. At a water–air surface, for example, the number of water molecules escaping into the air is dependent on the temperature of the water. The higher the temperature, the greater the speed of the water molecules and thus the greater the number escaping into the air. From this one might say that evaporation is dependent only on the temperature of the water. This is not true because we have considered only one side of the equation. The other side concerns the ability of the air to accept or absorb the escaping molecules. Again, temperature plays an important part in that the ability of the air to absorb moisture depends heavily on its temperature. The warmer the air, the more moisture it can absorb before becoming saturated. Now if we were to move saturated air over the water surface discussed, it would not be able to accept the water molecules escaping from the water and, although this would not prevent them from escaping, an equal number of molecules would be moving from the air to the water through the process called condensation.

In this way both processes, evaporation and condensation, can and do occur in nature at the same time. However, since we are usually concerned with the changes taking place, we look for the net effect. In the situation just described, saturated air over a warm water surface, the net effect is zero. Neither the air nor the water is changing. If we were to substitute unsaturated air in our example, the *net* effect would be evaporation. The air would gain moisture and the water should lose some moisture. On the other hand, if we were to go back to our saturated air and lower the temperature of the water, the *net* effect would be condensation. The air would lose moisture to the water.

There are other factors further complicating the moisture exchange process. We discussed moving the saturated air and replacing it with less saturated, or drier, air. This, of course, does occur in nature. Wind moves the air over the water surface, for example, and if the air is unsaturated, it will continue to absorb the evaporated moisture provided the air moves fast enough to prevent its becoming saturated. The wind plays the role of transporting the moist air away and replacing it with drier air. The process might be compared to a freight train of partly filled grain cars moving under a loading chute. If the train moves too slowly, the cars will fill up and be unable to carry off as much grain as is being fed to them. However, once the train reaches a speed at which the cars will not become filled, it is able to carry away all the grain and an increase in speed will not change its ability to do so; similarly, with the wind effect on evaporation. It is very important that there is some air movement but the importance of wind velocity diminishes once the critical velocity has been reached.

Another complicating factor influencing moisture exchange is atmospheric pressure, although it has a much lesser influence than temperature or wind. Essentially, the lower the atmospheric pressure, the less the air's ability to hold moisture. This factor is not significant with the pressure changes that normally take place in the lower atmosphere but does have some significance when we consider the pressure change that takes place with changing altitude. This is considered in the discussion of atmospheric stability.

## MEASURING HUMIDITY

Humidity, that is, the amount of moisture in the atmosphere, can be measured in a number of different ways. Absolute humidity, as the term implies, is a measure of the amount of water in a certain volume of air, usually expressed in grams per cubic meter. A related term, absolute humidity at saturation, indicates the weight of water that the same parcel of air will contain when it is fully saturated. As noted earlier, the amount of water air can hold is dependent on its temperature. Thus there is a value of absolute humidity at saturation for each temperature (Table 3.2). However, the ability of the air to lower the moisture content of forest fuels, a most important factor in forest fire weather, is best expressed by a measure known as relative humidity. Relative humidity is the expression in percent of the amount of moisture in the air as a ratio of the maximum amount that could be held at that particular temperature and atmospheric pressure. It gives in one figure the drying or wetting ability of a certain parcel of air and, for this reason, is the measure most used in fire weather and fire danger measurement.

A third measurement of air moisture is the dew point. Since all air has some moisture in it and since we have shown that as that air becomes cooler it is able to hold less and less moisture, it follows that if the air parcel continues to cool, it will reach a temperature at which the water contained in it becomes the maximum amount it can hold. This, in fact, happens in nature. When it does, the air is said to be saturated and the temperature at

*Table 3.2.  Dew Point, Vapor Pressure, and Absolute Humidity*

| Dew Point (Temperature) °C | Vapor Pressure (Saturation) mm of Hg | Absolute Humidity (Saturation) gm/m³ |
|---|---|---|
| −40 | 0.15 | 0.18 |
| −30 | 0.37 | 0.44 |
| −20 | 0.9 | 1.07 |
| −10 | 2.2 | 2.4 |
| 0 | 4.6 | 4.8 |
| 10 | 9.2 | 9.4 |
| 20 | 17.8 | 17.2 |
| 30 | 32.5 | 30.5 |
| 40 | 56.1 | 52.0 |
| 50 | 92.2 | 88.0 |

which this occurs is known as the dew point. This name comes from the fact that if the air continues to cool below this temperature, some of the moisture must condense out. If this occurs with air in contact with cool ground or objects on it, dew forms. There are, as might be expected, direct relationships between these different measures of atmospheric humidity. For example, when air is saturated, its temperature is the dew point temperature, its relative humidity is 100 percent, and its absolute humidity is the absolute humidity at saturation for that temperature and pressure. For a more detailed explanation of these relationships the reader is referred to Countryman (1971).

There is another aspect of air humidity and its saturation in particular that is important in fire weather. This is its role in the formation of cloud and fog. They are essentially the same thing but form in a somewhat different way. Both result from oversaturated air, but air can reach that state in the following basic ways. First, air can absorb moisture by evaporation until it reaches its saturation point. In nature this commonly happens to air lying immediately over a water surface. If this air then moves over a land mass that is cooler than the air, the air cools below the dew point and the excess moisture condenses out as fog or low cloud. This is a common occurrence along sea coasts and on the leeward side of large lakes, and thereby influences the fire climate and fire danger in those areas.

The second way in which condensation commonly takes place is through the process of cooling by lifting. Most clouds, including thunderstorms, form in this way and the process is known as adiabatic cooling. There are several basic ways in which air is forced to rise in the atmosphere. One is thermal lifting where local heating of the earth's surface in turn heats the air in contact with it. The warm air, being more buoyant than the surrounding cooler air, will rise. Second, air moving as a wind is forced to rise over mountains and higher land masses. This is called orographic lifting. Third, where cold and warm air masses meet, known as a front, the warmer air, again being more buoyant, is lifted and this is called frontal lifting. All three processes occur regularly in the atmosphere, continually resulting in clouds and precipitation wherever the lifting is sufficient to cool the air below its saturation point.

**Humidity Measuring Instruments**

There are several different instruments for measuring atmospheric humidity based on various physical principles. The type of instrument most commonly used in fire weather measurement is the psychrometer and a more portable variation, the sling psychrometer. A psychrometer consists of a pair of thermometers, one of which measures air temperature in the normal way, whereas the other has its bulb covered by an absorbent cloth wick which, during measurements, is kept wet. When the relative humidity of the air is less than 100 percent, the *wet bulb* is cooled by evaporation to a temperature that is dependent on the evaporative power of the air or, in other words, its relative humidity. The difference between the dry and wet-bulb temperatures, known as the wet-bulb depression, can be applied in an equation to determine the relative humidity of the air. The calculation need not be used, however, inasmuch as tables, slide rules, and computer programs have been produced from which the relative humidity can be read once the two temperature measurements have been obtained. Since, as we have noted earlier, the relationship changes with pressure, which may also be expressed as altitude, different tables are required for various altitudes.

The ordinary psychrometer is usually mounted in an instrument shelter where it is shaded from the sun yet exposed to air movement. This is important inasmuch as an accurate measurement of relative humidity can be obtained only if the thermometers are in the shade and the wet bulb is ventilated. For this reason, when a psychrometer is used, the wet bulb must be fanned before a reading is made. Psychrometers known as aspirated psychrometers are available. These instruments are equipped with mechanically or electrically driven fans to ensure that the optimum amount of air flows past the wet bulb.

They and the sling psychrometer have the advantage of being portable. The latter, in particular, is often used in field locations and on the fire line. It is a special form of wet and dry-bulb psychrometer where the thermometers are set in a frame attached to a swivel handle. Readings are made by first wetting the wick on the wet-bulb thermometer and then whirling the instrument briskly (about 200 revolutions per minute) in a shaded spot and observing, as before, the readings of the two thermometers. Again, readings should be made in the shade or if none is available, in the shade of the observer's body. The instrument should be whirled and observations noted until there

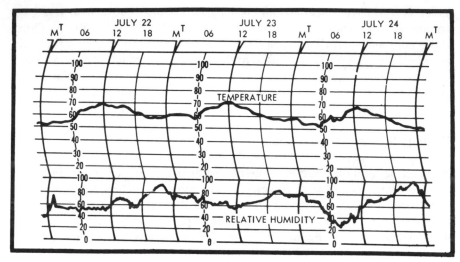

***Figure 3.5.***    Typical temperature and relative humidity traces from a hygrothermograph chart.

is no change in the readings. In using this instrument, the observer should be careful not to strike it on any object and must ensure that the wick is kept wet throughout the observations.

Humidity may also be measured by a recording instrument, the hygrograph or, more currently, by an instrument that records both humidity and temperature, the hygrothermograph. This instrument provides a continuous record of relative humidity and temperature on a chart mounted on a clockwork-driven drum. In the hygrograph relative humidity is determined by a different principle than we have discussed before. This principle is that certain filaments, including human hair, change in length in response to changes in relative humidity in close to a linear relationship. Thus by placing such a filament under a certain tension and attaching one end to a lever which is, in turn, attached to a pen arm, it is possible to record the change in filament length, and thus the relative humidity and its changes on a chart. A typical chart is shown in Figure 3.5.

Other humidity-measuring instruments commonly used in remote-reporting weather stations or upper-air soundings use moisture sensors that are based on relationships between humidity and the chemical or electrical characteristics of sensor elements. The use of remote-reporting weather stations in forest fire weather measurement is dealt with in a later section.

## CLOUDS AND PRECIPITATION

As discussed under the section on humidity, clouds normally form in the atmosphere when air containing water vapor (as all air does) is lifted thermally, orographically, or frontally to a height where it reaches saturation. Clouds form by processes called condensation and sublimation. Condensation, as when steam forms over a kettle, is the change in state of the gas water vapor to liquid water, whereas sublimation is the change of the gas to solid ice. Although we say that these changes occur at certain temperatures, in fact, another factor is required to trigger the change. This factor is the presence of particles in the air that act as condensation nuclei or sublimation nuclei depending on the change taking place. These particles can be any small foreign objects commonly found in the air such as dust, salt, or smoke particles, and they simply provide a surface to which the water molecules may cling. Most nuclei are hygroscopic and begin to absorb moisture at relative humidities below 100 percent. As condensation proceeds, small chaplets are formed and these increase in size until they reach about 1 mm in diameter. Larger drops cannot develop from condensation alone and, since chaplets are not large enough or heavy enough to produce precipitation, a large proportion of clouds formed do not precipitate. Thus some other process must take place in the cloud to cause these very small condensation droplets to cluster together to form drops large enough to fall as precipitation. One such process occurs when the cloud is a few degrees below the freezing temperature. In such clouds it is common to find both water droplets, called supercooled since they continue to exist as a liquid even though their temperature is below freezing, and ice crystals. Inasmuch as there is a difference between water vapor pressure and ice vapor pressure at the same temperature, water molecules tend to be drawn to the ice crystals and the latter will proceed to grow in size until they are large enough to fall as snow or, if they fall into a warmer temperature, melt and continue to fall as rain. A second process forming precipitation is coalescence where, as droplets move about in a cloud, they collide and join together to form larger drops and so on until the drops are large enough to fall as rain. Combinations of these two processes result in the different familiar forms of precipitation such as sleet, hail, snow pellets, and large snowflakes.

## Kinds of Clouds

Clouds, from ancient times, have been classified and named by their appearance and by how high they are. There are many different types and subtypes but there are really four basic classes: low, middle, high, and thunderstorm clouds that have considerable vertical development.

Since there are many excellent cloud atlases with color photographs depicting the many different types of clouds (e.g., Schaefer and Day 1981), and since good photographs are able to describe the special characteristics of the clouds much better than words, we refer the reader to one of these atlases and confine ourselves to a general description.

Low clouds are layer clouds with their base within about 2000 m of the earth's surface. The most common is the stratus cloud which is a thin layer

100 to 1000 m thick resembling fog but is, in reality, a cloud formed near the surface of the ground by advection of cold moist air.

Middle clouds, designated by the prefix "alto," are clouds having their bases at altitudes varying from about 2000 to about 5000 m. The most common types in this class are altostratus and altocumulus. Altostratus appears as a high mist or film, whereas altocumulus is broken up into cloudlets or ridges having a wave pattern.

High clouds, designated by the prefix "cirro," have their bases between 5000 and 15,000 m. Because they are so high they are usually made up of ice crystals. They are thin wispy clouds sometimes forming as a thin veil over the whole sky (cirrostratus), or as small cloudlets (cirrocumulus) that may form in ripples across the sky.

The fourth type of clouds is those having significant depth or vertical development. They are known as cumulus clouds or, when fully developed, cumulonimbus, and are often formed by convective lifting during warm weather and so are often associated with fire behavior. In fact, cumulus clouds have been observed to form over large forest fires atop the convection column produced by the fire. Cumulus clouds are significant to forest fire weather in that they are indicative of air turbulence and instability.

As noted, the fully developed cumulus cloud is the well-known thunderhead or cumulonimbus that commonly produces lightning, rain, hail, and strong winds or even tornados. They have extensive vertical development, up to 20,000 m or more, and represent a tremendous concentration of energy. Some of this energy is converted to electric discharges or lightning, nature's primary forest fire ignition source.

## LIGHTNING

The atmosphere during clear weather exhibits a positive electrical charge in relation to the earth's surface with an upward gradient of about 100 volts per meter. When a cumulus cloud begins to build up within this gradient, it upsets this normal gradient, possibly through the updrafts and downdrafts that form in the cloud. All the causes of these changes are not well understood, but they result in a build-up of negative charge in the base of the cloud and positive charge near the top. As the cloud develops, the negative charge at the cloud base induces a positive charge on the surface of the earth beneath the cloud and on all objects in contact with the earth. When the potential difference between the cloud and the earth is sufficient to produce a cloud-to-ground stroke, an initiating stroke, called a stepped leader, begins in the cloud and moves downward in a zig-zag path until it reaches the earth. At this point a number of strong return strokes or pulses flash back up the path created by the stepped leader (Figure 3.6). The strength and duration of these return strokes are factors determining whether the stroke will cause a fire in the forest. The other important factors are the dryness and flammabil-

**Figure 3.6.** Lightning is a frequent forest visitor in many fire climates. Photo by Project Skyfire, U.S. Forest Service.

ity of the tree or other object "struck" by the lightning stroke (Figure 3.7). Several types of lightning counters or detectors have been developed to assist fire control agencies to determine where lightning is occurring in their regions. These are more fully discussed in the section on applications of fire weather later in this chapter.

Cloud-to-ground lightning represents only one-quarter to one-third of all lightning strokes in a cumulonimbus cloud but they are the only ones that matter to the forest firefighter. Other strokes within a cloud or from one cloud to another result from other differences in electrical potential within and between clouds. Instruments have been developed that register only cloud-to-ground strokes and can thus pinpoint strikes that are likely to cause fires.

## WIND

Wind is one of the most variable and most important of the weather factors influencing forest fires. It acts in several ways. As we have seen earlier, it assists in drying fuel by providing the means of carrying off the evaporated moisture. Wind also supports and increases combustion by ensuring a continued supply of air, by increasing radiation through the tilting of flames toward unburned fuel in advance of the flame front, and by carrying burning embers to ignite spot fires ahead of the main fire. Since wind direction and speed are paramount in determining how quickly a fire will spread and what direction it will take, they are obviously very important factors to consider

***Figure 3.7.***    Lightning can start fires in green trees as well as snags. Photo by Project Skyfire, U.S. Forest Service.

in both the control of wildfires and in the planning and conduct of a pre-scribed burn. Like many of the other weather factors we have examined, wind is the result of a series of complex forces that are constantly active in the air around us.

The atmosphere, being mainly a gas, is highly fluid and in constant motion about the earth. It has mass, however, and thus is affected by gravity and by the heating of the earth's surface. In very general terms, since the earth is hot at the equator and cold at the poles, there is a general rising of air at the equator and a subsiding at the poles. If the earth were stationary, this simple convective pattern would, no doubt, prevail but because of the rotation of the earth the air flowing toward or away from the pole tends to curve toward the right in the northern hemisphere and toward the left in the southern hemisphere in response to what is known as the Coriolis force. As air in

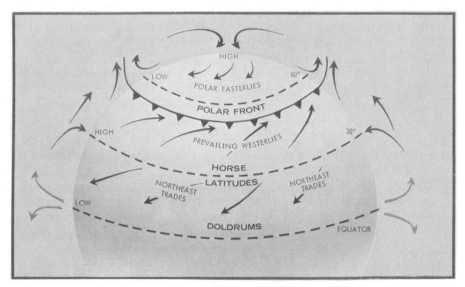

*Figure 3.8.* On a rotating earth with a uniform surface, the general circulation of the Northern Hemisphere would be composed of the northeast trade winds, prevailing westerlies, and polar easterlies.

Canada flows south, for example, the earth rotates under it so that its path, in relation to the earth, becomes curved toward the right and the flow becomes an easterly wind. This complicating factor combined with changes in pressure and exchanges of heat that occur simultaneously result in general air movement patterns (Figure 3.8) made up of, in the northern hemisphere, polar easterlies, prevailing westerlies, northeast trades, and areas of low wind activity known as the doldrums and the horse latitudes.

These are the general wind patterns but secondary patterns are superimposed on these broader patterns. They are caused by high and low pressure systems that develop in the atmosphere because of unequal heating mainly between water and land. A high pressure area may be considered as a dome of air where for various reasons air has "piled up," whereas a low pressure area may be thought of as a depression in the atmosphere. In each case, the pressure is an expression of the weight of air above a point on the earth's surface. Since nature deplores an imbalance, air tends to flow from a high to a low pressure area but, because of the various forces acting on the air including the Coriolis force, the wind in the northern hemisphere tends to spiral in a clockwise direction out from a high and spiral in a counterclockwise direction into a low. These vectors are reversed in the southern hemisphere.

High pressure areas tend to be relatively stationary, remaining for days or even weeks over the same area of land or ocean. During this time the air tends to take on the characteristics of the surface on which it rests—hot or

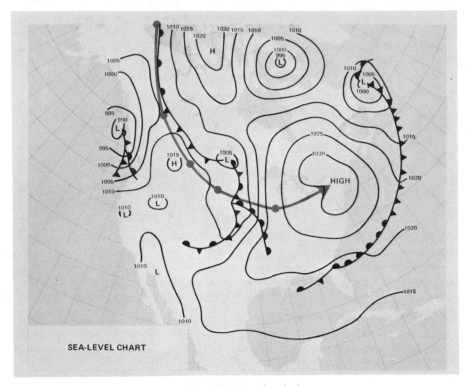

*Figure 3.9.*  Northern hemisphere.

cold, moist or dry. These stationary high pressure areas develop the air masses already discussed. When the high pressure cell does begin to move, it brings its characteristic mass of air with it.

If points having equal air pressure readings are joined by lines or isobars, as they are called, the high and low pressure systems can be drawn on a map. Weather maps are one of the main tools of the meteorologist. Figure 3.9 shows a typical fire season pattern in the northern hemisphere and Figure 3.10 one for the southern hemisphere. Some of the high and low pressure areas are relatively stationary like those shown in Figure 3.11, and result from the effect of large bodies of water or land. Other high and low systems move continually and these form the systems that result in rapidly changing weather. Fronts are shown on the weather map as broad lines with triangles designating cold fronts and semicircles warm fronts pointing in the direction toward which the front is moving. It is through the plotting and prediction of the movement of these systems that meteorologists predict wind velocities, directions, and changes in temperature and humidity that are so important in fire control.

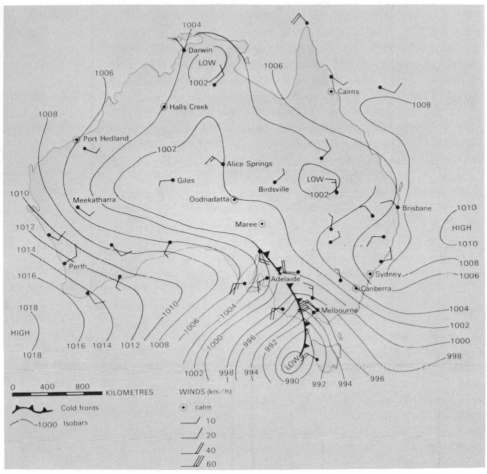

***Figure 3.10.***   Southern hemisphere.

## Wind Profiles

Most of the winds we consider as influencing forest fires are so-called *surface winds*—the winds we normally measure with handheld anemometers or those mounted on the tops of buildings or masts at forestry and airport weather stations. These are the winds normally used in describing weather and the climate of an area. In fact, winds generally change both speed and direction with height above ground. Where the atmosphere is well mixed, windspeed usually increases with altitude. The reason for this is relatively simple. In the upper troposphere the winds are free to move under the influence of pressure systems, whereas winds near the ground are interfered with and held back by ground obstructions such as mountains, buildings,

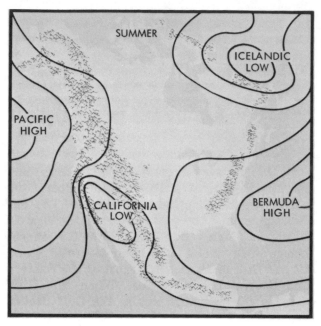

***Figure 3.11.*** Average July sea-level pressure pattern.

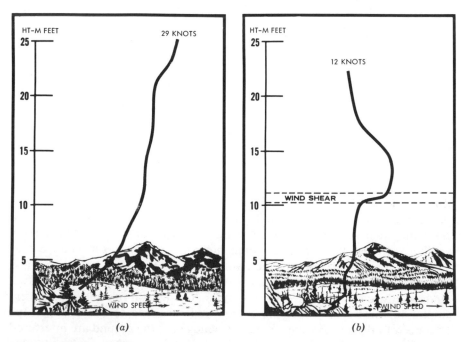

***Figure 3.12.*** Typical wind profiles. (*a*) In a well mixed atmosphere. (*b*) In an atmosphere with marked wind shear.

trees, or even low brush and grass. The depth of this influence is, of course, dependent on the height of the obstructions, and the layer of the atmosphere so influenced is called the friction or mixing layer. Winds above this layer are more consistent in speed and direction. However, where the atmosphere is not well mixed and is stratified into different layers, it is common to find different windspeeds and directions within the different layers, thus the fairly common sight of clouds at different levels traveling in different directions. When the varying windspeeds and directions are plotted against height above ground, the result is known as a *wind profile* (Figure 3.12). These wind profiles give an indication of how a convection column may form over a forest fire. A strong convection column is more likely to develop if the wind profile shows a *normal* increase in velocity with height above ground.

**Convective Winds**

Unless the general circulation produces winds of at least 5 to 10 m/sec at the 850 millibar level, they will have little or no effect at the surface and the winds on a fire will be of local origin (Ryan 1977).

If an area is not strongly influenced by general winds, local winds can be caused in a number of different ways. A common cause of such local winds is differential heating of the earth's surface. Where strong heating occurs, the air above that surface is warmed and, becoming buoyant, rises either up a slope or, over flat ground, as a bubble of air and if it is moist enough and rises high enough, as we have seen earlier, cumulus clouds may form. On occasion, the heated air may rise in a spiral motion producing whirlwinds. Where air is cooled over a cold ground surface, however, it tends to flow, like water, down any slope and pool in low areas.

A special type of convective wind is seen in the sea breeze and the land breeze. These air movements are experienced along the shores of large bodies of water. The flow is toward the land during the day, a sea breeze, and toward the water at night, a land breeze. The reason is that during the day the land surface becomes warmer than the water surface, usually by late morning, and as it becomes less dense it rises and is replaced by cooler air moving in from the water. At night the opposite effect takes place as the land surface cools more quickly than the water surface and cooled air flows from the land out over the water creating a land breeze. A land breeze usually begins several hours after sunset and ends just after sunrise when the land surface begins to warm up again. The intensity of sea and land breezes and their predictability depend on a number of factors. First, since they depend on a heating differential between the land and the water, general water temperatures and the ability of the land surface to absorb heat are important factors. Secondly, since these breezes are not generally strong, usually not more than 5 or 6 m/sec, they are frequently overpowered by general winds. However, in areas influenced by sea and land breezes, they can be important in forest fire control not only because of the predictability of wind shifts at specific times during the day, but also because some sea breezes as they move inland create turbulence at the interface with warmer air and this turbulence can create unusual fire behavior.

### Slope Winds

Another form of convective wind is the slope wind. During the day as the surface of a slope warms, the warmed air flows upslope; during the night as the surface cools, the cooled air flows down the slope. Since most sloped surfaces in nature are not perfectly flat but contain ridges and hollows, ravines, and the like, slope winds tend to follow the natural paths created by these irregularities. The cool air producing downslope winds at night, for example, may be likened to water flowing down through the drainage patterns of the surface and often pooling in the valleys, tending to gradually fill them during the night. As with sea and land breezes, slope wind intensities and predictability depend on local conditions and the influence of general winds, and a knowledge of their occurrence can be of considerable benefit when dealing with forest fires in hilly and mountainous terrain.

Wind, then, along with temperature, humidity, and precipitation is one of the major weather elements that strongly influences the ability of forest fuels to ignite and sustain combustion, and also fire behavior when these fuels have been ignited. The firefighter should be constantly aware of the winds in the vicinity of the fire. If an anemometer is not available, wind velocities in the forest can be estimated by observing the surroundings as shown in Table 3.3.

### ATMOSPHERIC STABILITY

Atmospheric stability is the measure of the tendency of the atmosphere to suppress or encourage vertical motion. It is easy to understand how the horizontal component of air movement (wind) affects a forest fire inasmuch as it is the only component that the earthbound firefighter can see and feel directly. However, the vertical component of air movement is equally important to forest fire behavior and good fire management requires a comprehensive understanding of atmospheric stability.

Consider a parcel of air encased in an infinitely expandable membrane. Since air pressure at any point above the surface of the earth represents the weight of air above that point, it follows that air pressure decreases with altitude. Air is a compressible fluid and expands and contracts in response to the pressure acting on it. Air follows the universal gas law that states that for any perfect gas the product of pressure, volume, and the reciprocal of the temperature is a constant. If we move our parcel of air upward in the atmosphere, the pressure on the parcel decreases and the air inside the parcel expands. This expansion requires energy that is obtained from the heat

*Table 3.3.   Modified Beaufort Scale for Estimating Windspeed*

| Wind Class | Range of Speeds m/s | Nomenclature |
|---|---|---|
| 1 | 0–1.5 | Very Light—Smoke rises nearly vertically. Leaves of quaking aspen in constant motion; small branches of bushes sway; slender branchlets and twigs of trees move gently; tall grasses and reeds sway and bend with wind; wind vane barely moves. |
| 2 | 1.5–3 | Light—Trees of pole size in the open sway gently; wind felt distinctly on face; loose scraps of paper move; wind flutters small flag. |
| 3 | 3–5 | Gentle Breeze—Trees of pole size in open sway very noticeably; large branches of pole size trees in the open toss; tops of trees in dense stands sway; wind extends small flag; a few crested waves form on lakes. |
| 4 | 5–8 | Moderate Breeze—Trees of pole size in the open sway violently; whole trees in dense stands sway noticeably; dust is raised in the road. |
| 5 | 8–11 | Fresh—Branchlets are broken from trees; inconvenience is felt in walking against wind. |
| 6 | 11–14 | Strong—Tree damage increases with occasional breaking of exposed tops and branches; progress impeded when walking against wind; light structural damage to buildings. |
| 7 | 14–17 | Moderate Gale—Severe damage to tree tops; very difficult to walk into wind; significant structural damage occurs. |
| 8 | 17 | Fresh Gale—Intense stress on all exposed objects, vegetation, buildings; canopy offers virtually no protection; wind flow is systematic in disturbing everything in its path. |

energy of the air within the membrane. Conversely, if the parcel of air is lowered in the atmosphere, the air pressure on the membrane increases and the air inside the parcel contracts. The energy for contraction has come from the outside air pressure rather than from the air within the parcel. Inasmuch as the energy level of the parcel has changed, its temperature will change. These temperature changes will occur even if no *heat* energy is gained or lost from the parcel itself by conduction, radiation, or convection. When temperature is changed without the gain or loss of heat, the process is called *adiabatic cooling* or *adiabatic heating*. When dry air rises or descends in the

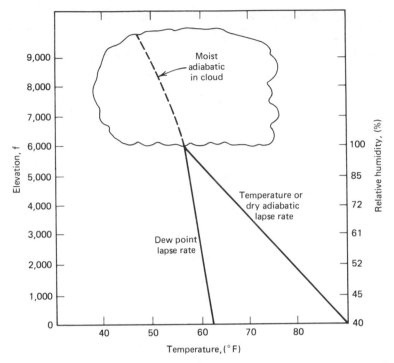

***Figure 3.13.*** Temperature lapse rates and humidity increase in a rising column of air.

atmosphere, the rate of adiabatic change is constant: 1°C for every 100 m change in altitude—cooling going up, warming coming down.

When the air contains moisture, and all air in nature does, the process is not quite so simple. When air is cooled to its dew point temperature, some water vapor will condense, releasing latent heat of condensation and partially offsetting the cooling due to adiabatic expansion. Similarly, when air is warmed above its dew point temperature, the free water droplets evaporate. This requires heat and reduces the temperature change that would occur under adiabatic compression. These changes that occur when air is saturated are not constant like the dry adiabatic rate, but vary according to the temperature and pressure of the air in the saturated parcel. The average value at the temperatures and pressures of most interest in forest fire management are about half that of the dry adiabatic rate or 0.5°C per 100 m (Figure 3.13).

A further complication occurs if we lift a parcel of air high enough that some water vapor not only condenses into fog droplets, but becomes dense enough to precipitate out of the parcel as rain or snow. Then if we bring the parcel back to the surface again, it will arrive both drier and warmer than when it left.

To illustrate the adiabatic processes, let us look at what happens when a parcel of air blown onshore from the ocean is lofted over a 2000 m range of mountains and down into a valley at sea level on the other side. Assume our parcel over the ocean to be at 25°C with a relative humidity of 50 percent and a dew point temperature of 14°C. As the air is pushed up the mountain slope the pressure drops, the parcel expands, and being unsaturated, its temperature drops at the dry adiabatic rate of 1°C/100 m. Since the volume of the parcel gets larger as it expands while the amount of water vapor within it is constant, the absolute humidity decreases and so does the dew point temperature. However, the dew point temperature falls more slowly than the adiabatic rate, in this instance 0.2°C/100 m. Therefore, at 200 m elevation the air temperature is 23°C and the dew point temperature is 13.6°C. At 1375 m the air temperature and the dew point temperature are both 11.25°C, the parcel is saturated, clouds begin to form, and the parcel now begins to cool at the moist adiabatic rate, in this instance 0.5°C/100 m. At the 2000 m summit the air is still saturated and has cooled to nearly 8°C but all the condensed water has been removed as precipitation or by canopy interception. As it starts down the other side, the air is compressed by the surrounding atmosphere and warms at the dry adiabatic rate of 1°/100m and arrives at the valley floor with a temperature of 28°C. Because of the water lost during the ascent, the dew point temperature has been lowered to 12°C and the relative humidity of the air is only 36 percent when it reaches the valley.

To assist in making these calculations, most meteorologists and fire behavior specialists rely on the adiabatic chart which presents the various temperature–pressure–moisture relationships of the atmosphere in graphic form. Adiabatic charts come in various formats and are readily available in most countries through the aircraft weather service. The serious student of fire behavior should obtain a supply of adiabatic charts and become thoroughly familiar with their use.

All the foregoing discussion has dealt with parcels of air as they are moved upward or downward through an already established atmosphere. This happens regularly in nature as evidenced by thermal cells, clouds, and, of course, the convection columns of forest fires which are discussed in detail in the section on large fire behavior. However, so far we have not discussed the properties of the atmosphere through which these parcels of air are moving. The properties of the surrounding air are also important in determining vertical motions.

The actual vertical temperature structure of the air at any given time does not follow the adiabatic lapse rate. In fact, the temperature may even increase with height rather than decrease. There are several reasons for this, the principal one being that the atmosphere gains and loses heat from a number of conductive, radiative, and convective sources and is, therefore, nonadiabatic. Then varying windspeeds and directions at different heights move air from different source regions in and out of a particular area. Frontal surfaces cause severe vertical discontinuities in the temperature profile. Figure 3.14 shows the actual temperature profiles measured during two large forest fires.

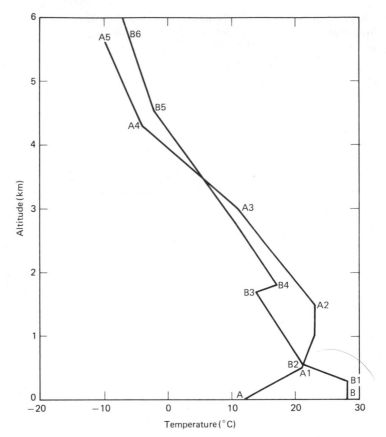

*Figure 3.14.*  Examples of atmospheric temperature profiles.

    Looking at these profiles, let us see what happens when a parcel of air or a
puff of smoke from a forest fire moves through any of the layers shown on
the profiles. First let us move a parcel of air along profile A from the surface
to 500 m. The air in the parcel starts at 12°C and, if it is not saturated, will
cool at the dry adiabatic rate of 1°C/100 m and arrive at the 500 m mark with
a temperature of 7°C. However, the air in the atmosphere around the parcel
has become warmer with height and at 500 m the ambient temperature is
21°C. The air in the parcel is 14°C colder than the air around it and thus
considerably denser. Unless supported mechanically, the parcel will tend to
sink back to its original location. The increase of temperature with height is
called an inversion because it is the inverse of the normal temperature–
height relationship. An inversion layer inhibits vertical motion and conditions are very stable within the layer. Inversion layers are characterized by
their depth and by their lapse rate (strength). An increase of less than 1°C/
100 m is called weak; one between 1 and 2.5°C/100 m is called strong; one

above 2.5°C, very strong. Inversion layers are most commonly formed on clear nights when the air in contact with the earth is cooled by conduction while the air at some distance above remains warm. This is why winds are generally lower and less gusty at night and is one of the reasons why forest fires tend to burn less vigorously at such times.

The layer of air in profile B, from point B to point B1, is called isothermal because the temperature remains the same at all heights. Isothermal layers are stable, the same as inversions, inasmuch as air displaced upward will be colder than the air around it and air displaced downward will be warmer.

The layers from A4 to A5 and B5 to B6 get cooler with height: 6°C in 1300 m for A3 to A5, and 5°C in 1500 m for B5 to B6. These layers too are stable since their lapse rates of 0.46 and 0.33°C/100 m, respectively, are both smaller than either the dry adiabatic rate of 1°C/100 m or the moist rate of 0.5°C/100 m. Within these layers all vertical motion will be damped, but not nearly so strongly as in an inversion.

The very deep layer from B4 to B5 has a temperature drop of 19°C in 2700 meters or 0.7°/100 m. This is a very common lapse rate in the upper atmosphere. The rate is less than dry adiabatic and thus resists vertical motion of unsaturated air, but greater than the moist adiabatic and thus accelerates the motion of saturated air. Once clouds begin to form they will continue to build until they reach the top of the conditionally unstable layer.

From A3 to A4 the lapse rate is 15°C in 1300 m or 1.2°/100 m, greater than either the dry or moist adiabatic rates. Any layer with a lapse rate greater than the dry adiabatic is absolutely unstable in that any parcel set in vertical motion will accelerate in its ascent or descent. Absolute instability means that vertical movement will accelerate but it does not mean that such motion will start automatically. In order for a parcel of air to initiate its own motion without an external force acting on it, the actual density of the parcel, not just its change in density with expansion or compression, must be less than the air around it. In order for air to have a positive density gradient, the lapse rate must exceed 3.5°C/100 m. This never occurs in nature except in tornados, and in a thin layer over intensely heated surfaces on calm days. The 3.5°C lapse rate is called autoconvective and is never exceeded in nature. Even over forest fires, where flame temperatures may exceed 1000°C, a good first approximation of convection column rise can be obtained by raising the ambient surface temperature 3.5°C and tracking a parcel of that temperature dry adiabatically until it intersects the sounding. This procedure, for example, predicts that the column from a fire at point B will rise above the isothermal layer at B1 (which it did) but will not penetrate the inversion layer B3 to B4 (which it did not).

Unstable atmospheres are associated with good visibility, gusty winds, turbulence, "bumpy" flying, dust devils, and strong convective activity with increased chances of short and moderate range spot fires and fire whirlwinds. Stable atmospheres are marked by haze layers, smooth flying, steady winds, and reduced fire convective activity but with chances of long range spotting under special circumstances. The effects of atmospheric stability on forest fire behavior are discussed in more depth in Chapter 4.

## FIRE WEATHER SERVICES

Because accurate weather forecasts are so crucial to successful forest fire control, most countries with severe forest fire problems have developed specialized meteorological services to assist the forestry agencies.

In the United States, the National Weather Service of the Department of Commerce provides fire weather forecasts and meteorological assistance on wildfires under the direction of a Federal Plan for a National Fire Weather Service. Under the plan, 1100 fire weather observing stations operated by federal, state, and private forestry organizations in forested areas report weather elements daily. These readings are used by fire weather forecasters in 44 offices around the country to prepare short and long-term forecasts and warnings of unusually high fire danger. The Fire Weather Service also operates 21 truck-mounted mobile weather stations that are deployed at major forest fires to provide on-the-spot forecasts and assistance.

In Canada, a special fire weather forecasting service is provided to forest fire control agencies by the Atmospheric Environment Service of Environment Canada. In addition to forecasts of weather elements of particular interest to fire officials, the Service also provides, if requested, daily Fire Weather Index (FWI) values as well as forecast FWI values for agency fire centers across Canada. They will also supply on-site consultation and field operations on large fires. These services are provided from a number of regional offices across Canada through an agreement reached between the Service and the requesting fire control agency prior to the beginning of the fire season. Monitoring of the Service is done by regional committees and national policies, standards, and levels of service are reviewed by a national steering committee with representatives of the Atmospheric Environment Service and the Canadian Forestry Service. In most regions, current and forecast FWI values are made available to local and national media for broadcasting to the public where they become a regular part of the radio and television weather forecasts during the fire season.

In the USSR, there is a large network of meteorological stations operated by the Hydrological-Meteorological Service with which the Forest Service negotiates an annual contract to supply the meteorological information needed for forest fire management. Each morning during fire season the Hydro-Met Service also supplies satellite imagery, 24-hour forecasts, and long-term forecasts and calculates the forecast fire danger indices for each district station. It is reported (Kourtz 1973) that many of the meteorological states are electronic remote-reporting stations.

In the Mediterranean region of France, a Regional Meteorological Center prepares special fire weather forecasts based on twice-daily readings from observation stations operated by the fire services (Orieux 1977). These are used by the fire services to prepare fire danger ratings and are also used to alert the general public to situations of unusual fire danger.

## BIBLIOGRAPHY

Beal, H. W. 1939. *Preliminary forest fire danger tables and fire control administration plans for the New Brunswick limits of the Bathurst Power and Paper Company, Limited.* Dom. For. Ser., Ottawa.

Countryman, C. M. 1971. *This humidity business.* U.S. For. Serv. Pacific Southwest Forest and Range Exp. Sta., Berkeley, Cal., unnumbered report.

Fischer, W. C. and C. E. Hardy. 1976. *Fire-weather observers' handbook.* U.S. For. Serv. Agric. Handbook No. 494.

Gisborne, H. T. 1933. The wood cylinder method of measuring forest inflammability. *J. For.* **31**:673–679.

Hornby, L. G. 1936. *Fire control planning in the northern Rocky Mountain region.* U.S. For. Serv. N. Rocky Mt. For. and Range Exp. Sta., unnumbered report.

Kourtz, P. H. 1973. *The USSR forest fire control operation as seen by the Canadian fire control delegation.* Env. Canada, For. Serv. Misc. Report FF-Y-2.

McArthur, A. G. 1976. *Fire danger rating systems.* F.A.O. Consultation on Fires in the Mediterranean Region, Rome 1976.

Orieux, M. 1977. *Forecasting of fire risks.* FAO-United Nations Tech. Report FO:FFM/77/3-02.

Ryan, W. C. 1977. A mathematical model for diagnosis and prediction of surface winds in mountainous terrain. *J. Appl. Met.* **16**:571–584.

Schaefer, V. J. and J. A. Day. 1981. *A field guide to the atmosphere,* Peterson Field Guide Series No. 26, Houghton Mifflin, Boston, 359 pp.

Schroeder, M. J. and C. C. Buck. 1970. *Fire weather—a guide for application of meteorological information to forest fire control operations.* U.S. For. Serv. Agric. Handbook No. 360.

Simard, A. J. 1973. *Forest fire weather zones of Canada.* Can. For. Ser., Dept. of the Environment, Ottawa.

Williams, D. E. 1963. *Forest fire danger manual.* Dept. of Forestry, Canada.

Wright, J. G. 1932. *Forest fire hazard research as developed and conducted at the Patawawa Forest Experiment Station.* Dom. For. Ser., Ottawa.

# CHAPTER FOUR

# *Fire Behavior*

To a combustion engineer, the chemical processes occurring in a forest fire are but little different than those in an industrial furnace. Gases and volatiles emitted by the heated solid fuel are mixed with air in varying proportions, undergo chemical reactions that produce simple gaseous end products that are, in turn, exhausted from the system and replaced with fresh fuel and air. The engineer's method of studying these processes is called stoichiometric analysis; it determines the weights of materials and quantities of energy entering and leaving the combustion reactions. Although a detailed presentation of stoichiometric analysis is beyond the scope of this book, a brief overview is helpful in understanding how a forest fire initiates and grows.

## STOICHIOMETRIC ANALYSIS

When wood burns stoichiometrically, that is, with exactly enough air to complete all reactions leaving only carbon dioxide, water, and the residual nitrogen from the air, six grams of air are supplied for every gram of wood burned. The stoichiometric flame temperature of burning wood is 1920°C and seven grams of combustion products are produced for every gram of wood burned. However, fires in the outdoors never burn stoichiometrically. If there is too little air supply, the chemical reactions do not go to completion, unburned hydrocarbons are carried off in the convective stream above the flame, and the flame temperature is lower than 1920°. This situation is common on large, intensely burning forest fires where air supply is limited except at the edges of the burning area. On the other hand, when there is an excessive air supply, much of the energy from the chemical reactions is used to heat the additional air, and again the flame temperature is below 1920°. This is always the case in small forest fires, and the more usual case even in large ones. There is a direct relationship between flame temperature and the amount of excess air (Smith and Stinson 1952).

$$E = \frac{2195 - 1.1435T_F}{T_F - T_A}$$

where    $E$ = fraction of excess air
   $T_F$ = flame temperature (°C)
   $T_A$ = ambient air temperature (°C)

Thus if the flame temperature is known, the amount of excess air, indrafts, and convection gases can be calculated. Flame temperatures in forest fires vary quite widely, but more or less predictably, from 1500°C in the hottest fires (Philpot 1965) to about 800°C in the coolest (Clements and McMahon 1980). Below 800°C there is sufficient excess air to dilute the distilled volatiles below their lower flammability limits. In building fires where air flow is restricted, flame temperatures may be as low as 500 to 600°C, the lower limit at which carbon particles emit visible radiation. Flame temperatures are roughly correlated with flame height and depth, and most headfires with flames 2 to 3 m high will have flame temperatures of 850 to 1000°C. To put this information to some practical use, let us look at the development of a small forest fire from its inception.

## DEVELOPMENT OF FIRE FROM A POINT SOURCE

We start with the simplest case: a single match dropped on a uniform forest floor of twigs and needles on a dry day with no wind. Suppose our litter layer to be 15 cm deep with a loading of 5t/ha. Flame from the burning match bathes the surface needles beneath and alongside it, and they pyrolyze and emit gases and volatiles that eventually begin to flame in their turn. Slowly the fire progresses away from its point of origin, laterally in all directions along the surface and downward into the fuelbed.

Initially, the fire is spread almost entirely by direct contact of the flames with unburned fuel ahead of and below it. However, as the area on fire gets larger and deeper, radiation, both from glowing embers within the fuelbed and from the flames above it, becomes more important in preheating the fuels ahead of the fire and shortening their ignition time. As a result the rate at which the fire edge moves outward constantly accelerates. Each ignition of new fuel adds to the total mass of burning fuel that lengthens the flames, adds to the radiant heat, and decreases the time to ignition of the next unit of fuel. By the time the fire beneath the initial point of ignition has reached the bottom of the fuelbed, the fire will typically be $\frac{3}{4}$ m to 1 m in diameter with flames 1 m or so in height, burning fuel at a rate of 1 kg/min and spreading outward at a rate of $\frac{1}{4}$ m/min. Heated air is lofted in a plume above the fire

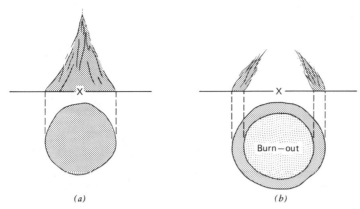

*(a)*             *(b)*

**Figure 4.1.** Initial stages of fire development under calm conditions on level ground. (*a*) Shortly after the start with flames drawing into the center of the flaming area. (*b*) After 10 to 15 min the fire has a doughnut shape and flames are leaning inwards.

and replaced by ambient air flowing in at the base. Indrafts to the perimeter will be on the order of 1 m/min—imperceptible to the onlookers but sufficient to cause the flames to tilt inward as shown in Figure 4.1*a*. Only two or three minutes have elapsed since the match was dropped.

This period from the time of ignition to the time when the area first ignited burns out is known as the first period of acceleration. It is of little consequence to fire suppression efforts since it is usually over long before firefighters arrive on the scene, but it is extremely important in some prescribed burning techniques as will be discussed in depth in a later chapter.

At this time our fire on the forest floor is little larger than a large campfire and not very impressive. However, in heavier fuels with longer residence times such as brush or slash, fires may grow as large as half a hectare with flames 4 or 5 m high during the first period of acceleration. Since air requirements depend on the burning rate of the fire as a whole, although air is supplied only from the perimeter, indraft velocities increase linearly with burning area provided that flame height stays constant. Indrafts of 10 to 15 m/min are common by the end of the first period of acceleration on fires in heavy fuels.

When the area originally ignited burns out, the fire rapidly begins to resemble a burning doughnut rather than a campfire (Figure 4.1*b*). Soon ambient air becomes available from inside the fire perimeter as well as outside. This greatly increases the excess air available for combustion and decreases flame temperature which, in turn, decreases both flame length and rate of forward spread and, eventually, the fire acts as a moving line of fire rather than a single unit. Even in a no-wind, no-slope situation the fire will tend to develop a head, rear, and flanks since inhomogeneities in fuel or simple surface roughness will cause certain portions of the line to advance faster than others. When this occurs, radiation from and convection into the

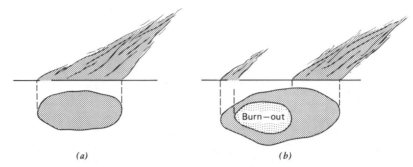

(a)                                            (b)

**Figure 4.2.**   Initial stages of fire development under windy conditions or on sloping ground. (*a*) Shortly after the start flames lean upslope or with the wind. (*b*) After center burnout the rear spreads slowly against the wind with low flame heights while the front begins to run with the wind.

advanced flame tends to speed up the movement of flames immediately adjacent to it.

Up to now we have been looking at a fire without the influence of wind or slope. When a fire is ignited on a slope or under windy conditions, air moves into the combustion zone preferentially from the downslope or upwind side, the flames are tilted upslope or downwind, and the fire rapidly assumes an oval shape as in Figure 4.2*a*. When the first period of acceleration is over, the head of the fire immediately begins a second period of acceleration (Figure 4.2*b*). In the no-wind fire the volatiles and combustion gases move nearly vertically and material produced at one edge of the fire has little influence on the other edge. However, under the influence of wind, the hot gases from the upwind edge are swept across the combustion zone and contribute to heating fuels ahead of the burning edge (Figures 4.3 and 4.4). Although wind increases the amount of excess air in the combustion zone and thus produces lower flame temperatures, flame lengths are greatly increased in wind-blown fires. The reasons for this are first, the flames tilted over the unburned fuel are much more effective radiators than are vertical

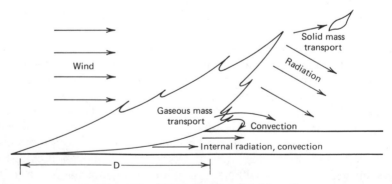

**Figure 4.3.**   Schematic of a wind-driven fire.

**Figure 4.4.** Photo of a wind-driven fire. Photo by U.S. Forest Service.

flames, because the radiating surface is closer to the fuel and because each fuel element can "see" much more of the flame surface. Second, and more important, the zone beneath the flames and above the fuel surface is highly turbulent. Convective eddies entrain flame gases and bring them into direct contact with fuels at some distance from the leading fire edge.

Because ignition in front of a wind-blown fire occurs more rapidly than it does for a no-wind fire, the actively burning zone at the head of the wind-driven fire is wider for fuels of a given residence time. Furthermore, the hot gases from large fuels farther behind the front also affect the rate of spread. Consequently, the effective combustion depth is much greater for a wind-blown fire burning in fuelbeds with mixed sizes of particles than would be the case in the same fuelbed with no wind. Wind also increases the glowing combustion rate of residual charred material adding still further to the rate of production of hot combustion products. In terms of Byram's fireline intensity equation, where intensity equals heat of combustion times fuel weight times rate of spread, wind acts to increase all three of the variables. The effective heat of combustion is increased by speeding up glowing combustion. The effective fuel weight is increased because larger size particles contribute to the fire front. The rate of spread is increased by directing more of the total heat output toward the fuels in advance of the fire. Consequently, the intensity of a wind-blown head fire increases disproportionately to its rate of spread and this, in turn, tends to increase the rate of spread even further. Fire spread equations such as those used in the United States and fire spread tables such as those used in Canada and Australia are based on observations of surface-burning fires that have reached steady state after the second period of acceleration. They should be used with caution in the initial stages of a fire since they will overpredict spread rates and do not provide for the increasing fire intensity that accompanies the second period of acceleration.

The second period of acceleration usually takes more time than the first period: the time varies directly with the size of fuel particles involved and to a lesser extent with wind velocity. Fires in grassland normally reach a steady state in 5 to 10 minutes (Luke and McArthur 1978), whereas fires in heavy logging slash may continue to accelerate for an hour or more.

Rates of spread on the flanks of a wind-blown fire are controlled by wind gustiness to the effective exclusion of any other factor. The wind at ground level is never absolutely constant in either speed or direction. Because of turbulence set up by surface roughness, the wind will be gusty and subject to rapid changes in direction. Flames on the flanks respond nearly instantaneously to these wind changes and flank fires spread erratically.

At the rear, fire behavior is more predictable. Wind tilts the flames away from the unburned fuel and also cools the flames by adding excess air. As a result spread is caused almost entirely by radiation from the embers and direct contact with burning gases in the fuelbed. Since wind enhances glowing combustion but cools and dilutes the flame gases, the net result is that the rate of rearward spread is primarily controlled by fuelbed variables and is virtually independent of windspeed.

Luke and McArthur (op. cit.) in their discussion of fire acceleration include the effects of diurnal changes in fuel moisture and wind. As we are defining fire acceleration, this is not strictly correct inasmuch as at any given moment the fire may be in a perfectly steady state with regard to the forces acting on it at that time. However, it is quite true that rates of spread change predictably with changes in fuel moisture and wind, and that a fire started when the humidity is falling and the wind picking up will accelerate its rate of spread faster and for a longer time than it would if weather conditions were constant. On the other hand, if fuel moisture is rising and the wind slacking off, the decrease in rate of spread caused by these factors may mask or even overcome the normal acceleration in rate of spread.

If the fire is burning in multilayered fuels or in fuels conducive to spotting, the second period of acceleration may be succeeded by a third period. Overstory brush or trees may become ignited, thus involving a completely new fuelbed and creating an essentially new fire. If the intensity during the second period of acceleration builds to a point where the fire perturbs the surface wind field inducing severe turbulence, burning fuels may be lofted from the fire zone and deposited in unburned fuels ahead of the fire front producing spot fires. Spotting is a normal occurrence on most forest and grass fires once their intensity exceeds 300 to 500 kW/m. Spotting will have little effect on overall fire intensity or rate of spread provided that the distance of spot fires from the fire front is such that the front will arrive before the spot fires complete their first period of acceleration. However, as spot fire distances increase beyond this limit, the spot fires act to effectively deepen the active front and increase fire intensity and rate of spread in the same manner as do the tilted flames in the second period of acceleration. This added intensity may, in turn, produce even more spot fires at even longer distances and rapidly turn a manageable fire into a full scale blowup.

## TRANSITION TO A LARGE FIRE REGIME

The terms "small" and "large" fire have but little to do with fire size; rather, they refer to the vertical height to which the fire affects the normal wind field. Small fire behavior is governed by the properties of the fuelbed in which the fires burn and air movements within and a few meters above the fuelbed. Large fires, on the other hand, affect and are affected by atmospheric processes several hundred to several thousand meters above the fuelbed. Large fires are said to "make their own weather" because they can noticeably alter the temperature, humidity, and wind fields in their vicinity over what would be expected at that time and location without a fire nearby.

The extent to which a fire can remain separate from the ambient wind field depends on the height to which it can maintain a convection column where the products of combustion within the column have a sufficient density and velocity difference from the air outside the column that mixing is inhibited and the column acts as a flue for the stack gases produced by the fire in its later stages of growth. To a large extent this depends on the intensity of the fire being able to overcome the horizontal and mixing forces in the wind field through which the gases pass. This was recognized first by Byram in a chapter on fire behavior in a text by Davis (1959) and later in more simplified form by Rothermel and Anderson (1966). Fire size is also a consideration since the convection column boundary is actually a boundary layer between two fluids in turbulent motion and not a solid such as a brick chimney or metal flue. The larger the horizontal cross section of the column, the more isolated are the rising gases in the center from the turbulent edge effects. Atmospheric stability and general atmospheric circulations also play a role in convection column development. The most comprehensive models of convection column initiation presented to date are those of Small (Small and Brode 1980, Small et al. 1981).

The transition from a small fire to a large fire regime is typically sudden, 15 minutes or so at the most. This transition to convective dominance is marked by an increase in fire intensity, particularly by fuels burning well inside the fire edge, an increase in indrafts, the production of black smoke indicating incomplete combustion of the flame gases, and often an increase in the amount and distance of spot fires.

## LARGE FIRE BEHAVIOR

Although most large forest fires are controlled by large scale convective and advective motions (and we shall discuss these later in some detail) two types of large fires operate relatively independently of organized convection phenomena.

We have already seen that the transition to a large fire regime can be triggered by multiple spot fires produced at distances far enough from the fire front that they effectively serve to widen the front. This process is known as pseudo flame front production since it results in wider zones of active combustion than would otherwise be possible in the volume and mixture of fuel sizes existing in the fuelbed. Once the fire has formed an active column, the process may be extentuated with more spot fires being thrown to even greater distances as burning materials are ejected from greater heights on the column. The fire will then move in a series of surges, remaining relatively stationary as the spots are initiated, advancing almost instantaneously as they merge and produce new firebrands, and quieting again as the new brands start new spot fires. Pseudo flame front production is most common when ambient windspeeds are 2 to 4 m/sec to a considerable height, strong enough to discourage fire whirlwind formation but not sufficiently strong to favor very long distance spotting where the spot fires behave independently of the main fire.

Large fire behavior may also be controlled by topography, independent of convective activity. Generally, this occurs when a fire enters the mouth of a drainage basin with a strong upcanyon wind. The fire moves upcanyon pushed by the wind but slope effects cause the fire to burn rapidly to the ridge crests on both sides (Figure 4.5). The result is very rapid involvement of the entire drainage. If fire is held to one side of the drainage by a stream or other fire barrier, the uninvolved slope may be preheated by radiation from the opposite burning slope and if spot fires are thrown across the canyon, the preheated slope may flash over almost explosively.

Although pseudo flame front production and topographic influences can be important modifiers of large fire behavior under certain conditions, it is large scale convective motions that play a dominant role in controlling the behavior of most large fires. These motions result from the interactions at the semipermeous boundary between the primarily vertically moving fluid in the convection column and the primarily horizontally moving fluid of the ambient air. In these situations, although the total flow may be turbulent, organized motions may be expected within the flow field and such motions often occur in pairs (Cantwell 1981).

The height of the convection column and the rate of flow of the gases within it is determined by the atmospheric lapse rate and by the size and intensity of the fire. To a good first approximation, the base of the column can be considered to be the flame tips and the temperature can be considered

***Figure 4.5.*** Topographically controlled fire. Later this fire spotted across the ridge on the right and burned 7500 hectares. Photo by U.S. Forest Service.

to be 325°C, the piloted ignition temperature for cellulosic fuels. Temperature in the first hundred or so meters above the flame tips can be calculated from the formula $\Delta T = 3.9I^{2/3}/h$ (Alexander 1982, Puzdrichenko 1978),

where   $\Delta T$ = temperature rise above ambient (°C)
        $I$ = fireline intensity (kW/m)
       $h$ = height above flame tip (m)

The effective top of the column may be considered to be the height where the atmospheric temperature equals the autoconvective surface temperature lifted dry adiabatically (surface temperature at the fire site plus 3.5°C minus 1°C/100 m increase in elevation). Because of the rapid cooling and contraction of the combustion gases in the first few meters or tens of meters above the flame zone, the column is actually smaller than the diameter of the fire for a short distance. This is called the neck of the convection column. Above the neck the column expands because of air entrained from the edges (Figure 4.6). On most forest fires the column expands at a rather constant angle from the neck to the height where the water vapor within the column begins to

**Figure 4.6.** Convection column over a fire burning in mixed fuel sizes with light winds. Photo by U.S. Forest Service.

condense. The angle of expansion can vary from 6° on very intense fires in heavy fuels to 18° on low intensity fires in light fuels with 12° as a reasonable average. The average volume entrained at any altitude above the fire is thus:

$$V = \frac{H^2 \tan \alpha \, P}{2}$$

where   $V$ = average volume of air entrained
$H$ = altitude above the neck of the convection column
$\alpha$ = expansion angle of the column
$P$ = perimeter of the fire

Since the area of the fire varies as the square of the perimeter, it is evident that the amount of air entrained relative to the amount of convective gases decreases very rapidly as fire size increases. Entrainment also depends on fire intensity, atmospheric stability, windspeed, and wind turbulence.

If the power of the wind field at any altitude exceeds the square of the vertical momentum of the convection column at that same altitude, the column will be sheared off and the products of combustion together with any burning embers will be blown downwind (Figure 4.7). If this occurs at low enough altitudes, spot fires may be produced for some distance downwind of the fire. If both the fire intensity and the wind velocity are sufficiently strong

*Figure 4.7.*   Fractured convection column. Photo by U.S. Forest Service.

that the fracture zone is a region of high shear, horizontal roll vortices will often form at the edges of the fractured column with their axes parallel to the wind. Such "horizontal tornados" have been noted on many high intensity crown fires and may be a common mechanism of spot fire production in crown fires as well as a device for steering and limiting flame spread (Haines 1981). Horizontal roll vortices were prominent on a Michigan forest fire that burned 10,000 ha of pineland, 44 homes and cottages, and one firefighter (Simard et al. 1981).

Even if winds are not sufficiently strong to shear the column, they may be strong enough to tilt it so that the outer edge of the convection column overhangs unburned fuels ahead of the fire. Any embers thrown from the edge of the column may start spot fires ahead of the main fire. In addition, the area immediately below the column to the leeward of the prevailing winds is a preferential spot for the development of large-scale, tornadic fire whirls (Figure 4.8; Countryman 1971). Tornadic whirls are those that originate in or slightly below the convection column and stretch downward to touch the surface as opposed to flame whirls which originate in the combustion area and stretch upward independently of the convection column (Luke and McArthur op. cit.). Tornadic whirls are typically 10 to 50 m in diameter and generate updrafts and horizontal velocities of 50 to 100 m/sec. Such tornadic whirls have caused great property damage during forest fires in several countries and loss of life on at least one fire in the United States

**Figure 4.8.** Tornadic whirls beginning to form in the lee of a tilted convection column. Photo by U.S. Forest Service.

(a)

**Figure 4.9.** Flame whirls can be produced (a) in the laboratory or (b) during forest fires. Crown copyright photos by Philip Thomas.

**Figure 4.9.** *(Continued)*

(Chandler 1960). Tornadic whirls are similar to, and may be caused by, the same mechanism as the horizontal roll vortices that form over fractured convection columns (Church et al. 1980).

The flame whirl is a much more common phenomenon in forest fires than are tornadic whirls and its causes and effects are much better understood. There has been extensive study and modeling of flame whirls in liquid fuels (Emmons and Ying 1968) and substantiating data for flame whirl behavior in forest fuels (Martin et al. 1976). Flame whirls are produced when rising parcels of flame gases entrain and concentrate vorticity from the surrounding environment (Figure 4.9). This can occur most readily when the atmosphere in the lowest layers is highly unstable, as on hot summer days, and, paradoxically, on cold, clear, calm nights when the temperature differences between the fire gases and the ambient air are greatest. Flame whirls have diameters of tens of centimeters to a maximum of 10 m and extend vertically from 10 to 300 m. Both rotary motion and ascent velocities are quite high within the flame zone, but the high rotational scouring of the fuelbed and ground surface is not evident in flame whirls as it is in tornadic whirls. Combustion rates in the fuels beneath the whirl increase from 1.5 to 5 times depending on fuel moisture content, with lower moisture content fuels exhibiting the greatest increase in combustion rate. When flame whirls migrate outside of the fire area, they may spread fire through direct flame contact for a few seconds, but the base of the flame in the whirl rises rapidly and most flame whirls have dissipated within 100 m or so of the fire edge. Flame whirls are seldom a serious hazard to firefighters but they may be a significant contributor of spot fires.

Another type of organized flow is the eddy formation in the lee side of strong convection columns. As mentioned previously, strong convection columns act as solid barriers to light or moderate winds, and eddy circulations form on the lee side of the columns just as they do on the lee sides of tree trunks when wind is blowing through the forest or a fire is moving up a slope (Figure 4.10). These eddies serve to translate momentum and turbulence downward from the stronger winds at higher elevations to lower levels. Consequently, winds on the lee side of the fire are usually stronger and gustier than those on the windward side. The increase in gustiness is important to fire behavior because it causes the fire to spread in surges rather than at a steady forward velocity. This occurs because the higher velocity wind gusts tilt the flames into fresh unburned fuel. The increased combustion rate from the new fuel increases flame length and the increased flame depth creates added buoyancy so that the flames are straightened and forward rate slows until either a new wind gust or burnout of the fuel causes the flames to tilt forward again and start a new cycle. When the residence time of the fuelbed is synchronous to the timing of wind gusts, the results can be awesome. On fires burning downslope in brush fuels under the influence of downslope winds the effect can resemble breakers on a beach, though in this instance the waves are flames 10 to 15 m high.

### Spot Fire Determinants

Throughout this discussion of fire behavior we have emphasized the importance of the spotting process. Spotting has been studied for many years, and although the process is conceptually easy to visualize, a quantitative understanding of it is still elusive.

A firebrand or burning ember is lofted into the rising stream of flame and combustion gases, rises in the convection column until it is ejected into the ambient wind field, and falls under the influence of gravity while being moved laterally by the wind until it lands on the surface. If the firebrand has sufficient energy left when it lands, a spot fire will result. The maximum spotting distance will result when the firebrand leaves the convection col-

*Figure 4.10.* Eddy circulations form on the lee side of tree trunks. Photo by Bluford Muir.

umn at the exact height where it will land with just sufficient energy remaining to produce ignition. Most early research was concentrated on determining the fall rates, burning times, and aerodynamic properties of various types of firebrands (Tarifa et al. 1965). It was nearly 20 years later before anyone tackled the much more intractable problem of determining the forces that lift the brand in the convection column to the point where it is ejected (Albini 1979). There are still many unknowns about the process of firebrand initiation and, particularly, about the fields of motion within the flame zone and the convection column above it. Research is still needed to develop a comprehensive and reliable model of the spotting process.

### Crown Fire Behavior

The classic, and practically the only, study of crown fire behavior is that of Van Wagner (1977). For a full explanation the reader should consult the original source, but a brief synopsis is given here.

Within the crown space only two properties, foliar bulk density and foliar moisture content, determine how much heat is required to produce sustained flaming within the crown. Assuming that the heat to initiate crowning comes

*Figure 4.11.* In a passive crown fire the surface fire advances first. Photo by U.S. Forest Service.

originally from a fire burning on the surface, then the height of the crown base above the surface is the third important variable.

With crown bulk density, moisture content, and height above the surface as fixed quantities, a surface fire intensity can be calculated that will just induce crowning (i.e., a solid continuous flame within the crown space). At this minimum level, however, there is insufficient heat transferred horizontally through the crown or upward from the leading edge of the surface fire to sustain horizontal spread through the crowns. The leading edge of the crown fire lags behind the leading edge of the surface fire. This is a passive crown fire representing the torching of individual trees rather than a moving flame front (Figure 4.11).

At a somewhat higher surface fire intensity, the heat transferred to the crowns will be sufficient that the heat supplied by the burning crowns plus the heat from the surface fire will cause fire to spread horizontally through the crowns at the same rate as the surface fire. However, the heat from the burning crowns alone is not sufficient to sustain horizontal crown spread. The crown fire and surface fire are effectively coupled and move together as a unit. This is termed an active crown fire.

If sufficient heat is produced within the crown volume itself to permit horizontal spread, then flame will move through the crowns without regard to the surface fire. This is termed an independent crown fire. Van Wagner shows that this can only occur with an appreciable flame angle and convective heat transfer through the crown space. Independent crown fires are thus possible only on steep slopes or in strong winds.

In summary, a forest fire's initial growth is by direct flame contact, a convective process. As the fire grows, radiation becomes more dominant and the rate of fire spread accelerates. If the fire's intensity becomes sufficiently great to produce a convection column stronger than the ambient wind field, large scale convective processes come into play and fire behavior is governed by conditions in the atmosphere high above the firefighter on the ground. When conditions are right, these forces can produce massive fire whirls, large-scale spotting, crown fires, and similar extreme fire behavior characteristics that are usually summarized in the literature by the term "blowup."

The foregoing, we hope, has demonstrated to the reader how very complex the behavior of a wildfire can be and why the battle to control one is still as much an art as a science. Not only are there many more variables influencing the behavior of a wildfire as compared to the combustion engineer's model, but many of the more influential variables are in a constant state of change, changes that are to some extent predictable. Those fire officials responsible for planning the control strategy for a particular wildfire must have a clear understanding of fire behavior and potential fire behavior under the circumstances in which they find themselves. An increasing proportion of this essential knowledge can be gained through comprehensive fire management courses, but experience on a variety of wildfires is still extremely valuable.

## BIBLIOGRAPHY

Albini, F. A. 1979. *Spot fire distances from burning trees—a prediction model*. U.S. For. Serv. Gen. Tech. Report INT-56, 73 pp.

Alexander, M. E. 1982. *Calculating and interpreting forest fire intensities*. Can. For. Serv. Unnumbered Report, 33 pp.

Cantwell, B. J. 1981. Organized motion in turbulent flow. *Ann. Rev. Fluid Mech.* **13**:457–515.

Chandler, C. C. 1960. *Fire behavior on the Decker Fire*. U.S. For. Serv. Unnumbered Report, 14 pp., illus.

Church, C. R., J. T. Snow, and J. Dessens. 1980. Intense atmospheric vortices associated with a 1000 MW fire. *Bull. Am. Met. Soc.* **61**(7):682–695.

Clements, H. B. and C. K. McMahon. 1980. Nitrogen oxides from burning forest fuels examined by thermogravimetry and evolved gas analysis. *Thermochim. Acta* **35**:133–139.

Countryman, C. M. 1971. *Fire whirls—why, when and where.* U.S. For. Serv. Unnumbered Report, 11 pp.

Davis, K. P. 1959. *Forest fire control and use.* McGraw-Hill, New York, 584 pp.

Emmons, H. W. and Ying, S. J. 1967. *The fire whirl.* Proc. 11th Symp. (Int.) on Combustion, Comb. Inst., Pittsburgh, pp. 475–488.

Haines, D. A. 1981. *Horizontal roll vortices and crown fires.* U.S. For. Serv. Unnumbered Report, 31 pp., illus.

Luke, R. H. and A. G. McArthur. 1978. *Bushfires in Australia.* CSIRO Division of Forest Research, Canberra, 359 pp., illus.

Martin, R. E., D. W. Pendleton, and W. Burges. 1976. Effect of fire whirlwind formation on solid fuel burning rates. *Fire Tech.* **12**(1):33–40.

Philpot. C. W. 1965. *Temperatures in a large natural fuel fire.* U.S. For. Serv. Res. Note PSW-90, 14 pp., illus.

Puzdrichenko, V. D. 1978. *The effect of thermodynamic atmospheric state and area under fire on smoke train formation.* Ezdatelesvo Akademee, Moscow, 43 pp.

Rothermel, R. C. and H. E. Anderson. 1966. *Fire spread characteristics determined in the laboratory.* U.S. For. Serv. Res. Paper INT-30, 34 pp., illus.

Simard, A. J. and others. 1981. *The Mack Lake Fire.* U.S. For. Serv. Unnumbered Report, 91 pp., illus.

Small, R. D. and H. L. Brode. 1980. *Physics of large urban fires.* Pacific Sierra Res. Corp. Report PSR 1010, 51 pp.

Small, R. D., D. A. Larson, and H. L. Brode. 1981. *Analysis of large urban fires.* Pacific Sierra Res. Corp. Report 1122, 169 pp.

Smith, M. L. and K. W. Stinson. 1952. *Fuels and combustion.* McGraw-Hill, New York, 329 pp.

Tarifa, C. A., P. P. Notario, and F. G. Moreno. 1965. *On the flight paths and lifetimes of burning particles of wood.* Proc. 10th Symp. (Int.) on Combustion, Comb. Inst. Pittsburgh, pp. 1021–1037.

Van Wagner, C. E. 1977. Conditions for the start and spread of crown fires. *Can. J. For. Res.* **7**:23–34.

# CHAPTER FIVE

# *Fire Behavior Prediction*

In the preceding four chapters we have systematically reviewed the processes of combustion and the interactions of fuels, weather, and topography that make forest fires burn as they do. However, although the understanding of why a fire is burning in a certain manner may be of academic interest to the fire manager, it is the manager's ability to predict how that fire will behave in the future that makes fire behavior knowledge useful.

There are two kinds of fire behavior predictions and it is important to distinguish between them. A *fire danger rating* is an estimate of burning conditions anticipated over a large area at a particular time, usually early afternoon of the following day. A *fire behavior forecast* is an estimate of the rates of spread and other fire behavior characteristics to be expected on a particular wildfire or prescribed fire over some future time period, usually the next work period or planned burning period. A fire danger rating is generalized for fuel type and topography. A fire behavior forecast is site specific. Though they may use the same input data, and even process the data through the same equations, the two are not interchangeable unless the relationships between the rating standard and such other variables as fuel type and quantity, insolation, slope, and the diurnal cycle of temperature and humidity are known. When these interrelationships have been precisely studied, fire danger ratings can be used for site-specific predictions with fair reliability (Cheney 1968), but when they are not, reliance on fire danger tables can give misleading results (Deeming et al. 1972).

Fire danger rating as a system for integrating weather elements was discussed briefly in Chapter 3. In this chapter we examine the history and technology of fire danger rating as a means of predicting forest fire behavior.

## FIRE DANGER RATING

The day-to-day measurement of fire danger has become a fire management tool in numerous forested countries around the world but originated and was perfected mainly in Australia, North America, and the USSR.

It is not surprising that development took place in this way. First, danger rating is more applicable to temperate and Mediterranean climates where frequent weather fluctuations strongly influence flammability, as opposed to tropical climates where there is a definite wet and dry season but little change in day-to-day weather. Second, the areas mentioned are those where the forest industry was in a state of rapid growth in the early part of this century and organized fire control systems were essential.

As noted earlier, in the United States and Canada forest fire danger rating systems were developed more or less independently, beginning about 1920, although there was continuing correspondence between the two groups of researchers involved. Although the systems presently used in the two countries are different, they naturally do have some similarities. In a comparison of the two, Van Wagner (1975) describes these differences and similarities.

One fundamental difference is the basis on which each was constructed. The United States system is based on the mathematics and physics of fuel moisture and heat exchange as they affect fuel moisture variations (Deeming et al. op. cit.) and on laboratory experiments that measured the influence of various fuel and weather factors on fire behavior in needle litter fuelbeds (Rothermel 1972). The Canadian system, in contrast, was largely developed, like the Australian, from statistical analyses of large quantities of field data. The tables (Anon. 1970) were empirically constructed by putting together weather, fuel moisture, and fire behavior data gathered over several field seasons at selected locations. The fire behavior data were provided by small test fires that were allowed to burn for two minutes. Lawson (1972) prepared an interpretative guide and later, Van Wagner reduced the tables to a set of equations and described the system (Van Wagner 1974), and the system was coded for computer (Kourtz 1967).

Both the United States and Canadian systems interpret the moisture level of a wide range of forest fuel sizes through the use of three representative classes of fuels having different drying rates. Their moisture content is estimated daily; they both include a fire rate-of-spread component based largely on wind velocity and a component to represent the effect of long-term drying on fuel availability; both produce an index representing fire intensity. In the United States system it is the Burning Index (BI) and in the Canadian system, the Fire Weather Index (FWI). Both also have a number of other indices that can be used to indicate the level of other fire factors such as ignition possibility and rate of spread.

Another important difference between the two systems lies in the way the final output is presented. The American system gives an array of BIs for a range of different fuel types, nine in all. The user chooses one of the fuel types typical of his or her area to begin danger rating calculations. The Canadian system resembles the Australian system in that it has a single universal index, the FWI which, given the same weather parameters and so on, will give the same FWI value regardless of location and fuel type. It represents fire intensity in one standardized fuel type. It, in effect, is a measure of fire intensity potential and provides the means to compare fire weather and fire climate in different parts of the country. To obtain a true measure of local conditions, the range of FWIs falling into the various categories of low, moderate, high, very high, and extreme is determined by local fire experience, which is, of course, tied to local fuel types.

In Australia, a number of different fire danger rating systems have been in use but the one most universally accepted was developed by McArthur (1966, 1976) mainly for the eucalypt forests of that country. McArthur designed a meter based on fire behavior data measured at some 800 test fires in typical fuels that were allowed to burn for 30 to 60 minutes. Thus, like the Canadian system, it is an empirical derivation based strictly on field measurements. The tabulated indices for the various Australian fire danger meters have been reduced to equations (Noble et al. 1980) and programmed for use on a pocket calculator (Crane 1982). The Australian system has also been tested and is operationally used in the Mediterranean region of Spain.

There have been several danger rating systems developed in the USSR but the one that is most widely used is a relatively simple ignition index (*P*) based on the work of Nesterov (1949) and calculated as follows:

$$P - \sum_{i=1}^{W} (t_i - D_i) \cdot t_i$$

where   $P$ = ignition index
     $W$ = number of days since the last rainfall >3 mm
     $t$ = temperature °C
     $D$ = dew point temperature °C

The calculations are begun in the spring on the first day the temperature exceeds freezing (0°C) after the snow has melted. The ignition index increases each day until a rainfall of more than 3 mm occurs at which time the index drops back to zero and the process begins again. The system also utilizes a danger class breakdown and the approximate class boundaries are:

| Class | Ignition Index (*P*) |
|---|---|
| Nil | 0–300 |
| Moderate | 301–1000 |
| High | 1001–4000 |
| Extreme | 4001 + |

Class boundaries, however, are adjusted for various regions through the plotting of 10 years of fire experience vs. the index. The upper limit of the "Nil" class (300 in the example) is set at that value of the index at which no fires have occurred in the 10-year period and the upper limit of the "Moderate" class is set at the index value that would include 25 percent of all fires. The upper limit of the "High" is set at that index value that would include 65 percent of all fires.

Although a considerable amount of research has been undertaken in the USSR on fire weather, fire behavior, and related fields, no operational use is made of the resulting indices except for the system just discussed and it is used strictly as an ignition index to provide a measure of the chance of a fire starting in the area served by the weather station.

A modification of the Nesterov system was proposed by Gritsenko (1962) based mainly on the summing of daily vapor pressure deficit at 0900 local time beginning from the day that snow cover disappears. Called the Forest Fire Danger Index (FFDI), it was based on the accumulated vapor pressure deficit corrected for precipitation over the past four days, obtained from a table provided, and for season, also obtained from a table. There is no evidence that Gritsenko's system was ever used operationally.

A Swedish fire danger rating system known as the *Angstrom Index* has been used as an indicator of expected fire starts in parts of Scandinavia. It is the simplest of all fire danger rating systems in current use.

$$I = \left(\frac{R}{20}\right) + \left[\frac{(27 - T)}{10}\right]$$

where   $I$ = angstrom Index
$R$ = relative humidity (%)
$T$ = air temperature (°C)

The index is interpreted as:

| | |
|---|---|
| $I > 4.0$ | Fire occurrence unlikely |
| $4.0 < I < 2.5$ | Fire conditions unfavorable |
| $2.5 < I < 2.0$ | Fire conditions favorable |
| $I < 2.0$ | Fire occurrence very likely |

The index ignores the effects of precipitation and wind, and does not accurately reflect the relationship between relative humidity, temperature, and fuel moisture. Its primary virtue is simplicity. It is the only fire danger rating that can be calculated mentally without resorting to pencil and paper.

In France, drought and wind are considered to be the most important variables for rating fire danger (Orieux 1974). The degree of drought is determined by the formula:

$$D = Cd^{(-\Sigma E/C)}$$

where   $D$ = drought index
$C$ = available water capacity of the soil
$E$ = potential evaportranspiration according to Thornthwaite (1948)

The index is calculated daily and combined with the forecast wind velocity to determine the level of fire danger for the coming day.

All these systems developed in various countries, although varying in appearance and complexity, have the common objective of obtaining a relatively simple and comparable measure of the flammability of forest fuels from day to day. Some of them have been adapted for use in other countries such as the Australian meter used in Spain. A modified Canadian system has been used in parts of Spain, in Mexico, Venezuela, Chile, and Argentina to some degree. The Swedish Angstrom Index is used in Portugal and several former Portuguese possessions. As mentioned at the beginning of this section, it is important in most forested areas to have good weather observations, but it is much more important to have some system that can make use of the weather information in a way that will give the fire control agency optimum assistance in decision making.

The selection of a rating area to be represented by a single fire danger index and the selection of how many weather stations to install and where to install them is perhaps as critical to the utility of a fire danger rating system as is the selection of the system itself. Because weather elements forecast for a single time, usually midafternoon, are used to predict the fire danger for the entire rating area for the whole day, the rating area must be climatically uniform. This is true because the weather elements are used to predict fuel moisture, and fuel moisture depends on antecedent as well as current weather. If diurnal variations in weather across the rating area are not the same, fires will behave differently even though they are burning in the same fuel type under the identical weather conditions of the moment.

Within a climatically uniform area, fire danger can be expected to vary with latitude, altitude, day length, aspect, and fuel type. Since it is usually economically impossible to establish and maintain enough weather stations to stratify these many variables, standard practice is to specify the exposure of the station and to correct the reading when extrapolating to locations that vary from the standard (Burgan 1976, Just 1977, Stockstad and Barney 1974). Even at locations with specified fuel type and exposure in a uniform climate, there will still be variations in fire danger between reporting stations. King and Furman (1976) find in a study of 300 fire danger rating stations in the western United States that station spacings of 8 to 65 km were needed to ensure index readings within one point of each other. This means that the rating area to be represented by a single weather station with a probable error of one burning index unit can vary from 5000 to 33,000 hectares depending on the climate and fuel type.

Fire danger ratings are most often used to guide presuppression activities and in writing prescriptions for prescribed fires. Once a protection organization has accumulated 5 to 10 seasons of fire danger rating records, the expected fire load can be predicted quite accurately by comparing the fire danger index with past experience. This information, in turn, can be used to guide such diverse actions as scheduling of aerial detection patrols, manning secondary lookouts, instituting emergency prevention activities, mobilizing extra stand-by crews and equipment, and closing or curtailing woods operations.

Because fire danger ratings are derived from studies of the behavior of surface fires following their second peak of acceleration, they can be used to predict fire intensity and rate of spread of fires after their initial stages, and of all fires burning under weather conditions sufficiently mild that the third, or convective, stage of acceleration is never reached. Consequently, fire danger ratings are often used to prepare dispatchers' guides for initial attack, and by Fire Behavior Officers to predict fire spread on larger fires during periods when the fire is spreading as a strictly surface phenomenon (Rothermel 1981).

## FIRE BEHAVIOR FORECASTS

Perhaps more than any other single skill, the ability to accurately forecast fire behavior marks the distinction between the successful forest firefighter and the failure. Beginning with the sizeup by the first firefighter on the scene, all decisions on the tactics to be used and the disposition of forces will be based on estimates of the future spread and intensity of the fire. Overestimation leads to excessive burned area because of unnecessary indirect lines and to unnecessarily high suppression costs because of excessive manpower and equipment. Underestimation leads to excessive burned area because of lost line, to unnecessarily high suppression costs because of nonproductive effort, and, occasionally, to tragedy because of failure to recognize the lethal potential of a seemingly quiet sector. An accurate fire behavior forecast results in firelines prepared in the right places at the right times with a minimum of suppression forces, thus minimizing both cost and damage.

In one way, predicting fire behavior on a going fire is easier than either fire danger rating or writing a prescription for a prescribed burn. The fire is already there and its present behavior is observable and measurable. Prediction involves only the determination of how the fire's present behavior will change as it encounters new combinations of fuels, weather, and topography. Fire services throughout the world have developed simple rules of thumb to assist firefighters in recognizing the changes to be expected as burning conditions change.

### Fire Behavior Rules of Thumb

#### *Fuel Loading*

Both rate of spread and flame height will vary linearly with fuel loading in the same fuel type; for example, when fuel loading doubles, rate of spread and flame height will also double. This rule is strictly accurate only in fuelbeds that are near their optimum packing ratio and in which the degree of compaction is not greatly affected by loading. For very fine fuels such as grasses and reeds, rate of spread increases more rapidly than loading: for example, spread rate triples when loading doubles (Sheshukov 1970), whereas in very large fuels or densely packed fuelbeds, spread rate is little affected by loading.

#### *Fuel Moisture*

At fuel moistures below 5 percent, fires in fine and large fuels tend to spread at equal rates. At fuel moisture between 5 and 10 percent, fires in fine fuels spread more rapidly than those in large fuels. Above 10 percent, the rates tend to equalize again and at moistures above 15 percent, fires in heavy fuels will continue to burn and spread, whereas those in fine fuels will extinguish themselves.

There is no simple rule of thumb equating change in flame length or rate of spread to fuel moisture changes within a given fuel type.

#### *Wind*

Rate of spread will double for each 4 meters per second increase in wind speed. This rule is valid for fires in loosely compacted surface litter. Grass fires increase their rates of spread faster than this, particularly at higher windspeeds (McArthur 1965), whereas fires in heavy or compacted fuels are less affected.

#### *Slope*

1. Rate of spread doubles for every 10° increase in slope (McArthur 1962).
2. Rate of spread doubles for every 15° increase in slope up to 30° and every 10° thereafter (Chandler 1963).
3. Rate of spread increases tenfold on slopes above 35° (Sheshukov op. cit.).

Actually, the effect of slope on fire spread is a function of the packing ratio of the fuelbed (Albini 1974). Consequently, fires in loosely packed fuels such as grass are affected more than those in dense duff. Table 5.1 gives some representative values.

*Table 5.1.  Effect of Slope on Rate of Fire Spread*

| Fuel Type<br>Packing Ratio<br>Slope° | Grass<br>0.001 | Loose Litter<br>0.01<br>Relative Rate of Spread | Tightly Packed Litter<br>0.1 |
|:---:|:---:|:---:|:---:|
| 0 | 1.0 | 1.0 | 1.0 |
| 10 | 2.3 | 1.7 | 1.3 |
| 20 | 6.6 | 3.8 | 2.4 |
| 30 | 15.0 | 8.0 | 4.5 |
| 40 | 30.1 | 15.8 | 8.4 |
| 50 | 60.5 | 30.8 | 15.9 |
| 60 | 126.7 | 64.0 | 32.6 |

### Spotting Distances

Algorithms are available for calculating spot fire distances under given situations (Albini 1979, 1981), but they are too complex to qualify as rules of thumb as they require a handheld calculator to be useful in real time.

If a fire danger rating system is available for the fuel types representative of the fire area, then direct comparison of the indices computed for current weather and predicted weather is usually the most accurate method for predicting fire spread and intensity. Virtually all fire danger rating systems have one index that is purported to be directly proportional to rate of spread and several have intensity indices directly proportional to flame length.

Once a fire enters the third stage of acceleration and becomes convection dominated, fire behavior prediction is much more complex and much more difficult. The fire's behavior is influenced largely by winds aloft, upper level stability, and by interactions between the main fire and spot fires or between various parts of the fire itself. Both upper air conditions and fire interactions are difficult to identify for an observer on the ground near the fireline. Fire spread will be in very rapid "runs," typically lasting from one to four hours, and ending at well defined changes in fuel type or topography. The task of fire behavior prediction on the convection-dominated fire is not one of predicting the rate of spread, but rather of predicting when fire runs can be expected to start and where they can be expected to stop.

## TRANSITION TO CONVECTIVE DOMINANCE

To a distant observer in an aircraft or on a lookout tower, the transition to convective dominance is immediate and obvious. The color of the smoke turns markedly darker, indicating incomplete combustion; the edges of the convection column become quite distinct with a "rolling" motion at the lower edges resembling a heavy swell on a calm sea. Soon the column

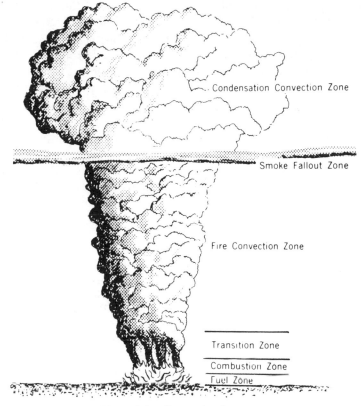

*Figure 5.1.*  Convective fire zones.

organizes into the six zones described by Countryman (1969; Figure 5.1) though the first two and sometimes three zones may not be apparent at a distance.

I.  *Fuel Bed Zone.*   Extends from the ground to the top of the fuelbed. The vertical dimensions may vary from less than 1 cm to many meters, depending on the kinds of fuel involved.

II.  *Combustion Zone.*   The actively flaming area in and above the fuel zone. Vertical height varies, but is usually less than 30 m above the fuelbed.

III.  *Transition (Turbulence) Zone.*   Lies between the combustion zone and the more organized flow of the main convection column. Both upper and lower boundaries are indefinite. In most fires, this zone does not extend more than 30 to 60 m above the combustion zone.

IV.  *Fire (Thermal) Convection Zone.*   The area between the top of the transition zone and the base of the convection column cap. Energy for the convection in this zone comes chiefly from the fire, although some condensation of water vapor is also likely. Vertical height of this zone may vary from less than 300 m in some fires to more than 5000 m in others.

V.   *Smoke Fallout Zone.*   A relatively thin zone at the base of the convection cap. This thin layer of smoke spreading out from the convection column is characteristic of towering convection columns.

VI.   *Condensation Convection Zone.*   The area from the smoke fallout zone to the top of the convection column. The column usually widens abruptly to form a "cap." It is usually light in color as a result of the condensed water vapor or ice crystals. Heat from condensation is the chief source of energy for convection in this zone. This zone is not found in all fires. Its formation depends on air mass characteristics as well as on size and energy output of the fire. The vertical length of this zone is variable. At times it may approach the length of the fire convection zone.

To the firefighter on the line, these changes in the convection column are not so apparent. However, the transition to convective dominance is equally impressive at close quarters. The first sign is usually that the flames seem to straighten up and lengthen. Then previously unburned fuels inside the perimeter begin to flame. If the fire is between the firefighter and the sun, the sky will seem to darken as the blacker smoke rises. The noise level of the fire increases appreciably and flames may pulsate at intervals of 10 to 20 sec. Flareups and torching become more common if trees are present and the indraft can be distinctly felt on the back of one's neck. Despite the indraft, spot fires are likely a short distance across the fireline as embers are thrown out from the turbulent zone. More embers will be ejected on the downwind side of the fire and they will land farther away from the perimeter. As the spot fires grow and coalesce, the center of fire activity shifts downwind and/or upslope and the fire has begun a run.

With the beginning of a run, the area actively flaming at the same time increases dramatically and so does the size of the convection column above it and the temperature difference between the hot gases inside the column and the air outside it. Because of the difference in temperature, and thus in density, the column begins to act like a solid object with most of the outside air deflected around it rather than entrained into it.

At this point the behavior of the fire will be governed by the wind and temperature fields for several thousands of meters above the fire and any one of several things may happen.

If upper winds are low and the atmosphere is neutral or moderately unstable, the run will continue to be steered by surface wind and slope with little change in behavior unless the humidity profile is such that condensation begins at a low level. In this instance the latent heat of condensation may cause the column to resemble a small thunderhead with associated downdrafts and turbulence (Figure 5.2).

If there is a strong inversion at any height above the fire, convective activity will weaken soon after the top of the column reaches the inversion.

***Figure 5.2.***    The convection column above a large fire often resembles a cumulus cloud. Photo by U.S. Forest Service.

The lower the inversion, the more marked the effect, and, if the inversion is less than 1000 m above the fire, convection may be slowed sufficiently that the fire will return to a normal surface type.

However, if there is a weak inversion above the fire with a strong wind above the inversion, as sometimes happens at night and early morning in mountainous country (Baughman 1981), the convection column may pierce the inversion and mechanical turbulence will bring the upper winds to ground level in the lee of the column. Fire spread will increase immediately and dramatically. This is a particularly dangerous situation if the upper winds are from a different direction than the surface winds, since the flank of the fire may become the head with little advance warning.

This same situation, a low level wind jet with lighter winds above and below it can occur without the presence of an inversion, most often shortly ahead of a cold front or low pressure trough. Fire behavior will be the same as in the previous case—development of a strong convection column and mechanical translation of the jet winds to ground level. This phenomenon was first documented in the United States by George Byram (1954).

When winds increase continuously with height, the top of the convection column is usually sheared off before reaching full development. This reduces the amount of turbulence and the increase in windspeed at ground level, but is highly favorable to long distance spotting if the fire is burning in a fuel type capable of producing firebrands with long residence times. If the fire is very intense, which requires either very heavy ground fuels or a crown fire in standing timber, *Benard cells* may form along the outer edges of the sheared column. Benard cells are horizontal roll eddies formed in pairs and rotating downward on the outer edges and upward at the center. The downward rotation may reach the surface and affect the rate of combustion of the crown fire (Haines 1981, Schaefer 1957). The physics of vortex formation over fires is very well explained in an article by Church, Snow, and Dessens (1980).

With foehn type winds or other wind profiles with high velocities at the ground and decreasing winds aloft, fire spread is a surface phenomenon even though there may be strong vertical development of the convection column. Fire whirlwinds may develop at the leading edges of the run, particularly when the lower atmosphere is highly unstable. These fire whirls may pose an acute safety threat to firefighters but are normally not a factor in fire spread since surface winds are already driving the fire at a rapid rate.

## FIRE BEHAVIOR FORECASTS ON LARGE FIRES

As previously stated, on a large forest fire where transition to convective dominance is possible, prediction of when major runs may be expected to occur and where they may be expected to stop is vital to a successful fire control effort. This is true because the head of a convectively dominated fire is not controllable with any presently known technology and even flank attacks are often unsuccessful because of spot fires. The wise commander marshals forces along the line where the run is expected to stop or slow down and prepares to take aggressive action as soon as burning conditions ease. A miscalculation on the location leaves firefighters stationed embarrassingly far in front of a now quiet fire or, even more embarrassingly, scrambling to get out of the way of a juggernaut that shows no signs of slowing down.

Since the key factor in establishing convective dominance is the power output of the fire relative to the power output of the wind field, the elements to look for in predicting the onset of a run are those that will cause high intensity burning.

Heavy fuels and living fuels contribute disproportionately to fire intensity when they are dry enough to burn. Prolonged drought will lower these fuel moistures to critical levels and their time lags are so long that they will not recover appreciable moisture at night. At high latitudes conifer foliage moisture may also be extraordinarily low in early spring when transpiration is high during the day but water uptake by the roots is inhibited by low soil temperatures. Fires may burn quietly in early morning, but as the fine fuels dry, the rate of spread increases and more and more heavy fuels with long burning times become involved. Eventually, the fire's intensity may pass the critical level triggering a run. This phenomenon has been noted ever since the beginnings of organized fire control and formed the intellectual basis for the various "Get 'em by 10 AM" policies followed by many forest fire organizations.

Another mechanism by which fuels can become critically dry and burn with unusual intensity is to be cooked by a surface fire spreading under mild burning conditions. If a large area has been burned in this manner and then burning conditions become more favorable, the area may become reignited and burn as a crown fire that may carry far past the edge of the original burn. This is quite common in peat and marsh fires and some areas may reburn four or five times over the course of a few weeks as successive layers of fuel dry out.

Since fireline intensity is directly proportional to rate of fire spread, anything producing a sudden increase in rate of spread will also increase the probability of convective dominance. As we have already seen in Table 5.1, changes in slope are more effective than anything except major wind shifts in altering rates of spread. Any time a fire moves from level ground to a steep hillside, spread will increase and a full scale run is possible.

Topographic features other than slope may also influence fire behavior. A fire on one slope of a narrow V-shaped canyon may radiate sufficient heat to the opposite slope to predry fuels and lead to very rapid spread should the fire spot across the canyon. Narrow canyons also serve to channel winds, particularly nighttime downcanyon winds, and sharp bends or intersecting side drainages set up eddies in the wind field that may carry embers across the canyon. This was the direct cause of the Basin Fire in California doubling in size in a six-hour period (Chandler 1961). Lakes or other large bodies of water often develop a strong inversion layer a meter or so above the surface on clear hot days. Under the influence of light winds, burning material may ride for considerable distances along the surface of the denser air at the top of the inversion, causing spot fires on the opposite shore at distances many times those where the trajectory is over land. Ridges are important not only because of the abrupt change in slope but because the upper lee slope is a zone of turbulence when strong winds are blowing across the ridge. Often firelines are best located on the lee side of a ridge where advantage can be taken of the upslope winds caused by the roll eddy as the wind crosses the ridge crest. Determining how far down the slope the upslope component can be depended on is difficult since the size of the eddy depends both on the windspeed and the turbulence characteristics of the wind field. Dropping too far downslope may place the fireline in a zone of extreme and erratic turbulence. Saddles tend to channel winds, as do canyons, as well as set up lateral and vertical eddies. Although broken topography makes line construction arduous, the many abrupt changes in slope and the variation in fuel types with changing aspect usually preclude a fire making a long sustained run and the hectarage burned per day in broken country is less than it would be on the plain.

Fuel continuity is necessary for a sustained high intensity fire run. When a fire enters a markedly different fuel type it must progress through the initial cycles of acceleration before reaching a steady state rate of spread. This is true regardless of whether the transition is from a faster burning fuel to a slower burning one or vice versa. In the latter case, however, spread rates during the initial acceleration period may be as rapid as the convective-dominated spread rate in the slower burning fuel, so the effect of the change may not be readily apparent. Since all fuel types tend to burn alike as fuel moisture decreases, the effect of fuel continuity is most marked under easy burning conditions and tends to disappear as conditions grow more severe.

A fire with an energy output sufficient to establish convective dominance is little affected by strictly surface phenomena such as slope winds or changes in humidity or insolation. The surface weather phenomena that influence the behavior of large fires are those that have a major effect on the wind field, usually extending to a considerable height. The passage of a dry cold front is the most formidable of such phenomena since the influx of cold air above the fire increases thermal instability and turbulence, the wind shifts 90° turning the long axis of the fire into the front, and the air behind the front is drier than the air in which the fire had been burning so that fuel moistures will decrease for some time after the frontal passage. Although rates of spread are not extreme following frontal passages (1.5 to 5 km/hr are normal), hectarage burned can be very large because of the wide front. The Gaston Fire in South Carolina burned nearly 35,000 hectares in 10 hours following the passage of a dry cold front (DeCoste et al. 1968). Passage of a sea breeze front resembles a micro cold front except that it is much shallower, usually only a few hundred meters in depth, and the air behind the front is more moist than the air it displaces, leading to an increase in fuel moistures over time. The strength of the sea breeze is related to the difference between the water temperature and the air temperature at the coast. The onshore vector of the sea breeze front is approximately $\frac{2}{3}$ m/sec/°C difference in temperature between the water and the air. The distance inland to which the front will penetrate is determined by the strength of the front and the direction and strength of the synoptic pressure gradient. Although the probability of occurrence of a sea breeze front can be predicted from the pressure gradients on a weather map, the timing is subject to significant local variation. When sea breeze fronts are likely, a weather watch should be established a few kilometers to seaward of the fire to give warning of an approaching front. A large fire may be exposed to several sea breeze fronts during the course of its history. Unpredicted advances and retreats of the sea breeze front were responsible for the 6000 hectare extent of the Dandenong fires north of Melbourne in 1964 (Whittingham 1964).

Foehn winds are relatively easy to forecast but virtually impossible to counter. When an area is exposed to winds in excess of 40 m/sec with relative humidities below 5 percent, it is not unusual for a fire to spread at rates of 8 to 15 km/hr burning 2000 to 3000 ha/hr from the moment of ignition (Lewis 1958). Forecasting problems are often encountered as the foehn is weakening, when the downslope winds are kept aloft by surface heating but often resurface in late afternoon or at night. This is a common phenomenon in southern California (called a "sundowner"), and cost the lives of four firefighters on the Romero Fire in 1971. The best way to be alert to this possibility is to maintain close watch on the wind direction and speeds at ridgetops and lookout towers in the vicinity of the fire. These exposed locations are often under the influence of the foehn even though it has not reached the surface at lower elevations.

Upper level phenomena that affect large fire behavior are more difficult to predict, or even to observe, than are the surface weather phenomena since winds aloft and radiosonde observations are scarce compared to surface observations. Even in countries with advanced meteorological networks, upper level observation stations are so widely spaced that significant events can occur unrecorded. On every large fire where aerial service is available it is prudent to take aerial temperature and humidity soundings twice daily from the surface to at least 4500 m. This can easily be done by helicopter with a handheld psychrometer. For some phenomena of interest to fire behavior prediction, clouds make excellent indicators. Cirrus streaks or lenticular clouds are warnings of high winds aloft. Cumulus clouds are certain indicators of thermal instability, and unusual cumulus activity in the morning is a clear warning of possible thunderstorm activity later in the day.

Cumulus clouds in themselves can affect fire behavior. A growing cumulus cloud signals a region of strong updrafts that increase toward the top of the cloud. If a cumulus cloud drifts over the convection column of an established fire, the column becomes essentially a part of the cloud. The increased updraft produces stronger indrafts at the surface with a consequent increase in fire intensity. Since the cloud cell is moving faster than the fire, the convection column will become tilted at an angle between the fire and the moving cloud. At some point the buoyancy forces of the fire gases will overcome the shear forces in the convection column and the fire will form a new vertical column. If the fire was burning intensely enough to entrain firebrands into the tilted column, they will be released simultaneously when the new column is formed and create a line of spot fires downwind.

Cumulonimbus clouds, particularly with virga, signal strong downdrafts from the cloud base. The downdrafts, being much colder than the air at the ground surface, tend to follow surface contours after they reach the ground.

The result is a strong downslope wind resembling a foehn that may extend up to 10 or 12 km out from the base of the cloud cell that produced the downdraft. Thunderstorm downdrafts have been responsible for unanticipated runs by many large fires, the most notable being the Mann Gulch fire in Montana in 1949 where 13 firefighters were burned to death (Granger 1949).

Except for thunderstorm downdrafts, all of the upper level weather phenomena mentioned (strong winds aloft, marked thermal instability, and subsidence) can occur in clear air with no cloud indicators. Probably the most troublesome of these is the low pressure trough which has effects similar to, but less violent than, the passage of a dry cold front. Because the trough does not extend to the surface, there are no visible indications of its passage save for a slight increase in windspeed and gustiness. The passage of a trough will have little effect upon a surface fire, but a fire that has already developed a strong convection column will increase markedly in intensity because of the greater instability of the air aloft within the trough. There is also the possibility of mechanical translation of upper level winds to the surface depending on the depth and strength of the trough. There is little that a fire behavior forecaster at a fire can do to predict the passage of low level troughs except to rely on synoptic meteorologists at headquarters or the National Weather Service.

Although the existence and strength of an upper level inversion layer cannot be determined from cloud indicators, it is easily measured by an aircraft sounding and, if aircraft are not available, can be estimated by observing the behavior of the smoke from the fire itself. The convection column will flatten out at the base of the inversion and spread laterally beneath it (Figure 5.3). The height of this drift smoke layer thus marks the height of the inversion base. The depth of the inversion cannot be known without a temperature sounding, but the strength can be estimated rather closely by noting the depth to which the center of the convection column rises above the inversion base: the greater the penetration, the weaker the inversion. The breaking of an inversion and the subsequent increase in fire intensity can often be forecast by taking regular notice of changes in the top of the convection column. In an active fire the top will usually start to visibly pulsate 30 minutes to an hour before the inversion breaks up.

Smoke is not only a good indicator of fire activity and a visual cue to atmospheric processes, but smoke from a large fire is also a significant modifier of the microclimate in the fire's vicinity. In the daytime smoke can significantly reduce incoming solar radiation, reducing the temperature increase during the day to half of that forecast for a clear day with a corresponding increase in relative humidity and fuel moisture. At night smoke is even more effective in blocking outgoing radiation and the temperature decrease will be from $\frac{1}{3}$ to 10 percent of that predicted for a clear night, with consequently lower humidities and fuel moistures, and higher fire intensities. Slope winds, both day and night, will be weak or nonexistent under a

***Figure 5.3.***    Fire burning beneath a strong inversion layer. Photo by Craig Chandler.

smoke cloud. Weather forecasts made from locations other than the fire scene should always be modified to take account of smoke effects.

On a large fire, interactions between various parts of the fire may be more important in determining overall fire behavior than any external influences. The convection column over a large fire is not a simple stack or chimney with all the combustion products rising within it to be replaced by fresh air at the base. Rather, the column, particularly in the transition region between the high temperature flames and the purely convective zone where chemical reactions cease to influence the thermal gradient, is a region of extremely turbulent flow (Figure 5.4) with flame flashes, hot and cold bubbles, high velocity updrafts and downdrafts, and eddy circulations that constantly form, decay, and then reform again elsewhere. The sudden onset of high

**Figure 5.4.**    The lower portion of the convection column is a region of highly turbulent flow. Photo by U.S. Forest Service.

intensity combustion at one sector of a fire may trigger increased fire activity at another widely separated location or, conversely, may slow or change the direction of the fire at yet another site. This occurs because the increase in convection over one portion of the fire area within the influence of the total convection column affects the motions of the column as a whole. This is most vividly evident when two separate columns, as from the main fire and a large spot fire, merge at some height above the fires. The combined draft is greater than that of either of the fires separately and the junction zone where the two columns coalesce moves rapidly downward toward the surface creating a gradient flow that pulls the two fires together. With intense fires and an unstable atmosphere this mechanism can operate when the fires are a kilometer or more apart.

Predicting the behavior of small fires is like two-dimensional algebra—if a fire is spreading at 3 m/min in light brush when the humidity is 30 percent and the wind is 3 m/sec, how far will it go in 4 hours if the humidity is expected to drop to 20 percent, the wind pick up to 5 m/sec, and the fuel type changes to grass 300 m downwind from the fire's present location? Predicting the behavior of large fires is like three-dimensional chess—the head will cross two drainages in one afternoon if the sea breeze front arrives after 1 PM when the west slope is exposed to full insolation, but will only run to the ridgeline if the front arrives in the morning, and no head will develop if the offshore gradient strengthens and keeps the sea breeze from penetrating the fire area. The successful fire officer must be capable of both kinds of prediction.

# BIBLIOGRAPHY

Albini, F. A. 1974. *Fire behavior estimation*. U.S. For. Serv. Nor. For. Fire Lab., Unnumbered Report, 67 pp., processed.

Albini, F. A. 1979. *Spot fire distances from burning trees—a predictive model*. U.S. For. Serv. Gen. Tech. Report INT-56, 73 pp.

Albini, F. A. 1981. *Spot fire distances from isolated sources—extensions of a predictive model*. U.S. For. Serv. Res. Note INT-309, 9 pp.

Anon. 1970. *Canadian forest fire weather index*. Can. Dept. Fish. & For., Can. For. Serv.

Baughman, R. G. 1981. *Why windspeeds increase on high mountain slopes at night*. U.S. For. Serv. Res. Paper INT-276, 6 pp.

Burgan, R. E. 1976. *The effect of latitude and season on index values in the 1977 NFDR system*. U.S. For. Serv. Gen. Tech. Report RM-32, pp. 70–74.

Byram, G. M. 1954. *Atmospheric conditions related to blowup fires*. U.S. For. Serv. Sta. Paper SE-35, 34 pp.

Chandler, C. C. 1963. *Prediction of fire spread following nuclear explosions*. U.S. For. Serv. Res. Paper PSW-5, 110 pp., illus.

Chandler, C. C. 1961. *Fire behavior of the Basin fire*. U.S. For. Serv., Unnumbered Report, 83 pp.

Chency, N. P. 1968. Predicting fire behavior with fire danger tables. *Aust. For.* **32**(2):71–79.

Church, C. R., J. T. Snow, and J. Dessens. 1980. Intense atmospheric vortices associated with a 100 MW fire. *Bull. Amer. Met. Soc.* **61**(7):682–694.

Countryman, C. M. 1969. *Project flambeau—an investigation of mass fire (1964–1967)*. Final Report Vol. 1. U.S. For. Serv., 68 pp., illus.

Crane, W. J. B. 1982. Computing grassland and forest fire behavior, relative humidity and drought index by pocket calculator. *Aust. For.* (in press).

DeCoste, J. H., D. D. Wade, and J. E. Deeming. 1968. *The Gaston fire*. U.S. For. Serv. Res. Paper SE-43, 36 pp., illus.

Deeming, J. E. et al. 1972. *National fire-danger rating system*. U.S. For. Serv. Res. Paper RM-84, 165 pp.

Granger, C. M. 1949. *Report of board of review. Mann Gulch fire*. U.S. For. Serv., Unnumbered Report, 23 pp., processed.

Gritsenko, M. V. 1962. A new scale for forest fire danger. *Meteorologiya i Gedrologiya* 3.

Haines, D. A. 1981. *Horizontal roll vortices and crown fires*. U.S. For. Serv., Unnumbered Report, 37 pp.

Just, T. E. 1977. *Fire control problems of the Wallum with particular reference to cooloola*. Queensland Dept. For. Tech. Paper No. 3, 15 pp., illus.

King, R. M. and R. W. Furman. 1976. *Fire danger rating network density*. U.S. For. Serv. Res. Paper RM-177, 4 pp.

Kourtz, P. H. 1967. *Forecasting forest fire danger by computer*. Canada Dept. For. and Rural Dev., For. Branch, Ottawa, Info. Report FF-X-7, 10 pp.

Lawson, B. D. 1972. *An interpretive guide to the Canadian forest fire behavior rating system*. Can. For. Serv. BCP-3-72.

Lewis, A. 1958. *Special report—the Gale fire*. U.S. For. Serv., Unnumbered Report, 7 pp.

McArthur, A. G. 1962. *Control burning in Eucalypt forests*. Aust. For. and Timber Bur. Leaflet No. 80, 31 pp., illus.

McArthur, A. G. 1965. *Weather and grassland fire behavior*. Aust. For. and Timber Bur. Leaflet No. 100, 23 pp.

McArthur, A. G. 1966. *Forest fire danger meter, Mk4.* For. and Timber Bur., For. Res. Dist. Canberra.

McArthur, A. G. 1976. *Fire danger rating systems.* FAO Consultation on Fires in the Mediterranean Region, Rome 1976.

Nesterov, V. G. 1949. *Combustibility of the forest and methods for its determination,* USSR State Industry Press, 1949.

Noble, I. R., G. A. V. Bary, and A. M. Gill. 1980. McArthur's fire-danger meters expressed as equations. *Aust. J. Ecol.* **5**:201–203.

Orieux, A. 1974. Conditions meteorologiques et incendies en region mediterraneenne. Rev. For. Fr. n. n° special, *Incendies de Forest* **1**:122–129.

Rothermel, R. C. 1972. *A mathematical model for predicting fire spread in wildland fuels.* U.S. For. Ser. Res. Paper INT-115, 40 pp.

Rothermel, R. E. 1981. *How to predict the behavior of forest and range fires.* U.S. For. Serv. Intermtn. For. Exp. Sta., 256 pp., processed.

Schaefer, V. J. 1957. The relationship of jet streams to forest wildfires. *J. For.* **55**(6):419–425.

Sheshukov, M. A. 1970. *Effect of the steepness of the slope on the propagation of fire.* Lesnoye Khozyaystvo, pp. 50–54.

Stockstad, D. S. and R. J. Barney. 1974. *Conversion tables for use with the national fire danger rating system in the Intermountain area.* U.S. For. Serv. Res. Note INT-12, 6 pp.

Thornthwaite, C. W. 1948. An approach toward a rational classification of climate. *Geog. Rev.* **38**:55–94.

Van Wagner, C. E. 1974. *Structure of the Canadian forest fire weather index.* Can. Dept. Environment., Can. For. Serv. Pub. 1333, 44 pp.

Van Wagner, C. E. 1975. *A comparison of the Canadian and American forest fire danger rating systems.* Can. For. Serv., Petawawa Forest Exp. Sta. Info. Report PS-X-59, 19 pp.

Whittingham, H. E. 1964. Meteorological conditions associated with the Dandenong Bush Fires of 14–16 January, 1964. *Aust. Met. Mag.* **44**:10–37.

# CHAPTER SIX

# *Ecological Principles and Their Relationship to Fire*

Every living being is surrounded by materials and forces that constitute its environment and through which it meets its needs. Nothing can escape its environment. No animal or plant can live completely sealed off from the world; all living things must make exchanges with their environment in terms of (1) energy, (2) matter, and (3) waste elimination.

All living beings are interdependent. All living creatures must absorb energy more or less continuously to fuel their life processes. Most plants absorb this energy directly from the sun. Other organisms absorb it indirectly by feeding on plants or on other animals. The cycle of who eats what and is eaten by whom is called a trophic chain and is used by ecologists to measure the flow of energy through the ecosystem. In addition to the direct relationships between food producers and consumers, every natural ecosystem contains species linked by complex hereditary bonds of coadaptation and mutual interdependence to a degree where neither can function without the other. All animals depend directly or indirectly on plants. Many plants depend on animals, as, for example, those that depend on insects for pollination. Some green plants can live independently for periods, deriving their energy from the sun and their nutritional supply from the soil, but as soon as the young plants start to grow, competition develops. For each living organism there are other living organisms that are necessary or disadvantageous. Ecology is the science that studies the relationships between living organisms and their environment. For more detailed discussion, the reader should consult the authoritative writings of Clark (1959), Clements (1928), Daubenmire (1968a), Margalef (1974), Odum (1959), and Whittaker (1970).

Communities are assemblages of plants or animals inhabiting the same area. Communities are fundamentally the result of interactions between two phenomena: the different tolerances of the various taxonomic groups for the environment or ecological amplitudes, and the heterogeneity of the environment. The physical restrictions acting on the community must be considered together with those acting on the individual. Organisms react to each other and also to the environment so that the organisms and the physiographic conditions of the habitat form an ecological complex or, more briefly, an ecosystem.

## ECOSYSTEMS AND THEIR FUNCTIONS

An ecosystem is a part of the biosphere that can be considered a relatively autonomous entity with respect to neighboring ecosystems and whose structure and functioning can be analyzed independently of its neighbors. In very general terms, an ecosystem comprises a set of living things, plant and animal, that constitutes a biocenosis (also called biotic community) and the physical environment of the living organisms, sometimes called the biotope, so that the following relationship can be described:

$$ecosystem = biocenosis + biotope$$

An ecosystem cannot continue to exist if one or more of its component parts disappear. If, for example, the trees that make up a forest should disappear, the community will cease to be a forest for as long as there are no trees.

The equilibrium of ecosystems is maintained by factors that mutually interact. Light plays a role in controlling the growth of the trees in a forest but, at the same time, the trees determine the amount of light that penetrates. In the same way, the minerals and oxygen dissolved in the water of a pond affect the growth of aquatic organisms living there, but the activity of the organisms also alters these factors. Plant growth reduces the level of mineral salts, whereas animal respiration consumes oxygen and increases the carbon dioxide content of the water. This observation leads to consideration of the factors limiting the lives of organisms and ecosystems. Every animal or plant tends to grow, reproduce, and propagate itself until it is stopped by some environmental influence. The factor that stops the growth or dissemination of an organism is called the limiting factor. When we consider factors separately in order to distinguish and measure the effect of each one, we must realize that in nature no factor ever acts alone. Animals and plants are subject to many influences at the same time, and the effect of one factor is often modified by the action of others.

Although the characteristics of the environment generally play a role in determining the type of community that forms, the community also determines many of the characteristics of the habitat. As a community develops in a previously bare area, most of the original conditions change and new ones appear. No progress can be made toward understanding the role of the physical factors that determine the distribution of communities unless a clear distinction is made between the primary or intrinsic characteristics of the habitat and the secondary or extrinsic characteristics resulting from biological activity.

It is difficult to define the concept of ecosystem strictly, because the term is applied to a number of entities that may appear quite different.

An ecosystem can extend over a large area as does a forest or savanna and thus be difficult to delimit, but its structure is spatially repetitive and so it can, on one level, be considered homogeneous. In such a case, even superficial examination allows one to recognize immediately the major characteristics of the plant portion of the population—the plant community— and to have an idea of its homogeneity. Indeed, the plant portion of a community is generally the most important, the one with the greatest continuity and the most regular throughout the year. Recognition and definition of the animal portion—the animal community—is more difficult, as species are usually represented by a small number of individuals that move freely from one type of community to another. However, the animals have numerous interrelationships with the plants. Although plant distribution is controlled mainly by the physical factors of the environment, animal distribution is more often determined by the types of food and shelter offered by the vegetation.

An ecosystem thus may be defined with reference essentially to the most visible and abundant organisms. Practically speaking, this is the upper level of vegetation in the case of terrestrial environments. In a second acceptance of the term, an ecosystem is an entity that, though irregular, is clearly delimited in space. The biotic communities of ponds or shorelines are often cited as typical examples. The shore is different from the center of the body of water and the various depths are different from each other, but the shoreline or pond forms a functional biological entity whose various constituent organisms have innumerable interrelationships and form a stable and relatively autonomous population. In the same sense of a well-defined entity, smaller communities such as the organisms populating a dead tree can be regarded as ecosystems. However, such small communities have limited autonomy and persist for a very short time. It seems preferable to regard them as portions of larger ecosystems.

Every ecosystem has a specific structure that corresponds to the list of living beings, both plant and animal, it contains. Every community is limited in both time and space.

To draw up a complete list of the organisms constituting an ecosystem is often very difficult, especially since microscopic organisms such as bacteria, fungi, and protozoans are difficult to detect. As a result, researchers often consider only a fraction of the population. Such lists, even if they are limited to the plant community, animal community, or to the upper plant layers, for instance, are nonetheless valuable in the characterization of a biotope because the presence or absence of one or more given organisms is often a precise indicator of important ecological factors. They remain, on the other hand, entirely insufficient as a basis for study of the complete functioning of an ecosystem.

The organisms of a community are not just piled into the available space; they occupy sites that are usually well-defined, although in the case of mobile animals the sites may vary with time. Such localization plays an essential role in the life of the community because it permits or prevents the meeting of various species and determines their relationships. It is the basis of the trophic relationships existing between organisms and thus the basis of the very functioning of the ecosystem.

Various types of horizontal distribution are possible for the individuals belonging to a given species. Regular distributions are rare and related to the existence of territorial behavior in which each individual does not tolerate neighbors of the same or a different species except at a certain distance. Random distribution implies infrequent interactions between individuals and homogeneity of environmental factors. Cluster distributions are by far the most frequent.

The components of an ecosystem are arranged in three-dimensional space, and the vertical distribution of organisms is the basis of a diversification of structure that is too often underestimated: stratification. At any given point on a vertical line, the physical environment is unique. There are sharp discontinuities, such as the passage from air to ground or air to water, and there are progressive gradients of pressure, light intensity, oxygen content, or content of other chemical substances. Such gradients exist in the air, the soil, and the water. Together, the discontinuities and gradients define *strata* characterized by a certain distribution of plant and animal organisms. Broadly speaking, there are two essential strata: the upper stratum, where there is sunlight and where autotrophic organisms can develop, and the lower stratum, which is dark and where only heterotrophs can live.

In terrestrial environments the transition between the two strata is abrupt, at the level of the ground. In deep aquatic environments where light is gradually absorbed by the water, the transition from the light to the dark stratum is, on the contrary, gradual. Within these major strata, gradients of various factors introduce additional subdivisions, some clearly separate and others less so. Conditions are, however, very different depending on whether the environment is air, soil, or water.

There are some air-dwelling organisms that can be found at great distances above the ground, but they spend only brief periods of their lives there. The atmosphere does not provide sufficient support for permanent existence. Only the presence of vegetation enables terrestrial environments to support stable existences on the surface of the soil. Vegetation is thus the

*Figure 6.1.*   The forest ecosystem has several vertical strata. Photo by Minnesota Department of Natural Resources.

essential characteristic and at the same time the cause of stratification. It is in forests that the greatest number of, and best-differentiated, strata are found: from top to bottom—the tree layer, shrub layer, herb, and moss layers (Figure 6.1). In grassland communities such as prairies, steppes, and savannas there are only two principal strata above ground level: the herb layer and the surface of the soil.

The concept of community implies a degree of homogeneity in structure and species composition within a given area. When two communities come in contact, a transition zone, wide or narrow, usually arises. This is known as an ecotone.

Several types of ecotone can be recognized: (1) the transition between two contiguous communities may be abrupt, as a result of an abrupt discontinuity in environmental conditions; (2) it may be abrupt because of species interaction, particularly competition between organisms, even though there appears to be a continuous gradient of environmental factors; and (3) the ecotone may be an area in which one community shades gradually into another, reflecting gradual changes in complex factors.

The physical and chemical characteristics of the environment of any biotic community are only rarely constant over time. The alternation of day and night and the succession of the seasons introduce continual variations. Living beings react to these environmental changes, so that a biocenosis can sometimes change considerably over the course of time.

The alternation of day and night imparts a rhythm of vital importance to the lives of animals and plants. The succession of the seasons at higher latitudes also brings considerable variations in temperature, light, rainfall, and, concomitantly, of all other environmental factors. The reactions of living organisms to these variations are diverse. During the day they consist mainly of movement in the case of mobile forms, but there are also sleep, feeding, and rest rhythms. Seasonal variations also affect the activity of some long-lived species, triggering hibernation or torpor, burrowing, shedding of leaves, and change of state. They determine the demographic cycle of most species, particularly short-lived ones; the least favorable season is spent in the state of egg or seed. Seasonal changes may bring about disappearance of the species or major reduction in numbers. Seasonal changes may set off migrations over greater or lesser distances, that is, regular changes in biocenosis, among animals—birds, mammals, fish, amphibians, and insects. Seasonal periodicity plays a determining role in the lives of most ecosystems. It causes a succession of populations on the same territory with only selected components persisting. In temperate climates the winter biocenosis seems very sparse and consists in large part of organisms in a state of inactivity—trees, rhizomes, and animals rendered dormant by the cold. With spring, some species begin to multiply actively and others take their places in summer and fall. The diversity of the ecosystem is greatly enhanced by this succession, which results in the multiplication of habitats just as stratification does.

Another important aspect of the variation over time in the composition of biocenoses is their transformation over the years owing to the effect of either changing external factors or internal determinism. Geological history shows that the surface of the earth has undergone profound changes over the ages. Continual upsets are still occurring, with new surfaces emerging, old ones being submerged by landslides, volcanic activity, flood, fire, and so on. Variations of this type have been studied mainly with respect to the plant world where they are more obvious and, therefore, easier to follow. A bare area is gradually covered with groups of plants. The pioneer species are those that reach reproductive maturity rapidly and produce large numbers of easily transported seeds or spores. Succeeding species are slower maturing, longer lived, and better able to modify a site to suit their physiological requirements. Eventually, the site will be occupied by a climax community which is considered to be in equilibrium, albeit relative, with environmental

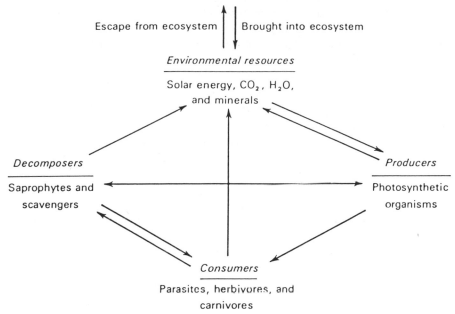

*Figure 6.2.* Trophic–dynamic interrelations in the ecosystem. Only three trophic levels (producer, consumer, decomposer) are diagrammed (from Daubenmire 1968a).

conditions. Such a sequence of communities is called a succession. As succession proceeds, an increasing number of species will coexist within the ecosystem, each occupying a specialized niche. Species diversity brings stability to the system since the welfare of the community as a whole is less dependent on any single component.

All living organisms require food. The trophic relationships between the various species of an ecosystem are referred to as food chains or, more appropriately, food webs, since the interrelationships are numerous. A predator often takes many different types of prey, and its prey may vary over its lifetime. Conversely, an animal or plant may be preyed upon by a wide variety of animals and parasites.

However simple the biocenosis, the food web is always highly complex. Its structure is best appreciated by considering a few broad categories, called trophic levels (Figure 6.2). The first level is that of the primary producers, essentially, the green plants that generate living matter from minerals and light energy. They are consumed by herbivores, which make up the primary consumer level. These, in turn, serve as food for carnivores and parasites, which form the secondary consumer level. There may be an additional level consisting of third-order consumers—carnivores that prey on carnivores. Bacteria and fungi are often placed in a class by themselves, the reducers, which use the organic matter from the remains of other living things.

To characterize the functioning of the ecosystem in terms of bioenergy, it is important to measure energy transfer or energy flow between the various components. Energy transfer is defined by its intensity (the quantity of energy transferred in a given period that corresponds to the concept of biological productivity, and also by its yield), the ratio between the energy actually used and the energy extracted. Biological productivity can be defined as the quantity of living matter produced in a given time period and a given area. The quantity of living matter is often expressed as a weight, but it is preferable to use the energy equivalent in calories as this allows more accurate comparisons between biochemically different products and facilitates evaluation and calculation of yield.

When species food habits are known, it becomes possible to draw up a general outline of the food web or at least to establish the main components of the successive trophic levels. Insertion of the energy balances of the various groups into the web or levels provides a representation of the trophic structure of the whole system and of the flow of energy in the system. The degree of detail known about the food web will determine the degree of detail with which energy flow in the system can be depicted.

The structure and functioning of the food web, which involves exchanges not only of energy but also of matter, is manifest in the biochemical cycles of some of the constituent elements of living matter such as carbon, nitrogen, phosphorus, and sulfur, and also calcium, sodium, and potassium. These biochemical cycles illustrate well the details of ecosystem functioning. Because of the relatively constant composition of living matter, the carbon cycle has characteristics directly related to those of energy flow. However, it comprises an essentially abiotic phase in the form of humus and organic matter not found in soil and an inorganic phase in the form of atmospheric $CO_2$ and carbonates in soil and water. The nitrogen cycle is even further removed from energy flow owing to the accumulation, in plants only, of tissues formed essentially of lignin and cellulose and nearly free of nitrogenous material. The nitrogen cycle includes a complex mineral phase in which nitric, nitrous, and ammoniacal forms succeed each other, as well as the phase of atmospheric nitrogen, subject to fixation and entry into the cycle through bacterial action.

The living part of an ecosystem consists of a community of organisms whose interactions are not limited to producer–consumer, prey–predator, or host–parasite relationships. The trophic categories are not simply juxtapositions of more or less interchangeable organisms, all more or less of equal importance to one another. All mature natural ecosystems are formed of a varying number of coadapted, mutually interdependent species, each of which has a role in the community.

Besides trophic relationships there are many other interactions that link the members of a biotic community. Many plants depend on insects and vertebrates for fertilization and transport of seeds to sites favorable for germination. The frequency of these nonalimentary interactions between the members of a biocenosis increases with the number of member species.

The cohesion of an ecosystem is ensured by the complementarity of interests of its component species. These interests are affected by two types of constraints, external and internal.

External constraints constitute what are generally referred to as the limiting factors of the system. These determine its limits in space and its temporal structure, and they affect the rate of renewal of its living components. The most important of these are temperature, precipitation, altitude, latitude, light, oxygen content, and mineral nutrients.

Most endogenous constraints are more difficult to recognize in a mature natural ecosystem where homeostasis is generally excellent. However, as soon as successions are considered over time it becomes possible to see some of the internal regulatory mechanisms. Some of these function to limit the size of species populations so that they do not exceed the capacity of the environment. The socio-ecological factors serving to regulate birth and death rates depending on species density are examples of this type. There are also interspecies mechanisms of internal regulation, the effect of which is to prevent or limit competition at a given trophic level. This seems to be the function of the chemical substances secreted by many plants which can prevent the growth of rival species (antibiosis and allelopathy). Certain animal pathogenic agents that cause only minor damage in their habitual hosts but can produce high mortality among similar forms may have a similar ecological role.

Species do not persist solely in terms of the persistence of their individual members but also at the level of populations and communities through given reproductive and regulatory modes. Individuals are born, grow, mature, and then die. Their only function is to ensure the continuity of the species. A species may disappear locally if the continuity of its life cycle is interrupted through diminished ability of the population to respond to ecological changes. Living beings compete with one another for food, light, water, space, and so on. The first occupants modify environmental conditions in such a way that new species may have difficulty in establishing themselves. In the end, the species best adapted to colonize an environment will constitute organized communities.

## SUCCESSION

After a community undergoes a disturbance of whatever extent or origin, a series of changes occurs. The appearance of a defined sequence of communities in an area is called an *ecological succession*. The term succession is thus used to describe the changes that can be observed in an area when different communities replace one another.

Theoretically, a community maintains itself more or less in equilibrium, but no community can be truly stable because the members of the community are never in complete equilibrium with each other or the physical environment. Changes in the environment appear over the course of time, produced by climatic or physiographic changes and also by the activity of animals and plants themselves. These habitat modifications can entail such a degree of change that the existing community is replaced by a new community.

Over the course of time, changes appear in the nonliving components of the ecosystem. These environmental transformations are due in part to the activities of the organisms themselves and in part to phenomena independent of the community proper. The former influences are referred to as autogenic, producing an autogenic succession (Tansley 1935), and the latter as allogenic, producing an allogenic succession. Normally, both forces are active at the same time but one or the other is generally stronger.

Autogenic influences depend on the species composition and structure of the community because each species contributes individually to the total effect. Even if the dominant species exercise a preponderant influence, subordinate species often have a role to play. Such influences are seen, for example, in the accumulation of soil due to the production of organic matter by plants and changes in soil structure and moisture. Cycling of nutrients can be greatly affected through preferential uptake or stocking of certain nutrients by some species. Autogenic influences also affect light and temperature; a further example is seen in the toxins emitted by the roots of various plants that prevent renewal of their own species or prevent other species from becoming established.

Allogenic forces affect succession but they are not due to the activity of the organisms in the community. Examples are forest fires, the pasturing of domestic animals, or the clear-cutting of an entire forest.

There are two types of succession, primary and secondary. The immediate cause determining the origin of a succession is the denuding of an area. New situations allowing species establishments are produced by:

1. Physiographic phenomena which create the following primary successions for the most part.
   a. Erosion by water, wind, or glaciers.
   b. Deposits left by these agents and by volcano activity.
   c. Emergence of new, bare surfaces.
   d. Submersion, creating submerged surfaces.
2. Climatic phenomena which create mainly the following secondary successions.
   a. Drought.
   b. Wind.
   c. Fire caused by lightning.

3. Biotic factors which create mainly the following secondary successions.
   a. Human destruction of communities through agriculture, forestry, open-pit mining, toxic fumes from factories, fire, and war.
   b. Activity of animals, leading to overgrazing, trampling, and creation of mounds or burrows.
   c. Destruction of plants through attacks by insects and parasitic fungi.

## Primary Succession

Primary succession arises in bare areas in which there have never been living organisms or in which the existing flora and fauna have been completely destroyed by the disturbance. They may be observed in moraines exposed by glacial retreat, or new islands and surfaces that have undergone intense erosion; further examples are provided by the colonization of lakes or ponds, river banks, debris, rocks, dunes, and recently deposited volcanic ash or lava. Substrates relatively untouched by the effects of time are thus constantly subject to invasion by immigrant species.

Such habitats are not favorable to the growth of most plants, so that the pioneer species must be adapted to survive harsh conditions. Water elimination phenomena are the main control over the possibility of invasion of new surfaces. Whatever the initial habitat conditions, vegetative cover tends to improve them while making the environment more hospitable to other species.

Striking and classic examples of primary successions are provided by the successions developing in lakes, ponds, and on rocks. According to the classic works of Clements (1916, 1936), Daubenmire (1968a), Odum (op. cit.), and Oosting (1958), community sequence in a primary succession begins with low plant cover, with few species and a simple structure, and progresses to communities of taller plants with numerous species and a complex structure. First to appear are flat, clinging forms such as lichens, mosses, and algae. Annual herbaceous species then become established. They give way to perennial herbaceous species and small woody plants; then bushes with a few scattered trees or arborescent populations uniform in age with little undergrowth appear. Finally there develops a tree cover with undergrowth and soil cover with various strata.

## Secondary Succession

When a natural area is disturbed to such an extent that the existing community is destroyed and the succession regresses, the new sequence of communities that appears is called a secondary succession. This situation arises when the principal species of a community have been destroyed by fire,

**Figure 6.3.** (*a*) Although the land may appear completely barren after an intense forest fire, (*b*) the soil contains the seeds of its secondary succession. Photos by U.S. Forest Service.

parasitic disease, tornadoes, floods, or human activities such as agriculture or forestry. The secondary succession can appear at any stage of the primary succession since the catastrophes that create secondary bare areas often do not destroy all the preexisting vegetation, and relict species can be mixed with the invading species. However, if fire sweeps a grassland area during the summer and new shoots arise from the subterranean organs of the same plants (as would occur in the next growing season), the burned surface cannot be said to belong to a stage of the succession.

The essential distinction between primary and secondary successions resides in the fact that the pioneer communities of a secondary succession benefit from the soil previously occupied by living organisms (Figure 6.3). The soil already contains humus, permitting activity by microorganisms; the mineral content of rocks has been altered by acid secretions; the soil contains dormant seeds and spores; roots and worm galleries penetrate the soil layers, letting air and water enter. As the roots and litter of a devastated community decay, nutrients become much more abundant, raising the nutritive potential of the environment. In the primary succession, by contrast, the soil is nearly sterile and structureless, some nutrients can be grossly deficient, and the rate of development of vegetation is governed by the rate at which the limiting factors are overcome.

According to the postulate proposed by Clements (1936) and his followers, community succession leads to a climax; the concept of succession is inseparable from that of climax.

The species that have successfully invaded a biotope dominate the scene for a period and constitute an "autonomous" community. However, in the course of time conditions change and the members of the existing community cannot compete successfully with new arrivals. A new community succeeds the first one. By modifying their environments, successive communities create conditions that do not allow them to continue to exist but which permit the establishment of another community, and so on until a community develops that cannot be replaced by another if all environmental factors remain stable. The final community that can maintain itself indefinitely in a biotope is called the climax.

The authors cited believe that given sufficient time, all areas in the same climatic region would give rise to the same type of climax community. The climax community is determined mainly by the climate. On limited areas that have special soil or physiographic conditions, or that undergo repeated disturbances, different types of climax communities can arise. The process is considered to be deterministic.

At present there are numerous objections to this model and it is felt that not all successions necessarily lead to a climax. If disturbances are part of the normal environment, the term climax loses all meaning because all the species that persist are climax species. In addition, no community can be completely stable. Because the component species are of different ages and have different lifespan potentials, there are always weak or overmature individuals that disappear and others that take their places. Young individuals can quickly replace them. Openings in the vegetation cover or the soil allow the establishment of new individuals or species that were previously excluded. Thus all communities are characterized by constant change rather than by stability. The concept of climax is fundamentally a postulate of stability. However, all ecosystems are in a state of constant change; over the course of time they are subject to natural constraints and disturbances and they have their own dynamics. The recurrent fire cycle in many forest types is a representative example. Fire cycles are discussed more fully in the section on fire-dependent ecosystems.

The establishment of a pioneer community on a bare surface and its replacement by other communities as the succession progresses depends mainly on the existence of means of dispersal that allow new species to reach the area. The means by which animals and plants can invade new areas are extremely varied. Nonmobile forms can be transported by wind or water over large distances, or they may be transported by animals. (Some plant species possess vegetative means of regeneration.) As a result, new species invade the area where the disturbance occurred or the preexisting species become reestablished.

At present, it seems that no single dynamic model can explain all successions. The model of Clements, called the facilitation model by Connell and Slatyer (1977) because of its stress on changes within successional areas facilitating the establishment of new species, or the floristic relay by Egler (1954) because of the sequence of stages, can exist in some situations but not in all. Egler's "initial floristic composition" model in which surviving underground plant organs allow a destroyed community to reappear immediately seems to play a greater role in many situations. Where there is total plant cover, the opposite of the facilitation model seems to occur. In the course of a succession a community can prevent the arrival of other species through innumerable means of defense, although occupation of space is usually sufficient to prevent such invasion. This process has been called the inhibition model by Connell and Slatyer (op. cit.).

To invade or simply to establish themselves, species use two types of means which have been called the r and K strategies. The two letters come from symbols used in population dynamics equations by MacArthur and Wilson (1967). Plants which have high seed production with respect to their mass are known as r strategists, whereas those producing few seeds with respect to their mass are called K strategists. Generally, species with a pronounced r strategy are early successional species, whereas species with a pronounced K strategy are associated with climax stages. The r and K terminology, although currently in vogue, is of rather limited usefulness with regard to vegetation dynamics. Recent work has suggested that there is a continuum between the two strategies or that, in fact, other types of fundamental strategies exist (Grime 1977).

The appearance of a plant community on a bare surface normally involves three processes: immigration, establishment, and multiplication.

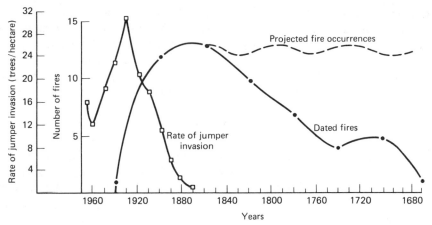

*Figure 6.4.* Frequency of fires and rate of western juniper invasion of the Owyhee Plateau (from Burkhardt and Tisdale 1976).

Immigration is the arrival of living organisms (disseminule or propagule) that can reproduce in a habitat where the species was not already represented. Establishment includes the seed germination phase, survival of seedlings, and growth of the plant. Many organisms that arrive in an area cannot live and thrive there. Fire often prevents the establishment of woody species (Figure 6.4). *Juniperus occidentalis* is an example of a fire-sensitive species. Before the arrival of the first settlers, stands of this species in southwestern Idaho were apparently restricted by periodic fires to rocky hillsides where the fires were less intense. With more active fire control over the last century, the juniper has spread into areas from which it was formerly excluded by fire (Burkhardt and Tisdale 1976). Multiplication is the increase in the number of individuals living in an area, ensuring perpetuation of the immigrant plants.

Working against strong dispersal pressures are barriers that slow or prevent the progression of some species. Ecological barriers can be either physical or biological. Some barriers are too wide to be crossed; others prevent unfavorable local conditions and cannot serve as relay stations. Large stretches of salt water or arid land may act as obstacles to dispersal. Mountain chains constitute barriers preventing the spread of plants or animals that require heat to survive.

Biological barriers are more difficult to detect, but they can also be effective in preventing the propagation of some species. The effect of biological barriers is perhaps more easily perceived when the barrier is competition between large plants. Dense tufts of grasses can prevent the invasion of a prairie by trees. As long as plants are disseminated in a bare area, they do not exert any effects on each other but need only deal with the physical conditions of soil and climate (and, sometimes, herbivorous animals). In environments with severe conditions this situation can persist indefinitely but, normally, the number of individuals increases until there are interrelationships that exercise a powerful influence on the establishment and development of future arrivals. These interrelationships can be advantageous, disadvantageous, or neutral. Usually the benefit consists of shelter, moisture, or shade provided by established plants. However, most of the time competition arises between species or individuals for water, food, light, heat, oxygen, space, carbon dioxide, and nutrient elements in the case of plants.

The genetic ability of species to deal with crowded conditions varies greatly and the ability of a given type of organism to compete is subject to environmental modification, so that it varies from one place to another. In addition, the intensity of competition varies with the seasons. For animals, the presence of certain plants is generally a prime factor in determining which species can become established. Vegetation must offer shelter and food.

The belief that natural ecosystems become more diversified and, therefore, more stable with time after a disturbance is widely held and regularly repeated in ecology. It is at final maturity that communities have the greatest stability. Both empirical and theoretical attempts have been made to demonstrate the quantitative relationships between diversity and stability. Unfortunately, it is difficult to establish a causal relationship between diversity and stability, especially since the word "stability" is subject to several different interpretations. Orians (1975) describes seven types of stability; others are possible. There are conflicting schools of thought with regard to stability. According to the classic theory, stability increases as succession proceeds. The second theory holds that plant communities are more stable the more they resist disturbances and the more quickly they return to their original states. A biotic community has to undergo a disturbance to prove its stability. The climax is thus not very stable because to return to its former state of vegetation it has to go through several successive stages.

Species diversity is not necessarily greater in advanced successional stages. As shown in Figure 6.5, it may be high a few months after a disturbance such as fire (Shafi and Yarranton 1973, Trabaud and Lepart 1980). The absence of disturbance may result in a fall-off of species diversity in communities considered to be climactic or close to climax; there are few plants adapted to the very shady environments of the end of a succession. Recurrent disturbances may even maintain diversity.

## FIRE-DEPENDENT ECOSYSTEMS

An ecosystem may be said to be fire dependent when its continued existence depends on the periodic occurrence of fires. If fires occur with sufficient regularity as in the African savannas, the Mediterranean shrublands, or the open pine forests in many parts of the world, these ecosystems may remain stable for millennia. They are then known as fire communities, even though in

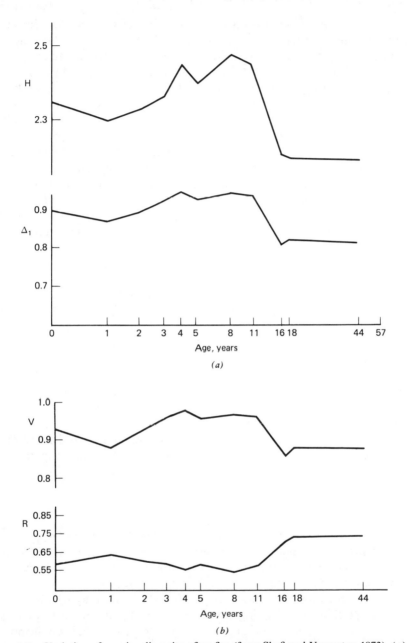

***Figure 6.5.*** Variation of species diversity after fire (from Shafi and Yarranton 1973). (*a*) The information measure of diversity **H'** and the probability of interspecific encounter, $\Delta_1$, at sites burned at various times in the past. (*b*) Evenness *V* and redundancy *R* at sites burned at various times in the past.

the line of ecological succession in the absence of fire they would be displaced by other species. For each individual species within the fire-dependent ecosystem, survival strategy depends on whether fire frequencies are such that fires can be expected to occur several times or only once during the normal lifetime of the individual. If fires will occur frequently, the species must develop characteristics that will allow the individuals to survive fire, at least until they reach sexual maturity. When fires can only be expected once in a lifetime, the survival of the individual is unimportant and species survival depends on ensuring immediate and prolific reproduction following fire. In this latter situation it is also advantageous for the species to ensure that a fire *does* occur during the lifetime of the individuals so that their postfire reproductive advantage can be realized. Consequently, fire-dependent ecosystems tend to be highly flammable and their flammability tends to increase over time. Fire protection in a fire-dependent ecosystem is not a static process. As protection succeeds and fire-free intervals get longer, the flammability of the ecosystem increases. As a result, a constantly increasing fire protection effort is required simply to keep the average area burned constant. Once fire protection efforts have been fixed at some constant level, the average annual burned area will increase until ecosystem flammability and available firefighting force reach equilibrium. When large areas of Siberian taiga were first provided with modern fire protection in the 1960s and 1970s, the successes were dramatic. Area burned in some districts dropped from 10 to 20 thousand hectares per year to 10 to 20 hectares. This trend will inevitably be reversed by the year 2000 unless fire suppression efforts are continuously expanded. In the United States, the constantly increasing budgets required to maintain burned area at the levels achieved by the mid1960s have resulted in policy changes that emphasize hazard reduction and ecosystem maintenance over conventional fire control activities.

## FIRE ADAPTATIONS

To survive fire most species have adaptive traits that allow them to regenerate and reproduce. What is an "adaptive trait"? Dobzhansky (1956) gives the following definition: "An adaptive trait, then, is an aspect of the development pattern which facilitates the survival and/or reproduction of its carrier in a certain succession of environments." It is difficult to say which traits are due to adaptation, as all living things possess organs or parts of organs adapted to the various disturbances and constraints of their environments (climatic conditions, and physical and biological disturbances). All living organisms display adaptations to the environment in which they live and its factors because they can live and reproduce there.

The adaptive traits used by living beings can be explained from three points of view: physical (physiological), ecological, and evolutionary. Thus the physical explanation of the serotinous cones of softwoods can be found by considering the physical properties of the material binding the bracts together. An ecological explanation can be provided by considering the quantity of seed liberated after a fire and disseminated by the animals feeding on it. The evolutionary explanation must be sought in the position of the pines possessing such cones with respect to other pines in the system. The pines with serotinous cones must have evolved genotypically in a fire environment. All these approaches represent attempts to understand the adaptation acquired by the species, but not all have been studied systematically and they do not afford an overall explanation of the phenomenon. In this section only fire-adaptive traits are considered.

Since fires can appear at any stage in plant development, adaptive traits can exist throughout the biological cycle.

Which traits should be regarded as adaptations to fire? One species may have a number of traits that can be considered to have reciprocal effects with a view to ensuring fire adaptation. Some of these traits may be more pronounced and have special significance directly related to the passage of fire. The time–temperature relationships for the coagulation of protoplasm are universal, and protoplasm coagulation defines lethality for the individual cell. Consequently, strategies for protecting the individual plant from fire injury are those that protect vital tissues from absorbing lethal amounts of heat. These consist of imposing insulating layers between the vital tissues and the external heat source, or of minimizing the amount of fuel on or adjacent to the plant thus reducing the heat load to which the vital tissues are subjected during fire. The former is a much more common strategy for most fire-dependent species.

The effectiveness of bark in insulating the cambial layer depends on bark thickness, thermal conductivity, density, heat capacity, thermal diffusivity, moisture content, thermal absorptivity, and the combustion properties of the bark itself. A full review of these considerations can be found in Spalt and Reifsnyder (1962).

Buds can be protected by covering them with layers of succulent nonflammable foliage (this adaptation is epitomized by *Pinus palustris*), by burying them deep within branch axils or heartwood pockets on the main stem (exemplified by many species of *Eucalyptus*), or locating them on the underground roots where sprouting is chemically induced after fire or other injury to the aboveground plant parts. This latter trait is common to many shrub species and to a few trees such as *Populus*.

Fuel minimization can occur by reducing the volume of small diameter stems and leaves or needles, by developing thick, fleshy photosynthetic and reproductive organs, or by reducing competitive herbaceous and shrub vegetation (allelopathy). Since these adaptations are almost always found in plants from arid regions, and since the adaptations serve to conserve available moisture as well as protect the plant from fire, it is not at all certain that they were truly developed in response to fire. However, they serve to preferentially perpetuate the species following fire and thus fit our definition of a fire adaptation. Traits relating to sexual or asexual reproduction can be closely associated with the frequency and intensity of fire and thus be adaptive traits. They may be grouped into the following categories (Gill 1977, 1981):

1. Vegetative survival of perennials through sprouts which may appear at various times in the life cycle depending on the position of the dormant buds and their protection by soil or bark.

2. Sexual reproduction promoted by increased stimulation of flowering after fire.

3. Increased seed liberation and dispersal due to fire.

4. Stimulation of germination by fire.

Survival of perennials after fire depends on the survival of buds having vascular connections with the roots. If the buds survive but the foliage of the plant is entirely destroyed, the buds produce new shoots. This is called sprouting.

Small woody plants generally have thin bark. They resist fire through production of shoots by subterranean organs protected from fire by the soil. Not only is soil a good insulator, that is, it does not conduct heat well, but also it receives only a small proportion of the heat produced by the burning vegetation (Packham 1971, Trabaud 1979). To have organs buried in the ground is an effective protection against fire. This phenomenon is universal and is found in many species in different parts of the world. Mooney and Dunn (1972) find that nearly 50 percent of small woody species in California and Chile sprouted after fire. Kruger (1977) finds that 65 percent of South African fynbos species behaved in the same fashion. Naveh (1974a) in Israel and Trabaud (1980a) in the south of France find that nearly all the woody species of these regions produce sprouts after fire. Protection of buds by soil and production of shoots when the leaves have been destroyed by fire is a very effective fire-survival mechanism. Perennial herbs, grasses, and ferns such as *Pteridium aquilinum* behave in the same manner (Daubenmire 1968b, Vogl 1974).

Most trees of the California chaparral (Hanes 1971) and of the European garrigues and maquis (Trabaud and Lepart op. cit.) produce sprouts. With the exception of perhaps 12 to 15 species, all eucalyptus have lignotubers (McArthur 1968). These woody protuberances begin as small swellings at the level of the axillae of the cotyledons and the first leaves of the seedlings. As the plant grows, the lignotuber enlarges and gradually buries itself in the soil. In small eucalypts subject to frequent burning, as in mallee formations, the lignotubers can grow continuously. This organ is a source of living buds that can survive fire owing to their subterranean position.

Bark, like soil, is an effective insulator (Hare 1961, Martin 1963), but the thickness of the bark is the most important factor determining the fire resistance of the tree. Many eucalypt species possess fire-resistant bark (Gill and Ashton 1968, Vines 1968). So does *Quercus suber*, whose branches produce large quantities of shoots after fires that are not too severe. *Pinus ponderosa* in the western United States (Weaver 1974) and *P. palustris, P. eeliottii*, and *P. taeda* in the southeastern United States (Komarek 1974) also have bark that protects the cambium and ensures the survival of the tree. The leafy shoots arise from dormant buds underneath the bark of the trunk or branches.

Sprouting is thought to be an ancient adaptation which appears only when the foliage is destroyed by an external agent. As long as the leaves are alive an inhibiting factor prevents the buds from becoming active, but when the foliage disappears so does the inhibition and the dormant buds produce sprouts (Gill 1977).

Fire can stimulate resistant plants to produce inflorescences. This has been observed particularly in geophytic monocotyledons and studied in *Xanthorrhoea australis*.

Plants of the genus *Xanthorrhoea* are widespread in the parts of Australia with a Mediterranean climate and also in southern Australia. *X. australis* is a plant about 2.5 m in height, with few branches and a thick trunk. The trunks are well protected from fire by a sleeve of densely arranged persistent leaf bases. Gill (1977, 1981) and Gill and Ingwersen (1976) have done careful studies of the mechanism of induction of flowering by fire in this species. Of the burned plants, 87 percent had produced inflorescences 4 to 7 months after the fire. Of the 30 control plants, only 37 percent had produced inflorescences 7 to 10 months after the beginning of the experiment, which the authors consider to be an unusually high proportion (Figure 6.6). The data indicate that fire season plays an extremely important role by affecting initiation of inflorescence and reproductive potential. The authors conclude that spring and summer burnings result in abundant production of inflorescences, whereas fall and winter burnings result in production of few inflorescences.

The flowering of plants such as *X. australis* immediately after fire and their virtual failure to do so beforehand is an extreme example of this type of adaptive trait. However, this behavior is also exhibited by many fire-resistant plants, mostly geophytes and especially Monocotyledons: Amaryllidaceae, Liliaceae, and Orchidaceae. Gill (1977) cites numerous observations made on species belonging to these families in South Africa, Australia, California, and Israel. However, the trait is not limited to Monocotyledons. Gill (1981) also cites three families of Dicotyledons (Proteaceac, Loranthaceae, and Droseraceae), certain genuses of which have the ability to flower abundantly only after fire.

The causes of these responses to fire are unknown. A change in the diurnal temperature variation after fire could act as a stimulus, or an increase in the amount of light reaching the soil could heat the floral primordia and cause flowering in this way. The disappearance of shrubs could promote pollination of geophytes, since the pollinating agents such as insects and

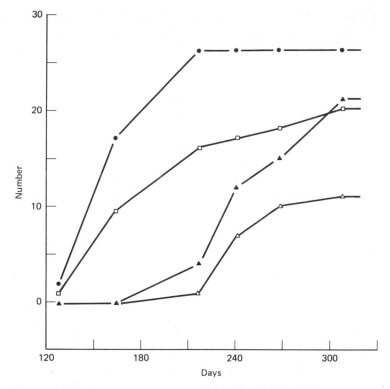

*Figure 6.6.* The effect of four treatments: burned (●), clipped (□), ethylene treatment (▲), and control (Δ) on the rates of appearance of primordial inflorescences in *X. australis* (from Gill and Ingwersen 1976).

wind could reach the flowers without having to overcome the obstacle of scrub, or could perceive them better in the case of insects.

Retention of seeds by the plant and stimulation of dispersal by fire is also an adaptive trait. If seedlings cannot establish themselves, annual liberation of seeds by perennials will not ensure reproduction. If, however, seed liberation coincides with the appearance of highly favorable germination conditions, reproduction is ensured. Thus many species possess dehiscent woody fruits that release their seeds shortly after fire.

A number of pine species possess cones that dehisce only after fire or under the effect of fire. In North America, *Pinus banksiana* possesses such serotinous cones, as does *P. contorta*, the lodgepole pine. The bracts of the cones of these species are held closed by a resin or wax sensitive to high temperatures. It melts as fire passes, allowing the seeds to fall. *P. contorta* is a particularly interesting example because its cones vary from the serotinous to the freely dehiscent type. In forests subject to frequent fires serotinous cones are common, whereas in stands where fire is less frequent, the cones are freely dehiscent (Brown 1975, Lotan 1975, 1976).

An analogous example is provided by *Banksia ornata* (Proteaceae) a shrub that is often dominant in the Mediterranean heaths of southeastern South Australia and western Victoria. The woody follicles of this species do not appear until the plant is five to seven years old (Specht et al. 1958). After fire burns a mature stand, there is generally massive release of seeds and establishment of seedlings. If the stands have not reached sufficient maturity to ensure reproduction when a fire occurs, the species may be eliminated from the areas it occupied.

*Eucalyptus* can release a few seeds each year. In the absence of fire, seed discharge occurs two to four years after maturity but, depending on the damage done to the trees, liberation of seeds can be greatly increased after a fire. Seed liberation is most marked after the most intense fires (Cremer 1962, Mount 1969).

The seeds released by the fruits that open due to fire often fall into an excellent seedbed. The ashes provide nutrients. The lack of foliage above increases the amount of light reaching the soil to promote seedling germination and growth, whereas the dead trees that still stand provide some shade to moderate the harshness of sun and wind, and thus reduce evaporation and sun-scorch.

As a corollary, the accumulation of seeds in the soil and stimulation of their germination by fire can be an adaptive trait. In the same way, fire can remove the obstacles to seed germination that cause accumulation of viable seeds in the soil.

The high level of seed germination in recently burned plant communities can generally be attributed to the liberation of seeds retained by the plants or to the germination of seeds buried in the soil for many years. In some cases seeds may be transported to the burned area from sources in unburned neighboring areas. The germination of seeds stored in the soil has been attributed to two principal causes: the structure of the seed envelope and allelopathy.

Seed response to high temperatures depends on the duration of exposure to heat. Long periods of exposure to relatively low temperatures give the same result as short exposures to higher temperatures, whether the response is germination or death of the seed. This has been observed for forest species of eastern Australia (Floyd 1966), the Scottish moors Whittaker and Gimingham 1962), the southeastern United States (Martin and Cushwa 1966, Martin et al. 1975), and the garrigues of southern France (Vuillemin and Bulard 1981). In nature, the response of the stock of buried seed depends not only on the properties of the seed but also on the characteristics of the fire, that is, its effect on soil temperature and its duration (Christensen and Kimber 1975), and on the position of the seeds in the soil (Trabaud 1970, 1980a and b, Moore and Wein 1977).

After a fire, many annual or biannual herbaceous species germinate and flower abundantly, to disappear in two or three years. This has been observed in the California chaparral (Muller et al. 1968), in Australia (Specht et al. op. cit.), South Africa (Kruger op. cit.), Israel (Naveh 1974), and France (Trabaud and Lepart op. cit.). Muller et al. (op. cit.) and Christensen and Muller (1975) have conducted more extensive research on this type of phenomenon. They conclude that the profuse flowering and growth of herbaceous species after fires in California is due to the removal of a chemical inhibition agent acting on seeds buried in soil produced by the woody cover. The research of Muller and colleagues on allelopathic phenomena in the Californian chaparral shows that light, water, and mineral nutrients are not limiting factors for germination. However, ligneous extracts affect seed germination, and seeds of herbaceous species subjected to temperatures of 80°C for one hour showed an increased rate of germination. These authors conclude that heat is not necessary for germination but stimulates it by removing the inhibiting factor. As soon as the woody plants become reestablished, seed inhibition is reinstated but the seeds remain viable until another fire occurs. This allelopathic phenomenon often does not occur where there is very strong competition for light and space by perennials, so that the annuals and biannuals cannot persist (Trabaud 1970, 1980a).

Of the adaptive traits presented, some can coexist in the same plant whereas others are mutually exclusive. Plants in which seed release and dispersal is associated with fire generally retain their seeds on the plant. Some plants with vegetative resistance can reproduce by means of seed, whereas others cannot. Some plants produce large quantities of seed but cannot regenerate vegetatively. The significance of these traits must be considered together with the life cycle of the species and the fire regimes: type, season, frequency, and intensity.

## VARIABILITY OF FIRE

These adaptive traits have been considered in connection with the appearance of a single fire, but an individual plant may be subjected to several fires. Fire recurrence is very important because it can have important consequences for the successful survival of a population or species. The significance of adaptive traits must be considered in the context of the life cycle of the species and the fire cycles to which the species is subjected. This approach also permits consideration of species that are not endowed with such adaptive traits but that still continue to survive and reproduce in communities subject to fire. It also leads to consideration of the size of the fire and the weather conditions preceding or following fire.

The timing and periodicity of fires are of extreme importance in the lives of plant communities as these factors affect plant survival and flowering, whereas fire intensity affects the resistance of woody plants and seed liberation and germination.

**Season of Fire Occurrence**

The timing of the fire plays a very important role in triggering the appearance of inflorescences and the reproductive potential of *Xanthorrhoea australis* (Gill 1977). Six months after an experimental fire, individuals burned in spring and summer had produced abundant inflorescences while individuals burned in fall and winter produced few. Less than five percent of the unburned plants had produced inflorescences.

Most fires in the eastern portion of the South African fynbos occur in summer, but in the southern part many fires start in winter, with a small peak in summer (Kruger op. cit.). Despite this periodicity in fire frequency distribution, fires may occur at any season. When fires occur in fall, populations of *Watsonia pyramidata*, a geophyte, react strongly with at least half the branches producing inflorescences. In populations burned in spring, the number of plants that flower remains the same as in unburned populations or may diminish slightly. In unburned populations only about five percent of the branches flower annually (Kruger op. cit.). As each inflorescence produces about 700 seeds, fall fires have enormous influence on *Watsonia* populations.

The season in which fires occur may affect community phytomass. In experiments on the effect of fires repeated at two-year intervals in spring and fall on the structure of *Quercus coccifera* garrigue (Trabaud 1980a) fall fires produced a change in the structure of the community. The phytomass of woody plants diminished with fall fires, whereas the phytomass of herbaceous plants increased (Figures 6.7 and 6.8). When fires were ignited in spring, the woody species always constituted the major part of the residual phytomass, as in unburned plots.

In Texas fire season was of considerable importance in *Hilaria mutica* communities. Perennial herbaceous species survived spring fires and were thus able to constitute stable populations. Spring fires were unfavorable to annual grasses which had germinated after the winter rains and were destroyed by the fire before they could produce seed. Perennial species were still dormant at this time and could sprout from stumps after a fire (Wright 1969, 1973, 1974).

**Fire Size**

The size of the burned area is also an important ecological factor affecting recolonization. For instance, if many plants cannot regenerate by sprouting and depend on the transportation of diaspores by wind or animals and if the burned area is extensive so that seed carriers must cover large distances, some species will not become established immediately or the first species to arrive will be the ones that become established. The weight and aerodynamic properties of fruits or seeds play a determining role.

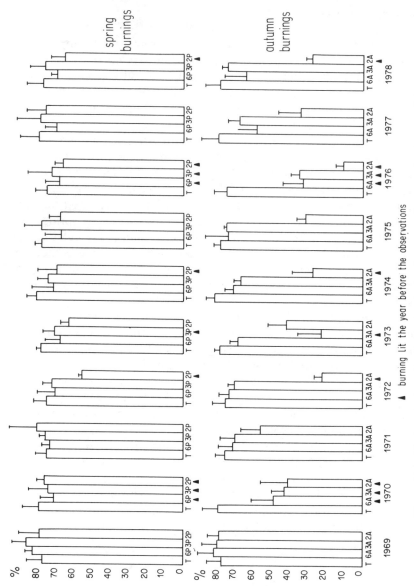

*Figure 6.7.* Changes in the ratio of the quantitative frequency from woody plants to the total vegetation quantitative frequency of a *Quercus coccifera* garrigue according to different prescribed fire regimes (Trabaud 1980).

The replacement of *Pinus resinosa* (red pine) forests and *P. strobus* (eastern white pine) forests by *P. banksiana* (jack pine) is thought to be due to the fact that the first two species release seeds every year so that their seeds would be destroyed by high temperatures during fires or, if the seed-bearing plants were far from the burned area, seeds could not be transported there. The jack pine, by contrast, because of its serotinous cones does not release its seeds until a fire occurs or directly afterwards, so that even burned trees can ensure regeneration (Ahlgren 1974).

Burned surfaces more than 60 m distant from a source of *Picea mariana* (black spruce) or *P. glauca* (white spruce) seed may not receive any seed to ensure recolonization because the seeds of these plants are for all practical purposes not disseminated farther than this. *Populus tremuloides* (quaking aspen), *P. balsamifera* (balsam poplar), and to a lesser degree *Betula papyrifera* (paper birch) can invade these areas because their seeds can be dispersed far from the point of origin and, in addition, these trees can sprout (Zasada 1971).

Animal reaction can vary depending on the size of the fire. The larger the burned area, the fewer interactions there are between burned and intact vegetation, while small fires create a large variety of biotopes. The size and shape of a burned area determine in part the number of new habitats that can be used by animals. Animals can invade new habitats and proliferate because they have relatively few contacts with other animals belonging to their own species or other species. A small fire may not cause enough change to have a significant impact on wildlife. Burned areas over 200 m wide in heather moors are not occupied by the *Lagopus* (red grouse) because of the absence of cover. The population of *Dendragapus* (blue grouse), however, is greater in large burned areas than in small ones (Bendell 1974).

## Fire Intensity

The intensity of a fire varies according to the amount, moisture content, and structure of the fuel. In communities where the strata are largely separated fires may be confined to the ground, whereas if there is continuous vertical distribution of fuel, more intense fires may occur. It is often very difficult to establish clearly the degree of intensity of a fire. Some authors judge intensity from observed effects on vegetation or soil, others from temperature recordings, and others from physical intensity using the index of Byram. Forest fire intensity can vary from 20 to over 60,000 kW m$^{-1}$ (Luke and McArthur 1978).

Response to fire varies considerably depending on the natural role of fire in the ecosystem. Thus in communities rarely subject to fire with highly fire-sensitive species such as the swampy *Chamaecyparis thyoides* (white cedar) forest of the southeastern United States, a surface fire can create a more intense disturbance than do crown fires in the California chaparral or *Pinus contorta* forests (Christensen 1981), where intense fires may merely stimu-

Figure 6.8.

**Figure 6.8.** Influence of the fire season and frequency upon the structure of a plant community. (*a*) Unburned *Quercus coccifera* garrigue (30 years old, last wildfire in 1951). (*b*) Garrigue burned every six years in spring (six years after the second burn). (*c*) Garrigue burned every two years in autumn (two years after the sixth burn). Photos by Louis Trabaud.

late reproduction of the same species and cause little change in floristic composition.

In *Pseudotsuga menziesii* (Douglas fir) forests, forest fire intensity varies from low-intensity surface fires to high-intensity crown fires. There is evidence that high-intensity crown fires occurred in Douglas fir forests before the arrival of settlers in that the first Europeans on the west coast found extensive immature stands of uniform age, just like those that arise in the wake of intense fires. In extreme weather conditions with strong winds, crown fires swept large areas of Douglas fir forest; otherwise, surface fires of relatively low intensity occurred (Kilgore 1981).

In Australia intense crown fires kill trees and shrubs by raising the temperature of meristemic tissue to lethal levels. The aboveground parts of shrubs, small trees, and ferns are totally reduced to ashes, but some arborescent ferns, Cycadaceae, and palms can survive. Only the trunks of the large eucalypts, dead or living remain. The lower parts of the upper crowns of the eucalypts may be scorched, with flames killing the trees where they reach the trunk which is protected only by thin bark (Ashton 1981). In low-intensity fires the vegetation suffers little damage despite some damage to the understory. Species that regenerate vegetatively sprout abundantly.

Fire intensity also affects the soil. In the chaparral, intense fires (700°C) completely destroy all organic matter on the soil surface. During an intense fire maximum temperatures at depths of 2.5 cm may reach 150°C and are high enough to destroy all organic matter by distillation. Fires of moderate intensity, with surface temperatures of 430°C, are capable of destroying most of the litter. Low-intensity fires (250°C) remove about 85 percent of the litter from the soil surface but only the humic acids are altered at 2.5 cm depth (DeBano et al. 1977).

## Depth of Burn

Subterranean survival organs (roots, rhizomes, seeds, and so on) are situated at various depths (Moore and Wein op. cit., Trabaud 1980a). The depth to which a fire burns is generally related to surface intensity and to litter and soil moisture content. If a fire burns deeply, these organs will be killed and the reestablishment of the species will be rendered more difficult or delayed. If the fire is superficial and does not destroy these organs, the vegetation can take hold again quickly and recovery will be almost immediate.

In *Pinus strobus* (eastern white pine) forests, McConkey and Gedney (1951) observe that root injuries caused by wildfires are more serious than crown lesions. In areas where more than 75 percent of superficial main roots were killed or seriously damaged by fire but only one-third or less of the crown was scorched, mortality in the three years following the fire was: small trees (5 to 15 cm diameter), 100 percent; medium-sized trees (17 to 27 cm), 60 percent; large trees (> 30 cm), 40 percent. However, where less than 25 percent of the root system was injured, even if more than two-thirds of the crown was scorched, mortality was lower: small trees, 80 percent; medium-sized trees, 46 percent; large trees, 14 percent.

In the forests of the low plains of the same region, shrubs and deciduous trees possess dormant survival buds situated in the deep organic layer. A single fire that burns deeply can destroy nearly all the vegetation competing with *Pinus rigida* (pitch pine). In New Jersey, a fire during the very dry period at the end of summer or beginning of fall can burn deeply enough to kill the buds on the shrubs and trees and hinder competition with the pines (Little 1974, Little and Moore 1953). The number of pine seedlings per hectare was 16,750 to 17,250 where the fire had burned deeply, but only 500 to 1850 per hectare when the fire had not burned deeply. On the second site, the trees and shrubs sprouted and the sprouts competed strongly with the small numbers of pine seedlings. Where the fire had burned deeply, most of the deciduous trees and shrubs did not sprout, so that the fire had not only prepared better conditions for the germination and establishment of the pines but also had in large part eliminated the competing species.

Shearer (1975), in a study of the effects of prescribed burning on the establishment of *Larix occidentalis* (western larch), uses the mortality rate of roots of nonresinous species as a reference from which to judge the effectiveness of the burn. Root mortality varied according to depth. At 1 cm mortality varied from 100 to 25 percent and was directly related to surface fire intensity. At 10 cm the rate was only 10 percent. However, during a wildfire that occurred when the soil was very dry, nearly 100 percent of the roots in the upper centimeter were killed and 70 percent of those between 8 and 10 cm died. The depth of burn may also cause changes in soil microbe populations.

The changes are most marked in superficial soil layers. The depth at which an effect can be detected increases with the intensity of the fire. Bacterial populations in the upper 3 cm of burned soil were superior to those of unburned soil seven months after a fire in the northwestern United States. No change was noted after low-intensity fires (Wright and Tarrant 1957). In the southern United States, the bacterial population in the fermentation and humus layers increased after burning but did not change significantly below the organic layer (Jorgensen and Hodges 1970, 1971).

## Frequency of Fire

Fire frequency affects the floristic composition of ecosystems by selecting the species that will continue to form part of the vegetation of an area. A species cannot survive if fire occurs too often, too early, or too late in its life cycle. For instance, in any given area the survival of species which do not sprout may be threatened if fire occurs before they have produced and accumulated seed, or if it occurs after they have disappeared and the seed stock is exhausted.

Over the distribution of *Pinus contorta* (lodgepole pine), the most probable interval between two fires varies from a maximum of 500 to less than 100 years. In some areas there may only be a few years between fires. Regionally, fire frequency varies depending on the dryness of the summer and how much lightning there is; locally, it varies depending on factors such as slope, exposure, and altitude (Brown op. cit.).

In a review of the effects of fire on the pine barrens of New Jersey, Little (op. cit.) observes that wildfires occurring at intervals of 8 to 12 years easily eliminated *Pinus echinata* (shortleaf pine) and the associated oaks over one to two centuries. In the same area there are stands of *P. rigida* and bushy oaks (*Quercus ilicifolia, Q. marilandica*). Some species are of normal height, while others do not exceed 3 m. This difference is thought to be related to fire history in the region. The first type of formation is thought to be overrun by fire only every 16 years or so, whereas the bushy forms and the forms issued from sprouts are thought to have undergone very intense fires every eight years.

In *Pinus ponderosa* forests the intervals between fires are highly variable.

Weaver (op. cit.) analyzes the data of various authors and concludes that fires occur at an average interval of 14 to 18 years in Oregon, 8 to 10 years in the Californian Sierra Nevada, every 10 years in Washington, and as frequently as every 4 to 5 years in Arizona.

Of Mediterranean-type ecosystems, the California chaparral is one of the best studied. Keeley (1981) feels that the most common fire frequency was between 20 and 30 years. Some authors (Hanes op. cit.) feel that fire is necessary to keep a population vigorous and healthy. Old populations over 60 years are decadent and show signs of degeneration. In a *Quercus coccifera* garrigue in southern France, the regular occurrence of fire every two years in fall changed the structure of the community but not the floristic composition (Trabaud 1980a).

Simard (1975) prepared a map of Canada, using fire occurrence data to delineate zones of varying historic fire frequency. In this publication, fire frequency is expressed in terms of probable number of fires per 1000 square kilometers per year. Simard found that these probability values varied from 0 to 73 in various provinces.

### Pre- and Postfire Weather Conditions

The atmospheric conditions that play principal roles before and after fires are not the same. Before a severe fire, weather conditions play the major role, determining its appearance (Van Wagner 1977), whereas after the fire, climatic conditions affect the establishment of animal or plant species. Wade and Ward (1973) observe that a cold front passed over the *Pinus serotina* (pond pine) forest of the Air Force bomb range in North Carolina three days before a very large and destructive fire, bringing in cold dry air. The relative humidity was already low, continued to drop, and remained below 60 percent for the next three days with daily minimums as low as 2.5 percent. The day the fire broke out, temperatures had risen to 21°C by 11 o'clock, although it was only March. The low relative humidity, high temperature, and strong winds contributed to the establishment of dry conditions favorable for fire. The day the fire started, the drought index was 54, the build-up index 28, and the spread index 36.

In *Pinus clausa* (sand pine) forests in Florida, Hough (1973) observes that weather conditions before severe fires are always similar: low precipitation in fall and spring, up to 200 mm less than normal; low relative humidity (25 to 35 percent); high winds (14 to 32 km/h). Large fires were also associated with passage of weather fronts or unstable air masses.

A notable fire in forests of *Larix occidentalis, Abies lasiocarpa,* and *Picea engelmannii* on Mount Sundance in southern Idaho was ignited by lightning three weeks before the conflagration (Finklin 1973). During these three weeks it was hot and dry in the area with no rain. The build-up index reached 348 the day of maximum extent of the fire. Two low pressure areas passed over the region during this period (Figure 6.9). The fire was really fanned

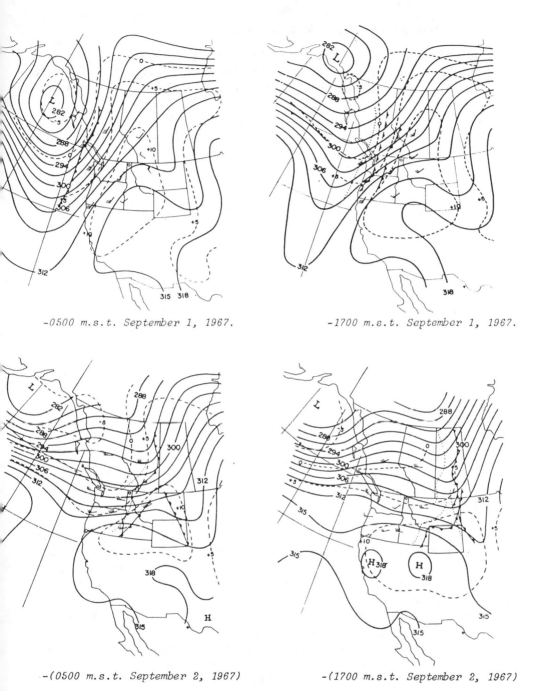

-0500 m.s.t. September 1, 1967.

-1700 m.s.t. September 1, 1967.

-(0500 m.s.t. September 2, 1967)

-(1700 m.s.t. September 2, 1967)

**Figure 6.9.** Analyses of 700 mb. conditions September 1, 1967 through September 2, 1967, and superimposed surface-map positions of fronts. Height contours are labeled in tens of meters, isotherms (dashed lines) in °C. Wind reports are plotted in standard symbolic form, with speeds to nearest 5 knots: tail of arrow (containing "barbs") points in direction from which wind is blowing; each full barb denotes 10 knots of speed (a half barb, 5 knots), a pennant 50 knots. Frontal positions 6 hours earlier are indicated by dotted lines (from Finklin 1973).

161

into action by southwesterly winds of 32 to 40 km/h, with gusts to 56 km/h. A dry cold front had passed by before the lows. The passage of fronts before periods of high fire hazard has also been noted in Australia (Luke and McArthur op. cit.).

After a fire, it is climatic conditions that principally affect recolonization. A long drought can prevent the appearance of some plants or kill them after they appear. Heavy rain can cause severe erosion, washing away much of the superficial soil layer (Wells et al. 1979) and with it the diaspores it contains. Therefore, some of the plants that could reestablish themselves are eliminated and the conditions for species reappearance are altered.

The black color of burned vegetation and soil increases the amount of heat received by an area and hence the temperature of the soil surface. The vigorous and immediate regrowth of vegetation after fire has been attributed by several authors to this temperature increase (Ahlgren and Ahlgren 1960, Anderson 1973, Daubenmire 1968b). Minimum temperatures are generally lower and maximums higher in burned than unburned areas (Trabaud 1980a). Relative humidity is lower because of the more intense sunlight and increased windspeed. These environmental modifications indirectly produce changes in wildlife (Bendell op. cit.). Fire also modifies the effect of snow. A forest floor receives less snow than the ground in a burned area because tree crowns intercept some of the load. When snow melts on the foliage of trees, the droplets of water that fall reduce the depth of the snow layer on the ground below. Inasmuch as temperatures fluctuate less in a forest and winds are weaker, any crust that forms tends to remain. Snow also lasts longer in a forest than in a burned area because the trees protect the snow from direct sunlight and insulate the frozen ground and the snow above.

## FIRE CYCLES

Lightning and volcanic activity have been causes of fire since there has been fuel to burn everywhere in the world and no one can deny their importance but human development has profoundly changed the natural frequency of fire. Unfortunately, fire frequency before and since the dawn of history is known only for a small number of geographic regions. Fire frequency has been estimated mainly from scars left by fires on trees (Arno 1976, Weaver op. cit.) or by means of paleoecological techniques which can focus on longer periods (Byrne et al. 1977, Swain 1973, Wright 1974) by examining pieces of charcoal included in the varves of sediments.

The fire cycle depends on the frequency, intensity, season, and distribution pattern of fire. Fire frequently plays a major role in determining vegetation structure, but vegetation structure largely determines fire intensity. There can be various combinations of intensity and frequency: frequent low-intensity surface fires, infrequent low-intensity surface fires, or infrequent high-intensity surface fires, all the way to infrequent high-intensity crown

**Table 6.1.** *Some Ecosystem Types and their Fire Cycles*

| Bioclimatic Zones Ecosystem Types | Site | Fire Frequency (Years) |
|---|---|---|
| *Tundra* | | |
| Tundra | Canada, Alaska | 500 |
| Alpine tundra | Rockies | 300 |
| Alpine tundra | New England | 1000+ |
| *Boreal Forest* | | |
| Open forest of *Picea* and lichens | Alaska, Yukon | 130 |
| Open *Picea* forest | Northwest Territories (NWT) | 120 |
| Closed forest of *Picea* and *Betula* or *P. mariana* | Alaska, Yukon | 100 |
| Forest of *Picea mariana* and *P. glauca* | NWT | 100 |
| *Picea* forest | British Columbia | 100 |
| *Picea mariana* forest | Ontario | 100 |
| *Picea mariana* forest | Hudson Bay | 150 |
| Open *Picea mariana* forest | Quebec | 150 |
| *Picea glauca* forest and flood plains | Alaska, Yukon | 200+ |
| *Picea glauca* forest and flood plains | NWT | 200+ |
| *Picea mariana* and *Abies* forest | Newfoundland | 150 |
| *Picea mariana* and *Pinus banksiana* forest | Quebec | 100 |
| *Picea mariana* and *Pinus banksiana* forest | Ontario | 60 |
| Open *Pinus banksiana* forest | NWT | 25–100 |
| *Pinus contorta* forest | British Columbia | 50 |
| *Pinus contorta* and *Picea* forest | Alberta | 50 |
| Mixed forest | Alberta | 50 |
| *Subalpine Forest* | | |
| *Pinus contorta* forest | Alberta | 25–50 |
| *Pinus contorta* forest | Montana | 25–150 |
| *Pinus contorta* forest | Wyoming | 25–75 |
| *Pinus contorta* forest | Colorado | 100 |
| *Pinus contorta* forest | Sierra Nevada, California | 100–300 |
| *Pinus contorta, Picea, Abies* forest | Alberta | 55–100 |
| *Pinus contorta, Picea, Abies* forest | Montana | 35–150 |
| *Pinus contorta, Picea, Abies* forest | Wyoming | 150 |
| *Picea* and *Abies* forest | Montana | 300+ |
| *Abies balsamea* and *Picea rubens* forest | New England | 1000+ |
| *Populus tremuloides* forest | Colorado | 100 |
| *Laurentians and Great Lakes* | | |
| *Picea mariana* forest | Minnesota | 150 |
| *Pinus banksiana, Picea mariana* forest | Minnesota | 50 |
| *Populus, Betula, Abies* forest | Minnesota | 80 |

**Table 6.1** *(Continued)*

| Bioclimatic Zones Ecosystem Types | Site | Fire Frequency (Years) |
|---|---|---|
| *Pinus resinosa, P. strobus* forest | Minnesota | 20–180 |
| *Pinus banksiana* barrens | Great Lakes | 15–60 |
| *Pinus rigida, P. echinata* barrens | New Jersey | 10–20 |
| *Pinus strobus, Tsuga,* and deciduous forest | New Hampshire | 250 |
| *Acer saccharum, Betula lutea, Tsuga,* and *Pinus strobus* | Great Lakes | 350 |
| Mixed forest | Minnesota | 60–70 |
| *Populus* savanna-woodland | Minnesota, Manitoba, Saskatchewan, Alberta | 10 |
| *Temperate Acadian Forest* | | |
| *Picea rubens, Tsuga,* and *Pinus* forest | New Brunswick | 150 |
| *Acer saccharum, Tsuga,* and *Pinus* forest | New Brunswick | 300 |
| Deciduous forest | NE United States, SE Canada | 100–500 |
| *Moist Temperate Forest* | | |
| *Pinus palustris* and *Andropogon* forest | SE United States | 3 |
| *Pinus* savanna-woodland | SE United States | 20–50 |
| *Nothofagus* and *Atherosperma* rainforest | Tasmania | 300 |
| Mixed *Eucalyptus regnans, E. fastigata* forest | Tasmania | 150–200 |
| Sclerophyllous forest (*Eucalyptus, Pomaderris, Olearia*) | Tasmania | 100 |
| *Eucalyptus* heath | Tasmania | 50–70 |
| Grasslands | Tasmania | 10–25 |
| *Grasslands* | | |
| Prairie | Missouri | 1 |
| Annual or perennial grassland | Central North America | 5–25 |
| Swamps and marshes | SE United States | 30–100 |
| *Dry Temperate Forest* | | |
| Mixed coniferous forest | California | 7–10 |
| Mixed coniferous and *Sequoia* forest | California | 10–100 |
| *Pinus ponderosa* forest | Sierra Nevada, California | 5–10 |
| *Pinus ponderosa* forest | Arizona | 5–10 |
| *Pinus ponderosa* forest | Oregon | 15–20 |
| *Pinus ponderosa* forest | Washington | 10 |

**Table 6.1** *(Continued)*

| Bioclimatic Zones<br>Ecosystem Types | Site | Fire Frequency<br>(Years) |
|---|---|---|
| *Mediterranean Vegetation* | | |
| Evergreen chaparral (*Adenostoma, Quercus*) | California | 20–50 |
| Deciduous chaparral (*Salvia, Encelia* coastal sage scrub) | California | 30–100 |
| *Cupressus forbesii* forest | California | 50–100 |
| *Pinus (P. attenuata, muricata, coulteri, sabiniana, jeffreyi)* forests | California | 20–40 |
| *Steppes and Semiarid Desert Areas* | | |
| Desert scrub | Arizona, California | 50–100 |
| Scrub steppe | W. United States | 100–300 |
| *Pinus* and *Juniperus* woodland | W. United States | 100–300 |
| *Tropical Vegetation* | | |
| Moist evergreen scrub | Florida | 20–30 |
| Tropical forest | Tropical and equatorial areas | Never Burns |

fires. Variable cycles also exist in which frequent low-intensity fires alternate with infrequent high-intensity blazes.

There are many reasons for this variability but it is primarily due to the different frequencies of ignition and different fuel characteristics of the phytomass. The fire-frequency amplitude that can be supported by an ecosystem without change in floristic composition or structure is wide; fire frequency is not the same in a grassland as in a coniferous or deciduous forest. Fire frequency also depends on the site of the community, whether it is in the boreal zone or the tropics where vegetative growth and recovery occur at different rates. The main point is that fire frequency has shaped the evolution of vegetation, and any change in the fire cycle of a community will automatically entail a change in its floristic composition and structure.

The successive repetition of fires is important to understand because it can markedly affect the survival possibility of an individual, population, or species after fire. The season of fire appearance and its effects with regard to plant survival and flowering, and the importance of fire intensity with regard to tree response and seed germination have already been mentioned. The significance of an adaptive trait must be considered in the context of the cycle of the species itself and of the fire cycle to which the species is exposed. This context also enables consideration of species that do not possess "classic" adaptive traits but continue to survive and reproduce in fire environments. The time lapse in a fire cycle is highly variable. Some species or types of vegetation such as grasses or the North American prairie and the African savannas can support a fire every year, whereas for other species or types such as boreal or subalpine forest, the natural fire cycle is 300 years or more. Table 6.1 gives an idea of fire frequency amplitude for several well-studied communities (data excerpted from Heinselman 1981, Keeley op. cit., Noble and Slatyer 1981, Wein 1978).

When fire is too frequent and the natural fire cycle is disturbed, irreversible changes in community composition may appear, and communities adapted to the new fire cycle become established. In the wettest parts of Tasmania where natural fires occur no more than once every 300 years, the forest is dominated by *Nothofagus* and *Atherosperma*. When fire frequency drops to every 200 years, three species of *Eucalyptus* invade and overtake the two types just mentioned. If fire occurs once or twice per century, a low forest of *Pomaderris, Olearia,* and *Acacia* will replace *Nothofagus*. If fire occurs every 10 to 20 years, low *Eucalyptus* will invade and dominate the site. Areas where fires are still more frequent become covered with grasses (Jackson 1968). This example provides an excellent illustration of the importance of the fire cycle and of how necessary knowledge of it is to an understanding of ecosystems.

# BIBLIOGRAPHY

Ahlgren, C. E. 1974. Effects of fire on temperate forest: North Central United States. In T. T. Kozlowski and C. E. Ahlgren, Eds., *Fire and Ecosystems*, Academic, New York, pp. 195–223.

Ahlgren, I. F. and C. E. Ahlgren. 1960. Ecological effects of forest fires. *Bot. Rev.* **26**:483–533.

Anderson, R. C. 1973. *The use of fire as a management tool on the Curtis prairie*. Proc. Ann. Tall Timbers Fire Ecol. Conf. **12**:23–35.

Arno, S. F. 1976. *The historical role of fire in the Bitterroot National Forest*. U.S. For. Serv. Res. Paper INT-187, 29 pp.

Ashton, D. H. 1981. Fire in tall open forests (wet sclerophyll forests). In A. M. Gill, R. H. Groves, and I. R. Noble, Eds., *Fire and Australian Biota*, Aust. Acad. Sci., Canberra, pp. 339–366.

Bendell, J. F. 1974. Effects of fire on birds and mammals. In T. T. Kozlowski and C. E. Ahlgren, Eds., *Fire and Ecosystems*, Academic, New York, pp. 73–138.

Brown, J. K. 1975. *Fire cycles and community dynamics in lodgepole pine forests*. Proc. Symp. Monogr. Lodgepole Pine Ecosyst., Wash. State Univ. Coop. Ext. Serv. Publ., pp. 429–456.

Burkhardt, J. W. and E. W. Tisdale. 1976. Causes of juniper invasion in southwestern Idaho. *Ecology* **57**:472–684.

Byrne R., J. Michaelsen, and A. Souter. 1977. *Fossil charcoal as a measure of wildfire frequency in southern California: a preliminary analysis*. Proc. Symp. Environ. Consequences Fire Fuel Manage. Medit. Ecosyst. U.S. For. Serv. Gen. Tech. Report WO-3, pp. 361–367.

Cayford, J. H. 1970. *The role of fire in the ecology and silviculture of jack pine*. Ann. Tall Timbers Fire Ecol. Conf. Proc., **10**:221–244.

Christensen, N. L. 1981. *Fire regimes in southeastern ecosystems.* Proc. Conf. Fire Regimes and Ecosyst. Properties, U.S. For. Serv. Gen. Tech. Report WO-26, pp. 112–136.

Christensen, N. L. and C. H. Muller. 1975. Effects of fire on factors controlling plant growth in *Adenostoma* chaparral. *Ecol. Monogr.* **45**:29–55.

Christensen, P. E. and P. C. Kimber. 1975. *Effect of prescribed burning on the flora and fauna of southwest Australian forests.* Proc. Ecol. Soc. Aust., **9**:85–106.

Clark, G. L. 1959. *Elements of ecology.* Wiley, New York, 535 pp.

Clements, F. E. 1916. *Plant succession.* Carnegie Inst. Wash. Pub. 242, 512 pp.

Clements, F. E. 1928. *Plant succession and indicators.* H. W. Wilson, New York, 434 pp.

Clements, F. E. 1936. Nature and structure of the climax. *J. Ecol.* **24**:252–284.

Connell, J. H. and R. O. Slatyer. 1977. Mechanisms of succession in natural communities and their role in community stability and organization. *Am. Nat.* **111**:1119–1144.

Cremer, K. W. 1962. Effects of fire on seedshed from *Eucalyptus regnans. Aust. For.* **29**:252–262.

Daubenmire, R. 1968a. *Plant communities.* Harper and Row, New York, 300 pp.

Daubenmire, R. 1968b. *Ecology of fire in grasslands. Advances in Ecological Res.*, Vol. 5, Academic, London, pp. 209–266.

DeBano, L. F., P. H. Dunn, and C. E. Conrad. 1977. *Fire's effect on physical and chemical properties of chaparral soils.* Proc. Environ. Consequences Fire Fuel Manage. Medit. Ecosyst., U.S. For. Serv. Gen. Tech. Report WO-3, pp. 65–74.

Dobzhansky, T. 1956. What is an adaptive trait? *Am. Nat.* **90**:337–347.

Egler, F. E. 1954. Vegetation science concepts. I: Initial floristic composition, a factor in old field vegetation development. *Vegetatio* **4**:412–417.

Finklin, A. I. 1973. *Meteorological factors in the Sundance fire run.* U.S. For. Serv. Gen. Tech. Report INT-6, 46 pp.

Floyd, A. G. 1966. Effects of fire on weed seeds in wet sclerophyll forests of northern New South Wales. *Aust. J. Bot.* **14**:243–256.

Gill, A. M. 1977. *Plant trait adaptive to fires in Mediterranean land ecosystems.* Proc. Symp. Environ. Consequences Fire Fuel Manage. Medit. Ecosyst., U.S. For. Serv. Gen. Tech. Report WO-3, pp. 17–26.

Gill, A. M. 1981. Adaptive responses of Australian plant species to fires. In A. M. Gill, R. H. Groves, and I. R. Noble, Eds., *Fire and Australian Biota*, Aust. Acad. Sci., Canberra, pp. 243–272.

Gill, A. M. and D. H. Ashton. 1968. The role of bark type in relative tolerance to fire in three central victorian eucalypts. *Aust. J. Bot.* **16**:491–498.

Gill, A. M. and F. Ingwersen. 1976. Growth of *Xanthorrhoea australis* R. Br. in relation to fire. *J. Appl. Ecol.* **13**:195–203.

Grime, J. P. 1977. Evidence for the existence of three primary strategies in plants and its relevance to ecological and evolutionary theory. *Am. Nat.* **111**:1169–1194.

Hanes, T. L. 1971. Succession after fire in the chaparral of southern California. *Ecol.* **48**:259–264.

Hare, R. C. 1961. *Heat effects on living plants.* U.S. For. Serv. Occ. Paper 183, 32 pp.

Heinselman, M. L. 1970. The natural role of fire in northern conifer forests. *Naturalist* **21**:15–23.

Heinselman, M. L. 1981. *Fire intensity and frequency as factors in the distribution and structure of northern ecosystems.* Proc. Conf. Fire Regimes and Ecosyst. Properties, U.S. For. Serv. Gen. Tech. Report WO-26, pp. 7–57.

Hough, W. A. 1973. *Fuel and weather influence wildfires in sand pine forests.* U.S. For. Serv. Res. Paper SE-106, 11 pp.

Jackson, W. O. 1968. *Fire, air, water and earth. An elemental ecology of Tasmania.* Proc. Ecol. Soc. Aust. **3**:9–16.

Jorgensen, J. R. and C. S. Hodges. 1970. Microbial characteristics of a forest soil after twenty years of prescribed burning. *Mycologia* **62**:721–726.

Jorgensen, J. R. and C. S. Hodges. 1971. *Effects of prescribed burning on microbial characteristics of soil.* Prescribed Burning Symp. Proc., U.S. For. Serv. Southeastern For. Exp. Stn., pp. 107–116.

Keeley, J. E. 1981. *Reproductive cycles and fire regimes.* Proc. Conf. Fire Regimes Ecosyst. Properties, U.S. For. Serv. Gen. Tech. Report WO-26, pp. 231–277.

Kilgore, B. M. 1981. *Fire in ecosystem distribution and structure: western forests and shrublands.* Proc. Conf. Fire Regimes Ecosyst. Properties, U.S. For. Serv. Gen. Tech. Report WO-26, pp. 58–89.

Komarek, E. V. 1974. Effects of fire on temperate forests and related ecosystems: southeastern United States. In T. T. Kozlowski and C. E. Ahlgren, Eds., *Fire and Ecosystems*, Academic, New York, pp. 251–277.

Kruger, F. J. 1977. *Ecology of Cape fynbos in relation to fire.* Proc. Symp. Environ. Consequences Fire Fuel Manage. Medit. Ecosyst., U.S. For. Serv. Gen. Tech. Report WO-3, pp. 230–244.

Little, S. 1974. Effects of fire on temperate forests: northeastern United States. In T. T. Kozlowski and C. E. Ahlgren, Eds., *Fire and Ecosystems*, Academic, New York, pp. 225–250.

Little, S. and E. B. Moore. 1953. *Severe burning treatment tested on lowland pine sites.* U.S. For. Serv. Stn. Paper NE-64, 11 pp.

Lotan, J. E. 1975. *The role of cone serotiny in lodgepole pine forests.* Proc. Symp. Manage. Lodgepole Pine Ecosyst., Wash. State Univ., Coop. Ext. Serv. Publ., pp. 471–495.

Lotan, J. E. 1976. *Cone serotiny. Fire relationships in lodgepole pine.* Tall Timbers Fire Ecol. Conf. Proc. **14**:267–278.

Luke, R. H. and A. G. McArthur. 1978. *Bushfires in Australia.* Dept. For. and Timber Bur., CSIRO Div., For. Res., Canberra, 359 pp.

MacArthur, R. H. and E. O. Wilson. 1967. *The theory of island biogeography,* Princeton Univ. Press, Princeton, 203 pp.

McArthur, A. G. 1968. *Fire resistance of eucalypts.* Proc. Ecol. Soc. Aust. **3**:83–90.

McConkey, T. W. and D. R. Gedney. 1951. *A guide for salvaging white pine injured by forest fires.* U.S. For. Serv. Res. Note NE-11, 4 pp.

Margalef, R. 1974. *Ecologia,* Omega S.A., Barcelona, 951 pp.

Martin, R. E. 1963. Thermal properties of bark. *For. Prod. J.* **13**:419–426.

Martin, R. E. and C. T. Cushwa. 1966. *Effects of heat and moisture on leguminous seeds.* Tall Timbers Fire Ecol. Conf. Proc. **5**:159–175.

Martin, R. E., R. L. Miller, and C. T. Cushwa. 1975. Germination response of legume seeds subjected to moist and dry heat. *Ecology* **56**:1441–1445.

Mooney, H. A. and E. L. Dunn. 1972. Land use history of California and Chile as related to the structure of the sclerophyll scrub vegetations. *Madrono* **21**:305–319.

Moore, J. M. and R. W. Wein. 1977. Viable seed populations by soil depth and potential site recolonization after disturbance. *Can. J. Bot.* **55**:2408–2412.

Mount, A. B. 1969. *Eucalypt ecology as related to fire.* Tall Timbers Fire Ecol. Conf. Proc. **9**:75–108.

Muller, C. J., R. B. Hanawalt, and J. K. McPherson. 1968. Allelopathic control of herb growth in the fire cycle of California chaparral. *Bull. Torr. Bot. Club* **95**:225–231.

Naveh, Z. 1974a. *The ecology of fire in Israel.* Tall Timbers Fire Ecol. Conf. Proc. **13**:131–170.

Naveh, Z. 1974b. Effects of fire in the Mediterranean region. In T. T. Kozlowski and C. E. Ahlgren, Eds., *Fire and Ecosystems*, Academic, New York, pp. 401–434.

Noble, I. R. and R. O. Slatyer. 1981. Concepts and models of succession in vascular plant communities subject to recurrent fires. In A. M. Gill, R. H. Groves, and I. R. Noble, Eds., *Fire and Australian Biota*, Aust. Acad. Sci., Canberra, pp. 311–335.

Odum, E. P. 1959. *Fundamentals of ecology* 2nd ed., W. B. Saunders, Philadelphia, 546 pp.

Oosting, H. J. 1958. *The study of plant communities* 2nd ed., N. H. Freeman, San Francisco, 440 pp.

Orians, G. H. 1975. Diversity, stability and maturity in natural ecosystems. In Van Dobbin and L. McConnell, Eds., *Unifying Concepts in Ecology*, Junk., The Hague, pp. 139–150.

Packham, D. R. 1971. Heat transfer above a small ground fire. *Aust. For. Res.* **5**:19–24.

Shafi, M. I. and G. A. Yarranton. 1973. Diversity, floristic richness, and species evenness during a secondary (post-fire) succession. *Ecology* **54**:897–902.

Shearer, R. C. 1975. *Seedbed characteristics in western larch forests after prescribed burning.* U.S. For. Serv. Res. Paper INT-167, 26 pp.

Simard, A. J. 1975. *Wildland fire occurrence in Canada.* Can. For. Serv. Unnumbered Pub. (map).

Spalt, K. W. and W. E. Reifsnyder. 1962. *Bark characteristics and fire resistance: a literature review.* U.S. Forest Serv. So. For. Exp. Stn. Occ. Paper 193, 19 pp., illus.

Specht, R. L., P. Rayson, and M. E. Jackman. 1958. Dark Island health (Ninety Miles Plain, South Australia), VI Pyric succession: changes in composition, coverage, dry weight and mineral nutrient status. *Aust. J. Bot.* **6**:59–88.

Swain, A. M. 1973. A history of fire and vegetation in northeastern Minnesota as recorded in lake sediments. *Quater. Res.* **3**:383–396.

Tansley, A. G. 1935. The use and abuse of vegetational terms and concepts. *Ecology* **16**:284–307.

Trabaud, L. 1970. Quelques valeurs et observations sur la phytodynamique des surfaces incendiées dans le Bas-Languedoc. *Natur. Monspel.* **21**:231–242.

Trabaud, L. 1974. *Experimental study on the effects of prescribed burning on a* Quercus coccifera L. *garrigue.* Tall Timbers Fire Ecol. Conf. Proc. **13**:97–129.

Trabaud, L. 1977. *Comparison between the effects of prescribed fires and wildfires on the global quantitative development of the kermes-scrub oak* (Quercus coccifera L.) *garrigues,* Proc. Symp. Environ. Consequences Fire Fuel Manage. Medit. Ecosyst., U.S. For. Serv. Gen. Tech. Report WO-3, pp. 271–282.

Trabaud, L. 1979. Etude du comportement du feu dans la garrigue de chêne kermès à partir des températures et des vitesses de propagation. *Ann. Sci. For.* **36**:13–38.

Trabaud, L. 1980a. *Impact biologique et écologique des feux de végétation sur l'organisation, la structure et l'évolution de la végétation des zones de garrigues du Bas-Languedoc.* Thèse Doctorat Etat. Univ. Sci. Tech. Languedoc, Montpellier, 288 pp.

Trabaud, L. 1980b. Influence du feu sur les semences enfouies dans les couches superficielles du sol d'une garrigue de chêne kermès. *Natur. Monspel.* **39**:1–12.

Trabaud, L. and J. Lepart. 1980. Diversity and stability in garrigue ecosystems after fire. *Vegetatio* **43**:49–57.

Van Wagner, C. E. 1977. Conditions for the start and spread of crown fires. *Can. J. For. Res.* **7(1)**:23.

Vines, R. G. 1968. Heat transfer through bark and the resistance of trees to fire. *Aust. J. Bot.* **16**:499–514.

Vogl, R. J. 1974. Effects of fire on grasslands. In T. T. Kozlowski and C. E. Ahlgren, Eds., *Fire and Ecosystems*, Academic, New York, pp. 139–194.

Vuillemin, J. and C. Bulard. 1981. Ecophysiologie de la germination de *Cistus albidus* et *C. monspeliensis*. *Natur. Monspel.* **46:**1–11.

Wade, D. D. and D. E. Ward. 1973. *An analysis of the air bomb range fire.* U.S. For. Serv. Res. Paper SE-105, 38 pp.

Weaver, H. 1974. Effects of fire on temperate forests: western United States. In T. T. Kozlowski and C. E. Ahlgren, Eds., *Fire and Ecosystems*, Academic, New York, pp. 279–319.

Wein, R. W. 1978. The role of fire in the degradation of ecosystems. In M. W. Holdgate and M. J. Woodman, Eds., *Breakdown and Restoration of Ecosystems*, NATO Conf. Series, Plenum, New York, pp. 193–209.

Wells, C. G. and others. 1979. *Effects of fire on soil. A state-of-the-knowledge review.* U.S. For. Serv. Gen. Tech. Report WO-7, 36 pp.

Whittaker, E. and C. H. Gimingham 1962. The effects of fire on regeneration of *Calluna vulgaris* (L.) Hull. from seed. *J. Ecol.* **50:**815–822.

Whittaker, R. H. 1970. *Communities and ecosystems,* MacMillan, London, 162 pp.

Wright, E. and R. F. Tarrant. 1957. *Microbial soil properties after logging and slash burning.* U.S. For. Serv. Res. Note PNW-157, 5 pp.

Wright, H. A. 1969. Effects of spring burning on tobosa grass. *J. Range Manage.* **22:**425–427.

Wright, H. A. 1973. *Fire as a tool to manage tobosa grasslands.* Tall Timbers Fire Ecol. Conf. Proc. **12:**153–167.

Wright, H. A. 1974. Range burning. *J. Range Manage.* **27:**5–11.

Wright, H. E. Jr. 1974. Landscape development, forest fires and wilderness management. *Science* **186:**487–495.

Zasada, J. C. 1971. Natural regeneration of interior Alaska forests—seed, seedbed, and vegetative reproduction considerations. In C. W. Slaughter, R. J. Barney, and G. M. Hausen, Eds., *Proc. Symp. Fire in Northern Environ.*, U.S. For. Serv. Pacific Northwest Forest and Range Exp. Stn., pp. 231–246.

# CHAPTER SEVEN

# *Fire Effects on Soil, Water, and Air*

The effects of fire on the chemical and physical properties of forest soils will vary from nil to profound depending on the type of soil, the moisture content of the soil, the intensity and duration of the fire, and the timing and intensity of postfire precipitation. In completely mineral soils, heat transfer takes place through conduction and vapor transport downward from the exposed surface, whereas soils with a high organic content may actually support combustion to a significant depth. In addition to natural peatlands, many landfills and other reclaimed lands contain buried combustible debris that may become subject to spontaneous ignition or be ignited by a mild surface fire. Such underground fires are quite difficult to extinguish and may burn for several years.

Soil moisture content affects both specific heat and thermal conductivity, and thus determines to a large degree how much and how fast heat is conducted downward through the soil. Table 7.1 shows the specific heat and thermal conductivity of some common soil constituents. It not only requires more heat to increase the temperature of moist soil by a given amount but, except for clays, the heat is dissipated more rapidly into the lower layers of soil thus minimizing the surface temperature rise.

The most important aspect of soil moisture is its high heat of vaporization which prevents the temperature in any layer of soil from rising above 100°C until the moisture has been evaporated or driven downward into deeper soil layers. The heating of moist soil is a complex process because of both vapor and free moisture diffusion and models have been tested and verified only under the simplest sets of assumptions (Aston and Gill 1976).

The moisture content of the litter and duff layers is usually more important than the moisture of the mineral soil itself. If moisture gradients are so

*Table 7.1. Specific Heats and Thermal Conductivities of Common Soils and Soil Materials*

| | Specific Heat (Cal/gm°C) | | Conductivity (Cal/cm²sec) (°C/cm) $\times$ $10^{-4}$ | |
|---|---|---|---|---|
| Material | Oven Dry | Fully Saturated | Oven Dry | Fully Saturated |
| Sand | 0.20 | 0.72 | 7.85 | 12.85 |
| Clay | 0.20 | 0.82 | 24.00 | 16.85 |
| Granite | 0.20 | — | 68.15 | — |
| Charcoal | 0.37 | 0.92 | 1.80 | 13.15 |
| Duff | 0.42 | 0.90 | 1.20 | 12.85 |
| Water | — | 1.00 | — | 14.45 |

steep that the surface litter will burn but the lower layers of duff will not, the soil temperature, even at the surface, remains below 100°C and there are virtually no effects on soil chemistry or physics. Prescribed fires for hazard reduction are timed to take advantage of such situations since 75 percent or more of the total fuel loading can be removed with minimum alteration of the natural soil and site conditions.

## SOIL TEMPERATURE AND HEATING

Sometimes, as when burning for seedbed preparation with a species that requires mineral soil for germination, complete incineration of the litter is desired. In order to minimize soil damage fires should be planned for an intensity just sufficient to burn off the duff layer, but with a minimum of excess heat for conduction into the soil. To achieve such a result requires a knowledge of the amounts, size classes, and moisture distribution in the aboveground fuels as well as the moisture gradient within the duff. One practical method of obtaining such information is the planar intercept technique (Brown 1974). Observations in several forest types have shown that lower duff layers will not burn at moisture contents above 120 percent and will burn independently at moisture contents below 40 percent. Within these limits, duff burnout depends on the amount of heat received from the burning of other fuels above the duff. Several prediction equations have been developed by Canadian and American researchers to aid in developing prescriptions for duff removal (Muraro 1977, Sandberg 1980).

Wildfire severity can also be rated by how severely litter has been reduced and mineral soil exposed (Wells et al. 1979). A lightly burned area will be characterized by "black ash," the charred remnants of the litter and duff layer. Maximum temperatures at the soil surface will have been between 100 and 250°C and temperatures 1 to 2 cm below the surface will not have exceeded 100°C. A moderate burn will have a significant amount of bare soil

*Figure 7.1.* Severely burned areas are characterized by white ash. Photo by U.S. Forest Service.

where the overlying litter and duff have burned completely away. Surface temperatures are typically in the 300 to 400°C range, with temperatures of 200 to 300 at 1 cm depth, 60 to 80 at 3 cm, and 40 to 50 at 5 cm. A severely burned area is characterized by "white ash," the fluffy ash layer left after the complete combustion of heavy fuels (Figure 7.1). Where mineral soil is exposed it has changed color from the heat. Surface temperatures will have been 500 to 750°C, well above the ignition temperature of organic materials. Penetration of heat below the surface depends largely on the duration of the fire immediately above it, but temperatures are typically 350 to 450°C in the first 2 cm, 150 to 300 at 3 cm and 100°C or less at 5 cm.

Even the most intense forest fire will rarely have a direct heating effect on the soil at depths below 7 to 10 cm. However, the changed microclimate due to the removal of litter and duff, opening of the canopy by killing overstory shrubs and trees, and darkening of the soil surface by residual soot and charcoal can increase insolation and cause temperature increases of 10°C or more at depths of 10 cm over the course of a summer until revegetation again shades the surface. Surface temperatures are altered even more drastically. Maximum summer soil surface temperatures following a fire in high elevation fir in central Washington State increased 26°C and even the mean daily temperatures increased 6°C (Fowler and Helvey 1978).

## CHEMICAL PROPERTIES AND NUTRIENT CYCLING

Fire affects the chemical properties of soils, directly by decomposition of clay minerals and indirectly by converting complex organic structures into simple inorganic residues which, in turn, react with the minerals in the soil. The ash from most plant materials is high in basic ions such as calcium, potassium, and magnesium. This tends to raise the $pH$ of acid soils, especially sandy soils that are poorly buffered. Ash deposits generally do not increase the alkalinity of alkaline soils since the soil is already rich in the released elements and they tend to leach out rather than to become bound to the soil minerals. The degree to which soil $pH$ is altered depends also on the prefire fuel loading and fire intensity since these factors determine the quantity of ash made available to the soil.

Increase of soil $pH$ following fire is a consistent effect that occurs as a result of basic cations released by the combustion of organic matter. The degree to which $pH$ is shifted and the length of time it remains higher than under prefire conditions are a function of the original soil $pH$ and organic matter content, the amount of ash produced and its chemical composition, and the amount of local precipitation (Grier 1975, Lutz 1956, Metz et al. 1961, Wells 1971). In western North America hot slash fires in coniferous forests may commonly raise the $pH$ one to two units from about 5 or 6 to 7 or more (Isaac and Hopkins 1937, St. John and Rundel 1976, Tarrant 1956). In eastern pine forests where fire intensity is lower much smaller increases occur. Soils under *Pinus taida* stands of South Carolina subject to annual burning for 20 years changed $pH$ from 4.2 to 4.6 in the upper mineral soil, whereas burning at 4 to 5 year intervals did not affect $pH$ (Wells op. cit.). After 14 years of annual burning of stands of *P. resinosa* and *P. strobus* in Connecticut, mineral soil $pH$ increased from 4.3 to 5.0 (Lunt 1950). Varying frequencies of fire in *P. resinosa* stands in Minnesota increased $pH$ of mineral soil from 5.3 to 5.5 (Alban 1977). Christensen (1977) finds no $pH$ change following fire in *P. palustris* savannas. Rangeland fires where small amounts of organic matter are consumed produce no significant changes in soil $pH$ (Owensby and Wyrill 1973). In southern France, Trabaud (1980) does not find any significant changes of $pH$ in a soil of a garrigue burned at various fire regimes.

Fire can alter the mineralogy of certain soils, particularly those with a high clay fraction. Many of the clay minerals such as mica, calcite, kaolinite, and smectite decompose at temperatures between 400 and 800°C, well within the ranges reached in intense forest fires. The result is a shift toward larger particle sizes and higher erodibility in burned soils since the clay fraction is reduced, whereas the sand and silt fractions are relatively unaffected (Wells 1981).

The fate of organic matter and nitrogen is of primary interest because of their importance to soil physical properties and nutrient release. Severe burns such as those caused by wildfire or pile burning can result in nearly complete destruction of organic matter and cause changes in the physical,

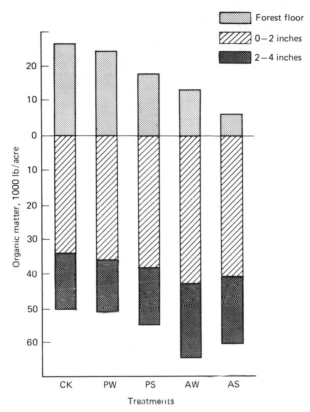

*Figure 7.2.* Organic matter in the forest floor, 0 to 2 and 2 to 4 inches of mineral soil for check (CK), periodic winter (PW), periodic summer (PS), annual winter (AW), and annual summer (AS) treatments after 20 years. Organic matter and nitrogen in the forest floor (From Wells 1971).

chemical, and biological properties of the upper layers of mineral soil (Neal et al. 1965). If combustion of organic matter is complete, all contained nitrogen is lost to the atmosphere. Oxidation is usually incomplete, however, and the extent of nitrogen loss is proportional to the intensity of the burn and the kind of fuel consumed.

Cooper (1971), Stone (1971), and Wells (1971) present the effects of burning on nutrient availability. Periodic prescribed underburning reduces the amounts of organic matter on the surface, but the organic matter content of the upper layers of soil (0 to 5 in depth) may increase by up to 30 percent. The principal effect of burning is often a redistribution, not a reduction, of organic matter in the profile (Figure 7.2; Wells 1971). Reduction in the amount of surface residue can be accompanied by a decrease in the total amounts of P, K, Ca, and Mg in the forest floor, and these nutrients are carried into the mineral soil where available P and exchangable K, Ca, and Mg increase.

Under periodic prescribed burning as practiced in the southeastern

United States, most of the yearly addition of nitrogen in litter is volatilized by fire (Stone op. cit.). However, after 20 annual burns, the nitrogen content lost from the forest floor was compensated for by an approximately equal increase in nitrogen in the upper layer of mineral soil. The increases in soil nitrogen were attributed to increased rates of nitrogen fixation brought about by an increase in $p$H (Stone op. cit., Wells 1971). Overall conclusions from several studies were that prescribed burning had no deleterious effects on chemical and physical soil properties and did not decrease soil productivity.

Severe burns usually occur in small scattered patches. Only here will all organic matter be destroyed to a depth of several centimeters. Knight (1966), from burning experiments in the laboratory, reports 25 to 64 percent loss of nitrogen from forest floor material at temperatures of 300 to 700°C. Nitrogen concentration of residual material increased, but the total amount of nitrogen decreased. Decay fungi will be destroyed in burned areas but can survive in underlying roots.

Accumulation of residues in forests from which fire has been excluded constitutes a fire hazard. For this reason, very light burns may be made periodically. Burning of surface material occurred naturally at intervals of about 5 to 15 years in sequoia and ponderosa pine forests before white settlement. Prescribed burning to remove the duff or surface litter of needles, leaves, twigs, and the like is practiced at about 5-year intervals in pine plantations of the south. Prescribed burning in conjunction with clearcutting has been used to prepare seed beds for loblolly pine (*Pinus taeda*) in the upper Piedmont of South Carolina and in mixed stands of shortleaf pine (*P. echinata*) and hardwoods. Effects of such light burning are (1) to stimulate germination of seeds of certain species, (2) to remove the competitive herbaceous understory, and (3) to provide ash as a source of newly available nutrients. Although nitrogen of the burned duff is lost to the air, this loss may be compensated for through nitrogen fixation by *Azotobacter* and other nitrogen-fixed bacteria when the ash is leached into the soil.

Loblolly pine stands burned annually in the lower coastal plain of South Carolina showed an increase in nitrogen of 23 kg/ha/yr. The nitrogen fixation rate in burned forest floor samples increased whenever soil moisture was above field capacity and temperatures were between 25 and 35°C (Jorgensen and Wells 1971).

Numerous studies on the effects of slash burning on chemical, physical, and microbial properties of forest soils have been conducted in the Douglas fir region (Morris 1970, Neal et al., op. cit., Tarrant op. cit.). Conflicting results obtained under different conditions have contributed to the controversy surrounding the effects on burning. Many of the differences can be explained by wide variations in the intensity of burning. In general, burning increases the amounts of available nutrients in the surface soil with the possible exception of nitrogen. Some studies report significant nitrogen loss, but others report small losses or no effect. Loss of nitrogen and release of other nutrients are associated with a decrease in organic matter content of the forest floor. On severely burned sites, organic matter content of the soil may also be reduced. Detrimental effects on soil physical properties are confined to severely burned areas, and a number of studies have shown that only 3 to 8 percent of the total area is severely burned in a typical broadcast slash burn (Dyrness and Youngberg 1957, Tarrant op. cit.).

Nutrients released by broadcast burning may accumulate in the lower layers of the forest floor or move into the mineral soil. These increases in nutrient availability for cycling and utilization, however, may also increase nutrient vulnerability to loss by leaching. Grier and Cole (1971) find that slash burning causes substantial increases in the concentrations of nutrient ions entering the soil. Downward movement was also increased, but most of the nutrients were retained in the surface 40 cm of soil, and only insignificant amounts were leached from the rooting zone of the profile. Nutrients contained in the ash from piled slash will be concentrated in small areas.

Nitrogen is readily volatilized by heating during a fire. DeBell and Ralston (1970) observe volatile losses of nitrogen of 58 to 85 percent in a study of a variety of forest fuel types. White et al. (1973) find that 100 percent of the nitrogen in plant and litter material could be lost at temperatures above 500°C. At temperatures of 400 to 500°C they find potential losses of 75 to 100 percent, at 300 to 400°C, losses of 50 to 75 percent, and at 200 to 300°C, losses up to 50 percent. Below 200°C they observe no measurable nitrogen volatilization.

DeBano and Conrad (1978) report that 10 percent of the total nitrogen from plant, litter, and upper soil layers is lost in a prescribed chaparral burn. In a later study with chaparral soils and litter layers alone they find that about 67 percent of the total nitrogen is lost during intense burns over dry soils but less than 25 percent is lost when soil and litter are moist (DeBano et al. 1979). In England, Allen (1964) simulated fires in *Calluna*-dominated heaths and reports that approximately 70 percent of the nitrogen in plant phytomass is volatilized at temperatures of 500 to 800°C. Christensen (op. cit.) finds a 70 pecent loss of nitrogen during burning from the phytomass of a *Pinus palustris* savanna in North Carolina.

Despite major volatilization of nitrogen in fires, the available forms of nitrogen are commonly higher on burned than unburned sites. This condition results from the rapid mineralization of litter and associated enrichment of the soil (Christensen and Muller 1975, DeBano and Conrad op. cit., Garren 1943, St. John and Rundel op. cit., Stark and Steel 1977, Wells 1942). The nature of this enrichment is highly variable, however, due to complex interactions of volatiles and changes in chemical form (Lewis 1974). Orme and Teege (1976) report variable increases in available forms of nitrogen depending on the seasonality and severity of fires in northern Idaho. Cool spring burns increased soil concentrations of nitrate and ammonium by 3 and 1.5 times, respectively, whereas more severe fall burns increased nitrate by 20 times and ammonium 3 times. In a study in North Carolina Christensen (op. cit.) finds only 1 percent of the nitrogen in ash added to pine savanna soils following fire to be in extractable forms. He suggests that ash may act as a reservoir for gradual mineralization and release of available forms, but that this reservoir is subject to leaching effects.

Phosphorous cycles are also affected by fire. Significant quantities of phosphorus in litter and plant canopies are often lost during fires, apparently transported away as fine ash particles. Christensen (op. cit.) estimates a 46 percent loss of total phosphorus from standing biomass of a southern pine savanna. Lloyd (1971) also shows high losses due to fire in English heaths, but Allen (op. cit.) finds no effect. DeBano and Conrad (op. cit.) find only a 2 percent loss of total phosphorus from the plant, litter, and upper soil horizon following a chaparral fire. They suggest that virtually all the total phosphorus in the standing crop phytomass was added to the soil as ash.

Available forms of phosphorus in soil generally increase following fires. Wagle and Kitchen (1972) find a 32-fold increase in available soil phosphorus after a prescribed burn in *Pinus ponderosa* stands, but Campbell et al. (1977) report much smaller increases for this forest type. St. John and Rundel (op. cit.) find small increases following fire in a mixed conifer forest, but the relationship of burned to unburned plots showed a definite seasonal cycle. Larger increases in available phosphorus in burned chaparral soils are found by Christensen and Muller (op. cit.) but their seasonal data does not show any clear pattern. Viro (1974) reports small increases in soluble phosphorus for the first three years following fire in the boreal forests of Scandinavia. Similar results are found by Trabaud (op. cit.) for scrub oak garrigues in southern France (Figure 7.3). Despite this general pattern of increased availability of phosphorus, exceptions have been described (Isaac and Hopkins op. cit.). Some of these apparently contradictory results may be explained by differential binding of phosphate ions in soils and by variations in fire intensity. Very hot fires such as those studied by Isaac and Hopkins increase losses of phosphorus. White et al. (1973) suggest that the greatest phosphorous availability occurs in soils heated to less than 200°C, although Hoffman (1966) finds the greatest availability after heating to 200 to 300°C.

Numerous studies in different ecosystems have documented increases in exchangeable potassium in postfire soils (Austin and Basinger 1955, Hatch 1960, Hoffman op. cit., Isaac and Hopkins op. cit., Lewis 1974, St. John and Rundel op. cit., Stark 1977, Trabaud op. cit.). Studies on chaparral soils have also reported large initial increases in potassium following fire. Christensen and Muller (op. cit.) record 43 kg ha$^{-1}$ of potassium added as ash, increasing extractable soil potassium over 50 percent. Christensen (op. cit.) finds that 60 percent of the potassium in the standing crop of vegetation was returned to the soil as ash. This increased potassium concentration was

---

*Figure 7.3.* Changes through years of the phosphorus and potassium levels of the upper soil layer of a *Quercus coccifera* garrigue according to different prescribed fire regimes: spring burns (P), autumn burns (A), burns every six years (6), burns every three years (3), burns every two years (2), and control (T). (From Trabaud, 1980.)

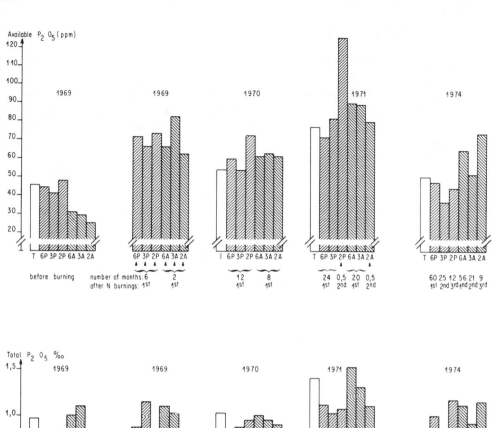

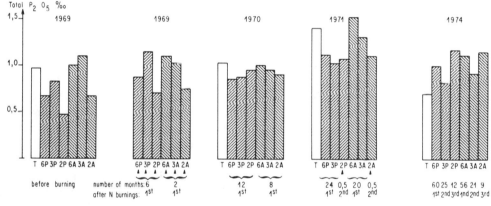

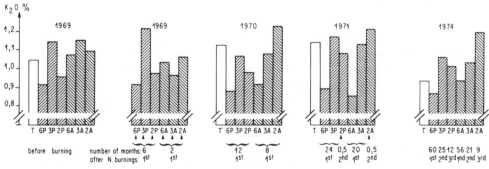

*Figure 7.3.*

rapidly reduced to levels comparable to unburned soils within a few months. However, a few studies have recorded small decreases in total potassium following fire (Campbell et al. op. cit., DeBano and Conrad op. cit., Orme and Teege op. cit., Reynolds and Bohning 1956). Studies by White et al. (op. cit.) suggest that fire temperatures above 500°C may cause volatilization of potassium.

Calcium and magnesium commonly behave quite similarly under fire conditions. Numerous studies have reported increases in calcium and magnesium following fire (Austin and Basinger op. cit., Hatch op. cit., Lewis 1974, St. John and Rundel op. cit., Scotter 1963, Stark op. cit.). A few studies have found no change or an actual decrease in soil concentration of these cations (Christensen and Muller op. cit., Trabaud op. cit., Viro op. cit.). These latter results are probably related to changes in the cation exchange capacity that is commonly decreased by fires as the organic matter content of soil is reduced. DeBano and Conrad (op. cit.) find that 45 kg ha$^{-1}$ of calcium and 5.3 kg ha$^{-1}$ of magnesium are transported to soil as ash following a chaparral fire, but even larger amounts (67 kg ha$^{-1}$ and 32 kg ha$^{-1}$, respectively) are lost through postfire runoff and debris erosion.


## SOIL MICROORGANISMS

Severe burns such as wildfire and slash pile burns can sterilize the upper soil and change soil properties (Neal et al. op. cit.). However, reinoculation by windblown dust and debris soon follows; when moisture is sufficient, microbial populations can increase for a few weeks until an equilibrium is reached. Insofar as burning changes the soil properties, the microorganisms having the advantage in a burned soil will differ from those having the advantage before burning, since for the most part effects of fire are indirect through the physical and chemical changes induced. These changes vary in degree and duration by intensity of burn, soil and climatic characteristic of the site, and kind of vegetation that invades an area after the fire.

When the combustion of organic matter is complete, the end products are largely carbon dioxide, water, and ash, plus some nitrogen derived from nitrogenous materials. With both wildfires and prescribed burning, oxidations in much of the affected area are usually incomplete and produce a wide variety of products (Hall 1972). Many of these, including carbon monoxide and hydrocarbons, are like those entering the atmosphere from trees and other plant life and from microbial decomposition of vegetation remains. In effect, fire compresses these normally occurring processes into a shorter time. Most of the residual products, including carbon monoxide and hydrocarbons, are consumed by certain species of bacteria and microfungi, and the elements are eventually recycled in the biosphere.

Most of the nitrogen is in fallen and decaying leaves of the duff; much less nitrogen is in wood and bark. Wildfires or broadcast burning that consumes the duff results in loss of most of this nitrogen to the atmosphere. DeBell and Ralston (op. cit.) find that 62 percent of the nitrogen in pine litter and green needles is released by burning. They theorize that since only minor amounts of ammonia and other nitrogen compounds appear in the combustion gases, the majority of the nitrogen is volatilized as nitrogen gas. The nitrogen remaining in the soil is subject to microbial transformation into ammonium and nitrate, which is available to plant roots. These forms of nitrogen disappear from the soil by assimilation and in the case of nitrates by leaching.

Neal et al. (op. cit.) find that Douglas fir slash burning significantly reduced water-holding capacity during the first year of study. Soil $pH$ was increased in amounts ranging from 0.3 to 1.2 units. Increases in ammonium nitrogen were found up to six months after burning, but nitrate nitrogen was low at all times during the first year of study. Kjeldahl nitrogen declined, but total carbon increased by 1 to 2 percent; thus the C/N ratio appreciably widened. Numbers of bacteria significantly increased but fluctuated with seasonal changes. The percentage of *Streptomyces* among the bacteria was not markedly influenced. The mold population, however, was significantly reduced. In this instance the initial effects of slash burning on physical, chemical, and microbial properties of the soil appeared beneficial to fertility. The increase in soil of ammonium nitrogen may have resulted from partial sterilization that eliminated certain competitors or antagonists, and residual humus, perhaps thermally altered, became a suitable substrate.

Prescribed burning in a jack pine (*Pinus banksiana*) stand on a sandy loam soil in Minnesota immediately decreased numbers and activity of most microorganisms (Ahlgren and Ahlgren 1965), but these increased abruptly after the first rainfall. Depth and extent of burned area and the effects on various species were influenced by fire intensity and moisture conditions. Numbers and activity of organisms were generally lower the second growing season after burning, but some effects, especially a greatly increased *Streptomyces* population, were still evident in the third growing season.

From a study of microbial characteristics of a South Carolina forest soil after 20 years of prescribed burning, Jorgensen and Hodges (1970) find few indications that the burning adversely altered the composition of the saprophytic, sporeforming microfungi, or reduced the number of bacteria and actinomyces to the extent that soil metabolic processes were impaired.

Greene (1935) finds that eight years of annual grass-burning under a longleaf pine (*Pinus patustris*) stand in Mississippi increased soil organic matter and nitrogen, originating chiefly from roots rather than from tops of plants. Growth of grass and leguminous plants on burned areas was more than twice that on unburned areas.

Fire typically increases $pH$ significantly and this effect favors bacterial population growth over fungal population growth. It has been frequently hypothesized that the high soil nitrification rates commonly observed following fire result from increased activities of populations of *Nitrosomonas* and *Nitrobacter* (Ahlgren and Ahlgren 1960, Christensen and Muller op. cit., St.

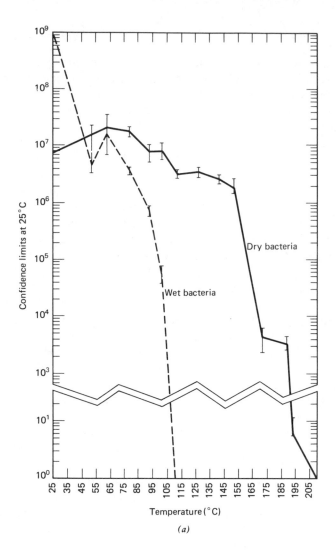

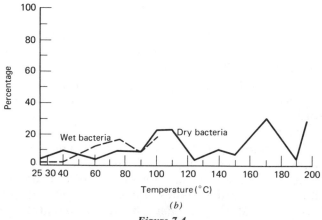

*(b)*

182            *Figure 7.4.*

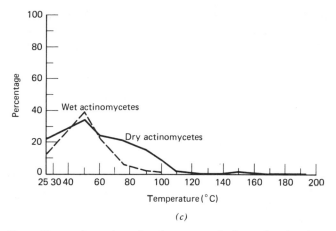

*(c)*

**Figure 7.4.** Heat effect on bacteria and actinomycetes in dry and moist chaparral soil subjected to various 30-minute heat treatments in an oil bath. (*a*) Survival of heterotrophic bacteria and actinomycetes. (*b*) Percentage of bacteria colonies forming spores. (*c*) Survival of actinomycetes (From Dunn and DeBano 1977).

John and Rundel op. cit.). Experimental studies with chaparral soils by Dunn et al. (1979), however, show that populations of *Nitrosomonas* and *Nitrobacter* remained low for 12 months following fire. They hypothesize that heterotrophic nitrifiers were of primary importance in these soils in the first year following fire.

For bacteria, which are generally more resistant to heating than fungi, the water content of bacterial spores is important, with moderately dry spores more heat resistant than either very wet or very dry spores (Murrel and Scott 1966). Lethal temperatures for heterotrophic bacteria in chaparral soils are reached at 210°C in dry soil, but most are killed by temperatures above 150°C (Figure 7.4; Dunn and DeBano 1977). In wet soil, rapid death begins at 50°C and no bacteria survive beyond 110°C. Ahlgren and Ahlgren (1965) report corresponding lethal temperatures for bacteria in forest soils. Nitrifying bacteria appear to be somewhat more sensitive to soil heating than typical heterotrophic bacteria. Dunn and DeBano (op. cit.) report that *Nitrosomonas* and *Nitrobacter* group bacteria were killed in dry soil at temperatures of 140°C, but at only 75 and 50°C, respectively, in wet soil. This sensitivity of nitrifying bacteria to heating may be significant in recovery of low nitrogen ecosystems following fire. Actinomycetes behave very similarly to bacteria in chaparral soils with death at 125°C in dry soil and 110°C in wet soil. However, some studies have reported that these microorganisms are generally more resistant to heating than bacteria (Bollen 1969).

In Australia, Renbuss et al. (1973) studied changes in the microbial population of the ash-bed soil produced by burning a log pile. All depths to 20 cm were found to maintain a temperature of at least 100°C for more than six hours. Microbial assays immediately after the fire showed that the ash-bed soil was apparently sterilized down to 25 cm. Bacteria rapidly recolonized the soil and shortly after the fire their number exceeded those of unheated soil. Actinomycetes and fungi recolonized the ash-bed soil more slowly. The early bacterial and fungal recolonizers were shown to include many types not detected in untreated soil. About a year was required for this distinctive ash-bed microflora to revert to that of the untreated soil.

## PLANT–SOIL–WATER RELATIONS

Forest fires can affect hydrologic processes indirectly but profoundly by altering the physical and chemical properties of the soil, converting organic ground cover to soluble ash, and modifying the microclimate through removal of overhead foliage. To understand these effects we need to review the steps in the hydrologic cycle.

Just as a human being traveling through life, the fate of precipitation depends on the company it meets once it leaves its nursery in the clouds. When rain falls on a forest in leaf, raindrops are intercepted by the foliage and fine twigs. Once the foliage is saturated, water drips from the leaves as drops which may be smaller or larger than the original raindrops. Some water also runs down the surface of the twigs and branches to the stem and down the stem to the ground. During its stay on the tree the water is subject to evaporation.

The interception storage capacity on foliage is approximately 150 percent of the dry weight of the foliage for all species. For many forest and shrub stands this amounts to 1 to 2 mm of rain for each canopy layer. Evaporation losses depend on storm duration and intensity, and on the surface/volume ratio of the foliage. As a generality, broadleaved vegetation will cause interception losses of 20 to 30 percent for storms with about 10 mm of rainfall, and conifers will have interception losses about half as great.

Interception losses can be negative (net gains in precipitation) when the precipitation is very finely divided as in fogs or mists. In some coastal areas of the world fog drip may supply half of the annual moisture available for plant growth.

Once the rain passes through the forest canopy, it reaches the forest floor and is absorbed by litter and duff until they are saturated and allow the excess to filter down to mineral soil. The water-holding capacity of duff and litter depends heavily on the degree of decomposition of the material, ranging from 150 percent of dry weight in freshly fallen foliage to 500 percent of dry weight for decomposed humus.

On reaching mineral soil, some water adheres to the individual mineral particles, some is retained by surface tension in the smaller capillary openings, and some infiltrates downward through larger pores and openings until it reaches the water table. If the rate of water supply at the soil surface is greater than the infiltration rate, the excess will flow across the surface under the force of gravity.

After the rain is over, moisture is lost from the soil by evaporation from the surface and drawn from the deeper layers of soil through plant roots to supply the water needed for transpiration processes in the forest above.

Forest fires can affect all these processes from interception to transpiration and thus affect the amount and quality of water reaching the watershed, leaving the watershed, and utilized by people hundreds of kilometers away.

### Fire and Hydrologic Processes: Onsite Effects

Forest fires will decrease interception to the extent that aerial foliage has been removed by the fire. Theoretically, this would result in increased soil moisture and available water, particularly from short-lived, low-intensity storms. However, in actuality the opening up of the forest floor to increased insolation and wind increases evaporation to a much greater extent than can be compensated for by decreased interception, so that the net effect of canopy removal is less available moisture from small storms and no discernible difference from large ones.

Removal of the surface litter and duff by fire has a much more important bearing on soil–water relations than removal of the overstory. A typical pine litter layer will hold 0.5 mm of precipitation in retention storage for every centimeter of litter bed depth. Thus removal of 10 cm of litter frees 5 mm of water for soil percolation or overland flow. In older soils with deep compact humus layers, moisture retention may be 10 times that of the surface litter resulting in the loss of 5 mm of water storage capacity for each centimeter of humus burned. Unless the entire litter layer is removed to mineral soil, this moisture release is achieved with little or no effect on evaporation or other hydrologic processes.

In intense fires where all litter and duff are removed and organic materials are incinerated or charred to some depth in the soil itself, the effects on soil–water relations are drastic and usually quite negative. Raindrops striking the bare surface cause a physical dislocation of the finer mineral particles (rain splash) that infiltrate the larger pores, clog them, and reduce porosity. Reduction in organic matter within the soil decreases its water storage capacity. In clay soils heat may result in colloidal aggregation and greatly decreased infiltration rates. All these effects result in overland flow being initiated by smaller storms and increased overland flow from larger storms resulting in increased surface erosion compared to prefire levels (Figure 7.5).

Surface erosion on severely burned slopes is most serious where soils are inherently highly erosive (grenodiorite, granite, pumice, and other single grain soils) and where high-intensity precipitation can be expected. Rothacher and Lopushinsky (1974) find that in eastern Washington one year after a severe fire sedimentation from three watersheds ranged from 41 to

**Figure 7.5.** Removal of all surface litter can result in severe surface erosion. Photo by Lee Talbot.

127 m³ whereas before fire they produced practically no sediment. This increased sedimentation largely resulted from accelerated channel cutting caused by increased streamflow rather than increased surface erosion. In 1953 Sartz estimated erosion from 81.3 cm of rain removed an average of 0.3 cm of soil after a severe fire on steep slopes in Oregon. The second year after fire, a cover of vegetation had been reestablished that provided effective control against further sheet erosion on most of the area.

Surface erosion on severely burned areas also occurs as dry ravel from steep slopes (Figure 7.6). Mersereau and Dyrness (1972) estimate over 340 m³ of soil moved by dry ravel during parts of two summer seasons from the over 60 percent slopes of a 96 ha slash-burned watershed (55 percent bare soil after burning). They find that slope steepness, aspect, and vegetative cover have a strong influence on accelerated surface erosion. After broadcast burning, soil movement was 4.5 times greater on 80 percent than on 60 percent slopes, almost 3.5 times greater on south slopes than on north slopes, and 46 times greater on bare 80 percent slopes than on vegetated 60 percent slopes.

Soil movement following fire is usually related to the intensity of the burn. Intense fires increase runoff and/or erosion (Connaughton 1935, Holland 1953), whereas low-intensity fires leave some litter on the soil surface and have little or no effect on surface runoff and erosion (Agee 1973, Biswell and Schultz 1957). Thus it appears that cover (live vegetation plus litter) is by far the most important variable related to soil erosion (Orr 1970, Wright et al. 1976). A cover of 60 to 70 percent is considered necessary for soil stability on steep sloped watersheds. This usually requires two to four years after fires (DeByle and Packer 1972, Orr op. cit., Wright et al. op. cit.).

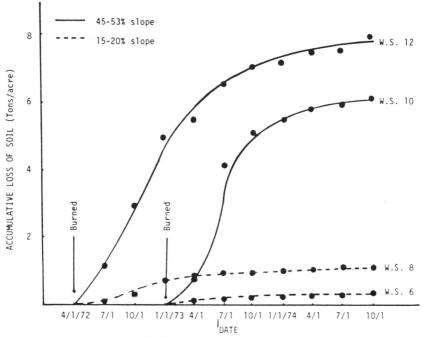

*Figure 7.6.* Accumulative loss of soil from burned watersheds for moderate and steep slopes in relation to date (From Wright et al. 1976).

In Southern California, fire has been thought to have some influence on landslides through its effect on infiltration. Reduced infiltration rates prevent soil water logging and make slopes less susceptible to mass movement, at least temporarily. Rice and Foggin (1971) suggest that when the roots of fire-killed vegetation on a nine-year old burn began to rot, there was a period when susceptibility to landslides was worse than immediately after fire or with full vegetative cover. Usually, because of destruction of water-using vegetation, fire can be expected to increase soil moisture content resulting in more rapid saturation during the recharge period. Studies by Klock and Helvey (1976) in Oregon show that in the fall, one year after a fire, the upper 1.2 m of soil profile contained 12.7 cm more water than was contained in the soil during the same period before fire.

Another phenomenon leading to increased erosion following intense fires has been noted on certain soils (DeBano 1981). Research has shown that hot fires often leave a nonwettable layer of soil. The hydrophobic compounds which lead to the formation of water-repellent soil layers occur in accumulated litter on the soil surface before a fire. When hot fires consume this litter and produce steep thermal gradients in the upper soil, an efficient distillation process occurs that leads to the volatilization and subsequent condensation of these hydrophobic compounds on individual soil particles at

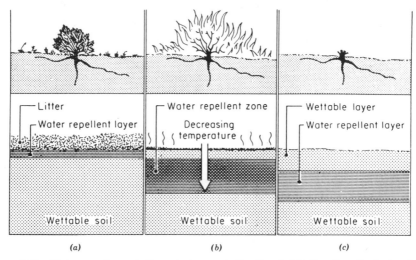

**Figure 7.7.** Water repellency before, during, and after fire. (*a*) Before fire, the hydrophobic substances accumulate in the litter and mineral soil immediately beneath it. (*b*) Fire burns the vegetation and litter, causing the hydrophobic substances to move downward along temperature gradients. (*c*) After fire a water-repellent layer is located below and parallel to the soil surface on the burned area (From DeBano et al. 1977).

some depth in the soil profile (Figure 7.7). The greater the intensity of the fire, the greater the nonwettability. This condition results in decreased infiltration and increased surface runoff and erosion. Nonwettability can persist for several years. The formation of water-repellent soil layer has been shown to be an important effect of fires in California, Arizona, and Oregon (Campbell et al. op. cit., DeBano et al. 1967, 1977, DeByle 1973, Dyrness 1976, Salih et al. 1973, Scholl 1975).

The extent of surface erosion as a result of increased overland flows following fire depends on storm intensity rates, the nature of the soils, and the steepness and length of slopes. At the one extreme, on poorly consolidated granitic soils on steep slopes in southern California with heavy convective showers, erosion rates following fires are 35 times those of unburned areas in the first year after the burn and 12 times the preburn rate in the following year (Rowe et al. 1954). More than a decade must pass before the watershed is restored to its normal hydrologic function. At the other extreme, many studies of soil movement following fires in the southeastern coastal plain of the United States have failed to show any measurable increase in erosion.

Even though percolation is usually reduced as a result of burning, soil moisture storage is generally increased following severe fires because of the reduction in transpiration losses after vegetation is killed. These effects can be very dramatic in semi-arid climates where, following fires, springs will flow that have been dry for decades and stream levels will rise appreciably.

These results are usually short-lived, however. In areas where moisture is the limiting factor to plant growth invading species will utilize all the soil moisture available within a very few years of even the hottest fire.

## Downstream Effects

The integrated effects of fire on the hydrologic processes in a forested watershed result in a tendency toward a moderately increased annual streamflow, a markedly increased peak stormflow, and some decrease in water quality. The magnitude of these effects depends on fire size and intensity, soil type, and the size and topography of the watershed. The trade-off between increased water yield and decreased water quality will depend on the water requirements and economic considerations of each particular case. For example, if water storage facilities are not available, peak stormflows may be lost to the ocean, or even result in undesirable flooding, whereas if water storage facilities are available, increased siltation may cost more to remove than the value added by the extra water.

Sediment loads are always increased to some extent by any fire sufficiently intense to bare mineral soil. Erosive effects are inordinately sensitive to fire size. In southern California the amount of soil loss *per hectare* was almost directly proportional to the area burned. That is, compared to a 1 hectare fire, 100 times as much soil was lost from a 10 hectare burn and 10,000 times as much from a 100 hectare fire of the same intensity (Storey and DeBano 1968). These values represent an extreme case, since southern California mountain soils are among the most erosive in the world, but in all instances, total soil loss following fire will be exponentially related to fire size.

In the first few storms following a forest fire stream chemistry will be altered by the addition of bicarbonates, nitrates, ammonium, and organic nitrogen as a result of percolation of the most easily dissolved ash constituents. These are not usually sufficiently concentrated to pose a health hazard to humans or animals, but they may contribute to eutrophication or algal blooms under marginal conditions. Other soil and ash elements are released more slowly and seldom pose a problem to downstream water quality. However, fine silts and clays may infiltrate gravel beds and seriously interfere with spawning grounds for fish.

Water chemistry studies conducted by Tiedemann (1973) and Tiedemann et al. (1978) show that before the fire, nitrate-N concentration in streams ranged from less than 0.005 ppm during periods of relatively low flow to 0.016 ppm during spring runoff. During the first spring runoff period after the fire, nitrate-N concentration increased to a peak of 0.095 ppm and during the following summer and fall declined to prefire background levels. During the winter, nitrate levels then began to increase, and during the second spring runoff after the fire, nitrate-N concentration peaked at 0.500 ppm. Although this concentration is considerably above the prefire background levels, it is substantially below Federal water quality standards. After the fire, measurements made on a nearby unburned watershed showed that before spring runoff the concentration of nitrate-N increased to 0.067 ppm; by the time of peak spring runoff, the concentration had declined to background levels.

Average Ca concentration of stream water for three watersheds in the same area declined from 8.8 ppm before the fire to 7.3 ppm one year after the fire, and to 5.0 ppm two years after the fire. Average Mg concentrations for the same periods were 1.5 ppm before the fire, 1.3 ppm and 0.9 ppm one and two years after the fire. Na concentration declined from 2.9 ppm before the fire to 2.3 ppm two years after the fire. These declines in concentration apparently resulted from dilution caused by increased runoff.

Other studies show an increase in nitrate-N in stream flow following fire (Brown et al. 1973, Helvey et al. 1976, Kimmins and Feller 1976, Longstretch and Patten 1975), whereas Lotspeich et al. (1970), McColl and Grigal (1977), and Wright (1976) find no changes in surface water levels of nitrate or organic-N.

There is a general agreement among studies that bicarbonate in soil solution and streamflow is increased as a consequence of burning (DeByle and Packer op. cit., Grier and Cole op. cit., Kimmins and Feller op. cit., Longstretch and Patten op. cit., Tiedemann et al. op. cit.).

Some studies of soil leachates show increased levels of total phosphate after burning, indicating accelerated mobilization of phosphorus (Knighton 1977, McColl and Grigal 1975, Smith 1970). DeByle and Packer (op. cit.) report increased mobilization of total phosphate from clearcut and burned areas. McColl and Grigal (op. cit.) find that total phosphate increased in overland flow from burned areas. However, increases were not sufficient to alter quality of stream or lake water. Stark (op. cit.) finds increased concentrations of total phosphate in soil water from 0 to 55 cm with hot burns ($> 300°C$ at the soil surface) compared to light burns (200 to 300°C). These patterns of elemental concentration would be related to the quality of ash produced, which was a function of burn intensity.

Several watershed studies (Brown et al. op. cit., Kimmins and Feller op. cit., Longstretch and Patten op. cit., Lotspeich et al. op. cit., McColl and Grigal op. cit., Wright op. cit.) have shown that fire does not affect stream water $PO_4$–P levels. In contrast to results of these studies, Tiedemann et al. (op. cit.) find that total phosphate levels in streams from burned watersheds are 2 to 3 times greater than in a stream from an unburned watershed.

Cations are perhaps the best indicators of chemical water quality constituents. Fire substantially alters the form and distribution of cations, placing them in a vulnerable position for removal by runoff and leaching. Studies of soil solutions and surface runoff following a fire indicated increased levels of cations such as Ca, Mg, K, Na, and Mn (DeByle and Packer op. cit., Grier and Cole op. cit., Knighton op. cit., Lewis 1974, McColl and Grigal op. cit., Smith op. cit., Stark op. cit.). Cation leaching from ash layers was related to water percolation through the ash. Many results indicated that the soil system maintains a high degree of retentive power for cations.

Watershed studies provide an integrated view of the effects of fire on cation concentrations and losses. Johnson and Needham (1966) conducted the first watershed study of effects of fire on chemical water quality. They find no specific effect of fire on the ionic composition of stream water following a forest fire in California. They postulate that, because of the acidic nature of the soil, the cations leached into the soil were absorbed on the exchange complex rather than washed directly into the stream. They conclude that increased runoff resulting from transpiration reduction masked concentration effects.

Helvey et al. (op. cit.), Tiedemann (op. cit.), and Tiedemann et al. (op. cit.) observe that concentration of major cations is inversely proportional to flow. McColl and Grigal (op. cit.), in contrast, find significantly increased concentrations of K attributed to an interaction of fire and soils derived from lacustine glacial sediments. Snyder et al. (1975) observe that K, Ca, and Mg were higher in stream water at a burned site than at a point above the burn. Below the burn and after passage through a buffer strip, there were only slight differences in Ca and Mg compared to the stream location above the burn. Maximum and mean concentrations of Ca, Mg, and K increased following slash burning in western Oregon. Similarly, Ca and K concentrations increased after burning in chaparral of Arizona (Longstretch and Patten op. cit.).

From the variability of responses exhibited by cations among the various studies, it is apparent that we presently have insufficient information to adequately predict effect of fire on concentrations of cation in streamflow.

A secondary effect of fire on stream quality is increased water temperatures that may occur when streamside vegetation is burned exposing the stream and its banks to direct sunlight. Higher temperatures and direct sunlight can drastically alter the habitat for many stream biota including game fish and their food sources.


## FOREST FIRES AND AIR POLLUTION

If a forest were composed solely of cellulose and if forests burned stoichiometrically, then a 1-hectare fire in a fuel loading of 50 tonnes per hectare would produce 92 tonnes of carbon dioxide, 27 tonnes of water vapor and vitiate 273 million liters of air in the process. There would be no visible smoke during the fire, but a cumulus cloud cap would form at the altitude where the water vapor cooled below its saturation temperature.

But forests are not composed of pure cellulose nor do they burn stoichiometrically, and the air above a forest fire carries away a large variety of products in addition to carbon dioxide and water vapor. As a result of preignition pyrolysis and incomplete combustion, forest fire plumes contain a bewildering array of solid, liquid, and gaseous intermediate hydrocarbons and inorganic residues. Ryan and McMahon (1976) have identified 60 hydrocarbons in the $C_4$ to $C_{12}$ class alone in the smoke from a fire in pine needles from a single species. Considering that intermediate range hydrocarbons make up only one-third of the total hydrocarbon content in the smoke (3 percent is composed of higher hydrocarbons and nearly two-thirds are lower hydrocarbons such as methane, ethylene and alkynes) and that hydrocarbon emissions only range from 0.5 to 2 percent of the total dry weight of fuel burned, the variety of species is startling. A thorough review of smoke chemistry can be found in Sandberg et al. (1979) and we confine ourselves here to an overview of the general processes involved.

Much of the destructive distillation of wood that evolves tars and other complex hydrocarbons takes place at temperatures lower than the ignition temperature of the mixture of air and volatiles escaping from the wood surface. Many of these are carried upward in the convective plume and escape before ignition occurs. Even after gas phase ignition, many of the reactions in the flame zone are not complete due to oxygen deficits caused by local turbulence, and some of the lower molecular weight species condense and synthesize larger molecules. As the surface of the solid fuel chars and erodes, particles of carbon and ash are carried through the flame zone to the convection column above, where they act as nuclei for the absorption of gaseous and liquid combustion products. It is these small particles of condensed hydrocarbons, charcoal, and ash that are the primary adverse ingredients in forest fire smoke. Particles smaller than 5 to 10 microns in diameter will remain suspended in the atmosphere until washed out by rain or intecepted by tree foliage or other solid objects. Particulates less than 2 to 3 microns in diameter will penetrate deeply into the lungs when inhaled and 50 percent of those smaller than 0.1 microns will be deposited on the tissues of the lower respiratory tract (Southern Forest Fire Laboratory Staff 1976). Particulates between 0.3 and 0.8 microns are the most effective in scattering visible light and contribute the most toward degradation of visibility in smoke.

Intensive investigations in widely separated parts of Australia and the United States show that particulate emissions are largely independent of the type of fuel burned. More than half of the total mass of particles consists of tar droplets and the rest of crystalline ash and carbon particles that may also contain absorbed hydrocarbons. About 90 percent of the particulate mass is less than 1 micron in diameter, only 15 percent is in the high light scattering range of 0.3 to 0.8 microns, and the median diameter is 0.1 microns.

Since all the particulate constituents except inorganic ash are the products of incomplete combustion, it is not surprising that the emission yield of particulates from forest fires will vary markedly with fire intensity and other burning characteristics.

Emission rates are in inverse proportion to the reaction intensity of the fire. Emission rates are about eight times higher during the smoldering phase of a fire than during the flaming phase. Because in head fires the flaming

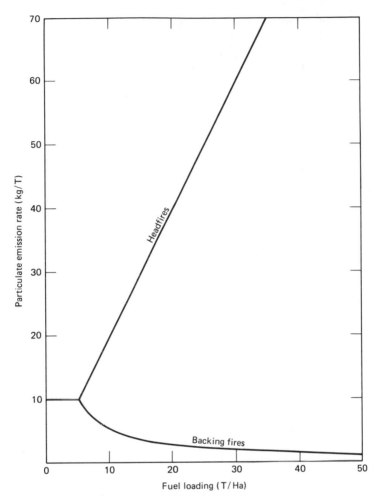

*Figure 7.8.* Emission rate vs. fuel loading.

phase moves rapidly through the fuelbed leaving a greater amount of fuel for residual smoldering, emissions from headfires are about three times those of backing fires where flaming combustion is less intense but more complete. Emission rates in heading fires also increase with fuel loading, though whether this is because of decreased oxygen availability or changes in the proportion of flaming to smoldering combustion due to increased fuel loads is not clear. This relationship is reversed (emission rates vary inversely with fuel loading) in backing fires, again for reasons that are not fully clear.

As a rough rule of thumb, particulate emissions will be 10 kilograms per tonne of fuel burned for fuel loadings up to 5 tonnes per hectare for both backing and heading fires. For higher fuel loadings multiply (for headfires) or divide (for backing fires) by 0.2 times the total fuel loading (Figure 7.8).

For example, the emission rate of particulates from a headfire burning 15 t/ha would be 10 × 0.2 × 15 = 30 kg/t, while a backing fire in the same fuel would produce 10 ÷ (0.2 × 15) = 3.33 kg/t. Hydrocarbon emission rates can be considered to be 70 percent that of particulates.

## Atmospheric Transport of Smoke

The motion of the wind field, particularly near the earth's surface, is highly turbulent. This means that the local motion of any windborne particle at any given instant of time is essentially random, that is, unpredictable. However, over a long period of time we know that the average movement of the particle will be close to that of the average movement of the wind field itself. That is, if we released a no-lift balloon in an easterly wind of 10 k/hr, the most likely place to start looking for the balloon after 1 hr would be 10 km to the west of the release point. We would not be shocked, however, if the balloon were found a half-kilometer or so from where we started our search. If we release a swarm of balloons, or a cloud of particles as in a puff of smoke, we would expect to find them clustered around the mean value of the wind vector and dispersed around that point of a degree correlated with the level of turbulence in the wind field. Thus for forest fire smoke, the mean wind field determines where the convective plume will go and the coefficient of diffusion determines the width of the plume and the concentration of particles within it at any point on the trajectory.

Although some of the smoke from a forest fire leaves as a wind-blown plume at or near ground level analogous to our no-lift balloons, much of it is entrained in the active convection column of the fire and lifted to a considerable height before being transported passively downwind. The amount of smoke produced during the convective lift phase of a fire is determined largely by fire intensity and wind velocity, varying from virtually none during grass fires in high winds to about 90 percent during high-intensity burning of heavy logging debris on calm days. In order to predict overall smoke movement and concentration, both the convected smoke and the smoke advected along the ground must be accounted for since the windspeed and direction will most probably be different at the two levels.

Two methods are available for determining the height at which the convected smoke will be traveling essentially horizontally. If no temperature soundings are available, the following formulas are recommended (Southern Forest Fire Laboratory Staff op. cit.):

$$H = 0.01Q^{3/4}U^{-1} \quad \text{when} \quad Q < 1.40 \times 10^6$$
$$H = 0.085Q^{3/5}U^{-1} \quad \text{when} \quad Q > 1.40 \times 10^6$$

For weak inversion conditions

$$H = 0.92Q^{1/3}U^{-1/3}$$

For strong inversion conditions

$$H = 0.76Q^{1/3}U^{-1/3}$$

where   $H$ = height of plume rise (m)
   $Q$ = average total heat release rate of the fire (cal/sec)
   $U$ = transport windspeed (m/sec). Transport windspeed is the arithmetic average of all windspeeds within the mixing layer.

If a temperature sounding can be obtained near the fire area, a more accurate estimate of plume rise can be obtained from the formula:

$$\Delta T = 10.75Q^{2/3}\left(\frac{r_0}{r_1}\right)^2$$

where   $\Delta T$ = difference in temperature (°C) between the convection plume and the dry adiabat of the surface temperature at the fire site
   $Q$ = average heat release rate of the fire (kW/m²)
   $r_0$ = effective radius of the fire. $r_0 = \sqrt{A/\pi}$ where $A$ = the area flaming at any given time
   $r_1$ — radius of the plume at any selected height. $r_1 = H \tan \alpha + r_0$ where $H$ = selected height (meters) and $\alpha$ = the half-angle of the plume. The plume half-angle can be measured or estimated. Plume half-angles vary from 6 to 18° depending on fire intensity. The more intense the fire, the smaller the half-angle.

In practice, the temperature difference is calculated and plotted for a number of different heights, usually at points of significant change in the sounding. The plume will cease to rise when the difference between the plume temperature and the sounding temperature (°C; *not* the dry adiabat) is numerically equal to the windspeed (m/sec) at that altitude (*not* the transport windspeed). The formula was developed for circular fires and overestimates for fires with linear shapes. For line fires, the preferred formula is (Alexander, personal communication):

$$\Delta T = \frac{3.9\ (I)^{2/3}}{H}$$

where   $I$ is the fireline intensity in kW/m.

In all instances, as stated in Chapter 4, the effective top of the plume will not be higher than the altitude where the ambient temperature equals the surface autoconvective temperature lifted dry adiabatically.

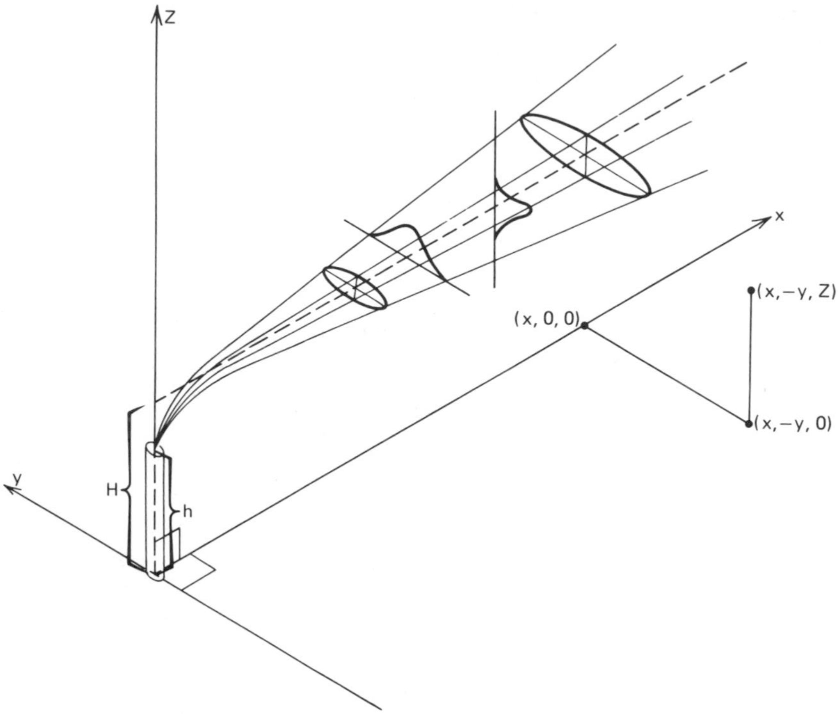

**Figure 7.9.** Coordinate system showing Gaussian distributions in the horizontal and vertical.

None of the preceding formulas are accurate if the plume rises sufficiently to form its own cumulus cloud cap. When condensation occurs, much of the smoke drifts off just below the condensation level, called the *Smoke Fallout Zone* by Countryman (1969) and the rest forms nuclei for the cloud droplets. The cap then behaves like any other cumulus cloud and the nucleating smoke particles are rained out or evaporated out when the cloud reaches drier layers of air.

Once the plume has reached its maximum rise height and becomes completely dominated by the local wind field, dispersion is normally calculated by the modified Gaussian equation of Turner (1970):

$$C = \frac{Q}{\pi U \sigma_y \sigma_z} \exp \frac{(-Y^2)(-Z^2)}{(\sigma_Y 2)(\sigma_Z 2)}$$

where   $C$ = mean concentration of aerosol
   $Q$ = emission rate of aerosol
   $\sigma_y$ and $\sigma_z$ = standard deviations of concentration in the $Y$ and
      $Z$ dimensions (see Figure 7.9)

The principal difficulty with using the Gaussian model is that the standard deviation terms depend very heavily on the atmospheric stability in the lower kilometer of the atmosphere where observations are scattered and difficult to obtain. Consequently, these values are determined empirically and subject to misuse when applied to situations other than those from which they were derived.

### Smoke Management

Smoke management is the application of knowledge of fire behavior and meteorological processes to minimize air quality degradation during prescribed fires. Smoke management includes the development of fire prescriptions and ignition techniques that maximize combustion efficiency and minimize emission rates; utilization of early and thorough mop-up to reduce residence time and smoldering; burning when winds will carry smoke away from sensitive areas; coordinating all landowners within a given airshed so that an overload from multiple sources is avoided.

Two directly opposing strategies are available when developing prescriptions to minimize smoke pollution. Backing fires can be used to the maximum extent possible in order to minimize emission rates and thus produce the least possible amount of smoke. This will normally mean burning on the driest end of the allowable prescription in order to achieve an acceptable rate of spread and maximize the area burned within the time available. It also means burning under unstable atmospheric conditions since backing fires produce the lowest convective heat outputs and have the lowest energies for lofting plumes.

If backing fires cannot be prescribed, either because of too large an area to be burned or fuels with too long a residence time to complete the burn within an acceptable time period, then the objective should be to lift the smoke as high as possible so as to achieve maximum dilution before it again reaches ground. This can be accomplished by aerial ignition or very rapid strip head firing and is a common practice when burning heavy accumulations of logging slash in the western United States. The convection column so produced has sufficient strength to attain a satisfactory height under neutral stability conditions and can often pierce weak inversions. Because the fires produced by mass ignition are quite intense, it is a dangerous practice to use when the atmosphere is unstable.

Mop-up is critical in avoiding smoke pollution. Smoldering material has eight times the particulate emission rate of flaming fuel. Much of the smoldering occurs after the convective lift phase of the fire and smoke is advected close to the ground. Smoldering often occurs during the evening and night hours when the atmosphere is at its most stable and there is a minimum of turbulence and dilution of pollutants.

One cannot make an omelet without breaking eggs and one cannot have a fire without making smoke. But neither fact should be used as an excuse for riding roughshod over the sensibilities of one's neighbors. Smoke from forest fires can be more than a nuisance. It can reduce visibility along highways, close airports, and cause serious loss of tourist revenue to resorts. Burning prescriptions should be written to minimize smoke emissions, and burning should only be conducted when actual and predicted winds will steer the smoke away from centers of population.

## BIBLIOGRAPHY

Agee, J. K. 1973. *Prescribed fire effects on physical and hydrologic properties of mixed-conifer forest floor and soil.* Water Res. Center, Univ. Calif. Contrib. Report 143, 57 pp.

Ahlgren, I. F. and C. E. Ahlgren. 1960. Ecological effects of forest fires. *Bot Rev.* **26**:483–533.

Ahlgren, I. F. and C. E. Ahlgren. 1965. Effects of prescribed burning on soil microorganisms in a Minnesota jack pine forest. *Ecol.* **46**:306–310.

Alban, D. H. 1977. *Influence on soil properties of prescribed burning under mature red pine.* U.S. For. Serv. Res. Paper NC-139, 8 pp.

Allen, S. E. 1964. Chemical aspects of heather burning. *J. Appl. Ecol.* **1**:347–367.

Aston, A. R. and R. M. Gill. 1976. Coupled soil moisture, heat and water vapour transfers under simulated fire conditions. *Aust. J. Soil Res.* **14**:55–66.

Austin, R. C. and D. H. Basinger. 1955. Some effects of burning on forest soils of western Oregon and Washington. *J. For.* **53**:275–280.

Biswell, H. H. and A. M. Schultz. 1957. Surface runoff and erosion as related to prescribed burning. *J. For.* **55**:372–375.

Bollen, G. J. 1969. The selective effect of heat treatment on the microflora of a greenhouse soil. *Neth. J. Plant Pathol.* **75**:15–163.

Brown, G. W., A. R. Gahler, and R. B. Marston. 1973. Nutrient losses after clear-cut logging and slash burning in the Oregon coast range. *Water Resource Res.* **9**:1450–1453.

Brown, J. K. 1974. *Handbook for inventorying downed woody material.* U.S. For. Serv. Gen. Tech. Report INT-16, 24 pp., illus.

Campbell, R. E. and others. 1977. *Wildfire effects on a ponderosa pine ecosystem: an Arizona case study.* U.S. For. Serv. Res. Paper RM-191, 12 pp.

Christensen, N. L. 1977. Fire and soil-plant nutrient relations in a pine-wiregrass savanna on the coastal plain of North Carolina. *Oecologia* **31**:27–44.

Christensen, N. L. and C. H. Muller. 1975. Effects of fire on factors controlling plant growth in *Adenostoma* chaparral. *Ecol. Monogr.* **45**:29–55.

Connaughton, C. A. 1935. Forest fires and accelerated erosion. *J. For.* **33**:751–752.

Cooper, C. F. 1971. *Effects of prescribed burning on the ecosystem.* Prescribed Burning Symp. Proc., U.S. For. Serv., pp. 152–160.

Countryman, C. M. 1969. *Project flambeau . . . an investigation of mass fire (1964–1967). Final Report,* Vol. I. OCD-PS-65-26, 68 pp., illus.

DeBano, L. F. 1981. *Water repellent soils: a state-of-the-art.* U.S. For. Serv. Gen. Tech. Report PSW-46, 21 pp., illus.

DeBano, L. F. and others. 1967. *Soil wettability and wetting agents . . . our current knowledge of the problem.* U.S. For. Serv. Res. Paper PSW-43, 13 pp.

DeBano, L. T., P. H. Dunn, and C. E. Conrad. 1977. *Fire's effect on physical and chemical properties of chaparral soil.* Proc. Symp. Environ. Consequences Fire Fuel Manage. Medit. Ecosyst., U.S. For. Serv. Gen. Tech. Report WO-3, pp. 65–74.

DeBano, L. F. and C. E. Conrad. 1978. The effect of fire on nutrients in a chaparral ecosystem. *Ecol.* **59**:489–497.

DeBano, L. F., G. E. Eberlein, and P. H. Dunn. 1979. Effects of burning on chaparral soils. Soil Nitrogen: *Soil Sci. Soc. Am. J.* **43**:504–509.

DeBell, D. S. and C. W. Ralston. 1970. Release of nitrogen by burning light forest fuels. *Soil Sci. Soc. Am. Proc.* **34**:935–938.

DeByle, N. V. 1973. Broadcast burning of logging residues and water repelling of soil. *Northwest Sci.* **47**:77–87.

DeByle, N. V. and P. E. Packer. 1972. *Plant nutrient and soil losses in overland flow from burned forest clearcuts*. Natl. Symp. Watersheds in Transition, pp. 296–307.

Dunn, P. H. and L. F. DeBano. 1977. *Fire's effect on the biological properties of chaparral soils*. Proc. Symp. Environ. Consequences Fire Fuel Manage. Medit. Ecosystems. U.S. For. Serv. Gen. Tech. Report WO-3, pp. 75–84.

Dunn, P. H., L. F. DeBano, and G. E. Eberlein. 1979. Effects of burning on chaparral soils II: soil microbes and nitrogen mineralization. *Soil Sci. Soc. Am. J.* **43**:509–514.

Dyrness, C. T. and C. T. Youngberg. 1957. The effect of logging and slash burning on soil structure. *Soil Sci. Soc. Am. Proc.* **21**:444–447.

Dyrness, C. T. 1976. *Erodibility and erosion potential of forest watersheds*. Int. Symp. For. Hydrol., Pergamon, New York, pp. 559–611.

Fowler, W. B. and J. D. Helvey. 1978. *Changes in the thermal regime after prescribed burning and selected tree removal*. U.S. For. Serv. Res. Paper PNW-234, 17 pp., illus.

Garren, K. H. 1943. Effects of fire on vegetation of the southeastern United States. *Bot. Rev.* **9**:617–654.

Greene, S. W. 1935. Effect of annual grass fires on organic matter and other constituents of virgin longleaf pine soils. *J. Agric. Res.* **50**:809–822.

Grier, C. C. 1975. Wildfire effects on nutrients distribution and teaching in a coniferous ecosystem. *Can. J. For. Res.* **5**:599–607.

Grier, C. C. and D. W. Cole. 1971. Influence of slash burning on ion transport in a forest soil. *Northwest Sci.* **45**:100–106.

Hall, J. A. 1972. *Forest fuels, prescribed fire, and air quality*. U.S. For. Serv. Pac. N.W. Exp. Sta., 44 pp.

Hatch, A. B. 1960. *Ash bed effects in western Australia forest soils*. Bull. For. Dept. W. Aust. 64, 20 pp.

Helvey, J. D., A. R. Tiedemann, and W. B. Fowler. 1976. *Some climatic and hydrologic effects of wildfire in Washington State*. Proc. Tall Timbers Fire Ecol. Conf. **15**:201–222.

Hoffman, G. R. 1966. Ecological studies of *Funaria hygrometrica* heather in eastern Washington and northern Idaho. *Ecol. Monogr.* **36**:157–180.

Holland, J. 1953. Infiltration on a timber and a burn site in northern Idaho. U.S. For. Serv. Res. Note 127, 3 pp.

Isaac, L. A. and H. G. Hopkins. 1937. The forest soil of the Douglas fir region and the changes wrought upon it by logging and slash burning. *Ecol.* **18**:264–273.

Johnson, C. M. and P. R. Needham. 1966. Ionic composition of Sagehen Creek, California, following an adjacent fire. *Ecol.* **67**:636–639.

Jorgensen, J. R. and C. S. Hodges. 1970. Microbial characteristics of a forest soil after twenty years of prescribed burning. *Mycologia* **62**:721–726.

Jorgensen, J. R. and C. G. Wells. 1971. *Apparent nitrogen fixation in soil influenced by prescribed burning*. Soil Sci. Soc. Am. Proc. **35**:806–810.

Kimmins, J. P. and M. C. Feller. 1976. *Effect of clearcutting and broadcast slash burning on nutrient budgets, streamwater chemistry and productivity in western Canada*. Proc. 16th IUFRO World Conf., Oslo, Norway, pp. 186–197.

Knight, H. 1966. Loss of nitrogen from the forest floor by burning. *For. Chron.* **42**:149–152.

Knighton, M. D. 1977. Hydrologic response and nutrient concentrations following spring burns in an oak-hickory forest. *Soil Sci. Soc. Am. J.* **41**:627–632.

Lewis, W. M., Jr. 1974. Effects of fire on nutrient movement in a South Carolina pine forest. *Ecol.* **55**(5):1120–1127.

Lloyd, P. S. 1971. Effects of fire on the chemical status of Luloceous communities of the Derbyshire Dales. *J. Ecol.* **59**:261–273.

Longstretch, D. J. and D. T. Patten. 1975. Conversion of chaparral to grass in central Arizona. Effects on selected ions in watershed runoff. *Am. Midland Natur.* **93**:25–34.

Lotspeich, F. B., E. W. Mueller, and P. J. Frey. 1970. *Effects of large scale forest fires on water quality in interior Alaska,* USDI Fed. Water Poll. Control Adm., Alaska Water Lab., College, Alaska, 115 pp.

Lunt, H. A. 1950. *Liming and twenty years of litter raking and burning under red and white pine.* Soil Sci. Am. Proc. **15**:381–390.

Lutz, H. J. 1956. *The ecological effects of forest fire in the interior of Alaska.* USDA Tech. Bull. 1133, 121 pp.

McColl, J. G. and D. F. Grigal. 1975. Forest fire effects on phosphorus movement to lakes. *Sci.* **188**:1109–1111.

McColl, J. G. and D. F. Grigal. 1977. Nutrient changes following a forest wildfire in Minnesota. Effects in watershed with differing soils. *Oikos* **28**:105–112.

Mersereau, R. C. and C. T. Dyrness. 1972. Accelerated mass wasting after logging and slash burning in western Oregon. *J. Soil and Water Conserv.* **27**:112–114.

Metz, L. T., T. Lotti, and R. A. Klawitter. 1961. *Some effects of prescribed burning on coastal plain forest soil.* U.S. For. Serv. Sta. Paper SE-133, 10 pp.

Morris, W. G. 1970. Effects of slash burning in overmature stands of the Douglas fir region. *For. Sci.* **16**:258–270.

Muraro, S. J. 1977. *The prescribed fire predictor.* Fire Control Notes **13**:26, Can. For. Assn. of British Columbia.

Murrell, W. G. and W. J. Scott. 1966. The heat resistance of boetinal spores at various water activities. *J. Gen. Microbiol.* **43**:411–425.

Neal, J. L., E. Wright, and W. B. Bollen. 1965. *Burning Douglas fir slash: physical, chemical and microbial effects on the soil.* Oregon State Univ., For. Res. Lab. Res. Paper 1, 32 pp.

Orme, M. L. and T. A. Teege. 1976. *Emergence and survival of redstem* (Ceanthus sanguineus) *following prescribed burning.* Proc. Tall Timbers Fire Ecol. Conf. **14**:391–420.

Orr, H. K. 1970. *Runoff and erosion control by seeded and native vegetation on a forest burn: Black Hills, South Dakota.* U.S. For. Serv. Res. Paper RM-60, 12 pp.

Owensby, C. E. and J. B. Wyrill. 1973. Effect of range burning on Kansas Flint Hills soils. *J. Range Manage.* **26**:185–188.

Renbuss, M., G. A. Chilvers, and L. D. Pryer. 1973. *Microbiology of an ashbed.* Proc. Linn. Soc. New South Wales **97**:302–310.

Reynolds, H. G. and J. W. Bohning. 1956. Effects of burning of a desert grassland range in southern Arizona. *Ecol.* **37**:769–777.

Rice, R. M. and G. T. Foggin. 1971. Effect of high intensity storms on soil slippage on mountainous watersheds in southern California. *Water Res.* **7**:1485–1496.

Rothacher, J. and W. Lopushinsky. 1974. *Soil stability and water yield and quality.* U.S. For. Serv. Gen. Tech. Report PNW-24, 23 pp.

Rowe, P. B., C. M. Countryman, and H. C. Storey. 1954. *Hydrologic analysis used to determine effects of fire on peak discharge and erosion rates in southern California watersheds.* U.S. For. Serv. Unnumbered Report, 49 pp., illus.

Ryan, P. W. and C. K. McMahon. 1976. *Some chemical and physical characteristics of emissions from forest fires.* 69th Annual Meeting Air Poll. Contr. Assoc., Paper No. 76-2.3, 15 pp.

St. John, T. U. and P. W. Rundel. 1976. The role of fire as a mineralizing agent in a Sierra coniferous forest. *Oecologia* **25**:35–45.

Salih, M. S. A., F. K. Taha, and G. F. Payne. 1973. Water repellency of soils under burned sagebrush. *J. Range Manage.* **26**:330–331.

Sandberg, D. V. 1980. *Duff reduction by prescribed underburning in Douglas fir.* U.S. For. Serv. Res. Paper PNW-272, 18 pp., illus.

Sandberg, D. V. and others. 1979. *Effects of fire on air: a state-of-knowledge review.* U.S. For. Serv. Gen. Tech. Report WO-9, 40 pp.

Sartz, R. S. 1953. Soil erosion on a fire-denuded forest area in the Douglas fir region. *J. Soil Water Conserv.* **8**:279–281.

Scholl, D. G. 1975. *Soil wettability and fire in Arizona chaparral.* Soil Sci. Soc. Am. Proc. **39**:356–361.

Scotter, G. W. 1963. Effects of forest fires on soil properties in northern Saskatchewan. *For. Chron.* **39**:412–421.

Smith, D. W. 1970. Concentration of nutrients before and after fire. *Can. J. Soil Sci.* **50**:17–29.

Snyder, G. G., H. F. Haupt, and G. H. Belt, Jr. 1975. *Clearcutting and burning slash alter quality of stream water in northern Idaho.* U.S. For. Serv. Res. Paper INT-168, 36 pp.

Southern Forest Fire Laboratory Staff. 1976. *Southern forestry smoke management guidebook.* U.S. For. Serv. Gen. Tech. Report SE-10, 140 pp.

Stark, N. M. 1977. Fire and nutrient cycling in a Douglas fir/larch forest. *Ecol.* **58**:16–30.

Stark, N. M. and R. Steele. 1977. Nutrient content of forest shrubs following fire. *Am. J. Bot.* **64**:1218–1224.

Stone, E. L., Jr. 1971. *Effects of prescribed burning on long-term productivity of coastal plain soils.* Proc. Symp. Prescribed Burning. U.S. For. Serv. SE For. Exp. Stn., pp. 115–129.

Storey, T. G. and E. A. DeBano. 1968. *The southern California study of fire-caused watershed damage—twenty years later.* U.S. For. Serv. Unnumbered Report, 18 pp.

Tarrant, R. F. 1956. Effects of slash burning on some soils of the Douglas-fir region. *Soil Sci. Am. Proc.* **20**:608–611.

Tarrant, R. F. and E. Wright. 1955. *Growth of Douglas fir seedlings after slash burning.* U.S. For. Serv. Res. Note PNW-115, 3 pp.

Tiedemann, A. R. 1973. *Stream chemistry following a forest fire and urea fertilization in northcentral Washington.* U.S. For. Serv. Res. Note PNW-203, 19 pp.

Tiedemann, A. R., J. D. Helvey, and T. D. Anderson. 1978. Stream chemistry and watershed nutrient economy following wildfire and fertilization in eastern Washington. *J. Environ. Qual.* **7**:580–588.

Trabaud, L. 1980. *Impact biologique et écologique des feux de végétation sur l'organisation, la structure et l'évolution de la végétation des garrigues due Bas Languedoc.* Thèse Doct. Etat. Univ. Sci. Tech. Languedoc, Montpellier. 288 pp.

Turner, D. B. 1970. *Workbook of atmospheric dispersion estimates.* U.S. Environ. Prot. Agency. Pub. No. AP-26, 84 pp.

Viro, P. J. 1974. Effects of forest fire on soil. In T. T. Kozlowski and C. E. Ahlgren, Eds., *Fire and Ecosystems,* Academic, New York, pp. 7–45.

Wagle, R. F. and J. H. Kitchen. 1972. Influence of fire on soil nutrients in a ponderosa pine type. *Ecol.* **53**:119–125.

Wells, B. W. 1942. Ecological problems of the southeastern United States coastal plain. *Bot. Rev.* 8:533–561.

Wells, C. G. 1971. *Effects of prescribed burning on soil chemical properties and nutrient availability.* Proc. Prescribed Burning Symp. U.S. For. Serv. NE For. Exp. Stn., pp. 86–89.

Wells, C. G. and others. 1979. *Effects of fire on soil: a state-of-knowledge review.* U.S. For. Serv. Gen. Tech. Report WO-7, 34 pp.

Wells, C. G. 1981. Some effects of brushfires on erosion processes in coastal southern California. In *Erosion and Sediment Transport in Pacific Rim Steeplands.* IAHS Pub. No. 132, Christchurch.

White, E. M., W. W. Thompson, and F. R. Gartner. 1973. Heat effects on nutrient release from soils under ponderosa pine. *J. Range Manage.* 26:22–24.

Wright, H. A., F. M. Churchill, and W. C. Stevens. 1976. Effects of prescribed burning on sediment, water yield, and water quality from dozed juniper lands in central Texas. *J. Range Manage.* 29:294–298.

Wright, R. F. 1976. The impact of forest fire on the nutrient influxes to small lakes in northeastern Minnesota. *Ecol.* 57:649–663.

# CHAPTER EIGHT

# *Fire Effects on Wildlife*

Fire in the natural environment has a profound effect on the wildlife of an area. Of particular interest are the animals' immediate and long-term reactions to a fire. Environmental changes such as those caused by fire, flooding, deforestation, or afforestation determine the representation and abundance of certain animal species. As fire is one of the natural factors of environmental change, its effects on animals must be examined.

More generally, we must consider how a particular species could have evolved in an environment in which fire was a frequent occurrence, how this species adapted to fire conditions, and in what way the animals interact with their fire-changed environment.

Of course, the effects of fire vary considerably. The fact that fire brings many different environmental changes makes it difficult to correlate fire with response of animals. Fires may vary in intensity, duration, frequency, location, shape, and extent. Their effects may differ with season, nature of the food, and properties of the site and soil. Added to these sources of variation are the effects of humans; a fire may have vastly different results in a natural forest as compared to fire over the same area after logging or some other use by people. Thus it may be wise to consider each fire as a special case and remember that animals will probably respond differently in each instance.

## INFLUENCE OF ANIMALS ON FIRE BEHAVIOR

Fire affects wildlife habitat; conversely, animals may indirectly increase or decrease the probability of fire as well as the intensity of any fire that occurs (Figure 8.1).

Insects very frequently cause enormous damage when they attack a forested area, weakening and thinning out the stands and leaving many dead or diseased trees that, being dry, are much more flammable. Eventually, the

*Figure 8.1.* Debris from beaver cuttings can increase the fire hazard. Photo by Michigan Department of Natural Resources.

tree trunks fall, increasing the fire hazard considerably. This is what happened in *Abies balsamea* and *Picea* forests in southeastern Canada and New England in 1825 and 1922 (Flieger 1970) and, more recently, in *Pinus contorta* forests in south-central Oregon (Geiszler et al. 1980). These authors mention an unusual association between a fungus and a coleopteran attack as the cause of increased susceptibility to fire. In mature pine forests (80 to 150 years) when trees are weakened by the fungus *Phaeolus schweintzii,* the mountain pine beetle *Dendroctonus ponderosae* multiplies rapidly. The resulting population explosion results in the killing of many trees, which contributes additional fuel to feed new fires. The surviving trees emerge injured; they are infested by the fungus and about 100 years later they are attacked anew by *Dendroctonus* (Figure 8.2).

Large herbivores such as deer, elk, bison, moose, and some rodents, beavers, for example, can alter the composition of a stand of plants when they browse, particularly when they choose certain plants over others (Bailey and Poulton 1968). In this way they affect fire probability and influence fire behavior. Large herds of grazing herbivores can sometimes reduce the fuel supply. Campbell (1954) shows that livestock grazing breaks up potential fuel and establishes trails through the forest that can be used as firebreaks.

In the western United States and throughout most of Canada, lightning is the leading cause of fire. Squirrels make trees more vulnerable to lightning

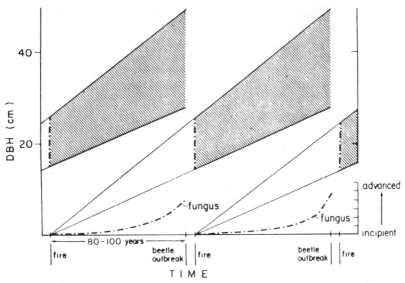

*Figure 8.2.* Conceptual model on the interaction between fire, fungus, and the mountain pine beetle in a lodgepole pine forest of south-central Oregon. Wedge represents equal age-class trees; shaded portion represents fungal infection; dashed lines represent stage of fungal decay in the living trees (from Geiszler et al. 1980).

by mutilating their tops (Keith 1965). Some squirrels create middens of cone scales around trees (Rowe 1970). These, along with tiny shavings from the nests of green woodpeckers, increase flammability.

## IMMEDIATE REACTIONS OF ANIMALS TO FIRE

The immediate reactions of animals to fire are fairly limited, although very large, intense fires can kill all types of wildlife including such huge animals as elephants (Brynard 1971). Fires do not usually sweep through great expanses all at once. Mobile animals can take temporary shelter in unburned or already burned areas. Less active species must take refuge in or beneath the soil. Small mammals can easily escape the destructive impact of fire by burrowing deep underground. Ground-dwelling fauna and species that temporarily go below ground for shelter have nothing to fear since the heat from the fire penetrates only a few centimeters into the soil.

Birds have to fear only for the safety of their nests and many birds species take advantage of a fire to catch escaping insects that are normally well camouflaged in their habitat. Some raptors momentarily turn into insectivores when a fire passes. Reptiles generally have hiding places in wet areas or underground. In the dry season on the African grassland the presence of some lizard populations is indicated only by their eggs buried in the ground

(Gillon 1974). Batrachians take to ground or leave the savanna for the wet lowlands as soon as the dry season starts.

The reaction of animals to fire depends on habitat attachment, mobility, ability to find shelter, and sensitivity to smoke and heat.

## Avoidance Behavior

Whether an animal will choose to flee, burrow, or simply remain near a fire depends largely on the fire's intensity and rate of spread as well as the familiarity of the individual or the species to fire. In ecosystems where mild surface fires with short return periods are the rule, such as the southern United States and parts of Australia, most species are adapted to fire as a regular occurrence. In the boreal forest, by contrast, fires are only experienced once in several generations and the individual's response depends on the perceived threat.

In the great fire that raged in Siberia for two months in 1915, squirrels (*Sciurus*), bears (*Ursus*), and elk (*Alces*) were seen swimming across large rivers to escape the fire (Udvardy 1969). In contrast to this scene of confusion, Hakala et al. (1971) describe how a family of swans (*Cygnus*) continued moving in a small lake while the forest burned to the shore. A small group of caribou (*Rangifer*) rested on the ground while encircled by fire and later moved away. Vogl (1967, 1973) reports similar calm behavior by birds and mammals in fires in Wisconsin.

In a fire with a great deal of smoke and little flame, the Carolina grasshopper *Dissoteria carolina* tends to crawl up stems or twigs into the dense smoke and remain motionless. In a fire with little smoke and high flames, however, it will hop and make short flights just ahead of the flames. Komarek (1969) observed green katydids taking flight in front of a head fire. Some grasshoppers such as the red-legged grasshopper usually do not start to move away until the flames are very close.

Sun-loving Hemiptera (Pentatomids) nimbly climb grass plant stalks and take off (D. Gillon 1972). After the fire they return to colonize the burned area. Among the winged adults, shade-loving species are affected the most, so that after the fire the heliophilic insects comprise a larger proportion of the general population. Adults and nymphs have been found burned by flames.

Crickets, particularly the common garden cricket (*Acheta* sp.), advance before the fire. Many may be killed by the fire but others take refuge under the debris or in the soil, for they may frequently be seen crawling over a still warm burn. The common wolf spider (*Lycosa rabida*) has been seen moving away or digging through the earth after passage of the fire. Spider webs have been found in burned-over areas the morning after a fire.

Ants (*Camponotus abdominalis floridana, Iridomyrmex humilis, Pheidole megacephala, Paratrechina longicornis, P. bourbonica,* and *Anoplolepis longipes*) can be killed by flames if they are caught away from their nest. After a fire they usually move their eggs and larvae to form new colonies in unburned areas. Often fire is not intense enough to kill off an entire colony. In frequent fire areas the acacia ant (*Pseudomyrmex* sp.) clears away vegetation and debris around its colony to keep it from being burned.

Fire triggers a variety of responses among the higher animals—some panic and flee the fire, others move calmly away from it, and others actually draw nearer the fire. The response is related to the animal's mobility and the extent of the fire.

Snakes usually avoid fire by taking refuge in burrows or rocky crevices. Komarek (1969) found two water moccasins (*Agkistrodon piscivorus*) that had been killed by fire. He notices, however, that southern diamond-back rattlesnake (*Crotalus admanteus*) populations did not seem to be reduced by annual fires in southern Georgia or northern Florida. He also states that he had never seen a rattlesnake killed in a fire. Quite the contrary; these reptiles were seen sunning themselves in holes in old trunks or burrows on still-blackened burns, where the ground was warmer.

Komarek (1969) also observed cotton rats (*Sigmodon*), some carrying young, running before a fire. He believes that the cotton rat could sense the fire and, therefore, escape in time. As the adult cotton rats could sense the direction from which the fire was coming, they uttered little cries to call their young, and thus saved them. Komarek (1963) trapped cotton rats before and after a fire. He did not find a single one killed in the burn and the lack of change in the capture rate allowed him to conclude that the fire had not caused any losses. He states that many cotton rats went into burrows or holes and escaped the fire. Mice (*Peromyscus*), chipmunks (*Eutamias*), shrews (*Sorex*), and wood rats (*Neotoma*) may flee quite far from a fire (Tevis 1956). Some wood rats go from shelter to shelter before disappearing into the thick of the forest. Other species of wood rats behave as if reluctant to leave their homes and linger before running from the clear-cut stand, whereas others, panic-stricken, remain immobile until the flames have almost reached them or actually singed their fur. This tendency to remain in their own area reveals the close relationship between a habitat type and an animal species and shows how the behavior of a species can make it vulnerable to fire. Tevis (op. cit.) trapped *Peromyscus* the day following a fire and found that the number of animals caught was less than before the fire. In his view, the fire and the flight of the animals caused the drop in the number of trapped individuals. Several of the wood rats managed to escape by burrowing into unburned areas or taking flight, then returning right after the fire. Two and a half weeks after the fire, Tevis trapped twice the number of rats as before the fire. Similar results are obtained by Tester (1965) with *Peromyscus* and *Clethrionomys,* and by Sims and Buckner (1973) with *Peromyscus.*

## Fire Mortality

Fire as a direct cause of mortality has been studied by a number of investigators.

The direct effect of fire on arthropods in the African savannas depends mainly on the layer in which they live. Surface-dwellers are barely affected (80 percent of arachnids and cockroaches have been found alive the day after a fire). Forty percent of carabids, Lygaeidae, Gryllidae, Tetrigidae, mantises, and myriapods have been found alive, whereas insects living in the higher part of the grass suffer considerable losses. The day after a fire not even 10 percent of acridians, grasshoppers, Corridae, and Homoptera were found alive (Gillon and Pernes 1968, Gillon 1974). Another direct consequence of fire is a decrease in the average size of animals in almost all arthropod genera. This is due to escape by flight of the winged adults—the largest individuals in each species—and to the smaller animals' greater facility for finding a temporary hiding place.

The ability of animals, particularly small mammals, to survive a fire depends mainly on the decrease in ground temperature just a few centimeters from the heat of the fire (Ahlgren and Ahlgren 1960, Cooper 1961, Lawrence 1966, Martin 1963, Smith 1968, Trabaud 1979). Small mammals cannot support an air temperature in excess of 62°C, the value found by Howard et al. (1959) to be fatal to caged rats and mice. Apparently, however, most burrowing animals are killed by suffocation rather than by high temperatures (Chew et al. 1958, Lawrence op. cit.). Lawrence speculates that animals may suffocate when caught in burrows without an adequate supply of fresh air and that as the soil warms, the vapor pressure of water increases, making the air within a burrow hot and humid. Birds and mammals hold their body temperatures against a rising ambient temperature by evaporative cooling. Should the temperature in a burrow exceed the upper lethal temperature for the mammal and evaporation cooling become impossible because of high vapor pressure of water, death from heat stroke will result.

Howard et al. (op. cit.) placed caged mammals (*Citellus, Peromyscus, Rattus*) and snakes in rocky crevices and underground burrows before starting a fire. Although the animals were not allowed to react freely to the fire, about half of them, including all the snakes, survived. A similar experiment was performed by Lawrence (op. cit.), who placed caged mice in burrows under a chaparral fire in California. When the burrow was open at one end only, all the *Peromyscus truei* died. But when the burrow was a tunnel open at both ends, presumably allowing adequate ventilation, all the *Microtus californicus* survived.

Although there is evidence that some game animals have been killed by fire, and some investigators consider fire capable of killing many wild animals (Greene 1935, Lutz 1956), it is commonly held that vertebrates are rarely killed in fires, with a very small, practically negligible number of deaths. Doerr et al. (1970), Keith and Surrendi (1971), Phillips (1965), Sims

*Figure 8.3.* A fast moving fire run can trap even the fleetest animal. Photo by U.S. Forest Service.


and Buckner (op. cit.), Stoddard (1963), Tester (op. cit.), Tevis (op. cit.), and Vogl (1967) believe that fire is not a direct cause of mortality in vertebrates. The experiences of these investigators are largely colored by their fire backgrounds. Those working primarily with prescribed fires and small wildfires rarely see a dead animal. Those who study conflagration aftermaths see many (Figure 8.3). Since most of the hectarage burned is in high-intensity fires, while the preponderant number of fires are of low intensity, wildlife mortality per hectare is undoubtedly higher than the scientific literature would suggest.

### Animals Attracted to Fire and Smoke

The attraction of the moth to the flame is a staple topic of fables in all parts of the world, but many animals besides Lepidoptera are also attracted by fire.

Some flying insects are attracted to heat, smoke, or burned trees so that for some time a population may increase during and immediately following a fire.

Some dipteran species behave in specific fashions. Komarek (1969) writes that the common blue dragonfly (*Pantala flavescens*), the giant dragonfly (*Ajax junius*), the brown dragonfly (*Erythemis simplificollis*), and the small dragonfly (*Lespes vigilax*) arrive at certain times of day and of the year and are attracted only to some types of fire. He also points out that smoke flies (*Microsania*) are attracted by the odor of smoke. He lists nine species of *Microsania* with this characteristic in the United States, Canada, New Zealand, Australia, Belgium, England, and Zaire.

Komarek believes that these insects display positive fumatropism, which he considers related to mating behavior; the smoke stream serving as a marker for mating swarms.

Some coleopterans, the fire beetles or firebugs, are attracted by heat. Buprestids such as the fire beetles (*Merimna atrata* in Australia, and *Melanophila atrata* and *M. acuminata* in the United States) are attracted by fire (Komarek 1969). These animals possess infrared radiation-detecting organs that can locate forest fires at great distances (100 to 160 km). This positive phototactism characteristic is related to mating; the female lays her eggs in charred wood. Fire beetles have been observed to alight on still-glowing tree trunks or stumps (Linsley 1943).

Many birds and mammals are attracted by fire so as to feed on fleeing animals. Birds, in particular, show little fear of fire; some are actually attracted by the smoke. Komarek (1969) lists 85 species of North American birds and mammals that are attracted to fire and/or smoke as well as 34 African species of birds and 22 northern Australian bird species. These include North American, African, and Australian birds such as the eagle, vulture, kite, and falcon that hunt small animals fleeing before the fire. Such species include the king vulture (*Sarcoramphus papa*), caracara (*Caracara cheriway*), drongo (*Picurus asimilis*), grey hornbill (*Lophoceros nasutus*), lilac-breasted roller (*Coracias caudata*), fire-bird (*Merops nubicus*), kite (*Milvus aegyptius*), African cattle egret (*Bubulcus ibis*), sacred ibis (*Threskiornis aethiopicus*), loggerhead shrike (*Lanius ludovicianus*), phoebe (*Sayornis phoebe*), wood pewee (*Contopus virens*), king bird (*Tyrannus tyrannus*), tree swallow (*Irdoprocne bicolor*), rough-winged swallow (*Stelgidopteryx ruficollis*), purple martin *Progne subis*), and flycatchers, swallows, and kestrels. Stoddard (1963) makes the same observation concerning the red-tailed hawk (*Buteo jamaicensis*), the sparrow hawk (*Falco sparverius*), and the purple martin (*Progne subis*), which take advantage of the flames to catch fleeing animals, particularly insects. Quail (*Colinus*) and turkey (*Meleagris*) often gather on the burns before the smoke clears, where they find a more ready source of food. Howard et al. (op. cit.) saw quail (*Lophortyx californicus*), bushtit (*Psaltriparus minimus*), and a thrasher (*Toxostoma*) leaving a fire site. They found at least five bird species feeding on the burn during a brushfire in California.

Kites and eagles (*Milvus migrans, Butastur rufipennis*) of the African grasslands are attracted by fire; flying ahead of the flames, they catch insects, birds, lizards, and rodents (Y. Gillon 1972, Handley 1969).

African carnivores such as the lion (*Panthera leo*), the leopard (*Panthera pardus*), and the cheetah (*Acinonyx jubatus*) hunt alongside fire in savannas (Komarek 1969).

Some herbivores apparently eat ash or wood charcoal. Among these are the snowshoe hare (*Lepus americanus*) cited by Grange (1965), the cotton rat (*Sigmodon hispidus*), and the Virginia and white-tailed deer (*Odocoileus virginianus*) cited by Komarek (1969). Numerous species seek out recent burns where they eat ash or burned plant parts for their high mineral content. Many herbivores also wallow in fresh ashes to rid themselves of ticks and other vermin.

Komarek (1967) also notes that various primates such as the gorilla, pan, and gibbon are attracted by wildfires and abandoned campfires. In his 1969 article, he observes that this attraction can also be seen in the Philippines tarsier (*Tarsier carbonarius*) and the Colobus monkey (*Colobus polykomos*) of Ceylon.

## INDIRECT EFFECTS OF FIRE ON ANIMAL BEHAVIOR

Some animal species react favorably to the environmental changes wrought by fire, although others find a habitat that has become inhospitable. Each burn has its own local climate and microclimate which may affect wildlife. Postfire vegetation is not identical to prefire plant life in structure or composition. Generally, animals can adapt to most habitat changes. Bendell (1974) lists several factors that determine the distribution and representation of animal species after a fire.

### Habitat Modification

Blackening of the ground and removal of vegetation increases heat input to the soil and thereby directly or indirectly influences insects, birds, and mammals. Vigorous plant growth due to warmer temperatures improves the food after winter burns. Blackening of the ground and exposure of light-colored mineral soil will change the input and reflectance of light. Shade-loving species leave a burn; light-loving species are attracted to it. As a general rule, higher temperature maxima and lower minima are found in a burned than in an unburned area. Changes in temperature and wind also affect relative humidity and some animals are sensitive to this.

The layers of a forest greatly modify the speed of winds that blow through them. After logging and fire there may be an increase in the frequency and velocity of winds over the burn. A cold wind may greatly increase heat loss from birds or mammals. Stoddard (1962) writes that in the southeastern United States summer winds might make burned areas cooler and, therefore, better habitat for birds.

***Figure 8.4.*** After fire, fallen trees may impede animal movement. Photo by U.S. Forest Service.

Snow can cut off access to a customary food source. Early spring melt and greening of a burn may explain its attraction for some species of wildlife.

Perhaps the greatest change made by fire that affects birds and mammals is the destruction of trees and large shrubs, so that for some time most growth is close to the ground. Animals may be either attracted or repelled by a burned forest.

After some fires, particularly when followed by snag-felling operations, the land may be a jungle of fallen trees that obstruct movement (Figure 8.4). Some investigators report, however, that wildlife can move more freely to seek their requirements on a burn than was possible before the fire, particularly in areas with heavy undergrowth (Austen 1972, Lemon 1968b). The amount of litter and the hardness of the soil may be modified by fire and afterwards by the action of logging and firefighting equipment. Removal of litter may make foods that were concealed by it available to birds and mammals (Hurst 1971, Stoddard 1931).

Fires rarely burn evenly and they usually result in a larger mosaic of old and new cover. They create a new cover type consisting of stumps, burned trunks, and clearings. Topography may also cause variations in fire behavior, plant cover renewal, and wildlife response. The type of plant cover within the burn may determine where animals live and affect their density. Biswell et al. (1952) recommend spot burns of one or two hectares in a checkerboard pattern to open up dense chamise brushland for black-tailed deer (*Odocoileus hemionus columbianus*), game birds, and mammals in California.

Size of burn is important. In Australia, Mount (1969) observes that areas burned by bush fires may be so large that forest animals will not move into them. Small burns and their edges are used because animals can readily retreat to nearby unburned forest. In the opinion of Bendell (1974), the size of a burn may determine the growth of populations that move into it by providing new and unlimiting resources releasing genotypes that will expand in numbers when free from the interference of previously established genotypes that tend to keep populations in check.

The size of a burn, its edge, and interspersion with cover types beyond the burn are structural features that may be important in the response of birds and mammals. Edges between cover types and interspersion of cover types are related in that a number of small fires in an area will create more edge and interspersion than one large burn. As burns become larger, the amount of edge and interspersion becomes less in proportion to the amount of open burn. The edge between a burned and unburned area may be very abrupt and occur within a few meters. On Vancouver Island Robinson (1958) considers that small fires (80 to 120 ha) produced a large number of burned and unburned areas and that deer, blue grouse, and moose were more numerous than in large burns (400+ ha).

The vast mosaic of forests of different sizes, shapes, and edges created by fire provides heterogeneity of environments, thereby benefiting most animals. Bendell (1974) reports that on a burn in the herb and shrub stage of succession, white-crowned sparrows (*Zonotrichia*), towhees (*Pipilo*), and robins (*Turdus*) were common residents. In another burn in the young tree stage, western tanagers (*Piranga*), warbling vireos, and thrushes (*Ixoreus*) were found. A fire may permit a species to increase until it encroaches on surrounding plant communities.

## Biota Modification

Animals are adapted to particular kinds of food, and the abundance and distribution of wildlife may depend on the supply of the appropriate kind of food. The concentration of plants near the ground after a fire will affect mammals, particularly the large forms, more than the birds, because the former cannot feed much beyond their standing height. Edwards (1954) describes the dramatic change in mammalian life, particularly the increase of moose and deer, with burning of mature conifer forest and the subsequent growth of herbs and shrubs in Wells Gray Park, British Columbia. The current number and winter distribution of caribou (*Rangifer*) appear to be due to the destruction of their main winter food, arboreal and ground lichens (mainly *Cladonia*) by fire (Cringan 1957, Edwards op. cit., Scotter 1971).

Munro and Cowan (1947) list some of the birds that disappeared from, and those that appeared on, logged and burned areas on Vancouver Island. As might be expected, some insectivorous birds that fed in coniferous foliage were lost, whereas some seed- and fruit-eating, ground-dwelling birds flourished in the new habitat. Seed-eating birds and mammals increased dramatically, at times by ingress, when a burn yielded large amounts of this kind of food (Ahlgren 1966, Cook 1959, Lawrence op. cit.).

Severe and repeated burning may reduce production of grasses, herbs, and shrubs and, in turn, grazing and browsing wildlife. However, the hardiness of some plants may be greatly increased after a fire. They may become more prolific because of an increased input of nutrients released by ash (Ahlgren and Ahlgren op. cit., Hayes 1970, Humphrey 1962, Komarek 1967, Vogl 1969). This may lead to a qualitative and quantitative increase in food supply. Siivonen (1957) equates the variation and abundance of European grouse species (*Tetrao, Urogallus, Tetrastes,* and *Lagopus*) to the beginning of spring plant growth.

The life cycles of some herbivores are related to fire-induced changes in food types, as well as the quantity and quality of feed. Bendell (1974) cites a study by Gates, who measured the amount of deer food present on logged and burned areas in the summer with years after disturbance. After logging and burning, levels of protein, fats, ash, crude fiber, and nitrogen-free extract in foods were adequate for deer through the first 14-year stages of forest growth. Food nutritional value was highest in the first years following the fire. On the basis of pellet counts Gates found that deer use was concentrated on the new areas from immediately after logging and burning until about six years later when numbers declined gradually.

Miller (1964) agrees that fire improves food quality by increasing the protein and phosphoric acid content of the most commonly used species. Protein content apparently increased from 5 percent before the fire to 42 percent after the fire (new shoots), and phosphoric acid content increased by 78 percent.

Fire may cause specific types of food to disappear or may destroy shelter required by two or more species which must then compete for what is left after the fire. A classic example is provided by Jasper and Banff ungulates (Flook 1964). Before the fire, elk (*Cervus*) were not particularly numerous, whereas mule deer (*Odocoileus*), moose (*Alces*), and bighorn sheep (*Ovis*) were abundant. Each species lived separate from the other although in a common habitat. Following large fires that led to the formation of herb and shrub communities, the elk population increased and occupied areas used by other ungulates. Since elk are strong competitors with mule deer for food and shelter and with bighorn sheep and moose for food, the mule deer, bighorn sheep, and moose populations declined. In this case, fire affected interspecific competition by favoring one mammalian species to the detriment of the other three.

Cover type can greatly affect predator–prey relationships. In Africa burning thick grassland affects predation and local prey distribution, for game

*Table 8.1.   Comparison of Parasitic Infections (%) in Blue Grouse 5 and 12 Years after Wildfire (from Bendell 1974)*

| | Adults | | Chicks | |
|---|---|---|---|---|
| Parasite | 5 years | 12 years | 5 years | 12 years |
| Blood | (12)[a] | (174) | (16) | (89) |
| *Trypanosoma* | 10 | 77 | 6 | 20 |
| *Haemoproteus* | 83 | 97 | 50 | 66 |
| *Leucocytozoon* | 42 | 85 | 19 | 38 |
| *Microfilaria* | 40 | 80 | 0 | 0 |
| Negative | 17 | 0 | — | — |
| Gut | (20) | (103) | (33) | (107) |
| *Dispharynx* | 0 | 4 | 0 | 64 |
| *Cheilospirura* | 0 | 22 | 0 | 10 |
| *Yseria* | — | — | — | — |
| *Rhabdometra* | 10 | 39 | 62 | 21 |
| *Ascaridia* | 21 | 14 | 12 | 4 |
| *Plagiorhynchus* | 0 | 0 | 0 | 50 |
| External | | | | |
| *Ceratophyllus* | 0 | 11 | 0 | 0 |
| *Lagopoecus* | 5 | 38 | 3 | 20 |
| *Ornithomyia* | 10 | 2 | 6 | 7 |

[a] Sample size.

will not enter cover that provides concealment to predators in ambush (Brynard op. cit.).

A prey moving into an open burn may be exposed to predators that are new to it or that operate more effectively in the new habitat. For example, some blue grouse moved onto the lowlands of Vancouver Island after logging and burning, whereas others lived in the alpine and subalpine forests (Bendell 1974). In the lowland burns grouse must face a number of predators such as marshhawk (*Circus*), fox (*Vulpes*), and raccoon (*Procyon*) that are rare or absent on the uplands. However, they escape from some upland predators such as the marten (*Martes*).

After a fire, infestations of external and internal parasites may be reduced, to the benefit of the host animals (Brynard op. cit., Isaac 1963, Lovat 1911, Stoddard 1931).

Fowle (1946) sampled parasites in a population of blue grouse five years after a wildfire that burned virtually everywhere to mineral soil; Bendell (1955) sampled the same area 12 years later. Differences in kind of parasites and frequency of infection were striking (Table 8.1). The fire apparently reduced the number of parasites shortly after the fire when the habitat was cleansed, but 12 years later the parasites had time to become established. More species of parasites and greater frequency of infection were found with longer times after burning. Four new parasites had appeared by 12 years, and two of them (*Plagiorynchus* and *Dispharynx*) caused severe damage to chicks. Parasite increase was felt to be due to the change in cover, which favored increase of populations of intermediate hosts, particularly the sowbug (*Porcellio*), which develops in a wetter microclimate. Although fire changed the ecology of most grouse parasites, they had few effects on the grouse population, which remained stable over the seven-year sample (Bendell 1955, 1974).

## ADAPTATIONS TO FLAMMABLE ENVIRONMENTS

Many plant formations are flammable and some of them depend on repeated fire for their very existence (Ahlgren and Ahlgren op. cit., Daubenmire 1968, Heinselman 1971, Hodgson 1968, Kayll 1968, Komarek 1968, Lutz op. cit., Mount 1964, Mutch 1970, Niering et al. 1970, Rowe op. cit., Shafi and Yarranton 1973, Swan 1970, Thilenius 1968, Trabaud 1980). Some investigators have shown that certain wildlife species that depend on fire-generated habitat have evolved to exploit burned areas (Handley op. cit., Lemon 1968a, Miller 1964, Wells 1965).

The relative stability of the number of species and populations in burned areas is a vivid demonstration of the adaptability of animal species and also has theoretical implications in terms of evolution. In undisturbed environments such as tropical forests, there tends to be a larger number of species adapted to specific niches that are stable and persistent (MacArthur et al. 1962, Orians 1969). Where habitats are frequently modified by fire, selection may be for a few broadly adapted species rather than many species that are specialists (Catling and Newsome 1981, Dunbar 1968, Martin 1960, Shafi and Yarranton op. cit.). Unfortunately, fire blurs the separation of habitats and brings species of wildlife together so that the hypothesis cannot always be tested. However, when plant communities are frequently modified by fire, selection must be for a species that is capable of adapting to a broader range of circumstances.

Under these conditions, there should be a tendency for large size (Bock and Lynch 1970, Martin 1960). In addition to size other factors have been considered by some authors. The ability to run or fly quickly for long distances, burrowing, storing food, kinds of camouflage, pressing flat to avoid detection, and migration are adaptations to flammable habitat (Bendell and Elliott 1966, Handley op. cit., Komarek 1962).

At the population level, species adaptation to a rapidly changing environment seems to include a high, variable birth rate and a high dispersal rate (Bendell 1974). Species with these characteristics can adapt immediately and profit by environmental change.

# EFFECTS OF FIRE ON VARIOUS CLASSES OF ANIMALS

## Invertebrates

The effects of fire on invertebrates vary greatly with fire type, plant community affected, and region.

In regions where fires are not particularly severe, the direct effects of heat are apparently less important than subsequent environmental changes. Rice (1932) finds living organisms under charred forest debris on the ground after a fire. In New Jersey pine barrens, Buffington (1967) observes a decrease in soil fauna which he attributes to the loss of incorporated and unincorporated organic matter that reduced the food input for small organisms and, therefore, for their predators. The arthropod population decreased by 50 percent, with an 80 percent reduction in the number of taxa.

In order to properly interpret recolonization data, we must consider how long it takes for animals to reoccupy the burn—the factor of mobility. In the southeastern United States, Metz and Farrier (op. cit.) find that the mesofauna of a forest recovered in under 43 months. In the prairies, Rice (op. cit.) finds that in the prewinter period after a burn the numbers of many species decreased but increased again with the return of spring and new vegetation growth.

In a South Carolina loblolly pine forest (*Pinus taeda*) the soil fauna was reduced one-third by fire (Pearse 1943). Representation of all species remained identical in burned and unburned areas except for earthworms, whose numbers fell sharply and ants, whose numbers increased. In longleaf pine forests (*P. palustris*) Heyward and Tissot (1936) observe 5 times more ground organisms in the Ao horizon of a burned soil, and 11 times more organisms in the first 5 cm of an unburned mineral soil. The decrease was due to the drought caused by postfire xeric soil conditions.

In Africa, Coults (1945) finds that all organisms in the first 2 cm of mineral soil survived the fire. However, Gillon (1974) observes that in grassland soils fauna have a hard time surviving after a fire because of soil dryness and lack of food and litter. Shade-loving animals that live under grasses survive fire relatively unscathed but have difficulty in adapting to the new sunny, drier environment. One month after fire more than half the arachnids, cockroaches, Tetrigidae, crickets, and carabids had disappeared (Gillon and Pernes op. cit.). Conversely, the density of sun-loving species that had fled the fire increased again after their return to the burned grassland. One of the most remarkable adaptations to a burned environment is the abrupt melanism exhibited by some invertebrates, mainly acridians; this probably acts as a camouflage for escaping predators, especially birds, which have easier access to food when the plant cover disappears.

Earthworm populations are significantly reduced by fire. Pearse (op. cit.) reports a 50 percent decrease after burning pine forest litter (*Pinus taeda*).

In *P. palustris* stands, Heyward and Tissot (op. cit.) note that populations were four times greater in the first 0 to 5 cm of an unburned mineral soil than in the corresponding portion of a burned soil. Earthworms, which had not been particularly abundant in the Ao horizon before the fire, decreased further afterward. In an Illinois prairie earthworm populations were lower in burned soil (Rice op. cit.). Earthworm populations in springtime were similar in the burned and unburned area when the moisture content of the soil was identical. In mid-April and in May, however, as the moisture content increased in the unburned prairie soil and decreased in the burned soil, the earthworm population grew in the unburned area. The decrease in moisture content was connected with increased evaporation due to the lack of surface vegetation. As earthworms live mainly in the humus and mineral layers, they are more sensitive to reduced moisture content than to heat from a fire. This decrease was also noted in Africa by Phillips (op. cit.).

The snail populations of the southern United States were reduced by fire (Heyward and Tissot op. cit.). Ahlgren (1974) also mentions that snails disappeared for at least three years after a fire in a northern Minnesota *Pinus banksiana* forest. After fires, a large number of empty, bleached shells were found in the garrigues of southern France. It is not certain whether their former inhabitants had been killed by the fire or before the fire. In Africa, Phillips (op. cit.) remarks on the reduction in the number and species of snails and slugs following fires.

Chilopod and diplopod populations are generally reduced by fire, sometimes by as much as 80 percent (Heyward and Tissot op. cit., Pearse op. cit., Rice op. cit.). The larger number of chilopods founds in the unburned areas is apparently related to the larger population of other arthropods because chilopods are predators (Heyward and Tissot op. cit.).

Spiders, particularly ground-dwelling species, are seriously affected by fire. Population decreases of 9 to 31 percent in burned as compared to unburned areas have frequently been mentioned (Buffington 1967, French and Keirle 1969, Heyward and Tissot op. cit., Rice op. cit.). Only Hurst (op. cit.) notes an increase in ground and wolf spiders after burning of powerline rights of way in Mississippi.

Although they vary in number with region, acarians may comprise one of the largest groups of ground-dwelling animals. Heyward and Tissot (op. cit.) consider that in *Pinus palustris* stands, acarians constitute about 71 to 93 percent of the unburned-ground fauna and 30 to 72 percent of the burned-ground fauna, depending on soil depth. All investigators agree that acarian populations are reduced by burning (Heyward and Tissot op. cit., Metz and Farrier op. cit., Pearse op. cit., Rice op. cit.). Metz and Farrier find a sizable reduction in the acarian population (Figures 8.5 and 8.6). Only 24 hours after the burn there were no more than 30 percent of the animals left in the first 7 cm of mineral soil. The reduction was not as marked in the humus layer, however. Prefire population levels were restored in less than 43 months. In

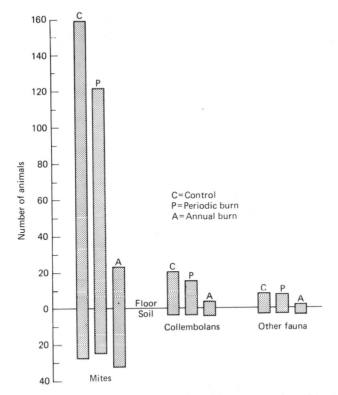

*Figure 8.5.* Average number of animals extracted per 20-sq cm sample on 3 treatments for 10 sampling days (from Metz and Farrier 1971).

South Africa the cattle tick population is higher in unburned than in burned areas (Phillips op. cit.).

Collembola populations are generally reduced by fire (Heyward and Tissot op. cit., Metz and Farrier op. cit.). These authors note that 24 hours after a fire there was a decrease in the population of Collembola living on the forest floor, but little effect on mineral soil dwellers. In three or four years the prefire population levels were reestablished.

Some termites can survive fire in shallow soils. Certain species apparently resist heat quite well. In New Jersey pine barrens, Buffington (op. cit.) finds *Reticulotermes* living under charred debris. However, Heyward and Tissot (op. cit.) notice a reduction in the number of termites in *Pinus palustris* after a fire.

Fire in prairies and grasslands leads to an increase in grasshopper and leafhopper densities (Hurst op. cit., Rice op. cit.). This can be attributed to recolonization of the burns by fire survivors returning from unburned areas. Higher daytime temperatures and good regrowth of grass plants after the fire may also be contributing factors. On the African savanna, fire affects various

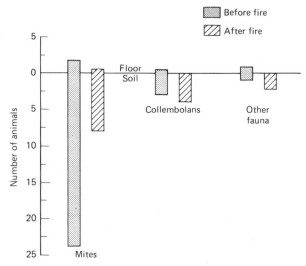

*Figure 8.6.* Average number of animals extracted per 20-sq cm sample immediately before and 24 hours after an annual summer burn on June 15 and 16, 1970 (from Metz and Farrier 1971).

acridian species differently. Some are almost completely destroyed by fire; others are barely affected. Yves Gillon (1972) believes that periodic grassland fires maintain specific diversity of this group.

Some acridians exhibit melanism when they live on burned soil (Komarek 1969).

Since many grasshoppers winter as larvae in the upper soil layers, spring burns have been recommended as a means of destroying them to improve agriculture (Komarek 1970). Such burns would also destroy leafhoppers, which are vectors of some plant viruses (Cantlon and Buell 1952).

Ants, except for those caught away from their nests, are the least affected of all insects by fire because of their adaptability to the heat and drought in the upper layers of the soil. In addition, their social organization and habitat fit them for rapid colonization of burned areas.

Pearse (op. cit.) mentions a one-third reduction in ant populations due to burning. Buffington also observes a reduction in the number of ants in burned soil in the New Jersey pine barrens. The decrease was not as large as for other soil arthropods, however. Two species, *Solenopsis molesta* and *Lasius flavus*, were much more numerous on burned land. This increase is probably due to their preference for a more xeric habitat and to their habit of gathering dry seeds. In a *Pinus radiata* plantation in Australia, French and Keirle (op. cit.) observe that ants, like most other insects, were killed by fire. However, the ants were among the first to colonize the area and were frequently found very early in the study burns.

Rice (op. cit.) finds that ant populations were one-third higher in burns than in unburned areas. Heyward and Tissot (op. cit.) find a great deal more ants in burned 0 to 5 cm mineral soil layers of southern United States pine forest than in similar unburned areas. The population of the fire ant (*Solenopsis*) increased after burning of powerline rights of way (Hurst op. cit.). This increase was felt to be due to the rapid colonization of the burned area and the survival of the ants in the upper soil layers.

In the African grasslands the impact of fire on Hemiptera varies with the season. After a winter fire, the decline in the number of Pentatomidae species is much higher than after a springtime fire (D. Gillon 1972). The longer after the fire, the larger the increase in the number of Pentatomidae (Figure 8.7). There is no decrease in specific diversity. Fire is not actually believed to be destructive in itself; it merely simplifies the habitat, maintaining the population of sun-loving Pentatomidae. In the absence of fire the dominant population trend is to shade-loving species. Thus fire seems to maintain the population balance of Pentatomidae on the savanna.

Phillips (op. cit.) reports a reduction in the number and type of litter and soil invertebrates such as Coleoptera, Lepidoptera, and Diptera. Fire is often used to control the tse-tse fly (*Glossina morsitans*, and *G. swynnertoni*) in transSaharan Africa.

Most Coleoptera genera decrease as a result of forest fire but less so in prairies and grasslands. This is partly because temperatures are lower in grassland fires than in forest fires. Rice (op. cit.) mentions a 15 percent decrease in Coleoptera populations immediately after a fire, followed by rapidly recolonization. A 60 percent decrease is found in southern United States pine forests by Pearse (op. cit.) and Heyward and Tissot (op. cit.). Buffington (op. cit.) finds four times more Coleoptera in unburned areas and Ahlgren (1974) finds fewer Coleoptera on burns than in unburned areas three months after a prescribed burning in *Pinus banksiana* forests in Minnesota. However, there was an increase in the number of Coleoptera on a burned Minnesota plain (Tester and Marshall 1961). Hurst (op. cit.) notes an increase in the number and biomass of Coleoptera on burned powerline rights of way.

Forest fires frequently cause problems related to insect attacks on trees. The damage done by bark beetles and wood borers is frequently cited (Mitchell and Martin op. cit.). Trees that are injured or scorched are attacked by the mountain pine beetle (*Dendroctonus ponderosae*), the pine engraver (*Ips pini*), the Douglas fir tussock moth (*Orgyia pseudotsugata*), the western pine beetle (*Dendroctonus brevicomis*), and the red turpentine beetle (*D. valens*; Figure 8.8).

However, prescribed burning can reduce the number of insects of these species or prevent dramatic population explosions (Mitchell and Martin op. cit.). *Ips pini,* for example, is attracted by logging debris in the areas where it winters. Careful prescribed burning of the debris can cause the pine engraver beetle population to decrease. The worse the tree tops are scorched,

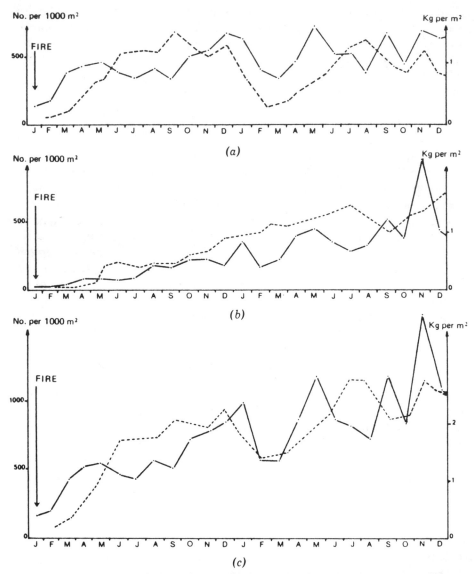

**Figure 8.7.** Monthly development of the level of pentatomids (solid lines) compared to that of the quantity of vegetation (dashed lines) during the year following fire, and the following year, if fire doesn't occur (Roland 1967). (*a*) Development of heliophilous pentatomids compared to that of living vegetation. (*b*) Development of sciaphilous pentatomids compared to that of the dead vegetation. (*c*) Development of all pentatomids compared to that of the total vegetation (from Gillon 1972).

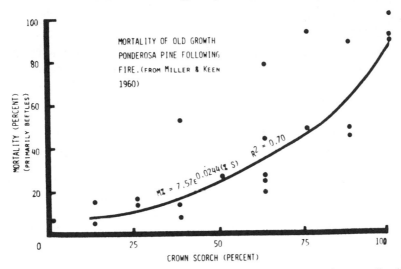

*Figure 8.8.* Relation between crown scorch in wildfires and ponderosa pine mortality due to attack from the western pine beetle (regression established from data by Miller and Keen 1960). The 30 percent variance unaccounted for probably reflects varying weather conditions and beetle populations (from Mitchell and Martin 1980).

the greater the mortality of *Pinus ponderosa* due to attacks by *Dendroctonus brevicomis*. However, Williams et al. (1980) find that prescribed burning caused a 53 percent decrease in the likelihood of outbreaks of *Orgyia pseudotsugata* in the northwestern states. There was a decrease of 85 percent in central Oregon and 82 percent in northwestern Washington. Simmons et al. (1977) find that in the Great Lakes states prescribed burning was more effective than insecticide in controlling the maple leaf cutter *Paraclemensia acerifoliella*, whose pupae develop in forest soil. Miller (1978) recommends prescribed burning to control attacks of the red pine cone beetle *Conophtorus resinosae* on *P. resinosa* cones.

The use of prescribed burning as a measure for controlling Coleoptera populations has been well established (Haig 1938). Populations of *Pelycyphorus densicollis* and *Eleodes hispitabris* were reduced after a brush fire in the state of Washington (Rickard 1970). In Australia carabid and scarabid populations were reduced in *Pinus radiata* stands, but were the first insects to recolonize the burns (French and Keirle op. cit.).

Insects that may be destroyed or at least controlled by fire are mainly those that lay their eggs or exist in immature forms in forest soils. If fire is to be used for controlling a pest, the insect's life cycle must be known in considerable detail so that fire can be used when most opportune. In the conclusion to their study, Mitchell and Martin (op. cit.) list a number of beneficial effects of fire for controlling insect populations.

## Fish

The ecological impacts of fire on fish must obviously be indirect. They generally have to do with changes in habitat or environment or with the chemical retardants used in firefighting.

Damage to fish habitat may also be caused by increases in soil erosion, increased velocity of flow, changes in nutrient content, and the removal of streamside vegetation. Lyon et al. (1978) refer to studies in which sediment input into watercourses was seen to result in a reduction in the average size of deposit of fine matter that smothered eggs, prevented egress of fry, and increased losses due to predation, and reduction in populations of preferred food species such as mayflies, caddis flies, and stoneflies.

Eggs may be crushed or dislodged because of the faster current and the smaller size of the pieces of gravelstones. Erosion may turn the gravelstones around, affecting eggs or fry. Disappearance of vegetation along banks often increases erosion, destroys some habitats, and raises water temperature. The latter factor increases biological oxygen demand by the fish and also decreases available oxygen. An increase of fish diseases is another consequence that can be expected from habitat deterioration due to higher temperatures. Many cold water species have narrow temperature tolerance limits and die out the summer following a fire (Figure 8.9).

An increase in nutrients is another common result of fire. The concentration of chemicals rarely attains toxic levels and the effect on productivity is generally beneficial. Thus increased algae production at the lowest level of the food chain can increase biomass and further diversify the insect larvae population.

The retardants used in firefighting are aqueous chemical concentrates. At some concentrations most soluble chemicals can injure or kill fish, so a retardant may damage fish if it is spilled directly into the watercourse (Van Meter and Hardy 1975). Fire retardants seem to have their most serious ecological impact on aquatic rather than terrestrial ecosystems. Ammonia $NH_3$ is the most toxic compound for fish according to McKee and Wolf in Douglas (1974). Table 8.2 shows data for a number of aquatic organisms, mainly fish, under a variety of conditions. Some aquatic organisms are highly sensitive to sodium dichromate and to a lesser extent to ammonia and sodium thiosulfate. Ammonia concentrations as low as 0.3 ppm are lethal to trout fry, whereas concentrations of 75 ppm are extremely lethal to adult trout. In tests cited in Douglas (op. cit.), fish exhibit greater tolerance to Fire-Trol (which is based on ammonium sulfate) than Phos-Check (which has an ammonium phosphate base). There may be some synergistic or antagonistic impact on the toxicity of the chemical compounds of these retardants.

The use of chemical additives such as phosphorus and nitrogen in diammonium phosphate speeds up eutrophication. These nutrients increase algal growth, resulting in detritus formation which, in turn, leads to an increase in

*Figure 8.9.* Cold water species such as trout cannot survive increased water temperatures following fire. Photo by Leland Prater.

breakdown products and a correlated drop in oxygen levels. Although productivity increases, specific diversity decreases. Species such as trout that cannot tolerate low concentrations of oxygen disappear; species such as catfish that can tolerate such low concentrations of oxygen prosper.

## Batrachians and Reptiles

The literature provides scant information on the ecological effects of fire on these groups, although reptiles have apparently attracted most of the attention that has been paid to this topic. Kahn (1960), studying the impact of burning chaparral on the western fence lizard (*Sceloporus occidentalis*), notices that the spring following the fire this species reproduced in both the burned and the unburned areas. He finds little difference between the type of food ingested in burned and unburned areas and observes no postfire move-

*Table 8.2.    Concentration of Various Retardant Components Reported to be Toxic or Lethal to Aquatic Life (from McKee and Wolf, 1963 in Douglas 1974)*

| Concentration of Compound (mg/l) | Time of Exposure | Organism |
|---|---|---|
| *Ammonia* (NH$_3$) | | |
| 90 (soft H$_2$O,20°C) | 96 hr TL$_m$ | *Phya heterostropha* (snail) |
| 134 (hard H$_2$O,30°C) | 96 hr TL$_m$ | *Phya heterostropha* |
| 320 (soft H$_2$O,28°C) | 5 days | *Havicula seminulum* (diatom) |
| 350 (hard H$_2$O,30°C) | 5 days | *Havicula seminulum* |
| 0.3–0.4 | — | Trout fry |
| 0.7 | 390 min | Rainbow trout |
| 75.7 | less than 4 min | Trout |
| *Ammonium sulfate* | | |
| 66 (distilled H$_2$O) | 17 days | Bluegills |
| 420–500 | 1 hr | Orange-spotted sunfish |
| 1290 | 96 hr TL$_m$ | Mosquito fish |
| *Sodium dichromate* | | |
| 0.016 | Toxic threshold | *Daphnia magna* |
| 0.05 | Lethal in 6 days | *Daphnia magna* |
| *Sodium thiosulfate* | | |
| 8400 | Toxic threshold | *Polycelis nigra* (flatworm) |
| 520 | Immobilization | *Daphnia magna* |
| *Sodium silicofluoride* | | |
| 5 | 120 hr | Minnows |
| 24,000 | 96 hr TL$_m$ | Mosquito fish |

ment of individuals inhabiting the burned areas toward the unburned areas and vice versa. He postulates that lizards survive fire by burrowing underground or hiding under stones.

Lillywhite and North (1974) observe that fire could temporarily increase the carrying capacity of lizards in burned chaparral in southern California and that they are not as numerous in older chaparral communities with dense brush as in recently burned areas. Lillywhite et al. (1977) also mention the tendency of the western fence lizard to perch on charred twigs during the first two years after the fire. The number of individuals of five lizard species caught in old chaparral was significantly lower than that for individuals caught in a recently burned chaparral area (Figure 8.10). Lillywhite (1977) believes that burned chaparral provides an optimum environment for lizards. Food resources seem to be much more diversified, abundant, and available in recently burned areas with richer plant life.

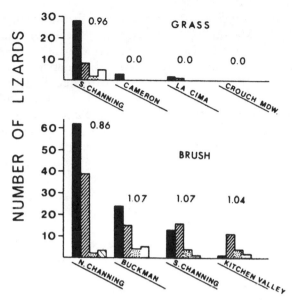

*Figure 8.10.* Total numbers of lizards captured at grass (upper) and brush (lower) locations May 28 to July 8, 1974. Black = side-blotched lizards (*Uta stansburiana*); heavy crosshatch = western fence lizards (*Sceloporus occidentalis*); heavy stipple = western whiptails (*Cnemidophorus tigris*); light crosshatch = western skinks (*Eumeces skiltonianus*); light stipple = coast horned lizards (*Phrynosoma coronatum*). Numbers indicate Shannon & Weaver's (1949) diversity index $H' = p_i \log_e P_i$, where $P_i$ are proportions of each species in the sample. N. Channing and Buckman are the burned areas (from Lillywhite 1977).

According to Lyon et al. (op. cit.), alligators keep almost exclusively to the burned shores along the swamps and bayous of the southern States. In southeast Asia, snakes (*Zamenis, Zaocys,* and *Naja*) and a lizard species (*Varanus*) escape fire by sliding into termite holes (Wharton 1966). Stoddard (1963) observes that although some species of snakes may be killed by rapidly advancing fires, most of them escape by moving into hollows in the ground.

The only Australian data come from Catling and Newsome (op. cit.), reporting on a study by Cogger in an area that had burned nine years earlier in a mallee of central New South Wales. The Mallee Dragon (*Amphibolurus fordi*) was found in a two-year count to be much more abundant in the burn. At the end of the count, however, the number of individuals in the burned and unburned areas was similar.

### Birds

Fire affects birds indirectly by modifying their habitat. Some species are disadvantaged by the disappearance of shrubs and trees but others are favored by the creation of clearings with vegetation close to the ground.

One of the most striking differences due to fire in avian populations is commented on by Marshall (1963) concerning the mountains of southern Arizona. In the part of the range nearest Mexico he observes birds that prefer open land such as the sparrow hawk, roadrunner, screech owl, Cassin's king bird, curved-billed thrasher, brown towhee, harlequin quail, common nighthawk, purple martin, violet-green swallow, robin, western bluebird, eastern bluebird, Mexican junco, and chipping sparrow. Species most numerous in Arizona were birds that live in brushland or dense forest such as elf owl, ash-throated flycatcher, bluegray gnatcatcher, black-throated gray warbler, Scott's oriole, and rufous-sided towhee. The same tree species were dominant on either side of the Mexican–American border. Marshall imputes the difference in bird populations to fire, writing that stringent firefighting practices are not observed in Mexico as they are in the United States.

Some species have a strong attraction to recent burns. Stoddard (1963) mentions robins, bluebirds, sparrows, flickers, woodpeckers, mourning doves, pine warblers, golden plovers, and Eskimo curlews. He points out that jacksnipes, frequently found in large numbers in burns, are rarely found in brushland.

Fire may cause some birds to disappear because the amount of litter or the consistency of the forest floor is modified by fire. Thus the disappearance of the sparrow (*Passerculus* and *Passerherbulus*) and the bobolink (*Dolichonyx*) appears to be due to the reduction by fire of the forest cover consisting of logs and debris. Some woodpeckers (Picidae) peck on stumps to attract their mates. The destruction of stumps by fire or logging can cause the woodpeckers to leave an area. Sometimes woodpeckers enter a burn, however, because of the new food source provided by insects attacking dead trees (Blackford 1955, Koplin 1969).

Lawrence (op. cit.) has provided invaluable data on bird populations after a controlled burn in Sierra Nevada chaparral. The breeding bird density was found to be higher in burned chaparral and grassland than in unburned areas. An increase in available food seems to be the cause of this increase. There was more seed available and plants that grew after the fire were more productive of seed. Similarly, there were more insects. As a result, total bird numbers did not change but species composition did.

The number of bird species found in a 17-year-old chaparral was essentially the same as in burned areas (Wirtz 1977). The author notes, however, that small changes in numbers could be found (Figure 8.11). Thus species such as the scrub pay (*Aphelocoma coerulescens*), wrentit (*Chamaea fasciata*), and brown towhee (*Pipilo fuscus*) appeared in smaller numbers in the burned areas and others were never seen at all. However, the rufous-sided towhee (*Pipilo erythrophthalmus*) and Bewick's wren (*Thryomanes bewickii*) were more abundant in the burned areas and the lazuli bunting (*Passerina amoena*), lark sparrow (*Chondestes grammacus*), and black-chinned sparrow (*Spizella atrogularis*) clearly preferred the burned chaparral. Diver-

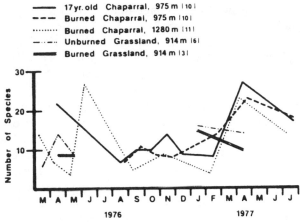

——— 17yr. old Chaparral, 975 m |10|
— — — Burned Chaparral, 975 m |10|
·········· Burned Chaparral, 1280 m |11|
—··—·· Unburned Grassland, 914 m |6|
▬▬▬ Burned Grassland, 914 m |3|

*Figure 8.11.* Species of birds present in burned and unburned habitats, March 1976 to July 1977, and number (10) of species breeding in the spring of 1977 (from Wirtz 1977).

sity was about the same in 17-year-old chaparral and the burned area except during the breeding season, when diversity was higher in the burned than the unburned chaparral.

In Yellowstone National Park, Taylor (1973) finds an increase in the number of bird species for the first 25 years after a fire, followed by a decrease in the older communities.

In Europe Walter (1977), studying warblers (*Sylvia*) in Sardinia, finds *Sylvia sarda* and *S. undata,* two fire-dependent species, living in open areas. *S. melanocephala* and *S. cantillans* could adapt to fire but were not dependent on it, whereas *S. atricapilla* could not tolerate fire and lived only in old brushland or forest. Walter believes that the latter species must have been seriously disturbed by the impact of humans in Sardinia.

In Western Australia it was found that there were more birds in forests that burned every 5 or 7 years than in forests that had not burned for 40 years, although specific composition seemed the same (Catling and Newsome op. cit.). The authors conclude that without fire the total number of birds, although not the number of species, declines in lower layers as the forest ages. Thus the number of birds counted declines after wildfires in sclerophyll eucalypt forests. In general, however, an increase was noticed within two years after a fire (Christensen and Kimber 1975, Kimber 1974) because of ingress from drier forests of some species such as the scarlet robin (*Petroica multicolor*). The authors think that the number of birds in a forest is higher when fire intensities are low. Finally, the ground parrot (*Pezoporus wallicus*) is found only in the southern Australian coastal heathlands. According to Catling and Newsome (op. cit.), if this heath is not burned periodically the parrot cannot live there. After a fire they note that birds stayed away from the burn for nine months but after the third year when the heath had once again grown to knee height, the prefire population level was reestablished.

Waterfowl may stay away from swamps when they are obstructed by dense marsh plants or encroaching terrestrial plant forms. Burning creates open areas where seed plants can grow; waterfowl use them for food (Givens 1962, Vogl 1967, 1969).

Miller (1963), studying wildlife on the coast of the Gulf of Mexico and in Wisconsin, and Vogl (1967) in Wisconsin think that fire affords better access to food for waterfowl by making edible plants available and destroying weeds and undesirable plants; burning delays succession by slowing encroachment of arboreal vegetation such as *Salix* and *Alnus,* and increases nesting by ducks. Following burning *Phragmites* marshes in Manitoba, Ward (1968) notes a higher frequency of nesting ducks. Buckley (1958) makes the same observation in Alaska, where he finds duck density increased from 8.1 to 12.8 per km². 

Early spring fires may destroy mallard and woodcock nests and eggs (Vogl 1967). Fires before May 10 affect mainly mallard and pintail (Ward op. cit.). Ward says, however, that fires after May 10 destroyed nests of all species, so he recommends that prescribed burning be started no later than April 20, when the mallard and pintail start nesting. According to him, the shoveler, blue-winged teal, and gadwall nest in postfire growth. Vogl (1967) mentions that four mallard chicks hatched out of seven charred eggs five days after a fire. He says that when the nests are completely destroyed by fire, the birds build new nests. Destruction of nests and the later hatching apparently result in an increase in the bird population because the nestlings are less likely to be killed by frost or predators (crows). According to Miller (1963), the Canada goose profits by marsh burning. Similarly, the blue goose is attracted to recent burns from fires between late September and January (Perkins 1968).

According to Miller (1963), the prairie chicken (*Tympanuchus c. cupido*) prefers to inhabit areas where the woody plant cover is under 25 percent. Sharp (1970) says that the eastern prairie chicken formerly inhabited an area where fire played an important role by maintaining a mosaic of various community types, including discontinuous forests. Studying breeding in the prairie chicken, Westemeier (1973) reports that burns were favorite display grounds. Prescribed burning rejuvenated old sods and nest densities increased the second year after the fire, with 1 nest per 0.3 ha. Seed production was increased by burning so that nest density was significantly higher, increasing from 1 nest per 37.2 ha in unburned areas to 1 nest per 2.4 ha in the second, third, and fourth years after fire. Vogl (1967) believes that fire is essential to good prairie chicken management.

In the coastal plains of Texas and southwest Louisiana, the decrease in Attwater's prairie chicken (*Tympanuchus cupido attwateri*) is partly due to the increase in human population, the number of farms, oil wells, and pastureland, and also to the growth of brush and other natural vegetation in the absence of fire (Lehman 1965). This author states that in the case of the adult, fire mortality is low because this species flies away from fire. Accordingly, fire destroys only eggs or nestlings. Chamrad and Dodd (1973) notice greater nesting density of Attwater's prairie chicken in burns about one year after the burn and they find that prescribed burning clearly improved food amount and quality.

According to Soutiere and Bolen (1973), fire has little impact on mourning dove (*Zenaidura macroura*) populations. These birds respond neither positively nor negatively to fire and if trees are destroyed, they nest on the ground. Biswell et al. (op. cit.) find, however, that mourning doves responded positively to opening of the California chaparral. Populations were smaller in dense brushland and higher in recently burned areas, with the highest densities in open brush. Kirsch and Kruse (1973) also note that the number of mourning dove nests was comparable in burned and unburned areas but that more young were hatched in the burns. They made the same observation for other birds such as the ring-necked pheasant *Phasianus colchicus,* the upland plover *Bartramia longicauda,* the American bittern *Botaurus lentiginosus,* the willet *Catoptrophorus semipalmatus,* the killdeer *Chadrius vociferus,* and eight duck species.

Wild turkey (*Meleagris gallopavo*) habitat is improved by periodic fires as long as they occur outside of nesting season. The turkey nests on the ground, often in highly flammable cover (Figure 8.12).

In South Africa two francolin species, the greywing *Francolinus africanus* and the redwing *F. levaillantii,* inhabit communities that are maintained by fire (Mentis and Bigalke 1981). Without fire, plant debris accumulates and the francolin populations decline. This process begins about one year after the fire in areas below 1800 m in altitude and three years in areas above 2200 m in altitude. Francolins need a habitat constituted by a mosaic of small burns. When the burns are too large, bird density decreases. When large areas are burned in spring, spring and fall bird densities are always lower the first year after the fire than the second. After the spring fires, birds prefer unburned to burned areas. However, this preference reverses in autumn.

The blue grouse (*Dendragapus obscurus*) population of mature forest is low (Redfield et al. 1970), but the species quickly invades breeding grounds created by logging or fire, in which case spectacularly high densities can be attained—about 1 pair per 0.4 ha in spring (Bendell 1955). This increase is short-lived, however, since a relatively stable period (about 20 years) is followed by a rapid population decline as the regenerating forest grows thicker (Figure 8.13). Thus Redfield et al. (op. cit.) find that maximum population levels are reached when the forest cover is between 0 and 50 percent and that beyond the 70 percent level populations decrease rapidly. Relative density would, therefore, be 2.5/ha in mature forest, 27.5/ha in the 20 years following burning, declining again to 2.5/ha 25 years after the disturbance. Bendell (1974) believes that there may be a relationship between size of burn

*Figure 8.12.* (*a*) The wild turkey often (*b*) nests in highly flammable ground cover. Photos by U.S. Forest Service.

and breeding density of blue grouse. However, grouse populations are not dependent exclusively on fire. They are as large in logging areas as in burns. They may also occupy strips of unburned forest within burned areas.

In Scotland red grouse (*Lagopus lagopus scoticus*) populations have been managed for decades by periodic burning on the moor of *Calluna vulgaris*, their main dietary source (Lovat op. cit., Miller 1964). High population densities can occur when the moors are burned in narrow strips on a regular basis or by spot burning in a 3 to 7-year rotation (Miller 1963) or a 10 to 12-year rotation (Miller 1964). Miller et al. (1970) manipulate grouse populations by fertilizing and burning moors. In fertilized areas the heather grew better and the number of grouse doubled. The authors conclude that territorial behavior of grouse was determined by food quality. With burning, the total number of grouse increased but density did not remain high. In a 1968 experiment, Picozzi (1968) surveys the number of burns and concludes that the average number of grouse on a moor is positively correlated with the

*Figure 8.12.*    (*Continued*)

average number of fires and the base status of the underlying rock. Bendell (1974) disagrees, however, stating that densities of red grouse may change in response to heather burning and seem to be limited by food quality or amount of cover, or both.

According to Miller (1963), the ruffed grouse (*Bonasa umbellus*) needs a habitat consisting of a mosaic with 0.1 ha cach of brush and grassland. The ruffed grouse lives in wetter burns than the blue grouse, with dense *Salix* and *Alnus* populations (Bendell 1974). As the two grouse species eat the same food in summer and as there is apparently no evidence that one species significantly affects the other, Bendell concludes that the relative humidity of the various sites probably determines local distribution of the ruffed and blue grouse. He finds, however, that if the burns are too large, the chicks could be killed by wind chill and this could cause the total ruffed grouse population to decline.

Gullion (1967) states that early spring melt in burns causes early greening due to the beneficial affect of ash, so that more young are hatched, increasing bird populations. He mentions that the ruffed grouse profits by burning because the number of litter-dwelling insects increases, providing essential food for nestlings.

Doerr et al. (op. cit.) find no difference before and after a fire in occupa-

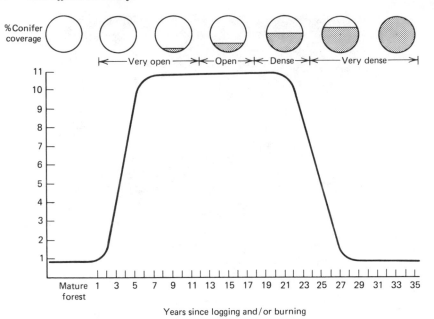

*Figure 8.13.* A generalized curve for growth, stability, and decline of blue grouse populations following logging and/or burning of the mature forest. Population density is low in the mature forest but rapidly builds to a stable density. The terms very open, open, dense, and very dense refer to structure of the vegetation as outlined in Bendell and Elliott (1966). Fluctuations in the general level of the population do occur but have not been included in this diagram (from Redfield et al. 1970).

tion of breeding grounds. However, within 48 hours of the fire, egress of birds led to a 50 percent decrease in the number of individuals, with females comprising almost two-thirds of the emigrants. In the year of the fire, the increase in numbers did not occur on the burned area at the beginning of summer due to reproductive failure. The immediate postfire population level persisted with little change for approximately a year. One and two years later, spring populations were identical on the burn but only half the prefire level (Figure 8.14). The nearly complete reproductive failure of the fire year was due to nest destruction by fire. Vogl (1967) notices a similar pattern. Reproductive success returned to normal the year after the fire. Adult mortality after and before the fire was similar.

Similarly, with the eastern ruffed grouse (*Bonasa u. umbellus*), Sharp (op. cit.) believes that fire destroys encroaching vegetation, favoring nesting as this grouse nests on mineral soil. Burn period is important. Fires occurring before the egg-laying season in April have no appreciable effect on nesting sites, but mid-April fires destroy clutches and fire after mid-May kills chicks. Fires should be set at the right time to destroy excess litter and debris. This

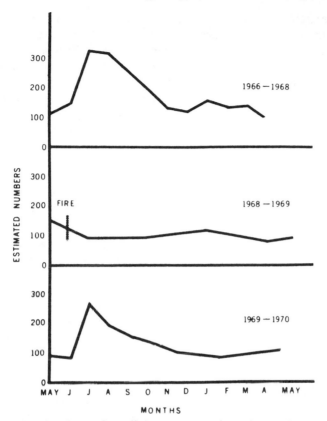

*Figure 8.14.* Population curves for ruffed grouse on main study area for two years before (average of 1966–1967 and 1967–1968) and two years after the May 1968 fire. Estimates based on King strip/censuses and marked-unmarked ratios in May (from Doerr et al. 1970).

measure affords good browsing sites, rejuvenates plant life that grouse feed on, and eradicates plant diseases. An unburned area could support one grouse per four ha or more, whereas a burn could support one grouse per ha. However, Sharp (op. cit.) believes that rotation burning is preferable to annual burning.

The sage grouse (*Centrocercus urophasianus*) needs small burns in the 0.5 to 4 ha range. It nests in dense sagebrush (Klebenow 1973). According to this investigator, repeated burning would be injurious to the sage grouse, as would large-scale fires with high temperatures that completely destroy all vegetation.

The sharptail grouse (*Pedioecetes phasianellus*) needs open spaces, such as plains dotted with a few trees here and there and vegetative cover under 40 percent. Vogl (1967) confirms this finding, reporting that 80 percent of clutches found were in open land, 14 percent on burn edges, and only 5 percent more than 450 m into the forest. The number of nests was found to be similar in burned and unburned areas by Kirsch and Kruse (op. cit.), but clutches were found to be more abundant in burns. However, Bendell (1974) judges overly large burned areas to be harmful to sharptailed grouse in that chicks are killed by cold and wind chill.

On the basis of Canadian studies (Rowe and Scotter 1973), the sharptailed grouse prefers recent burns, whereas the spruce grouse *Canachites canadensis* prefers old spruce forests. Hakala et al. (op. cit.) confirm this for Alaska, stating that fire reduces the carrying capacity for grouse clutches by 56 percent.

Fire is an important factor in the maintenance of bobwhite quail (*Colinus virginianus*) habitat. As this quail cannot penetrate dense forests, it disappears as the forest ages. Burning of undergrowth allows the bird to move about and feed (Hurst op. cit., Stoddard 1931). Fire maintains grassy and woody plants preferred by quail (Miller 1963) and stimulates seed production (Komarek 1971). The latter author observed bobwhite quail feeding on very recent burns. Hurst (op. cit.) finds that burns exposed to sun and wind are drier and hotter. He believes that sun and wind improve quail habitat, particularly for chicks. However, Stoddard (1963) reports that quail need small unburned patches in the middle of burns. The wild turkey *Meleagris gallopavo* has the same needs as quail, according to Miller (1963) and Stoddard (1963).

In a Texas study, Renwald et al. (1978) find that quail preferred the type of cover offered by *Ziziphus obtusifolia* bushes to all other woody plants throughout the year. The ziziphus bushes hold back much of the windblown litter, creating an isolated winter microhabitat favorable to quail. Within five or six months after a burn, quail use the large ziziphus bushes that have survived the fire. Renwald et al. observe that burns provided 15 percent more food than unburned areas, but the disappearance of all bushes due to fire could cause all the benefits of fire to be lost. This is why they suggest keeping at least 10 large *Prosopis glandulosa* and 4 large ziziphus per ha as resting areas.

The Kirkland's warbler (*Dendroica kirklandi*) is an extremely rare bird that apparently depends completely on periodic fire because it nests only in early successional stages of *Pinus banksiana* forests (Handley op. cit., Miller 1963, Stoddard 1963).

The California condor (*Gymnogyps californianus*) is another fire-dependent species nearing extinction because of fire-related habitat changes. According to Cowles (1967), the California condor needs calcium to form eggshell and for the young to grow. This calcium can come only from the bones of small animals (such as rabbits, squirrels, rats, and snakes), not from the viscera or muscles of large carrion (such as horses or deer) that the condor may find. Without fire the chaparral becomes denser, excluding small animals that the condor depends on for survival. Thus lack of fire may be one of the causes of the decrease in condor populations.

## Mammals

The effect of fire on mammals varies with habitat. According to Taylor (op. cit.), the number of mammal species in Yellowstone National Park increases in the first 25 years after fire and decreases in older communities. As with birds, some mammalian groups or species have been studied in greater detail than others.

Reactions of smaller rodents to fire differ with the extent to which plant cover is destroyed. Udvardy (op. cit.) believes that the wood mouse (*Apodesmus*) avoids light, whereas the ground squirrel (*Spermophilus*) prefers full sunlight. According to Gashwiler (1970) and Tevis (op. cit.), burning following logging operations is often followed by ingress of ground squirrels (*Citellus*). However, Terril and Crawford (1946) impute the absence of tree squirrels (*Sciurus*) from burns to the lack of nesting sites.

Loss of cover leads to a change in microclimate. Several investigators observe that after a fire the red-back vole (*Clethrionomys*) disappeared abruptly (Ahlgren 1966, Beck and Vogl 1972, Gashwiler op. cit.). The cause is generally considered to be the rise in temperature as a result of the removal of plant cover. This seems perfectly reasonable since the red-back vole prefers a cool climate.

The amount of litter and the consistency of the ground cover can be altered by fire. Many authors believe that the disappearance of the vole (*Microtus*) is due to the reduction by fire of the tangle of tree trunks and debris from the forest floor (Cook op. cit., Gashwiler op. cit., Sims and Buckner op. cit., Tester and Marshall op. cit.). However, *Peromyscus* did appear and its population increased after the forest litter had been burned (Sims and Buckner op. cit., Tester op. cit.). Potter and Moir (1961) observe fewer mammal burrows in burned areas than in unburned ones. Burned ground had lost part of its A horizon and the clay mineral soil had been hardened by heat.

Ahlgren (1966) observes the relationship between vegetation and small mammal populations and hypothesizes that the main factor in their population variations is food. Thus during three consecutive years of trapping following a fire, deer mouse populations were significantly higher in burns than in unburned areas. This increase was related to the larger volume of seeds shed from burned jack pines or exposed in the upper soil layers. In mixed oak woods in Pennsylvania, Fala (1975) notes that prescribed burning led to an apparent reduction in the number of small herbivorous rodents during two growth seasons. On the other hand, insectivorous deer mice (*Peromyscus* spp.) returned to the burns within a month after the fire.

Lillywhite (op. cit.) studies the impact of the transformation of chaparral into grassland and relates that the specific diversity of rodents was highest in chaparral that had been opened up by fire, and that diversity and total density were significantly higher in burned chaparral (Figure 8.15). Wirtz (op. cit.) observes the rapid return of such burrowers as the Pacific kangaroo

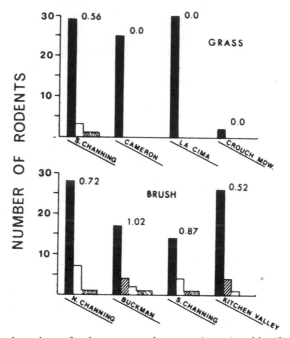

**Figure 8.15.**    Total numbers of rodents captured at grass (upper) and brush (lower) locations May 28 to June 7, 1974. Black = deer mice (*Peromyscus maniculatus*); white = brush mice (*P. boylei*); heavy crosshatch = California mice (*P. californicus*); heavy stipple = agile kangaroo rats (*Dipodomys agilis*); light stipple = dusky-footed woodrats (*Neotoma fuscipes*); light crosshatch = California pocket mice (*Perognathus californicus*); horizontal dash = western harvest mouse (*Reithrodontomys megalotis*); vertical dash = Botta's pocket gopher (*Thomomys bottae*). Numbers as in Figure 8.10. N. Channing and Buckman are the burned areas (from Lilly-white 1977).

rat (*Dipodomys agilis*) and the California pocket mouse (*Perognathus californicus*), most of which were able to survive fire; the temporary loss of some chaparral dwellers such as the wood rat (*Neotoma fuscipes* and *N. lepida*) and the brush mouse (*Peromyscus boylii*), followed by a slow return several months later; ingress of species not normally found in mature chaparral, such as the deer mouse (*Peromyscus maniculatus*), harvest mouse (*Reithrodontomys megalotis*), and California vole (*Microtus californicus*). The California pocket mouse and deer mouse are species that are generally found only in burned areas. Cook (op. cit.) and Lawrence (op. cit.) reach similar conclusions. Rodent diversity was essentially the same 1 year as 17 years after a fire. This would appear to indicate that fire in chaparral can alter species composition but does not lead to a decrease in diversity.

The kangaroo rat (*Bettongia penicillata*) prefers to shelter in *Casuarina* thickets, which are maintained at this stage by fire every seven years (Catling and Newsome op. cit.). These authors also mention that small native mice (*Pseudomys*) live only on heath in which fire is frequent. They find that small rodents are generally more numerous in the first years after a fire whatever the environment; only the moist upland heath remains problematic for these two investigators (Figure 8.16).

In northern forests snowshoe hare (*Lepus americanus*) prefer to inhabit very early stages of a succession shortly after a fire. Grange (op. cit.) says that the maximum population was attained about 10 years after fire. Eleven years after a fire, snowshoe density was an exceptionally high 20 hares per ha. However, density decreased immediately after a fire in Alberta and territorial distribution changed as the hares abandoned burns for more thickly vegetated areas. The population decrease is due to the egress of young hares, apparently the result of intraspecific competition generated by cover reduction. In the long term, however, fire had no effect on population trends in the study years. Only one year after the fire, the burn population returned to normal (Keith and Surrendi op. cit.).

In Australia, two rare possums are considered to be linked to fire. *Burramys parvus* and *Gymnobelideus leadbeateri* are always found in burned forest because they nest in fire-killed trees and feed on young shoots (Catling and Newsome op. cit.). According to these authors, if there were no fire there would be no possums.

Kangaroos and wallabies (*Macropus* spp.) have been seen in large numbers in the first years after fires (Catling and Newsome op. cit., Christensen and Kimber op. cit.). However, most results show varying tendencies.

Barren-ground caribou (*Rangifer tarandus groenlandicus*) are very sensitive to the ecological impact of fire. In winter they avoid open burns, not only because they are exposed to high winds (Scotter 1971) but also because the snow tends to be deep and crusty (Pruitt 1959). The disappearance of part of the caribou's food from the winter range has a more dramatic impact yet. Lichens are the main winter forage for caribou. Following fire, one of the most obvious effects on the winter range is the reduction in the amount of forage available. Both terrestrial and arboreal forage plants are affected (Scotter 1970, 1971). Lichens are more fire-sensitive than other caribou food as they regenerate more slowly. According to Scotter, fire reduces the potential carrying capacity of winter caribou range, whereas it increases that of moose (Figure 8.17). Moose prefer young forests (0 to 50 years old), while caribou prefer mature forests (over 50 years). This, then, is an example of two species, each of which occupies a specific ecological niche where any sudden change will profoundly alter living conditions, favoring one species to the detriment of the other. Destruction of slow-growing arboreal lichen by fire in particular leads to a severe shortage of winter forage for caribou, so that during migrations this species may be diverted from its usual trails (Scotter 1971).

The woodland caribou (*Rangifer tarandus caribou*) has the same needs as the barren-ground caribou. Its winter forage consists mostly of lichens and the increasing extent of forest fires in the far north as a result of settlement appears to be a cause of the decrease in the population of this species (Cringan op. cit.).

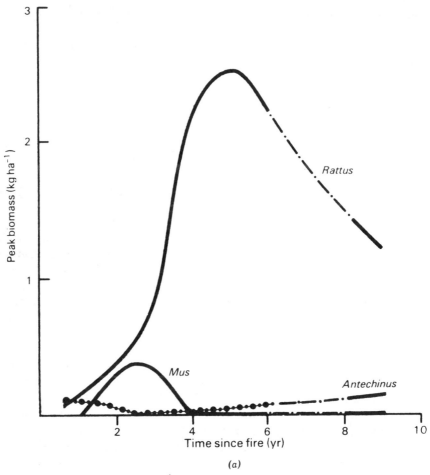

*(a)*

***Figure 8.16.***   Peak biomass (kg ha$^{-1}$) per year after fire for small mammals in Nadgee Nature Reserve, southern New South Wales. The end points represent values immediately before the fire transposed to times since previous fires. (*a*) Wet habitats (dune swale and swamp). (*b*) Moist upland heath. (*c*) Dry sclerophyll forest (from Catling and Newsome 1981).

Deer (*Odocoileus*) generally prefer burned areas free from debris to dense forest or to areas with unburned logging debris, and they prefer burns under six years of age. On the basis of a deer pellet count, McCulloch (1969) finds that deer preferred the edges of a burn to either the center or to unburned forest.

In California Biswell et al. (op. cit.) recommend spot burns of 1 to 2 ha in a checkerboard pattern to open up dense chamise for black-tailed deer (*Odocoileus hemionus columbianus*). Compared to larger burns or to dense brushland, the small burns had more deer use per square mile and produced heavier does; does had a higher frequency of ovulation, more fawns at heel,

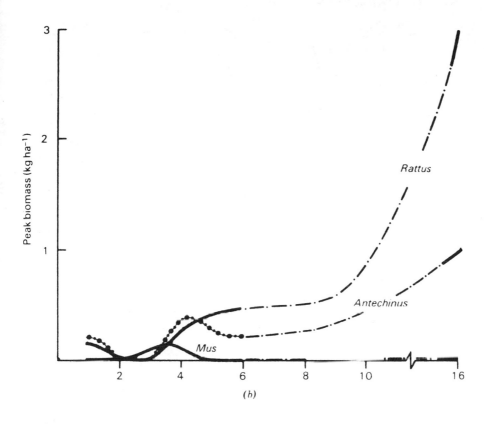

(b)

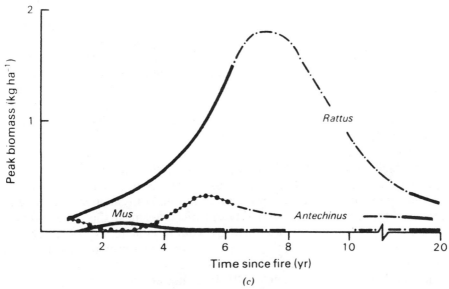

Time since fire (yr)

(c)

**Figure 8.16.** (Continued)

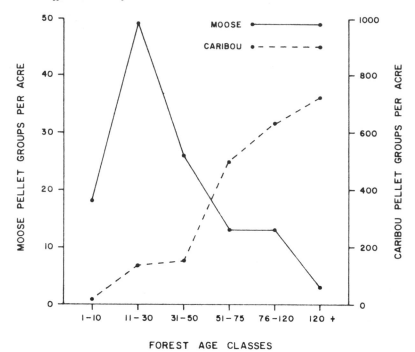

**Figure 8.17.**    Average number of caribou and moose pellet groups per acre in upland forests by age classes (from Scotter 1970).

and wintered in better condition. The better performance of deer was explained by the enhanced nutritive value of plants growing in the openings. Hendricks (1968) says that old decadent brush only produces about 56 kg/ha available feed at a protein count of about 1 percent, whereas after burning the same area will produce 2250 kg/ha at 6 percent protein content, over 240 times the original nutrient value. According to Miller (1963) and Hendricks (op. cit.), black-tailed deer are closely associated with the earliest stages of succession. In the opinion of these authors, forest fires increase the deer population to 20 times the preburn rate.

The ideal terrain for deer consists of small burns with a good food supply interspersed with brushland for protection (Biswell et al. op. cit., Hendricks op. cit.). Fires that cover too wide an area (over 400 ha) are not as attractive to deer, who will feed in the burned areas but do not remain there, going to chaparral for protection. Taber and Dasmann (1957) make the same observations after comparing an area burned by wildfire with an area of spot burns and with unburned chaparral. The population density of the burned area initially increased then declined, whereas the density of the unburned area remained low but stable. Bendell (1974) cannot find a relationship between the postfire stages where food would seem to be more abundant than population and concludes from this that deer population changes little as a result of fire.

White-tailed deer (*Odocoileus virginianus*) prefer early stages of succession with easily accessible browse plants (Vogl 1967). Fire keeps plant forms low to the ground and yields succulent young shoots (Miller 1963, Vogl 1967). These two investigators state that prescribed burning puts bushes within the animals' reach and increases feed production of browse plants, maintaining deer population at a high level. Kirsch and Kruse (op. cit.) note that in burned areas does had more fawns at heel.

Like the white-tailed deer, mule deer (*Odocoileus hemionus*) are generally found in the early stages of succession characteristic of burned areas. Fire stimulates rapid regeneration of deciduous shrubs, which increases the amount of available food. As trees regenerate and their crowns thicken, carrying capacity decreases (Rowe and Scotter op. cit.). Prescribed burning could help regenerate bushes and permit seed production of the redstem ceanothus, one of the forage plants used by the mule deer (Miller 1963).

Rocky Mountain elk or wapiti (*Cervus canadensis*) are attracted by freshly burned tracts. Young twigs and buds of their favorite food—brush plants—provide abundant winter forage within easy browsing reach. Leege (1968) finds that in Idaho elk herds are the most numerous and best provided for 20 years after large wildfires. Elk can reach plants 2 m high. As vegetation ages, the bushes grow too high for the animals to reach, so that the number of herds declines. Leege states that before a fire elk can reach only 28 percent of browsable plants, whereas after a fire they can reach 100 percent of the plants and 90 percent two years later (Figure 8.18).

Fire generates stands of *Salix, Betula,* and *Populus,* leading to an increase in the moose (*Alces alces*) population (Miller 1963); moose are considered to be favored by fire. Leopold and Darling (1953) observe, however, that fires do not always produce birch and willow, which constitute a good habitat for moose. Some burns returned almost immediately after the fire to a spruce forest type.

According to Miller (1963) and Spencer and Hakala (1964), the increase in the moose population is confined to a 10-year period following fire (Figure 8.19). Dense forest stands produce little forage to maintain large moose herds. Twenty years after fire most forage is too high for the moose to reach. Spencer and Hakala conclude from this that by improving grazing conditions, fire made it possible for moose populations to increase whereas the prefire tendency had been toward a decline due to deterioration of winter forage land. From the point of view of moose management, fires in the Kenai Peninsula were generally beneficial because they produced winter browse plants in sufficient quantity to sustain large moose herds. But Bendell (1974) disagrees with this conclusion; in his opinion there is no connection between moose population and forest fires.

Food seems likely to be the cause of the increase in the moose population

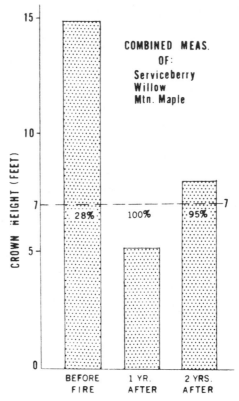

*Figure 8.18.*   The decrease in shrub height and increase in browse availability after burning. The number in each column under the 7 ft line is the percentage of the browse that can be reached by elk (from Leege 1968).

in burned areas. Amount and quality of browse plants are probably superior in the burned areas. Cowan et al. (1950) find higher ascorbic acid and protein content and more total carbohydrates in forage in the early stages (used by moose) than in old stands. Rowe and Scotter (op. cit.) come to the same conclusion.

Other ecological factors can act concurrently with fire to explain moose behavior. Scotter (1971) says that in winter moose avoid open burns because of increased windspeed, and moose (like deer) leave burns with a deep cover of light snow for surrounding forest where the snow is shallow and crusty (Kelsall and Prescott 1971). This occurs even when the burn contains an abundant supply of the animal's favorite food. Buckley (op. cit.) stresses the importance of edges between burn and forest as a factor in the increase in the moose populations in the Kenai Peninsula.

In his study on two wild bovid species, banteng [*Bos* (*Bibos*) *sondaicus*] and gaur [*Bos* (*Bibos*) *gaurus*], Wharton (1966, 1968) says that the gaur lives

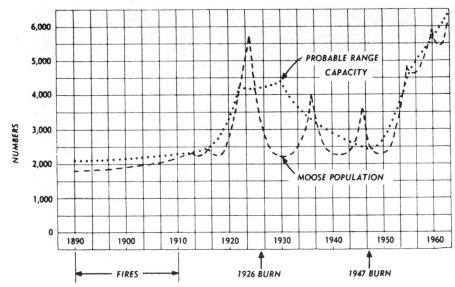

*Figure 8.19.* Estimated population and probable range capacity 1890 to 1960 of moose in the Kenai Peninsula (from Spencer and Hakala 1964).

in unburned south Asian jungle but grazes on burns, browsing young grass shoots such as *Imperata cylindrica*. Banteng, on the other hand, prefer grasslands amidst deciduous forest. The natives burn the savannas to establish garden plots for their shifting agriculture. After the humans leave, the two bovid species graze on these lands. The banteng and gaur are closely linked with grazing areas that are modified by human intervention.

Many fur-bearing species are markedly affected by fire. Recurrent fires in some parts of the northern forest have caused *Populus* and *Salix* to replace coniferous forest, favoring beaver (*Castor canadensis*), for which these trees are an important food source (Rowe and Scotter op. cit.). However, the burn area must not be too large because then there would be no food (Viereck 1973).

Marten (*Martes americana*) and fisher (*Martes pennanti*) are sensitive to fire (Figure 8.20). These two species are almost never found in fire-generated white birch or poplar stands; stands at a later stage in the succession such as spruce forest provide better habitat (Rowe and Scotter op. cit., Viereck op. cit.). Edwards (op. cit.) writes, concerning British Columbia, that fire reduces the marten population for decades. Mink (*Mustela vison*) generally inhabit lakeshores or marshes and riverbanks. Fire appears to be beneficial to this species. Ward (op. cit.) considers that controlled burning is beneficial to the muskrat (*Ondatra zibethicus*) as well as to mink and beaver. Like Vogl (1967), he observes an increase in the muskrat population in frequently burned marshes. Perkins (1968) makes similar comments concerning the coastal marsh areas of Louisiana with reference to the Louisiana muskrat

***Figure 8.20.***   The fox and the fisher are two furbearers who prefer late successional stages as habitat. Photo by Tony Quinkert.

(*Ondatra z. rivalicius*) and nutria (*Myocastor coypus*), and recommends prescribed burning as a standard management procedure.

The red squirrel (*Tamiasciurus hudsonicus*) is wiped out by fire for 10 to 25 years (Ward op. cit.) because it only inhabits coniferous forests mature enough to produce cones.

The ermine (*Mustela erminae*) prefers fire-sensitive sites but its behavior is influenced mostly by the impact of fire on prey species. Population increases have been observed during the first decade after a fire.

Black bears (*Ursus americanus*) have been observed browsing blueberries on recent burns (Rowe and Scotter op. cit., Viereck op. cit.). Blueberries may comprise up to 50 percent of the bear's diet.

In conclusion, fire is a major dynamic force that can modify the living conditions of many species of wildlife. Some animals are favored by fire, while others are not. The balance changes continually with time. Although some evidence of fire mortality has been related, the commonly held opinion is that vertebrates are rarely killed by fire. Effect on invertebrate populations are both short-term and long-term depending on whether eggs or larvae are destroyed by the fire and on the successional changes in food and plant cover.

The effects of plant succession on animal populations cannot be generalized. Plant growth and species changes generate a dynamic environment in which only those species that can adapt to changing conditions can survive.

# BIBLIOGRAPHY

Ahlgren, C. E. 1966. Small mammals and reforestation following prescribed burning. *J. For.* **64**:614–618.

Ahlgren, I. F. 1974. The effect of fire on soil organisms. In T. T. Kozlowski and C. E. Ahlgren, Eds., *Fire and Ecosystems,* Academic, New York, pp. 67–72.

Ahlgren, I. F. and C. E. Ahlgren. 1960. Ecological effects of forest fires. *Bot. Rev.* **26**:483–533.

Austen, B. 1972. *The history of veld burning in the Wankie National Park, Rhodesia.* Tall Timbers Fire Ecol. Conf. Proc. **11**:99–111.

Bailey, A. W. and C. E. Poulton. 1968. Plant communities and environmental interrelationships in a portion of the Tillamook burn, northwestern Oregon. *Ecol.* **49**:1–12.

Beck, A. M. and R. J. Vogl. 1972. The effects of spring burning on rodent populations in a brush prairie savanna. *J. Mammal.* **53**:336–346.

Bendell, J. F. 1955. Disease as a control of a population of blue grouse, *Dendragapus obscurus fuliginosus* (Ridgway). *Can. J. Zool.* **33**:195–223.

Bendell, J. F. 1974. Effects of fire on birds and mammals. In T. T. Kozlowski and C. E. Ahlgren, Eds., *Fire and Ecosystems,* Academic, New York, pp. 73–138.

Bendell, J. F. and P. W. Elliott. 1966. Habitat selection in blue grouse. *Condor* **68**:431–446.

Biswell, H. H. and others. 1952. Management of chamise brushlands for game in the north coast region of California. *Calif. Fish and Game* **38**:453–484.

Blackford, J. 1955. Woodpecker concentration in a burned forest. *Condor* **57**:28–30.

Bock, C. E. and J. F. Lynch. 1970. Breeding bird populations on burned and unburned conifer forests in the Sierra Nevada. *Condor* **72**:182–189.

Brynard, A. M. 1971. *Controlled burning in the Kruger National Park—history and development of a veld burning policy.* Tall Timbers Fire Ecol. Conf. Proc. **11**:219–231.

Buckley, J. L. 1958. *Effects of fire on Alaskan wildlife.* Soc. Am. For. Proc. **58**:123–126.

Buffington, J. D. 1967. Soil arthropod populations of the New Jersey pine barrens as affected by fire. *Entomol. Soc. Am.* **60**:530–535.

Campbell, R. S. 1954. Fire in relation to forest grazing. *Unasylva* **8**:154–158.

Cantlon, J. E. and M. F. Buell. 1952. Controlled burning—its broader ecological aspects. *Bartonia* **76**:48–52.

Catling, P. C. and A. E. Newsome. 1981. Responses of the Australian vertebrate fauna to fire—an evolutionary approach. In A. M. Gill, R. H. Groves, and I. R. Noble, Eds., *Fire and Australian Biota,* Aust. Acad. Sci., Canberra, pp. 273–310.

Chamrad, A. D. and J. D. Dodd. 1973. *Prescribed burning and grazing for prairie chicken habitat manipulation in the Texas coastal prairie.* Tall Timbers Fire Ecol. Conf. Proc. **12**:257–276.

Chew, R. W., B. B. Butterworth, and R. Grechmann. 1958. The effects of fire on the small mammal population of chaparral. *J. Mammal.* **40**:253.

Christensen, P. E. and P. C. Kimber. 1975. *Effect of prescribed burning on the flora and fauna of southwest Australian forests.* Proc. Ecol. Soc. Aust. **9**:85–106.

Cook, S. F., Jr. 1959. The effects of fire on a population of small rodents. *Ecol.* **40**:102–108.

Cooper, C. F. 1961. The ecology of fire. *Sci. Am.* **204**:150–160.

Coults, J. R. H. 1945. The effects of veld burning on the base exchange capacity of soil. *S. Afr. J. Sci.* **61**:218–224.

Cowan, I. McT., W. S. Hoar, and J. Hatter. 1950. The effect of forest succession upon the quantity and upon the nutritive values of woody plants used as food by moose. *Can. J. Res. Sect. D* **28**:249–271.

Cowles, R. B. 1967. *Fire suppression, faunal changes and condor diets*. Tall Timbers Fire Ecol. Conf. Proc. **7**:217–224.

Cringan, A. T. 1957. *History, food habits and range requirements of the woodland caribou of continental North America*. Trans. N. Am. Wildl. Conf. **22**:485–501.

Daubenmire, R. F. 1968. Ecology of fire in grasslands. *Ecol. Res.* **5**:209–266.

Doerr, P. D., L. B. Keith, and D. H. Rusch. 1970. *Effects of fire on a ruffed grouse population*. Tall Timbers Fire Ecol. Conf. Proc. **10**:25–46.

Douglas, G. W. 1974. *Ecological impact of chemical fire retardants: a review*. Can. For. Serv. Report NOR-X-109, 33 pp.

Dunbar, M. J. 1968. *Ecological development in polar regions*. Prentice-Hall, N.J.

Edwards, R. Y. 1954. Fire and the decline of a mountain caribou herd. *J. Wildl. Manage.* **18**:521–525.

Fala, R. A. 1975. Effects of prescribed burning on small mammal populations in a mixed-oak clearcut. *J. Forest.* **73**:586–587.

Flieger, B. W. 1970. *Forest fires and insects: the relation of fire to insect outbreak*. Tall Timbers Fire Ecol. Conf. Proc. **10**:107–116.

Flook, D. R. 1964. Range relationship of some ungulates native to Banff and Jasper National Parks, Alberta. In D. J. Crisp, Ed., *Grazing in Terrestrial and Marine Environments*, Blackwell, Oxford, pp. 119–128.

Fowle, C. D. 1946. The blood parasites of the blue grouse. *Sci.* **103**:708–709.

French, J. R. and R. M. Keirle. 1979. Studies in fire-damaged radiata pine plantations. *Aust. For.* **33**:175–180.

Gashwiler, J. S. 1970. Plant and mammal changes on a clearcut in west central Oregon. *Ecol.* **51**:1018–1026.

Geiszler, D. R. and others. 1980. Fire, fungi, and beetle influences on a lodgepole pine ecosystem of south central Oregon. *Oecologia* **68**:239–243.

Gillon, D. 1972. *The effects of bushfire on the principal pentatomid bugs (Hemiptera) of an Ivory Coast savanna*. Tall Timbers Fire Ecol. Conf. Proc. **11**:377–417.

Gillon, D. and J. Pernes. 1968. Etude de l'effet du feu de brousse sur certains groupes d'arthropodes dans une savane pré-forestière de Côte d'Ivoire. Ann. Univ. Abidjan **7**:113–197.

Gillon, Y. 1972. *The effect of bushfire on the principal acridid species of an Ivory Coast savanna*. Tall Timbers Fire Ecol. Conf. Proc. **11**:419–471.

Gillon, Y. 1974. *La vie des savanes*, Centre ORSTOM, Dakar, 28 pp.

Givens, L. S. 1962. *Use of fire on southeastern wildlife refuges*. Tall Timbers Fire Ecol. Conf. Proc. **1**:121–126.

Grange, W. 1965. *Fire and tree growth relationship to snowshoe rabbits*. Tall Timbers Fire Ecol. Conf. Proc. **4**:110–125.

Greene, S. W. 1935. Effect of annual grass fires on organic matter and other constituents of virgin longleaf pine soils. *J. Agr. Res.* **50**:809–822.

Gullion, G. W. 1967. *Factors affecting ruffed grouse population in the boreal forests of northern Minnesota, USA*. Proc. 8th Int. Congr. Game Biol. 1967, Finn. Game Res. **30**:103–117.

Haig, I. T. 1938. Fire in modern forest management. *J. For.* **25**:1045–1051.

Hakala, J. B. and others. 1971. Fire effects and rehabilitation methods—Swanson-Russian Rivers fires. In *Fire in Northern Environment*, U.S. For. Serv., PNW For. and Range Exp. Stn., pp. 87–99.

Handley, C. O. 1969. *Fire and mammals*. Tall Timbers Fire Ecol. Conf. Proc. **9**:151–159.

Hayes, G. L. 1970. Impacts of fire use on forest ecosystems. In *The Role of Fire in the Intermountain West*, Intermt. Fire Res. Council, Montana, pp. 99–118.

Heinselman, M. L. 1971. The natural role of fire in northern conifer forests. In *Fire in the Northern Environment,* U.S. For. Serv. PNW For. and Range Exp. Stn., pp. 61–72.

Hendricks, J. H. 1968. *Control burning for deer management in chaparral in California.* Tall Timbers Fire Ecol. Conf. Proc. **8**:219–234.

Heyward, F. and A. N. Tissot. 1936. Some changes in the soil fauna associated with forest fire in the longleaf pine region. *Ecol.* **17**:659–666.

Hodgson, A. 1968. Control burning in eucalypt forests in Victoria, Australia. *J. For.* **66**:601–605.

Howard, W. E., R. L. Fenner, and H. E. Childs, Jr. 1959. Wildlife survival in brush burns. *J. Range Manage.* **12**:230–234.

Humphrey, R. R. 1962. *Range ecology,* Ronald Press, New York, 235 pp.

Hurst, G. A. 1971. *The effects of controlled burning on arthropod density and biomass in relation to bobwhite quail brood habitat on a right-of-way.* Tall Timbers Conf. Ecol. Anim. Contr. Habitat Manage. Proc. **2**:173–183.

Isaac, N. 1963. *Fire, a tool, not a blanket rule in Douglas fir ecology.* Tall Timbers Fire Ecol. Conf. Proc. **2**:1–17.

Kahn, W. C. 1960. Observation on the effect of a burn on a population of *Sceloporus occidentalis. Ecol.* **41**:358–359.

Kayll, A. J. 1968. *The role of fire in the boreal forest of Canada.* Petawawa For. Exp. Stn., Can. Dept. For. and Rural Dev. Info. Report PS-X-7, 15 pp.

Keith, J. O. 1965. The Abert squirrel and its dependence on ponderosa pine. *Ecol.* **46**:150–163.

Keith, L. B. and D. C. Surrendi. 1971. Effects of fire on a snowshoe hare population. *J. Wildl. Manage.* **35**:16–26.

Kelsall, J. P. and W. Prescott. 1971. *Moose and deer behavior in snow in Fundy National Park, New Brunswick.* Can. Wildl. Serv. Report **15**:1–17.

Kimber, P. C. 1974. *Some effects of prescribed burning on jarrah forest birds.* Proc. 3rd Fire Ecol. Symp., Monash Univ. and For. Comm., Vict., Melbourne, pp. 49–57.

Kirsch, L. M. and A. D. Kruse. 1973. *Prairie fires and wildlife.* Tall Timbers Fire Ecol. Conf. Proc. **12**:289–304.

Klebenow, D. A. 1973. *The habitat requirements of sage grouse and the role of fire in management.* Tall Timbers Fire Ecol. Conf. Proc. **12**:305–316.

Komarek, E. V. 1962. *The use of fire: an historical background.* Tall Timbers Fire Ecol. Conf. Proc. **1**:7–10.

Komarek, E. V. 1963. *Fire, research and education.* Tall Timbers Fire Ecol. Conf. Proc. **2**:181–187.

Komarek, E. V. 1967. *Fire and the ecology of man.* Tall Timbers Fire Ecol. Conf. Proc. **6**:143–170.

Komarek, E. V. 1968. *Lightning and lightning fires as ecological forces.* Tall Timbers Fire Ecol. Conf. Proc. **8**:169–197.

Komarek, E. V. 1969. *Fire and animal behavior.* Tall Timbers Fire Ecol. Conf. Proc. **9**:161–207.

Komarek, E. V. 1970. *Insect control—fire for habitat management.* Tall Timbers Conf. Ecol. Anim. Contr. Habitat Manage. Proc. **2**:157–171.

Komarek, E. V. 1971. *Effects of fire on wildlife and range habitats.* Prescribed Burning Symp. Proc., U.S. For. Serv. Southeastern For. Exp. Stn., pp. 46–52.

Koplin, J. R. 1969. The numerical response of woodpeckers to insect prey in a subalpine forest in Colorado. *Condor* **71**:436–638.

Lawrence, G. E. 1966. Ecology of vertebrate animals in relation to chaparral fire in the Sierra Nevada foothills. *Ecol.* **47**:278–291.

Leege, T. A. 1968. *Prescribed burning for elk in northern Idaho.* Tall Timbers Fire Ecol. Conf. Proc. **8:**235–253.

Lehman, V. W. 1965. *Fire in the range of Attwater's prairie chicken.* Tall Timbers Fire Ecol. Conf. Proc. **6:**127–143.

Lemon, P. C. 1968a. Effects of fire on an African plateau grassland. *Ecol.* **49:**316–322.

Lemon, P. C. 1968b. *Fire and wildlife grazing on an African plateau.* Tall Timbers Fire Ecol. Conf. Proc. **8:**71–88.

Leopold, A. S. and F. F. Darling. 1953. *Effects of land use on moose and caribou in Alaska.* Trans. N. Am. Wildl. Conf. **18:**553–562.

Lillywhite, H. B. 1977. Effect of chaparral conversion on small vertebrates in southern California. *Biol. Conserv.* **11:**171–184.

Lillywhite, H. B. and F. North. 1974. Perching behavior of *Sceloporus occidentalis* in recently burned chaparral. *Copeia* 1974:76–81.

Lillywhite, H. B., G. Friedman, and N. Ford. 1977. Color matching and perch selection in lizards in recently burned chaparral. *Copeia* 1977:115–121.

Linsley, E. G. 1943. Attraction of melanophila beetles by fire and smoke. *J. Econ. Entomol.* **36:**341–342.

Lovat, L. 1911. Heather burning. In A. S. Leslie, Ed., *The Grouse in Health and Disease,* Comm. of Inquiry on Grouse Disease, Smith, London, pp. 392–413.

Lutz, H. J. 1956. *Ecological effects of forest fire in the interior of Alaska.* USDA Tech. Bull. No. 1133, 212 pp.

Lyon, L. J. and others. 1978. *Effects of fire on fauna. A state-of-knowledge review.* U.S. For. Serv. Gen. Tech. Report WO-6, 22 pp.

MacArthur, R. H., J. W. MacArthur, and J. Preer. 1962. On bird species diversity, II. Prediction of bird census from habitat measurements. *Am. Nat.* **96:**167–174.

McCulloch, D. Y. 1969. Some effects of wildfire on deer habitat in pinyon-juniper woodland. *J. Wildl. Manage.* **33:**778–784.

Marshall, J. T. 1963. *Fire and birds in the mountains of southern Arizona.* Tall Timbers Fire Ecol. Conf. Proc. **2:**135–141.

Martin, N. D. 1960. An analysis of bird population in relation to forest succession in Algonquin Provincial Park, Ontario. *Ecol.* **41:**126–140.

Martin, R. E. 1963. *A basic approach to fire injury of tree stems.* Tall Timbers Fire Ecol. Conf. Proc. **2:**151–162.

Mentis, M. T. and R. C. Bigalke. 1981. The effect of scale burn on the densities of grassland francolins in the Natal Drakensberg. *Biol. Conserv.* **21:**247–261.

Metz, L. J. and M. H. Farrier. 1971. *Prescribed burning and soil mesofauna on the Santee Experimental Forest.* Prescribed Burning Symp. Proc., U.S. For. Serv. Southeastern For. Exp. Stn., pp. 100–105.

Miller, G. R. 1964. The management of heather moors. *Advan. Sci.* **21:**163–169.

Miller, G. R., A. Watson, and D. Jenkins. 1970. *Responses of red grouse population to experimental improvement of their food.* Brit. Ecol. Soc. Symp. **10:**323–325.

Miller, H. A. 1963. *Use of fire in wildlife management.* Tall Timbers Fire Ecol. Conf. Proc. **2:**18–20.

Miller, W. E. 1978. Use of prescribed burning in seed production areas to control red pine cone beetle. *Environ. Entomol.* **7:**698–702.

Mitchell, R. G. and R. E. Martin. 1980. *Fire and insects in pine culture of the Pacific Northwest.* Proc. 6th Conf. Fire For. Meteor., Soc. Am. For., pp. 182–190.

Mount, A. B. 1964. The interdependence of the eucalypts and forest fires in southern Australia. *Aust. For.* **28:**166–172.

Mount, A. B. 1969. *Eucalypt ecology as related to fire.* Tall Timbers Fire Ecol. Conf. Proc. **9:**75–108.

Munro, J. A. and I. McT. Cowan. 1947. *A review of the bird fauna of British Columbia.* Brit. Col. Prov. Mus., Spec. Publ. **2:**1–285.

Mutch, R. W. 1970. Wildland fires and ecosystems—a hypothesis. *Ecol.* **51:**1046–1051.

Niering, W. A., R. H. Goodwin, and S. Taylor. 1970. *Prescribed burning in southern New England: introduction to long-range studies.* Tall Timbers Fire Ecol. Conf. Proc. **10:**267–286.

Orians, G. H. 1969. The number of bird species in some tropical forests. *Ecol.* **50:**783–801.

Pearse, A. S. 1943. Effects of burning over and raking off litter on certain soil animals in the Duke Forest. *Am. Midl. Nat.* **29:**405–424.

Perkins, C. J. 1968. *Controlled burning in the management of muskrats and waterfowl in Louisiana coastal marshes.* Tall Timber Fire Ecol. Conf. Proc. **8:**269–280.

Phillips, J. 1965. *Fire—as master and servant. Its influence on the bioclimatic regions of Trans-Saharan Africa.* Tall Timbers Fire Ecol. Conf. Proc. **4:**7–109.

Picozzi, N. 1968. Grouse bags in relation to the management and geology of heather moors. *J. App. Ecol.* **5:**483–488.

Potter, L. D. and D. R. Moir. 1961. Phytosociological study of burned deciduous woods, Turtle Mountains, North Dakota. *Ecol.* **42:**468–480.

Pruitt, W. O., Jr. 1959. Snow as a factor in the winter ecology of the barren-ground caribou (*Rangifer arcticus*). *Arctic* **12:**159–179.

Redfield, J. A., F. C. Zwickel, and J. F. Bendell. 1970. *Effects of fire on numbers of blue grouse.* Tall Timbers Fire Ecol. Conf. Proc. **10:**63–83.

Renwald, J. D., H. A. Wright, and J. T. Flinders. 1978. Effects of prescribed fire on bobwhite quail habitat in the Rolling Plains of Texas. *J. Range Manage.* **31:**65–69.

Rice, L. A. 1932. The effect of fire on the prairie animal communities. *Ecol.* **13:**392–401.

Rickard, W. H. 1970. Ground dwelling beetles in burned and unburned vegetation. *J. Range Manage.* **23:**293–294.

Robinson, D. J. 1958. Forestry and wildlife relationships on Vancouver Island. *For. Chron.* **34:**31–36.

Rowe, J. S. 1970. *Spruce and fire in northwest Canada and Alaska.* Tall Timbers Fire Ecol. Conf. Proc. **10:**245–254.

Rowe, J. S. and G. W. Scotter. 1973. Fire in the boreal forest. *J. Quat. Res.* **3:**444–464.

Scotter, G. W. 1970. *Wildfires in relation to the habitat of barren-ground caribou in the taiga of northern Canada.* Tall Timbers Fire Ecol. Conf. Proc. **10:**85–105.

Scotter, G. W. 1971. Fire, vegetation, soil, and barren-ground caribou relations in northern Canada. In *Fire in Northern Environment,* For. Serv. PNW For. and Range Exp. Stn., pp. 209–230.

Shafi, M. I. and G. A. Yarranton. 1973. Diversity, floristic richness and species evenness during a secondary (post-fire) succession. *Ecol.* **54:**897–902.

Sharp, W. M. 1970. *The role of fire in ruffed grouse habitat management.* Tall Timbers Fire Ecol. Conf. Proc. **10:**47–61.

Siivonen, L. 1957. The problem of the short-term fluctuation in numbers of Tetraonids in Europe. *Pap. Game Res.* **19:**1–64.

Simmons, G. A. and others. 1977. Preliminary test of prescribed burning for control of maple leaf cutter (Lepidoptera: Incurvariidae). *Great Lakes Entomol.* **10:**209–210.

Sims, H. R. and C. H. Buckner. 1973. The effect of clearcutting and burning of *Pinus banksiana* forests on the populations of small mammals in southeastern Manitoba. *Am. Midl. Natur.* **90:**228–231.

Smith, D. W. 1968. *Surface fires in northern Ontario.* Tall Timbers Fire Ecol. Conf. Proc. **8**:41–54.

Soutiere, E. C. and E. G. Bolen. 1973. *Role of fire in mourning dove nesting ecology.* Tall Timbers Fire Ecol. Conf. Proc. **12**:277–288.

Spencer, D. L. and H. B. Hakala. 1964. *Moose and fire on the Kenai.* Tall Timbers Fire Ecol. Conf. Proc. **3**:11–33.

Stoddard, H. L., Sr. 1931. *The bobwhite quail, its habits, preservation, and increase,* Ch. Schreives and Sons, New York, 555 pp.

Stoddard, H. L., Sr. 1962. *Use of fire in pine forests and game lands of the deep southeast.* Tall Timbers Fire Ecol. Conf. Proc. **1**:31–42.

Stoddard, H. L., Sr. 1963. *Bird habitat and fire.* Tall Timbers Fire Ecol. Conf. Proc. **2**:163–175.

Swan, F. R. 1970. Post-fire response of four plant communities in south-central New York State. *Ecol.* **51**:1074–1082.

Taber, R. D. and R. F. Dasmann. 1957. The dynamics of three natural populations of the deer *Odocoileus hemionus hemionus. Ecol.* **38**:233–246.

Taylor, D. L. 1973. Some ecological implications of forest fire control in Yellowstone National Park, Wyoming. *Ecol.* **54**:1394–1396.

Terril, H. V. and B. T. Crawford. 1946. Using den boxes to boost squirrel crop. *Missouri Conserv.* **7**:4–5.

Tester, J. R. 1965. Effects of a controlled burn on small mammals in a Minnesota oak savanna. *Am. Midl. Natur.* **74**:240–243.

Tester, J. R. and W. H. Marshall. 1961. *A study of certain plant and animal interrelations on a native prairie in northwestern Minnesota.* Univ. Minn., Mus. Nat. Hist. Occas. Paper **8**:1–151.

Tevis, L., Jr. 1956. Effect of slash burn on forest mice. *J. Wildl. Manage.* **20**:405–409.

Thilenius, J. F. 1968. The *Quercus garryana* forests of the Willamette Valley, Oregon. *Ecol.* **49**:1124–1133.

Trabaud, L. 1979. Etude du comportment du feu dans la garrigue de chêne kermès à partir des températures et des vitesses de propagation. *Ann. Sci. For.* **35**:13–38.

Trabaud, L. 1980. *Impact biologique et écologique des feux de végétation sur l'organisation, la structure et l'évolution de la végétation des zones de garrigues du Bas-Languedoc.* Thèse Etat. Univ. Sci. Tech. Languedoc, Montpellier, 288 pp.

Udvardy, M. D. F. 1969. *Dynamic geography with special reference to land animals.* Van Nostrand-Reinhold, Princeton, N.J.

Van Meter, W. P. and C. E. Hardy. 1975. *Predicting effects on fish of fire retardants in streams.* U.S. For. Serv. Res. Paper INT-166, 16 pp.

Viereck, L. A. 1973. Wildfire in the taiga of Alaska. *Quat. Res.* **3**:465–495.

Vogl, R. J. 1967. *Controlled burning for wildlife in Wisconsin.* Tall Timbers Fire Ecol. Conf. Proc. **6**:47–96.

Vogl, R. J. 1969. One-hundred and thirty years of plant succession in a southeastern Wisconsin lowland. *Ecol.* **50**:248–255.

Vogl, R. J. 1973. Effects of fire on plants and animals of a Florida wetland. *Am. Midl. Natur.* **89**:334–347.

Walter, H. 1977. *Effects of fire on wildlife communities.* Proc. Symp. Environ. Consequences Fire Fuel Manage. Medit. Ecosyst., U.S. For. Serv. Gen. Tech. Report WO-3, pp. 183–192.

Ward, P. 1968. *Fire in relation to waterfowl habitat of the delta marshes.* Tall Timbers Fire Ecol. Conf. Proc. **8**:255–267.

Wells, P. V. 1965. Scarp woodlands, transplanted grassland soils, and concepts of grassland climate in the Great Plains Region. *Sci.* **148**:246–249.

Westemeier, R. L. 1973. *Prescribed burning in grassland management for prairie chicken in Illinois.* Tall Timbers Fire Ecol. Conf. Proc. **12**:317–338.

Wharton, C. H. 1966. *Man, fire and wild cattle in north Cambodia.* Tall Timbers Fire Ecol. Conf. Proc. **5**:23–65.

Wharton, C. H. 1968. *Man, fire and wild cattle in Southeast Asia.* Tall Timbers Fire Ecol. Conf. Proc. **8**:107–167.

Williams, J. T., R. E. Martin, and S. G. Pickford. 1980. *Silvicultural and fire management implications from a timber type evaluation of tussock moth outbreak areas.* Proc. 6th Nat. Conf. Fire For. Meteorol., Soc. Am. For., pp. 191–196.

Wirtz, W. O., II 1977. *Vertebrate post-fire succession.* Proc. Symp. Environ. Consequences Fire Fuel Manage. Medit. Ecosyst., U.S. For. Serv. Gen. Tech. Report WO-3, pp. 46–57.

# CHAPTER NINE

# *Fire Effects on Vegetation*

Fire is such an ancient, universal phenomenon that it has played an important part in creating many of the vegetative communities and much of the landscape in the world. In fact, fire has affected the vegetation of the entire globe. Just how ancient fire is cannot be known for certain but there can be no doubt that its first occurrence predates mankind by a considerable margin; it may even be older than any existing terrestrial vegetation (Anonymous 1973, Komarek 1973). Lightning is one of the natural causes of fire in all corners of the globe, from the tundra to the tropical forest (Arnold 1964, Komarek 1964, 1966, 1967, 1968, 1972, Requa 1964, Taylor 1969). Other natural phenomena may also have caused fires, such as volcanic eruption, spontaneous combustion (Viosca 1931), and sparks produced in rockslides (Hennicker-Gotley 1936). Fire has always been a natural, regularly occurring, part of plant succession that permits the rejuvenation of some populations and creates a mosaic of plant communities that develop over time and vary with location.

However, man's appearance on the scene disturbed this balance of nature. Humans used and abused fire for agricultural, religious, and personal needs. This, in combination with cutting, grazing, and farming activities, followed by the abandonment of many areas, shaped much of the plant life that exists today.

The continued action of fire has led to the evolution of a large number of fire-adapted communities, some of which actually depend for their maintenance on the regular occurrence of fire.

## RELATIONSHIP BETWEEN FLAMMABILITY AND VEGETATION

Combustion of plant fuels is a typical example of the process of chemical oxidation. Although fire is generally regarded as an aspect of environmental

255

physics, the biological nature of the structural and chemical properties of the fuels permits natural selection that affects the fire-adaptive traits of plants in ecosystems in which fire occurs.

Three stages can be identified in the combustion of wood fuels. In the preheating, or endothermic, stage the fuel absorbs heat as the temperature rises to ignition, leading to a loss of water and molecular breakdown that releases volatile compounds. As the temperature increases, the exothermic stage is attained when pyrolysis of the cellulosic fuels begins, releasing heat and flammable volatiles. This is when the fuel's structural and chemical properties become extremely important in determining combustion behavior.

Several structural properties have a significant effect on fire probability, rate of fire spread, and fire intensity. Fuel load and surface-to-volume ratio can be used for estimating fuel energy release. Particle density (specific weight or weight per unit volume) affects flammability and fire spread (Brown 1970a, Fons 1946, 1950). In conifers density varies considerably among species and to a lesser extent among populations of a given species in different geographical locations. The surface-to-volume ratio provides an invaluable indicator of both flammability and combustion, since heat transfer by radiation, conduction, and convection varies with surface area. This ratio varies greatly with fuel type. Generally, the plants with the highest ratios are the most flammable, and most of these species belong to fire-prone communities. Conifers have surface-to-volume ratios in the neighborhood of 54 to 99 $cm^2/cm^3$, and highly flammable grasses have values in the range of 189 to 380 $cm^2/cm^3$ (Brown 1970b, Montgomery and Cheo 1971).

Porosity of the fuelbed (ratio of bed volume to fuel volume) is another structural parameter that gives a positive linear correlation with fire spread over a wide range of values (Rothermel and Anderson 1966). Higher porosity permits increased heat transfer by convection and increased oxygen circulation, thereby greatly affecting fire spread. If porosity is too high, however, insufficient heat is produced to ignite the unburned particles. Therefore, low fire-intensity and fire-spread values are obtained when porosity is extremely high or, conversely, very low. Fire is most intense and spreads fastest in formations with medium porosity such as grasslands, shrublands, and slash.

Flammability is greatly influenced by fuel moisture content; a high fuel moisture significantly reduces flammability (Countryman 1974, Montgomery and Cheo op. cit., Olsen 1960, Trabaud 1976). However, the relative ability of fine fuels to change their moisture content rapidly is more significant. This property may determine the appearance of combustion. Moisture balances can be calculated from air temperature and relative humidity (Fosberg and Schroeder 1971) and be used as indicators of flammability.

The nature of the chemical compounds in the fuels determines the temperature at which volatile fuel compounds are released. Various organic compounds affect the real heat of combustion of the gases released in pyrolysis. Inorganic compounds also affect plant flammability (Broido 1966, Broido and Nelson 1964). Mutch and Philpot (1970) showed that silica must be taken into account and that plants with the highest ash content without silica are the least flammable. A high concentration of sodium and/or potassium (and probably of other anionic compounds as well) likely has less effect on pyrolytic properties (Philpot 1970). The phosphorus content of fuel is inversely correlated with flammability. Philpot also finds good positive correlation between maximum volatilization and the phosphorus and calcium contents of plant fuels. Lindenmuth and Davis (1973) show that fire spread is positively correlated with the phosphorus content of Arizona oak chaparral. The role of phosphorus in determining flammability is also discussed by Countryman and Philpot (1970), and Rothermel (1976).

Since terpenes, fats, oils, and waxes with a high energy value constitute a high proportion of the volatile fuel components of plant tissues, the flammability of these tissues can vary considerably even when the overall heat of the total fuel is low (Philpot 1969a, 1969b). These high-energy compounds are extremely important from the point of view of flammability, for they easily facilitate ignition at relatively low temperatures and because most of the time they are at or near the surface of the plant parts, leaves in particular. Live fuels in chaparral with a moderate to high ether extractive content will burn at moisture contents well over 100 percent, whereas dead fuels will not burn at moisture contents above 30 percent (Rothermel op. cit.). This is probably due to the loss of volatile high energy compounds soon after death. Philpot (1969b) finds a linear correlation between the maximum burning rate of *Populus tremuloides* leaves and ether extractive content. The essential oils (terpenes) in eucalyptus leaves facilitate flammability by increasing temperature rise in the first stages of combustion (Pompe and Vines 1966). Addition of these oils significantly increases the heat release by relatively nonflammable leaves (King and Vines 1969). Philpot (1969a) finds a linear correlation between the total heat energy released by *Adenostoma fasciculatum* and its ether extractive content.

The ether extractives contain many secondary components, including methylated flavonoids, sesquiterpenes, waxes, triterpenes, and esterified phenol acids (Rundel 1981). Volatile monoterpenes and amines are probably also present at the leaf surfaces; these external compounds are very flammable at high temperatures. Some benzene–ethanol extractives are volatile at temperatures under 300°C. They contain resins, sugars, and other, easily soluble compounds.

Shafizadeh et al. (1977) obtained ether and benzene–ethanol extractives from foliage of various species. The total extractive content varied from 13 to 45 percent in broadleaf species and was about 30 percent in all coniferous species tested. Between 100 and 500°C, most of the combustion gases were from ether and benzene–ethanol extractives. These authors believe that both types of extractives play a significant role in the initiation of combustion at lower temperatures, whereas at higher temperatures the ether extractives increase fire intensity.

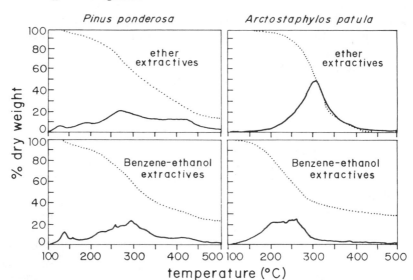

**Figure 9.1.** Thermal decomposition characteristics of ether and benzene alcohol extractives of *Pinus ponderosa* and *Arctostaphylos patula*. Both total weight loss (dotted line) and weight loss at a given temperature (solid line) are indicated. Adapted from Shafizadeh et al. (1977).

Thermal analysis of the ether and benzene–ethanol extractives of foliage from *Pinus ponderosa* and *Arctostaphylos patula* (Figure 9.1) shows that the ether extractives are volatilized in the 100 to 500°C temperature range (Shafizadeh et al. op. cit.). In *P. ponderosa* volatilization occurs gradually throughout the temperature increase, peaking around 270°C. In *Arctostaphylos* volatilization is slow at low temperatures with a sharp sudden peak at 300°C. The benzene–ethanol extractives decompose gradually at low temperatures between 200 and 300°C. The compounds in ether extractives can play a significant role in causing ignition at relatively low temperatures as well as increase fire intensity at higher temperatures.

Only a few authors have analyzed seasonal variations in ether extractives. Richards (1940) observes changes in ether extractive content with time. No research has been done, however, on the physiological significance of seasonal variation. Hough (1973) finds that the ether extractive concentration of *Pinus clausa* was highest (12 to 14 percent) when the leaf moisture content was lowest, during the maximum burning period. Philpot (1969a) comments that the ether extractive content of *Adenostoma fasciculatum* varied considerably with the season but he cannot obtain a good correlation between the maximum extractive content and the maximum lightning fire occurrence season—in fact, he finds that the variation was practically inverse.

Considering species flammability from the evolutionary point of view, plants can be grouped into three broad categories, namely, those that can resist fire with practically no damage, those that regenerate rapidly after defoliation, and those that are killed by fire.

Plants that can resist or survive fire have certain adaptive traits that afford the greatest fire-survival probability. Such plants have thick bark that insulates the cambium from the heat of the fire (Gill and Ashton 1968, Hare 1965, Martin 1963, Vines 1968) and they tend to be tall; their height minimizes the possibility of crown fire. According to Rundel (op. cit.), the long needles in conifers and in some species with comparable leaf structure produce a well-ventilated litter that facilitates ground fires, thus preventing excessive fuel build-up that could induce crown fires or lethal cambium damage. In vegetative-reproducing species the structural and chemical properties of the plants are often such as to enhance flammability, and stands of all ages and states of health experience fire. The preservation of fine dead fuel matter on a plant, as Specht et al. (1958) and Gill and Ingwersen (1976) find in *Xanthorrhoea australis,* Moore and Keraitis (1971) observe in *Eucalyptus macrorhyncha,* and Rundel and Parsons (1979) see in *Adenostoma fasciculatum,* is a frequent structural property of such species. High concentrations of ether extractives with a high-energy value are frequent, typical chemical components of the species in question—Philpot (1969a) finds 10,000 cal/g for *Adenostoma.* Species that are likely to be fire-killed produce dense, even-aged stands in which senescence occurs nearly simultaneously, leading to intense but infrequent fires. The chemical components of species of the latter category are probably not very significant.

Frequent fire helps maintain fire-adapted species and ecosystems such as many grassland types and pine forests. In communities with a low soil nutrient content fire may lead to the rapid decomposition and recycling of minerals. Under such conditions, natural selection may have led to a structural and chemical composition that favors high flammability and thus helps maintain a variety of stages and species in the community. In this case chemical compounds that ignite at low temperatures can be significant. Postignition fire intensity will be greatly affected by the structure and energy content of the fuels permitting heat transfer.

According to Rundel's hypothesis, foliage structure and shape have traditionally been considered a phytosynthetic adaptation (distribution of foliage area) or an adaptation to water requirements. The ecological interpretation of chemical properties of foliage has been concerned primarily with the problems of herbivores and allelopathy. Rundel proposes, however, that assuming that fire-adapted plant species may present reproductive modifications (sprouts from root systems, serotinous cones, fire-stimulated germination) and anatomical adaptations for survival (thick bark, epicormic buds), such species may have evolved structural and chemical modifications that can have a biological effect on natural fire frequency. Other authors such as Jackson (1968), Mount (1964), and Mutch (1970) had already advanced similar hypotheses in light of the fact that many properties favor flammability in a large number of plants that belong to communities in which fire occurs frequently.

## ADAPTATIONS TO FIRE BY VASCULAR PLANTS

In a way, the fire-adaptive properties of plants include all the characteristics that ensure that species inhabiting a fire environment can survive through their life cycles.

### Protection of Buds

Postfire regeneration is often considerable. Depending on fire intensity, trees may resprout from buds that were protected by the bark when the crown was burned, or a tree may survive apparently unharmed if its foliage did not burn. A shrub may be completely destroyed by a fire but survive through sprouting from buds buried in the ground. Similarly, rhizome-forming herbaceous plants may grow new leaves from protected basal meristems and reconstitute their photosynthetic elements.

Good examples of the role of bark thickness in bud protection can be found in dry eucalypt forests in Australia and in *Quercus suber* forests in Europe. Trees can survive and produce new leaves even after intense crown fires. In some cases in eucalypts, recovery can be quite rapid. Gill (1978) shows that 5 to 7 m high *E. dives* produced its prefire leaf area within a year even though the fire had completely destroyed the crowns of the trees. Within three years the normal branching system had recovered. Bark thickness is apparently important for bud protection (Gill and Ashton 1968, Hare op. cit., Kayll 1966, Martin op. cit., McArthur 1968, Reifsnyder et al. 1967, Stickel 1941, Vines op. cit.).

Soil is an effective insulating material and soil temperatures during fires are low in relation to the total heat released by the fire (Beadle 1940, Packham 1970, Trabaud 1979). Many plants (Filicineae, Cycadaceae, and Angiosperms) with underground regenerative organs such as rhizomes produce buds. Some Dicotyledons have root buds; some shrubby Dicotyledons have buds at the base of the stems. In some cases such buds can be so numerous as to form lignotubers, a local woody swelling. Lignotubers are very common in stressed *Eucalyptus*. Gill (1981) believes them to be an adaptive mechanism for surviving stressful conditions such as fire. Similar organs were described for African plants (White 1977); in the case of Brazil Eiten (1972) calls such forms xylopods and considers them a fire-survival mechanism. In many bushes and shrubs, sprouting from the base is frequent after crown fires but such sprouts can come from regions in which no swelling occurs. This is particularly true of species that regenerate by means of root suckers or rhizomes, such as *Quercus coccifera* in the Mediterranean basin (Trabaud 1980a).

The ability of buds to survive fire also depends on what Naveh (1974) calls a plant's "vitality." Young plants are particularly vulnerable to fire unless they possess special adaptive mechanisms or traits. Vitality may be lessened in older stands (Kayll and Gimingham 1965). However, vitality may change with physiological stage and season. Survival is also affected by fire intensity (Naveh 1974) and frequency. Grano (1970) finds that the number of hardwoods in a southeastern pine forest understory in the United States was reduced by high fire frequency—11 annual fires killed 85 percent of the stock, whereas biennial fires killed only 59 percent.

Some plants survive fire because their buds are protected by tufted leaves at ground level or high on the tree. Among this type are the fire-resistant *Pandanus* in Hawaii (Vogl 1969) and *Xanthorrhoea* in Australia (Gill and Ingwersen op. cit.). These dry leafy tufts provide good insulation in the trunk region, whereas the thick moist crown region affords excellent protection to apical buds. After burning of Monocotyledon tufted crowns, foliage grows back by intercalary growth. Dicotyledons develop new leaves but old Monocotyledon leaves keep growing from protected bases. This is why Monocotyledons are often the first plants to produce new greenery after fire. Examples include *Xanthorrhoea* described by Specht ct al. (op. cit.) and by Gill and Ingwersen (op. cit.), and most tussock grasses.

All these protective mechanisms vary over time so that a plant's susceptibility to fire varies through its life cycle. Young trees have very thin bark, mature ones have very thick bark, and overmature trees have thinning bark. The apices of some plants may appear at ground level at germination, then be buried during growth. One or another of these mechanisms appears in regions where fire is frequent, regardless of fire intensity or season. Fires operate a selection among plant forms that adopt those genetic traits that allow them to survive fires and other environmental stresses.

## Stimulation of Flowering

Among fire-resistant plants, the strange phenomenon of fire-stimulated flowering has been widely observed. These plants are generally Monocotyledons, although a few examples are described for Dicotyledons (Gardner 1957). The most frequently mentioned examples are in the Graminaceae, Orchidaceae, Iridaceae, Amaryllidaceae, Xanthorrhoeaceae, and Liliaceae families.

In the tussock grasslands of mountainous New Zealand regions, a dominant species, *Chionochloa rigida,* is stimulated to flower by fire. Fire usually causes both the number of flowering tussocks and the number of inflorescences per tussock to increase. This phenomenon has been amply studied by Mark (1965a,b) and Rowley (1970).

Increased flowering has also been observed in North American grasses (Daubenmire 1968, Wein and Bliss 1973). Old (1969) finds that burning an Illinois prairie caused a tenfold increase over normal flowering. Postfire weather has a considerable effect on graminoid behavior in such widely separated locations as Illinois and New Zealand.

There are many examples of fire-stimulated flowering among terrestrial Orchidaceae: Naveh (1974) for Israel; Hall (1959) for South Africa; Gill (1980) for Australia; Trabaud (personal observation) for southern France. In South Africa, flowering of Amaryllidaceae, Iridaceae, and Liliaceae geophytes after fire is characteristic (Kruger 1977). In Australia *Xanthorrhoea* spp. provide examples of fire-induced flowering (Gill and Ingwersen op. cit.).

In *X. australis* the period of inflorescence emergence has been changed by fire; this also seems to be common in other species. Kruger (op. cit.) reports that fire-induced flowering of *Asparagus* was much earlier than normal. This was equally true for *Watsonia* in South Africa and *Chionochloa* (Mark 1965a,b) in New Zealand. Such observations suggest that species' reactions are a result of genotypic or phenotypic variation.

Many mechanisms seem to be involved in the process of inducing flowering as a result of fire. However, the results are similar because prolific flowering is followed by increased seedling production. This may be due to the greater production of seeds, or low predation of seeds on the plant or after dispersal. Mark (1965a) finds that seed production is greater in the many flowers of burned plants than in the sparse flowers of unburned ones. Gill (1981) suggests that the abundant flowering of *X. australis* at irregular intervals could be an important factor in seed production in correlation with the cycle of a predator, *Hyaletis latro*.

### Seed Retention and Fire-Stimulated Dehiscence

For many shrubs and trees, retention of seeds on the plant is an important aspect of the life cycle. This is particularly true when fire-sensitive plants are affected because stored seeds become the means by which the species survives. *Eucalyptus regnans* in Australia is a typical example of this mode of adaptation.

Mountain ash (*E. regnans*) is a very large tree in which regeneration occurs after fire only if there are mature trees in the burned stands. Fires normally occur every two or three hundred years, although they have been known to occur as frequently as 15 to 20-year intervals. This is about when fruiting begins. After a fire kill, regeneration of the species depends on the tree's bearing seeds at the time of the fire. To explain this type of regeneration, Gill (1981) advances a number of tempting hypotheses, which are examined in the following paragraphs.

The study of flower and capsule production in *E. regnans* has led to the development of three hypotheses concerning seed storage, all of which are based on the assumption that the species must maintain an adequate stock of seeds on the tree at any time in order to regenerate after a fire. The hypotheses are as follows: (1) the seed stock is necessary to counterbalance varia-

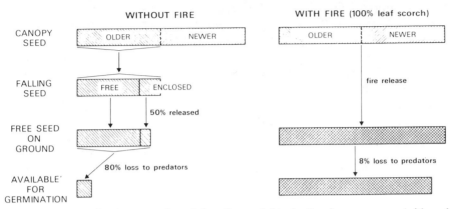

*Figure 9.2.* Tentative interpretation of data for seed fate in *Eucalyptus regnans* (with and without a crown-scorching fire) using data from Ashton (1975), Christensen (1971), and Cunningham (1960; from Gill 1981).

tions in seed input caused by biennial flowering, (2) seed storage is necessary to maintain seed input when the soil is poorly fertilized, and (3) seed storage is necessary to maintain seed supply during a drought when flowering is inadequate.

To grasp the significance of seed storage, we must follow the complete reproductive cycle from seed production to germination, with and without fire (Figure 9.2).

Seeds that are formed in a good flowering year seem to be released gradually over the following two years (Cunningham 1960). In this way variations in seed dispersal are less pronounced than fluctuations in the number of flowers produced. Without fire, half of the seeds may be considered lost each year. About 75 percent of the seeds fall; the rest remain in the capsules. Cockatoos and parrots eat or waste 30 percent of the viable seeds (Ashton 1975). Of the capsules that fall intact to the ground, 50 percent may open and release seeds (Cunningham op. cit.). Seeds on the ground are sometimes carried away by ants and other insects; Cunningham estimates that 80 percent of the free seed is lost.

After a crown-scorching fire, all the seeds in the crown may be released—this is half the year's seed production. If the entire crown is scorched, the seeds will usually be released within a few days. In the absence of any studies of losses to insects, Gill considers that the rate of loss must be the same as it would be without fire, approximately 8.2 percent. These results suggest that the amount of seed available for germination after a fire is much greater than in normal dispersal without fire. On this basis, Gill evolves the next hypothesis: (4) in a fire, enough seed is stored in the crown and then released to fall on the ground to satisfy predators so that there is a larger stock of seed available for germination.

Seedlings that germinate in the unburned forest die rapidly because of the lack of sufficient light, attacks by fungi, and browsing by animals (Ashton and MacAuley 1972). However, in seedlings produced after a fire the chances of survival are greatly increased because of adequate light and nutrients (ash). This observation leads Gill to develop another hypothesis: (5) the fire-stimulated dehiscence of crown-stored seeds permits seedling development in a physically and chemically enriched habitat.

In some pine species cones remain closed unless the heat produced by a fire opens them. A good example of pine cone serotiny is *Pinus contorta*. In young trees of this species the cones always seem open, whereas in older trees the cones may be open or closed (Lotan 1975). Serotiny can vary considerably within a stand according to altitude. For *P. contorta* and *P. banksiana*, bark thickness seems to be correlated with the extent of serotiny. The thicker the bark, the lower the serotiny. Serotiny is also correlated with the frequency of fires; the lower the fire frequency and intensity, the lower the serotiny (Lotan 1976). High fire intensities could be expected to favor serotinous genotypes since seeds of open-coned trees would be preferentially destroyed by fire. According to Naveh (1975), Mediterranean populations of *P. halepensis* and *P. brutia* have serotinous cones.

Many other genera produce seeds that are stored on the plant, then dispersed immediately following a fire. In Australia, examples are found among Cupressaceae, Casuarinaceae, Proteaceae, and Myrtaceae (Gardner op. cit.); in South Africa this type of seed storage and dispersal is found in Proteaceae (Williams 1972).

## Ground Storage of Seed with Germination Stimulated by Fire

There is no information on the morphology, physiology, or ecology of seeds stored in the ground that appear after a fire. There is little information on the effects of fire on seed germination, although Muller et al. (1968) show that California annuals appearing after fire depend on the allelopathic effects of germination inhibition and the uncovering of seeds by fire.

To illustrate this fire-related trait, Gill chooses the example of *Acacia cyclops,* originally found in western Australia and later spread to South Africa. This plant has become a problem of particular interest with respect to the conservation of native species in the Cape of Good Hope region (Taylor 1977). This species stores large amounts of seed in the ground (up to $250 \times 10^6$/ha) and is propagated rapidly by fire at the expense of indigenous flora. The germination of *A. cyclops* seeds has been studied by Jones (1963) for South Africa and by Christensen (1978) for Australia. Jones finds that heat increases germination; Christensen cannot obtain any increase in seed germination through heating in comparison with control seeds. The basic difference between the African and Australian *A. cyclops* habitats seems to be a result of fire frequency. Taylor (1977) observes that South African vegetation frequently burned; Christensen and Kimber (1975) point out that *A. cyclops* populations in western Australia rarely burned.

Floyd (1966) presents data illustrating the relationship between duration of exposure and temperature. Long periods of low temperatures brought about the same germination rate as short periods of high temperature. Field data gathered by Christensen and Kimber (op. cit.) suggest that severe fires bring about germination but destroy large stores of seeds enclosed in the ground. The effects of fire on germination have also been studied with respect to California (Keeley 1977), Australia (Floyd 1966, 1976), Brazil (Rizzini 1976), and France (Trabaud 1970, 1980b).

## CONSEQUENCES OF SELECTION OF FIRE-ADAPTIVE TRAITS

Many vital attributes of species may be regarded as fire-adaptive traits. In addition to those already mentioned, other possibilities include seed burial, plant longevity, chemical composition (see preceding section), flowering period, and leaf fall period. Many adaptive mechanisms may facilitate the survival or reproduction of plants that live in a fire-prone environment.

An adaptive trait is a property of a species' life cycle and the fire regime is a selective mechanism in a fire-prone environment. Fire intensity, frequency, and season as well as fire type are important for survival. Flowering, dehiscence, and seed germination may be profoundly altered by fire intensity. However, fire should be considered only one environmental factor among many that may have produced the same results. Thus flowering induced by fire may be only one of the phenomena that initiate large-scale fruit production. Periodic flowering may be essential for preventing heavy loss due to predation but seed storage is imperative if seed sources are not available at the time of the fire. Flowering behavior seems to be a more general phenomenon but fire induces flowering as, it seems, it induces germination of dispersed seeds. Other, local, environmental factors may also come into play.

Janzen (1967) shows that some Central American swollen-thorn acacias survive fire because of their root suckers. Ants form colonies in the sprouts and eliminate vegetation around the base of the plant, thereby lessening the likelihood of the plant's being killed by fire.

Most fire-adaptive traits seem to have evolved genetically. Some plants apparently have been subjected to a process of selection such that they develop rhizomes with flowering at ground level or underground for the purpose of surviving fires (Carlquist 1976, Rourke and Weins 1977).

### Reproductive Cycles and Fire-Adaptive Behavior

In order to survive a disturbance, species utilize various strategies that are adapted to their environment. Thus the frequency of a given disturbance, say, fire, may lead to the selection of certain vital attributes and, consequently, favor different modes of growth. It follows that the mode of reproduction, that is, the life cycle parameters that are immediately responsible for the perpetuation of the population, will be greatly affected by differing fire frequencies.

After a fire, plants can either reproduce (generally sexually) or regenerate (production of new plant parts: regrowth of branches, new sprouts, or underground organs). Species may use whichever method of survival environmental conditions or the extent of fire damage dictates.

In order to determine the evolutionary impact of fire frequency on survival strategies and reproduction, however, the effect of selection must be distinguished from other environmental parameters. If we say that fire has operated a selective influence in the evolution of a species, we must provide better evidence than mere observance of occasional wildfire occurrence. The periods of time without fire may be critical for survival and resiliency of a species (i.e., the species' ability to reestablish). How has this problem been solved in various plant forms?

Most grasslands are maintained by fire (Daubenmire op. cit., Vogl 1974). When the formations are not burned, there is invasion by woody plants (Bragg and Hulbert 1976). In temperate and tropical regions alike, dominant grassland species are hemicryptophytes with rhizomes that allow the plants to resist fire successfully. The relatively small caryopses, large awns, and the persistent pubescences of the seeds of some species (*Andropogon*) enhance their ability to invade recent burns. Regeneration from basal buds after the destruction of aboveground parts is well developed in most perennials. After a fire seed production is generally abundant (Daubenmire op. cit., Hadley and Kieckhefer 1963, Vogl 1974, West 1971). Some species can propagate by seeds and stolons or rhizomes, with the organs varying according to the fire intensity. Many herbaceous plants can survive fire by means of regenerating underground organs. In this case there is inter and intraspecific variability in regeneration such as in *Liatris*, an American prairie forb. Schall (1978) finds that after a fire there is a loss of juvenile plants but an increase in the number of seedlings. In a frequently burned grassland the dominant survival strategy consists of perennials which, because they can regenerate from underground organs, can appropriate more space and keep it for long periods.

Other species are fire tolerant, such as *Epilobium angustifolium* and *Pteridium aquilinum*. They are examples of strategies adapted to periodic intense fires that do not destroy the parent populations but open up adjacent areas.

Annual grasslands are common in Mediterranean climates. The increased frequency of fire due to human intervention is probably the main reason for their development (Wells 1962). However, frequent fire is not necessary to maintain the grasslands and how long they last depends on their neighbors since some communities nearby may have the ability to invade their territory (Wells 1962, Westman 1976). Although annual grasses are not well adapted for surviving annual fires, they do possess traits that allow them to survive frequent fire such as effective seed burial mechanisms that store seeds underground, safe from the fire's heat. In some Mediterranean climatic regions, California in particular, no herbaceous plant seeds can germinate unless the shrub cover has been destroyed by fire; then many herbaceous species proliferate. Germination of these species begins after the first winter rains following the fire. The biological cycle is completed in spring. Most of these species are annuals and do not survive into the second year after the fire (Keeley et al. 1981). Annual grasslands are a most resilient herbaceous community that exists independently of the fire regime.

Swamp vegetation frequently regenerates by means of stolons or rhizomes but is, nevertheless, very sensitive to the heat produced by fire. Garren (1943) observes that swamp species are killed by dry-season fires because roots close to the soil surface are killed. However, most swamplands in the southeastern United States experience fire every 30 to 100 years. Fire destroys the woody and marshy vegetation, leaving room for underwater aquatic plants (Cypert 1972). Tundra wetland species regenerate rapidly after a fire, except a very severe one (Wein and Bliss op. cit.).

Mediterranean sclerophyllous vegetation types exist on all continents except Antarctica and are quite similar in many respects. California chaparral has been studied in considerable detail. It consists of 1.5 to 3 m high shrubs distributed in a mosaic that is determined by fire. Some species can live a very long time, while others such as *Ceanothus* live no more than 40 to 60 years (Keeley and Zedler 1978, Schlesinger and Gill 1978; Figure 9.3).

Seed production in chaparral species varies widely from year to year, depending mostly on precipitation. There is no indication that fertility decreases with age (Keeley 1977, 1981, Keeley and Keeley 1977) and dispersal can be accomplished by wind, gravity, or animals. Build-up of seeds in the ground also varies greatly. Most species (*Adenostoma, Ceanothus,* and *Arc-*

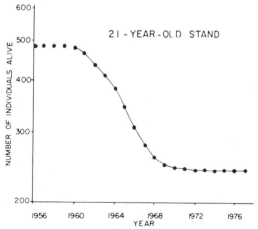

**Figure 9.3.**  Density of live *Ceanothus megacarpus* shrubs after fire in 1955 (from Schlesinger and Gill 1978).

*tostaphylos*) need the intense heat produced by fire in order to germinate (Hadley 1961, Quick 1935, Stone and Juhren 1953), but others, not requiring the stimulus of heat, can germinate promptly. After a fire there is an abundance of seedlings of *Adenostoma fasciculatum, Ceanothus,* and *Arctostaphylos* species, all from seeds stored in the ground and germinating the year following the fire. Most chaparral species (except for some *Ceanothus* and *Arctostaphylos* species) sprout after fire. These two strategies characterize the response of different species to fire frequencies—those that produce seeds are adapted to infrequent fires whereas those that sprout from the trunk can resist repeated fires (Keeley 1981). Dominant chaparral species as well as dominant garrigue species (Trabaud 1980a) are those that adopt both strategies and can regenerate by means of either seeds or sprouts; in addition, they have burls at the base of their trunks.

Lignotubers and burls are also found in shrubs in other Mediterranean regions, including Australian mallee, where they may be highly developed (Gill 1975, 1981), and in South Africa, where they are quite common (Kruger op. cit.). They are rarely found outside Mediterranean regions. Lignotubers supply a reservoir of carbohydrates to sustain the plant if defoliation occurs during dormancy. Since lignotubers are not necessary for sprouting, they are not necessarily closely related to fire; they are a fire-adaptive trait that is related to the Mediterranean climate.

The few woody Dicotyledons that cannot regenerate by sprouting reproduce by seed production according to Keeley (1981). These are fire-type species because they are very common in chaparral, mallee, and fynbos but practically absent from Chilean matorral, a Mediterranean region with low natural fire frequency.

In coastal sage scrub, fire is less frequent and species produce seeds that germinate without the aid of fire. All species can produce healthy shoots from the caudex or the root system (Keeley 1981).

On the coastal plain of the southeastern United States there grows a scrub species that is said to originate in pine forests that were destroyed by frequent fires at a given period. Fires in these regions are now infrequent (Webber 1935). All species of this type regenerate vigorously from the roots after a fire. However, fires are not very intense because the vegetation is always quite moisture-laden and there are practically no herbaceous species. These scrub plants differ from chaparral types in that seeds are not stored and germination does not require the stimulus of fire. Although not as fire-specific as in chaparral, they do exhibit good resistance to high fire frequency.

In desert communities shrubs can throw out new shoots from the base after a fire. Some species are healthier than others in this respect (Box et al. 1967). Fires are rare and most species produce seeds that can germinate in the absence of fire. In the brush steppes dominated by *Artemisia tridentata* and *Larrea tridentata* most species cannot regenerate vegetatively after a fire and many seeds are killed by fire (Mueggler 1956); therefore, when fire is frequent, the brush steppe is replaced by herbaceous formations (Houston

1973). If 80 years go by without a fire occurring, the *Artemisia* populations reestablish. This steppe type is not fire-resilient.

Many species grow in the forests of northeastern North America such as *Rubus, Vaccinium, Lonicera, Rosa, Rhus, Sassafras, Crataegus,* and *Symphoricarpus* that can reproduce by means of stolons and rhizomes. Most species have brilliantly colored fleshy fruits that are very attractive to birds. Many species have viable seeds stored in the ground for long periods of time (Moore and Wein 1977). When an opening is created by fire or another disturbance these species quickly invade the clearings, thus they use less energy to grow vegetatively but a great deal more for seed production.

Before European settlement, the Sierra Nevada forests of California experienced frequent fires, every 5 to 10 years or so (Kilgore 1973). Some of these fires were due to lightning, whereas others were probably set by Indians (Kilgore and Taylor 1979). According to Keeley (1981), these forests evolved under the influence of a temporal fire-frequency mosaic, meaning that there were periods when surface fires were frequent, followed by periods with no fire and ending in destructive crown fires. The trees apparently reflect the mosaic, with the dominant ones being long-lived (300 to over 600 years) and producing seeds by the age of 40 years that could be dispersed by wind. Vegetative regeneration (shoots) is practically unknown in these species, which are very sensitive to fire as juveniles. In order to survive fires, they must be at least 20 years old. Once they attain maturity, these trees can passively resist fire because of their thick bark, and their seeds need an unobstructed area of mineral soil such as one finds after a fire. *Abies concolor*, however, is very sensitive to fire and cannot survive a fire of much intensity. The mixed conifer forests present various adaptations to frequent and to infrequent fire regimes.

The case of *Pinus contorta* is slightly different, in that in those parts of the Sierra Nevada where fires are infrequent the cones are not serotinous, whereas in the Rocky Mountains where fires are more frequent (Komarek 1967, Loope and Gruell 1973), the cones are serotinous (Brown 1975, Lotan 1976) so that they can reestablish after a fire.

Southern California chaparral conifers illustrate variable fire-adaptive traits. *Cupressus forbesii* has serotinous cones but long fire-free periods are required for seed production (Zedler 1977). Chaparral pines with serotinous cones exhibit similar behavior to cypress but are more resilient when fires are frequent (Vogl 1973). *Pseudotsuga macrocarpa* does not have serotinous cones but can throw shoots; like cypress, however, it is not resilient in frequent fires.

The seeds of pines (*Pinus edulis, P. quadrifola*) and junipers (*Juniperus occidentalis, J. scopulorum*) of the pinyon–juniper woodland in the Rocky Mountains are dispersed by birds and can remain dormant underground for long periods. None of these species can regenerate vegetatively after fire.

The pine species of eastern North America (*Pinus echinata, P. taeda*) resist surface fires very well; even seedlings and saplings of *P. echinata* can regenerate from the base after a fire. These two species are quite resilient in frequent fires because the juveniles can resprout and the mature trees have a thick, fire-resistant bark. Two other pines, *P. elliottii* and *P. palustris,* show similar adaptations, other than the ability to regenerate vegetatively. The maximum fire adaptability occurs in the most localized pines, *P. rigida* and *P. serotina,* which can throw out shoots at any age and produce seeds very early (at the age of three or four); they also have serotinous cones (Little 1974).

The dominant boreal conifers (*Pinus banksiana, Picea glauca, P. mariana*) are closely associated with fire; they produce seeds that germinate very rapidly after a fire and quickly invade burned areas. Only *Abies balsamea* cannot resist fire and can regenerate only in the absence of fire. On the other hand, *Populus tremuloides* is an aggressive pioneer and rapid invader (Viereck 1973).

Deciduous broadleaf forests grow in temperate climates in both hemispheres. Forest fires are rare; in North America, such fires are a result of drought and cover vast areas (McLean and Wein 1977). There is considerable evidence that North American forests burned in previous centuries (Cwynar 1978, Frissell 1973, Lorimer 1977). However, eastern American forests are a fairly stable type within a matrix in which severe local disturbances and occasional widespread fires occur. On the basis of structure or floristic composition, it can be seen that a variety of survival strategies has been involved. Generally, pioneers produce numerous light seeds that are borne by the wind and germinate where they fall. Others produce fleshy fruits that attract birds so that the trees can colonize clearings as the seeds can remain dormant longer. Finally, mature forest species yield large fruits such as acorns and beechnuts.

To understand the evolutionary role of fire in ecosystems it is necessary to know the history of these ecosystems. Adaptive strategies are the product of evolution and genetic control. The vital attributes selected as a result of fire do not necessarily involve resilience; annuals are resilient and can survive annual fires but they are not specifically adapted to fire. Frequency and extent of fire are also important because they exert the greatest force of selection; they are related to fire probability in terms of time and space.

The type of growth strongly affects strategy. To illustrate this point, grasslands and shrublands are subject to fires whose frequency and extent are predictable; grasses can reappear, flower, and produce seeds in a few months, but shrubs cannot. Some trees have unique fire-resistant traits such as thick bark and natural branching. For a given member of a given population, the process of postfire sprouting is another reproductive tactic shared by several fire-adapted species.

### Vital Attributes and Persistence

To characterize species according to their response to disturbance or environmental stress and predict changes over time as vegetation grows, scien-

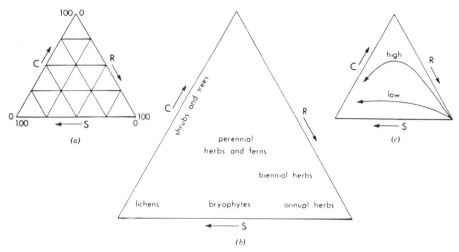

***Figure 9.4.*** Triangular model of Grime (1977). (*a*) The three primary strategies, competitive, C, stress tolerant, S, and ruderal, R, are each shown on an axis. (*b*) The approximate distribution of selected life forms and taxa in relation to the three primary strategies. (*c*) The course of successional change in high and low productivity environments (from Grime 1977).

tists have attempted to determine traits that allow species to withstand upheaval. These are the vital attributes.

One of the first classifications was done by MacArthur and Wilson (1967). It stresses the evolutionary strategies of each species. There are the r strategies in generalist and opportunist species, and the K strategies in specialist and equilibrial ones. Many authors have since attempted to explain succession in terms of species movement on the basis of these strategies (Colinvaux 1973, Drury and Nisbet 1973, Loucks 1970, Pickett 1976). Opportunistic species are adapted to dispersal and colonizing unoccupied areas, whereas the slower-growing equilibrial species occupy habitats and remain there but do not produce many means of dispersal.

Later, Grime (1974, 1977) proposes a new classification in which he describes three primary strategies in terms of a species ability to compete and to tolerate stress and disturbance (Figure 9.4). These strategies result from the interactions between stress intensity and disturbance in a given habitat. In habitats where stress and disturbances are of low intensity and infrequent, the competition (C strategy) is the best. Species that use this strategy have a low reproductive rate but occupy more space. Habitats where stress is of low intensity and disturbance is of high intensity are associated with species that use ruderal strategies (R); such species have a short life expectancy but rapid growth and large reproductive effort. Finally, habitats where stress is of high intensity and disturbance of low intensity are associated with plants that adopt a stress-tolerant (S) strategy; such species have low growth rates and exploit favorable conditions on a temporary basis. According to Grime, high stress and low disturbance inhibit plant establishment; this assertion is debatable, however (Trabaud and Lepart 1980).

Grime (1977) considers that his R strategy corresponds to MacArthur and Wilson's r selection and that his S strategy corresponds to their K selection; highly competitive species occupy an intermediate position.

Noble and Slatyer (1977, 1980) and Noble (1981) suggest that plants be characterized in terms of the vital attributes associated with the method of reproduction and of persistence after a disturbance. The vital attributes are:

Method of arrival or persistence of propagules at the site after a disturbance.

Conditions in which the species establish and grow to maturity.

Time taken to reach critical stages in the (individual's) life history.

Noble and Slatyer recognize four critical events in the life history of a species: the juvenile stage, when the majority of the members of a population in a site are immature; the mature (adult) stage, when the majority of the members of the population are mature (although there may be juvenile individuals present as well); a propagule stage, when the species is present in propagule form only (seeds, bulbs, dormant roots, etc.); an extinct stage, when the species is not present at the site in any form. Using these four events, Noble and Slatyer define 10 primary vital attributes (Table 9.1);

**Table 9.1.  Vital Attributes Associated with the Method of Persistence during and Immediately after a Disturbance (from Noble 1981)**

*Propagule Based*

| D | Species with highly *d*ispersed propagules. |
|---|---|
| S | Species with a long-lived propagule store, e.g., a long-lived seed store in the *s*oil. |
| G | A special case of S, in which the entire seed store either *g*erminates or perishes at a disturbance. |
| C | Species with a short-lived propagule store, e.g., seed stored in the *c*anopy. |

*Vegetative Based*

| V | Species that resprout but must pass through a ju*v*enile stage before becoming mature again, e.g., a species that coppices from the stem base or lignotuber (burl). |
|---|---|
| U | Species that are virtually *u*naffected by the disturbance. |
| W | A special case of U, in which individuals at the adult stage are virtually unaffected, but those at a juvenile stage are killed (*w*iped out). |

*Combinations*

Correspond to D, S, and G except that the adult stages are virtually unaffected by the disturbance.

**Table 9.2.    Vital Attributes Associated with the Conditions for Establishment (from Noble 1981)**

| | |
|---|---|
| T | Species that can establish and grow to maturity both immediately after a disturbance and for an indefinite period thereafter (i.e., *to*lerant). |
| I | Species that can establish only immediately after a disturbance (i.e., *i*ntolerant). |
| R | Species that cannot establish at the site immediately after a disturbance, but can do some time later (i.e., they have some *r*equirements that must be filled, e.g., shade, before they can establish). |

there is a second group of vital attributes that describes the conditions in which a species that has propagules available at a site can establish and grow to maturity (Table 9.2). The authors recognize two stages of community development after a disturbance during which competition for resources is often low, and one stage during which competition intensifies as the community closes. Although 30 behavioral types can be described on the basis of the vital attributes, Noble and Slatyer recognize only 14 distinct patterns (Figure 9.5).

Propagules with a short life expectancy that are stored so as to be able to survive a fire (vital attribute C) represent a simple persistence model that does not require a specialized mode of dispersal, long-term storage, or sprouting ability. However, species with this vital attribute cannot persist on a site without frequent disturbances. If the fire-free period is shorter than the time required for a species to attain maturity, the species will become extinct locally. Once established, a species with T or R vital attributes can persist on a site for an indefinite period between disturbances. CT and CR attribute species can persist in situations when the period between disturbances is rarely very short but often quite long, whereas CI species are confined to

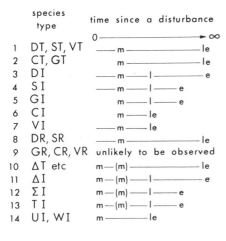

*Figure 9.5.* Life stage parameter characteristics for each of the species types. The species types are grouped on the basis of similar patterns of behavior in replacement sequences. The critical events are the time to reach reproductive maturity (m), the longevity of the species population (l), and the longevity of its propagule pool (e; from Noble 1981).

sites where the disturbance frequency range is small. S attribute species can persist for short occasional periods between two fires by using the common pool of propagules. Many understory shrubs in forest where fires occur belong to the SI type. Species with the D vital attribute have the ability to disperse their propagules highly as long as there is an appropriate mosaic that can provide the source of adult individuals; these species have a constantly available propagule pool. This attribute seems to be the ideal persistence type. Many pioneer species and fire weeds belong to the D type.

Vegetative resprouting is very common in fire-prone environments. Wells (1969) says that the ability of chaparral species to sprout is an original trait and that the restriction to regeneration by seed production is a result of the loss of this trait. Many chaparral, heath, maquis, and garrigue species belong to type VI. Some species can regenerate through seedlings but according to Noble (1981), the ability to sprout and to store seeds for a short time is another attribute of type V species. Type VI species have the advantage over type CI ones in fire-prone environments because they can regenerate during short intervals between fires. Long fire-free periods favor regeneration by seedlings. Type VT species have a very good ability to persist and become dominant because they can regenerate vegetatively immediately after a fire, an attribute that gives them the competitive edge over seedlings because after regenerating they can persist indefinitely. *Pteridium aquilinum, Quercus coccifera,* and *Imperata* sp. are examples.

Fire frequency can be the main determinant of strategy type. The system proposed by Noble and Slatyer (1977, 1980) emphasizes methods of persistence and time of regeneration after a disturbance such as fire, but pays less attention to postregenerative growth and competitive interaction. This is because in environments with recurrent fire, conditions requiring the ability to persist and regenerate occur more frequently, whereas competitive interactions among adults cannot be completed before the next fire.


## EXAMPLES OF FIRE-PRONE ECOSYSTEMS

### Boreal Forest

The dominant characteristic of the boreal forest is its vastness with stands comprising few species, where pine and spruce are the main types. Other trees only play the role of companions.

Among tree species in the boreal coniferous forest, the white pine (*Pinus strobus*), red pine (*P. resinosa*), and jack pine (*P. banksiana*) are frequently referred to as typical postfire species. Many authors conclude that these species do not reestablish independently without the aid of fire, either in a natural forest or after logging (Ahlgren 1959, 1960, 1970, Beaufait 1960a,b, Van Wagner 1970; Figure 9.6). The high flammability of the needles of these pines in the form of litter increases the fire probability. The cones can open

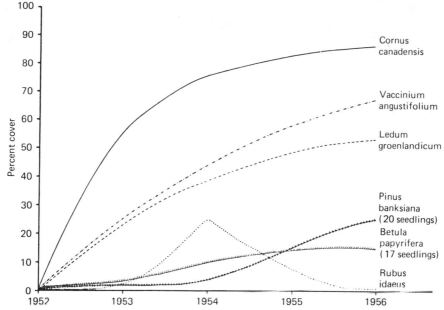

***Figure 9.6.*** Graph showing percent of cover by various species in a sample 1/1000 acre burned plot for five years after the fire (from Ahlgren 1959).

only at a fairly high temperature, which means that when a fire occurs, although it may destroy the entire stand, it causes the cones to open and release seeds to the ground from which a new forest grows. In this way, fire maintains the same specific composition of the stand.

Pure red pine stands are considered the most flammable because their crown structure is ideal for the spread of crown fires, and their highly compact litter burns rapidly (Van Wagner op. cit.).

The species with the most remarkable adaptation to fire is the jack pine (*Pinus banksiana*). This pine has serotinous cones that remain closed for several years. The seeds retain their capacity for germination for many years (as many as 20, according to Ahlgren 1959). In a fire the heat destroys the resin that keeps the scales of the cone closed, and seeds fall in profusion after the fire. The optimum temperature for opening cones is 50 to 60°C (Beaufait 1960a, Cayford 1963, 1970). In addition, Beaufait observes that seeds can resist temperatures in the 370° to 540°C range if they are of short duration.

These authors believe that serotiny is a fire-adaptive mechanism of the jack pine acquired through the process of natural selection as a result of frequent fires. However, the cones of white and red pine, which are not serotinous, are easily damaged or destroyed by crown fire. The fire adaptation of the jack pine goes much further, making the forest almost monospecific. Since the closed cones contain viable seeds for a long period, the seeds are soon available for germination after fire. The white and red pine, on the other hand, do not store their seeds but disperse them every year; therefore, seedlings are at the mercy of fire. As a result, with fire after fire, the jack pine wins out over the other pines.

Other conifers also belong to the boreal forest region; their adaptive mechanisms allow them to survive fire or constitute postfire stands. After a fire, the mineral soil (or a thin humus layer) is a favorable habitat for spruce germination.

The white spruce (*Picea glauca*) disperses its seeds in autumn. If a fire occurs in summer leaving seed-bearing trees standing, a white spruce stand can reestablish. The black spruce (*P. mariana*) is much more dependent on fire. It has semiserotinous cones that can store seeds for several years and that are opened by heat. Also, black spruce cones are located close to the middle of the crown, where they are least damaged by fire (Ahlgren 1974). Seeds are dispersed during the year following the fire. When the seed-bearing trees are located near swamps, black spruce establishes rapidly in the burned marshy area replacing tamarack (*Larix laricina*), according to Johnston (1971).

## Chaparral

Chaparral is a type of vegetation that is created by fire and that is remarkably suited for persisting despite recurring fires. It is also the most flammable vegetation type in the United States. For this reason and on account of the growth of the population of southern California, it presents a very considerable fire hazard. On the basis of ancient evidence, Biswell (1974) estimates that chaparral lands have experienced fire for over 100,000 years. One of the main reasons is the Mediterranean climate, with virtually rainless summers that desiccate ground and vegetation, high daytime temperatures, and low relative humidity, along with high Santa Ana winds from the inland.

The first fires were undoubtedly caused by lightning (Biswell op. cit., Show and Kotok 1923), so fire has always been naturally associated with chaparral. However, in more recent times lightning-caused fires in unforested areas are much less numerous than those due to man. Before the first settlers arrived, the Indians used to light fires. When the Europeans came to California, fires became both more numerous and more destructive. Miners and loggers used to set fires to facilitate mining and burn debris.

From this it can be seen that chaparral is well adapted to periodic fires. Many shrub species sprout from stumps, others from rhizomes, and propagules are produced when the plant is quite young. The propagules can remain dormant in the ground litter for a long time. In addition, some species have developed traits that make them highly flammable and thus dependent on fire for maintenance and optimum growth. Conversely, frequent fires depend on the fuels that feed the flames (Countryman and Philpot op. cit., Nord and Countryman 1972, Philpot 1969a).

Chaparral species sprout quickly; this enables them to grow and spread rapidly, giving them an advantage over species that can reproduce only by means of seeds, because shoots soon become larger and more vigorous than seedlings. This ability to sprout may be regarded as a fire-adaptive trait. Another such trait is the ability of chaparral seed to remain dormant yet viable in the ground litter for long periods (Quick op. cit.). Two more adaptive mechanisms are the production of heat-resistant seeds (Sampson 1944, Stone and Juhren 1951), and its converse, the production of seeds that require heat to germinate (Went et al. 1952).

Chamise (*Adenostoma fasciculatum*) does not sprout as vigorously as other species. Old chamise is much more sensitive to fire than young plants. Old plants cannot produce new sprouts but they can produce seeds; the fact that chamise populations can reproduce in two ways (sprouting and seed production) leads to the growth of healthy young stands in place of senescent ones and could prove to be a better adaptation to fire.

Postfire succession in chaparral has been the subject of many investigations (Biswell 1963, Hanes 1971, Hanes and Jones 1967, Horton and Kraebel 1955, Patric and Hanes 1964, Sampson op. cit., Stone and Juhren 1951, Sweeney 1956, 1967, Vogl and Schorr 1972). Postfire vegetation types can be easily predicted from a knowledge of fire types at the time of the fire. In practice, what occurs is autosuccession (Hanes op. cit.; Figure 9.7). Few new species appear; however, some species that had stored seeds underground for some years may germinate even though their parent plants died many years earlier.

When a fire occurs in stands of vigorously sprouting species like *Arctostaphylos glandulosa* and *Quercus dumosa*—the most widespread species after chamise—these species emerge from the fire as strong and as numerous as before, eventually regaining their prefire density and coverage (Biswell 1974). Hanes (op. cit.) believes that fire is necessary to keep stands strong and healthy; old stands (over 60 years) show signs of degeneration.

## Mediterranean Shrublands

Most communities of the Mediterranean Basin are fire prone. *Quercus ilex* resists fire fairly well; after a fire, woodlands recover without any major floral or structural change (Trabaud 1980, Trabaud and Lepart 1980; Figures 9.8 and 9.9).

*Quercus suber,* or cork oak, is more typical of forests that can resist fire passively. If fire is neither frequent nor intense, open *Q. suber* forests can be maintained without intervention.

A special case is that of the conifer forests belonging to the most flammable ecosystems in the region. *Pinus halepensis* and *P. brutia* make up great forests in the Mediterranean lands. Both pines reproduce only by seeds (Naveh 1974, Trabaud 1970, 1980) which are dispersed by cones that often burst during a fire. After a fire, pine forests are colonized by a great number

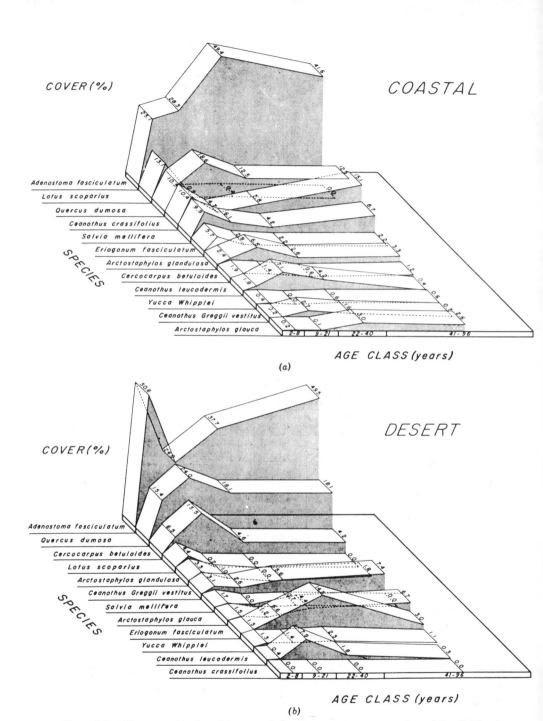

**Figure 9.7.** Changes with time in cover of the 12 most common species of the California chaparral after fire (from Hanes 1981). Species are ranked according to their values at two to eight years. Percentages are based on mean values in each age class. (*a*) Coastal exposures. (*b*) Desert exposures.

**Figure 9.8.** *Quercus ilex* woodland 18 years after a wildfire. *Q. ilex* regenerated from sprouts. Photo by Louis Trabaud.

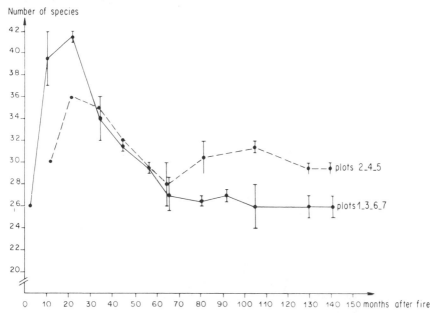

**Figure 9.9.** Floristic richness of dense *Quercus ilex* woodlands (from Trabaud and Lepart 1980).

**Figure 9.10.**  *Pinus halepensis* forest 15 years after a wildfire. *P. halepensis* reproduced by seeds. Photo by Louis Trabaud.

of pine seedlings that become a new pine forest (Figure 9.10). Because the seeds can germinate in mineral soil in areas exposed to full light where competition is less severe and minerals are abundant, these pine forests are perpetuated almost indefinitely.

The *Quercus coccifera* garrigue is the most typical example of a stand due partly to fire and maintained by fire. The garrigue covers about two million hectares in the western Mediterranean Basin; in the eastern Basin the species is *Q. calliprinos* (Le Houerou 1974). In about five years following fire, the *Q. coccifera* garrigue resumes its prefire aspect (Trabaud 1974, 1980). The garrigues are maintained in balance for centuries by periodic burning of a pyrostable vegetation type. The root system of *Q. coccifera* is very strong although shallow and after a fire the species can regenerate by sprouting from the base or by means of root suckers. As seedlings are rarely observed, the species apparently spreads vegetatively under the stimulus of fire.

The Ericaceae of the maquis all produce vigorous sprouts but can also regenerate by means of seeds, so that they dominate the early successional stages of burned maquis (Naveh 1974, Le Houerou op. cit.).

Some swards are maintained by or are created by recurring fire. Naveh (1974), speaking of the Near East, mentions such species of *Oryzopsis miliacea, Hyparrhenia hirta,* and *Andropogon distachium* in which inflorescence growth is stimulated by fire. These species form grasslands identical to the *Brachypodium ramosum* swards of the western Basin (Trabaud 1980, Trabaud and Lepart 1980).

## The South African Fynbos

Fynbos, which is the typical Mediterranean vegetation type of South Africa, will burn at any season of the year, weather permitting. From about the fourth year after burning it will have accumulated sufficient fuel to burn again.

Natural fires caused by lightning must have occurred at intervals of from 6 to 40 years (Bands 1977) because if they had occurred regularly at more frequent intervals, many seed-regenerating species would have been eliminated (Kruger op. cit.). However, even after a long period during which every effort has been made to exclude fires, there are few areas of fynbos older than 40 years. As might be expected, fuel loads increase with age and many of the living shrubs are themselves highly flammable such as *Stoebe* spp. Fire hazard, fuel load, and potential fire intensity are positively correlated with postfire age of the veld.

Most unscheduled fires occur in summer in the Western Cape winter rainfall area and in midwinter in the Southern Cape constant rainfall zone, when warm desiccating berg winds create conditions of extreme fire hazard (Bands op. cit.). The Eastern Cape with its predominantly summer rain experiences most fires in winter, although spring is also a time of considerable hazard. Fire seasons are not well defined, however, and no month has been entirely free of fires in any fynbos region over any 10 years of record (Bands op. cit.). Lightning fires tend to occur in spring and autumn.

Periodic fires are necessary to maintain the full range of fynbos species, many of which complete only part of their postfire development cycle before producing seeds and drying; they reappear at the same phase of the cycle after the next fire (Kruger op. cit.). Most fynbos plants resprout after a fire and many species exhibit pronounced positive reproductive responses to fire, sexually through increased flowering, but sometimes through enhanced vegetative reproduction as in *Watsonia pyramidata* and *Cliffortia lineari-folia.* The degree of response ranges from apparent complete reliance on periodic fire for reproduction through to indirect responses in shrubs that demonstrate increased vigor following fire. In some instances fire may induce flowering much earlier than normal (e.g., *Asparagus* spp.). All species observed to date mature and produce enough seed to ensure their survival in a period of 10 to 15 years (*Protea repens* and *Erica mauretanica*). The fauna of the fynbos ecosystem has also adapted to periodic fire and, as with the flora, many animal species complete only some developmental cycles after a fire. Thus recurring fire maintains a high specific diversity in fynbos.

## Australian Heath

Mediterranean heath communities in southern Australia exist in deep sandy soil that is extremely poor in nutrients coupled with a Mediterranean climate that receives about 500 to 600 mm of rainfall, mainly in winter. Fire has probably occurred more often in Australia than in most other shrubland regions since the arrival of the Europeans about 150 years ago (Gill and Groves 1981). Fuel loads become sufficient to sustain a fire within five years, sometimes earlier if rainfall is favorable. In southern California, by contrast, 20 years is the mean time required for fuels to build to hazardous levels.

Fire kills and consumes all vegetation above ground level. Shortly after a fire, a number of plants sprout from underground root systems. The first two or three years after the fire, Cyperaceae, restiods, some geophytes, and *Xanthorrhoea australis* dominate (Specht et al., op. cit.). There are few annuals, especially grasses, and these appear only during the first year after a fire; after this, they are never as abundant as in chaparral. The first five or six years after fire, shrubs such as *Casuarina pusilla* and some *Leptospermum*, which can regenerate by basal sprouting, dominate. About the tenth year, the small woody species that reproduce by seed dispersal become more numerous. Most of these are proteaceous types like *Banksia ornata*. If the habitat exists without fire for 25 to 35 years, *C. pusilla* and *B. ornata* become overmature and are not replaced. The senescent stage is attained about 40 to 50 years after fire. This general pattern is essentially the same as for fynbos except that in Australia, Epacridaceae shrubs never seem to dominate in the same way as fynbos *Erica* does three to six years after a fire. About 30 years later, *B. marginata* and *X. australis* dominate (Figure 9.11). *B. marginata* resprouts from the base and can maintain its position in the community by forming suckers. Specht et al. (op. cit.) never observed new *X. australis* seedlings, but as the individual plants are quite long-lived, mortality in recurring fires is apparently compensated for by vegetative regeneration. In some cases the senescent stage of the Australian heath is associated with an increase in the number of tall shrubs such as *Leptospermum laevigatum* or some *Eucalyptus* spp. Where this change occurs, and only there, the Australian Mediterranean heath can be considered a stage in the succession toward woods dominated by *B. serrata* or *Eucalyptus baxteri*, or tall *Leptospermum laevigatum* thickets.

In this quick survey we have seen that many vegetation species are related to fire. We must remember that fire is also involved in other parts of the world, though its role there is sometimes not so well known. Every year, fires occur in some region of all the continents save Antarctica.

From this we conclude that fire, whether caused by nature or man, has had a profound effect on the vegetation types of the world. Any time and

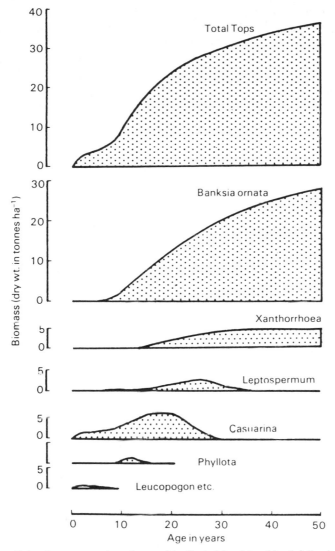

*Figure 9.11.* Secondary succession observed in Dark Island heathland following fire (from Specht et al. 1958).

anywhere there has been an appropriate combination of fuels, fire conditions, and sources of fire, vegetation has burned. Thus, more and more, fire is being regarded as a part of the evolutionary cycle of an ecosystem. Actually, fire does not cause all that much damage to an ecosystem or so seriously interfere with the time scale of nature, but most people consider fire a destructive force because of the economic damage it can do. In fact, fire only slows down, halts, or rejuvenates the development of an ecosystem.

The existence of properties that favor the appearance, resistance, or dependency of species on fire suggests that fire operates as a selective force. The combustibility, increase in organic matter, and dependence on fire exhibited by many species lead to the conclusion that fire is not entirely exogenous. It well may be considered as the product of the structure and floristic composition of a plant community as well as of the environment.

## BIBLIOGRAPHY

Ahlgren, C. E. 1959. Some effects of fire on forest reproduction in northeastern Minnesota. *J. For.* **57**:194–200.

Ahlgren, C. E. 1960. Some effects of fire on reproduction and growth of vegetation in northeastern Minnesota. *Ecol.* **41**:431–445.

Ahlgren, C. E. 1970. *Some effects of prescribed burning of jack pine reproduction in northeastern Minnesota.* Misc. Rep. Univ. of Minnesota Agr. Exp. Stn. 94, For. Ser. 5, 14 pp.

Ahlgren, C. E. 1974. Effects of fires on temperate forests: North Central United States. In T. T. Kozlowski, and C. E. Ahlgren, Eds., *Fire and Ecosystems,* Academic, New York, pp. 195–223.

Aikman, J. M. 1955. *Burning in the management of prairie in Iowa.* Proc. Iowa Acad. Sci. **62**:53–62.

Anonymous. 1973. Prehistoric forest fires. *Sci. News* **103**(6):89.

Arnold, K. 1964. *Project Skyfire lightning research.* Tall Timbers Fire Ecol. Conf. Proc. **3**:121–130.

Ashton, D. H. 1975. Studies on flowering behavior in *Eucalyptus regnans* F. Muell. *Aust. J. Bot.* **23**:399–411.

Ashton, D. H. 1981. Fire in tall open forests (wet sclerophyll forests). In A. M. Gill, R. H. Groves, and I. R. Noble, Eds., *Fire and Australian Biota,* Aust. Acad. Sci., Canberra, pp. 339–366.

Ashton, D. H. and B. J. MacAuley. 1972. Winter leaf spot disease of seedlings of *Eucalyptus regnans* and its relation to forest litter. *Trans. Brit. Mycol. Soc.* **58**:377–386.

Bands, D. P. 1977. *Prescribed burning in Cape Fynbos catchment.* Proc. Symp. Environ. Consequences Fire Fuel Manage. Medit. Ecosys., U.S. For. Serv. Gen. Tech. Report WO-3, pp. 245–56.

Beadle, N. C. W. 1940. Soil temperatures during fires and their effects on the survival of vegetation. *J. Ecol.* **28**:180–192.

Beaufait, W. R. 1960a. *Influence of shade level and site treatment, including fire, on germination and early survival of* Pinus banksiana. Michigan Dept. Conserv., For. Div. Tech. Publ. 1, 79 pp.

Beaufait, W. R. 1960b. Some effects of high temperatures on the cone and seeds of jack pine. *For. Sci.* **6**:194–198.

Biswell, H. H. 1963. *Research in wildland fire ecology in California.* Tall Timbers Fire Ecol. Conf. Proc. **2**:63–97.

Biswell, H. H. 1974. Effects of fire on chaparral. In T. T. Kozlowski, and C. E. Ahlgren, Eds., *Fire and Ecosystems,* Academic, New York, pp. 321–364.

Box, T. W., J. Powell, and D. L. Drawe. 1967. Influence of fire on south Texas chaparral communities. *Ecol.* **48**:955–960.

Bragg, T. B. and L. C. Hulbert. 1976. Woody plant invasion of unburned Kansas bluestem prairie. *J. Range Manage.* **29**:19–24.

Broido, A. 1966. Thermogravimetric and differential thermal analysis of potassium bicarbonate contaminated cellulose. *Pyrodynamics* **4**:243–251.

Broido, A. and M. Nelson. 1964. Ash content: its effect on combustion of corn plants. *Sci.* **146**:652–653.

Brown, J. K. 1970a. *Physical fuel properties of ponderosa pine forest floor and cheatgrass.* U.S. For. Serv. Res. Paper INT-74, 16 pp.

Brown, J. K. 1970b. Ratios of surface area to volume for common fine fuels. *For. Sci.* **16**:101–105.

Brown, J. K. 1975. *Fire cycles and community dynamics in lodgepole pine forests.* Proc. Symp. Monogr. Lodgepole Pine Ecosyst., Wash. State Univ., Coop. Ext. Serv. Publ., pp. 429–456.

Byrne, P. J. 1977. *Prescribed burning in Australia: the state of the art.* 5th Meeting, Aust. For. Council Res. Working Group **6**, 21 pp.

Carlquist, S. 1976. *Alexgeorgea,* a bizarre new genus of Restionaceae from Western Australia. *Aust. J. Bot.* **24**:281–295.

Cayford, J. H. 1963. *Some factors influencing jack pine regeneration after fire in southeastern Manitoba.* Can. Dept. For. Pub. 1016, pp. 5–16.

Cayford, J. H. 1970. *The rold of fire in the ecology and silviculture of jack pine.* Tall Timbers Fire Ecol. Conf. Proc. **10**:221–244.

Christensen, P. 1978. *The concept of fauna priority areas.* Vict. For. Comm., Monash Univ. Fire Ecol. Conf. Proc. **3**:66–73.

Christensen, P. and P. C. Kimber. 1975. *Effect of prescribed burning on the flora and fauna of northwest Australian forest.* Proc. Ecol. Soc. Aust. **9**:85–106.

Christensen, P., H. Recher, and J. Hoare. 1981. Responses of open forest to fire regimes. In. A. M. Gill, R. H. Groves, and I. R. Noble, Eds., *Fire and Australian Biota,* Aust. Acad. Sci., Canberra, pp. 367–394.

Cochrane, G. R. 1966. Bushfires and vegetation regeneration. *Vict. Nat.* **83**:4–10.

Colinvaux, P. A. 1973. *Introduction to ecology,* Wiley, New York, 621 pp.

Countryman, C. M. 1974. Moisture in living fuels affects fire behavior. *Fire Manage.* **35**:10–14.

Countryman, C. M. and C. W. Philpot. 1970. *Physical characteristics of chamise as a wildland fuel.* U.S. For. Serv. Res. Paper PSW-66, 16 pp.

Cunningham, T. M. 1960. *The natural regeneration of* Eucalyptus regnans. Univ. Melbourne Sch. For. Bull. 1.

Cwynar, L. D. 1978. Recent history of fire and vegetation from laminated sediment of Green Leaf Lake, Algonquin Park, Ontario. *Can. J. Bot.* **56**:10–21.

Cypert, E. 1972. *Plant succession on burned areas in Okefenokee swamp following fires of 1954 and 1955.* Tall Timbers Fire Ecol. Conf. Proc. **12**:199–217.

Daubenmire, R. 1968. *Ecology of fire in grasslands. Advances in ecological research,* Vol. 5, Academic, London, pp. 209–266.

Drury, W. H. and I. C. T. Nisbet. 1973. Succession. *J. Arnold Arb.,* **54**:331–358.

Eiten, G. 1972. The cerrado vegetation of Brazil. *Bot. Rev.* **38**:201–341.

Floyd, A. G. 1966. Effect of fire upon weed seeds in the wet sclerophyll forests of northern New South Wales. *Aust. J. Bot.* **14**:243–256.

Floyd, A. G. 1976. Effect of burning on regeneration from seeds in wet sclerophyll forest. *Aust. For.* **59**:210–220.

Fons, W. L. 1946. Analysis of fire spread in light forest fuels. *J. Agric. Res.* **72**:93–121.

Fons, W. L. 1950. Heating and ignition of small wood cylinders. *Ind. & Chem.* **42**:2130–2133.

Fosberg, M. A. and M. J. Schroeder. 1971. *Fine herbaceous fuels in fire danger rating.* U.S. Forest Serv. Res. Note RM-185, 7 pp.

Frissell, S. S., Jr. 1973. The importance of fire as a natural ecological factor in Itasca State Park, Minnesota. *J. Quat. Res.* **3**:397–407.

Gardner, C. A. 1957. The fire factor in relation to the vegetation of western Australia. *West. Aust. Natur.* **5**:166–173.

Garren, K. H. 1943. Effects of fire on vegetation of southeastern United States. *Biol. Rev.* **9**:617–654.

Gill, A. M. 1975. Fire and the Australian flora: a review. *Aust. For.* **38**:4–25.

Gill, A. M. 1978. Crown recovery of *Eucalyptus dives* following wildfire. *Aust. For.* **41**:207–214.

Gill, A. M. 1980. Adaptive response of Australian vascular plant species to fire. In A. M. Gill, R. M. Groves, and I. R. Noble, Eds., *Fire and Australian Biota*, Aust. Acad. Sci., Canberra, pp. 243–272.

Gill, A. M. 1981. Fire adaptive traits of vascular plants. In *Fire Regimes and Ecosystem Properties,* U.S. For. Serv. Gen. Tech. Report WO-26, pp. 208–230.

Gill, A. M. and D. H. Ashton. 1968. The role of bark type in relative tolerance to fire of three central Victorian eucalypts. *Aust. J. Bot.* **16**:491–498.

Gill, A. M. and R. H. Groves. 1981. *Fire regimes in heathland and their plant ecological effects.* In R. L. Specht, Ed., *Heathlands and Related Shrublands of the World,* Elsevier, Amsterdam, pp. 61–84.

Gill, A. M. and F. Ingwersen. 1976. Growth of *Xanthorrhoea australis* R. Br. in relation to fire. *J. Appl. Ecol.* **13**:195–203.

Grano, C. X. 1970. *Eradicating understory hardwoods by repeated prescribed burning.* U.S. For. Serv. Res. Paper SO-56.

Grime, J. P. 1974. Vegetation classification by reference to strategies. *Nature* **242**:344–347.

Grime, J. P. 1977. Evidence for the existence of three primary strategies in plants and its relevance to ecological evolutionary theory. *Am. Natur.* **111**:1169–1194.

Hadley, E. B. 1961. Influence of temperature and other factors on *Ceanothus megacarpus* seed germination. *Madrono* **16**:32–138.

Hadley, E. B. and B. J. Kieckhefer. 1963. Productivity of two prairie grasses in relation to fire frequency. *Ecol.* **44**(2):389–395.

Hall, A. V. 1959. Observations on the distribution and ecology of Orchidaceae in the Muizenberg Mountains, Cape Peninsula. *J. So. Africa Bot.* **25**:265–278.

Hanes, T. L. 1971. Succession after fire in the chaparral of southern California. *Ecol. Monogr.* **41**:27–52.

Hanes, T. L. and H. W. Jones. 1967. Postfire chaparral succession in southern California. *Ecol.* **48**:259–264.

Hare, R. C. 1965. Contribution of bark to fire resistance of southern trees. *J. For.* **63**:248–251.

Hennicker-Gotley, G. R. 1936. A forest fire caused by falling stones. *Indian For.* **62**:422–423.

Horton, J. S. and C. J. Kraebel. 1955. Development of vegetation after fire in the chamise chaparral of southern California. *Ecol.* **36**(2):244–262.

Hough, W. A. 1973. *Fuel and weather influence wildfires in sand pine forests.* U.S. For. Serv. Res. Paper SE-106, 19 pp.

Houston, D. B. 1973. Wildfires in northern Yellowstone National Park. *Ecol.* **54**:1111–1117.

Jackson, W. O. 1968. *Fire, air, water and earth, an elemental ecology of Tasmania.* Proc. Ecol. Soc. Aust. **3**:9–16.

Janzen, D. H. 1967. Fire, vegetation structure, and the ant–acacia interaction in Central America. *Ecol.* **48**:26–35.

Johnston, W. F. 1971. Broadcast burning slash favors black spruce reproduction on organic soil in Minnesota. *For. Chon.* **47**(1):33–35.

Jones, R. M. 1963. Studies in the autecology of the Australian acacias in South Africa. IV. Preliminary studies of the germination of seed of *Acacia cyclops* and *Acacia cyanophylla*. *So. Afr. J. Sci.* **59**:296–298.

Kayll, A. J. 1966. *A technique for studying the fire tolerance of living tree trunks*. Can. Dep. For. Publ. 1012, 22 pp.

Kayll, A. J. and C. H. Gimingham. 1965. Vegetative regeneration of *Calluna vulgaris* after fire. *J. Ecol.* **53**:729–734.

Keeley, J. E. 1977. Seed production, seed populations in soil and seedling production after fire for two congeneric pairs of sprouting and nonsprouting chaparral shrubs. *Ecol.* **59**:820–829.

Keeley, J. E. 1981. *Reproduction cycles and fire regimes*. Proc. Conf. Fire Regimes and Ecosyst. Properties, U.S. For. Serv. Gen. Tech. Report WO-26, pp. 231–277.

Keeley, J. E. and S. C. Keeley. 1977. Energy allocation patterns of sprouting and nonsprouting species of *Arctostaphylos* in the California chaparral. *Am. Midl. Natur.* **98**:1–10.

Keeley, J. E. and P. H. Zedler. 1978. Reproduction of chaparral shrubs after fire: a comparison of the sprouting and seedling strategies. *Am. Midl. Natur.* **99**:142–161.

Keeley, S. C. and others. 1981. Post-fire succession of the herbaceous flora in southern California chaparral. *Ecol.* **62**:1608–1621.

Kilgore, B. M. 1973. *Impact of prescribed burning on a Sequoia mixed conifer forest*. Tall Timbers Fire Ecol. Conf. Proc. 1972, **12**:345–375.

Kilgore, B. M. and D. L. Taylor. 1979. Fire history of a Sequoia mixed conifer forest. *Ecol.* **60**:129–142.

King, N. K. and R. G. Vines. 1969. *Variation in the flammability of the leaves of some Australian forest species*. C.S.I.R.O. Div. Appl. Chem., 14 pp.

Komarck, E. V. 1964. *The natural history of lightning*. Tall Timbers Fire Ecol. Conf. Proc. **3**:139–183.

Komarek, E. V. 1966. *The meterological basis for fire ecology*. Tall Timbers Fire Ecol. Conf. Proc. **5**:85–125.

Komarek, E. V. 1967. *The nature of lightning fires*. Tall Timbers Fire Ecol. Conf. Proc. **7**:5–41.

Komarek, E. V. 1968. *Lightning and lightning fires as ecological forces*. Tall Timbers Fire Ecol. Conf. Proc. **8**:169–197.

Komarek, E. V. 1972. *Lightning and fire ecology in Africa*. Tall Timbers Fire Ecol. Conf. Proc. **11**:473–511.

Komarek, E. V. 1973. *Ancient fire*. Tall Timbers Fire Ecol. Conf. Proc. **12**:219–241.

Kruger, F. J. 1977. *Ecology of Cape fynbos in relation to fire*. Proc. Symp. Environ. Consequences Fire Fuel Manage. Medit. Ecosyst., U.S. For. Serv. Gen. Tech. Report WO-3, pp. 230–244.

Le Houerou, H. N. 1974. *Fire and vegetation in the Mediterranean Basin*. Proc. Ann. Tall Timbers Fire Ecol. Conf. **13**:237–277.

Lindenmuth, A. W. and J. R. Davis. 1973. *Predicting fire spread in Arizona's oak chaparral*. U.S. For. Serv. Res. Paper RM-101, 11 pp.

Little, S. 1974. Effects of fire on temperate forests: northeastern United States. In T. T. Kozlowski and C. E. Ahlgren, Eds., *Fire and Ecosystems,* Academic, New York, pp. 225–250.

Loope, L. L. and G. E. Gruell. 1973. The ecological role of fire in the Jackson Hole area, northwestern Wyoming. *J. Quat. Res.* **3**:426–433.

Lorimer, C. G. 1977. The presettlement forest and natural disturbance cycle of northeastern Maine. *Ecol.* **58**:139–148.

Lotan, J. E. 1975. *The role of cone serotiny in lodgepole pine forest*. Manage. Lodgepole Pine Ecosyst. Symp. Wash. State Coop. Ext. Serv., pp. 471–495.

Lotan, J. E. 1976. *Cone serotiny—fire relationships in lodgepole pine.* Tall Timbers Fire Ecol. Conf. Proc. **14**:267–277.

Loucks, O. L. 1970. Evaluation of diversity, efficiency, and community stability. *Am. Zool.* **10**:17–25.

MacArthur, R. H. and E. O. Wilson. 1967. *The theory of island biogeography,* Princeton Univ. Press, 203 pp.

Mark, A. F. 1965a. Effects of management practices on narrow-leaved snow tussock, *Chionochloa rigida. N.Z. J. Bot.* **3**:300–319.

Mark, A. F. 1965b. Flowering, seeding, and seedling establishment of narrow-leaved snow tussock, *Chionochloa rigida. N.Z. J. Bot.* **3**:180–193.

Martin, R. E. 1963. *A basic approach to fire injury of tree stems.* Tall Timbers Fire Ecol. Conf. Proc. **2**:151–162.

McArthur, A. G. 1968. *The fire resistance of eucalypts.* Ecol. Soc. Aust. Proc. **3**:83–90.

McDaniel, S. 1971. *The genus* Sarracenia *(Sarraceniaceae).* Tall Timbers Res. Sta. Bull. 9, 36 pp.

McLean, D. A. and R. W. Wein. 1977. Nutrient accumulation for post-fire jack pine and hardwood succession patterns in New Brunswick. *Can. J. For. Res.* **7**:562–578.

Montgomery, K. R. and P. C. Cheo. 1971. Effects of leaf thickness on ignitibility. *For. Sci.* **17**:475–678.

Moore, C. W. E. and K. Keraitis. 1971. Effect of nitrogen source on growth of Eucalyptus in sand culture. *Aust. J. Bot.* **19**:125–141.

Moore, J. M. and R. W. Wein. 1977. Viable seed populations by soil depth and potential site recolonization after disturbance. *Can. J. Bot.* **56**:2408–2412.

Mount, A. B. 1964. The interdependence of the eucalypts and forest fires in southern Australia. *Aust. For.* **28**:166–172.

Mount, A. B. 1969. *Eucalypt ecology as related to fire.* Tall Timbers Fire Ecol. Conf. Proc. **9**:75–108.

Mueggler, W. F. 1956. *Is sagebrush seed residual in the soil of burns or is it windborn?* U.S. For. Serv. Res. Note INT-35, 10 pp.

Muller, C. J., R. B. Hanawalt, and J. K. McPherson. 1968. Allelopathic control of herb growth in the fire cycle of California chaparral. *Bull. Torr. Bot. Club* **95**:225–231.

Mutch, R. W. 1970. Wildland fires and ecosystems: a hypothesis. *Ecol.* **51**:1046–1051.

Mutch, R. W. and C. W. Philpot. 1970. Relation of silica content to flammability in grasses. *For. Sci.* **16**:64–65.

Naveh, Z. 1974. Effects of fire in the Mediterranean region. In T. T. Kozlowski and C. E. Ahlgren, Eds., *Fire and Ecosystems,* Academic, New York, pp. 401–434.

Naveh, Z. 1975. The evolutionary significance of fire in the Mediterranean region. *Vegetatio* **29**:199–208.

Noble, I. R. 1981. *Predicting successional change.* Proc. Conf. Fire Regimes and Ecosyst. Properties, U.S. For. Serv. Gen. Tech. Report WO-26, pp. 278–300.

Noble, I. R. and R. O. Slatyer. 1977. *Postfire succession of plants in Mediterranean ecosystem.* Proc. Symp. Environ. Consequences Fire Fuel Manage. Medit. Ecosyst., U.S. For. Serv. Gen. Tech. Report WO-3, pp. 27–36.

Noble, I. R. and R. O. Slatyer. 1980. The use of vital attributes to predict successional changes in plant communities subject to recurrent disturbances. *Vegetatio* **43**:5–21.

Nord, E. C. and C. M. Countryman. 1972. *Fire relations: wildlands shrubs: their biology and utilization.* Proc. Int. Symp. Utah State Univ., U.S. For. Serv. Gen. Tech. Report INT-1, pp. 88–97.

Old, S. M. 1969. Microclimate, fire and plant production in an Illinois prairie. *Ecol. Monogr.* **9**:355–384.

Olsen, J. M. 1960. Cistus, *fuel moisture and flammability*. U.S. For. Serv. Res. Note PSW-159, 6 pp.

Packham, D. R. 1970. Heat transfer above a small ground fire. *Aust. For. Res.* **5**:19–24.

Patric, J. H. and T. L. Hanes. 1964. Chaparral succession in a San Gabriel Mountain area of California. *Ecol.* **45**(2):353–360.

Philpot, C. W. 1969a. *Seasonal changes in heat content and ether extractive content of chamise.* U.S. For. Serv. Res. Paper INT-61, 10 pp.

Philpot, C. W. 1969b. *The effect of reducing ether extractives on the burning rate of aspen leaves.* U.S. For. Serv. Res. Note INT-92.

Philpot, C. W. 1970. Influence of mineral content on the pyrolysis of plant materials. *For. Sci.* **16**:461–471.

Pickett, S. T. A. 1976. Succession: an evolutionary interpretation. *Am. Natur.* **110**:107–119.

Pompe, A. and R. G. Vines. 1966. The influence of moisture on the combustion of leaves. *Aust. For.* **30**:231–242.

Quick, C. R. 1935. Notes on the germination of *Ceanothus* seeds. *Madrono* **3**:135–140.

Quick, C. R. 1962. Resurgence of a gooseberry population after fire in mature timber. *J. For.* **60**:100–103.

Reifsnyder, W. E., L. P. Herrington, and K. W. Spalt. 1967. *Thermophysical properties of bark of shortleaf, longleaf and red pine.* Yale Univ. Sch. For. Bull. 70.

Requa, L. E. 1964, *Lightning behavior in the Yukon.* Tall Timbers Fire Ecol. Conf. Proc. **3**:111–119.

Richards, L. W. 1940. Effects of certain chemical attributes of vegetation on forest inflammability. *J. Agr. Res.* **60**:833–838.

Rizzini, C. T. 1976. Influence of temperature on the germination of seeds from the cerrado. *Rodriguesia* **28**:341–384.

Rothermel, R. C. 1976. Forest fires and the chemistry of forest fuels. In *Thermal Use and Properties of Carbohydrates and Lignin,* Academic, New York, pp. 245–259.

Rothermel, R. C. and H. E. Anderson. 1966. *Fire spread characteristics determined in the laboratory.* U.S. For. Serv. Res. Paper INT-30, 34 pp.

Rourke, J. and D. Weins. 1977. Convergent floral evolution in South African and Australian Proteaceae and its possible bearing on pollination by nonflying mammals. *Ann. Mo. Bot. Gard.* **64**:2–17.

Rowley, S. 1970. Effect of burning and clipping on temperature, growth, and flowering of *narrow-leaved snow tussock*. *N.Z.J. Bot.* **8**:264–282.

Rundel, P. W. 1981. *Structural and chemical components of flammability.* Proc. Conf. Fire Regimes and Ecosystem Properties. U.S. For. Serv. Gen. Tech. Report WO-26, pp. 183–207.

Rundel, P. W. and D. J. Parsons. 1979. Structural changes in chamise (*Adenostoma fasciculatum*) along a fire induced gradient. *J. Range Manage.* **32**:462–466.

Sampson, A. W. 1944. *Plant succession on burned chaparral lands in Northern California.* Bull. 685. Univ. of Calif. Agric. Exp. Sta., Berkeley, 144 pp.

Schall, B. A. 1978. Age structure in *Liatris acidola* (Compositae). *Oecologia* **32**:93–100.

Schlesinger, W. H. and D. S. Gill. 1978. Demographic studies of the chaparral shrub *Ceanothus megacarpus* in the Santa Ynez Mountains, California. *Ecol.* **59**:1256–1263.

Shafizadeh, F., P. P. S. Chin, and W. F. Degroot, 1977. Effective heat content of green forest fuels. *For. Sci.* **23**:81–89.

Shea, S. R., G. B. Peet, and N. P. Cheney. 1981. The role of fire in forest management. In A. M. Gill, R. H. Groves, and I. R. Noble, Eds., *Fire and Australian Biota,* Aust. Acad. Sci., Canberra, pp. 443–470.

Show, S. B. and E. I. Kotok. 1923. The occurrence of lightning storms in relation to forest fires in California. *Monthly Wea. Rev.* **51**(4):175–180.

Specht, R. L., P. Rayson, and M. E. Jackman. 1958. Dark Island heath (Ninety Miles Plain, South Australia). VI. Pyric succession: changes in composition, coverage, dry weight and mineral nutrient status. *Aust. J. Bot.* **6**:59–88.

Stickel, P. W. 1941. *On the relation between bark character and the resistance to fire.* U.S. For. Serv. NE For. Exp. Sta. Tech. Note 39, 2 pp.

Stone, E. C. and G. Juhren. 1951. The effect of fire on the germination of the seed of *Rhus ovata. Am. J. Bot.* **38**:368–372.

Stone, E. C. and G. Juhren. 1953. Fire stimulated germination. *Cal. Agric.* **7**:13–14.

Sweeney, J. R. 1956. Responses of vegetation to fire. A study of the herbaceous vegetation following chaparral fires. *Bot. Publ. Univ. Calif.* **28**:143–250.

Sweeney, J. R. 1967. *Ecology of some "fire type" vegetation in northern California.* Tall Timbers Fire Ecol. Conf. Proc. **7**:110–125.

Taylor, A. R. 1969. *Lightning effects on the forest complex.* Tall Timbers Fire Ecol. Conf. Proc. **9**:127–150.

Taylor, H. C. 1977. *Aspects of the ecology of the Cape of Good Hope Nature Reserve in relation to fire and conservation.* Proc. Symp. Environ. Consequences Fire Fuel Manage. Medit. Ecosyst., U.S. For. Serv. Gen. Tech. Report WO-3, pp. 483–487.

Trabaud, L. 1970. Quelques valeurs et observations sur la phyto-dynamique des surfaces incendiées dans le Bas-Languedoc (Premiers résultats). *Naturalia Monspeliensia Ser. Bot.* **21**:231–242.

Trabaud, L. 1974. *Experimental study on the effects of prescribed burning on a* Quercus coccifera L. *garrigue: early results.* Tall Timbers Fire Ecol. Conf. Proc. **13**:97–129.

Trabaud, L. 1976. Inflammabilité et combustibilité des principales espèces de la garrigue. *Oecol. Plant.* **11**:117–136.

Trabaud, L. 1979. Etude du comportement du feu dans la garrigue de chêne kermès à partir des températures et des vitesses de propagation. *Ann. Sci. For.* **36**:13–38.

Trabaud, L. 1980a. *Impact biologique et écologique des feux de végétation sur l'organisation, la structure et evolution de la végétation des zones des garrigues du Bas-Languedoc.* Doct. Etat. Univ. Sci. Tech. Languedoc. Montpellier, 288 pp.

Trabaud, L. 1980b. Influence du feu sur les semences enfouies dans les couches superficielles du sol d'une garrigue de chêne kermès. *Natur. Monspel.* **39**:1–12.

Trabaud, L. and J. Lepart. 1980. Diversity and stability in garrigue ecosystems after fire. *Vegetatio* **43**:49–57.

Van Wagner, C. E. 1970. *Fire and red pine.* Tall Timber Fire Ecol. Conf. Proc. **10**:211–220.

Viereck, L. A. 1973. Wildfire in the taiga of Alaska. *Quat. Res.* **3**:465–495.

Vines, R. G. 1968. Heat transfer through bark, and the resistance of trees to fire. *Aust. J. Bot.* **16**:499–514.

Viosca, P. 1931. Spontaneous combustion in the marshes of southern Louisiana. *Ecol.* **12**:439–444.

Vogl, R. J. 1969. *The role of fire in the evolution of the Hawaiian flora and vegetation.* Tall Timbers Fire Ecol. Conf. Proc. **9**:5–60.

Vogl, R. J. 1973. Ecology of knobcone pine in the Santa Ana Mountains, California. *Ecol. Monogr.* **43**:125–143.

Vogl, R. J. 1974. Effects of fire on grasslands. In T. T. Kozlowski and C. E. Ahlgren, Eds., *Fire and Ecosystems,* Academic, New York, pp. 139–194.

Vogl, R. J. and P. K. Schorr. 1972. Fire and manzanita chaparral in the San Jacinto Mountains, California. *Ecol.* **53:**1179–1188.

Wagener, W. W. 1961. Post-fire incidence in Sierra Nevada forests. *J. For.* **59:**739–747.

Webber, H. J. 1935. The Florida scrub, a fire-fighting association. *Am. J. Bot.* **22:**244–361.

Wein, R. W. and L. C. Bliss. 1973. Changes in arctic *Eriophorum* tussock communities following fire. *Ecol.* **54:**845–852.

Wells, P. V. 1962. *Vegetation in relation to geological substratum and fire in the San Luis Obispo Quadrangle.* Calif. Ecol. Monogr. **32:**79–103.

Wells, P. V. 1969. The relation between mode of reproduction and extent of speciation in woody genera of the California chaparral. *Ecol.* **23:**264–267.

Went, F. W., G. Juhren, and M. C. Juhren. 1952. Fire and biotic factors affecting germination. *Ecol.* **33:**351–364.

West, D. 1971. *Fire, man and wildlife as interacting factors limiting the development of climax vegetation in Rhodesia.* Tall Timbers Fire Ecol. Conf. Proc. **11:**121–145.

Westman, W. E. 1976. Vegetation conversion for fire control in Los Angeles. *Urban Ecol.* **2:**119–137.

White, F. 1977. The underground forest of Africa: a preliminary review. *Gard. Bull. Singapore* **29:**57–71.

Williams, I. J. M. 1972. A revision of the genus *Leucadendron* (Proteaceae). *Contr. Bol. Herb.* **3:**1–425.

Zedler, P. H. 1977. *Life history attributes of plants and the fire cycle: a case study in chaparral dominated by* Cupressus forbesii. Proc. Symp. Environ. Consequences Fire Fuel Manage. Medit. Ecosyst. U.S. For. Serv. Gen. Tech. Report WO-3, pp. 451–458.

# CHAPTER TEN

# *Fire as a Natural Process in Forests*

Fire was a shaper of landscapes long before our ancestors first learned to nurture burning embers in their caves. Evidence of free-burning fire has been found in petrified wood and in coal deposits formed as early as the Paleozoic era (Komarek 1971). Wherever climate permits the growth of plants, lightning provides the match that will sooner or later set them afire. Following ignition, the fire's behavior will depend on the quantity and arrangement of the fuel through which it spreads and the ever-changing weather. The behavior of the fire, in turn, has a profound influence on the type of vegetation that will rise from its ashes. Everywhere outside of the tropical rainforest, vegetative communities have evolved and adapted to particular fire cycles of frequency and intensity, and in their evolution have developed mechanisms for perpetuating that fire cycle. It is important to understand these basic interactions between fire and the forest ecosystems because, as many foresters have learned to their sorrow, man's attempts to manage the forest resource have often changed the natural fire cycle to such an extent that neither the native nor the introduced species can be protected to harvest age.

Climate, which is the distribution of weather elements over long periods of time, has been known to be the primary determinant of vegetation patterns since the Greeks began their explorations six centuries before Christ. However, it was not until 1900 that Wladimir Koppen developed a mathematical system of climatic classification that tied climatic regions directly to plant distributions. Koppen's work has been extended and elaborated by many scientists since 1900, but his original theories are still the backbone of most schemes for linking climatic and botanical features.

Reduced to its simplest form, Koppen's classes can be depicted as 10

293

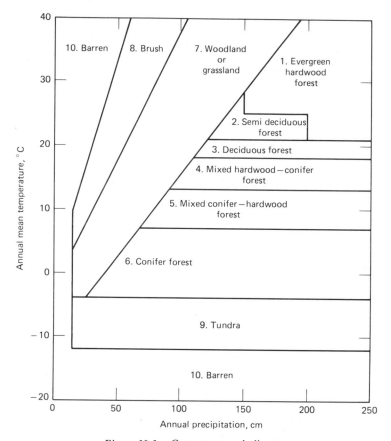

***Figure 10.1.***   Cover type and climate.

potential cover types distinguishable on the basis of annual mean temperature and total annual precipitation. These cover types and their relationship
to the climatic factors are shown in Figure 10.1.

For fire management purposes we need to know more than merely the
general cover type. We would like to know as much as possible about fuel
loading—understory and litter as well as overstory—and also as much as
possible about when and how intensely fires can be expected to burn.

Since litter accumulation is largely a function of winter temperature and
summer moisture, we first distinguish six winter climates on the basis of the
mean temperature of the coldest three months. Table 10.1 shows these classifications. In addition, a seventh category, "arctic," is established for climates where the mean temperature of the warmest three months is below
7°C. Such climates are too cold to grow sufficient vegetation to sustain forest
fires.

The distribution of moisture throughout the year can be determined by a

***Table 10.1.*    *Winter Climates***

| Class | $T^a$ | Litter Accumulation |
|---|---|---|
| 1. Frost Free | >16 | None |
| 2. Mild | 10 to 15.9 | Very Low |
| 3. Cool | 4.5 to 9.9 | Low |
| 4. Short Cold | −1 to 4.4 | Moderate |
| 5. Long Cold | −7 to −1.1 | Heavy |
| 6. Very Cold | <−7 | Very Heavy |

[a]Mean temperature of coldest three months, °C.

modified version of Thornthwaite's evapotranspiration index (Thornthwaite 1948). In this version:

$$M = (PR) - F$$

where  $M$ = Monthly moisture index
$P$ = Total monthly precipitation (cm)
$R$ = Total monthly days with precipitation
$F$ = Evapotranspiration factor

The evapotranspiration factor is determined from the formula:

$$\ln F = \frac{(0.14 T^{0.89})(L)}{12}$$

where  $T$ = Mean monthly temperature (°C)
$L$ = Mean monthly day length (hr)

Both the evapotranspiration factor and the monthly moisture index are taken to be zero whenever the monthly mean temperature is 0°C or below.

When the monthly moisture index is negative, evapotranspiration exceeds moisture input and forest fires are probable sometime during the month.

Because only a limited amount of moisture can be carried over a 30-day period, the monthly moisture index is limited to a maximum value of 100 (all values greater than 100 are listed as 100).

By summing the monthly moisture index values for all months having a positive index, four classes of aridity are derived that relate to density of understory cover and the rate of litter decomposition as shown in Table 10.2.

The length of the average fire season is obtained by simply counting the number of months with negative moisture indices. No negative months indicates no fire season, 1 to 4 months a short fire season, and 5 to 12 months a long fire season.

**Table 10.2.  *Aridity Classification***

| Class | $\Sigma M^a$ | Understory Density | Litter Decomposition Rate |
|---|---|---|---|
| A. Very Humid | >500 | Dense | Rapid |
| B. Humid | 251–500 | Moderate | Moderate |
| C. Nonhumid | 11–250 | Scattered | Slow |
| D. Arid | <11 | Vegetation insufficient to carry fire | |

$^a$Total annual moisture index, negative values omitted.

The possible combination of 10 cover types, 7 winter climates, 4 aridity classes, and 3 lengths of fire season equals 840 fuel–fireclimate classes—a formidable number with which to contend. Even eliminating the "barren" fuel class, the "arctic" winter climate, and the "arid" aridity class as being unimportant to fire management still leaves 486 cells in the matrix. However, this complexity is more apparent than real because the meteorological variables used to identify the fuel and climatic types are highly correlated and most combinations such as "evergreen hardwood forest with a cold winter" or "humid brushland" are impossible. In a study of 3000 airfield records as compiled by the World Meteorological Organization, only 100 individual fuel–fireclimate classes were represented and the great majority of stations fell into fewer than 50 classes. About a dozen classes encompass the major forest fire problem areas. In this chapter we look in depth at these major fuel–fireclimate classes with examples from around the world.

In addition to indicating cover type and fuel accumulation, climatic data can be used to estimate forest fire potential. A pair of semiempirical equations expand the fireclimate categorization to include a monthly estimate of the behavior of fires that do start. These have proven reasonably accurate over a wide range of fireclimates.

The probability that a forest fire can be started on a random day of any given month can be determined by:

$$P_M = P_0 - .25\,(P_0 - P_{M-1}) \quad \text{if } P_0 > P_{M-1}$$

where
$P_M$ = Probability of fire start on a random day in month $M$
$P_{M-1}$ = Probability of fire start on a random day in month $M-1$
$P_0$ = Conditional probability of fire start on a random day in month $M$

$$P_0 = 1 - \left\{ \frac{[D + (0.394R)]/N}{0.00412L \times 10^{0.0308T}} \right\}$$

where  $D$ = Number of days in the month with precipitation of 0.25 cm or more

$R$ = Total monthly precipitation (cm) or snowfall (cm), whichever is greater

$L$ = Mean day length (hr)

$T$ = Mean monthly temperature (°C)

$N$ = Number of days in the month

By starting calculations with the wettest month of the year, $P_{M-1}$ is known to be greater than $P_M$ and the necessity to iterate beyond 12 months is avoided. Negative values of $P_0$, $P_M$, and $P_{M-1}$ are carried for computation purposes but displayed as zero since the concept of negative probability is meaningless.

The behavior of fires in the absence of wind (wind data is seldom available in climatological summaries) can be estimated by determining the effects of temperature and humidity on fire intensity and rate of spread.

$$B = \frac{IS}{60}$$

where  $B$ = Burning Index

$I$ = Intensity component

$S$ = Spread component

and

$$I = (110 - 1.373H) - (20.4 - 0.054T)$$

where  $H$ = Humidity Index

$T$ = Monthly mean maximum temperature (°C)

and

$$S = 124 \times 10^{-0.0142H}$$

where  $H = 100 \times (10^{0.0308D}/10^{0.0308T})$

$D$ = Monthly mean dew point temperature (°C).

The Burning Index is correlated with fire behavior as follows:

| BI | Fire Behavior |
| --- | --- |
| 1–19 | Creeping fire only |
| 20–39 | Surface fire only |

40–59    Running fire, occasional torching of tree crowns

60–79    Hot running fire, spot fires, and torching common

80+    Crown fire likely

Thus by using only readily available climatic data, it is possible to derive considerable information about the forest fire potential of any area in the world.

In the remainder of this chapter we discuss the climate and cover types of those parts of the world that have forest fire problems, actual or potential. Coverage is complete except for parts of Oceania and Central and Southern Asia where forest fire data are unavailable.

## BOREAL FORESTS

In the belt between the Arctic Circle and approximately latitude 50° north lie more than three-fourths of the world's reserves of coniferous timber and one-third of the forested area of the world. There is no equivalent resource in the southern hemisphere.

Its floristic homogeneity is no less prominent. Trees and shrubs of the understory belong to a very few genera with vicariant species. This is due to the relative proximity of lands that have undergone the same climatic vagaries since the end of the Tertiary.

In boreal forests, the climatic year is divided into two well separated seasons: a long hard winter where the coldest month has a mean temperature varying between −6 and −50°C, and a very short summer (one to three months with temperatures higher than 10°C) where the hottest month reaches 16 to 17°C. The frost-free period does not exceed 120 days. The soil thermal regime also follows these wide seasonal oscillations. Where the annual mean temperature remains below 0°C and the snow cover is too thin, soils remain perpetually frozen (permafrost). Then only the superficial layer thaws and the shorter the summer, the more shallow the thawed depth. In spite of low average precipitation (250 to 600 mm), water is never lacking since evaporation is also low. At a depth of 1 m, soil moisture content is practically constant year-round. When drainage is poor, soils become wetter and covered by bogs and swamps.

These forests of *Picea, Pinus, Larix,* and *Abies* are almost invariably "born of fire" in the sense that there are virtually no second generation stands of climax species self-reproduced without the aid of fire. On the more moist sites fires typically recur in 200 to 250 year cycles during times of abnormal drought, burning fiercely and covering very large areas. The largest forest fire complex ever recorded, 14.25 million hectares, burned in Siberia during the summer of 1915 (Shostakovich 1925). Individual fires larger than a half million hectares have not been unusual in any of the boreal forests during this century (Lutz 1956). On these high-intensity burn sites, all standing trees are usually destroyed. The forest regenerates as an even-aged stand, either directly or through a successional series, depending on the availability of stored seed or seed sources. On drier sites, fire cycles may be as short as 40 to 65 years. Since it takes about 50 years for fuels to accumulate in sufficient quantity to ensure tree mortality, not all trees are killed in these fires. Consequently, scattered survivors are left and the forest regenerates as an uneven-aged stand often of mixed species such as *Betula-Pinus* or *Picea-Thuja-Larix*. If the fire cycle is a natural one (lightning caused) rather than human-caused, there is a tendency for specialized "fire types" to evolve and dominate the sites. This is particularly true at the southern margins of the boreal forest and is typified by the jack pine (*Pinus banksiana*) and lodgepole pine (*P. contorta*) whose serotinous cones require fire to release their seed and whose ability to withstand any degree of heat short of incineration ensures an ample seed supply immediately following fire (Figure 10.2).

Fire is also partly responsible for maintaining stands of *Picea mariana*, *Populus tremuloides*, and *Betula papyrifera* in the boreal forests of Canada and Alaska (Scotter 1972). The reasons for the high incidence of fire in the boreal forest are low precipitation combined with long daylight hours during the fire season (usually May to September), the high flammability of lichens such as reindeer moss (*Cladonia rangiferina*), and the high incidence of lightning, particularly the so-called "dry lightning storms," thunderstorms accompanied by little or patchy precipitation.

The Russians, who own most of it, divide the northern land mass into several natural zones (Tseplyaev 1961).

The polar desert (Fireclimate Type 10) is covered with ice and snow throughout most of the year. Vegetation is limited to sparse lichens and mosses with a few scattered pockets of grassy plants. Fuels are too discontinuous to permit fire spread regardless of weather conditions.

The tundra type (Fireclimate Type 9, Table 10.3) covers a vast region of the northern hemisphere north of the boreal conifer forests. For fireclimate purposes, tundra includes the northern portions of what silviculturists would classify as taiga, the distinction being that the stunted spruce and other conifers at the northern limits of their range resemble shrubs in their fire behavior rather than forests.

Inasmuch as permafrost is always close to the surface in the tundra, this type is usually marshy in the summer and fires are uncommon in normal years. The tundras are treeless due to the marshiness and the shallow depth available for root development above the permafrost. Because of the long day length, fires can cover large acreages during exceptionally dry periods and since growth and revegetation processes are slow in the arctic, tundra fires are very damaging when they do occur.

The tundras are subdivided by their plant cover into mossy, lichen, or shrubby tundras. The different types of tundra are:

**Figure 10.2.**    *Pinus banksiana* cones are opened by heat from a crown fire releasing seed for the next generation of forest. Photo by U.S. Forest Service.

Shrub thickets, especially near altitudinal and latitudinal limits of the trees, with deciduous shrubs lower than 2 m high (willows; *Salix glauca, S. laponum;* birches: *Betula nana, B. glandulosa;* alders: *Alnus crispa, A. tenuifolia*).

Heathers with low woody plants (30 to 50 cm) with narrow, thick leaves such as *Empetrum nigrum, Vaccinium uliginosum, V. vitis-idaea, Cassiope tetragona*, and *Loiseleuria procumbens*.

Marshes or swamps with Graminaceae, Cyperaceae, Juncaceae.

Huge areas almost exclusively covered by mosses or lichens.

All these types are often mixed together. Usually they are sparse and open communities interspersed with large rocky areas. Fires are rare in the tundra (Wein and Bliss 1973), but particularly devastating when they occur because of the long time required for vegetation to become reestablished. In lichen tundra, for example, it may take more than a century for a burned area to recover sufficiently to sustain reindeer populations.

Conifer forests (Fireclimate Type 6, Table 10.4) occupy the higher

Table 10.3. Fireclimate of Yakutsk, USSR, 62°05' N, 129°45' E, Elev. 105 m

| Month | Max T°C | Min T°C | DPT°C | Precip (cm) | Snow (cm) | Days Precip | Day Length (hr) |
|---|---|---|---|---|---|---|---|
| Jan | −39.5 | −43.9 | −44.8 | 1.5 | 18 | 4.6 | 5.8 |
| Feb | −31.7 | −39.4 | −38.9 | 1.0 | 12 | 3.9 | 8.7 |
| Mar | −15.6 | −28.9 | −26.1 | 1.0 | 12 | 2.9 | 11.6 |
| Apr | −1.1 | −13.9 | −13.9 | 1.0 | 10 | 2.2 | 14.6 |
| May | 11.1 | −0.6 | −3.9 | 2.0 | 4 | 2.6 | 17.5 |
| Jun | 21.7 | 8.3 | 6.1 | 3.2 | 0 | 2.9 | 19.5 |
| Jul | 24.4 | 11.7 | 10.6 | 4.0 | 0 | 3.0 | 18.7 |
| Aug | 21.1 | 8.9 | 8.9 | 3.3 | 0 | 2.8 | 15.7 |
| Sep | 11.1 | 1.1 | 1.1 | 2.6 | 0 | 3.0 | 12.7 |
| Oct | −3.9 | −11.1 | −11.1 | 2.1 | 21 | 4.3 | 9.8 |
| Nov | −26.1 | −31.7 | −32.2 | 1.9 | 23 | 6.0 | 7.0 |
| Dec | −38.3 | −42.8 | −44.0 | 1.3 | 16 | 4.6 | 5.4 |
| Annual | −5.6 | −15.0 | — | 24.9 | — | — | — |

Cover Type 9: Tundra
Very Cold Winter, Nonhumid, Short Burning Season
Very Heavy Litter, Scattered Shrubs

| Month | Jan | Feb | Mar | Apr | May | Jun | Jul | Aug | Sep | Oct | Nov | Dec |
|---|---|---|---|---|---|---|---|---|---|---|---|---|
| Fire Prob. | 0 | 0 | 0 | 0 | 0 | 0.02 | 0.53 | 0.64 | 0.45 | 0 | 0 | 0 |
| Burning Index | 0 | 2 | 10 | 19 | 29 | 32.0 | 24.0 | 17.0 | 9.0 | 2 | 0 | 0 |

*Table 10.4. Fireclimate of Fort Smith, Canada, 60°1′ N, 111°58′ W, Elev. 200 m*

| Month | Max T°C | Min T°C | DPT°C | Precip (cm) | Snow (cm) | Days Precip | Day Length (hr) |
|---|---|---|---|---|---|---|---|
| Jan | −20.6 | −30.0 | −22.8 | 1.4 | 13.2 | 1.6 | 6.6 |
| Feb | −16.7 | −28.3 | −21.7 | 1.7 | 16.8 | 2.1 | 9.0 |
| Mar | −7.8 | −21.7 | −12.8 | 1.7 | 17.0 | 2.1 | 11.7 |
| Apr | 3.3 | −10.0 | −5.0 | 1.3 | 9.9 | 1.6 | 14.4 |
| May | 13.9 | 1.1 | 1.7 | 2.5 | 1.8 | 3.1 | 16.9 |
| Jun | 20.0 | 6.1 | 6.7 | 3.6 | 0.0 | 4.0 | 18.6 |
| Jul | 23.3 | 8.9 | 10.6 | 5.1 | 0.0 | 5.1 | 18.0 |
| Aug | 20.6 | 6.7 | 8.3 | 4.2 | 0.0 | 4.5 | 15.4 |
| Sep | 12.2 | 1.1 | 3.9 | 3.9 | 2.8 | 4.2 | 12.7 |
| Oct | 3.9 | −4.4 | 0.6 | 2.4 | 13.7 | 3.1 | 10.0 |
| Nov | −8.3 | −16.1 | −15.0 | 2.2 | 21.3 | 2.9 | 7.5 |
| Dec | −17.2 | −26.1 | −25.0 | 2.2 | 21.3 | 2.8 | 5.9 |
| Annual | 7.8 | 2.8 | — | 107.6 | — | — | — |

Cover Type 6: Conifer Forest
Very Cold Winter, Nonarid, Short Burning Season
Very Heavy Litter, Scattered Shrubs

| Month | Jan | Feb | Mar | Apr | May | Jun | Jul | Aug | Sep | Oct | Nov | Dec |
|---|---|---|---|---|---|---|---|---|---|---|---|---|
| Fire Prob. | 0 | 0 | 0 | 0 | 0 | 0.24 | 0.48 | 0.52 | 0.25 | 0 | 0 | 0 |
| Burning Index | 0 | 0 | 0 | 0 | 17 | 22.0 | 20.0 | 17.0 | 5.0 | 0 | 0 | 0 |

latitudes of the northern hemisphere and higher elevations in both hemispheres outside the tropics. In areas with continental climates, fire seasons are short but, because of the long summer day lengths at high latitudes, severe. Forest fire is the natural harvester of conifers, and large acreages burn nearly every year in Alaska, Canada, and Siberia. Undergrowth is scattered to moderate, but litter accumulates throughout the life of the stand since the cold winters inhibit decay.

The taiga is the northernmost zone of true forest. Except for its northernmost limits where *Salix, Betula,* and *Populus* predominate, the taiga is an exclusively coniferous forest with no admixture of nonconiferous species except for *Betula* and *Populus.* In North America the taiga is almost exclusively covered with *Picea, P. glauca* being the climax type on well drained soils with *P. mariana* as a dominant on poorly drained sites and as a fire subclimax of *P. glauca.* In Eurasia the taiga contains a richer mixture of coniferous species including *Pinus, Larix, Picea, Abies,* and *Thuja,* both singly and in various mixtures. In general, "dark taiga" (*Picea, Abies,* and *Thuja* mixtures) occupy the sites of heavy soils and poor drainage, whereas "light taiga" (*Pinus* and *Larix*) dominates on sandy soils. As in the tundra, permafrost is a notable feature of the taiga, and a particularly important one with regard to fire. For once a fire has burned over an area, increased insolation falling on the blackened surface may melt the permafrost to a sufficient depth to expose the surviving stand to a severe windthrow hazard. Consequently, even relatively "light" fires in the taiga often result in complete elimination of the forest stand. Because of the slow build-up of fuel and because of the wet nature of the ground due to permafrost, natural fire cycles in the taiga are quite long.

The number of fires reported in the interior Alaskan taiga is only 2.7 per million hectares protected in contrast to 415 per million in the "lower 48" states. However, the area burned per fire in Alaska averages 1800 hectares vs. only 12 hectares in the rest of the United States. Consequently, the return period for Alaskan fires is 206 years, almost identical to that of the rest of the United States (201 years). Inasmuch as the number of fires has greatly increased since settlement, whereas the average fire size has been reduced by improved fire protection, it is likely that the natural fire cycle of 200 to 250 years has remained little changed (Barney 1971).

Recovery following fire is largely dependent on fire intensity. On severely burned sites, especially where deep organic soil layers have been burned during droughts, succession is usually set back to the shrub stage, and reestablishment of conifer stands takes several decades. In areas of complete crown removal, but where soil destruction is not complete, *Populus* and *Betula* will regenerate from suckers, and conifers will gradually replace them, either from prefire stored seed sources or from airborne seed from adjacent stands. Where burns are patchy or where crown removal is incomplete, restocking of conifers from seed is usually rapid since regeneration conditions are normally favorable.

South of the taiga, beyond the reach of permafrost, lies the true boreal forest which is often distinguishable from the taiga only by the fact that hardwoods other than birch and aspen mix with the predominant conifers.

Therefore, due to the slight floristic differences that exist between the taiga and the true boreal forest, they are described together.

### Eurasia

In Eurasia from Scandinavia to the Ienissei River, the forest is dense in the south, progressively becoming clearer toward the north, whereas the height of trees decreases. The dominant species are spruce (*Picea excelsa*) or "dark taiga" which grows on heavy soils with poor drainage; *Pinus sibirica* (more frost-hardy than spruce) and *Abies sibirica* play a rather important role in western Siberia. *Pinus silvestris* and also *Betula* spp. or "light taiga" grows in many varied situations but mainly on sandy soils, or they appear when spruce forest has been destroyed by cutting or wildfire.

East of the Ienissei River the world's most severe winters combined with very cool summers restrict the vegetation to *Larix dahurica*. Here the understory flora are particularly poor because of permanent darkness due to the tree crowns and the low nutrient level of podzolic soils. Shrubs are the most characteristic element, most of them belonging to the Ericaceae family: *Vaccinium myrtillus, V. vitis-idaea,* and *Empetrum nigrum.*

*Pinus silvestris* occupies all the areas too dry or too moist for spruce. The *P. silvestris* forest is an open forest; it forms a part of the pioneering formations of the taiga. In areas where spruce forest has been destroyed, *P. silvestris* (Scots pine) invade, until the time when spruce, which has begun to grow in the shade protected from an excess of evaporation, overtop them. At that time, if conditions are good for spruce, its shade gradually eliminates the pine. Because of the open crowns, abundant light reaches the soil in a Scots pine forest and the understory is relatively abundant, mainly constituted of lichens of the *Cladonia* genus.

The larches (*Larix decidua* and *L. dahurica*), owing to their deciduous needles and strong frost-hardiness, spread into areas with continental climates with hard and severe winters. *L. decidua* buds are frozen by temperatures of $-40°C$ whereas *L. dahurica* can withstand temperatures down to $-70°C$. The main species that constitute the understory of the open forests of *Larix* are: *Betula nana, Arctostaphylos uva-ursi, Vaccinium* spp., and several kinds of lichens.

Everywhere, the taiga is interspersed by bogs and marshes of *Sphagnum* mosses (*S. recurrum, S. cuspidatum,* and *S. rubellum*) of *Eriophorum vaginatum, Erica tetralix, Calluna vulgaris, Vaccinium uliginosum,* and *Ledum palustre.*

In the taiga of Scandinavia fire incidence is markedly higher than in Alaska. The region as a whole averages 13 fires per million hectares protected—ranging from 6.5 per million in Sweden to 22 fires per million hectares in Finland. Because of intensive and sophisticated fire protection, average fire sizes are quite small, 6.25 hectares per fire for the region as a whole, with a low of 1.6 hectares in Norway and a high of 9.0 in Sweden. Return periods are longer than either harvest cycles or even the natural longevity of the species. In Scandinavia fire is no longer a consequence in the natural ecosystem of the taiga.

Although the USSR does not release anything except fragmentary statistics on forest fire losses, fire is known to play a significant role in the taiga, particularly in Siberia. Return periods in the Siberian taiga are undoubtedly shorter, and perhaps only half as long as the 200 to 250 years estimated for Alaska.

### North America

In North America the boreal forest or taiga stretches in a broad transcontinental belt from Newfoundland across central and northern Canada to Alaska. As shown in Figure 10.3, it is predominantly a coniferous forest, mossy-floored or with low herbs and shrubs, interspersed with numerous small lakes and ponds (Rowe 1972, Rowe and Scotter 1973, Viereck 1973). Usually the boreal forest is divided into three parts: a closed forest in the south, an equally extensive subarctic open lichen-woodland in the central part, and a mosaic of forest-and-tundra patches in the north.

In North America, this vast region with its relatively uniform forest type covers the area between Quebec, Alaska, and the Great Lakes. The vegetation of the region has been and still is shaped by fire (Kayll 1968). It has been determined from charcoal layers in soil profiles that over 95 percent of all forests in the region have burned at least once (Ahlgren 1974). Almost all the forests in northeastern Minnesota have burned at one time or another in the last 300 to 400 years (Heinselman 1970, 1973). Most natural, even-aged stands of pine grew as a result of the great fires that have swept the region. This is also true of herbaceous communities (graminoids and ferns) that have developed following recurring fires (Vogl 1964).

The mature forest pattern in the south shows *Abies balsamea* (balsam fir) dominant on well-drained sites in eastern Canada changing centrally and westward to a preeminence of *Picea glauca* (white spruce), with *P. mariana* (black spruce) and *Larix laricina* (tamarack) on poorly drained sites, including those underlain by permafrost and on north-facing slopes. *Pinus banksiana* (jack pine) is usually present on dry sites except in the extreme east where it is absent. Inextricably woven into the patterns are the effects of fires, which in the east favor black spruce, paper birch (*Betula papyrifera*), and jack pine over balsam fir and in the west give advantage to *Populus tremuloides* (trembling aspen), jack pine, or lodgepole pine, black spruce, and birch over white pine. The white birch (*Betula papyrifera*) and the aspen (*Populus tremuloides*) form abundant suckers after a fire (Lutz op. cit., Maini and Horton 1966) and produce many seedlings, permitting rapid colonization. The increased ground heat around the rhizomes during the first year after the fire apparently enhances shoot production (Horton and Hop-

***Figure 10.3.*** Typical fuels and topography of central Canada. Photo by Ontario Dept. of Lands and Forests.

kins 1965). In Alaska a long-term fire cycle of 40 to 60 years can probably maintain a mixed birch–spruce community.

Northward, the boreal forest is dominated by black spruce, reflecting both the increase in frequency of peaty or shallow, cold substrate and the prevalence of fire, whereas in the northwest Rocky Mountain region (Alberta foothills, northern British Columbia, and the Yukon Territory) *Pinus contorta latifolia* (lodgepole pine) clothes the sites of burned-out black spruce, white spruce, and upper altitude stands of *Abies lasiocarpa* (alpine fir). Southward, where the deciduous tree component increases, the soils are generally deeper and more fertile; here black spruce is unimportant compared to aspen, white spruce, and *Populus balsamifera* (balsam poplar) which forms extensive stands on the flood plains of the major rivers.

On the broad expanses of the foothills and upland regions are extensive areas of open stands of white spruce and black spruce with different willows (*Salix*), *Betula glandulosa* (resin birch), ericaceous shrubs, *Cladonia* lichens, feather mosses, and *Sphagnum* mosses (Figure 10.4). Throughout the taiga, the forest stands are interspersed with bogs of many types. These bogs vary from the rich grass and sedge types to oligotrophic sphagnum bogs. A tussock sedge type with sphagnum mosses and low ericaceous shrubs (especially *Ledum groenlandicum*—Labrador tea—and *Chamae-*

**Figure 10.4.** *Cladonia* lichen understory is a typical forest floor of the taiga in Manitoba, Canada. Photo by Canadian Forest Service.

*daphne calyculata*) is particularly extensive. These bogs, with widely scattered black spruce and tamarack, are commonly referred to as "muskeg."

Grasslands are uncommon, but in some areas, especially in the foothills, *Calamagrostis canadensis* and *Festuca altaica* occur on windy sites. Areas repeatedly burned at lower elevations also sometimes develop into meadows dominated by *C. canadensis, Rosa acicularis,* several species of *Carex,* and many herbaceous species.

Fire has always played, and will continue to play, an important role in the boreal forest from both the plant and animal points of view. The major species of the forest are very well adapted to fire, even fire dependent. The cones of jack pine, for example, will not open until they have been subjected to high temperatures, and the seed of birch and poplar are very light and can be carried long distances on the wind to regenerate burned areas. Large fires are common to the boreal forest for several reasons.

A high proportion of the fires are lightning caused which means they are widely distributed over vast areas of relatively inaccessible forest. These same northern forests have a low density of human habitation and thus the resources are not available to take the prompt detection and suppression action necessary to ensure that fires, once ignited, will not spread into conflagrations. Also, these forests, being inaccessible, have low immediate timber value and, to some degree, it is preferable to let fire take its natural course in recycling the forest.

Fires in the boreal forest of Canada's Northwest Territories average 2.2 per million hectares with an average size of 2400 hectares per fire and a return period of 190 years. Because 97 percent of the fires in the Northwest Territories are lightning caused, and because firefighting efforts are limited by policy to protection of communities of over 25 persons, these figures are probably the most representative available for natural fire regimes at latitude 60 to 70° North (Murphy et al. 1980).

Because of the importance of fire in the boreal forest, interests in the use of prescribed fire is high and a number of seminars and workshops on that subject and fire effects have been held (Fire in the Northern Environment, Fairbanks, 1971; Canadian–Alaska Seminar on Research Needs in Fire Ecology and Fire Management in the North, Anchorage and Fairbanks, 1975; Fire Ecology in Resource Management, Edmonton, 1977; Symposium on Fire in the Northern Circumpolar Ecosystems, Fredericton, 1979). As noted earlier, fire in the boreal forest also has a strong influence on wildlife and a number of papers have been given at these seminars concerning what might better be called the influence of *fire exclusion* on wildlife since wildlife, like the tree species, are well adapted to the natural fire cycle of that forest.

## TEMPERATE FORESTS

Temperate forests (more properly referred to as the phytocenoses of temperate regions) are primarily found:

Throughout western Europe and east to the Urals, reappearing in the Caucasus.

In the temperate region of North America, from south of the boreal forest to the Atlantic Ocean, the Gulf of Mexico, and the Pacific Ocean.

In South America, in limited parts of Patagonia, the Andes, southern Chile, and Tierra del Fuego.

In Australia, covering a large part of the Central Desert's periphery, and in New Zealand.

In most of Japan and along the entire eastern side of continental Asia.

Owing to the vast differences between the communities involved, much like the phytocenoses in the Mediterranean area, it is preferable to describe the main characteristics and fire relationships of this vegetation by geographic region.

### Europe

The forests of the European temperate zone extend approximately from 40 to 55° latitude along the ocean shores, but only to 50° within continental Russia.

The climate features a mild winter (January temperatures ranging from $-5$ to $+5°$ C) of short duration. Summers are normally cool (July temperatures of between 15 and 21°C). The intermediate seasons (spring and fall) are long and characterized by alternating warm and cold spells.

Precipitation varies between 500 and 1000 mm in the plains and hills where these forests grow. Although precipitation is more abundant during the winter in oceanic climates and during the summer in continental regions, there is no dry season because summer overcast serves to reduce evaporation in the first case and because of low winter temperatures in the second case.

Snow plays a fairly small ecological role. It forms a durable but thin mantle only in the continental area or in the mountains. During the winter, the ground is rarely frozen for many consecutive weeks (there is no permafrost) and only exceptionally to a depth greater than 20 cm.

Under these weather conditions, the ground receives a sufficient water supply year-round, the fire season is bimodal in the spring and fall, and severe fires occur only during periods of exceptional drought. The average number of fires in the temperate forests of Europe is 167 per million hectares. The average fire size is 0.97 hectares and the return period is over 6000 years. In intensively managed forests such as those of central France and Germany, the average fire size is less than 0.5 hectares. Even in Poland where the average fire size is over twice that of Germany, the return period in temperate forests exceeds 4000 years.

The European temperate forest is classified as Fireclimate Type 5: Mixed Conifer–Hardwood Forest (Table 10.5). It is not very diversified, comprising two principal types dominated by deciduous species: beech forests and oak forests (Becker et al. 1980, Ellenberg 1963, Michalko 1967, Tomaselli 1973).

The beech (*Fagus silvatica*) is the dominant tree in the plains, low plateaus, and lesser mountain ranges of central and western Europe wherever there is a sufficiently oceanic climate (Figure 10.5). The limit of this area extends from the mouth of the Vistula to Galicia. Farther east, *Fagus silvatica* yields its place to the various *Quercus* and to *Carpinus betulus*.

Within the area thus defined, the *Fagus silvatica* forest forms a mosaic with other types of forests, particularly those dominated by *Quercus robur, Carpinus betulus, Quercus robur-Castanea sativa,* or *Pinus silvestris.* Such forests appear whenever the rocks, slopes, drainage, or exposure are not ecologically suitable for *Fagus silvatica.* However, *Fagus silvatica* is capable of prospering on a variety of soils, from rendzinas to leached soils.

On rendzinas, *Fagus silvatica* is often associated with *Fraxinus excelsior.* The undergrowth is rich in geophytes: *Mercurialis perennis, Allium ursinum,* and *Pulmonaria offinalis.* The optimum conditions for *Fagus silvatica* are on slightly acid brown soils. *Acer pseudoplatanus* and *Tilia cordata* are usual companions. *Anemone nemorosa* is the most typical geophyte. The tree trunks are tall and slender, particularly when trees are tightly spaced. A thick brown carpet of fallen and decomposed leaves covers the ground. The *Fagus silvatica* forest also grows on leached or even podzolic soils. The

*Table 10.5.  Fireclimate of Cherbourg, France 49°39′ N, 1°28′ W Elev. 140 m*

| Month | Max $T$°C | Min $T$°C | $DPT$°C | Precip (cm) | Snow (cm) | Days Precip | Day Length (hr) |
|---|---|---|---|---|---|---|---|
| Jan | 8.3 | 4.4 | 2.8 | 8.4 | 0 | 8.9 | 8.4 |
| Feb | 8.9 | 3.9 | 2.2 | 7.4 | 0 | 8.3 | 9.9 |
| Mar | 10.0 | 5.0 | 2.2 | 7.0 | 0 | 11.7 | 11.8 |
| Apr | 12.2 | 6.1 | 10.0 | 5.1 | 0 | 6.0 | 13.6 |
| May | 15.6 | 9.4 | 10.0 | 4.8 | 0 | 5.8 | 15.2 |
| Jun | 17.8 | 11.7 | 10.0 | 4.6 | 0 | 5.1 | 16.2 |
| Jul | 19.4 | 13.9 | 11.7 | 4.8 | 0 | 5.3 | 15.8 |
| Aug | 20.0 | 14.4 | 12.2 | 7.6 | 0 | 7.4 | 14.4 |
| Sep | 16.3 | 12.8 | 10.6 | 7.4 | 0 | 7.2 | 12.4 |
| Oct | 15.0 | 10.0 | 7.8 | 11.6 | 0 | 9.1 | 10.6 |
| Nov | 11.7 | 7.2 | 4.4 | 13.0 | 0 | 9.5 | 9.0 |
| Dec | 9.4 | 5.0 | 2.8 | 13.2 | 0 | 10.7 | 8.0 |
| Annual | 13.9 | 8.9 | — | 94.9 | — | — | — |

Cover Type 5: Mixed Conifer–Hardwood Forest
Cool Winter, Humid, No Burning Season
Dense Understory, Little Litter

| Month | Jan | Feb | Mar | Apr | May | Jun | Jul | Aug | Sep | Oct | Nov | Dec |
|---|---|---|---|---|---|---|---|---|---|---|---|---|
| Fire Prob. | 0 | 0 | 0 | 0 | 0.24 | 0.44 | 0.52 | 0.28 | 0 | 0 | 0 | 0 |
| Burning Index | 0 | 1 | 4 | 0 | 0.0 | 4.0 | 3.0 | 4.0 | 2 | 2 | 1 | 0 |

**Figure 10.5.**   *Fagus silvatica* (European beech) is the dominant tree of central and western Europe. This is a pure stand in the French Pyrenees. Photo by Louis Trabaud.

companion trees are *Quercus petraea* and *Q. robur;* the undergrowth species are *Luzula albida, Deschampsia flexuosa, Pteridium aquilinum,* and *Vaccinium myrtillus.* Fires are confined to short periods in the fall when leaves are freshly fallen, or when the litter is exposed to full sun before the trees leaf out in the spring.

On rich soils with low drainage and abundant precipitation, the beech forest is replaced by a forest of *Fraxinus excelsior* and *Acer pseudoplatanus,* with *Ulmus montana* also present.

Mixed oak forests are found in the areas of western and central Europe where edaphic conditions or dryness prevent the development of beech forests, and in eastern Europe where dryness is combined with late frosts.

On calcareous rock, *Quercus robur* and *Carpinus betulus* forest replaces the beech. On sandy rock is a forest of *Quercus robur*, more or less durably associated with *Betula verrucosa*.

The oak forest understory is more abundant and varied than that of beech forests. Many geophytes and hemicryptophytes are frequent in oak forests, as well as many Gramineae and more or less heliophilic shrubs (*Rubus* and *Crataegus*). Tall shrubs grow well in the relatively light shade: *Corylus avellana, Acer campestre, A. pseudoplatanus, Tilia platyphyllos,* and *T. cordata*. Because of the denser undergrowth and consequent fuel accumulation, fires are more frequent and more severe in oak forests than in other types of deciduous forests.

The various species of oak do not have the same thermal requirements. *Quercus robur* (*Q. pedunculata*) ranges farthest to the north and east, reaching the Urals and latitude 60° in southern Finland and northern Scotland. Conversely, *Q. petraea* (*Q. sessiliflora*) extends to the east in a manner analogous to the beech. *Q. pubescens* extends from the shores of the Mediterranean to Nancy and Bohemia. *Q. cerris* ranges from the Atlantic to the Jura and Moravia.

The chestnut (*Castanea sativa*) has often been planted in various parts of southern and eastern Europe.

At their southernmost point on the Russian plain, these forests are broken into a steppe-forest mosaic.

Throughout the region deforestation has resulted in heathlands, comprising more or less tightly spaced low shrubs of a xeromorphic nature, with small leaves or sometimes needles. The most common species belong to the heath group: *Calluna vulgaris,* various species of the genus *Erica;* another large group belongs to the Papilionaceae family (*Ulex europaeus, Cytisus scoparius, C. purgans,* and *Genista* spp.). *Molinia coerulea* and *Erica tetralix* heathlands are found in the most marshy areas, and waterlogged soils feature a continuous boggy cover, comprising clumps of *Eriophorum vaginatum, E. angustifolium,* and *Scirpus caespitosus*. Peat moss is interspersed here and there.

Although most of the heathlands in the temperate region are the result of intensive grazing and repeated fires, a few coastal areas, particularly in northern Europe, have heathlands maintained by their exposure to the wind. Heath burns vary intensely whenever dry conditions occur and many of the heath species show fire adaptations similar to those of Mediterranean shrublands. Ireland, which has more heath and less forest than any other European temperate forest region also has the highest fire rate: 380 fires per million hectares with an average fire size of nearly 4 hectares.

In the mountains (Alps, Pyrenees, Carpathians) the altitudinal tiers of vegetation correspond remarkably to the zonal distribution. *Fagus silvatica* forests grow at the base of the mountains, between 600 and 1300 m. *Abies alba* forests occur from 1300 to 1600 m. From 1600 to 2300 m, forests of *Picea abies, Larix decidua, Pinus silvestris, P. cembra,* and *P. uncinata* grow. Above the tree line, the vegetation consists of various creeping shrubs (e.g., *Rhododendron* and *Loiseleuria procumbens, Vaccinium uliginosum, Juniperus nana,* and *Arctostaphylos uva-ursi*). These plants also grow in the southern tundra. Because of the decrease in average temperature with elevation and year-round precipitation, fires in these European conifer forests are much less common than farther north in the boreal forests.

## North America

In North America the temperate forest extends across the entire continent from coast to coast between the boreal forest to the north and the tropical and desert vegetation to the south. Its floristic richness is incomparably greater than that of the European temperate forest (Braun 1950, Curtis 1959, Daubenmire 1952, Gleason and Cronquist 1964, Oosting 1958).

In the eastern part of the area the deciduous forest predominates. Precipitation varies from 750 to 2000 mm. Summers are long, warm, and humid. Northward, winters are severe but still shorter than the summer. The annual minimums range from −20 to −30°C for the northern limit to −8°C in the southern part; mean temperatures in January range from 0 to −10°C toward the northern limit to +10°C in the southern limit.

The southeastern region extends eastward from the Appalachians to the ocean. It can be divided into two sections, one being the Piedmont Plateau east of the Appalachians and the other the coastal plain that extends eastward and southward from New Jersey to the Gulf of Mexico and eastern Texas.

Lightning is the most ancient natural cause of fires in this region (Komarek 1964, 1968, 1973), responsible for an average of more than 1370 fires per year (Taylor 1969). Then man entered the picture. Human intervention, however, was not restricted to short seasons; fires could be set in winter or during a long drought, even when lightning fires were not possible. When the first settlers arrived, they saw a vast stretch of pine forest of the parkland type, broken only by rivers and hollows. The understory of this forest was regularly cleared by fires caused by lightning or set by Indians.

Fireclimate Type 3 (Deciduous Forest, Table 10.6) predominates in the southern portion of the temperate forest, Type 4 (Mixed Hardwood–Conifer) in the central region, and Type 5 (Mixed Conifer–Hardwood) in the north. Throughout the eastern United States, fall is the predominant fire season with a short fire season in the spring during years of unusual drought.

Natural fire frequency is greater in the North American temperate forest than it is in the boreal forest. Frequency varies with latitude, ranging from 10 to 25-year intervals at the northern limit to 2 to 5 years at the southern. In all parts of the range, fires are more frequent in stands composed of conifers or mixed hardwood–conifer stands than they are in pure hardwood stands. Throughout the entire temperate forest, surface fires were the rule with crown fires a rare event confined solely to coniferous stands. In recent

*Table 10.6. Fireclimate of Texarkana, Arkansas, 32°27′ N, 93°59′ W, Elev. 120 m*

| Month | Max T°C | Min T°C | DPT°C | Precip (cm) | Snow (cm) | Days Precip | Day Length (hr) |
|---|---|---|---|---|---|---|---|
| Jan | 13.9 | 2.2 | 2.8 | 12.6 | 3.6 | 8.6 | 10.1 |
| Feb | 15.6 | 3.3 | 3.9 | 9.4 | 0.5 | 7.1 | 10.9 |
| Mar | 19.4 | 6.7 | 5.6 | 10.5 | 0.0 | 6.9 | 11.8 |
| Apr | 24.4 | 11.1 | 10.0 | 14.4 | 0.0 | 7.4 | 12.9 |
| May | 28.3 | 16.1 | 16.7 | 10.5 | 0.0 | 6.9 | 13.7 |
| Jun | 32.8 | 20.6 | 20.0 | 10.1 | 0.0 | 6.7 | 14.2 |
| Jul | 34.4 | 22.2 | 21.1 | 10.5 | 0.0 | 6.9 | 14.1 |
| Aug | 35.0 | 21.7 | 20.6 | 7.7 | 0.0 | 5.6 | 13.2 |
| Sep | 32.2 | 18.3 | 17.8 | 6.6 | 0.0 | 4.5 | 12.2 |
| Oct | 26.7 | 12.2 | 12.2 | 7.4 | 0.0 | 4.9 | 11.3 |
| Nov | 18.9 | 5.6 | 5.6 | 11.0 | 0.0 | 6.7 | 10.3 |
| Dec | 14.4 | 3.3 | 2.8 | 12.0 | 0.0 | 8.3 | 9.8 |
| Annual | 24.4 | 12.2 | — | 122.7 | — | — | — |

Cover Type 3: Deciduous Forest
Cool Winter, Very Humid, Short Burning Season
Dense Understory, Little Litter

| Month | Jan | Feb | Mar | Apr | May | Jun | Jul | Aug | Sep | Oct | Nov | Dec |
|---|---|---|---|---|---|---|---|---|---|---|---|---|
| Fire Prob. | 0 | 0 | 0 | 0 | 0.14 | 0.36 | 0.44 | 0.54 | 0.56 | 0.33 | 0 | 0 |
| Burning Index | 13 | 15 | 24 | 26 | 15.0 | 20.0 | 22.0 | 27.0 | 27.0 | 27.0 | 22 | 15 |

decades crown fires have become more common as a result of excessive logging and a build-up of ground fuels following fire exclusion.

On the higher mountains of the Appalachians, as far south as the Great Smoky Mountains, the forest is similar to that of the boreal forests. However, *Picea rubens* (red spruce) takes the place of *P. glauca* (white spruce), and farther south *Abies fraseri* (Fraser fir) replaces *A. balsamea* (balsam fir) with *Betula alleghaniensis*.

Throughout the Appalachians and Cumberland Plateaus, numerous species of forest grow in varying combinations. *Fagus grandifolia, Aesculus octandra, Magnolia acuminata, Tilia heterophylla, Liriodendron tulipifera, Acer saccharum, Quercus alba,* and *Tsuga canadensis* are the most abundant trees. Because of the late springs and wet summers fires are rare.

The northward extension of the mixed forest shows an increasing importance of *Fagus grandifolia* (beech) and *Acer saccharum* (sugar maple). This forest type stretches along an area west of the Alleghenies from New York to Ohio and up into Wisconsin and southwestern Ontario between Lakes Huron, Erie, and Ontario. Associated trees include *Acer rubrum* (red maple), *Ulmus americana* (American elm), *Quercus rubra* (northern red oak), and *Prunus serotina* (black cherry). The natural range of *Fagus grandifolia* does not extend to the northwest limits of the deciduous formation. *Tilia americana* (American basswood) replaces it in Wisconsin and Minnesota.

Between the northern boreal forest and the deciduous forest lies a transitional community of which *Tsuga canadensis* (hemlock) is an important and constant member, together with *Fagus grandifolia* and *Acer saccharum*, and in lesser numbers *Betula alleghaniensis* (yellow birch), *Pinus strobus* (white pine), *Tilia americana, Fraxinus americana* (white ash), *Quercus rubra,* and other species. This community, known in Canada as the Great Lakes–St. Lawrence Forest Region (Hosie 1969, Rowe op. cit.), extends from northwestern Minnesota through the Lake States into southern Manitoba, Ontario, Quebec, and New Brunswick. This area was once occupied by beautiful pine forests, now mostly decimated by land clearing, fire, and lumbering. *P. strobus* tended to occur on sites with more favorable moisture conditions than the sand plains and ridges occupied by *P. resinosa* (red pine). Throughout this area many bogs are occupied by *Larix laricina, Picea mariana,* and *Thuja occidentalis* groves. Fires occur in the spring and fall. Severe fire weather in the spring coincides with the presence of the "Hudson's Bay High," a stagnant weather system that brings high temperatures and low humidities to the Lake States area. Fall fires are rarely damaging except following years of unusual summer drought.

The slopes and uplands of the mountains that extend from southern New England to Georgia were once occupied by the oak–chestnut forest. *Castanea dentata* was almost completely eliminated by blight. *Quercus prinus* (chestnut oak) and *Q. coccinea* (scarlet oak) are important species everywhere, with *Liriodendron tulipifera, Quercus rubra,* and *Q. alba,* and different *Caryas*. Through the foothills of the mountains this community grades into the oak–hickory forest of the bordering Piedmont Plateau.

*Pinus rigida* (pitch pine) is the important successional species throughout the area, but southward *P. virginiana* and *P. echinata* (Virginia and shortleaf pines) increase and *P. strobus* is locally abundant. Fire tends to favor the pines and prescribed fire is an important management tool throughout the type.

In all directions from the deciduous forest center except northward along the mountains, precipitation decreases and becomes less effective. This results in dominance by the drought-resistant oak–hickory forest, which occurs as a fringe on rugged topography or poor sites. Oak–hickory forests range through the Piedmont Plateau and the Atlantic coast to the coastal plain of Texas and Oklahoma. The dominants of oak–hickory forest are not the same throughout its range, but several species occur consistently. *Quercus alba, Q. rubra, Q. velutina, Q. stellata* (post oak), *Q. marilandica* (blackjack oak), *Carya cordiformis, C. ovata, C. tomentosa,* and *C. laciniosa* are trees that may be found anywhere in this type. Typical subordinate species are *Oxydendrum arboreum* (sourwood), *Cornus florida* (dogwood), *Nyssa sylvatica* (black gum), and *Liquidambar styraciflua* (sweet gum). Other oaks and hickories with more restricted ranges may be in association and produce local variations. *Q. imbricaria* (shingle oak) should be added from Arkansas and eastern Oklahoma northward. *Q. macrocarpa* (bur oak) is the characteristic tree of sometimes extensive savannalike transition from forest to grassland from Texas to Minnesota. Fire was once used extensively to improve grazing opportunities on oak–hickory sites, but its use has died out with the decline in open range grazing.

On sites where moisture may be exceptionally favorable (along rivers, on flood plains) stands a forest of *Fagus grandifolia, Acer saccharum, Quercus phellos* (willow oak), *Q. lyrata* (overcup oak), *Q. michauxii* (swamp chestnut oak), and *Carya ovata* (shagbark hickory).

The lowlands grow stands of *Liquidambar styraciflua, Liriodendron tulipifera, Platanus occidentalis, Betula nigra, Acer rubrum, Ulmus* spp., *Fraxinus* spp., and *Celtis* spp. Fires are rare in these wetland types but devastating when they do occur.

Because of the large amount of abandoned croplands throughout the eastern and southern ranges of the oak–hickory forests, pine stands are conspicuous.

The coastal plain extends from New Jersey down into Florida along the Gulf of Texas. *Pinus virginiana* (Virginia pine) predominates in the northern Piedmont, *P. rigida* (pitch pine) in the pine barrens of New Jersey, and *P. taeda* (loblolly pine), *P. echinata* (shortleaf pine), *P. elliottii* (slash pine), and *P. palustris* (longleaf pine) are dominant in the more southern states. Fire maintains pine dominance, usually in open stands with the highly flammable *Aristida stricta* (wire grass) a common ground cover. These stands owe their origin and maintenance to their resistance to fire.

*Pinus palustris*, like all the other pines of the southeastern United States, needs mineral soil for germination. In the seedling stage leaves can be attacked by a fungus (*Scirrhia acicola*); the disease can be eradicated by burning the infected needles before spring growth. The buds are protected from fire by long needles and scales. The bark of the young pine resists heat and is quite thick for a young tree. Once the tree has reached the sapling stage it is virtually fire resistant.

A number of authors (Komarek 1974, Wahlenberg 1936, 1946) have observed that *Pinus palustris* is a temporary forest stand type that without human intervention or the occurrence of fire would become a mixed deciduous forest. Therefore, any management system that maintains *P. palustris* forests inhibits natural evolution. Fire may be considered a natural means of controlling pine regencration, thus prescribed burning is widely used in forest management.

Frequently, *P. palustris* forms open forests with a grassy cover of *Andropogon scoparius* and *A. tener*. Like the denser forests, this population is maintained by fire. It is in a relative balance only when fire occurs at fairly frequent intervals (Komarek 1974). Many studies (Campbell and Cassady 1951, Greene 1935, Grelen 1975, Grelen and Enghardt 1973, Grelen and Epps 1967, Grelen and Whitaker 1973, Lay 1956, 1957, 1967) have shown that burning increased the protein, phosphorus, and calcium content of the grasses, increased their palatability, and improved the composition of grazing lands by increasing the desirable herbaceous species (Figure 10.6). No significant effect of burning on edaphic properties was observed, but burning increased the mineral, nitrogen, and organic matter content of the soil.

*Pinus elliottii* was abundant in this region of the southeast. As a wetland tree, slash pine was not subjected to frequent fire. It does not resist fire well except at the sapling stage. After that, it can survive defoliation seemingly undamaged as long as the upper third of the crown has not been scorched and the fires do not occur in summer (Komarek 1974). Apparently, slash pine needles are less flammable than *P. palustris* needles. Slash pine forests have a highly flammable grass and brush understory with such plants as *Ilex glabra* and *Serenoa repens*.

*Pinus taeda* originally occupied the driest parts of the region. However, as a result of colonization, logging, and fire prevention, it has come to take over lands that used to be covered by *P. elliottii* and *P. palustris*. Loblolly pine is sensitive to fire until it reaches a height of 4 m. After that, its thick bark protects it well from heat. Prescribed burning is widely used to regenerate this species, which requires mineral soil to germinate (Lotti et al. 1960). Prescribed burning is also used to clear away invading deciduous understory once the *P. taeda* has reached maturity (Lotti et al. op. cit., Komarek 1974).

*Pinus clausa* is not fire resistant but it does have serotinous cones that open only in the presence of heat. This is the most fire-sensitive forest type in the region. Overly frequent or mistimed fire causes the gradual disappearance of the species.

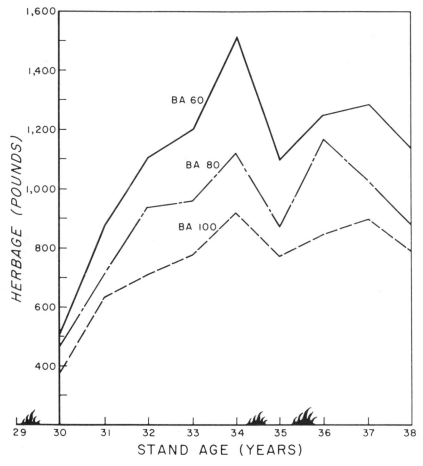

***Figure 10.6.***  Effects of burning on herbage production (from Grelen and Enghardt 1973).

On sand dunes near the coast and inland, *Quercus laevis* (turkey oak), *Q. stellata* var. *margaretta* (sand post oak), *Q. incana* (bluejack oak), and *Q. marilandica* are dominants. In this forest the sand is often bare, or covered only by a thin layer of litter.

Undrained shallow depressions form upland bogs or pocosins in which evergreen shrubs predominate. *Ilex glabra, Myrica cerifera, Cyrilla racemiflora, Persea borbonia,* and *Magnolia virginiana*, are representative of the numerous tall shrubs or small trees. With them are usually numerous ericaceous shrubs. *Pinus serotina* (pond pine) is very common. Their cones are serotinous and require the heat of intense fires to open. Seedlings germinate and grow well on mineral soil, which is exposed by fire. *P. serotina* can also sprout. Another fire-adaptive trait is the epicormic buds along the trunks and branches, which can produce new shoots after a fire (Komarek 1974, Little and Somes 1956).

Bamboo and cane species are frequently associated with *P. serotina* in the understory of open forests. These forests are regularly burned (Hilmon and Hughes 1965, Hughes 1966, Shepard et al. 1951). Regular, timely burning of the canes increases their nutrient value (higher protein content) and makes them more appetizing. In the absence of fire, the canes become inedible and if the absence of fire becomes permanent, the stands lose vigor, thin out, and die (Hughes op. cit.). Without fire, there is a build-up of highly flammable fuels and the fires that eventually do occur are among the most devastating in the entire region (Komarek 1974). *Sphagnum* is the usual ground cover. Burned-over pocosins often grow up to a persistent forest of *Chamaecyparis thyoides* (southern white cedar). These trees have been cut so systematically that they remain only in small stands or in remote areas.

The hammocks of Florida, in contrast with pocosins, are mesic habitats raised above surrounding wetter areas. Conspicuous trees are *Quercus virginiana* and *Sabal palmetto*.

Any shallow depression in the flatland of the lower coastal plain fills with water. Permanent standing water results in open marshes of *Mariscus jamaicensis* (saw grass). If flooding is not continuous, swamp forests develop. *Taxodium distichum* (bald cypress) occupies stream and lake margins where water normally remains most of the year. *Nyssa biflora, N. aquatica, Fraxinus profunda, F. caroliniana,* and *Acer rubrum* occupy swamps that are flooded only seasonally. The most severe fire problem in the southern United States occurs during drought years when these swamps dry out. The presence of peat and organic soils encourages deep ground fires that are literally impossible to extinguish until the water table is restored.

West of the prairies stand the Rocky Mountains. Their great height provides conditions for diversified vegetation zones. Precipitation rarely exceeds 1000 mm, but at high elevations snow can cover the ground for most of the year.

On the lowest part of the foothill zone of the Rockies, above the treeless plains and plateaus there is a broadleaved scrub. This zone is widest and best developed in the southern Rockies, narrows and becomes discontinuous in the central Rockies, then disappears entirely farther north. In the southern part, oaks (*Quercus gambelii, Q. gunnisonii, Q. undulata, Q. fendleri, Q. emoryi,* and *Q. utahensis*) are the largest and most conspicuous trees. North of Colorado, oaks are spotty, and *Cercocarpus montanus* (mountain mahogany) is dominant. Other important species include *Rhus trilobata, Purshia tridentata, Amelanchier* spp., and *Symphoricarpos* spp. Vegetation seldom forms a continuous cover but occurs in dense clumps, or even as isolated trees, separated by areas of grassland. Fires are common, but the trees and shrubs are prolific sprouters and soon reclaim the burned areas.

In the upper part of the foothill zone there is an open forest of pinyon–juniper type. The type extends from northern Mexico along the west slope of the Rockies to the Snake River in Idaho, beyond which it continues into southern Alberta with *Juniperus occidentalis* and *J. scopulorum* stands. Along the east slope, it extends to Colorado and northward up to Wyoming. The junipers include *Juniperus scopulorum, J. osteosperma, J. monosperma, J. occidentalis,* and *J. deppeana,* whereas the pines are mainly *Pinus edulis* and *P. monophylla.* The openings between trees support a grass cover (*Bouteloua, Stipa, Agropyron,* and *Poa*) together with a few shrubs (*Ceanothus, Cercocarpus, Purshia,* and *Artemisia*). Fire keeps this forest open. When fire is excluded the junipers tend to form a closed canopy with very little ground fuel. Then fire will only occur as high intensity crown fires during strong winds.

Above the pinyon–juniper forest *Pinus ponderosa* (ponderosa pine) constitutes a relatively open forest. The widely spaced trees provide little shade so that the ground cover is made up of grasses (*Festuca, Poa, Agropyron,* and *Muhlenbergia* are the most common genera). Climatically, the ponderosa pine forest falls into Fireclimate Type 7 (Open Woodland or Grassland, Table 10.7). Fires are frequent in dry summers, favored by the grass of the forest floor. They are rarely severe enough to kill the fire-resistant older trees. Fire acts as an effective thinning agent, keeping the forest open and the trees widely spaced. In the absence of fire, dense reproduction grows until stands reach 3 to 10 m in height at which time they stagnate, developing little growth in height or diameter. Tree ring studies of fire scars throughout the ponderosa pine type show that the return period before fire protection was 5 to 15 years and in some areas as short as 2 to 3 years. With the advent of modern firefighting the number of fires has increased to 356 per million ha, the average fire size reduced to 35 ha and the return period lengthened to 80 to 90 years resulting in significantly increased fuel loads in many areas. Ponderosa pine (*Pinus ponderosa*) forests are well adapted to periodic fire. The dry needles of this species form litter in which fire spreads readily. The frequency of fire is evidenced by the fire scars on old trees. Each time the tree is wounded, the cambium produces wood from the living part toward the middle of the scar. In this way the dates and number of the fires that occurred during a tree's life span can be determined accurately by counting the annual rings and the wounds. Weaver (1974) cites a study in which trees survived 25 fires at intervals of approximately 18 years; the average interval between fires was found to be 14.2 years. Weaver (1955) also discovered 8-year intervals in eastern Washington and 4-year intervals in Arizona (Weaver 1951). The regular occurrence of fire eliminated new or shrubby vegetation and helped maintain the ponderosa pine.

Periodic fires lead to the development of dispersed, even-aged stands comprising mosaics of stands of different ages. Fire prevents the understory from becoming too dense and creates clearings where new plants can establish undisturbed by fire for a period of time (Cooper 1960, Weaver 1951, 1967, 1974).

Where intervals between fires are long enough, species that resist fire less well than *P. ponderosa* can develop; examples are *Abies concolor* and

Table 10.7. *Fireclimate of Flagstaff, Arizona, 35°08' N, 111°40' W, Elev. 2140 m*

| Month | Max T°C | Min T°C | DPT°C | Precip (cm) | Snow (cm) | Days Precip | Day Length (hr) |
|---|---|---|---|---|---|---|---|
| Jan | 5.0 | −10.0 | −7.2 | 6.4 | 49.8 | 5.4 | 10.0 |
| Feb | 6.7 | −7.8 | −6.7 | 5.3 | 33.0 | 4.6 | 10.8 |
| Mar | 9.4 | −5.0 | −7.8 | 6.1 | 35.1 | 5.4 | 11.8 |
| Apr | 14.4 | −1.7 | −4.4 | 3.3 | 12.7 | 3.5 | 12.9 |
| May | 18.9 | 1.1 | −4.4 | 2.5 | 4.1 | 2.8 | 13.8 |
| Jun | 25.0 | 5.0 | −3.9 | 1.0 | 0.0 | 1.2 | 14.3 |
| Jul | 26.7 | 10.0 | 8.3 | 7.9 | 0.0 | 5.7 | 14.0 |
| Aug | 25.6 | 9.4 | 7.2 | 6.9 | 0.0 | 5.2 | 13.3 |
| Sep | 22.2 | 5.0 | 2.2 | 4.1 | 0.0 | 3.1 | 12.2 |
| Oct | 16.7 | −0.6 | −3.3 | 3.6 | 1.5 | 2.8 | 11.2 |
| Nov | 11.1 | −5.6 | −6.1 | 3.6 | 19.1 | 2.8 | 10.2 |
| Dec | 5.6 | −8.9 | −8.3 | 5.1 | 18.5 | 4.6 | 9.7 |
| Annual | 15.6 | −0.6 | — | 55.8 | — | — | — |

Cover Type 7: Woodland or Grassland
Long Cold Winter, Nonhumid, Short Burning Season
Scattered Shrubs, Heavy Litter

| Month | Jan | Feb | Mar | Apr | May | Jun | Jul | Aug | Sep | Oct | Nov | Dec |
|---|---|---|---|---|---|---|---|---|---|---|---|---|
| Fire Prob. | 0 | 0 | 0 | 0 | 0 | 0.57 | 0.34 | 0.37 | 0.46 | 0.36 | 0 | 0 |
| Burning Index | 17 | 21 | 39 | 48 | 71 | 99.0 | 45.0 | 45.0 | 54.0 | 54.0 | 39 | 24 |

*Libocedrus decurrens.* In an unusually dry year a fire can destroy these forests completely, followed by colonization by more resistant species. If fire is infrequent, shade-tolerant species invade the understory of the pine forests. These species are considered less commercially important than the pine.

Frequent periodic fires minimize the danger of a devastating fire, a fact that has been particularly noticed (Cooper op. cit., Weaver 1951) when fires had occurred regularly until recently. Thus controlled understory burning has been recommended, introduced, and used regularly for a number of years (Kallander 1969, Weaver 1967).

Along streams and moist sites, *Populus angustifolia* (narrowleaf cotton-wood) are found in association with *P. acuminata, P. sargentii, P. tremuloides* and *Acer negundo* (box elder).

Above the ponderosa pine zone, *Pseudotsuga menziesii* (Douglas fir) is the dominant tree, growing in dense stands. In the southern Rockies *Abies concolor* (white fir) and *Picea pungens* (blue spruce) are found in relatively small numbers and mostly on moist sites. In the north *Abies grandis* (grand fir) is an associate principally west of the continental divide and on west slopes. East of the divide, *Pseudotsuga menziesii* shares its dominance with *Picea glauca.* In the *Pseudotsuga* forest, fire results in the establishment of *Pinus contorta* or *Populus* spp.

On dry, exposed ridges in both the montane and subalpine zones, several stands of pines occur: *Pinus flexilis* var. *reflexa* in the south, *P. aristata* in northern Arizona, southern Colorado and Utah, *P. flexilis* more northward, then *P. albicaulis* takes over in the northern Rockies.

The forest of the subalpine zone is mainly dominated by *Picea engelmannii* (Engelman spruce) and *Abies lasiocarpa* (alpine fir) which grow in dense stands. In Montana and northern Idaho *Tsuga mertensiana* (mountain hemlock) is often found in this zone. Farther north near the boreal forest, *Picea glauca* and *A. lasiocarpa* may grow in association. The most conspicuous succession in the subalpine zone follows fire and may result in stands of *Pinus contorta* var. *latifolia* (lodgepole pine), *Populus tremuloides,* or *Pseudotsuga menziesii. Pinus contorta* is absent in the southern Rockies. The transition from subalpine forest to alpine tundra is usually occupied by trees having a dwarfed and twisted form known as "krummholz." *Pinus aristata* (bristle cone pine) occupies this position in the southern Rockies, *P. flexilis* (limber pine) in the central Rockies, *P. albicaulis* (whitebark pine) and *Larix lyallii* (alpine larch) in the northern Rockies. Lightning fires are common, but do not usually spread far because of cold damp nights and discontinuous fuels.

Between the Pacific Ocean and the Rocky Mountains stretches an area 10 to 300 km in width, 2400 km in length—the Pacific Region. The frost-free period is long and minimum temperatures are not severe. The annual minimum average ranges between −15°C for the northern part to −2°C for the southern parts. Precipitation is heavy, between 1250 and 2500 mm falling principally in winter. Southward, summer drought becomes an important factor, but it is compensated for by cloudiness. In the north and central parts snow is the usual winter precipitation. Trees are very high (50 to 90 m) with big trunks (2 to 6 m in diameter).

The coastal forest is predominantly Fireclimate Type 5 (Mixed Conifer–Hardwood, Table 10.8) forest. Return periods are long—from 50 to 200 years—and the dominant species are maintained by very large conflagration fires during drought years.

The coastal forest is represented by *Abies lasiocarpa, A. amabilis, A. procera,* and *Tsuga mertensiana* in the Cascades and into south British Columbia. This coastal forest is most fully represented in the Puget Sound and the Olympic Peninsula areas. The forest is constituted by *Tsuga heterophylla* (western hemlock), *Thuja plicata* (western arborvitae), and *Abies grandis* (grand fir). *Pseudotsuga menziesii,* which reaches its greatest size in this area, is relatively abundant and is the principal tree species in succession after fire (Figure 10.7). Douglas fir (*Pseudotsuga menziesii*) forests extend from Oregon and Washington along the Pacific coast to northern California, and inland to Idaho and Montana. In the southern part of the Rockies, Douglas fir is found mixed with ponderosa pine (*Pinus ponderosa*), which gradually takes over the dominant position in the forest regions of Arizona, New Mexico, and Colorado (Weaver 1974).

Fire has played an important part in the development and maintenance of Douglas fir forests for many centuries. Frequency was perhaps lower than in other, drier forests but under conditions of extreme drought intense fires raged, often turning into destructive crown fires. Isaac (1963) said that Douglas fir forests that had not burned for 500 years were rare and they had clearly evolved toward a more climax stage with *Tsuga heterophylla, Abies balsamea,* and *Thuja plicata.*

Lightning has from time immemorial been an important cause of fire (Taylor 1969). American Indians used to light fires. Then European settlers set fires to open up the country, or for other reasons. The most destructive fires in the coastal forests occurred in 1849, 1868, 1902, and 1933. The fire of 1849 destroyed about 200,000 ha (Weaver 1974). In 1902, about 400,000 ha were destroyed (Davis 1959) and in 1933, 142,000 ha were lost (Weaver 1974). Between 1933 and 1945, three fires occurred in the Tillamook region of northwest Oregon.

The occurrence of fire at regular intervals enables the Douglas fir to regenerate and spread afterwards, because this species cannot reproduce in a dense forest cover where seedlings of more shade-tolerant species such as *Thuja, Tsuga,* or balsam fir compete for space. Too frequent fire, however, is followed by establishment of intermediate stands of alder, fern, and bramble (Bailey and Poulton 1968, Neiland 1958).

North of the Puget Sound region, *Picea sitchensis* (sitka spruce) is increasingly important, with *Tsuga heterophylla* and *T. mertensiana.* Further northward in Alaska, the coastal and boreal forests meet and mix together.

*Table 10.8.  Fireclimate of Seattle, Washington, 47°26' N, 122°18' W, Elev. 130 m*

| Month | Max T°C | Min T°C | DPT°C | Precip (cm) | Snow (cm) | Days Precip | Day Length (hr) |
|---|---|---|---|---|---|---|---|
| Jan | 6.1 | 0.0 | 0.6 | 15.5 | 20.1 | 9.8 | 8.7 |
| Feb | 8.3 | 1.7 | 1.7 | 12.3 | 7.1 | 8.4 | 10.1 |
| Mar | 10.0 | 2.2 | 1.7 | 10.2 | 7.1 | 6.8 | 11.7 |
| Apr | 14.0 | 3.9 | 3.3 | 6.3 | 0.0 | 5.5 | 13.5 |
| May | 18.3 | 7.2 | 6.7 | 4.2 | 0.0 | 4.3 | 15.0 |
| Jun | 20.0 | 10.0 | 9.4 | 3.8 | 0.0 | 3.4 | 15.8 |
| Jul | 23.9 | 11.7 | 11.1 | 2.0 | 0.0 | 2.0 | 15.5 |
| Aug | 22.8 | 11.1 | 11.1 | 2.4 | 0.0 | 2.3 | 14.2 |
| Sep | 20.0 | 9.4 | 10.0 | 5.5 | 0.0 | 3.9 | 12.4 |
| Oct | 15.0 | 6.7 | 7.8 | 11.1 | 0.0 | 6.8 | 10.7 |
| Nov | 10.0 | 3.3 | 3.3 | 15.2 | 4.3 | 8.8 | 9.2 |
| Dec | 7.8 | 1.7 | 2.8 | 15.2 | 3.8 | 9.6 | 8.3 |
| Annual | 14.4 | 5.6 | — | 103.7 | — | — | — |

Cover Type 5: Mixed Conifer–Hardwood Forest
Short Cold Winter, Very Humid, Short Burning Season
Dense Understory, Moderate Litter

| Month | Jan | Feb | Mar | Apr | May | Jun | Jul | Aug | Sep | Oct | Nov | Dec |
|---|---|---|---|---|---|---|---|---|---|---|---|---|
| Fire Prob. | 0 | 0 | 0 | 0 | 0.30 | 0.54 | 0.75 | 0.76 | 0.37 | 0 | 0 | 0 |
| Burning Index | 0 | 1 | 5 | 11 | 15.0 | 11.0 | 20.0 | 15.0 | 10.0 | 3 | 1 | 0 |

**Figure 10.7.** *Pseudotsuga menziesii* (Douglas fir) is a principal fire type on the Pacific Coast of the United States and southern Canada. This virgin stand is located on the Rogue River National Forest in Oregon. Photo by U.S. Forest Service.

Southward, the forest is dominated by *Chamaecyparis lawsoniana* and *Pseudotsuga menziesii*. In northern Washington, southern British Columbia, and Idaho appears a forest made up of *Pinus monticola* (western white pine), *Larix occidentalis* (western larch) associated with *Tsuga heterophylla, Thuja plicata*, and *Abies grandis*.

Sequoia forests (*Sequoia sempervirens* and *Sequoiadendron giganteum*) cover a narrow uneven strip 10 to 50 km wide from southern Oregon to central California. The total range is over 1000 km long. These forests are created by and dependent for continued survival upon fire (Biswell 1961, Hartesveldt 1964, Kilgore 1970, 1972, 1973). Although sequoias always dominate mature stands, they are found mixed with other species, including *Pseudotsuga menziesii, Abies grandis*, and *Tsuga heterophylla*.

The two sequoia species cannot tolerate shade, so fire helps them by clearing away shade-bringing trees. They reproduce abundantly by seed production after a fire, so that many seedlings grow up (Kilgore 1973, Kilgore and Biswell 1971, Sweeney 1967). These species can also throw out shoots. They belong to the few conifer species that share this ability. The trees have many lateral roots close to the ground. By producing adventitious buds, they form a ring of sprouts about the base of the tree (Weaver 1974).

The primeval sequoia forest was a mosaic of sequoia-dominated forest ecosystems. Fire was an integral part of this environment, maintaining or renewing forests by eliminating other species. The sequoias survived the fires because of their thick bark, which could resist heat, but also because of their ability to produce sprouts from the base and trunk and to yield many seedlings that could easily germinate in the open terrain.

In the last 1100 years the average sequoia forest experienced 45 fires (Fritz 1930), but fires occur as frequently as 7 to 9-year intervals in the southern portion of their range (Kilgore 1972). These fires, set by Indian hunters or caused by lightning, periodically destroyed the understory without attacking the giant trees, which could develop freely. Since forest-fire protection began in the early twentieth century, the young trees of other species that used to burn before growing to full height have been able to grow until their crowns touch the lowest branches of their larger neighbors. If a fire occurs now in these almost impenetrable forests, the sequoias will probably burn. For this reason, the United States Forest Service, in cooperation with the National Park Service, has been following a program of controlled burning in various areas (Hartesveldt op. cit., Kilgore 1970, Kilgore and Briggs 1972).

On the montane zone of the Sierra Nevada, *Abies concolor* (white fir) is usually the dominant tree in the higher elevations, sometimes mixed in pine stands. Lower down, *Libocedrus decurrens* (incense cedar) predominates on the most favorable sites. *Pinus lambertiana* (sugar pine), *P. jeffreyi* (jeffrey pine), *P. ponderosa,* and *Pseudotsuga menziesii* are more abundant in the north than in the south, whereas *P. lambertiana* and *P. jeffreyi* are more frequent than *P. ponderosa* at upper elevations. Dense chaparral communities of species of *Arctostaphylos, Ceanothus, Rhamnus,* and so on may appear after fire and sometimes last for many years. *Sequoiadendron giganteum* are found in this zone at altitudes of 1350 to 1800 m southward from the latitude of San Francisco to the Kern River. *P. lambertiana, P. ponderosa,* and *Libocedrus decurrens* are common associates.

In the Cascade Mountains and the Sierra Nevada, *Abies magnifica* (red fir) is the dominant tree in the subalpine zone. Although *Pinus monticola* (western white pine) is constantly present, it is only a minor constituent. *P. contorta* (lodgepole pine) is often present especially in the margins of wet meadows. *Tsuga mertensiana* (mountain hemlock) and *Abies concolor* (white fir) occur in an extremely irregular pattern. The most abundant and most constantly represented shrubs are *Ribes viscosissimum* and *Symphoricarpos rotundifolius.* The herb flora is sparse; constant species are *Chrysopsis breweri,* and *Pedicularis semibarbata.* A yellow-green lichen,

*Evernia vulpina,* is present on the trees throughout the zone. At timberline the characteristic trees are *Pinus albicaulis, P. flexilis,* and *P. balfouriana.* On exposed bare rocky slopes, *Juniperus occidentalis* is common, especially on west slopes. Fires are seldom particularly damaging and in national park areas many fires in the subalpine zone are simply left to burn themselves out.

In the foothill zone and above the true chaparral the vegetation is characteristically formed by several oak woodlands (*Quercus wislizenii, Q. chrysolepis, Q. dunnii, Q. garryana,* and *Castanopsis chrysophylla*); common associates are *Arbutus menziesii, Aesculus californica,* and *Rhamnus californica.* In the upper part *Pinus sabiniana* (digger pine) and *Q. douglasii* (blue oak) are the dominants forming typical open or woodland stands. Fires are common and fuels rarely accumulate sufficiently to allow fire into the crowns.

## South America

Through the southern hemisphere, the temperate zone is situated between 35 and 50° latitude. There is a basic difference between the temperate zones of the southern and northern hemispheres: the oceanic climate applied to small continental or insular surfaces.

In South America, the temperate zone and the vegetation best corresponding to it are mainly located in southern Chile and in the Argentinian Andes. The major climate characteristics are heavy precipitation of 1000 to 3500 mm annually with very small temperature ranges; average maximum temperatures vary between 17 and 10°C, and average minimum temperatures vary between 7 and 5°C (except in the mountains, where temperatures can drop below 0°C). This zone is classified as Fireclimate Type 5: Mixed Conifer–Hardwood Forest (Table 10.9) and is normally without a fire season except at its northern edge where there is a short fire season.

The plant community most characteristic of this zone is the "valdivian" forest, dominated by *Nothofagus dombeyi* (called the coigue, an evergreen capable of growing to more than 45 m in height) and *Araucaria araucana* (di Castri 1968). The typical valdivian forest is quite dense, with trees up to 40 m in height; it is almost impenetrable owing to its lush understory. Found mainly in central Chile, it also occurs on the Argentinian slope of the Andes. It is not very sensitive to fire.

Inland (toward the northern portion of its range) and in the central valley, this forest loses much of its density, probably as a result of human activity, and resembles more of a park-forest dominated by *Nothofagus obliqua* and *Laurelia* spp. Near the coast, it is more humid, rich in epiphytes, with a dense undergrowth of *Chusquea* (Bambusae), ferns (e.g., *Lophosoria quadripinnata*), plus the addition of another tree, *Eucryptia cordifolia* (ulmo). *Drimys winteri* and *Embothrium coccineum* occur in the flood plains.

Farther south, the "Selva de Chiloe" appears, characterized by the ab-

*Table 10.9. Fireclimate of La Chamiza, Chile, 41°29' S, 72°51' W, Elev. 2 m*

| Month | Max T°C | Min T°C | DPT°C | Precip (cm) | Snow (cm) | Days Precip | Day Length (hr) |
|---|---|---|---|---|---|---|---|
| Jan | 20.0 | 11.1 | 12.2 | 2.8 | 0 | 2.2 | 14.6 |
| Feb | 20.0 | 11.1 | 12.2 | 10.5 | 0 | 8.2 | 13.6 |
| Mar | 17.8 | 9.4 | 11.1 | 11.1 | 0 | 10.5 | 12.3 |
| Apr | 15.6 | 8.3 | 10.0 | 24.8 | 0 | 9.8 | 11.0 |
| May | 13.3 | 6.7 | 8.3 | 32.5 | 0 | 17.3 | 9.9 |
| Jun | 11.1 | 6.1 | 6.7 | 27.5 | 0 | 18.1 | 9.3 |
| Jul | 10.6 | 5.0 | 6.1 | 8.8 | 0 | 9.0 | 9.5 |
| Aug | 11.7 | 5.0 | 5.6 | 8.9 | 0 | 8.7 | 10.5 |
| Sep | 13.3 | 5.6 | 6.7 | 8.2 | 0 | 10.7 | 11.8 |
| Oct | 15.0 | 6.7 | 8.3 | 4.3 | 0 | 5.2 | 13.1 |
| Nov | 16.7 | 8.3 | 9.4 | 3.1 | 0 | 3.1 | 14.2 |
| Dec | 18.3 | 10.0 | 11.1 | 8.0 | 0 | 8.1 | 14.8 |
| Annual | 15.6 | 7.8 | — | 150.5 | — | — | — |

Cover Type 5: Mixed Conifer–Hardwood Forest
Mild Winter, Very Humid, Short Burning Season
Dense Shrubs, Little Litter

| Month | Jan | Feb | Mar | Apr | May | Jun | Jul | Aug | Sep | Oct | Nov | Dec |
|---|---|---|---|---|---|---|---|---|---|---|---|---|
| Fire Prob. | 0.58 | 0 | 0 | 0 | 0 | 0 | 0 | 0 | 0 | 0.12 | 0.49 | 0.13 |
| Burning Index | 4.0 | 4 | 1 | 0 | 0 | 0 | 0 | 0 | 1 | 1.0 | 2.0 | 2.0 |

sence of *Nothofagus obliqua;* the conifers are *Podocarpus* (*P. nubigena*) and *Pilgerodendron uvifera* (Las Guaytecas cypress), *Laurelia.* On the islands in the Chilean archipelago, the forest is replaced by *Pernettya* (Ericaceae) and *Gleichenia* (Pteridophyta) formations; these are marshy heathlands. *Nothofagus antarctica, N. betuloides,* and *Drimys winteri* also grow on these islands in shrub form.

In the coastal Cordillera and the Andes Mountains, throughout both the ranges, occur low shrubby stands of *Nothofagus pumilio, N. antarctica,* and conifer forests (*Libocedrus chilensis,* and *Fitzroya cupressoides* which can reach 50 m in height and a diameter of 3 m).

From 45° of latitude southward, the subantarctic region stretches up to Cape Horn. Forests are dominated by *Nothofagus betuloides,* with *Embothrium coccineum, Maytenus magellanica, Drimys winteri,* and several conifers (*Pilgerodendron, Libocedrus,* and *Podocarpus*). In these forests epiphytes and the understory with *Chusquea* strongly disappear. The most frequent vegetation is a marshy tundra with tussock or cushion plants (*Donatia, Astelia,* and *Azorella*). Plant landscape in the mountains is mostly constituted by grass steppes with tussock grasses (*Stipa, Festuca,* and *Poa*) that form the "coironales," cushion Umbellifereae (*Laretia,* and *Azorella*). Vegetation is generally very sparse. In the ecotones of the Andean steppes the most common trees are conifers (*Araucaria araucana,* and *Libocedrus chilensis*) and deciduous *Nothofagus* (*N. antarctica,* and *N. pumilio*).

## Australia and New Zealand

Nearly 70 percent of the forests of Australia consist of eucalypts. More than 500 species of eucalypts grow under a wide range of climates from hot, dry inland plains to high mountain areas in the Australian Alps. The temperate area of Australia is found where precipitation amounts to more than 600 mm per year.

The tropical forest, an open type bordering on woodlands, occurs on Cape York Peninsula, in Northern Queensland, the Arnhem Land in the Northern Territory, and the Kimberleys of Western Australia where climate is monsoonal. *Melaleuca quinquenervia* (broadleaved paperbark) is widespread on the east coast of Australia where stands are commonly more than 25 m high. *Melaleuca* is extremely flammable and as an introduced exotic in southern Florida, United States of America, has become a major fire problem.

In the parts of eastern Australia where rainfall exceeds 1000 mm and the soil is relatively rich, a dense forest formation known as *rainforest* occurs. Rainforest covers about 1.8 million ha in a discontinuous belt and is of three main types: tropical and subtropical found along the coast and ranges of Queensland and New South Wales, and the temperate rainforest found from New South Wales to Tasmania. Small pockets of rainforest also occur in the Kimberleys (Western Australia) and the Northern Territory.

Cattle raising is the primary industry throughout most of this area and fire is widely used as a tool to remove dry unpalatable grass. Fires exceeding 50,000 ha are not uncommon. Fire incidence averages less than 2 fires per million ha, but the average fire size is nearly 400 ha. The computation of a return period for fires in these areas is impossible; there are few statistics for wildfires primarily because it is virtually impossible to tell the difference for various purposes including pasture improvement for rough rangeland grazing. These areas have been burned frequently, say, every one to five years, for perhaps the last 40,000 years first by Aboriginals and second by graziers in northern Australia.

Eucalypt forests grow best in the wetter areas of the continent. There are two main types of eucalypt forest, divided mainly on the basis of undergrowth characteristics. The wet eucalypt forests (or wet sclerophyll forest) are perhaps the most majestic forests. The dominant trees are usually over 30 m tall with a dense understory of moisture-loving plants such as tree-ferns, palms, and rainforest shrubs. A typical stand is dense, of uniform age, and of height up to 70 m with a well-developed understory. These two eucalypt species with *E. nitens* (shining gum) occupy about half a million ha of forest in Victoria. In 1939 major forest fires devastated this area. More than 20,000 square km were severely burned. Over a 25-year period in the Victoria wet sclerophyll forest, the average fire incidence has been 66 fires per million ha, the average fire size 353 ha, and the return period for severe fires 43 years. Temperate forest cannot endure such short return periods and large scale underburning programs have been instituted to reduce fire intensity and average fire size. Wet eucalypt forests fall into either Fireclimate Type 3 (Deciduous Forest) or Type 4 (Mixed Hardwood–Conifer Forest, Table 10.10). Dry eucalypt forests fall into Fireclimate Type 7: Woodland (Table 10.11).

The dry eucalypt forests are the most widespread. Hard-leafed shrubs are common as understory, whereas in the more open types the forest floor is carpeted with grass. These forests occur in high rainfall areas when soil is infertile, shallow, or rocky, as well in low rainfall areas of central Australia. Prescribed burning is largely used to protect these forests from hot summer fires. These forests show an infinite variety. They include stands over 60 m high in sheltered sites on the north coast of New South Wales, low *Eucalyptus haemastoma, E. micrantha* stands of the sandstone plateaus near Sydney, open *E. pauciflora* woodlands of the tablelands, and the dwarf mallee stands on shallow or low-nutrient soils. From the south of New South Wales to Victoria, the foothills and slopes of the ranges up to 1000 m in elevation support forests of *E. sieberi*. Again, the escarpment region supports forests with species like *E. obliqua*, and *E. fastigata*. The better tableland forests of New South Wales are most extensive on the northern part where *E. andrewsii* and *E. laevopinea* are important species. Also, the tablelands contain areas of *E. viminalis, E. dalrympleana, E. dives*, and *E. radiata, E. sideroxylon*, and *E. microcarpa* in mixtures that constitute open forests. The flora

*Table 10.10. Fireclimate of Perth, Australia, 31°56' S, 115°58' E, Elev. 20 m*

| Month | Max T°C | Min T°C | DPT°C | Precip (cm) | Snow (cm) | Days Precip | Day Length (hr) |
|---|---|---|---|---|---|---|---|
| Jan | 29.4 | 17.2 | 14.4 | 0.8 | 0 | 1.5 | 13.6 |
| Feb | 29.4 | 17.2 | 13.9 | 1.0 | 0 | 1.8 | 13.2 |
| Mar | 27.2 | 16.1 | 13.3 | 2.0 | 0 | 8.3 | 12.2 |
| Apr | 24.4 | 13.9 | 11.1 | 4.3 | 0 | 9.3 | 11.4 |
| May | 20.6 | 11.6 | 10.6 | 13.0 | 0 | 12.4 | 10.4 |
| Jun | 17.8 | 10.0 | 10.0 | 18.0 | 0 | 13.8 | 10.0 |
| Jul | 17.2 | 8.9 | 8.9 | 17.0 | 0 | 13.4 | 10.3 |
| Aug | 17.8 | 8.9 | 8.3 | 14.5 | 0 | 12.4 | 10.4 |
| Sep | 19.4 | 10.0 | 8.9 | 8.6 | 0 | 9.0 | 11.9 |
| Oct | 21.1 | 11.7 | 10.0 | 5.6 | 0 | 6.2 | 12.8 |
| Nov | 24.4 | 13.9 | 11.1 | 2.0 | 0 | 2.2 | 13.6 |
| Dec | 27.2 | 16.1 | 12.8 | 1.3 | 0 | 2.0 | 14.0 |
| Annual | 22.8 | 12.8 | — | 88.1 | — | — | — |

Cover Type 4: Mixed Conifer–Hardwood Forest
Mild Winter, Very Humid, Long Burning Season
Dense Shrubs, Little Litter

| Month | Jan | Feb | Mar | Apr | May | Jun | Jul | Aug | Sep | Oct | Nov | Dec |
|---|---|---|---|---|---|---|---|---|---|---|---|---|
| Fire Prob. | 0.89 | 0.89 | 0.62 | 0.38 | 0 | 0 | 0 | 0 | 0 | 0.19 | 0.65 | 0.82 |
| Burning Index | 30.0 | 32.0 | 24.0 | 22.0 | 10 | 4 | 5 | 8 | 11 | 13.0 | 22.0 | 27.0 |

*Table 10.11. Fireclimate of East Sale, Australia, 38°06' S, 147°09' E, Elev. 5 m*

| Month | Max T°C | Min T°C | DPT°C | Precip (cm) | Snow (cm) | Days Precip | Day Length (hr) |
|---|---|---|---|---|---|---|---|
| Jan | 24.4 | 11.7 | 12.2 | 4.7 | 0 | 5.1 | 14.5 |
| Feb | 23.9 | 12.8 | 13.3 | 4.8 | 0 | 5.2 | 13.5 |
| Mar | 22.8 | 11.1 | 12.2 | 5.6 | 0 | 9.8 | 12.3 |
| Apr | 19.4 | 8.3 | 9.4 | 4.3 | 0 | 9.3 | 11.0 |
| May | 16.1 | 6.7 | 7.8 | 4.9 | 0 | 9.5 | 10.0 |
| Jun | 13.9 | 4.4 | 6.7 | 4.6 | 0 | 5.9 | 9.4 |
| Jul | 13.3 | 3.3 | 5.0 | 4.2 | 0 | 5.5 | 9.6 |
| Aug | 15.0 | 3.9 | 5.6 | 4.3 | 0 | 5.6 | 10.6 |
| Sep | 17.2 | 5.0 | 7.2 | 5.6 | 0 | 6.4 | 11.8 |
| Oct | 18.9 | 7.8 | 8.9 | 6.3 | 0 | 6.9 | 13.1 |
| Nov | 20.6 | 8.9 | 9.4 | 5.6 | 0 | 6.3 | 14.1 |
| Dec | 22.8 | 10.6 | 10.6 | 5.0 | 0 | 5.4 | 14.7 |
| Annual | 18.9 | 7.8 | — | 60.1 | — | — | — |

Cover Type 7: Woodland or Grassland
Cool Winter, Humid, No Burning Season
Low Litter Weight, Moderate Shrubs

| Month | Jan | Feb | Mar | Apr | May | Jun | Jul | Aug | Sep | Oct | Nov | Dec |
|---|---|---|---|---|---|---|---|---|---|---|---|---|
| Fire Prob. | 0.53 | 0.48 | 0.26 | 0.32 | 0.02 | 0 | 0.05 | 0.15 | 0.08 | 0.17 | 0.30 | 0.45 |
| Burning Index | 17.0 | 11.0 | 11.0 | 10.0 | 5.0 | 2 | 5.0 | 8.0 | 10.0 | 10.0 | 13.0 | 17.0 |

and fauna of all these forests are rich and diverse. Stands of eucalypt forests contain other trees such as *Casuarina* spp. and *Acacia* spp., and *Angophora* spp. continues to have a marked influence on Tasmania's forests. Frequent grazing fires have strongly modified the understory of many of the original sclerophyll forests.

Cypress pine (*Callitris columellaris*) forests covering about 4.5 million ha are the most widely spread native conifers occurring in Australia's drier regions. Much of the area originally covered by *C. columellaris* was cleared for wheat farming and grazing. The trees develop best on deep sandy soils, grow very slowly, and are drought resistant but quite sensitive to fire. Cypress pine forests occur in New South Wales and southern Queensland west of the Great Dividing Range, and in the Northern Territory on large areas north of Katherine.

*Eucalyptus camaldulensis* (river red gum) forests rely on standing water rather than rain. They occur mainly near the inland streams, water-courses, and adjacent flood plains. The most important forests of *E. camaldulensis* are concentrated along the Murray River system with fine stands between Victoria and New South Wales. On the western plains *E. camaldulensis* forest forms a savanna woodland.

Even though Tasmania is not large, its forest types vary widely. There are temperate rainforests where soils are fertile as well as open savanna woodlands and dry and wet sclerophyll forests. Tasmania's prime hardwood forests are located in areas where rainfall varies from 1000 to 1300 mm per year. Early colonial settlement meant the destruction and burning of much forest. The frequency and intensity of fires has had and continues to have a marked influence on Tasmania's forests. Frequent grazing fires have strongly modified the understory of many of the original sclerophyll forests.

Rainforest is dominated by noneucalypt tree species such as *Nothofagus cunninghamii* (myrtle beech). Commonly associated conifers include *Phyllocladus asplenifolius*, *Dacrydium franklinii*, and *Athrotaxis selaginoides*. The most continuous areas of this forest are formed at higher elevations where the mean annual rainfall exceeds 1500 mm. Exceptionally severe droughts are necessary before these forests can burn. In the drier sclerophyll forests eucalypt species such as *E. obliqua*, *E. delegatensis*, *E. viminea*, *E. sieberi*, and *E. globulus* are the most common. Conifer forests made up of *Dacrydium franklinii* (huon pine) stretches on the riverine areas of the west coast of the island, but they range from small shrubs to trees and occur in a wide variety of locations and rainfall areas. In the mountains, shrublands of *E. coccifera* are common.

A considerable portion of Tasmania's vegetation consists of moor, sedge, or heath. Moor and sedge are common in areas of high rainfall on poor soils with bad drainage; heath is usually found on poor coastal sands.

For Tasmania as a whole, fire incidence averages 60 per million ha with an average fire size of 165 ha and a return period of slightly over 100 years. These figures are misleading, however, because no subdivision by forest type is available. The return period of the rainforest is undoubtedly much longer, since rainforest or even temperate hardwood forests cannot long survive return periods shorter than 1000 years. As eucalypts require fire for natural regeneration, it seems that the return period in these areas must have been something less than 300 years prior to European colonization otherwise the species would not exist as they do. The sclerophyll forests are probably subject to return periods of 50 to 75 years as is typical of the sclerophyll forests on the main subcontinent, and the heatherlands to much shorter return periods.

In the southern island of New Zealand where precipitation is higher than 2000 mm per year, forests of *Nothofagus* (*N. menziesii*) occur in the southwestern slopes. In the other parts of the archipelago the forests are dominated by conifers such as *Agathis australis, Dacrydium cupressinum*, and *Weinmannia racemosa*. The understory is dense with many *Podocarpus*, Proteaceae, Lauraceae, and tree-ferns (such as *Cyathea smithii*). In drier areas and above timberline tussock grasslands are constituted by tuft grasses of *Poa, Festuca* (*F. novae-zelandiae*), and *Chionochloa* (*C. rigida*).

Everywhere in Australia and New Zealand many North American pines (mainly, *Pinus radiata*) have been planted on large areas. These pine plantations represent the principal fire control problem in New Zealand.

## MEDITERRANEAN ECOSYSTEMS

Mediterranean type vegetation exists on five continents in areas extremely distant from one another: southern Europe, Near East and North Africa around the Mediterranean Sea, California and the northern part of Baja California in North America, part of central Chile in South America, the occidental part of South Africa, and the western and central parts of southern Australia. All these areas are located on the coasts of oceans or seas.

The Mediterranean ecosystems are of unusual importance to fire managers because the natural return period—15 to 35 years—is long enough for fuels to accumulate to conflagration proportions, yet short enough that each generation of landowners can expect to experience a fire. Where fire cycles are shorter, they are usually not so severe; where the cycles are longer, the chances of an individual property being wiped out are more remote.

The plants that constitute the phytocenoses, in spite of deep differences in composition of the flora, present convergences of form and adaptative traits to climate and fire. There are also physiognomic similarities: the dominant plants, whether trees or shrubs, have a tendency to be evergreen and to bear small, hard, thick, tough (sclerophyllous) leaves.

Plants living in separate but climatically similar areas often resemble each other to some extent. These similarities are attributed to the effects of similar environmental conditions on the evolution of each group. Convergence among plants is often seen in growth form, morphological details, and other features of the life history, and has been demonstrated in physiological processes as well (Mooney and Dunn 1970).

First of all, the lands with a Mediterranean climate and the ecosystems that have developed in them must be defined in climatic terms. If one attempts to focus on the characteristic core of a Mediterranean climate, two factors stand out: precipitation and temperature. The most distinctive involves the concentration of rainfall in the winter half-year, November through April in the northern hemisphere and May through October in the southern. Although at a large number of stations, especially in California and Chile, 80 or even 90 percent of the precipitation occurs in winter, so large a proportion rarely obtains around the Mediterranean Basin itself (Aschmann 1973).

The worldwide distribution of this singular climatic type shows a pattern of notable regularity, displaying a direct relationship to the general circulation of the world's atmosphere and its seasonal displacement. Areas of Mediterranean climate are found between latitudes 30 to 40°, both north and south of the equator on the west coasts of continents. On the northside of the Mediterranean Sea they extend into somewhat higher latitudes (45°), and into somewhat lower latitudes (27°) in western Australia.

Irregularity of total annual precipitation is one characteristic common to all areas with a Mediterranean climate (Aschmann 1973, Daget 1977, Emberger 1955). The concept of average annual rainfall is not of great significance in Mediterranean regions because the annual average can vary from 500 to 1500 mm. Hence dry and hot summers, and mild and rainy winters are the basic features of the Mediterranean climate.

All climatic classifications tend to be too broad to adequately delimit vegetation regions and are of limited value to agriculturalists (for whom most systems were devised) because they fail to take into account the different requirements of different crops (Gentilli 1971). Therefore, it is not surprising that simple classification does not cover all areas with a similar summer fire environment. In some areas with uniform rainfall, particularly southeastern Australia south of latitude 35°S, the summer rainfall is so erratic and ineffective on plant growth, and summer drought so characteristic that the climate is best thought of as a modified Mediterranean type (Leeper 1960). Certainly, these areas are prone to large summer fires of high intensity.

The reason for the high susceptibility of Mediterranean regions to fire is due principally to the climate and the vegetation adapted to that climate. The Mediterranean (and modified Mediterranean) climate is characterized by prolonged summer droughts with high temperatures and low atmospheric humidities and hot, strong summer winds. Although these factors are particularly favorable to the outbreak of fires, the climate has evolved a vegetation which is xerophilous, drought resistant, and highly flammable and which ensures abundant fuel available for combustion even after prolonged periods without rain.

The total quantity of rainfall that determines a dry or rainy season is not the most important phenomenon affecting the occurrence of fires. It is rather the amount and distribution of summer rainfall that plays the important role in fire frequency. A light rainfall of a few millimeters is enough to saturate the litter and temporarily lower the fire danger. The effects of a heavy shower are often less beneficial than the effects of small quantity of water well distributed over a longer period.

Another factor characteristic of Mediterranean climates is the foehn wind. These are generally high speed drying winds. In France they are called "mistral" or "tramontane." In Spain and Italy, they are the "tramontana." In Morocco, Algeria, and Tunisia when the hot and drying "sirocco" comes from the Sahara desert during the months of September and October, the relative humidity of the air falls below 30 percent and may get as low as 1 or 2 percent. In Israel these winds are called "sharav," in Greece and Yugoslavia they are the "bora" and "crivetz"; in southern California "Santa Ana." When these winds blow, the vegetation is more flammable. Throughout the Mediterranean, the largest and most destructive fires occur during the foehn wind outbreaks.

Moreover, the uneven topography of all these countries causes fires to spread faster and firefighting to be more difficult. As a matter of fact, except in Australia where the topography is characterized by moderate relief, the Mediterranean lands are singularly rugged.

It should also be added that the presence of millions of people (permanent or summer residents) living in these areas creates an everpresent potential for catastrophe.

The vegetation of the Mediterranean climate countries bears the brand of aridity. Except in better watered mountains, forests are scarce, and what few trees there are have evergreen persistent leaves. As most of the primeval forest was long ago destroyed by humans, it is now replaced by dense shrublands that constitute the greatest part of the present landscapes of these regions. Climatically, the Mediterranean ecosystems are primarily Fireclimate Type 8 (Brushland or Scrub, Table 10.12), but extend to Type 7 (Woodland) on the wet side and Type 10 (Barren) on the dry.

The names of the communities frequently quoted in literature well describe the kind of stands according to the structure and physiognomy of plants: in Europe we have the *maquis* and *garrigue* (Figure 10.8) in southern France, *macchia* in Italy, *xerovuni* and *phrygana* in Greece, *tomillar, matorral, encirar,* and *jaral* in Spain; in the Near East there are *choresh* and *batha* in Israel, and *gatha nabati* in Syria and Lebanon; in North Africa we find the *steppe* of Morocco and Algeria; in America there is *chaparral* in California, and *espinal* and *matorral* in Chile. Moreover, there are similar landscape types: the *fynbos* of South Africa, and the *scrub* or *bush (mallee* and *heathland)* in Australia.

Due to their great diversity, as compared to the boreal forest, it is more advisable to look at the different communities individually according to the world's geographical regions.

*Table 10.12. Fireclimate of Murcia, Spain, 37°56' N, 1°14' W, Elev. 75 m*

| Month | Max *T*°C | Min *T*°C | DPT°C | Precip (cm) | Snow (cm) | Days Precip | Day Length (hr) |
|-------|-----------|-----------|-------|-------------|-----------|-------------|-----------------|
| Jan | 15.6 | 4.4 | 3.3 | 1.3 | 0 | 1.4 | 9.1 |
| Feb | 17.2 | 5.6 | 3.9 | 2.3 | 0 | 2.9 | 10.8 |
| Mar | 19.4 | 7.2 | 5.6 | 2.3 | 0 | 3.0 | 12.0 |
| Apr | 22.2 | 9.4 | 7.2 | 3.6 | 0 | 4.6 | 13.4 |
| May | 26.1 | 12.8 | 9.4 | 2.8 | 0 | 3.7 | 14.9 |
| Jun | 29.4 | 16.1 | 12.8 | 1.3 | 0 | 1.4 | 16.3 |
| Jul | 32.8 | 18.9 | 15.0 | 0.3 | 0 | 0.1 | 14.9 |
| Aug | 32.8 | 19.4 | 16.7 | 0.5 | 0 | 0.3 | 13.4 |
| Sep | 29.4 | 16.7 | 15.5 | 3.3 | 0 | 4.2 | 12.0 |
| Oct | 25.0 | 12.8 | 11.7 | 3.3 | 0 | 4.2 | 10.8 |
| Nov | 20.0 | 8.3 | 5.6 | 5.1 | 0 | 5.7 | 9.1 |
| Dec | 24.4 | 14.4 | 11.7 | 2.0 | 0 | 1.8 | 14.3 |
| Annual | 23.9 | 11.7 | — | 28.6 | — | — | — |

Cover Type 8: Brush
Mild Winter, Nonhumid, Long Burning Season
Light Understory, Low Litter Weight

| Month | Jan | Feb | Mar | Apr | May | Jun | Jul | Aug | Sep | Oct | Nov | Dec |
|-------|-----|-----|-----|-----|-----|-----|-----|-----|-----|-----|-----|-----|
| Fire Prob. | 0.65 | 0.57 | 0.65 | 0.57 | 0.69 | 0.85 | 0.96 | 0.97 | 0.69 | 0.62 | 0.16 | 0.36 |
| Burning Index | 17.0 | 21.0 | 24.0 | 29.0 | 37.0 | 37.0 | 43.0 | 25.0 | 24.0 | 22.0 | 26.0 | 15.0 |

**Figure 10.8.** *Quercus coccifera*, the typical garrigue of southern France. Photo by Louis Trabaud.

### The Mediterranean Basin Region

The countries around the Mediterranean Sea are an ecological entity, subject to the influence of the Mediterranean climate. Wildfires in this region destroy about 200,000 ha of Mediterranean forest and garrigue annually (Le Houerou 1974). In our day lightning seems to play only a minor role in fires. According to Susmel (1973), lightning fires account for only about 2 percent of the annual toll of burned hectares. One of the characteristic features of plant communities on the periphery of the Mediterranean Basin is their floristic and ecological heterogeneity as compared to the other communities of temperate and cold regions. More than 40 principal forest species and at least 50 subordinate ones share in the composition of the forest (Quezel 1976); in northern and middle Europe, the values do not exceed 12 and 20, respectively. This heterogeneity is linked to numerous factors including the history, climate, physiognomy, geomorphology, and pedology of the areas. Plant species exhibit widely differing behaviors toward fire and there are many adaptations. Within a given species, there is a range of mechanisms for resisting fire depending on the intensity of the fire and the stages of growth and maturity of the species. Thus frequent summer or autumn fires have a greater inhibiting effect on sprouting and development of *Quercus ilex* or *Q. coccifera* than do the less intense but equally frequent fires of winter or spring (Trabaud 1970, 1974, 1980).

Many Mediterranean species can survive fires by means of such underground organs as bulbs, rhizomes, and tubercles. Some of these species are *Asphodelus cerasifer* (Trabaud 1974), *Ophrys* spp. (Naveh 1974, 1975), and *Brachypodium ramosum* (Trabaud 1974). The latter species seems quite unaffected by frequent burnings at any time in the fire season. Other species have strong root systems, such as *Quercus coccifera* in the western Basin and *Q. calliprinoss* in the eastern Basin. There are also species such as *Q. suber* that can resist fire because of their relatively thick bark.

The forests around the Mediterranean Basin have a tendency to organize at successive altitudinal levels from the sea up to the summit of the mountains. However, due to the interaction of all of the communities, they are described here according to their foliar types and according to Quezel's description (op. cit.).

### Coniferous Forests

These often occupy very wide areas on all the Mediterranean periphery. In the warmest areas *Pinus halepensis* and *P. brutia* are growing; the height of these trees is variable. *P. halepensis* (aleppo pine; Figure 10.9) is generally twisted and of middle height (10 to 15 m), whereas *P. brutia* has a slender trunk often reaching a height of 20 m. *P. halepensis* confines its range to the western part of the Basin (except in Italy where it is rare, and in the Tyrrhenian Islands) and to Greece. *P. brutia* is important mainly in Anatolia, Syria, and the Aegean islands.

Stands of *Pinus pinaster* var. *mesogeensis* occur sparsely everywhere around the Mediterranean Basin; the most noteworthy grow in Corsica (Quezel op. cit.). *P. pinea* is no more frequent; there are stands in France, but principally in Spain and in Italy. *P. nigra,* with its numerous ecological races, constitutes small forests scattered all around the Mediterranean periphery; locally, mainly in the eastern part, it grows in beautiful forests. Forests of *Cedrus* develop in the mountains (1500 to 2300 m) of North Africa (*Cedrus atlantica*) and the Near East (*C. libani*), and on the mountain crests of Cyprus (*C. brevifolia*). Some forests of North Africa are still in excellent condition, but human exploitation has ill-used most of them and more than half of the Mediterranean *Cedrus* forests remain only as scattered and disappearing remnants. In North Africa also, exceptionally dense forest of *Tetraclinis articulata* (Barbarian thuya) or of *Juniperus phoenicea* appear here and there.

Lastly, in spite of their rather small extent, the Mediterranean fir-forests are very worthwhile. *Abies cephalonica* is widespread in Greece where it forms important stands, rising in altitude from 500 to 2000 m in the mountains. A second group of firs, localized in the cold areas of the Mediterranean region and encountered from the west to the east, are *Abies pinsapo, A. maroccana, A. numidica,* and *A. cilicica* (Quezel op. cit.). Only this last species has a wide distribution. The trees can form beautiful forests (30 m high), and except for *A. pinsapo,* are always mixed with the cedars, usually on north-facing slopes or in narrow valleys. A third group of firs, occupying very small areas, is constituted by *Abies borisi-regis, A. equi-trojani,* and *A. bormulleriana.* These trees are found in mixed forests on the edges of the Mediterranean Region.

**Figure 10.9.** *Pinus halepensis* (Aleppo pine) forest near Barcelona, Spain. Photo by Louis Trabaud.

## The Sclerophyll Forests

These are mainly constituted of a few species of *Quercus* with persistent leaves and, more particularly, by *Quercus ilex, Q. suber, Q. calliprinos*. *Quercus ilex* (holly oak) is very abundant everywhere around the perimeter of the western Mediterranean where it occupies huge areas; it is still abundant in occidental Greece, on the verge of the Aegean Sea, and in the islands. It disappears farther east. In the countries on the north side of the Mediterranean Sea, *Q. ilex* rises from the seashore to an altitude of 900 to 1000 m. In North Africa, southern Spain, and locally in southern Italy and Greece, *Q. ilex* is rarely present under 400 m, but is common up to 1500 and 1800 meters. *Quercus suber* (cork oak) is also present in the western Mediterranean and extends westward in Spain and Portugal and eastward to

Dalmatia. Its ecological requirements are more demanding than those of *Q. ilex;* therefore, it is localized in the warmer and more humid zones on substrates without active calcium. *Q. suber* forests are rarely dense; most often they are found in open stands invaded by dense maquis. *Quercus calliprinos* also presents an important sylvatic element in the Near East, where it forms open forests that rise from an altitude of 200 up to 1200 m.

### Deciduous Forests

These are particularly numerous and complex in the Mediterranean and peri-Mediterranean areas. These forests are found in the cool and temperate parts of the region. Their importance is variable. In the northern part deciduous forests occupy huge areas, yet in the central and southern part their importance decreases, both due to human activity and the existence of a longer summer dry period: where these forests exist in the south, they are scattered and of small size. *Quercus pubescens* forests are the most widespread since they extend from Catalonia toward Greece, principally on the northern periphery of the Mediterranean Sea. Forests of *Ostrya carpinifolia, Carpinus orientalis, Fraxinus ornus,* and *Tilia cordata* stretch from the Maritime Alps (southeast of France) to the Balkans and as far as Anatolia. The other deciduous oak forests (mainly *Q. cerris, Q. frainetto,* and *Q. trojana*) form vast forests on the European edge of the Mediterranean Sea. Planted and favored by the natives, *Castanea sativa* (common chestnut) replaced these forests in many areas (principally on acid soils). South of the Mediterranean Sea, deciduous forests are less developed. *Quercus faginea* is present in pure stands in Spain and Portugal, and in North Africa mixed with *Q. toza* and *Q. afares.* In the Near East there are *Q. infectoria* forests.

Tall shrublands composed of *Olea europaea, Ceratonia siliqua,* and *Pistacia lentiscus* are found in the warmest regions everywhere on the Mediterranean periphery. However, they are more abundant in the southern part. These are mixed with *Rhus oxyacantha, R. pentaphylla,* and *Zizyphus lotus* in the western part and *Pistacia palaestina* and *Arbutus andrachne* in the eastern part. Where severely injured by overcultivation, they give way to open garrigues with *Poterium spinosum* in the east, or to xerophil swards with perennial Andropogonae, more particularly in Morocco and in Algeria in the west.

Most wooded areas have been so disturbed by tree felling and grazing that today only rare stunted and gnarled trees subsist scattered here and there; dominant vegetation is a low garrigue on calcareous soils and a denser and higher maquis on siliceous soils. The height of the maquis can reach 3 m and more. A multitude of community types exists, and only the most frequently encountered communities are quoted here (according to Tomaselli 1976).

In continental Spain and the Balearic Islands are found *Q. ilex* maquis (Figure 10.10; twisted and low trees, 2 to 4 m) as well as shrublands of *Q. coccifera* and *Calycotome spinosa.* Their homologue is *Calycotome villosa* shrubland in Portugal. Everywhere in the Mediterranean are several kinds of

***Figure 10.10.***    A dense, high maquis of *Quercus ilex* in Corsica. Photo by Louis Trabaud.

shrublands with *Erica arborea, E. scoparia,* several species of *Cistus, Rosmarinus officinalis, Olea europaea* var. *oleaster, Pistacia lentiscus, Rhamnus alaternus,* and *Juniperus oxycedrus.* In the northeast, the center, and south grow garrigues of *Rhamnus lycioides,* whereas shrublands of *R. oleoides,* and *Chamaerops humilis* (dwarf palm) spread in the northwest.

In France, the compact limestones are covered by huge areas (100,000 ha) of *Quercus coccifera* garrigues; garrigues of *Rosmarinus officinalis* are also present. Maquis of *Erica arborea* and *Arbutus unedo,* of *Erica scoparia,* or of *Calycotome villosa* with *Cistus monspeliensis* extend on acid substrates.

In Italy, there are shrublands with *Olea europaea* var. *oleaster* and *Pistacia lentiscus,* with *Chamaerops humilis.* In Puglie (southeastern part of the pennisula) and Sicily, *Q. calliprinos* garrigues are homologues to those of *Q. coccifera* in southern France. Other kinds of shrublands are *Myrtus communis, Arbutus unedo, Phillyrea media, Rhamnus alaternus, Calycotome spinosa, Genista aethnensis, Erica scoparia, E. arborea, Juniperus oxyce-drus,* and *J. phoenicea.*

These same types of shrublands are found in Greece and Turkey, with, in addition, shrublands of *Arbutus andrachne* and *Calycotome villosa*. A typi-cal community of Mediterranean Greece is the "phrygana" which rarely reaches 1 m high (Table 10.13). It consists of two principal communities dominated either by *Sarcopoterium spinosum* or by *Phlomis fruticosa* (Papanastasis 1977).

In Cyprus, most of the island vegetation is maquis, predominantly *Pis-tacia lentiscus,* except in the eastern part of the island where *Juniperus phoenicea* is the dominant species. Another important community is *Cistus incanus* var. *creticus.*

In North Africa, the same types of brushlands encountered in southern Europe stretch over the country and, in addition, on the "Hauts Plateaux" (Atlas mountains) one finds a steppe formed by a grass with long leathery leaves: *Stipa tenacissima.*

On the southern and eastern fingers of the Mediterranean Region, as precipitation decreases and desertic areas begin, communities become more and more open and give way to communities associated with desertic cli-mate.

In the Mediterranean countries, average fire sizes and return periods depend more on the degree and sophistication of the forest fire control effort than on fuels or climate. Table 10.14 lists average fire size for several coun-tries in the Mediterranean Basin.

## Southern California

In the part of California that profits by the Mediterranean climate, vegeta-tion, according to a physiognomic or a physiologic point of view, is similar to that of the Mediterranean Region of the old Continent. Dominant species often belong to the same genera as their Mediterranean homologues (Table 10.15).

As in the countries around the Mediterranean Sea, the primeval forest is only conserved on small areas, generally on north-facing slopes. Evergreen trees are dominant: *Quercus chrysolepis, Q. agrifolia, Arbutus menziesii, Castanopsis chrysophylla, Myrica californica,* and conifers: *Pinus radiata, Cupressus sargentii* (localized on the Coast Range serpentines), and *C. ma-crocarpa*. Many of these trees are adapted to survive fires by sprouting from stumps.

This ability exists not only for the hardwoods but also for several coni-fers, which is uncommon. Certain species possess other adaptations to fire such as *Cupressus sargentii* whose serotinous cones are opened by the heat from a forest fire.

An original feature of the coastal forest is the abundance of epiphytic lichens as a result of summer fogs. The majority of noncultivated lands in

*Table 10.13.   Fireclimate of Athens, Greece, 37°53' N, 23°43' E, Elev. 27 m*

| Month | Max T°C | Min T°C | DPT°C | Precip (cm) | Snow (cm) | Days Precip | Day Length (hr) |
|---|---|---|---|---|---|---|---|
| Jan | 12.2 | 5.6 | 2.8 | 5.6 | 0 | 6.8 | 9.7 |
| Feb | 12.8 | 6.1 | 4.4 | 4.1 | 0 | 5.2 | 10.6 |
| Mar | 15.6 | 7.8 | 3.3 | 3.6 | 0 | 4.6 | 11.8 |
| Apr | 19.4 | 11.1 | 6.7 | 2.0 | 0 | 2.7 | 13.0 |
| May | 25.0 | 15.6 | 10.0 | 2.0 | 0 | 2.7 | 14.0 |
| Jun | 29.4 | 19.4 | 11.7 | 1.5 | 0 | 1.7 | 14.6 |
| Jul | 32.8 | 18.9 | 15.0 | 0.3 | 0 | 0.1 | 14.9 |
| Aug | 32.2 | 22.2 | 15.0 | 1.0 | 0 | 1.1 | 13.5 |
| Sep | 28.3 | 18.9 | 13.9 | 1.5 | 0 | 2.6 | 12.3 |
| Oct | 23.3 | 15.6 | 11.1 | 4.3 | 0 | 5.1 | 11.1 |
| Nov | 17.8 | 11.1 | 10.6 | 7.1 | 0 | 7.1 | 10.0 |
| Dec | 13.9 | 7.8 | 6.7 | 7.1 | 0 | 8.1 | 9.5 |
| Annual | 21.7 | 13.9 | — | 40.3 | — | — | — |

Cover Type 8: Brush
Cool Winter, Nonhumid, Long Burning Season
Scattered Shrubs, Low Litter Weight

| Month | Jan | Feb | Mar | Apr | May | Jun | Jul | Aug | Sep | Oct | Nov | Dec |
|---|---|---|---|---|---|---|---|---|---|---|---|---|
| Fire Prob. | 0 | 0.06 | 0.35 | 0.64 | 0.77 | 0.86 | 0.94 | 0.93 | 0.84 | 0.53 | 0 | 0 |
| Burning Index | 8 | 5.0 | 17.0 | 19.0 | 29.0 | 42.0 | 43.0 | 40.0 | 29.0 | 17.0 | 2 | 2 |

*Table 10.14.    Average Fire Size in Hectares*

| | |
|---|---|
| Algeria | 37.1 |
| Cyprus | 13.0 |
| France | 13.2 |
| Greece | 79.0 |
| Israel | 4.2 |
| Italy | 11.9 |
| Portugal | 57.2 |
| Spain | 41.5 |
| Turkey | 38.5 |
| Yugoslavia | 12.4 |

southern California are occupied by chaparral or housing developments. Chaparral vegetation is made up of medium-sized evergreen-leaved shrubs belonging to some 40 species, different from those of the forest, which belong to such genera as *Arctostaphylos, Adenostoma,* and *Quercus.* Chaparral is periodically swept by wildfires, after which the shrubs regenerate from root sprouts which gives the brush a scrubby aspect. On a great part of its area, chaparral can be considered as a secondary formation in equilibrium with fire, analogous to the maquis or garrigue. On south-facing slopes and at the eastern limit of its range, conditions are so xeric that chaparral probably represents the climax (Biswell 1974, Zinke 1973).

In a rather narrow strip along the coast (in the Coast Range) a sage community with a lower height presents some physiognomic analogies with *Cistus* stands or tomillares of the Mediterranean Basin. The plants (*Salvia* and *Artemisia*) have thin woody stems and aromatic soft leaves. They produce numerous light seeds whose germination is stimulated by fire and whose growth is more rapid than that of shrubs.

In the valleys and foothills, grasslands or woodland savannas appear mainly dominated by several oaks: *Quercus chrysolepis, Q. douglasii, Q. wislizenii,* and *Q. engelmannii.*

The fact that almost all the plants of the southern California region are adapted to fire would tend to prove that wildfires constituted an ecological factor of chaparral even before the Indian settlement, as a matter of fact, numerous characteristic species have been present since the middle Miocene (Axelrod 1973).

Forest fires have been a predominant feature of the southern California scene since the days of the earliest explorers (Figure 10.11). Vancouver, attempting to map the coast below Los Angeles in 1793 wrote of immense columns of smoke that occasionally reduced the visibility from the ship to less than 30 m. Richard Dana in his book *Two Years Before the Mast* gives vivid description of the great fire of 1823 in the hills behind Santa Barbara. But with the increase in population density has come a marked increase in fire frequency. Return periods in southern California now range from 50 to

*Table 10.15.* Fireclimate of Riverside, California, 33°57' N, 117°26' W, Elev. 250 m

| Month | Max T°C | Min T°C | DPT°C | Precip (cm) | Snow (cm) | Days Precip | Day Length (hr) |
|---|---|---|---|---|---|---|---|
| Jan | 16.7 | 4.4 | 1.1 | 6.3 | 0 | 4.9 | 10.1 |
| Feb | 18.3 | 5.6 | 1.7 | 5.6 | 0 | 3.5 | 10.8 |
| Mar | 19.4 | 6.1 | 3.3 | 3.1 | 0 | 2.9 | 11.8 |
| Apr | 22.2 | 8.3 | 6.7 | 2.6 | 0 | 2.6 | 12.9 |
| May | 24.4 | 10.6 | 7.8 | 0.5 | 0 | 0.6 | 13.8 |
| Jun | 29.4 | 13.3 | 10.6 | 0.1 | 0 | 0.1 | 14.2 |
| Jul | 33.9 | 17.2 | 12.2 | 0.1 | 0 | 0.1 | 14.1 |
| Aug | 32.8 | 16.1 | 12.2 | 0.3 | 0 | 0.4 | 13.3 |
| Sep | 31.7 | 15.0 | 10.6 | 0.5 | 0 | 0.2 | 12.2 |
| Oct | 26.7 | 11.1 | 6.7 | 0.6 | 0 | 0.9 | 11.2 |
| Nov | 21.7 | 7.2 | 1.7 | 2.3 | 0 | 2.3 | 10.2 |
| Dec | 18.9 | 5.0 | -0.6 | 5.0 | 0 | 2.6 | 9.8 |
| Annual | 24.4 | 10.0 | — | 27.0 | — | — | — |

Cover Type 8: Brush
Mild Winter, Nonhumid, Long Burning Season
Scattered Shrubs, Little Litter

| Month | Jan | Feb | Mar | Apr | May | Jun | Jul | Aug | Sep | Oct | Nov | Dec |
|---|---|---|---|---|---|---|---|---|---|---|---|---|
| Fire Prob. | 0 | 0.07 | 0.45 | 0.63 | 0.87 | 0.96 | 0.99 | 0.97 | 0.97 | 0.93 | 0.67 | 0.24 |
| Burning Index | 32 | 36.0 | 34.0 | 31.0 | 37.0 | 48.0 | 63.0 | 58.0 | 60.0 | 54.0 | 54.0 | 51.0 |

***Figure 10.11.*** Large fires are commonplace in southern California. Here two fires are burning simultaneously north of San Diego. Photo by Craig Chandler.

as low as 15 years, and most older firefighters have fought fires twice on the same piece of ground.

### Central Chile

From the six Mediterranean regions of Chile described by di Castri (1968, 1973): per-arid, arid, semi-arid, subhumid, humid, and per-humid, only vegetation of the last five has sufficient continuity of fuel to carry fire. These six regions are located in zones from north to south and west to east.

The most northern vegetation is a semidesert (jaral) of chamaephytes and Cactaceae, whose density increases toward the coast and northern part. On hills and in the coastal valleys, where fogs have an influence, very dense communities of *Euphorbia lactiflua* and Cactaceae such as *Trichocereus coquimbensis* are found; they are similar to low woodland savannas of 2 to 3 m height and are some times too dense to penetrate. Savannas with chanar (*Geoffroea decorticans*) grow along rivers.

Further to the south the regular occurrence of fire associated with intense grazing has involved a transformation of open sclerophyllous forests with *Quillaja saponaria, Peumus boldus, Cryptocarya,* and *Beilschmiedia* into thorny scrubs in the Coast Ranges, whereas shrubby steppes occupy the coastal terraces. In the Central Plain steppes with *Acacia caven* (espinal) are the vegetation types that are, at the present time, most widespread and characteristic of the landscape. This *Acacia caven* steppe has resulted by degradation from a *Lithraea caustica* and *Quillaja saponaria* primeval forest.

*Proustia pungens* and *Trevoa trinervis* are both drought deciduous spring shrubs that are very common, either occurring in almost pure stands or among the evergreen sclerophylls listed. The widespread mixing of these diverse types leads to a general vegetation that diverges from its California counterpart.

Small deciduous forests of *Nothofagus obliqua* appear when allowed by atmospheric (fogs) or edaphic (humid soils) conditions.

In the far south, the landscape takes a forested, parklike appearance in which the preceding species are present but mixed with species common to the more southern humid regions such as: *Nothofagus* spp. (e.g., *Nothofagus dombeyi*), *Drimys winteri,* and *Araucaria araucana.*

Virtually all of the fires (96 percent of the number and 93 percent of the burned area) in Chile occur in the central section between 33 and 42° south latitude (Table 10.16). Because Chile is fortunately free from the foehn winds that plague the Mediterranean Basin and southern California, the average fire size is only 10.2 ha as opposed to 31 ha in the Mediterranean and 219 in southern California. The return period is 272 years, sufficient to warrant conversion to productive forests. However, fire incidence and fire sizes have both increased in the 750,000 ha of *Pinus radiata* plantations in

*Table 10.16. Fireclimate of Santiago, Chile, 33°27' S, 70°42' W, Elev. 520 m*

| Month | Max *T*°C | Min *T*°C | DPT°C | Precip (cm) | Snow (cm) | Days Precip | Day Length (hr) |
|---|---|---|---|---|---|---|---|
| Jan | 29.4 | 11.7 | 9.4 | 0.3 | 0.0 | 0.8 | 13.9 |
| Feb | 28.9 | 11.1 | 10.6 | 0.3 | 0.0 | 0.8 | 13.3 |
| Mar | 26.7 | 9.4 | 9.4 | 0.5 | 0.0 | 1.1 | 12.2 |
| Apr | 23.3 | 7.2 | 8.3 | 1.3 | 0.0 | 1.5 | 11.2 |
| May | 18.3 | 5.0 | 7.2 | 6.4 | 0.0 | 4.2 | 10.2 |
| Jun | 14.4 | 2.8 | 5.0 | 8.4 | 5.1 | 5.8 | 9.6 |
| Jul | 15.0 | 2.8 | 5.0 | 7.6 | 5.1 | 5.3 | 10.1 |
| Aug | 16.7 | 3.9 | 6.1 | 5.6 | 12.7 | 4.0 | 10.8 |
| Sep | 18.9 | 5.6 | 6.7 | 3.1 | 0.0 | 2.7 | 11.8 |
| Oct | 22.2 | 7.2 | 7.8 | 2.1 | 0.0 | 1.6 | 12.9 |
| Nov | 25.6 | 8.9 | 7.8 | 0.8 | 0.0 | 1.1 | 13.8 |
| Dec | 28.3 | 10.6 | 8.3 | 0.5 | 0.0 | 1.0 | 14.2 |
| Annual | 22.2 | 7.2 | — | 36.9 | — | — | — |

Cover Type 8: Brush
Cool Winter, Nonhumid, Long Burning Season
Scattered Shrubs, Low Litter Weight

| Month | Jan | Feb | Mar | Apr | May | Jun | Jul | Aug | Sep | Oct | Nov | Dec |
|---|---|---|---|---|---|---|---|---|---|---|---|---|
| Fire Prob. | 0.95 | 0.95 | 0.93 | 0.82 | 0.82 | 0 | 0 | 0 | 0.20 | 0.63 | 0.84 | 0.92 |
| Burning Index | 54.0 | 45.0 | 40.0 | 29.0 | 13.0 | 8 | 9 | 11 | 17.0 | 26.0 | 43.0 | 54.0 |

Chile where the return period is 166 years, a marginal figure for sustained capital investment.

## Southern Africa

The typical vegetation of the Cape Region is constituted by a broad category of sclerophyllous shrublands called *fynbos* (Table 10.17). This vegetation has an irregular L-shaped distribution stretching into the region near the coast along two major mountain chains. On the coastline the influence of the environment (sand dunes and winds) gives it a very low size (example at the Cape of Good Hope). Fynbos occupies some slopes on the Little Karoo Mountains.

Taylor (1972, 1977) has identified the following features particular to or characteristic of the fynbos: (1) the invariable presence of the family Restionaceae, and (2) normally dominant (or codominant) physiognomic elements: the restioid-wiry aphyllous hemicryptophytes, mainly of Restionaceae—and the ericoid element that comprises dwarf and low evergreen shrubs with small, hard, narrow-rolled leaves (Ericaceae as *Erica chamissonis, E. caffra,* etc.; Rhamnaceae, i.e., *Phylica;* Compositae, i.e., *Metalassia* and *Stoebe*). Another typical and often dominant growth form (not invariably present) is the tall broad-sclerophyllous shrub—Taylor's (1972) proteoid element—that normally comprises certain members of the Proteaceae (*Protea grandiflora, P. arborea, P. mellifera,* etc.). Native trees are absent or rare (Moll et al. 1980); the only real tree of the fynbos is *Leucadendron argenteum* (Proteaceae).

Three major types of fynbos are normally recognized, principally on habitat differences; these are coastal, mountain, and arid fynbos (Kruger 1977, Taylor 1972).

A wide range of structural formations is found in the fynbos zone, from low communities dominated by Restionaceae or Cyperaceae, or both, to tall (4 m), dense, broad sclerophyllous scrub. Taylor (1972) describes the manner in which these formations are loosely segregated in zones. A proteoid zone on the foothills and lower slopes, in which communities have an upper layer (1.5 to 3 m) of tall, broad sclerophylls, especially Proteaceae, an understory of ericoid shrubs and graminoid–restoid plants and a short graminoid–restoid layer with forbs. An ericoid–restoid zone occurs at upper elevations, where the broad sclerophyllous shrubs are sparse or absent. This pattern is rather diffuse and communities are intermingled in the region.

On marine sand dunes along the coast stretches the coastal fynbos. The restoid element still forms the matrix, but the ericoid element is very much in evidence (Taylor 1972, 1977).

The structure of arid fynbos is simple and open. Ericoid and restoid forms predominate.

Toward the Karoo area, other plant formation categories include two

Table 10.17.  *Fireclimate of Cape Agulhas, South Africa, 34°50' S, 20°01' E, Elev. 19 m*

| Month | Max T°C | Min T°C | DPT°C | Precip (cm) | Snow (cm) | Days Precip | Day Length (hr) |
|-------|---------|---------|-------|-------------|-----------|-------------|-----------------|
| Jan | 23.3 | 17.2 | 15.6 | 2.0 | 0 | 1.9 | 14.0 |
| Feb | 23.3 | 17.2 | 16.1 | 1.8 | 0 | 1.6 | 13.3 |
| Mar | 22.2 | 16.1 | 16.1 | 3.3 | 0 | 3.1 | 12.2 |
| Apr | 20.6 | 14.4 | 14.4 | 3.8 | 0 | 3.5 | 11.2 |
| May | 18.9 | 12.8 | 12.2 | 5.1 | 0 | 4.4 | 10.2 |
| Jun | 17.2 | 11.1 | 10.6 | 5.8 | 0 | 4.4 | 9.7 |
| Jul | 16.1 | 10.0 | 9.4 | 5.3 | 0 | 4.0 | 10.0 |
| Aug | 17.2 | 10.6 | 10.6 | 4.8 | 0 | 3.7 | 10.8 |
| Sep | 17.2 | 11.1 | 10.6 | 4.1 | 0 | 3.1 | 11.8 |
| Oct | 18.9 | 12.8 | 11.7 | 3.8 | 0 | 2.9 | 12.9 |
| Nov | 20.6 | 15.0 | 13.9 | 2.8 | 0 | 2.2 | 13.8 |
| Dec | 22.2 | 16.1 | 14.4 | 1.8 | 0 | 1.6 | 14.3 |
| Annual | 20.0 | 13.9 | — | 44.4 | — | — | — |

Cover Type 8: Brush
Mild Winter, Nonhumid, Long Burning Season
Scattered Shrubs, Little Litter

| Month | Jan | Feb | Mar | Apr | May | Jun | Jul | Aug | Sep | Oct | Nov | Dec |
|-------|-----|-----|-----|-----|-----|-----|-----|-----|-----|-----|-----|-----|
| Fire Prob. | 0.83 | 0.83 | 0.69 | 0.57 | 0.36 | 0.15 | 0.21 | 0.33 | 0.45 | 0.57 | 0.70 | 0.81 |
| Burning Index | 4.0 | 2.0 | 0.0 | 1.0 | 1.0 | 1.0 | 1.0 | 1.0 | 1.0 | 2.0 | 1.0 | 4.0 |

types of low narrow sclerophyllous shrublands (1 m) dominated by members of Asteraceae (*Elytropappus rhinocerotis* and *Eriocephalus*).

Adapted to, and apparently requiring periodic fires for the maintenance of its character and diversity (Kruger op. cit., Taylor 1972, 1977), very flammable fynbos is increasing its area with fire.

In addition to the fynbos, another type of ligneous formation is encountered in the Mediterranean zone of southern Africa. Evergreen mesophyll forest, apparently relictual, grows in moister rocky canyons, confined to ravines, and similarly scattered sites, covering a small fraction of the land area (Kruger op. cit.). In the upper layer these forests are constituted by trees with broad, hard, shiny leaves as *Podocarpus falcatus* and *P. latifolius;* in the understory: *Ocotea bullata, Platylopnus trifoliatus, Trichocladus crinitus, Cunonia capensis,* and *Olea capensis.* A few centuries ago, before the arrival of European settlement, these forests extended over areas occupied by the fynbos today.

Along the entire eastern coast of South Africa from Zululand through the Eastern Cape, state and private forest plantations are managed for pulpwood and timber products. Nearly one-half million ha are under organized fire protection. The average area burned annually is 3600 ha, or 0.8 percent, but in bad fire years such as 1980 the area burned may be more than triple the average. One fire on USUTO Pulp Company Land in Swaziland devastated 500 ha of juvenile plantations and burned three forest workers to death.

## Southern Australia

Australia is a large continental mass extending from 11 to 44°S. Although the climate varies from tropical and subtropical in the north to temperate and cool temperate in the south, the vegetation structure and floristics may appear remarkably similar in quite different climatic regions.

There is a marked rainfall gradient from the high rainfall areas of the southern, eastern, and northern coastal regions into the arid interior. Broadly, the structure of the vegetation formations vary according to this rainfall gradient. Tall dense forests are found in high rainfall regions; stunted open communities in the arid regions. The upper stratum of almost all perennial communities is evergreen and the structural characteristics of the vegetation change subtly along a continuum from humid to arid localities. Vegetation is classified on the basis of the life form height and projected canopy cover of the uppermost stratum (Specht 1970, 1981).

Under this structural classification the following climax formations can be recognized with the continuum from the humid to arid zones: (1) closed forest, (2) tall open forest, (3) open forest, (4) tall woodland, (5) woodland, (6) tall shrubland, (7) low shrubland, and (8) low open shrubland.

The genus *Eucalyptus* (with over 600 species) dominates all open forests and woodland formations, whereas species of *Acacia* predominate in the upper stratum of the arid and semi-arid areas. The hummock grass, *Triodia* spp., is often present as an understory in the more arid *Acacia* shrublands and may be found with few or no *Acacia* shrubs in the driest sites.

Apart from the closed forest formations (tropical and temperate rainforests) and the brigalow open forest (*Acacia harpophylla*), all other communities are fire prone and carry abundant flammable fuel. In the arid interior fuels may be sparse except after periods of exceptional rainfall when ephemeral grasses and forbs provide a continuous ground cover between the perennial vegetation and extraordinarily extensive fires can occur. In 1974 to 1975 prolific grass growth provided continuous fuel over much of inland Australia and more than 117 million ha burned (Luke and McArthur 1978).

Since the vegetation structure is similar in the open forest in both northern and southern Australia, forest fuels exhibit similar combustion characteristics. In the summer rainfall zone of northern Australia tall tropical grasses tend to dominate the understory. Fires are common but as the dry season occurs in the winter months, and as fuels are relatively light and winds rarely very strong, these fires never achieve the intensity exhibited by wildfires in the true Mediterranean regions of southern Australia. Further discussion of Australian vegetation types is restricted to these latter areas.

The forests are classified as *closed* forest (70 to 100 percent foliage projective cover) or *open* forest (30 to 70 percent projected foliage cover) (Specht 1970). In forestry literature the closed forest is equivalent to temperate rainforest and the tall open forest is separated into wet sclerophyll and dry sclerophyll forest. As this alternative terminology provides a useful subdivision for discussing the burning characteristics and vegetation responses to fire it is used here.

The temperate rainforest is a dense closed canopy layered forest 10 to 30 m high. It is characterized by Antarctic beeches (*Nothofagus* species) with *Eucalyptus* at the interface with more open communities. It occupies small remnant areas in New South Wales and Victoria and larger areas in Tasmania where it is associated with some of the few softwood (conifer) genera (*Dacrydium, Phyllocladus,* and *Athrotaxis*) native to Australia. The understory may contain a small tree or tall shrub stratum. Tree ferns (e.g., *Dicksonia antarctica*) usually exceed 2 m and ferns are common in the ground story. Grasses are absent or sparse. These forests are flammable only during periods of extreme drought.

Wet sclerophyll forests are tall (30 to 50 m) open forests, generally with two or three layers of shade-tolerant understory trees to 10 m; tree ferns are common usually over 2 m, and ferns, mosses, and liverworts are common in the ground strata. These forests accumulate large fuel loads that dry out during extended drought periods and can support extremely high intensity fires. The forests are fire sensitive and are killed outright by most fires. However, these forests require high intensity fires to regenerate and in the absence of fire are succeeded by the temperate rainforest communities.

In the southwest corner of Western Australia the karri forests (*E. diversicolor*) are commonly around 70 m and may reach 87 m. They grow in pure stands or in association with marri (*E. calophylla*). Although forests are killed by fires of high intensity (catastrophic fires appear to be the natural process by which degenerate, overmature forests are regenerated; White 1980), they have some resistance to fire and prescribed fire has been used to reduce fuel loads in mature forests (Shea et al. 1981).

Southeastern wet sclerophyll forests contain some of the tallest hardwoods in the world. Trees of mountain ash (*E. regnans*) over 107 m have been recorded (Hall et al. 1975) and this species is exceeded in height only by the redwoods of California. Many wet sclerophyll eucalypts and, particularly, *E. regnans* have very thin bark up to the spar stage, and most wet sclerophyll forests are managed with the complete exclusion of fire. One exception is alpine ash (*E. delegatensis*) which develops a thick fibrous bark on the lower bole and hazardous fuel loads can be reduced with careful application of low intensity prescribed fires (Shea et al. op. cit.).

Dry sclerophyll forests are communities where the dominant tree layer is of moderate height (10 to 30 m) and open (foliage projective cover 70 to 30 percent). In northern Australia the open forest grades into a woodland (foliage projective cover 30 to 10 percent) but in southern Australia practically all the original woodlands have been cleared or modified for agriculture and in many areas the only vestiges of the original native vegetation that remain are on the verges along roadsides. The dry sclerophyll forest has a well-developed layer of xeromorphic understory shrubs; grasses are abundant in other less dense forests and woodlands, but tend to be suppressed by litter accumulation in the denser forests although they may regenerate quite prolifically after fire has removed litter and opened the forest canopy. These forests cover large areas of southwest Western Australia, eastern Australia, and Tasmania. Many eucalypt species are represented in different forest associations but most contain species with rough fibrous bark (stringybarks). A typical dry sclerophyll forest is the jarrah-marri (*E. marginata–E. calophylla*) forest of Western Australia or the messmate–peppermint forests (*E. obliqua–E. radiata*) of Victoria and Tasmania. The forests are flammable in most seasons and the high spotting potential of the fibrous stringybarks promote the spread of high-intensity fires into the crowns for considerable distances ahead by spotting. However, most tree species are thick-barked and fire resistant and are seldom killed outright even by high-intensity fires. The understory species are highly flammable and may die out in prolonged protection from fire. Both plants and animals in the dry sclerophyll community are adapted to frequent fire, and coexist in a dynamic equilibrium determined by the frequency season and intensity of fire (Christensen et al. 1981).

Eucalypts are very well adapted to regenerate after fire. If the fire is intense, seedling regeneration is excellent. If the fire burns the foliage without killing the trees, epicormic sprouts appear in large numbers (Mount 1969). In order to survive in a fire environment, eucalypts need natural protective mechanisms from the seedling to the mature stage when the seeds are produced (Ashton 1981, Christensen et al. op. cit., Mount op. cit., Shea et al. op. cit.).

Seeds that are dispersed after a fire and that ensure regeneration are protected from fire in three ways. There is no fuel for crown fires (Mount op. cit.); capsules are located under the leaves so that in case a crown fire did occur the heat flow into the capsules would be lessened; the nature of the capsules, with their thick wood cover surrounded by wet living tissue, makes them especially resistant to fire.

In all but exceptionally intense fires when all the vegetation is burned, fire in a sclerophyll eucalypt forest generally destroys the foliage in the upper part of the crown mainly by radiant heat and burns up all the understory (Cochrane 1966). With the burning of understory vegetation the soil is exposed but the tree structure persists. In less intense fires some understory shrubs may be damaged but not destroyed; the litter is consumed. However, in regions with fires of low intensity and high frequency, *Eucalyptus* spp. produce seedlings that have lignotubers. These can survive frequent fires and quickly occupy the openings left by fires in the forest cover (Mount op. cit.).

It is worth mentioning that since all eucalyptus regenerate by seed production, seeds of the currently present species may have always been available after every major fire, so that the factors that predispose a forest to burn (i.e., fuel load and dryness) may provide flowering and seed production at a very early stage.

With the notable exception of *Eucalyptus regnans* or mountain ash, which is very sensitive to fire and normally killed by it, most sclerophyll eucalyptus sprout freely after a fire. These species are characterized by vigorous regeneration from dormant advantitious buds (Ashton op. cit., Christensen et al. op. cit., Cochrane op. cit., Mount op. cit.). Resprouting varies greatly depending on prefire and postfire species and climatic conditions. Intense fires produce an *ash bed* effect that often stimulates tree growth (Shea et al. op. cit.), hence stimulating the growth of *Eucalyptus marginata* (jarrah) found on poor soil.

Low-intensity fires do not effect circumference growth of *E. marginata* or *E. diversicolor* (karri). Byrne (1977) concludes from a long-term study of the effect of fire on a forest of *E. maculata* (spotted gum), *E. fibrosa* (ironbark), and *E. drepanophylla* (grey ironbark) in Queensland that tree circumference increased in the first years after fire, followed by a return to normal growth thereafter. Under good to optimal growth conditions, *E. goniocalyx* and *E. aleophora* develop thick trunk foliage. This also occurs in *E. radiata* although the process is slower. Regeneration of *E. obliqua* is not so dense along the main trunk; sprouting is relatively vigorous along the upper part of the main branches but is slower and not so dense as in the three species just mentioned. In *E. macrorhyncha* and *E. baxteri*, regeneration is limited; the trunks never become densely covered with twigs or leaves.

Other important communities of the Mediterranean (and modified Mediterranean) region of Australia are the sclerophyll heathlands, mallee open scrublands, *Acacia* tall scrublands (mulga), and the chenopod low scrublands.

Heathland communities may have tree (10 to 30 m) or small tree–tall shrub strata present above a dense low shrub layer (2 m). These communities are found on infertile soils in all subhumid parts of forest. On better sites these communities grade into dry sclerophyll forest. True heathlands may be found on both seasonally droughted and seasonally water-logged sites from lowland to alpine altitude and from coastal to inland locations.

Mallee scrublands are dominated by mallee species (multistemmed with a large lignotuber) of eucalypts 2 to 10 m high and occur in a belt from southern Western Australia through southern South Australia into northern Victoria and southwestern New South Wales. The mallee scrubs vary from open to thicket formations with ground flora or heaths or grasses. The spread of fire in these communities depends largely on the amount of grass cover between the mallee clumps, but under strong winds the high spotting potential of the mallee clump ensures that fire is spread from clump to clump across relatively sparse ground cover.

The mulga scrub is a landscape of low scattered trees (10 m) or tall shrubs of *Acacia aneura*. Emergent tall trees (10 m) are rare and there is little or no ground cover except after periods of exceptional rainfall. Other species of *Acacia* may replace mulga and genera such as *Eremophila, Santalum,* and *Grevillea* may form part of the scrub layer. Vast areas of mulga are found in all states except Victoria.

Areas of saltbush (*Atriplex* spp.) and blue brush (*Kochia* spp.) consisting of low (1 to 2 m) succulent shrubs form low shrublands in the Mediterranean climate area of Australia. They constitute a large area in the Nullabor Plain of Western and South Australia. These shrubs normally occur in scattered clumps, but as in the case of the mulga areas, the spaces between clumps are sometimes occupied by grasses and other ephemeral plants (Luke and McArthur op. cit.) which may become hazardous when they dry out after a year of exceptionally heavy rainfall.

In the 200 years of European settlement in southern Australia, agricultural development has imposed great changes on the landscape. First the savanna ecosystems were grazed by large numbers of sheep and cattle where formerly only a low grazing pressure had been exerted by kangaroos and other native marsupials. Later these systems were destroyed to make way for grain crops and improved pastures of introduced grasses and legumes. In the winter rainfall zone most of the crops and pasture plants have been introduced from regions of the world with a Mediterranean climate (Specht 1972). Even the major plantation species is the exotic *P. radiata* from the Mediterranean climate of California. With the aid of widespread applications of superphosphate and trace elements (Mn, Cu, Zn, Mo) and other macronutrients (K, S), agricultural development has established crops and improved pastures into vast areas previously dominated by woodlands and mallees with heathy understories on soils very poor in plant nutrients. As a result, the areas are carrying higher fuel loads than under native grasses and shrubs, and summer grass fires of high intensity are an increasing threat in improved pastoral lands (Cheney 1976).

## GRASSLANDS, SAVANNAS, AND WOODLANDS

The woodland–grassland type is found where precipitation is insufficient to maintain a closed canopied forest. Woodland–grassland occupies more surface area worldwide than any other cover type and examples are found in every winter fireclimate. This type is extremely diverse, ranging from the parklike oak woodlands of England through the African and South American savannas, to the steppes of Russia and the great plains of central North America. However, generalizations are possible. In fireclimates where precipitation is distributed evenly throughout the year and there is no natural fire season, woodlands predominate. In areas with a short fire season, the type of cover is directly correlated with the frequency of fire. Where fire has been deliberately used to encourage grazing, as is true in much of the world, the cover is nearly treeless. Where fire is excluded or suppressed, woodlands predominate. In fireclimates with a long burning season, fires will occur frequently enough to maintain a grass rather than a tree cover even when fire is not deliberately used for that purpose. In some cold winter fireclimates, even when potential evapotranspiration exceeds precipitation every month of the year, there is sufficient snow accumulation to allow a single cover of annual grasses in the spring.

Understory cover and density in the woodland–grassland type is more related to winter temperatures than to the aridity index, since the type covers a relatively narrow precipitation range. In frost-free and cool fireclimates, the low vegetation tends to be shrubby rather than grassy except where fire occurs with sufficient frequency to suppress the shrubs. In fireclimates with colder winters grass is the typical low cover.

Plant communities dominated by grasses cover vast areas in the interior plains of the continents at temperate and subtropical latitudes. In the latter case they often merge into savannas. All these communities have continuous herbaceous dominants where the subterranean organs are perennial and the aboveground material dries during summer for lack of moisture, and in winter due to cold.

### Eurasia

In this part of the world *steppe,* as the Russians call it, covers huge areas stretching from eastern Europe to Siberia (Table 10.18). In this zonal extension of the Eurasian grasslands, the lack of tropical grasses (except *An-*

*Table 10.18. Fireclimate of Odessa, USSR, 46°29' N, 30°38' E, Elev. 65 m*

| Month | Max T°C | Min T°C | DPT°C | Precip (cm) | Snow (cm) | Days Precip | Day Length (hr) |
|---|---|---|---|---|---|---|---|
| Jan | 0.0 | −5.0 | −4.4 | 5.2 | 31.0 | 10.8 | 8.9 |
| Feb | 1.1 | −3.9 | −3.3 | 4.7 | 18.8 | 7.2 | 10.1 |
| Mar | 6.1 | −0.6 | 0.0 | 2.2 | 4.3 | 6.6 | 11.8 |
| Apr | 14.4 | 5.6 | 4.4 | 2.4 | 1.1 | 5.7 | 13.3 |
| May | 20.6 | 11.1 | 10.0 | 3.5 | 0.0 | 6.0 | 14.8 |
| Jun | 25.6 | 14.4 | 12.8 | 3.3 | 0.0 | 4.9 | 15.5 |
| Jul | 27.8 | 16.7 | 14.4 | 7.2 | 0.0 | 5.3 | 15.3 |
| Aug | 27.2 | 16.1 | 14.4 | 3.3 | 0.0 | 4.0 | 14.0 |
| Sep | 21.7 | 12.2 | 11.1 | 3.9 | 0.0 | 4.1 | 12.4 |
| Oct | 15.6 | 7.2 | 7.8 | 1.5 | 0.0 | 3.2 | 10.8 |
| Nov | 8.9 | 3.9 | 4.4 | 4.0 | 3.2 | 6.7 | 9.4 |
| Dec | 3.3 | −1.1 | −0.6 | 6.2 | 12.5 | 9.9 | 8.6 |
| Annual | 14.4 | 6.7 | — | 47.4 | — | — | — |

Cover Type 7: Woodland or Grassland
Short Cold Winter, Nonhumid, Long Burning Season
Moderate Litter, Scattered Shrubs

| Month | Jan | Feb | Mar | Apr | May | Jun | Jul | Aug | Sep | Oct | Nov | Dec |
|---|---|---|---|---|---|---|---|---|---|---|---|---|
| Fire Prob. | 0 | 0 | 0 | 0.53 | 0.57 | 0.67 | 0.53 | 0.72 | 0.57 | 0.71 | 0 | 0 |
| Burning Index | 0 | 0 | 0 | 9.0 | 11.0 | 20.0 | 22.0 | 20.0 | 12.0 | 4.0 | 0 | 0 |

*dropogon ischaemum,* appearing in isolated patches on the hill slopes), and a gentle and smoothed topography lead to plant communities that are not so varied as in North America.

The principal grasses are numerous species of *Stipa, Koeleria gracilis,* and *Fetuca sulcata.* Other genera such as *Bromus riparius,* and *Poa pratensis* not encountered in America are frequent, as the drought-resistant grasses such as *Carex humilis.* Geophytes with bulbs or rhizomes are abundant. All this vegetation is of low height; very few are higher than 50 cm.

Some complex mosaic appear where the topography permits. Thickets of *Quercus* grow in well-drained valley bottoms where there is some moisture. On side slopes shrubs such as *Amygdalus nana,* and *Prunus* are frequently encountered.

In eastern Europe and the European USSR, virtually all of the steppe has been converted to cropland and receives intensive fire protection. However, in northeast Asia where the steppe is still utilized by nomadic herders, range fires still occur annually. In Mongolia fires have been sufficiently large that their smoke is discernable from meteorological satellites 850 km in space. Steppe fireclimates invariably fit in the Woodland–Grassland cover type and are nonhumid with long but not very intense burning seasons.

**North America**

In contrast to the grasslands in Eurasia, the herbaceous communities of North America are much more diverse. Grasses are dominant over an area extending from southern Saskatchewan and Alberta to eastern Texas and from eastern Indiana to the woodland zone of the Rocky Mountains (Table 10.19). The climatic eastern limit is not certain. The actual boundary was certainly pushed past its "natural" limits by repeated fires set by Indians (Gleason and Cronquist op. cit.). In addition to the central plains, natural grasslands occur in the Palouse region of Washington and the great valley of California. The North American grassland formation grows under a variety of conditions. This is possible because of the growth form of the species, their long period of dormancy, and the fact that their moisture requirements are critical primarily in spring and early summer.

The eastern transition to forest is marked by an annual precipitation of 750 to 1000 mm from Texas to Indiana, and 500 to 625 mm farther north. A great proportion of this amount falls as spring rain. Westward, however, as the total decreases to about 250 to 350 mm near the Rocky Mountains, rainfall is scanty and irregular and the amount falling in spring and summer also decreases. Temperatures are equally variable. In the north, the growing season is cool and short and temperatures below 0°C are frequent for long periods in winter. In the southern part of the area, frosts may be almost unknown, and high temperatures occur in summer. In all the regions late summer dry spells with high temperatures and drying winds lead to extreme fire danger periods. Because the American Great Plains are higher in eleva-

Table 10.19.  *Fireclimate of Dodge City, Kansas, 37°45'' N, 99°58' W, Elev. 790 m*

| Month | Max T°C | Min T°C | DPT°C | Precip (cm) | Snow (cm) | Days Precip | Day Length (hr) |
|---|---|---|---|---|---|---|---|
| Jan | 5.0 | −8.3 | −7.2 | 1.0 | 4.8 | 1.4 | 9.7 |
| Feb | 7.8 | −6.1 | −5.0 | 1.8 | 3.2 | 2.1 | 10.6 |
| Mar | 13.3 | −1.7 | −4.4 | 2.3 | 5.8 | 2.5 | 11.8 |
| Apr | 19.4 | 5.0 | 1.1 | 4.8 | 0.9 | 4.7 | 13.0 |
| May | 23.9 | 10.6 | 9.4 | 7.4 | 0.0 | 6.0 | 14.0 |
| Jun | 29.4 | 16.1 | 13.9 | 8.1 | 0.0 | 5.9 | 14.6 |
| Jul | 32.3 | 18.9 | 15.6 | 7.9 | 0.0 | 5.7 | 14.3 |
| Aug | 31.7 | 17.8 | 15.0 | 6.6 | 0.0 | 5.1 | 13.5 |
| Sep | 27.8 | 13.3 | 9.4 | 4.8 | 0.0 | 3.5 | 12.3 |
| Oct | 20.6 | 6.1 | 3.9 | 3.6 | 0.1 | 2.8 | 11.1 |
| Nov | 13.3 | −1.1 | −3.3 | 2.0 | 2.4 | 2.0 | 10.0 |
| Dec | 6.7 | −6.1 | −6.1 | 1.5 | 3.5 | 1.9 | 9.5 |
| Annual | 19.4 | 5.6 | — | 51.8 | — | — | — |

Cover Type 7: Woodland or Grassland
Short Cold Winter, Nonhumid, Short Burning Season
Moderate Litter, Scattered Shrubs

| Month | Jan | Feb | Mar | Apr | May | Jun | Jul | Aug | Sep | Oct | Nov | Dec |
|---|---|---|---|---|---|---|---|---|---|---|---|---|
| Fire Prob. | 0 | 0 | 0 | 0.35 | 0.33 | 0.45 | 0.54 | 0.58 | 0.60 | 0.53 | 0.44 | 0 |
| Burning Index | 17 | 19 | 42 | 45.0 | 27.0 | 32.0 | 37.0 | 37.0 | 46.0 | 37.0 | 36.0 | 19 |

tion than the European steppes, they are subject to greater extremes of temperature with consequently higher mean burning indexes. In contrast to the steppes, most of the plains rainfall comes from summer thundershowers and the fire season is shorter, though more intense.

This region is characterized by the prairie grassland, which American authors consider the result of recurring fires due to lightning or to Indian intervention well before the coming of the first Europeans (Aikman 1955, Humphrey 1962, 1963, Komarek 1965, Vogl 1974, Wright 1974a). According to these authors, fires were an integral part of the ecosystem, not a rare phenomenon. The grassland vegetation is particularly well adapted to recurring fire, and fire maintains this vegetation type, preventing the invasion of shrubs and trees.

Before man in general and Europeans in particular, prairie fires could sweep across vast areas with nothing to stop them, as there were no natural barriers (Vogl op. cit.). Dry grasses with their loosely arranged leaves and inflorescences are a highly flammable fuel source. Their structure also permits good air circulation, hence an increased oxygen supply.

Grassland flora is generally lacking in diversity. Fire conditions lead to the creation of monotypical grass stands. Fire stimulates vegetative reproduction by the dominant species, which are well adapted to fire and compete with less well adapted species, finally eliminating them altogether. Dense, almost pure grass stands, more particularly rhizomatic or turfy types, are the characteristic prairie vegetation forms. Martin and Cushwa (1966) show that heating increases the germination rate of some species and the production of seeds. Germination and establishment of seedlings in annuals and perennials are generally favored by fire (Cushwa et al. 1968, 1970, Ehrenreich and Aikman 1957).

The season in which a fire occurs is quite important. In Texas herbaceous perennials survive fire and form stable populations because the fire season is in the spring, a season unfavorable to annual grasses that, stimulated by winter rains, are destroyed in the growth process before they can seed. Perennials on the other hand are still dormant in spring, so they can resprout after a fire (Wright 1968, 1973, 1974b). The interval between fires is about three to six years, enough time for stalks, leaves, inflorescences, and litter to accumulate until the conditions that favor fire are attained once again (Dix 1960, Ehrenreich and Aikman 1963, Hadley and Kieckhefer 1963, Vogl op. cit.).

### Tall Grass Prairie

Sometimes called "true prairie," bunch grasses are the dominant species, for most of them grow higher than 2 m tall, but sod-forming species are also present. Because of the generally favorable climatic and soil conditions, the major part of the area is cultivated and little of the original vegetation remains today except in isolated patches. The dominant grasses are *Stipa spartea, Andropogon furcatus, A. gerardi,* and *Sorghastrum nutans* (tall grasses), *Andropogon scoparius* and *Bouteloua curtipendula* (medium grasses), *Bouteloua gracilis* and *B. hirsuta* (short grasses). Other species, commonly called forbs, are present in all grasslands.

## Mixed Grass Prairie

The mixed grasses occupy an area between that of the tall grasses and short grasses and the dominant species come from both these communities. Important dominants throughout the area are *Bouteloua gracilis, B. hirsuta,* and *Andropogon scoparius,* and except in the north, *Buchloe dactyloides.* In the northern part of the mixed prairie occur *Koeleria cristata, Stipa spartea,* and *S. comata. Andropogon furcatus,* and *Sporobolus cryptandrus* are other important species.

## Short Grass Plains

Westward from the mixed grass prairie to the woodland zone of the Rockies, the xeric short grasses are dominant. The most important species are *Bouteloua gracilis* and *Buchloe dactyloides,* except north of the Dakotas, where the latter is absent. In several places *Stipa comata, Agropyron smithii,* or *Aristida longiseta* mixes with the dominants.

Short grasses belonging to the genera of *Bouteloua* and *Aristida* extend on desert plains of western Texas, northern Mexico, and southern New Mexico and Arizona.

Although the grassland region is dominated by grasses, it is not totally treeless. There is a thin border of *Populus deltoides* var. *occidentalis* along most of the larger streams. A dwarf form of *Quercus macrocarpa* var. *depressa* occurs wherever the moisture conditions are favorable for tree growth.

## California

The hotter and drier sites especially in the central valley of California were once occupied mainly by grasslands that because of fire, grazing, and conversion to cropland have been eliminated except for relic stands. Various perennial bunch grasses dominated the scene. Throughout most of the area it appears that *Stipa pulchra* was the principal species except near the coast. What remains has been so heavily grazed that the native grasses are mostly gone, replaced by weedy annual grasses introduced from Europe. *Avena (A. barbata), Bromus, Festuca,* and *Hordeum* are the commonest of the weedy grasses.

## The Palouse Region

The rolling hills of the Palouse region, as well as most of eastern Washington and Oregon and a western part of Idaho supported prairie grasses before being cultivated for wheat production. The most important species are *Agropyron spicatum, Festuca idahoensis,* and *Elymus condensatus.* Probably the dominance of the annual *Bromus tectorum* results from fire and grazing as it does in the Great Basin.

## South America

The plant communities dominated by herbaceous plants in the southern hemisphere differ from those of the northern hemisphere in that freezing does not play the same role in limiting vegetative activity and in modifying soil water conditions (with the exception of the communities dominated by herbaceous plants in South Africa, where the winter is relatively cold because of the altitude; Table 10.20).

In South America, savannas occasionally take the place of forest, even in regions that receive 2000 or 3000 mm of rainfall a year, for example, on the large island of Marajo, at the mouth of the Amazon. These savannas assume three principal forms.

The *campos de varzea* are treeless savannas that are flooded during high-water periods. There is no forest because of the extent of this submersion. During low-water periods, the ground is covered with dense grass vegetation.

The *campinas* are also treeless savannas, but they have developed on sandy soils following the destruction of the dry forest (carrasco) by fire.

Some campos resemble parkland, for example, in the Obidos region of Brazil. Corridors of savanna cut through semideciduous forest; they have been opened in the forest mass by clearing and burning and are maintained by fire.

South of the Amazonian forest, the vegetative landscape involves the juxtaposition of forests and savannas, distributed on the basis of climatic conditions and the nature of the soil.

The *Orbinya speciosa* (babaçu) forest occurs in the state of Maranhao, between the selva and the caatinga of northeastern Brazil. *Orbinya speciosa* is a palm which grows to a height of 10 m; the present range of this type of palm is due to human land-clearing efforts. Palms growing in the extremely dark undergrowth of the tropical rainforest are left by those clearing the land; exposed to the light, they develop vigorously and multiply.

The *campos cerrados* cover immense areas of the Brazilian plateau between the Amazonian forest and the coastal zone. The campo cerrado, which is far more extensive than the *campo limpo* (treeless savanna) is a savanna dotted with trees or shrubs. Most of the trees are less than 10 m high (*Annona coriacea* and *Andira humilis*); they have gnarled trunks, thick bark, small crowns, and, in most cases, persistent xeromorphic leaves. They belong to species other than those of the rainforest. The herbaceous layer is composed of 90 percent grasses. The current range of the campos cerrados is the result of fire. In many regions, the cerradao, that is, a savanna woodland or even an open forest in which the crowns of the trees (*Copaifera langsdorfii*) ensure over 50 percent coverage and in which the clumps of herbs are discontinuous, exists only in isolated islands.

In Venezuela, on either side of the Orinoco, stretch hundreds of thousands of square kilometers of savannas, the Llanos. These grassy areas take a wide range of forms, from treeless savanna to tree savanna and

Table 10.20. *Fireclimate of Ciudad Bolivar, Venezuela, 7°07' N, 63°32' W, Elev. 60 m*

| Month | Max T°C | Min T°C | DPT°C | Precip (cm) | Snow (cm) | Days Precip | Day Length (hr) |
|---|---|---|---|---|---|---|---|
| Jan | 32.2 | 22.2 | 21.7 | 3.6 | 0 | 2.9 | 11.6 |
| Feb | 32.8 | 22.2 | 22.2 | 2.0 | 0 | 1.9 | 11.7 |
| Mar | 33.9 | 22.8 | 22.2 | 2.8 | 0 | 1.8 | 12.0 |
| Apr | 33.9 | 23.9 | 22.8 | 2.5 | 0 | 2.2 | 12.2 |
| May | 33.9 | 23.9 | 23.3 | 9.7 | 0 | 5.9 | 12.4 |
| Jun | 32.2 | 23.9 | 23.3 | 14.0 | 0 | 9.4 | 12.5 |
| Jul | 32.2 | 23.9 | 23.3 | 16.0 | 0 | 10.7 | 12.4 |
| Aug | 32.8 | 23.9 | 23.9 | 18.0 | 0 | 11.8 | 12.2 |
| Sep | 33.9 | 23.9 | 23.9 | 9.1 | 0 | 5.9 | 12.0 |
| Oct | 33.9 | 23.9 | 24.4 | 10.2 | 0 | 6.4 | 11.8 |
| Nov | 32.8 | 23.9 | 23.9 | 7.1 | 0 | 5.0 | 11.7 |
| Dec | 32.2 | 22.8 | 23.3 | 3.3 | 0 | 2.7 | 11.5 |
| Annual | 33.3 | 23.3 | — | 97.3 | — | — | — |

Cover Type 7: Woodland or Grassland
Frost Free Winter, Humid, Long Burning Season
No Litter, Moderate Shrubs

| Month | Jan | Feb | Mar | Apr | May | Jun | Jul | Aug | Sep | Oct | Nov | Dec |
|---|---|---|---|---|---|---|---|---|---|---|---|---|
| Fire Prob. | 0.77 | 0.85 | 0.88 | 0.84 | 0.50 | 0.20 | 0.12 | 0.02 | 0.50 | 0.45 | 0.58 | 0.79 |
| Burning Index | 11.0 | 12.0 | 16.0 | 14.0 | 12.0 | 7.0 | 7.0 | 7.0 | 10.0 | 8.0 | 7.0 | 7.0 |

parkland. The Llanos consist primarily of grasses (*Trachypogon* and *Axono-pus*), some of which grow to a height of 3 to 4 m (*Paspalum*), whereas others form a relatively smooth carpet (*Cymbopogon*). For many years the Llanos was explained by a hypothesis according to which the savannas were the result of a deciduous forest destroyed by fire. At the end of the dry season, the deciduous forest was flammable. Fires set in the neighboring savannas reached the forest, burning leaves and twigs and injuring saplings, mostly with fatal results, although large trees resisted. With an increase in light penetration to ground level, grass could become established, especially in openings and around the edges. The grass, in turn, could burn more easily the following years. Older trees were injured in the next fire and over the years many fell. The forest opened more and more, with practically no regeneration of tree cover. Gradually the grasses took over more space. This process has been termed *savanization*. A comparable process was alleged to take place for lands cleared for agriculture. After the land was abandoned, succession started with grass, and fire halted the natural progression toward forest.

The traditional argument in defense of this hypothesis is that the process was very lengthy and that the forest has been destroyed to the point of no return. The obvious absence of an immediate succession to forest as soon as burning was discontinued is often interpreted as a secondary effect of the changes in the soil over centuries of recurring fire. This interpretation is unfounded, however, as savanna soil is frequently the same as forest soil. According to Blydenstein (1968), the hypothesis that imputes the origin of the savannas to the recurring burning of the forest is difficult to support.

Moreover, the presence of characteristic trees forming a savanna park-land is typical of savannas in which fire occurs. These trees are never found in a forest and are not the remainder of a primeval forest (Budowski 1966, Vareschi 1962). The most typical species are *Curatella americana*, *Bow-ditchia virgiliodes*, and *Xylopia grandifolia* and some palms such as *Coper-nicia tectorum*.

In these tropical grasslands, the fireclimate is uniform year-long except for precipitation. The fire season is governed by the length of the rainy season. In most areas even the dry season climate is humid and burning indices remain low. The herbaceous vegetation of the Llanos is well adapted to recurring fire. The phenological development of the species from sprout-ing to flowering and seed dispersal takes place during the rainy season when there are no fires.

In southern Brazil from the Tropic of Capricorn southward appear com-munities dominated by herbaceous plants. Lassalle (1980) describes their principal characteristics.

In the northern portion of the Argentine provinces of Corrientes and Entre Rios, the landscape consists of savanna. *Schinopsis balansae* (quebra-cho colorado) and *Copernicia albida* (the caranday palm) form groves on a dense carpet of *Panicum*, *Paspalum*, and *Andropogon* (*A. lateralis*). Farther to the south and west in these provinces, and in Uruguay as well, the hills and plains are covered by grasslands; the dominant genera are *Eragrostris, Axonopus, Paspalum, Panicum, Setaria, Andropogon, Briza,* and *Stipa,* together with Leguminosae, Compositae, Verbenaceae, and Oxalidaceae. The campos are dominated by isolated groves of *Prosopis algarobilla* (nandubay), then *Celtis spinosa* (tala), *Butia yatay* (a palm tree), and *Acacia caven* (espinello).

In Chaco (500 to 800 mm of precipitation per year), parkland forests alternate with grasslands and savannas. The main species of these woodlands are *Schinopsis lorentzii* (quebracho colorado), *S. balansae* (quebracho chaqueno), and numerous Cactaceae (*Trichocereus,* and *Cereus*). Near Salta and Tucuman a typical tree appears: *Piptadenia macrocarpa* (cebil); in the southwestern part of the area, *Chorisia insignis* (palo borracho) is a strange tree with a swelling trunk that characterizes the landscapes; southward, a palm tree *Tritinax campestris* becomes abundant; westward *Prosopis alba* (algarrobo) and *Geoffraea decorticans* (chanar) appear. Chanar constitutes groves more or less isolated in the middle of grasslands; the trunk of the tree is surrounded by sprouts coming from its roots. Andropogonae (*Bothriochloa, Sorghastrum, Trachypogon,* and *Elyonurus*), Panicae (*Paspalum, Panicum, Axonopus,* and *Setaria*), Eragrosticeae (*Aristida*), and *Pappophorum* are mainly dominant in the grass communities of Southern Chaco; some shrubs such as *Vernonia, Baccharis, Sphaeralcea, Eupatorium,* and *Cestrum* grow there also.

From the Rio de la Plata southwestward a prairie stretches similar to that of North America; it is called Pampa (Table 10.21). It is a boundless grassy plain, crossed only by a few rivers. Total yearly precipitation ranges from 600 to 1000 mm. Most of the cold season is not very severe (8 to 12°C) in spite of the pampero, a cold wind blowing from the southwest. Frost is less severe than in the northern hemisphere. The xerophilous vegetation is composed of grasses with threadlike and tough leaves such as *Stipa tenuissima, S. trichotoma,* and *S. tenuis,* as well as *Bromus brevis, B. auleticus, Bothriochloa springfieldii, Cenchrus parviflorus, Digitaria californica,* and *Koeleria permollis.* Where soils are better, other grasses thrive; *Hordeum murinum, H. pusillum, H. leporinum, Piptochaetium montevidense, P. stipoides, Phalaris angusta, Briza subaristata, Stipa trichotoma, S. papposa,* and *Poa bonariensis,* with Compositae, Leguminosae, Plantaginaceae, Verbenaceae, Oxalidaceae, and Juncaceae. In the western part of the area inland dunes are covered by psammophilous species: *Spartina ciliata, Poa lanuginosa, Sporobolus rigens, Hyalis argentea* (olivillo), and *Panicum urvilleanum* (tupe), with *Cenchrus myosuroides* and other species of the genus *Digitaria, Setaria, Andropogon,* and *Stipa.* On the Atlantic coast, the vegetation of the dunes is rhizomatic with *Panicum racemosum, Poa lanuginosa, P. barrosiana, Calycera crassifolia,* and *Sporobolus rigens.* In the depressions that collect winter rains, the species are more hygrophilic, and include *Stipa formicarum, S. bavionensis,* and *Paspalum quadrifarium.* On the western

*Table 10.21. Fireclimate of Esquel, Argentina, 42°56′ S, 71°09′ W, Elev. 815 m*

| Month | Max *T*°C | Min *T*°C | *DPT*°C | Precip (cm) | Snow (cm) | Days Precip | Day Length (hr) |
|-------|-----------|-----------|---------|-------------|-----------|-------------|-----------------|
| Jan | 22.8 | 7.2 | 3.3 | 1.4 | 0.0 | 1.6 | 14.9 |
| Feb | 22.8 | 6.1 | 2.8 | 2.1 | 0.0 | 2.0 | 13.8 |
| Mar | 20.0 | 5.0 | 4.4 | 3.4 | 0.0 | 2.7 | 12.4 |
| Apr | 15.0 | 2.2 | 2.8 | 4.9 | 1.2 | 3.4 | 10.9 |
| May | 11.1 | 1.1 | 0.0 | 6.9 | 3.4 | 4.5 | 9.7 |
| Jun | 7.8 | −1.1 | 0.0 | 9.8 | 19.6 | 6.8 | 9.0 |
| Jul | 7.2 | −2.2 | 0.0 | 6.4 | 25.3 | 4.5 | 9.2 |
| Aug | 8.9 | −1.1 | 0.0 | 6.3 | 13.5 | 4.4 | 10.3 |
| Sep | 12.8 | 1.1 | −0.6 | 3.3 | 1.7 | 2.8 | 11.8 |
| Oct | 16.1 | 2.2 | 0.6 | 1.9 | 0.4 | 1.9 | 13.2 |
| Nov | 17.8 | 3.9 | 1.7 | 2.2 | 0.0 | 2.1 | 14.5 |
| Dec | 21.1 | 6.1 | 2.8 | 1.9 | 0.0 | 1.8 | 15.1 |
| Annual | 15.6 | 2.8 | — | 50.5 | — | — | — |

Cover Type 7: Woodland or Grassland
Short Cold Winter, Humid, Long Burning Season
Moderate Litter, Moderate Shrubs

| Month | Jan | Feb | Mar | Apr | May | Jun | Jul | Aug | Sep | Oct | Nov | Dec |
|-------|-----|-----|-----|-----|-----|-----|-----|-----|-----|-----|-----|-----|
| Fire Prob. | 0.85 | 0.74 | 0.57 | 0.12 | 0 | 0 | 0 | 0 | 0.37 | 0.71 | 0.71 | 0.80 |
| Burning Index | 51.0 | 54.0 | 32.0 | 17.0 | 1? | 3 | 2 | 6 | 22.0 | 31.0 | 34.0 | 45.0 |

border, and around to the mouth of the Rio Negro, *Prosopis caldenia* (calden) is the only tree, together with *Prosopis alba* (algarrobo) and *Schinus polygamus* (molle) to form groves, with undergrowths of *Condalia microphylla* (piquillin) and *Lycium tenuispinosum* (yauyin). Grasses such as *Stipa tenuis, S. dusenii, Piptochaetium napostaensis, Setaria mendocina, Bromus brevis, Hordeum murinum,* and *Aristida subulata* constitute the meadow species.

Farther south, Patagonia is a region covered by a grassy steppe dominated by *Stipa pinosa, S. humilis, Poa ligularis, Milium spinosum, Adesmia campestris,* and *Selenia filiganoides,* in the north; in the south, the grassy steppe is composed of *Festuca pallescens* (coiron blanco), *Poa ligularis, Agrostis leptotricha, A. pyrogaea, Festuca ovina, Elymus patagonicus,* Juncaceae, Compositae, and clumps of *Festuca argentina.* The center of Patagonia is covered with dwarf shrubs (*Chuquiraja avellanedae, Berberis cuneata,* and *Lycium ameghinoi*), grasses (*Stipa humilis, Poa ligularis, Festuca* spp., *Danthonia* spp., and *Hordeum* spp.), and a single type of tree, *Prosopis denudans.* Around the Golfo San Jorge, the vegetation is slightly different with *Trevoa patagonica* (malaspina) and *Colliguaya integerrima* (duraznillo).

These south temperate, high elevation grasslands share some of the fireclimate characteristics of both the North American great plains and the Eurasian steppes. Like the steppes they have a dry summer, but like the great plains they have a large amplitude of diurnal temperatures. This combination produces high burning indices and high fire probabilities summer-long.

## Africa

On all sides of the great tropical rainforest of the central interior, savanna woodlands and savannas cover immense areas of Africa (Figure 10.12).

The savannas are mixed formations of trees and herbs, the proportions varying from one area to another. There is a full range from herbaceous (treeless) savanna to savanna woodland which differs from true forest only in the persistence of a thick carpet of herbs. The African savannas are characterized by the dominance of rhizomatous Gramineae, the surface portions of which die during the dry season and regenerate every year from the reserves stored in their underground organs.

The essentially herbaceous formations that constitute the African savannas are maintained by fire; here as in other savannas, the succession is toward fairly open forest. With some exceptions, tropical grasslands appear to be secondary formations resulting from forest groupings destroyed by humans and fire, and maintained by fire. Within the savannas there are strips of dry forest that probably predate the establishment of the savannas. Although the savannas may be, in fact, secondary growth, the intervention of man and fire is so ancient that the savannas have probably been in place for a

*Figure 10.12.* Typical African savanna near Bouake, Ivory Coast. Photo by Louis Trabaud.

very long time. The animals of the savannas and the steppes are not forest animals; giraffes in particular cannot live in a forest. On account of their ecology and morphology, the savanna animals are probably the product of a long process of evolution in the fairly open plant landscapes that existed in ancient times and climates and, consequently, they are related to the ancient, natural origin of the savannas and steppes.

Kortlandt (1972) believes that the open savanna landscape might be the result of grazing by large wild herbivores in forest formations before these forests were cleared by human intervention at a time when these animals must have been more numerous than at present. Grassy clearings might have been formed in this way. There is no doubt that the ecological importance of the wild herbivores has often been neglected in historical interpretations of present-day vegetation formations. If such animals were truly responsible for the creation of grassy formations before humans arrived on the scene, it would be logical to assume that man-made fires could have ensured their maintenance to our time.

Finally, the action of fire may have had its effect in the remote past. Now almost all fires are set by humans; prehistoric man also may have set fires before they learned to practice agriculture, and even natural fires (Komarek 1972, Phillips 1974)—although unusual—may have reached the climax grasslands at the edge of the desert or the edaphic grasslands on rocky escarpments and spread into the neighboring forests.

During the dry season, the savanna is extremely flammable, and is swept each year by fires of natural and human origin. In most cases, the trees have achieved a balance with these fires through their forms and modes of life. The separation of the individual specimens characteristic of the landscape prevents the spread of crown fires, which create much higher temperatures than do surface fires. In addition, many savanna trees have trunks protected by cork bark.

A number of climatic conditions are common to the African savannas and savanna woodlands.

Temperatures show the same characteristics as in all the intertropical zone (Gillon 1974); high annual averages (over 25°C) and annual range of monthly averages less than the range between night and day (3 to 10°C). The average daily ranges vary, depending on the month, from 11 to 20°C in the Sahelian zone and from approximately 8 to 13°C in the subequatorial savanna. The minimum ranges occur during the rainy season and the maximum values during the dry season. The predominant fireclimate of the African savanna (frost-free, humid, long burning season, Table 10.22) is found in every country in Africa south of the Sahara desert. Isolated examples also occur in southeast Asia and elsewhere.

The amount of rain received by the savannas varies widely from one zone to another, and the only characteristic common to all savannas is the cyclic alternation of dry and rainy seasons. Comparisons of the length of the rainy season (from approximately two to eight months) are deceiving, since more rain may fall during the "dry" season alone in a subequatorial savanna than during the entire rainy season, and hence the year, in a Sahelian savanna. In the least rainy zones annual precipitation may reach 100 to 400 mm, whereas in the rainiest zones the amount of rain may reach 700 to 800 mm. At the extreme opposite, in the subequatorial savannas, annual rains may reach 2000 mm. Rainfall fluctuates considerably from one year to another; it may rise to double the previous year's level, or even higher in the Sahel.

The plant carpet of the savannas consists essentially of herbs, primarily Gramineae, and, secondarily, Cyperaceae. The Gramineae grow in clumps or patches, on the surface of which buds form and develop stems. This arrangement provides better protection for the plants against fires. Vegetative reproduction is common. The same genera of herbaceous plants are found throughout the entire savanna and savanna woodland zone, both north and south of the equator; the commonest are: *Pennisetum (P. purpureum), Imperata (I. cylindrica), Andropogon (A. schirensis, A. pseudapricus), Hyparrhenia (H. diplandra, H. lecomtii), Loudetia (L. simplex, L. demeusii, L. arundinacea), Brachiaria (B. brachylopha); Themeda triandra, Heteropogon contortus,* and *Hyparrhenia rufa* being found primarily in East Africa. During the rainy season, these herbs may form a dense carpet 3 to 3.50 m high.

*Table 10.22.  Fireclimate of Nairobi, Kenya, 1°19′ S, 36°55′ E, Elev. 1620 m*

| Month | Max T°C | Min T°C | DPT°C | Precip (cm) | Snow (cm) | Days Precip | Day Length (hr) |
|---|---|---|---|---|---|---|---|
| Jan | 25.0 | 12.2 | 12.8 | 3.5 | 0 | 3.1 | 12 |
| Feb | 26.1 | 12.8 | 12.2 | 4.0 | 0 | 3.5 | 12 |
| Mar | 25.0 | 13.9 | 13.9 | 11.4 | 0 | 7.8 | 12 |
| Apr | 23.9 | 14.4 | 15.6 | 21.1 | 0 | 9.9 | 12 |
| May | 22.2 | 13.3 | 15.0 | 13.0 | 0 | 8.3 | 12 |
| Jun | 21.1 | 11.7 | 12.8 | 4.5 | 0 | 3.5 | 12 |
| Jul | 20.6 | 10.6 | 12.2 | 1.4 | 0 | 1.2 | 12 |
| Aug | 21.1 | 11.1 | 12.2 | 2.1 | 0 | 1.7 | 12 |
| Sep | 23.9 | 11.1 | 12.2 | 2.5 | 0 | 2.0 | 12 |
| Oct | 24.4 | 12.8 | 12.8 | 5.7 | 0 | 4.0 | 12 |
| Nov | 23.3 | 13.3 | 14.4 | 11.5 | 0 | 7.6 | 12 |
| Dec | 23.3 | 12.8 | 14.4 | 6.8 | 0 | 5.8 | 12 |
| Annual | 23.3 | 12.8 | — | 87.2 | — | — | — |

Cover Type 7: Woodland or Grassland
Frost Free Winter, Humid, Long Burning Season
Moderate Shrubs, No Litter

| Month | Jan | Feb | Mar | Apr | May | Jun | Jul | Aug | Sep | Oct | Nov | Dec |
|---|---|---|---|---|---|---|---|---|---|---|---|---|
| Fire Prob. | 0.55 | 0.58 | 0.01 | 0 | 0 | 0.29 | 0.71 | 0.76 | 0.74 | 0.50 | 0 | 0.22 |
| Burning Index | 17.0 | 24.0 | 13.0 | 5 | 2 | 5.0 | 5.0 | 6.0 | 5.0 | 15.0 | 6 | 6.0 |

The trees, most of them deciduous, differ from those of the tropical rainforest. The trunks are gnarled and the bark is thick, thus offering effective protection against repeated fires; most, moreover, have the ability to throw out suckers: they send out shoots from the stump if the individual has been burned or killed. As with the herbaceous plants, the same genera appear both north and south of the Equator: *Acacia, Isoberlinia* (Caesalpiniaceae), *Brachystegia* (Caesalpiniaceae), *Colophospermum* (Caesalpiniaceae), *Monotes* (Dipterocarpaceae), and *Uapaca* (Euphorbiaceae).

Schnell (1976) has produced a major study on the vegetation of tropical Africa, from which we have drawn the principal characteristics of the savannas.

North of the Equator, a zonal arrangement with bands of vegetation becoming progressively poorer toward the north is evident in western and central Africa. Savanna woodlands and tree savannas are the most common formations: particularly savannas with *Vitellaria paradoxa* (*Butyrospermum paradoxum* subspp. *parkii*, the karite), with one tree every 20 or 30 m, tree savannas or savanna parks with *Isoberlinia* (*I. globifera, I. doka*) and *Uapaca* (*U. nitida, U. togoensis*), or *Monotes* (*M. dalzielii, M. kerstingii*) and savannas with *Borassus aethiopum*.

However, this zonal arrangement is frequently disrupted by the following influences.

Edaphic. Gallery forests penetrating deeply into the savanna zones.

Human. With increased pressure by grazing and fire, the savanna has advanced considerably at the expense of the forest. For example, the dry forest of Lower Casamance no longer exists except in relic form.

Climatic anomalies. Savannas exist as far as the coast in eastern Ghana and in Togo.

South of the Equator, in central Africa, littoral savannas sometimes forming thickets separate the forests of Gabon and the Congo from the coast. In the interior, the savannas of the Congo are situated in an extremely rainy equatorial-type climate zone. They correspond to the sandy soils of the Bateke plateau; probably they developed during a drier climatic phase and have been maintained by the poverty of the soil and by brush fires. To the east, in Zaire, along the very edge of the rainforest, there is a mosaic of relatively broad gallery forests and high savannas with few trees because of frequent intense brush fires.

Farther south, an extremely wide band of dry savanna woodland, occasionally opening into tree savanna, extends from the plateaus of the Angolan interior to Katanga and on to Lake Tanganyika and the southern shores of Lake Victoria. It cuts east Africa in half and reaches the Indian Ocean between 9 and 15° South latitude. The southern boundary extends beyond the Zambezi and almost to the Tropic of Capricorn in Rhodesia. The trees of which this savanna woodland is composed are primarily "miombos" *Brachystegia* (*B. spiciformis, B. boeghmii*) and *Isoberlinia* (*I. globifera, I. angolensis,* and *I. tomentosa*), although they include *Uapaca* (*U. nitida, U. kirkiana*) and *Monotes* (*M. katangensis, M. glaber*) as well. Along the northern boundary of this savanna woodland, large numbers of *Acacia* appear in the middle of the savannas; in the region of the Limpopo and Zambezi rivers, savanna woodland with *Colophospermum mopane* (mopane) dominates. Most of these trees lose their leaves for part of the dry season. The density of the trees is related to the quality of the soils. On good soils, cool and deep, we find true dry forest with an undergrowth of bushes of lianas and almost bare ground. Where the soil is poor, the forest is very open with sparse undergrowth and a short, thinly scattered herbaceous layer: the brush fires that sweep over it do little damage to the trees.

In east Africa, in the coastal zone of Tanzania and Mozambique, the savanna often resembles parkland. Palm groves, dominated by *Phoenix reclinata,* are very important in the south toward Natal, where the vegetation passes progressively into subtropical or Mediterranean types.

Inland, between the Orange River and the southern Transvaal, an immense prairie, the *Veld,* covers a plateau at an altitude of more than 1400 m. The grasses belong to the genera *Eragrostis* (*E. lehmanniana, E. curvula*), *Aristida* (*A. ciliata, A. obtusa*), and, more particularly, *Themeda* (*T. trianda*). There are no trees, except along the rivers, where *Acacia* serve as a reminder that the Veld is not far from the tropical savannas. On the high plateaus and to the west of Madagascar, the forest has been replaced by savannas with scattered trees.

### Australia

The main areas of natural grasslands in Australia are the arid tussock grasslands and arid hummock grasslands (Luke and McArthur op. cit.).

The arid tussock grasslands occupy large areas in the arid or semi-arid regions of Queensland, the Northern Territory, and small scattered areas in the Kimberley region of Western Australia. *Astrebla* spp. (Mitchell grass), a perennial tussock grass, is the main component; the intertussock spaces are occupied by annuals to a density determined by the amount of recent rains. When large amounts of dry fuel are present, there is a high fire hazard.

About one-quarter of Australia is occupied by perennial hummock grasslands belonging to the genera *Triodia* and *Plectrachne,* commonly called spinifex. The hummocks are up to 2 m in diameter and often contain dead material. The vegetation between tussocks is usually sparse except after heavy rains, when there may be a dense population of annuals.

Though they are not true grasslands or savanna woodlands, we can cite the brigalow (*Acacia harpophylla*) which extends as a belt lying to the west of the subhumid eucalypt woodland in the southern half of Queensland and extending into northern New South Wales. In their natural state *Acacia harpophylla* scrubs are closed communities in which the trees grow so close together that ground cover is normally sparse and fuel quantity is low. Brigalow is, therefore, fairly fire resistant but as several million hectares have been cleared and sown to pastures, vulnerability to fire has increased in this region.

## VEGETATION OF THE ARID AND SEMI-ARID REGIONS—BRUSHLAND AND SCRUB

Below an annual precipitation level of between 500 and 900 mm, depending on temperatures, there appears a mosaic of open savannas and of low brush forest composed of small deciduous thorntrees, with occasional succulent or cactaceous plants: this is the vegetation of the arid and semi-arid regions, formed of bushy steppes and of thorn scrubs.

Wherever rainfall is too scanty or too uncertain from year to year to support a full stand of grass, bush or scrub will occupy the site. Although limited in extent, this is a most important fire type wherever it occurs. The scrub type is too dry for tree growth and only marginal for grazing. Fires, often deliberately set to improve browse, burn fiercely during the long burning season and often spread to more desirable forests, agricultural areas, or settlements. Because the economic value of brushlands is low, and fires are difficult to fight in shrub cover, few countries are willing to invest in sufficient firefighting forces to adequately control brush and scrub fires.

Because brushlands occupy marginal sites in all climates, there is little variation between fireclimates although there is a tendency for shrub density to vary inversely with winter severity.

Even when normal rainfall is insufficient to sustain the continuous cover of vegetation needed to propagate fire, a rare heavy rain may be followed by a luxuriant cover of annual plants that become a fire hazard when they die and desiccate. Fire in the desert destroys valuable forage that may not appear again for several years.

Vast arid and semi-arid regions exist around the world. The Sahara extends eastward into the deserts of western and central Asia. The North American desert stretches to the western edge of the continent on either side of the border between the United States and Mexico. In South America, the continent is split diagonally from northern Peru to southern Argentina. Two other desert regions occur in the southern hemisphere: the desert of southwest Africa and the vast Australian desert. These deserts have different origins: the largest are related to the presence of high subtropical pressures; others owe their existence to their distance from the sea (continental deserts).

All deserts are characterized by the low quantity of precipitation and its wide variability from year to year. There is considerable disproportion between the quantities of water received and the intensity of evaporation. Thus only those plants capable of withstanding drought can survive in these climates. The vegetation of the arid and semi-arid regions consists of open formations, that is, formations in which bare ground appears between the plants. There are no forests, except in those rare areas where an underground body of water is capable of supporting trees on a permanent basis.

Despite some remarkable similarities of form which give plants of very different species a comparable appearance, floristic characteristics differ markedly from one continent to another. For instance, the succulents typical of the American desert are rarely found in Africa or western Asia. Each desert is thus unique in terms of its plant life. Because of the spacing between plants, fires are rare in the plant communities of the arid and semi-arid regions, although Humphrey (1962) notes fires in the North American "deserts". Fires also occur in the scrub formations of southern Africa and Australia (Luke and McArthur op. cit.)

## Asia

The types of vegetation in western Asia frequently show extreme contrasts. The relief, in fact, creates humid climates, characterized by forest formations, alongside or even within the arid regions. For instance, the fringe of Mediterranean vegetation that lines the seacoast from Syria to Israel stands in sharp contrast to the desert of the interior. In Asia Minor, the high plateaus of Anatolia receive less than 250 mm of precipitation and are occupied by the steppe (*Tamarix* and *Acacia*), whereas to the south and west the Taurus mountains are covered by Mediterranean forests, and to the northeast the extremely rainy Pontic mountains (over 2000 mm) possess luxuriant forests in which beeches (*Fagus orientalis*) and conifers shelter numerous evergreen shrubs (*Laurus cerasus,* and *Ilex*).

Similarly, the lovely terraced vegetation of the mountains of Armenia and the Caucasus contrasts with the steppe of the plains below to the north and south. In Iran, the northern slopes of the Elburz provide the setting for a magnificent beech forest (*Fagus orientalis*), whereas to the south we find the steppe and the alkaline deserts of the Kavir and the Lut. In the middle of the arid zone, islands of woodland of various extents cover part of the Zagros mountains, the Kopet Dagh in Iran, and the Hindu Kush in Afghanistan. The steppes are covered with bushes: *Artemisia* spp., *Stipa* spp., *Poa* spp. A few islands of forest remain in the foothills west of the Zagros (*Quercus brautii*, small xerophilic oaks). In the Negev (100 mm of rain), there is an aphyllous bush, *Haloxylon articulatum,* whereas the Dead Sea is ringed by halophilic plants: *Arthrocnemum glaucum, Suaeda monoica,* and *Tamarix tetragyna.*

### Central Asia

Along the southern border of the Russian prairie, the semi-arid regions of Kazakhstan are covered by a steppe dominated by *Artemisia pauciflora* together with *Kochia prostata* and *Statice gmelini.* Artemisia grows in tussocks 15 to 30 cm high, separated by patches of bare ground. In addition to the plants already cited, we find a number of species of *Tulipa* and *Ranunculus*. When the soil is sufficiently alkaline, *Anabasis salsa, Salicornia herbacea, Salsola* spp., and *Nitraria* or *Tamarix* bushes appear.

On sandy soils (e.g., to the east of Lake Balkhash), *Carex physodes* with its long rhizomes develops rapidly with the rain. In the Karakoram, south of the Amu-Dar'ya, the dryness of the summer is accentuated; along with the *Salsola* grow small bushes of *Calligonum* or *Aristida* (*A. pennata*), and shrubs, *Arthrophytum persicum* and *A. haloxylon*, which prefer slightly alkaline sandy soils, for example, the abandoned beds of old rivers. These may grow to a height of five or six meters and form an actual savanna woodland.

On the alluvial and clayey soils of Turkestan, the spring thaw and the occasional showers that accompany it see the appearance of *Poa bulbosa* and *Carex pachystylis*. By the end of May, these plants have dried up and the ground remains bare until the following spring. Along the courses of permanent or near-permanent rivers grow small forests of *Elaeagnus angustifolia*.

### North America

The major area of the North American "desert" extends from southeastern Oregon and southern Idaho southward through the Great Basin, including most of Nevada and Utah except high elevations, continues southward into southern California and western Arizona, down most of the peninsula of Baja California and, on the mainland, through Sonora as far south as the Yaqui River (Table 10.23). The highlands of eastern Arizona and western New Mexico interrupt the continuity of desert, but from south-central New Mexico, there is almost continuous desert through eastern Chihuahua and most of Coahuilia in Mexico (Oosting op. cit.).

In this area there are stabilized communities that occur throughout with minor variations in the least extreme environments. The vegetation is a complex mosaic of communities that may be of great or limited extent. Because the effects of biological reaction on environment are seemingly negligible, primary succession is hardly apparent. However, secondary succession does occur, especially after the often extensive fires in shrub types.

### *The Great Basin Desert*

This is a physiographic, climatologic, and vegetational unity that extends north from southern Nevada and southern Utah. The topography of the area is variable, but elevation is always higher than 1000 m. The meager rainfall (150 to 300 mm) increases with altitude and toward the east side of the Basin; it is greatest in winter and thus summers are very dry. Average temperatures are lower and the frost-free season is very short. It is a cold desert.

The two major communities are simple, with few dominants in each, and

*Table 10.23.  Fireclimate of Bishop, California, 37°22' N, 118°22' W, Elev. 1250 m*

| Month | Max T°C | Min T°C | DPT°C | Precip (cm) | Snow (cm) | Days Precip | Day Length (hr) |
|---|---|---|---|---|---|---|---|
| Jan | 11.7 | -6.1 | -7.2 | 4.2 | 13.2 | 4.0 | 9.8 |
| Feb | 13.9 | -3.3 | -7.2 | 2.5 | 6.1 | 2.7 | 10.7 |
| Mar | 17.2 | -1.7 | -8.9 | 2.1 | 1.8 | 2.3 | 11.8 |
| Apr | 22.2 | 2.2 | -6.7 | 0.8 | 0.8 | 0.9 | 13.0 |
| May | 26.1 | 5.6 | -4.4 | 0.7 | 0.0 | 0.7 | 14.0 |
| Jun | 31.1 | 9.4 | -2.2 | 0.2 | 0.0 | 0.5 | 14.5 |
| Jul | 35.0 | 12.8 | 2.2 | 0.2 | 0.0 | 0.5 | 14.3 |
| Aug | 33.9 | 11.1 | 0.6 | 0.3 | 0.0 | 0.5 | 13.4 |
| Sep | 30.6 | 7.8 | -1.7 | 0.5 | 0.0 | 1.2 | 12.2 |
| Oct | 24.4 | 2.2 | -4.4 | 0.8 | 0.0 | 1.4 | 11.1 |
| Nov | 17.8 | -3.3 | -6.7 | 1.3 | 1.5 | 1.6 | 10.1 |
| Dec | 12.8 | -6.1 | -7.8 | 2.2 | 7.6 | 2.5 | 9.5 |
| Annual | 23.2 | 2.8 | — | 15.8 | — | — | — |

Cover Type 10: Barren
Short Cold Winter, Nonhumid, Long Burning Season
Fuels Normally Insufficient for Burning

| Month | Jan | Feb | Mar | Apr | May | Jun | Jul | Aug | Sep | Oct | Nov | Dec |
|---|---|---|---|---|---|---|---|---|---|---|---|---|
| Fire Prob. | 0 | 0 | 0.22 | 0.72 | 0.88 | 0.95 | 0.97 | 0.97 | 0.93 | 0.87 | 0.66 | 0 |
| Burning Index | 48 | 59 | 85.0 | 99.0 | 107.0 | 117.0 | 117.0 | 119.0 | 115.0 | 98.0 | 77.0 | 57 |

often extend uninterrupted for many kilometers. The sagebrush community, dominated by *Artemisia tridentata* (common sagebrush) occupies wide areas in the northern portion of the Great Basin or at relatively high elevations. The shadscale community, with *Atriplex confertifolia* (shadscale) and *Artemisia spinescens* (bud sage) ranges through the south and at low elevations (Oosting op. cit.).

The controlling effect of salts on community structure is important. Zonal patterns around playa lakes are the same everywhere. Where flooding is periodic and salt content high, vegetation is absent or dominated by *Salicornia* spp. (samphire) or *Allenrolfea occidentalis* (iodine brush). With somewhat less salt, *Atriplex confertifolia* and *Sarcobatus vermiculatus* (greasewood) or *Kochia americana* (gray molly) are dominant. Away from the playas on soils with a minimum of salts, *Artemisia tridentata* may be the major species.

Many other species occur also. They are mostly shrubs with the same growth form. There are numerous species of *Atriplex* and *Artemisia*, *Chrysothamnus puberulus*, *Grayia spinosa*, *Coleogyne ramosissima*, *Eurotia lanata* (winter fat), and *Purshia tridentata* (antelope bitterbrush). Several species of *Ephedra* are characteristic. Grasses and other herbs occur in varying amounts with the sagebrush. Especially noteworthy are two perennial bunch-grasses, *Agropyron spicatum* (blue-bunch wheatgrass) and *Festuca ovina* (sheep fescue).

The Great Basin desert regularly experiences fire due to human intervention or lightning, not because human activity or lightning fires are more common there but because of the abundance and continuity of the plant fuel. *Aristida tridentata* and grasses like *Bromus tectorum*, *Agopyron spicatum*, or *Sitanion hystrix* take up large areas. These plants constitute very flammable fuels. These species produce seedlings or sprouts in abundance after a fire (Blaisdell 1953, Humphrey 1962, 1974, Wright and Klemmedson 1965). Shrub species are damaged by fire and herbaceous ones tend to dominate.

One of the areas in which fire has occurred most frequently and which has formed a pyrophytic landscape, is the desert grassland. Regular fires maintain ecosystems without woody plants such as *Hilaria mutica* grassland, *Bouteloua* spp. prairie, and *Aristida* spp. Woody plants are killed by fire and their regrowth is poor. Mesquite (*Prosopis juliflora* var. *velutina*, *Larrea tridentata*, and *Aplopappus tenuisectus*, which would tend to invade these stands, are killed by fire (Box 1967, Britton and Wright 1971, Cable 1965, 1967, 1973, Jamison 1962, Reynolds and Bohning 1956, Trlica and Schuster 1969, Wright 1969, 1974). In the absence of fire, woody species invade grasslands causing the loss of pasture; this is why ranchers use fire to maintain grazing lands.

### The Mojave Desert

The smallest of the American desert units lies almost entirely in California below and to the east of the southern end of the Sierra Nevada. Physiographic conditions are similar to the Great Basin but elevations are generally lower (300 to 1000 m). The irregular, meager precipitation is lower than 50 mm in Death Valley, and between 80 to 300 mm elsewhere.

Many of the same species as in the Great Basin are encountered in the Mojave Desert, their distribution controlled, here too, by soil texture and salt concentration. However, at the upper elevations (900 to 1200 m) and in the transition from sagebrush with maximum precipitation, *Yucca brevifolia* (Joshua tree) is conspicuous. With decreasing altitude and precipitation, *Larrea divaricata* (creosote brush) with *Franseria dumosa* (bur sage) in association becomes the major dominant. This community occupies 70 percent of the total area of the Mojave Desert (Oosting op. cit.).

### The Sonoran Desert

The lowlands around the Gulf of California in Mexico, Baja California, and southern California, which lie chiefly below 500 m, constitute this desert. Much of the area is made up of dunes and sand plains. The low plains are dominated by the *Larrea-Franseria* community with various associates. *Fouquieria splendens* (ocotillo) and *Encelia farinosa* are common. Margins of streambeds support a distinctive mixed community including species of *Prosopis* (mesquite), *Cercidium* (Palo verde), and *Olneya*. In the higher elevations of Arizona and northern Sonora (300 to 1000 m) there is a great mixture of species and life forms. Although numerous species characteristic of the other deserts are present, *Arcidium microphyllum* is dominant with numerous arborescent and columnar cacti, including *Carnegiea gigantea* (saguaro cactus), *Agave americana* (century plant), *Lemaireocereus schotii*, and many other *Opuntia* (Oosting op. cit.).

Extending from southern New Mexico southeastward to western Texas and down into Mexico, much of the Chihuahua Desert is interrupted by high mountains and lies between 1000 and 2000 m. Precipitation varies with altitude from 80 to 400 mm and falls largely in summer (July to September). The steppic vegetation presents several regional variations. Shrubs and semishrubs predominate with a great variety of inconspicuous stem succulents in association. *Fouquieria splendens* (ocotillo), which is found throughout the area, *Larrea tridentata* (creosote bush), and several *Prosopis* (mesquite) are the only species common in the Sonoran Desert that are also important and widespread here. A number of species are conspicuous because of size or unusual form. *Yucca, Nolina,* and *Dasylirion* are large semisucculents. *Agave* and *Hechtia* are particularly abundant leaf succulents. Leafless, green-stemmed trees, columnar cacti, and *Dasylirion longissimum* are examples of locally important species of striking appearance.

### South America

The vegetation of the arid or semi-arid regions occurs in various regions of South America. The first is located at the northern tip of Venezuela and in northeastern Brazil, where precipitation is extremely irregular and thickets of thornbushes (caatinga) cover most of the area. The second corresponds to a coastal desert edging the Pacific Ocean. The third is located in a zone of high-altitude steppes in the Andes. The fourth extends over the foothills in the Mendoza region of Argentina, and the fifth is situated in Patagonia (previously mentioned with the grasslands) where the vegetation consists largely of perennial grasses.

### Caatinga

This is the characteristic plant formation of Brazil's northeastern interior (sertao); precipitation is light (700 to 900 mm) and, more important, it is extremely irregular from year to year. The aridity is emphasized by the abundance of thornbushes and cacti *Opuntia, Cereus gounellei* (xique-xique), and various *Cereus* 4 or 5 m high. The appearance of the caatinga varies with the nature of the soil and the extent of human intervention. In some cases it is dry forest with small trees 7 to 10 m high and a dense undergrowth of bushes and shrubs. More frequently, the caatinga forms a thicket or scrub that may be either dense and impenetrable (the *carrascal*), or divided up into small clumps by bare spaces. Frequently, a bushy steppe with scattered thornbushes covers most of the area. The caatinga is occasionally interrupted by groves of palm trees in valley bottoms, particularly *Copernicia cerifera* (cernauba).

### Pacific Coast Desert

This desert begins some degrees from the Equator (Paita, at 5° South latitude, receives 30 mm of rain a year during the summer) and extends to central Chile (Coquimbo, 30°, 110 mm of rain during the winter). Rain is extremely rare throughout the entire central portion (southern Peru and northern Chile) but the proximity of the cold ocean waters (Humboldt current) produces fog. The vegetation is thus arranged in strips parallel to the shore (di Castri 1968).

Along the coast, the *lomas* have relatively dense winter vegetation consisting of ephemeral annuals or perennials (chamaephytes, Cactaceae, and geophytes) that develop when the soil is sufficiently dampened by the mist. Clumps of *Tillandsia* are abundant in areas where fogs lie most frequently.

East of this first strip, the influence of the coastal fog disappears and, since there is practically no precipitation, the land is absolute desert.

On the western slopes of the Andes between 1500 and 3000 m, the infrequent showers and higher humidity are enough to maintain a cactaceous steppe. In northern Chile vegetation is totally absent over most of this area with the exception of chamaephytes (*Adesmia* and *Atriplex*) in what are frequently dried-up streambeds. When the phreatic level is close enough to the surface, *Prosopis tamarugo* grows. Farther south, these semideserts generally consist of a fairly diverse floristic range of chamaephytes (*Ephedra andina* and *Atriplex atacamensis*). The density of the vegetation varies considerably: during particularly favorable years, the herbaceous stratum is almost continuous during the summer but, more frequently, the therophytes and geophytes remain latent. Very typical of this region is the presence of columniform Cactaceae (*Cereus* and *Orocereus*). Along the shores of small rivers we find abundant vegetation consisting of hydrophilic bushes, in particular, the genera *Tessaria* and *Baccharis*, and very thick tussocks of *Cortaderia* (Graminae) (di Castri 1968). Farther south, the vegetation takes on Mediterranean characteristics.

### High-Altitude Desert

This desert occupies the Andean highlands at altitudes of 3000 to 4500 m. Growing conditions are extremely difficult because of the combination of cold and aridity (average annual temperature 4°C; rainfall 100 to 400 mm). The most common form of vegetation is the *puna,* with clumps of hard grasses (*Festuca orthophylla,* ichu), a few thornbushes, and a number of acaulous plants with villous leaves. When the grasses (*Festuca* and *Stipa*) become thicker and form an almost continuous carpet, it is known as *jalca.* The vegetation generally shows very clear altitudinal zonation reflected in longitudinal strips from west to east. From the semidesert (*jaral*) and the belt of columniform cactaceae in the desert along the Pacific coast, the formations pass progressively to the *tolar, pajonal,* and *llaretal* (di Castri 1968).

The *tolar* is a bushy steppe generally on pebbly soil with discontinuous but frequently quite dense vegetation, consisting of resinous bushes (*Baccharis* and *Fabiana*) as much as 1 m high, and low Cactaceae (*Opuntia*). The *pajonal* is the true Andean steppe, dominated by tussocks of grasses (*Stipa* and *Festuca*). The physiognomy of the *llaretal* is established by the presence of large, cushion-shaped Umbelliferae, highly ligneous and resinous (*Laretia compacta* and *Azorella*).

In sheltered, moister areas often above 4000 m, shrubs (*Polylepis tomentolla; P. incana,* quenoa; *Prosopis ferox,* churquii; *Trichocereus pasacana,* cardon) form a dense scrub sometimes 8 to 10 m high (Lassalle op. cit.).

In central Argentina, a vast arid region stretches from the Andes to the Pampa, from the Chaco to Patagonia. Precipitation is low (less than 200 mm; all falling during the summer). The distribution of plant formations depends on both total rainfall and the nature of the soil. The most common plant community is the *Larrea divaricata* (jarilla) dwarf-shrub steppe (jarillal). Other species are *Larrea cuneiformis* and *L. nitida.* Other shrubs that also cover vast areas are *Cercidium praecox* (brea), *Prosopis alpataco* and the Cactaceae, genera *Opuntia* and *Cereus,* which give the landscape its characteristic appearance: this is the *solupal,* dominated by *Ephedra.* Various species of grasses appear after the rains: in the dunes, *Panicum urvilleanum* (tupe) and *Hyalis argentea* (olivillo); on alkaline soils, the halophytes (*Suaeda, Atriplex, Salicornia,* and *Heterostachys*).

## Africa

### Sahelian Steppe

South of the Sahara, the curve representing 150 mm of rainfall coincides largely with the disappearance of *Cornulaca monacantha* (had), a typical plant of the Sahara, and with the appearance of a Sudanese grass, *Cenchrus ciliaris* (cramcram), identifiable by its thorny spines. This isohyet may be considered the boundary between the desert and the Sahelian steppe. The zone receives 150 to 600 mm of rain. Whatever the total precipitation, the rainy season is short (three or four months) and extremely irregular from year to year.

The herbaceous plants of the steppe, in particular *Panicum* and *Aristida*, do not form a continuous cover as they do in the savannas but are widely spaced and in this open formation fires are unable to spread. The steppe is composed of shrubs or bushes and, since most of the trees have thorns, it is often described as a thorn steppe. In most cases, these are Combretaceae (*Combretum glutinosum*) or Mimosaceae (*Acacia tortilis* subsp. *raddiana*, *A. seyal*, and *A. senegal*). To the south along the edge of the savanna zone we find *Adansonia digitata* (baobab). In the valleys the bushes become denser and the vegetation may form an almost impenetrable thorn scrub of *Acacia nilotica* (Schnell op. cit.).

The steppe is 300 to 400 km across in the west; toward the east it becomes wider, particularly in east Africa where it almost completely encircles the Ethiopian massif. Somalia, in fact, receives little rain. The vegetation consists primarily of thornbushes, which vary in density depending on the nature of the soil: on lands capable of retaining water, *Acacia senegal*, *A. tortilis*, *A. etbaica*, *Balanites aegyptiaca*, and *Hyphaene thebaica* form open forests or thickets. Elsewhere we find bushy steppe. To the southeast in Tanzania, Kenya, and Uganda, the steppe is characterized by *Acacia hockii*, *A. senegal*, *Albizia coriaria*, and *Euphorbia candelabrum*, which form dense and sometimes impenetrable thickets 4 to 8 m high.

### Namib Desert

On the Atlantic coast of southern Africa, this area has extremely scattered vegetation, except along waterways. In the central portion, vegetation is practically absent.

### High Plateaus of the Karoo

These range from 600 to 1200 m, precipitation is still low (50 to 350 mm), and the altitude results in cool winters. The plant formation is a steppe with no real trees. It occasionally consists of tussocks of grasses (several *Aristida*: *A. ciliata*, *A. obtusa*, and *A. diffusa*), particularly on clayey soils. When the soil is alkaline, we find *Salsola*, *Atriplex halimus*, and *Tamarix* (Schnell op. cit.). However, over vast areas stretches a bushy scrub dominated by Compositae (*Pentzia, Pteronia, Pegolettia, Chrysocoma,* and *Eriocephalus*), Bignoniaceae (*Rhigozum*), thorny *Lycium,* thorny or succulent Mesembry-anthemaceae (*Aridaria, Hereroa,* and *Ruschia*), Crassulaceae (*Crassula* and *Cotyledon*), succulent Euphorbiaceae, and various *Aloe.*

### Kalahari Desert

This vast range which extends from the Orange River to the Zambezi is, in fact, a semi-arid region that receives between 200 and 500 mm of rain a year. The vegetation, known as *Thornveld* to South Africans, is a thorn steppe. In the northeastern portion of the Kalahari, the vegetation is relatively dense, composed of *Tarchonanthus camphoratus, T. minor, Olea africana, Rhus ciliata,* and *Grewia flava.* The rest of the area is characterized by savannas formed primarily of *Acacia giraffae* and *A. heteracantha, A. mellifera, Tar-chonanthus camphoratus,* and *Grewia flava.* A very open savanna of *A. giraffae* occupies the western part with *Boscia albitrunca* and *Rhigozum trichotomum* along the waterways (Schnell op. cit.). In the sandy region near the Zambezi, the sandy soils support dune vegetation with scattered *Boschia* and, in other areas, *Atriplex, Salsola, Eriocephalus,* and frequently, *Co-locynthis citrullus.*

To complete the picture of the African brushlands, we must mention the communities found in the high mountains of east Africa (from 2700 m to 3800 m and above), consisting of sclerophyllous brush with Ericaceae and stands of arborescent *Senecio* and large *Lobelia.* In the Ethiopian massif between 2700 and 3300 m appear low ligneous subalpine formations of *Erica arborea* and *Hypericum lanceolatum.* Above 3300 m, the landscape is characterized by *Erica arborea* and *Lobelia rhynchopetalum.* Farther south in the mountains of Kilimanjaro, Kenya, and Ruwenzori (from 3000 to 3500 m, stretch stands of suffrutescent Ericaceae: *Erica arborea, Philippia* (*P. longifolia, P. excelsa,* and *P. jaegeri*), *Vaccinium stanleyi;* from 3500 to 4000 m, the bushes become discontinuous and we find arborescent *Senecio* (*S. ad-nivalis, S. cottonii,* and *S. kilimandjari*) and giant *Lobelia* (*L. wollastonii* and *L. bequaertii*). The vegetation is frequently disturbed by humans and occasionally burned; its current range is probably due to the fires that have driven back the forest (Schnell op. cit.).

### Australia

There are few regions in central Australia that receive less than 150 mm of rain a year. However, precipitation is extremely irregular from year to year. In the north, the rain falls during the summer (November to March); in the south, precipitation occurs during the winter.

The most common plant formation in the semi-arid zones of central Australia is mulga scrub; shrubs (*Acacia aneura*) and various other deep-rooted bushy plants (*Cassia* and *Eremophila*) form more or less scattered clumps of vegetation. In the northern and northeastern portion, when rains exceed 500 mm, tropical savanna replaces the scrub. In the driest portions Acacia become rarer and are frequently found in the depressions between dunes; the landscape consists of grassy steppe dominated by *Triodia* (*T. basedowii*, spinifex). On the rocky platforms, *Triodia*, *Kochia*, and *Atriplex* occur in scattered locations. The latter two plants are also characteristic of the slightly alkaline clay plains (Luke and McArthur op. cit.).

On the southern border, in the zone of winter rains, *mallee scrub* represents the transition to plant landscapes of the Mediterranean type. This community of small *Eucalyptus*, all dwarf varieties (*E. dumosa* and *E. oleosa*), occurs primarily on the sandy soils west of the Murray River basin.

## FORESTS OF CHANGE—EXOTIC PLANTATIONS

A fire protection problem of growing world-wide significance is associated with the establishment of fast-growing exotic species in extensive plantations. There are two main types of plantation: the introduction of conifers on tropical hardwood sites, and the plantations of eucalypts on savanna or woodland sites. In a survey of 146 tropical countries the United Nations Food and Agriculture Organization found that softwood plantations had increased from 1.6 million ha in 1975 to 2.6 million ha in 1980, and were projected to be 6.5 million ha by the year 2000 (Lanly and Clement 1979). The area of eucalypts outside Australia and mainland China rose from 0.7 million ha in 1950 to 3.7 million ha in 1974 (Anon. 1976) and continues to increase rapidly.

Along with the plantations have come forest fire problems to countries which had never known them before. In the initial stages of a large plantation program fire presents few problems because areas are relatively small; a large workforce is engaged on establishment and in some areas a program of clean tending that may last for several years removes flammable fuels. As the areas expand and the plantations start to accumulate flammable fuels, the density of labor falls and some countries have found the means necessary for controlling multiple fires, or a single fire on a bad day, beyond them (Cheney 1970).

Establishing plantations increases the fire hazard in several ways. This may arise because the plantation species are more fire-prone than the vegetation they replace or due to changes in microclimate beneath the forest stand, but by far the most important are due to dramatic changes in fuel loads as the plantations develop and begin to be utilized (Figure 10.13).

When the native vegetation is cleared for plantation the increase in sunlight results in a marked increase in low vegetation (particularly, tall rank grasses in tropical areas). This may be clean tended in some areas but more often this vegetation remains and not only adds directly to the ground fuels, but also supports litter above the ground thereby keeping it drier and slowing the rate of litter decay. Litter decay in exotic plantations may be even slower

**Figure 10.13.**    Plantations are usually more fire-prone than the vegetation they replace. *Pinus elliottii* (slash pine) plantation in Florida. Photo by U.S. Forest Service.

than in the species' natural environment. Eucalypt litter breaks down mainly through disintegration by soil fauna rather than decay (Jacobs 1955). Overseas, the absence of suitable litter fauna and spectacular growth rates can also result in spectacular increases in accumulated fire fuels. In Zambia fuel loads beneath 5-year-old plantations of *E. grandis* were around 20 t/ha accumulating in only three years after clean tending and were expected to exceed 27 t/ha at age eight (Cheney 1970). In southern Brazil, litter in pine plantations accumulates at the rate of about 1 t/ha per year. By the time plantations are 10 to 15 years old, the hazard is extreme even during a normal fire season. More than 30,000 ha of plantations were lost to fire in the states of Parana and São Paulo in August and September 1981 (Goldammer 1982).

Intensive forestry practices may further increase undisturbed fuel accumulation rates. Heavy uncommercial thinnings, which may be essential in some areas to avoid droughting, lead to heavy loads of both fine and large fuel components. These residues make the task of fire suppression very difficult. Apart from the important changes in fuel loads, exotic fast-growing plantation species may be more fire-prone than the vegetation they replace. Conifers contain resins and waxes and their small needles and branches offer a large surface area for burning relative to their total mass. Thus they are more flammable and also more persistent and less compact than the hardwood litter they often replace. Eucalypt leaves also contain flammable oils and are naturally resistant to decay. However, those species that have flammable fibrous bark (stringybarks) can introduce a source of firebrands that dramatically influence fire behavior by massive short distance spotting not experienced in fires of other vegetation types.

Finally, microclimate changes associated with opening up a forest stand for planting can change the fire hazard significantly. In the tropics ground fuels exposed to direct solar radiation can be heated to 75°C, while fuels beneath a forest canopy are only 30 to 36°C. Similarly, the relative humidity in the open is often less than half that within the stand. These temperature and humidity relationships have an important influence on fuel moisture. On sunny days dead fuels in the open will have moisture contents one-third as high as those under a closed canopy. Consequently, fuels ignite more easily and fires spread more rapidly and burn more intensely than in the closed native forest. Often there is more wind movement in the plantation, particularly while it is young. This results in a drier site condition and a greater direct influence on the fire. The influence of microclimate changes on fuel accumulation has already been discussed.

In developing countries plantations are often afforded complete protection in areas where the natural forest burns infrequently (tropical hardwoods), or where the native vegetation is burned frequently (savanna woodlands) and fuels are naturally light. In both cases the risk of fire is high and the hazard to plantations with their increased flammability and high fuel loads dictates a need for intensive protection measures.

The degree of protection required usually depends on the chance of a conflagration occurring once or more per rotation. Protection measures must, by definition, be adequate to meet the "worst likely" combination of fire weather, fuel, and risk conditions. This implies there is a threshold on protection requirements below which it is pointless to budget. Rather than attempt to determine what level of protection expenditure a given enterprise can afford, this threshold must be determined at the outset and exposed as a requirement that the project must be capable of meeting economically (Cheney and Richmond 1980).

In mild climates or where fuel levels naturally remain low, it may be possible to provide protection by suppression forces alone. In severe fire climates and where heavy fuels accumulate, some fires will burn uncontrollably regardless of suppression expenditure. Protection planning may need to take into consideration factors such as species selection (fire-resistant species may be required if some level of burning is unavoidable), establishment practices, plantation layout and design (compartment size shape, intensity of access, provision of firebreaks or fuel breaks, and the distribution of size classes), fuel modification within the plantation, and suppression resources. This subject is treated in more detail in Volume II.

# BIBLIOGRAPHY

Ahlgren, C. E. 1974. Effects of fires on temperate forests: North Central United States. In T. T. Kozlowski and C. E. Ahlgren, Eds., *Fire and Ecosystems,* Academic, New York, pp. 195–223.

Aikman, J. M. 1955. *Burning in the management of prairie in Iowa.* Proc. Iowa Acad. Sci. **62**:53–62.

Anon. 1976. *Eucalypts for planting.* Draft 2nd ed. FO:Misc/76/10, FAO, Rome.

Aschmann, H. 1973. Distribution and peculiarity of Mediterranean ecosystems. In F. di Castri and H. A. Mooney Eds., *Ecological Studies 7, Mediterranean Type Ecosystems,* Springer-Verlag, Berlin, pp. 11–19.

Ashton, D. H. 1981. Fire in tall open forests (wet sclerophyll forests) In A. M. Gill, R. H. Groves, and I. R. Noble, Eds., *Fire and Australian Biota,* Aust. Acad. Sci., Canberra, pp. 339–366.

Axelrod, D. I. 1973. History of the Mediterranean ecosystems in California. In F. di Castri and H. A. Mooney, Eds., *Ecological Studies 7. Mediterranean Type Ecosystems.* Springer-Verlag, Berlin, pp. 225–277.

Bailey, A. W. and C. E. Poulton. 1968. Plant communities and environmental interrelationships in a portion of the Tillamook burn, Northwestern Oregon. *Ecol.* **49**:1–13.

Barney, R. J. 1971. *Wildfires in Alaska.* Proc. Fire Northern Environ. Symp., U.S. For. Serv., PNW. For. and Range Exp. Sta., pp. 51–60.

Becker, M., F. Le Tacon, and J. Timball. 1980. *Les plateaux calcaires de Lorraine. Types de stations et potentialités forestières,* Ecole Natl. Génie Rural Eaux et Forests, Nancy, 268 pp.

Biswell, H. H. 1961. The big trees and fire. *Natl. Parks* **35**:11–14.

Biswell, H. H. 1974. Effects of fire on chaparral. In T. T. Kozlowski and C. E. Ahlgren, Eds., *Fire and Ecosystems,* Academic, New York, pp. 321–364.

Blaisdell, J. P. 1953. *Ecological effects of planned burning of sagebrush-grass range on the Upper Snake River Plains.* U.S. Dept. Agric. Tech. Bull. No. 1075, p. 39.

Blydenstein, J. 1968. *Burning and tropical American savannas.* Tall Timbers Fire Ecol. Conf. Proc. **8**:1–14.

Box, T. W. 1967. *Brush, fire and West Texas rangelands.* Tall Timbers Fire Ecol. Conf. Proc. **6**:7–19.

Braun, E. L. 1950. *Deciduous forests of eastern North America.* Blakiston, Philadelphia, 596 pp.

Britton, C. M. and H. A. Wright. 1971. Correlation of weather and fuel variables to mesquite damage by fire. *J. Range Manage.* **24**:136–141.

Budowski, G. 1966. *Fire in tropical American lowland areas.* Tall Timbers Fire Ecol. Conf. Proc. **5**:5–22.

Byrne, P. J. 1977. *Prescribed burning in Australia: the state of the art.* 5th Meeting, Aust. For. Council Res. Working Group, **6**, 21 pp.

Cable, D. R. 1965. Damage to mesquite (*Prosopis juliflora*), Lehmann lovegrass (*Eragrostis lehmanniana*), and black grama (*Bouteloua eriopoda*) by a hot June fire. *J. Range Manage.* **18**:326–329.

Cable, D. R. 1967. Fire effects on semidesert grasses and shrubs. *J. Range Manage.* **20**(3):170–176.

Cable, D. R. 1973. *Fire effects in south western semidesert grass-shrubs communities.* Tall Timbers Fire Ecol. Conf. Proc. 1972, **12**:109–127.

Campbell, J. A. and J. B. Cassady. 1951. *Forage response to month of burning.* U.S. For. Serv. Res. Note SE-34, 4 pp.

Cheney, N. P. 1970. *Forest industries feasibility study, Zambia. Fire Protection of Industrial Plantations.* FO:SF/ZAM 5 Tech. Report 4, FAO, Rome.

Cheney, N. P. 1976. Bushfire disasters in Australia. *Aust. For.* **39**:245–268.

Cheney, N. P. and Richmond, R. R. 1980. *The impact of intensive forest management on fire protection with special regard to plantations of Eucalypts.* Paper presented at the 11th Comm. Forestry Conf., Trinidad, 22 pp.

Christensen, P., H. Recher, and J. Hoare. 1981. Responses of open forests (dry sclerophyll) to fire regimes. In A. M. Gill, R. H. Groves, and I. R. Noble, Eds., *Fire and Australian Biota*, Aust. Acad. Sci., Canberra, pp. 367–393.

Cochrane, G. R. 1966. Bushfires and vegetation regeneration. *Vict. Nat.* **83**:4–10.

Cooper, C. F. 1960. Changes in vegetation structure and growth of southwestern pine forests since white settlement. *Ecol. Monogr.* **30**:129–164.

Curtis, J. T. 1959. *The vegetation of Wisconsin.* University of Wisconsin Press, Madison, 657 pp.

Cushwa, C. T., M. Hopkins, and B. S. McGinnes. 1970. *Response of legumes to prescribed burns in loblolly pine stands of the South Carolina Piedmont.* U.S. For. Serv. Res. Note SE-140, 6 pp.

Cushwa, C. T., R. E. Martin, and R. L. Miller. 1968. The effects of fire on seed germination. *J. Range Manage.* **21**:250–254.

Daget, P. 1977. Le bioclimat méditerranéen: caractères généraux, modes de caractèrisation. *Vegetatio* **34**:1–20.

Daubenmire, R. F. 1952. Forest vegetation of northern Idaho and adjacent Washington, and its bearing on concepts of vegetation classification. *Ecol. Monogr.* **22**:301–330.

Davis, K. P. 1959. *Forest fire, control and use.* McGraw-Hill, New York, 584 pp.

di Castri, F. 1968. Esquisse écologique du Chili. In C. Delamare-Deboutteville and E. Rapoport, Eds., *Biologie de l'Amérique australe IV*, CNRS, Paris, pp. 7–52.

di Castri, F. 1973. Climatographical comparison between Chile and the western coast of North America. In F. di Castri and H. A. Mooney, Eds., *Ecological Studies 7, Mediterranean Type Ecosystems*, Springer-Verlag, Berlin, pp. 21–36.

Dix, R. L. 1960. The effects of burning on the mulch structure and species composition of grasslands in western North Dakota. *Ecol.* **41**:49–56.

Ehrenreich, J. H. and J. M. Aikman. 1957. *Effect of burning on seedstalk production of native prairie grasses.* Proc. Iowa Acad. Sci. **64**:205–212.

Ehrenreich, J. H. and J. M. Aikman. 1963. An ecological study of the effect of certain management practices on native prairie in Iowa. *Ecol. Monogr.* **33**:113–130.

Ellenberg, H. 1963. *Vegetation Mitteleuropas mit den Alpen*, E. Winer, Stuttgart, 943 pp.

Emberger, L. 1955. Une classification biogéographique des climats. *Rech. Trav. Lab. Bot. Geol. Zool. Fac. Sci. Montpellier* **7**:3–43.

Fritz, E. 1930. The role of fire in the redwood region. *J. For.* **29**:939–950.

Gentilli, J. 1971. Climatic regions. In H. E. Landsberg, Ed., *World Survey of Climatology*, Vol. 13, Climates of Australia and New Zealand, Elsevier, London, pp. 176–181.

Gillon, Y. 1974. *La vie des savanes*, O.R.S.T.O.M., Dakar, 28 pp.

Gleason, H. A. and A. Cronquist. 1964. *The natural geography of plants.* Columbia Univ. Press, New York, 4201(275–414).

Goldammer, J. G. 1982. Prescribed burning R&D in Brazil. *For. Fire News*, July 1982, p. 12.

Greene, S. W. 1935a. Effect of annual grass fire on organic matter and other constituents of virgin longleaf pine soils. *J. Agric. Res.* **50**:809–822.

Greene, S. W. 1935b. Relation between winter grass fire and cattle grazing in the longleaf pine belt. *J. For.* **33**:339–341.

Grelen, H. E. 1975. *Vegetative response to twelve years of seasonal burning on a Louisiana longleaf pine site.* U.S. For. Serv. Res. Note SO-192, 4 pp.

Grelen, H. E. and H. G. Enghardt. 1973. Burning and thinning maintain forage in a longleaf pine plantation. *J. For.* **71**:419–420.

Grelen, H. E. and E. A. Epps, Jr. 1967a. Season of burning affects herbage quality and yield on Pine-bluestem range. *J. Range Manage.* **20**:31–32.

Grelen, H. E. and E. A. Epps, Jr. 1967b. Herbage responses to fire and litter removal on southern bluestem range. *J. Range Manage.* **20**:403–404.

Grelen, H. E. and L. B. Whitaker. 1973. Prescribed burning rotations on pine bluestem range. *J. Range. Manage.* **26**:152–153.

Groves, R. H. 1977. *Fire and nutrients in the management of Australian vegetation.* Proc. Symp. Environ. Consequences Fire Fuel Manage. Medit. Ecosyst., USDA Forest Serv. Gen. Tech. Report WO-3, pp. 220–229.

Hadley, E. B. and B. J. Kieckhefer. 1963. Productivity of two prairie grasses in relation to fire frequency. *Ecol.* **44**:389–395.

Hall, N., R. D. Johnston, and G. M. Chippendale. 1975. *Forest trees of Australia,* Aust. Govt. Publ. Serv., Canberra.

Hartesveldt, R. J. 1964. Fire ecology of the giant Sequoia: controlled fire may be one solution to survival of the species. *Nat. Hist.* **73**:12–19.

Heinselman, M. L. 1970. The natural role of fire in northern conifer forests. *Natur.* **21**:15–23.

Heinselman, M. L. 1973. Fire in the virgin forest of the Boundary Waters Canoe Area, Minnesota. *Quater. Res.* **3**:329–382.

Hilmon, J. B. and R. H. Hughes. 1965. *Forest Service Research on the use of fire in livestock management in the South.* Tall Timbers Fire Ecol. Conf. Proc. **4**:261–275.

Horton, K. W. and E. J. Hopkins. 1965. *Influence of fire on aspen* (Populus tremuloides *and* P. grandidentata) *suckering.* Publ. Dept. For. Can. 1095, p. 19.

Hosie, R. C. 1969. *Native trees of Canada,* 7th ed. Canadian For. Ser., Dept. of Fisheries and Forestry.

Hughes, R. H. 1966. *Fire ecology of canebrakes.* Tall Timbers Fire Ecol. Conf. Proc. **5**:149–158.

Humphrey, R. R. 1962. *Range ecology.* Ronald Press, New York, 234 pp.

Humphrey, R. R. 1963. *The role of fire in the desert and desert grassland areas of Arizona.* Tall Timbers Fire Ecol. Conf. Proc. **2**:45–61.

Humphrey, R. R. 1974. Fire in the deserts and desert grassland of North America. In T. T. Kozlowski and C. E. Ahlgren, Eds., *Fire and Ecosystems,* Academic, New York, pp. 365–400.

Isaac, L. A. 1963. *Fire a tool not a blanket rule in Douglas fir ecology.* Tall Timbers Fire Ecol. Conf. Proc. **2**:1–17.

Jacobs, M. R. 1955. *Growth habits of the Eucalypts.* Comm. For. Timber Bur., Canberra.

Jameson, D. A. 1962. Effects of burning on a galleta-black grama range invaded by Juniper. *Ecol.* **43**:760–763.

Kallander, H. 1969. *Controlled burning on the Fort Apache Indian Reservation, Arizona.* Tall Timbers Fire Ecol. Conf. Proc. **9**:241–249.

Kayll, A. J. 1968. *The role of fire in the boreal forest of Canada.* Can. For. Br. Inf. Report PS-X-7, 15 pp.

Kilgore, B. M. 1970. Restoring fire to the Sequoias. *Nat. Parks and Conserv.* **44**:16–22.

Kilgore, B. M. 1972. Fire's role in a Sequoia forest. *Natur.* **23**:26–27.

Kilgore, B. M. 1973. *Impact of prescribed burning on a Sequoia mixed conifer forest.* Tall Timbers Fire Ecol. Conf. Proc. **12**:345–375.

Kilgore, B. M. and H. H. Biswell. 1971. Seedling germination following fire in a Giant Sequoia forest. *Calif. Agric.* **25**:8–10.

Kilgore, B. M. and G. S. Briggs. 1972. Restoring fire to high elevation forests in California. *J. For.* **70**:266–271.

Komarek, E. V. 1964. *The natural history of lightning.* Tall Timbers Fire Ecol. Conf. Proc. **3**:139–183.

Komarek, E. V. 1965. *Fire ecology, grassland and man.* Tall Timbers Fire Ecol. Conf. Proc. **4**:169–220.

Komarek, E. V. 1968. *Lightning and lightning fires as ecological forces.* Tall Timbers Fire Ecol. Conf. Proc. **8**:169–197.

Komarek, E. V. 1971. *Lightning and fire ecology in Africa.* Tall Timbers Fire Ecology Conf. **11**:473–516.

Komarek, E. V. 1972. *Lightning and fire ecology in Africa.* Tall Timbers Fire Ecol. Conf. Proc. **11**:473–511.

Komarek, E. V. 1973. *Ancient fire.* Tall Timbers Fire Ecol. Conf. Proc. **12**:219–241.

Komarek, E. V. 1974. Effects of fire on temperate forests and related ecosystems: southeastern United States. In T. T. Kozlowski and C. E. Ahlgren, Eds., *Fire and Ecosystems,* Academic, New York, pp. 251–277.

Koppen, W. 1900. Versuch einer Klassification der Klimate, Vorzugsweise nach ihren Beziehungen zur Pflanzenselt. *Geograph. Zeitschr.,* **6**:593–611, 657–679.

Kortlandt, A. 1972. *New perspectives on ape and human evolution.* Dept. Animal Psych. and Ethol., Amsterdam, 100 pp.

Kruger, F. J. 1977. *Ecology of Cape fynbos in relation to fire.* Proc. Symp. Environ. Consequences Fire Fuel Manage. Medit. Ecosyst. USDA For. Serv., Gen. Tech. Report WO-3, pp. 230–244.

Lanly, J. P. and J. Clement. 1979. Present and future natural forest and plantation areas in the tropics. *Unisilva* **31**(123):12–30.

Lassalle, J. E. 1980. Relevé écologique de la République Argentine. *Berichte Geobot. Inst. Eidg. Techn. Hochsch. Stift. Rubel* **47**:87–131.

Lay, D. W. 1956. Effects of prescribed burning on forage and mast production in southern pine forests. *J. For.* **54**:582–584.

Lay, D. W. 1957. Browse quality and the effects of prescribed burning in southern pine forests. *J. For.* **55**:342–347.

Lay, D. W. 1967. Browse palatability and the effects of prescribed burning in southern pine forests. *J. For.* **65**:826–828.

Le Houerou, H. N. 1974. *Fire and vegetation in the Mediterranean basin.* Tall Timbers Fire Ecol. Conf. Proc. **13**:237–277.

Leeper, G. W. 1960. Climates. In G. W. Leeper, Ed., *The Australian Environment,* CSIRO, Melbourne Univ. Press, Melbourne, pp. 19–28.

Little, S. and H. A. Somes. 1956. *Buds enable pitch and short-leaf pine to recover from injury.* U.S. For. Serv. Res. Paper NE-81, 14 pp.

Lotti, T., R. A. Klawitter, and W. P. Le Grande. 1960. *Prescribed burning for understory control in loblolly pine stands of the coastal plains.* U.S. For. Serv. Sta. Paper SE-116, 19 pp.

Luke, R. M. and A. G. McArthur. 1978. *Brushfires in Australia.* CSIRO Div. For. Res., For. and Timber Bur., Canberra, 359 pp.

Lutz, H. J. 1956. *Ecological effects of forest fire in the interior of Alaska.* U.S.D.A. Tech. Bull. No. 1133, 121 pp., illus.

Maini, J. S. and K. W. Horton. 1966. *Reproductive response of* Populus *and associated* Pteridium *to cutting, burning and scarification.* For. Branch, Dept. Pub. 1155, 20 pp.

Martin, R. E. and C. T. Cushwa. 1966. *Effects of heat and moisture on leguminous seed.* Tall Timbers Fire Ecol. Conf. Proc. **5**:159–175.

Michalko, J. 1967. Vegetation of the southern slopes of the Tribec and Hronsky Inovec Mountains. *Bull. Org. Mond. Sante* **36**:15–18.

Moll, E. J., B. McKenzie, and D. McLachlan. 1980. A possible explanation for the lack of trees in the fynbos, Cape Province, South Africa. *Biolog. Conserv.* **17**:221–228.

Mooney, H. A. and E. L. Dunn. 1970. Photosynthetic systems of mediterranean-climate shrubs and trees of California and Chile. *Am. Natur.* **104**:447–453.

Mount, A. B. 1969. *Eucalypt ecology as related to fire.* Tall Timbers Fire Ecol. Conf. Proc. **9**:75–108.

Murphy, P. J., S. R. Hughes, and J. S. Mactavish. 1980. *Forest fire management in the Northwest Territories.* Dept. Indian and Nor. Affairs, Canada unnumbered report, 164 pp., illus.

Naveh, Z. 1974. Effects of fire in the Mediterranean region. In T. T. Kozlowski and C. E. Ahlgren, Eds., *Fire and Ecosystems,* Academic, New York, pp. 401–434.

Naveh, Z. 1975. The evolutionary significance of fire in the Mediterranean region. *Vegetatio* **29**:199–208.

Neiland, B. 1958. Forest and adjacent burn in the Tillamook burn area of northwestern Oregon. *Ecol.* **29**:660–671.

Oosting, H. J. 1958. *The study of plant communities.* W. H. Freeman, San Francisco, 440 pp, (pp. 269–335).

Papanastasis, V. P. 1977. *Fire ecology and management of phrygana communities in Greece.* Proc. Symp. Environ. Consequences Fire Fuel Manage. Medit. Ecosyst., U.S. For. Serv. Gen. Tech. Report WO-3, pp. 478–482.

Phillips, J. 1974. Effects of fire in forest and savanna ecosystems of sub-saharan Africa. In T. T. Kozlowski and C. E. Ahlgren, Eds., *Fire and Ecosystems,* Academic, New York, pp. 435–481.

Quezel, P. 1976. *Les forêts du pourtour méditerranéen.* In Forêts et maquis méditerranéens, Notes Techniques MAB 2, UNESCO, Paris, pp. 9–34.

Quirk, W. A. and D. J. Sykes. 1972. *White spruce stringers in a fire patterned landscape in interior Alaska.* Proc. Symp. Fire North. Environ. PNW For. and Range Exp. Sta., pp. 179–197.

Reynolds, H. G. and J. W. Bohning. 1956. Effects of burning on a desert grass-shrub range in southern Arizona. *Ecol.* **37**:769–776.

Rowe, J. S. 1972. *Forest regions of Canada.* Canadian For. Serv., Dept. of Fisheries and the Environment, Publ. 1300, 172 pp.

Rowe, J. S. and G. W. Scotter. 1973. Fire in the boreal forest. *J. Quat. Res.* **3**:444–464.

Schnell, R. 1976. *Flore et végétation de l'Afrique tropicale,* Gauthier-Villars, Paris, Vol. 1, 468 pp., Vol. 2, 375 pp.

Scotter, G. W. 1972. *Fire as an ecological factor in boreal forest ecosystems of Canada.* Proc. Fire Environ. Symp. Denver, pp. 15–24.

Shea, S. R., G. B. Peet, and N. P. Cheney. 1981. The role of fire in forest management. In A. M. Gill, R. H. Groves, and I. R. Noble, Eds., *Fire in the Australian Biota,* Aust. Acad. Sci., Canberra, pp. 443–470.

Shepard, W. O., E. U. Dillard, and H. L. Lucas. 1951. *Grazing and fire influences in pond pine forests.* N.C. Agr. Exp. Sta. Tech. Bull. 97, 56 pp.

Shostakovich, V. B. 1925. Forest conflagrations in Siberia. *J. For.* **23**:365–371.

Specht, R. L. 1970. Vegetation. In G. W. Leeper, Ed., *The Australian Environment*, 4th ed., CSIRO, Melbourne Univ. Press, Melbourne, pp. 67–84.

Specht, R. L. 1972. *Vegetation of South Australia*, 2nd ed., Govt. Printer, Adelaide, 328 pp.

Specht, R. L. 1981. Major vegetation formations in Australia. In Allen Keast, Ed., *Ecological Biogeography of Australia*, pp. 163–297.

Susmel, L. 1973. *Sviluppi e problemi attuali del controllo degli incendi nella foresta mediterranea*. For. Res. Div. FAO, Rome, 92 pp.

Sweeney, J. R. 1967. *Ecology of some "fire type" vegetation in northern California*. Tall Timbers Fire Ecol. Conf. Proc. 7:110–125.

Taylor, A. R. 1969. *Lightning effects on the forest complex*. Tall Timbers Fire Ecol. Conf. Proc. 9:127–150.

Taylor, H. C. 1972. Fynbos. *Veld and Flora* 2:68–75.

Taylor, H. C. 1977. *Aspects of the ecology of the Cape of Good Hope Nature Reserve in relation to fire and conservation*. Proc. Symp. Environ. Consequences Fire Fuel Manage. Medit. Ecosyst., U.S. For. Serv. Gen. Tech. Report WO-3, pp. 483–487.

Thornthwaite, C. W. 1948. An approach toward a rational classification of climate. *Geograph. Rev.* 38:55–94.

Tomaselli, R. 1973. La vegetazione forestale d'Italia. *Collana Verde* 33:25–60.

Tomaselli, R. 1976. La dégradation du maquis méditerranéen. In *Forêts et maquis méditerranéens*, Notes Techniques MAB 2, UNESCO, pp. 35–76.

Trabaud, L. 1970. Quelques valeurs et observations sur la phyto-dynamique des surfaces incendiées dans le Bas-Languedoc (Premiers résultats). *Natur. Monspel. Ser. Bot.* 21:231–242.

Trabaud, L. 1974. *Experimental study on the effects of prescribed burning on a* Quercus coccifera L. *garrigue: early results*. Tall Timbers Fire Ecol. Conf. Proc. 13:97–129.

Trabaud, L. 1980. *Impact biologique et écologique des feux de végétation sur l'organisation, la structure et l'évolution de la végétation des zones des garrigues du Bas-Languedoc*. Doct. Etat. Univ. Sci. Tech. Languedoc. Montpellier, 288 pp.

Trlica, M. J. and J. L. Schuster. 1969. Effects of fire on grasses of the Texas High Plains. *J. Range Manage.* 22:329–333.

Tseplyaev, V. P. 1961. *The Forest of the U.S.S.R.,* Gosudarstvennoe Izdatel'stvo Sel'skokhozyaistvennoi Literatury, Moscow, 521 pp., illus.

Vareschi, W. 1962. La quema como factor ecologico en los Llanos. *Bol. Soc. Venezol. Ci. Nat.* 23:9–26.

Viereck, L. A. 1973. Wildfire in the Taiga of Alaska. *Quat. Res.* 3:465–495.

Vogl, R. J. 1964a. Vegetational history of Crex Meadows, a prairie savanna in northwestern Wisconsin. *Am. Midl. Nat.* 72:157–175.

Vogl, R. J. 1964b. The effects of fire on a muskeg in northern Wisconsin. *J. Wildlife Manage.* 28:317–329.

Vogl, R. J. 1964c. The effects of fire on the vegetational composition of bracken grasslands. *Trans. Wisc. Acad. Sci. Arts Lett.* 53:67–82.

Vogl, R. J. 1974. Effects of fire on grasslands. In T. T. Kozlowski and C. E. Ahlgren, Eds., *Fire and Ecosystems,* Academic, New York, pp. 139–194.

Wahlenberg, W. G. 1936. Effects of annual burning on thickness of bark in second growth longleaf pine stands at McNeill, Miss. *J. For.* 34:79–81.

Wahlenberg, W. G. 1946. Longleaf pine. II. Natural distribution of longleaf pine and the role of fire in its regeneration. *South. Lumber.* 172:64–66.

Weaver, H. 1951. Fire as an ecological factor in the southwestern ponderosa pine forests. *J. For.* 49:93–98.

Weaver, H. 1955. Fire as an enemy, friend and tool in forest management. *J. For.* **53**:499–504.

Weaver, H. 1967. *Fire and its relationships to ponderosa pine.* Tall Timbers Fire Ecol. Conf. Proc. **7**:127–149.

Weaver, H. 1974. Effects of fire on temperate forests: western United States. In T. T. Kozlowski and C. E. Ahlgren, Eds., *Fire and Ecosystems,* Academic, New York, pp. 279–319.

Wein, R. W. and L. C. Bliss. 1973. Changes in arctic *Eriophorum* tussock communities following fire. *Ecology* **54**:845–852.

White, B. J. 1980. Karri and Jarrah—mainstay of the west Australian timber industry. *For. and Timber* **16**:8–14.

Wright, H. A. 1968. Effect of spring burning on Tobosa grass. *J. Range Manage.* **22**:425–427.

Wright, H. A. 1973. *Fire as a tool to manage tobosa grasslands.* Tall Timbers Fire Ecol. Conf. Proc. **12**:153–167.

Wright, H. A. 1974a. Range burning. *J. Range Manage.* **27**:5–11.

Wright, H. A. 1974b. Effect of fire on southern mixed prairie grasses. *J. Range Manage.* **27**:417–419.

Wright, H. A. and J. O. Klemmedson. 1965. Effect of fire on bunchgrasses of the sagebrush-grass region in southern Idaho. *Ecol.* **46**:680–688.

Zinke, P. J. 1973. Analogies between the soil and vegetation types of Italy, Greece, and California. In F. di Castri and H. A. Mooney, Eds., *Ecological Studies 7. Mediterranean Type Ecosystems,* Springer-Verlag, New York, pp. 61–80.

# CHAPTER ELEVEN

# *Forest Fire Terminology and Conversion Factors*

## CONVERSION FACTORS USED IN FIRE MANAGEMENT

In this book we have used the metric units most commonly found in forest
fire practice. Because these may differ from the units common in engineering
practice and because some countries still use English standards of measurement, the following conversion factors may be helpful. They are not numerically exact but are sufficient for practical purposes.

*Length*

1 centimeter (cm) = 0.39 inches (in)
1 meter (m) = 3.3 feet (ft)
1 kilometer (km) = 3300 ft
$\qquad\qquad\quad$ = 0.62 miles (mi)
$\qquad\qquad\quad$ = 50 chains (ch)

*Area*

1 square centimeter ($cm^2$) = 0.16 $in^2$
1 square meter ($m^2$) = 10.8 $ft^2$
1 hectare (ha) = 10,000 $m^2$
$\qquad\qquad\quad$ = 2.5 acres (ac)
1 square kilometer ($km^2$) = 0.39 $mi^2$
$\qquad\qquad\qquad$ = 250 ac

*Volume*

  1 cubic centimeter ($cm^3$) $= 0.06$ $in^3$
  1 liter (l) $= 0.26$ gallons (gal)
          $= 0.035$ $ft^3$

*Mass*

  1 gram (gm) $= 0.035$ ounces (oz)
  1 kilogram (kg) $= 2.2$ pounds (lb)

*Heat (Energy)*

  1 calorie (cal) $= 0.004$ British Thermal Units (BTU)
                $= 4.2$ Joules (J)
  1 cal/$cm^2$ $= 3.7$ BTU/$ft^2$

*Temperature*

  degrees celsius (°C) $=$ degrees Kelvin (°K) $- 273$
                      $=$ [degrees Fahrenheit (°F) $- 32] \times \frac{5}{9}$

*Velocity*

  1 meter/second (m/sec) $= 3.3$ ft/sec
                        $= 2.2$ mi/hr
                        $= 3.6$ km/hr
  1 meter/minute (m/min) $= 0.055$ ft/sec
                        $= 3$ ch/hr

*Power*

  1 watt (W) $= 1$ J/sec
            $= 0.24$ cal/sec
            $= 3.4$ BTU/hr

*Pressure*

  1 kilopascal (KP) $= 0.15$ pounds/square inch (PSI)
                   $= 10$ millibars (mb)
                   $= 7.5$ millimeters of mercury (mm Hg)
                   $= 0.1$ meters of head (m water)

*Fuel Loading*

1 tonne/hectare (t/ha) $= 0.1$ kg/m$^2$
$= 0.45$ tons/acre (t/a)
$= 0.021$ lb/ft$^2$

*Heat Content*

1 cal/gm $= 1.8$ BTU/lb

*Irradiance*

1 kW/m$^2$ $= 0.24$ cal/cm$^2$sec
$= 5.3$ BTU/ft$^2$min

*Fireline Intensity*

1 kW/m $= 2.4$ cal/cm sec
$= 0.29$ BTU/ft sec

*Thermal Conductivity*

1 cal/cm$^2$sec(°C/cm) $= 240$ BTU/ft$^2$hr(°F/ft)

# Glossary of Terms

Fire terminology is not adequately standardized, even within the English-speaking countries of the world. The terminology used in this book follows the standards set by the Food and Agricultural Organization of the United Nations wherever possible. Terms in this glossary are taken from the following references in order of priority:

FAO Wildland Fire Management Terminology
Edited by C. Bentley Lyon. 1982.
FAO Terminology of Forest Science, Technology, Practice and Products
Edited by F. C. Ford-Robertson. 1971.
Am. Met. Soc. Glossary of Meteorology
Edited by R. E. Huschke. 1959.

ABSOLUTE TEMPERATURE: Temperature as measured on a scale (Kelvin temperature scale) independent of the thermodynamic properties of the working substance. Units are degrees Kelvin. The Kelvin scale is equal to the celsius scale plus 273.16 degrees ($0°C = 273.16°K$).

ACCELERANT: Any substance (such as oil, gasoline, etc.) that is applied to a fuelbed to expedite the burning process.

ACTIONABLE FIRE:
(1) Generally, any fire that requires suppression.
(2) More particularly, a fire started or allowed to spread in violation of law, ordinance, or regulation.

ACTIVITY FUELS: Fuels resulting from or altered by forestry practices such as timber harvest and thinning as opposed to naturally created fuels.

ADIABATIC: Without gain or loss of heat.

ADVANCING FRONT COMBUSTION STAGE: The period of combustion when a fire is spreading, usually accompanied by flaming combustion that releases heat to sustain the convection column.

ADVECTION: The transfer of atmospheric properties by the horizontal movement of air. Most commonly used in reference to the transfer of warmer or colder air.

AERIAL FUELS: The standing and supported forest combustibles not in direct contact with the ground and consisting mainly of foliage, twigs, branches, stems, bark, and vines.

AERIAL IGNITION: The igniting of wildland fuels by dropping incendiary devices or materials from aircraft.

AIR ATTACK: The direct use of aircraft in the suppression of wildfires.

AIRTANKER: A fixed wing aircraft fitted with tanks and equipment for releasing water or fire retardant chemicals on fires.

ALDS (Automatic Lightning Detection System): An electronic system that detects cloud-to-ground lightning strikes by their electrical discharges and plots their locations.

APHYLLOUS: Without leaves (as most cacti).

AREA IGNITION = SIMULTANEOUS IGNITION = FORCED BURNING: Igniting, throughout an area to be broadcast burned or backfired, a number of individual fires either simultaneously or in quick succession, and so spaced that they soon influence and support each other to produce fast spread of fire throughout the area.

ASPECT: The direction toward which a slope faces.

ATMOMETER: An instrument that provides an approximate measure of evapotranspiration by measuring the water loss from an artificial evaporating surface.

ATMOSPHERIC STABILITY: The degree to which the atmosphere resists turbulence and vertical motion.

AVAILABLE FUEL: The portion of the total fuel that would actually burn under various specified conditions.

AVAILABLE FUEL ENERGY: Energy released by the fuel which actually burns.

AVERAGE RELATIVE HUMIDITY: The mathematical average of the maximum and minimum relative humidities measured at a fire danger station from one basic observation time to the next.

AVERAGE TEMPERATURE: The mathematical average of the maximum and minimum dry-bulb temperatures measured at a fire danger station from one basic observation time to the next.

AVERAGE WORST DAY: The average fire danger of the highest 15 percent of the days occurring in the average worst fire year.

AVERAGE WORST FIRE YEAR: The third worst established fire season in the last 10, as determined by the sum of the daily fire danger or burning indices during the regularly financed fire season.

AZIMUTH:   The horizontal angle or bearing of a point, measured clockwise from the true (astronomic) north. Note: The azimuth plus 180° is termed the *back azimuth*.

BACKBURN:   Any prescribed fire burning against the wind. (In Australia, synonymous with backing fire.)

BACKFIRE:   A fire set along the inner edge of a control line to consume the fuel in the path of a forest fire and/or change the direction of force of the fires convection column. (In Australia, synonymous with backing fire.)

BACKING FIRE:   A prescribed fire or wildfire burning into or against the wind or down the slope without the aid of wind.

BACKING WIND:   A wind that changes direction in a counterclockwise motion.

BARRIER:   Any obstruction to the spread of fire—typically, an area or strip devoid of combustible material.

BASE AREA:   An area representative of the major fire problems on a protection unit. From the base area, the base fuel model and slope class are chosen.

BASE FUEL MODEL:   A representation of the vegetative cover and fuel in a base area. Used in the calculation of fire danger rating.

BASE OBSERVATION TIME:   The time established to take the fire danger observations. It should be at the time of day when the fire danger is normally the highest.

BASELINE:   In prescribed burning, the initial line of fire, usually set along a road, stream, or firebreak, that serves to contain subsequent burning operations.

BAYS (OF A FIRE):   Marked indentations in the fire perimeter.

BEAUFORT WIND SCALE:   A system of estimating and reporting wind speeds, invented in the early nineteenth century by Admiral Beaufort of the British Navy. It was originally based on the effects of various wind speeds on the amount of canvas that a full-rigged frigate of the period could carry, but has since been modified and modernized. In its present form for international meteorological use it equates (1) Beaufort force (or Beaufort number), (2) wind speed, (3) descriptive term, and (4) visible effects upon land objects or sea surface.

BELT WEATHER KIT:   A belt-mounted canvas case with fitted pockets for windmeter, compass, psychrometer, slide rule, water bottle, pencils, and book of weather report forms.

BLACK BODY:   A substance which absorbs all electromagnetic radiation incident upon it and emits all wavelengths with maximum possible intensity for any given temperature.

BLOW DOWN: An area of previously standing timber which has been blown over by strong winds or storms.

BLOW-UP: A sudden increase in fire intensity and rate of spread, sufficient to preclude immediate control or to upset existing suppression plans; often accompanied by violent convection.

BOUNDARY CONDITIONS: The temperature and relative humidity of the boundary layer.

BOUNDARY LAYER: The air in immediate contact with a fuel element.

BOUNDARY VALUE: The equilibrium moisture content commensurate with the boundary conditions and precipitation events of the preceding 24 hours.

BOX CANYON: A steep-sided, dead-end canyon.

BREAKOVER = SLOPOVER = BREAKAWAY = BREAKOVER FIRE:
(1) A fire edge that crosses a control line intended to confine the fire.
(2) The resultant fire.

BROADCAST BURNING:
(1) Allowing a prescribed fire to burn over a designated area within well-defined boundaries, for reduction of fuel hazard, as a silvicultural treatment, or both.
(2) Burning over an entire area.
(3) A prescribed fire set to burn slash left in situ (Australia).

BROWN & BURN: Application of an herbicide in order to desiccate living vegetation prior to burning.

BRUSH = SCRUB: A growth of shrubs or small trees usually of a type undesirable to livestock or timber management. A collective term that refers to stands of vegetation dominated by shrubby, woody plants or low growing trees.

BRUSH FIRE: A fire burning in vegetation that is predominantly shrubs, brush, and scrub growth.

BRUSH MANAGEMENT: Manipulation of stands of brush by manual, mechanical, chemical, or biological means or by prescribed burning.

BUILD-UP:
(1) The cumulative effects of long-term drying on current fire danger.
(2) The increase in strength of a fire management organization.
(3) The accelerated spreading of a fire with time.

BUILDUP INDEX: A number expressing the cumulative effect of daily drying factors and precipitation on fuels with a 10-day time lag constant.

BURN: An area over which fire has run.

BURNING CONDITIONS: The state of the combined factors of the environment that affect fire behavior in a given fuel association.

BURNING INDEX: A number related to the contribution that fire behavior makes to the amount of effort needed to contain a fire in a particular fuel type within a rating area. A doubling of the BI indicates that twice the effort will be needed to contain a fire in that fuel type as was previously required.

BURNING OFF: Generally, setting fire—with more or less regulation—to areas carrying unwanted vegetation such as rough grass, slash, and other fuels.

BURNING OUT: Setting fire so as to consume islands of unburned fuel inside the fire perimeter.

BURNING PERIOD: That part of each 24-hour period when fires spread most rapidly; typically from 10 AM to sundown.

BUYS BALLOT'S LAW: If a person stands with his back to the wind, the high atmospheric pressure is found to his right in the Northern Hemisphere.

BYRAM'S INTENSITY—See FIRELINE INTENSITY

CAMPAIGN FIRE = PROJECT FIRE: A fire normally of a size and/or complexity that requires a large organization and possibly several days or weeks to suppress.

CANDLE (CANDLING) = TORCH (TORCHING): A tree (or small clump of trees) is said to "candle" when its foliage ignites and flares up, usually from bottom to top.

CANDLE BARK = RIBBON BARK (AUSTRALIA): Long streamers of bark decorticated from some eucalypt species that form firebrands conducive to very long distance spotting.

CARDINAL DIRECTIONS: North, south, east, west, always to be used in giving directions and information from the ground or air in describing the fire (e.g., the west flank or east flank, not right or left flank).

CATFACE = CATSEYE (AUSTRALIA): A defect on the surface of a tree or log resulting from a wound where healing has not reestablished the normal cross section.

CEILING: The height above the earth's surface of the lowest layer of clouds or obscuring phenomena aloft.

CHAIN LIGHTNING: Lightning in a long zigzag or apparently broken line.

CHAMAEPHYTE—See LIFE-FORMS

CLEAN BURN = CLEAR BURN: Any fire, whether deliberately set or accidental, that destroys all aboveground vegetation and litter, along with the lighter slash, so exposing the mineral soil.

CLOUDY: Adjective class representing the degree to which the sky is obscured by clouds. In weather forecast terminology, expected cloud cover of about 0.7 or more warrants use of this term.

COMBUSTION: Consumption of fuels by oxidation, evolving heat and generally flame (neither necessarily sensible) and/or incandescence.

COMBUSTION PERIOD: Total time required for a specified fuel component to be completely burned.

COMMERCIAL FOREST LAND:   Land that is producing, or is capable of producing, crops of industrial wood and which is not withdrawn from timber use by statute or regulation.

COMPACTNESS—See FUEL COMPACTNESS

CONDITION OF VEGETATION:   Stage of growth, or degree of flammability of vegetation that forms part of a fuel complex. The term herbaceous stage is used when referring to herbaceous vegetation alone. In grass areas minimum qualitative distinctions for stages of annual growth are usually green, curing, and dry or cured.

CONDUCTION:   Transfer of heat through a solid material from a region of higher temperature to a region of lower temperature.

CONFINE A FIRE:   To restrict the fire within determined boundaries established either prior to the fire or during the fire.

CONFLAGRATION:   A raging, destructive fire. Often used to connote such a fire with a moving front as distinguished from a fire storm.

CONFLAGRATION THREAT = CONFLAGRATION POTENTIAL:   The likelihood that a wildfire capable of causing high damage will occur.

CONSTANT DANGER:   The resultant of all fire danger factors that are relatively unchanging in a given area (e.g., values at risk, topography, fuel type, and exposure to prevailing wind).

CONTAIN A FIRE:   To take suppression action as needed, which can reasonably be expected to check the fire's spread under prevailing conditions.

CONTINENTAL CLIMATE:   The climate that is characteristic of the interior of a land mass of continental size. Marked by large annual, daily and day-to-day ranges of temperature, low relative humidity, and irregular rainfall.

CONTROL A FIRE:   To complete control line around a fire, any spot fires therefrom, and any interior islands to be saved; burn out any unburned area adjacent to the fire side of the control lines; and cool down all hot spots that are immediate threats to the control line until the line can reasonably be expected to hold under foreseeable conditions.

CONTROL LINE:   A comprehensive term for all the constructed or natural fire barriers and treated fire edges used to control a fire.

CONTROLLED BURNING—See PRESCRIBED BURNING

CONVECTION:   As specialized in meteorology, atmospheric motions that are predominantly vertical, resulting in vertical transport and mixing of atmospheric properties; distinguished from advection. Convection, along with conduction and radiation, is a principal means of energy transfer.

CONVECTION COLUMN:   The thermally produced ascending column of gases, smoke, and debris produced by a fire. Note: On multiple-headed fires more than one convection column may be present.

CONVECTIVE ACTIVITY:   General term for manifestations of convection in the atmosphere, alluding particularly to the development of convective clouds and resulting weather phenomena, such as showers, thunderstorms, squalls, hail, and tornadoes.

CONVECTIVE-LIFT FIRE PHASE:   The phase of a fire when most of the emissions are entrained into a definite convection column.

COUNTER FIRE:   Fire set between main fire and backfire to hasten spread of backfire. Also called draft fire. The act of setting counter fires is sometimes called front firing or strip firing. (In European forestry, synonymous with backfire.)

COVER TYPE:   The designation of a vegetation complex described by dominant species, age, and form.

CREEPING FIRE:   A fire spreading slowly over the ground, generally with a low flame.

CRITICAL BURNOUT TIME:   Total time a fuel can burn and continue to feed energy to the base of a forward-traveling convection column.

CROWN:   The upper part of a tree or other woody plant, carrying the main branch system and foliage.

CROWN COVER:   The ground area covered by a crown as delimited by the vertical projection of its outermost perimeter.

CROWN FIRE:   A fire that advances from top to top of trees or shrubs more or less independently of the surface fire. Sometimes crown fires are classed as either running or dependent, to distinguish the degree of independence from the surface fire.

CROWN OUT:   With reference to a forest fire, to rise from ground level and begin advancing from tree top to tree top. To intermittently ignite tree crowns as a surface fire advances.

CROWN SCORCH:   Browning of the needles or leaves in the crown of a tree or shrub caused by heat from a fire.

DAILY ACTIVITY LEVEL:   In fire danger rating, a subjective estimate of the degree of activity of a potential man-caused fire source relative to that which is normally experienced. Five activity levels are defined: none, low, normal, high, and extreme.

DANGER CLASS:   A portion (i.e., a sector or segment) of a fire danger scale, identified by a qualitative or numerical term.

DANGER INDEX = FIRE DANGER INDEX:   A relative number indicating the severity of forest fire danger as determined from burning conditions and other variable facets of fire danger.

DANGER METER = FIRE DANGER METER:   A device for combining ratings of several variable factors into numerical classes of fire danger, the process of integration being termed a *fire danger rating.*

DANGER TABLES = FIRE DANGER TABLES:   A set of tables whereby current fire danger may be noted on a numerical scale, termed a (*fire*) *danger scale*—a tabular form of danger meter.

DEAD FUELS:   Fuels having no living tissue in which the moisture content is governed almost entirely by atmospheric moisture (relative humidity and precipitation), air temperature, and solar radiation.

DEEP-SEATED FIRE:    A fire burning far below the surface in deep duff, mulch, peat, or other combustibles as contrasted with a surface fire. A fire that has gained headway and built up heat in a structure so as to require greater cooling for extinguishment. Deep charring of structural members; a stubborn fire.

DENSE LAYER:    A layer of clouds whose ratio of dense sky cover to total sky cover is more than one-half.

DENSE SKY COVER:    Sky cover that prevents detection of higher clouds or the sky above it.

DENSITY ALTITUDE:    The pressure altitude corrected for temperature deviations from the standard atmosphere. *Density altitude* bears the same relation to *pressure altitude* as *true altitude* does to *indicated altitude*.

DESICCANT:    A chemical that, when applied to a living plant, causes or accelerates the drying out of its aerial parts.

DEW POINT:    The temperature to which a given parcel of air must be cooled at constant pressure and constant water-vapor content in order for saturation to occur.

DIFFICULTY OF CONTROL—See RESISTANCE TO CONTROL

DISPERSION:    In air pollution terminology, loosely applied to the removal (by whatever means) of pollutants from the atmosphere over a given area; or the distribution of a given quantity of pollutant throughout an increasing volume of atmosphere.

DRAFT FIRE—See COUNTER FIRE

DRAPED FUELS:    Needles, leaves, and twigs that have fallen from tree branches and have lodged on lower branches or brush. A part of aerial fuels.

DRIFT:    The effect of wind on smoke, or on a retardant drop.

DRIFT SMOKE:    Smoke that has drifted from its point of origin and has lost any original billow form.

DRIZZLE:    Precipitation composed exclusively of water drops smaller than 0.5 mm in diameter.

DROUGHT INDEX = DROUGHT CODE:    A numerical rating of the average moisture content of deep, compact organic layers.

DRY ADIABATIC LAPSE RATE:    The rate of decrease of temperature with height of a parcel of dry air lifted adiabatically through an atmosphere in hydrostatic equilibrium. Numerically equal to 9.767°C per km.

DRY-BULB TEMPERATURE:    The temperature of the air.

DRYING REGIME:    The response of fuel moisture content to a cyclically varying temperature/relative humidity combination.

DRY STORM:    A thunderstorm in which negligible precipitation reaches the ground.

DUFF:   Forest floor material composed of the L (litter), F (fermentation), and H (humus) layers in different stages of decomposition.

EARLY BURNING:   Prescribed burning early in the dry season before the leaves and undergrowth are completely dry or before the leaves are shed, as an insurance against more severe fire damage later on.

ECOTONE:   A transition zone between two or more biotic communities. Often of considerable linear extent but narrower than the adjoining community areas themselves. The ecotonal community commonly contains many of the organisms of each of the overlapping communities and, in addition, organisms that are characteristic of and often restricted to the ecotone. The number of species in the ecotone is usually greater than in the communities flanking it.

ECOTYPE:
   (1) A subdivision of a biological group that maintains its identity through isolation and/or environmental selection.
   (2) A locally adapted population of a species that has a distinctive limit of tolerance to environmental factors.

EDAPHIC:   Pertaining to the physical and chemical characteristics of soil without reference to climate.

EDDY:   Any circulation drawing its energy from a flow of much larger scale, and brought about by pressure irregularities as in the lee of a solid obstacle.

EMISSION FACTOR:   The amount of pollution released to the atmosphere per unit weight of dry fuel consumed during combustion. Expressed in kilograms per tonne.

EMISSION RATE:
   (1) The mass of a specified pollutant released to the atmosphere per unit mass of dry fuel consumed per unit time.
   (2) The quantity of pollutant released to the atmosphere per unit of time per unit length of fire front.

ENVIRONMENTAL LAPSE RATE:   The rate of decrease of temperature with elevation. The environmental lapse rate is determined by the distribution of temperature in the vertical at a given time and place and should be carefully distinguished from the *process lapse rate,* which is applied to an individual air parcel.

EPIPHYTE—See LIFE-FORMS:   A plant growing on, but not nourished by, another plant.

EQUILIBRIUM MOISTURE CONTENT (EMC):   The moisture content that a fuel particle will attain if exposed for an indefinite period in an environment of specified constant temperature and humidity. When a fuel particle has reached its EMC, the net exchange of moisture between it and its environment is zero.

ERICOID:   Concerning a plant, an organ, or an organism, that has characteristics belonging to the Ericaceae family species (dwarf and low evergreen shrubs with small, hard, narrow, rolled leaves).

ESCAPE ROUTE:    A route away from danger spots on a fire; should be pre-planned.

ESCAPED FIRE:    A fire which has exceeded initial attack capabilities.

EUTROPHIC:    Water rich in dissolved nutrients but with seasonal oxygen deficiency.

EUTROPHICATION:    The process of overfertilization of a body of water by nutrients that produce more organic matter than the self-purification processes can overcome. Often results in an undesirable stimulation of algal growth.

EXPOSURE:

(1) Property that may be endangered by a fire burning in another structure or by a wildfire. In general, property within 12 m of a fire may be considered to involve exposure hazard, although in very large fires danger may exist at much greater distances.

(2) Direction in which a slope faces, usually with respect to cardinal directions.

(3) The general surroundings of a site, with special reference to its openness to winds and sunshine.

EXTENDED FORECAST—See MEDIUM-RANGE FORECAST

EXTINCTION MOISTURE CONTENT:    That moisture content of a fuel beyond which a fire will not propagate itself and a firebrand will not ignite a spreading fire.

EXTINGUISHING AGENT:    A substance used to put out a fire by cooling the burning material, blocking the supply of oxygen, or chemically inhibiting combustion.

EXTRA BURNING PERIOD:    For any particular fire which is neither contained nor controlled, any 24-hour period following the termination of the first burning period.

EXTREME FIRE BEHAVIOR:    "Extreme" implies a level of wildfire behavior characteristics that ordinarily precludes methods of direct control action. One or more of the following is usually involved: high rates of spread, prolific crowning and/or spotting, presence of fire whirls, and a strong convection column. Predictability is difficult because such fires often exercise some degree of influence on their environment and behave erratically, sometimes dangerously.

EXTREME FIRE DANGER:    The highest fire danger class.

FINE FUEL MOISTURE:    The moisture content of fast-drying fuels which have a time lag constant of one hour or less. Includes grass, leaves, ferns, tree moss, draped pine needles, and small twigs.

FINE FUELS = FLASH FUELS:    Fuels such as grass, leaves, draped pine needles, fern, tree moss, and some kinds of slash that ignite readily and are consumed rapidly when dry.

FIRE AGENCY:   An official group or organization compelled and authorized under statutes of law with the responsibility for control of fire within a designated area or upon certain designated lands.

FIRE BEHAVIOR:   The manner in which a fire reacts to the variables of fuel, weather, and topography.

FIRE BEHAVIOR FORECAST:   A forecast of probable fire behavior, usually prepared by a fire behavior officer, in support of fire suppression or prescribed burning operations.

FIRE BELT:   A strip, cleared or planted with trees, maintained as a firebreak.

FIRE BOMBER—See AIRTANKER

FIREBRAND:   Any burning material such as leaves, wood, glowing charcoal, or sparks that could start a forest fire.

FIREBREAK:   Any natural or constructed discontinuity in a fuelbed utilized to segregate, stop and control the spread of fire or to provide a control line from which to suppress a fire.

FIRE CLIMATE:   The composite pattern of weather elements over time that affect fire behavior in a given region.

FIRE CLIMAX = PYRIC CLIMAX:   A (plant) community maintained by regular fires.

FIRE CONCENTRATION:

(1) Generally, a situation in which numerous fires are burning in a locality.

(2) More specifically, the number of fires per unit area or locality for a given period, generally a year.

FIRE CONTROL—See FIRE SUPPRESSION

FIRE CYCLE—See RETURN PERIOD

FIRE DANGER:   The resultant, often expressed as an index, of both constant and variable danger factors affecting the inception, spread, and difficulty of control of fires and the damage they cause.

FIRE DANGER INDEX—See DANGER INDEX

FIRE DANGER METER—See DANGER METER

FIRE DANGER RATING:   A fire management system that integrates the effects of selected fire danger factors into one or more qualitative or numerical indices of current protection needs.

FIRE DANGER RATING AREA:   A geographical area within which the fire danger can be assumed to be uniform. It is relatively homogeneous in climate, fuels, and topography.

FIRE DANGER STATION = FIRE WEATHER STATION:   A forest meteorological station specially selected, equipped, and operated to measure the daily variable factors of fire danger.

FIRE DAY:   A standard 24-hour period beginning at 1000 hours. During this period, most wildfires undergo a predictable speeding up and slowing down of intensity, depending primarily on the influence of weather and fuel factors.

FIRE EDGE:   Any part of the boundary of a fire at a given moment. Note: The *entire* boundary is termed the fire perimeter.

FIRE EFFECTS:   The physical, biological, and ecological impact of fire on the environment.

FIRE ENVIRONMENT:   The surrounding conditions, influences, and modifying forces of topography, fuel, and air mass that determine fire behavior.

FIREFIGHTER:   A person whose principal function is fire suppression.

FIREFIGHTING FORCES:   Qualified firefighters, together with their equipment and material, used to suppress wildland fires.

FIRE-FLOOD CYCLE:   The greatly increased rate of water run-off and soil movement from steep slopes that may follow removal of the vegetative cover by burning.

FIRE GUARD:
  (1) A general term for a firefighter, lookout, patrol, prevention guard, or other person directly employed for prevention and/or detection and suppression of fires.
  (2) An artificial barrier constructed for the purpose of protecting a high-value area from fires and to provide a control line from which to carry out fire suppression.

FIRE HAZARD:
  (1) A fuel complex, defined by volume, type condition, arrangement, and location, that determines the degree both of ease of ignition and of fire suppression difficulty.
  (2) A measure of that part of the fire danger contributed by the fuels available for burning.

FIRE HAZARDOUS AREAS:   Those wildland areas where the combination of vegetation, topography, weather, and the threat of fire to life and property create difficult and dangerous problems.

FIRE LANE:   A cleared way, broad enough to permit single-lane vehicular access in a remote area.

FIRE LINE:
  (1) A loose term for any cleared strip used in control of a fire.
  (2) A cleared permanent firebreak, generally of considerable width.
  (3) That portion of a control line from which flammable materials have been removed by scraping or digging down to the mineral soil.
  (4) A line cleared around an actionable fire, generally following its edge to prevent further spread of the fire and effectively control it.

FIRELINE INTENSITY (BYRAM'S INTENSITY):   The product of the available heat of combustion per unit area of ground and the rate of spread of the fire. The primary unit is kW/m of fire front.

FIRE LOAD: The number and size of fires historically experienced on a given unit over a given period (usually one day) at a given index of fire danger.

FIRE MANAGEMENT: All activities required to provide protection of burnable forest values from fire and the use of fire to meet land management goals and objectives.

FIRE MANAGEMENT AREA: One or more parcels of land with common fire management objectives.

FIRE MANAGEMENT PLAN: A statement, for a specific area, of fire policy and prescribed action. Note: May include maps, charts, tables, and statistical data.

FIRE PRESUPPRESSION: Activities undertaken in advance of fire occurrence to help ensure more effective fire suppression. Includes over-all planning, the recruitment and training of fire personnel, the procurement and maintenance of firefighting equipment and supplies, fuel treatment, and creating, maintaining, and improving a system of fuelbreaks, roads, water sources, and control lines.

FIRE-PROOFING: Treating fuels, timber, and so on with fire retardants so as to reduce the danger of fires starting or spreading (e.g., fire-proofing roadsides or campsites, or structural timber). Note: As the definition implies, the protection afforded is not absolute but relative.

FIRE PROTECTION: All activities to protect wildland from fire.

FIRE RETARDANT: Any substance (except water) that by chemical or physical action reduces the flammability of fuels or slows their rate of combustion (e.g., a liquid or slurry applied aerially or from the ground during a fire suppression operation.)

FIRE RISK:
(1) The chance of fire starting, as affected by the nature and incidence of causative agencies.
(2) Any causative agency.

FIRE ROTATION—See RETURN PERIOD

FIRE RUN: A rapid advance of a fire front characterized by a marked transition in intensity and rate of spread with respect to that noted both before and following the advance.

FIRE SCAR:
(1) A healing or healed over injury, caused or aggravated by fire, on a woody plant.
(2) The destructive mark left on a landscape by fire.

FIRE SEASON: The period(s) of the year during which fires are likely to occur, spread, and do damage to forest values sufficient to warrant organized fire control.

FIRE STORM:   Violent convection caused by a large continuous area of intense fire; often characterized by destructively violent, surface indrafts, a towering convection column, long-distance spotting, and sometimes by tornado-like vortices.

FIRE SUPPRESSION = FIRE CONTROL:   All the work and activities connected with fire-extinguishing operations, beginning with discovery and continuing until the fire is completely extinguished.

FIRE SUPPRESSION ORGANIZATION:

(1) The management structure, usually shown in the form of an organization chart, of the personnel collectively assigned to the suppression of a going fire.

(2) The supervisory and facilitating personnel so assigned.

FIRE TRIANGLE:   An instructional aid in which the sides of a triangle are used to represent the three factors (oxygen, heat, and fuel) necessary for combustion and flame production. When any one of these factors is removed, flame production ceases.

FIRE TYPE:   A vegetative ecotype that commonly follows or is otherwise dependent on fire.

FIRE WEATHER:   Weather conditions which influence fire starts, fire behavior, or fire suppression.

FIRE WEATHER FORECAST:   A weather prediction specially prepared for use in forest fire management.

FIRE WEATHER STATION—See FIRE DANGER STATION

FIRE WHIRL:   A spinning, vortex column of ascending hot air and gases rising from a fire and carrying aloft smoke, debris, and flame. Fire whirls range from a foot or two in diameter to small tornados in size and intensity. They may involve the entire area or only a hot spot within the fire area.

FIRE WOUND:   A fresh or healing injury of the cambium of a woody plant caused by fire.

FIRING = FIRING OUT:   The intentional setting of fires to fuels between the control line and the main body of fire in either a backfiring or burning out operation.

FIRING TECHNIQUE:   Any method of igniting a wildland area to consume the fuel in a prescribed pattern; for example, heading or backing fire, spot fire, strip-head fire, and ring fire.

FIRST ATTACK—See INITIAL ATTACK

FLAME:   A mass of gas undergoing rapid combustion, generally accompanied by the evolution of sensible heat and incandescence.

FLAME ANGLE:   The angle subtended by a flame to the horizontal surface as measured from behind the fire. (In Australia this angle is measured from the horizontal in front of the fire.)

FLAME DEPTH: The width of the zone within which continuous flaming occurs behind the fire edge.

FLAME HEIGHT: The height of flames measured vertically above the ground surface.

FLAME LENGTH: The length of flames measured along their axis at the fire front. Flame length is an indicator of fire intensity.

FLAMING COMBUSTION: Luminous oxidation of the gases evolved from the decomposition of the fuel.

FLAMING FRONT: That zone of a moving fire where the combustion is primarily flaming. Behind this flaming zone combustion is primarily glowing. Light fuels typically have a shallow flaming front, whereas heavy fuels have a deeper front.

FLAMING PHASE: That phase of a fire where the fuel is ignited and consumed by flaming combustion.

FLAMMABILITY: The relative ease with which a substance ignites and sustains combustion.

FLANK FIRE:
(1) A fire set along a control line parallel to the wind and allowed to spread at right angles to it toward the main fire.
(2) A firing technique consisting of treating an area with lines of fire set into the wind which burn outward at right angles to the wind.
(3) That part of the fire perimeter aligned parallel with the prevailing wind direction. See FLANKS OF A FIRE.

FLANKS OF A FIRE: Those parts of a fire's perimeter that are roughly parallel to the main direction of spread.

FLAREUP: Any sudden acceleration of fire spread or intensification of the fire or a part of the fire. Unlike blowup, a flareup is of relatively short duration and does not radically change existing control plans.

FLASH FUEL—See FINE FUELS

FLASHOVER:
(1) Rapid combustion and/or explosion of trapped, unburned gases. Usually occurs only in poorly ventilated areas. Can occur on wildland fires when gases are trapped in topographic pockets or accumulate over a broad area when there is a temporary lull in air movement.
(2) In structural fire terminology flashover occurs when radiation and convection from burning objects within an enclosure heat the walls and other objects within the enclosure to their ignition temperature and all flammable interior surfaces begin to flame. Flashover in a room is marked by a large increase in flame volume and a sudden, marked rise in gas temperature.

FLY ASH: Particulate matter emitted by a fire and larger than 10 microns in diameter with a consequently short residence time in the atmosphere.

FOEHN WIND: A warm dry wind on the lee side of a mountain range, the warmth and dryness of the air being due to adiabatic compression upon descending the mountain slopes.

FORB: Any herbaceous plant that is neither a grass nor at all like one (e.g., such weeds as geranium, buttercup, and sunflower).

FORCED BURNING—See AREA IGNITION

FORECAST AREA: The geographical area for which a fire weather forecast is specified.

FOREST:
(1) Generally, an ecosystem characterized by a more or less dense and extensive tree cover.
(2) More particularly, a plant community predominantly of trees and other woody vegetation growing more or less closely together.

FOREST FIRE—See WILDFIRE

FOREST PROTECTION: That branch of forestry concerned with the prevention and control of damage to forests arising mainly from human action (particularly, unauthorized fire, grazing and browsing, felling, fumes, and smoke) and of pests and pathogens, but also from storm, frost, and other climatic agencies.

FOREST RESIDUE: The accumulation in the forest of living or dead, mostly woody material that is added to and rearranged by man's activities such as forest harvest, cultural operations, and land clearing.

FREEZING RAIN: Rain that freezes upon contact with objects on the ground.

FRICTION: The resistance to relative motion between two bodies in contact.

FRONT—See HEAD

FUEL: Combustible material.

FUEL ARRANGEMENT: A general term referring to the spatial distribution and orientation of fuel particles within a fuelbed.

FUELBREAK: Generally wide (20 to 300 m) strips of land on which the native vegetation has been permanently modified so that fires burning into them can be more readily controlled.

FUEL CLASS: A group of fuels possessing common characteristics.

FUEL LOADING: The oven dry weight of fuel per unit area.

FUEL MANAGEMENT: The act or practice of controlling the flammability and reducing the resistance to control of forest fuels through mechanical, chemical, or biological means, or by fire.

FUEL MODEL: A simulated fuel complex for which all the fuel descriptors required for the solution of a mathematical fire spread model have been specified.

FUEL MOISTURE ANALOGUE: A device that emulates the moisture response of specific classes of dead fuels. Examples are basswood slats that represent the 1-h TL fuels and $\frac{1}{2}$ ponderosa pine dowels that represent the 10-h TL fuels. An analogue may also be constructed of inorganic materials.

FUEL MOISTURE CONTENT = FUEL MOISTURE = FM:   The water content of a fuel particle expressed as a percent of the over dry weight of the fuel particle.

FUEL MOISTURE INDICATOR STICK = FUEL MOISTURE STICK:   A specially manufactured stick or set of sticks of known dry weight continuously exposed to the weather and periodically weighed to determine changes in moisture content as an indication of moisture changes in wildland fuels.

FUEL TREATMENT:   Any manipulation (e.g., lopping, chipping, crushing, piling, and burning) of fuels for the purpose of reducing their flammability.

FUEL TYPE:   An identifiable association of fuel elements of distinctive species, form, size, arrangement, or other characteristics, that will cause a predictable rate of fire spread or difficulty of control, under specified weather conditions.

GEOPHYTE—See LIFE-FORMS

GLOWING COMBUSTION = SMOLDERING COMBUSTION:   Oxidation of a solid surface accompanied by incandescence, sometimes evolving flame above it.

GOING FIRE:   Any forest fire on which suppression action has not reached an extensive mop-up stage.

GRADIENT WIND:   Any horizontal wind velocity tangent to the contour line of a constant pressure surface (or to the isobar of a geopotential surface) at the point in question.

GRASSLAND:   Any land on which grasses dominate the vegetation.

GRAY BODY:   A substance which absorbs some fraction of electromagnetic radiation incident upon it independent of wavelength.

GREEN FUELS—See LIVING FUELS

GRID IGNITION:   A method of lighting prescribed fires where ignition points are set individually at a predetermined spacing through an area. If close enough, synonymous with AREA IGNITION.

GROUND FIRE:   Fire that burns the organic material in the soil layer (e.g., a "peat fire") and often also the surface litter and small vegetation.

GROUND FUEL:   All combustible materials below the surface litter including duff, tree or shrub, roots, punky wood, peat, and sawdust that normally support glowing combustion without flame.

GROUND TRUTH:   Verification at the site of what has been observed and/or measured from an aircraft, satellite, or other platform.

GUST:   An increase in wind speed of 19 km/hr or more that lasts for less than 1 min.

HAIL:    Precipitation composed of pieces of ice generally occurring when the surface air is above freezing.

HANGOVER FIRE = HOLDOVER FIRE = SLEEPER FIRE:

(1) A fire that remains dormant for a considerable time after it starts.

(2) A fire that starts up again after appearing to be extinguished.

HAZARD—See FIRE HAZARD

HAZARD REDUCTION—See FUEL TREATMENT

HAZE:    A suspension of minute dry particles that reduces horizontal visibility.

HEAD = (FIRE) FRONT:    That portion of a fire edge showing the greatest rate of spread (i.e., generally to leeward or upslope).

HEAD (HYDRAULICS):    The height to which an incompressible fluid will be lifted by the application of a specified force.

HEAD FIRE = HEADING FIRE:    A fire spreading or set to spread with the wind or uphill. If set, synonymous with LINE IGNITION.

HEAT LIGHTNING:    Nontechnically, the luminosity observed from ordinary lightning too far away for its thunder to be heard.

HEAT OF COMBUSTION:    The heat of reaction resulting from the complete burning of a substance and usually expressed as calories per gram.

HEAT RELEASE RATE:

(1) The total amount of heat produced per unit of fuel consumed per unit of time.

(2) The amount of heat released to the atmosphere from the advancing front combustion stage of a fire per unit of time.

HEAT TRANSFER:    The process by which heat is imparted from one body to another through conduction, convection, or radiation.

HEAT YIELD:    To a very close approximation, the quantity of heat per pound of fuel burned that passes through a cross section of the convection column above a fire that is burning in a neutrally stable atmosphere.

HEAVY FUELS:    Fuels of large diameter, such as snags, logs, and large branch-wood, or of a peaty nature, that ignite and burn more slowly than flash fuels.

HEMICRYPTOPHYTE—See LIFE-FORMS

HOLDOVER FIRE—See HANGOVER FIRE

HOT SPOT:    A particularly active part of a fire.

HOT-SPOTTING:    Checking the spread of fire at points of particularly rapid spread or special threat.

HUMAN-CAUSED RISK:    A number related to the expected number of firebrands originating from human activities to which a protection unit will be exposed during the rating day.

HYGROTHERMOGRAPH:    A recording instrument combining, on one record, the variation of atmospheric temperature and humidity content as a function of time.

IGNITION INDEX: A number related to the probability of a firebrand starting a fire.

INCENDIARY FIRE: A wildfire willfully set by anyone to burn, or spread to, vegetation or property not owned or controlled by that person, and without consent of the owner or his agent.

INDIRECT ATTACK = INDIRECT METHOD = INDIRECT FIRE SUPPRESSION: A method of suppression in which the control line is located some considerable distance away from the fire's active edge.

INITIAL ACTION:
(1) The steps taken after report of a fire and before actual firefighting begins.
(2) Resources initially committed to an incident.

INITIAL ATTACK = FIRST ATTACK:
(1) The first action taken to suppress a fire, whether it be by ground or air.
(2) Resources initially committed to an incident.

INSOLATION: Solar radiation received at the earth's surface.

INSTABILITY—See ATMOSPHERIC STABILITY

INVERSION: In meteorology, a departure from the usual increase or decrease with altitude of the value of an atmospheric property; also, the layer through which this departure occurs (the "inversion layer") or the lowest altitude at which the departure is found (the "base of the inversion"). Note: In fire management usage the term almost always means a *temperature inversion,* and describes a condition in which the temperature increases with height.

ISOBAR: A line on a weather map connecting points of equal atmospheric pressure.

JUMPING FIRE—See SPOTTING FIRE

KNOCK DOWN: To reduce the flame or heat on the more vigorously burning parts of a fire edge.

LADDER FUELS: Fuels which provide vertical continuity between strata. Fire is able to carry from surface fuels into the crowns with relative ease.

LAPSE RATE: The decrease of an atmospheric variable with height, the variable being temperature, unless otherwise specified.

LARGE FIRE:
(1) For statistical purposes, a fire burning more than a specified land area (e.g., 100 hectares or 300 acres).
(2) A fire burning with a size and intensity such that its behavior is

determined by interactions between its own convection column and weather conditions above the surface.

LAYER:

(Meteorology) An array of clouds or obscuring phenomena aloft whose bases are at approximately the same level.

(Ecology) A subdivision of vegetative cover based on plant height (e.g., shrub layer or litter layer).

LIFE-FORMS (a classification developed by Raunkiaer)*:

(Therophytes) Annuals in which the renewal bud is protected by a seed coat.

(Geophytes) Plants with perennating organs (buds, corms, tubers, and rhizomes) buried in the soil and therefore but little exposed to the influences of unfavorable seasons.

(Hemicryptophytes) Plants with surviving buds or shoot apices situated in the soil surface; vegetative buds at the level of the ground, so that their protection from climatic extremes depends on litter, dead organs or snow cover.

(Chamaephytes) Prostate plants or low shrubs with buds a little above the soil, but not over 25 cm above.

(Phanerophytes) Taller plants with vegetative buds located over 25 cm above the ground.

(Epiphytes) Plants growing perched upon other plants which differ from parasites in not deriving water or food from the supporting plant and from lianas in not having soil connections (as certain orchids, mosses, and lichens).

LIGHT BURN:    A degree of burn which leaves the soil covered with partially charred organic material; large fuels are not deeply charred.

LIGHTNING FIRE:    A wildfire caused directly or indirectly by lightning.

LIGHTNING FIRE OCCURRENCE INDEX:    A numerical rating of the potential occurrence of lightning-caused fires.

LIGHT WIND:    Wind speeds of less than 3 m/sec.

LINE FIRING:    Setting fire to only the border fuel immediately adjacent to the control line. See STRIP BURNING.

LINE IGNITION = LINE FIRE (AUSTRALIA):    Setting fire in a continuous line; usually at right angles to the wind direction.

LITTER:    The top layer of the forest floor composed of loose debris of dead sticks, branches, twigs, and recently fallen leaves or needles, little altered in structure by decomposition. (The L layer of the forest floor.)

LITTORAL:    Of, on, or along the shores of lakes and rivers and seas.

---

*Raunkiaer, C. 1934. *The life forms of plants and statistical plant geography*, Clarendon Press, Oxford, 632 pp.

LIVING FUELS: Naturally occurring fuels in which the moisture content is physiologically controlled within the living plant.

LOCAL WINDS: Winds generated over a comparatively small area by local terrain and weather. They differ from those which would be appropriate to the general pressure distribution or which possess some other peculiarity.

LONG-RANGE FORECAST: (Also called extended-range forecast.) A forecast for a period greater than five days (or a week) in advance.

LONG-TERM FIRE DANGER: The resultant of those factors in fire danger affecting long-term planning involving consideration of past records and conditions and probable future trends.

MACROCLIMATE: The general large-scale climate of a large area or country, as distinguished from the smaller scale mesoclimate and microclimate.

MARINE AIR: Air which has a high moisture content and the temperature characteristics of an ocean surface due to extensive exposure to that surface.

MARINE CLIMATE = MARITIME CLIMATE: A regional climate which is under the predominant influence of the sea, that is, a climate characterized by oceanicity; the antithesis of a continental climate.

MASS FIRE: A fire resulting from many simultaneous ignitions that generates a high level of energy output.

MEAN SEA LEVEL (MSL): The average height of the surface of the sea for all stages of the tide over a 19-year period. Note: When the abbreviation MSL is used in conjunction with a number of meters, it is taken to mean altitude *above* sea level.

MEDITERRANEAN CLIMATE: A type of climate characterized by hot, dry, sunny summers and cool, rainy winters. Basically, this is the opposite of a *monsoon* climate.

MEDIUM-RANGE FORECAST = EXTENDED FORECAST: A forecast for a period extending from about two days to five days or a week in advance; there are no absolute limits to the period embraced by this definition.

MESOCLIMATE: The climate of small areas of the earth's surface which may not be representative of the general climate of the district, such as small valleys, "frost hollows," and forest clearings. The mesoclimate is intermediate in scale between the *macroclimate* and the *microclimate*.

MICROCLIMATE: The fine climatic structure of the air space which extends from the very surface of the earth to a height where the effects of the immediate character of the underlying surface no longer can be distinguished from the general local climate (mesoclimate or macroclimate).

MICRON: A unit of length equal to one-millionth of a meter.

MIDDLE CLOUDS: Includes altocumulus, altostratus, nimbostratus, and portions of cumulus and cumulonimbus.

MINERAL SOIL:   Soil layers below the predominantly organic horizons; a soil that has little combustible material.

MODERATE BURN:   Degree of burn in which all organic material is burned away from the surface of the soil which is not discolored by heat. Any remaining fuel is deeply charred. Organic matter remains in the soil immediately below the surface.

MOIST ADIABATIC LAPSE RATE = SATURATED ADIABATIC LAPSE RATE:   The rate of decrease of temperature with height of an air parcel lifted in a saturation–adiabatic process through an atmosphere in hydrostatic equilibrium. This rate varies according to the amount of water vapor in the parcel and is usually between 3.6 and 9.2°C/1000 m.

MOISTURE OF EXTINCTION—See EXTINCTION MOISTURE CONTENT

MONSOON CLIMATE:   Type of climate characterized by dry winter–spring periods and wet summer–autumn periods.

MOPPING UP = MOP-UP:   Making a fire safe after it has been controlled, by extinguishing or removing burning material along or near the control line, felling snags, trenching logs to prevent rolling, and the like.

NATURAL BARRIER:   Any area where lack of flammable material obstructs the spread of forest fires.

NATURAL FIRE:   Any fire of natural origin, for example, caused by lightning, spontaneous combustion, or volcanic activity.

NATURAL FUELS:   Fuels resulting from natural processes and not directly generated or altered by forestry practices.

NONCOMMERCIAL FOREST LAND:   Land incapable of yielding crops of industrial wood because of adverse site conditions, or productive forest land withdrawn from commercial timber use through statute or administrative regulation.

NORMAL FIRE SEASON:
   (1) A season in which weather, fire danger, and number or distribution of fires are about average.

   (2) The period of the year that normally comprises the fire season.

OBSTRUCTION TO VISION:   Considered as occurring when the phenomenon restricts the visibility to 10 km or less.

OCCURRENCE INDEX (OI):   A number related to the potential fire incidence within a protection unit.

OLIGOTROPHIC:   Designating a lake, pond, soil, and the like, poor in nutrient minerals or organisms and rich in oxygen at all depths.

ONE-HOUR TIMELAG FUELS:   Fuels consisting of dead herbaceous plants and roundwood less than about 6 mm ($\frac{1}{4}$ in.) in diameter. Also included is the uppermost layer of needles or leaves on the forest floor.

ONE-HUNDRED HOUR TIMELAG FUELS:   Dead fuels consisting of roundwood in the size range of 2.5 to 7.5 cm (1 to 3 in.) in diameter and very roughly the layer of litter extending from approximately 2 cm ($\frac{3}{4}$ in.) to 10 cm (4 in.) below the surface.

ONE-THOUSAND HOUR TIMELAG FUELS:   Dead fuels consisting of roundwood 7.5 to 20 cm (3 to 8 in.) in diameter or the layer of the forest floor more than about 10 cm (4 in.) below the surface.

OVERHEAD:   Supervisory or specialist personnel working in some capacity related to the control of a going fire (or fires) but not including leaders of regularly organized crews and equipment operators while engaged in their regularly assigned duties.

PACKING RATIO:   The fraction of a fuelbed occupied by fuels, or the fuel volume divided by bed volume.

PARALLEL ATTACK = PARALLEL METHOD = PARALLEL FIRE SUPPRESSION:   A method of suppression in which fireline is constructed approximately parallel to, and just far enough from the fire edge to enable workers and equipment to work effectively, though the line may be shortened by cutting across unburned fingers. The intervening strip of unburned fuel is normally burned out as the control line proceeds, but may be allowed to burn out unassisted where this occurs without undue delay or threat to the line.

PARALLEL BURNING—See STRIP BURNING

PARTICULATE MASS CONCENTRATION:   The amount of particulate matter per unit volume of air (mg/m$^3$).

PARTICULATE MATTER:   Any liquid or solid particles suspended in or falling through the atmosphere. In air pollution usage the term is confined to particles less than 10 microns in diameter. See FLY ASH.

PARTS OF A FIRE:   On typical free-burning fires the spread is uneven, with the main spread moving with the wind or upslope. The most rapidly moving portion is designated the *head* of the fire, the adjoining portions of the perimeter at right angles to the head are known as the *flanks,* and the slowest moving portion is known as the *rear,* the *base* or the *back.*

PATROL:
(1) Generally, to travel over a given route to prevent, detect, and suppress fires.
(2) More specifically, to go back and forth vigilantly over a length of control line during and/or after construction, to prevent breakaways, control spot fires, and extinguish overlooked hot spots.
(3) A person or group of persons who carry out patrol actions.

PEAK FIRE SEASON:   That period of the fire season during which fires are expected to ignite most readily, to burn with greater than average intensity, and to create damages at an unacceptable level.

PEDOLOGY = SOIL SCIENCE

PERIMETER:   The exterior boundary of a fire area.

PHANEROPHYTE—See LIFE-FORMS

PHYTOCENOSIS = PLANT COMMUNITY

PILING AND BURNING:   Piling lopped slash resulting from logging and, subsequently, burning the individual piles.

PLANETARY BOUNDARY LAYER:   That layer of the atmosphere from the earth's surface to the gradient wind level (i.e., the friction layer).

PODZOL:   A soil characterized by a light-colored relatively infertile layer, poor in lime, iron, aluminum, and colloids. Found typically in coniferous forests in cool humid regions.

PRECIPITATION:   Any or all the forms of water particles, liquid or solid, that fall from the atmosphere and reach the ground.

PRECIPITATION DURATION:   The time that a precipitation event lasts. More precisely, for fire danger rating purposes, the length of time that fuels are subjected to liquid water.

PREIGNITION PHASE:   That phase of a fire when the fuel is heated to ignition temperature.

PRESCRIBED BURNING:   Controlled application of fire to wildland fuels in either their natural or modified state, under specified environmental conditions which allow the fire to be confined to a predetermined area and at the same time to produce the intensity of heat and rate of spread required to attain planned resource management objectives.

PRESCRIPTION:   A written statement defining the objectives to be attained as well as the condition of temperature, humidity, wind direction and speed, fuel moisture, and soil moisture under which the fire will be allowed to burn, generally expressed as acceptable ranges of the various indices, and the limit of the geographic area to be covered.

PRESSURE ALTITUDE:   The altitude, in the standard atmosphere, at which a given pressure will be observed. It is the *indicated altitude* of a pressure altimeter at an altimeter setting of 29.92 inches of mercury (1013.2 mb); therefore, it is the indicated altitude above the 1013.2 mb constant-pressure surface.

PRESSURE GRADIENT:   The rate of decrease (gradient) of pressure in space at a fixed time. The term is sometimes loosely used to denote simply the magnitude of the gradient of the pressure field.

PRESUPPRESSION—See FIRE PRESUPPRESSION

PREVENTION—See FIRE PREVENTION

PROBABILITY FORECAST:   A forecast of the probability of occurrence of one or more of a mutually exclusive set of weather contingencies, as distinguished from a series of categorical statements.

PROCESS LAPSE RATE—See ENVIRONMENTAL LAPSE RATE

PROJECT FIRE—See CAMPAIGN FIRE

PROTECTION—See FIRE PROTECTION

PROTECTION FOREST = PROTECTED FOREST:  An area, wholly or partly covered with woody growth, managed primarily to regulate stream flow, maintain water quality, minimize erosion, stabilize drifting sand, or exert any other beneficial forest influences.

PROTECTION UNIT:  A geographical area which is administratively defined and is the smallest area for which organized fire suppression activities are formally planned.

PUNK:  Partly decayed material such as old wood in which fire can smolder unless it is carefully mopped up and extinguished.

PYRIC CLIMAX—See FIRE CLIMAX

PYROLYSIS:  The thermal or chemical decomposition of fuel at an elevated temperature.

PYROPHYTE:  A species that is adapted to survive severe fires.

RADIATION:
(1) The propagation of energy in free space by virtue of joint, undulatory variations in the electric or magnetic fields in space (i.e., by electromagnetic waves).
(2) Transfer of heat through a gas or a vacuum other than by heating of the intervening space.

RAIN:  Precipitation composed of water drops with diameters of 0.5 mm or greater.

RATE OF SPREAD:  The relative activity of a fire in extending its horizontal dimensions. Note: Expressed as a rate of increase of the fire perimeter, as a rate of increase in area, or as a rate of advance of its head, depending on the intended use of the information.

RATE OF SPREAD METER:  A device that computes the probable rate of spread of a fire for different combinations of fuel moisture, windspeed, and other selected factors.

RATING PERIOD:  The period of time during which a fire danger rating value is considered valid or representative for administrative or other purposes. Normally, 24 hours extending from midnight to midnight.

REAR = BACK (AUSTRALIA):
(1) That portion of a fire spreading directly into the wind.
(2) That portion of a fire edge opposite the head.
(3) The slowest spreading portion of a fire edge.

REBURN:
(1) Repeat burning of an area over which a fire has previously passed but has left fuel subsequently ignitible.
(2) Also the area so reburned.

RECOVERY:
(1) The increase in fuel moisture as a result of increased relative humidity, usually occurring overnight.

(2) The process of vegetative reestablishment following a disturbance such as a fire.

RED FLAG WARNING:   A term used by fire weather forecasters to call attention to weather of particular importance to fire behavior. The purpose is to call attention of forecast users to special conditions of limited duration which may result in extreme burning conditions. In addition to being used when extreme burning conditions are expected, the term may be employed when a rapid weather change is expected to cause an important increase in danger without actually reaching the extreme stage.

REKINDLE:   Reignition due to latent heat, sparks, or embers, or due to presence of smoke or steam.

RELATIVE HUMIDITY:   The dimensionless ratio of the actual vapor pressure of the atmosphere to its saturation vapor pressure.

RENDZINA:   In the European terminology, a soil constituted upon a substrate or a bedrock very rich in lime and characterized by an $A_1$ layer black or strong brown, very rich in organic matter laying directly on a C calcareous layer, without intermediate layer.

RESIDENCE TIME:
   (1) The time required for the flaming zone of a fire to pass a stationary point; the width of the flaming zone divided by the rate of spread of the fire.
   (2) The time an emission component is in the air between emission and removal from the air or change into another chemical configuration.

RESIDUAL COMBUSTION STAGE:   The period when a fire is burning by glowing rather than flaming.

RESISTANCE TO CONTROL = DIFFICULTY OF CONTROL:   The relative difficulty of constructing and holding a control line, as affected by fire behavior and difficulty of line construction.

RESOURCES:
   (1) The personnel and equipment available for suppression of a wildfire.
   (2) The natural resources of an area, such as timber, grass, watershed values, recreation values, and wildlife habitat.

RETURN PERIOD:   The expected interval between fires for a particular ecosystem. Calculated by dividing the total area of the ecotype by the average annual area burned.

RIBBON BARK—See CANDLE BARK

RISK:
   (1) The chance of fire starting as determined by the presence and activity of causative agents.
   (2) A causative agent.
   (3) A number related to the potential number of firebrands to which a given area will be exposed during the rating day.

ROUNDWOOD:   Boles, stems, or limbs of woody material; that portion of the dead wildland fuels which are roughly cylindrical in shape.

RUN—See FIRE RUN

RUNNING FIRE:   A fire spreading rapidly with a well-defined head.

SATURATED ADIABATIC LAPSE RATE—See MOIST ADIABATIC LAPSE RATE

SATURATION VAPOR PRESSURE:   The vapor pressure of a system at a given temperature wherein the vapor of a substance is in equilibrium with its liquid or solid phase. Saturation vapor pressure is an intrinsic property of any pure substance and is a function of temperature alone.

SAVANNA:   Grassland, generally with a scattering of trees and/or shrubs.

SCORCH LINE = SCORCH HEIGHT:   The level up to which foliage has been browned by fire.

SCRUB—See BRUSH

SEA-LEVEL PRESSURE:   The pressure value obtained by the theoretical reduction or increase of station pressure to sea level.

SECONDARY WEATHER STATION:   A station at which insufficient weather measurements are taken to compute ratings of burning conditions. Secondary weather stations provide fill-in information on weather experience.

SEROTINOUS CONE:   In forest fire usage, a cone that remains closed on the tree for several years and requires heat from a fire to open the scales and release the seed.

SEVERE BURN:   Degree of burn in which all organic material is burned from the soil surface which is discolored by heat, usually to red. Organic material below the surface is consumed or charred.

SHRUB:   A woody perennial plant differing from a perennial herb in its persistent and woody stem(s), and less definitely from a tree in its lower stature and the general absence of a well-defined main stem.

SIMULTANEOUS IGNITION—See AREA IGNITION

SIZE UP:   The evaluation of a fire by the officer in charge to determine a course of action for suppression.

SKID TRAIL:   Any road or trail formed by the process of skidding logs from stump to landing.

SLASH:   Unusual concentrations of fuel resulting from such natural events as wind, fire, or snow breakage, or such human activities as logging or road construction.

SLASH DISPOSAL:   Treatment of slash to reduce the fire hazard or for other purposes.

SLEEPER FIRE—See HANGOVER FIRE

SLING PSYCHROMETER:   A hand operated instrument for obtaining wet and dry bulb temperature readings and, subsequently, relative humidity.

SLOPOVER—See BREAKOVER

SMOKE:    A term used when reporting a fire or probable fire in its initial stages. In fire control the following types of smokes are recognized: legitimate smoke, false smoke, drift smoke, intermittent smoke, smoke haze, and smoke column.

SMOKE COLUMN:    Smoke that is definable in vertical form.

SMOKE EPISODE:    A period when smoke is dense enough to be an unmistakable visual nuisance or hazard to driving or flying.

SMOKE HAZE:    Haze caused by smoke alone and not by water vapor, dust, or other suspended matter.

SMOKEJUMPER:    A firefighter who travels to fires by aircraft and parachute.

SMOKE PALL:    An extensive, thick blanket of smoke spreading more or less horizontally from a fire.

SMOKE-SENSITIVE AREA:    An area in which smoke from outside sources is intolerable, owing to heavy population, existing air pollution, or intensive recreation or tourist use.

SMOKE TARGET:    An area that may be adversely affected by smoke from a prescribed burn.

SMOLDERING FIRE:    A fire burning without flame and barely spreading.

SMUDGE:    A spot in a fire or along a fire's edge that has not yet been extinguished, and which is producing smoke; a term commonly used during the mop-up stage of a fire.

SNAG:    A standing dead tree or standing portion from which at least the leaves and smaller branches have fallen. Often called a *stub* if less than 6 m tall.

SPECIFIC HEAT:    The heat capacity of a system per unit mass, that is, the ratio of the heat absorbed (or released) by unit mass of the system to the corresponding temperature rise (or fall). Units are ergs (or calories) per gram per degree celsius.

SPOT BURNING:    A modified form of broadcast burning in which only the larger accumulations of slash are fired and fire is confined to these spots.

SPOT FIRE:    Fire set outside the perimeter of the main fire by flying sparks or embers.

SPOTTING:    Behavior of a fire producing sparks or embers that are carried by the wind and start new fires beyond the zone of direct ignition by the main fire.

SPOTTING FIRE = JUMPING FIRE:    A fire that spreads by spot fires, the process being termed *spotting*.

SPOT WEATHER FORECAST:    A special forecast issued to fit the time, topography, and weather of each specific fire (or site). These forecasts are issued upon request of the user agency and are more detailed, timely, and specific than zone forecasts.

STABILITY—See ATMOSPHERIC STABILITY

STANDARD ATMOSPHERE: A hypothetical vertical distribution of atmospheric temperature, pressure, and density which, by international agreement, is taken to be representative of the atmosphere for purposes of pressure altimeter calibrations, aircraft performance calculations, aircraft and missile design, ballistic tables, and so on. The air is assumed to obey the perfect gas law and the hydrostatic equation, which, taken together, relate temperature, pressure, and density variations in the vertical. It is further assumed that the air contains no water vapor, and that the acceleration of gravity does not change with height.

The current standard atmosphere, as adopted on November 7, 1952 by the International Civil Aeronautical Organization, comprises the following constants of interest to fire management personnel.

(1) Zero pressure altitude = 1013.250 mb.

(2) Temperature at zero pressure altitude = 15°C.

(3) Lapse rate of temperature in the troposphere = 6.5°C/km.

(4) Pressure altitude of the tropopause is 11 km.

(5) Temperature of the tropopause is −56.5°C.

STANDARD DRYING DAY: A day which produces the same net drying as experienced during a 24-hour period under laboratory conditions where the dry-bulb temperature is maintained at 27°C and the relative humidity at 20 percent.

STATE OF WEATHER: A code which expresses the amount of cloud cover, kind of precipitation, and/or restrictions to visibility being observed at the fire danger station at basic observation time.

STOICHIOMETRIC: A proportion of substances exactly right for a specific chemical reaction with no excess of any reactant or product.

STRATEGY: An overall plan of action for fighting a fire which gives regard to the most cost-efficient use of personnel and equipment in consideration of values threatened, fire behavior, legal constraints, and objectives established for resource management. Leaves decisions on the tactical use of personnel and equipment to line commanders in the suppression function.

STRENGTH OF ATTACK: The number of firefighters and/or machines with which a fire is attacked.

STRINGER: A narrow finger or band of fuel that connects two or more patches or areas of wildland fuel.

STRIP BURNING:

(1) Setting fire to a narrow strip of fuel adjacent to a control line and then burning successively wider adjacent strips as the preceding strip burns out.

(2) Burning only a relatively narrow strip or strips through an area of slash, leaving the remainder.

(3) Burning the slash on strips generally 30 to 90 m wide along roads or barriers so as to subdivide the slash area into blocks.

STRIP HEAD FIRING:   Setting a line or series of lines of fire near and upwind of a firebreak so they burn with the wind into the firebreak. A technique used to quickly burn out an area.

STRUCTURE FIRE:   A fire originating in and burning any part of or all of any building, shelter, or other structure, inhabited, worked in, or used by people to house or store equipment, livestock, feed, or other items, or used for amusement, recreational, business, or educational purposes.

SUNNY:   The adjective classification of the sky when $\frac{5}{10}$ or less of the sky is obscured by clouds.

SUPPRESS A FIRE:   Extinguish a fire or confine the area it burns within fixed boundaries.

SUPPRESSION—See FIRE SUPPRESSION

SUPPRESSION CREW:   Two or more firefighters stationed at a strategic location, either regularly or in emergency, for initial action on fires.

SUPPRESSION FIRING:   The various applications or uses of fire to speed up or strengthen control action on wildfires. Many terms are used for various types of suppression firing: burning out, backfire, line firing, counter firing, burned strip, and so on.

SURFACE FIRE:   Fire that burns only surface litter, other loose debris of the forest floor, and small vegetation.

SURFACE FUEL:   The loose surface litter on the forest floor, normally consisting of fallen leaves or needles, twigs, bark, cones, and small branches that have not yet decayed sufficiently to lose their identity. Also grasses, shrubs, and tree reproduction less than 1 m in height, heavier branchwood, down logs, stumps, seedlings, and forbs interspersed with or partially replacing the litter.

SURFACE WIND:   The wind measured at a surface observing station. This wind is customarily measured at some distance above the ground itself to minimize the distorting effects of local obstacles and terrain.

SYNOPTIC CHART:   In meteorology, any chart or map on which data and analyses are presented that describe the state of the atmosphere over a large area at a given moment in time.

TACTICS:   Determining exactly where and how to build a control line and what other suppression measures are necessary to extinguish the fire.

TEMPERATURE INVERSION—See INVERSION

TEN-HOUR TIMELAG FUELS:   Dead fuels consisting of roundwood 1.5 to 2.5 cm ($\frac{1}{4}$ to 1 in.) in diameter and, very roughly, the layer of litter extending from just below the surface to 2 cm ($\frac{3}{4}$ in.) below the surface.

TEST FIRE:   A controlled fire set to evaluate such things as fire behavior, efficiency in detection, or control measures.

THERMAL BELT:   An area of mountainous slope (characteristically the middle third) that typically experiences the least variation in diurnal temperatures, has the highest average temperatures, and thus the lowest relative humidity. Its presence is most evident during clear weather with light winds.

THEROPHYTE—See LIFE-FORMS

THIN LAYER:   A layer of clouds whose ratio of dense sky cover to total sky cover is one-half or less.

THIN SKY COVER:   Sky cover through which higher clouds or the sky can be detected.

THUNDERSTORM:   A localized storm characterized by one or more electrical discharges.

TIMELAG (TL):   The time necessary for a fuel particle to lose approximately 63 percent of the difference between its initial moisture content and its equilibrium moisture content.

TORCH (TORCHING)—See CANDLE (CANDLING)

TRANSPORT WINDSPEED:   A measure of the average rate of the horizontal transport of air within the mixing layer expressed in m/sec.

TROPHIC:   Having to do with the processes of nutrition. Trophic level: in biotic communities, organisms whose food is obtained from plants by the same number of feeding steps in a food chain are said to belong to the same "trophic level." Thus green plants occupy the first trophic level; plantcaters (i.e., herbivores), the second level; the carnivores (i.c., meat eaters) which eat the herbivores, the third level; secondary carnivores (i.e., carnivores that eat other carnivores), the fourth level.

UNDERBURNING:   Prescribed burning with a low intensity fire in activity-created or natural fuels under a timber canopy.

UNSTABLE AIR—See ATMOSPHERIC STABILITY

UPPER WINDS—See WINDS ALOFT

URBAN/WILDLAND INTERFACE:   That line, area, or zone where structures and other human development meets or intermingles with undeveloped wildland or vegetative fuels.

VAPOR PRESSURE:   The pressure exerted by the molecules of a given vapor. In a mixed gas system, the contribution of a particular vapor to the total pressure (i.e., its partial pressure). In meteorology, vapor pressure is used almost exclusively to denote the partial pressure of water vapor in the atmosphere.

VARIABLE DANGER = VARIABLE FIRE DANGER:   The resultant of all fire danger factors that vary from day to day, month to month, or year to year (e.g., weather, fuel moisture, foliage growth and condition, variable man-caused fire hazard, and variable risks of ignition).

VARIABLE VISIBILITY:   A condition when the prevailing visibility is less than

5 km and rapidly increases and decreases by one or more reportable values during the period of observation.

VARIABLE WIND DIRECTION: Wind direction which varies by 60 degrees or more during the period of time the wind direction is being determined.

VERTICAL ARRANGEMENT: The relative heights of fuels above the ground and their vertical continuity which influences fire reaching various levels or strata.

VERTICAL VISIBILITY: The distance that can be seen vertically upward into a surface-based obscuring phenomenon.

VICARIANT: One species which, in any given ecological situation, represents a different species found in a similar environment in another geographical location.

VIRGA: Streaks of water or ice particles falling out of a cloud but evaporating before they reach the ground.

VISIBILITY: The greatest distance at which selected objects can be seen and identified or its equivalent derived from instrumental measurements.

VISIBILITY DISTANCE: The maximum distance at which a smoke column of specified size and density can be seen and recognized as smoke by the unaided eye.

VISUAL RANGE: Maximum distance at which a given object can just be seen by an observer with normal vision.

VOLATILES: Readily vaporized organic materials which, when mixed with oxygen are easily ignited.

WEATHER ADVISORY: In aviation forecast practice, an expression of hazardous weather conditions not predicted in the area forecast as they affect the operation of air traffic.

WEATHERING: The action of natural atmospheric conditions on any material exposed to them. Weathering includes both physical and chemical changes.

WET BULB DEPRESSION: The difference between the wet and dry-bulb temperatures recorded by a psychrometer; used in conjunction with the dry-bulb temperature as a measure of the relative humidity of the air.

WET BULB TEMPERATURE: The temperature an air parcel would have if cooled adiabatically to saturation at constant pressure by evaporation of water into it, all latent heat being supplied by the parcel.

WILDFIRE = WILDLAND FIRE: Any fire occurring on wildland except a fire under prescription.

WILDLAND: An area in which development is essentially nonexistent, except for roads, railroads, powerlines, and similar transportation facilities. Structures, if any, are widely scattered and are primarily for recreation purposes.

WILDLAND FIRE—See WILDFIRE

WIND DIRECTION: The direction from which wind is blowing.

WINDFALL: A tree that has been uprooted or broken off by the wind.

WIND SHIFT: A change in the average wind direction of 45 degrees or more which takes place in less than 15 min if the windspeed during this period is 3 m/sec or greater.

WINDSPEED: The rate of horizontal motion of the air past a given point.

WINDS ALOFT = UPPER WINDS = UPPER-LEVEL WINDS: Generally, the windspeeds and directions at various levels in the atmosphere above the domain of surface weather observations.

WOODLAND: Plant communities in which trees, often small and characteristically short-boled relative to their depth of crown, are present but form only an open canopy, the intervening areas being occupied by a lower vegetation, commonly, grass.

XEROMORPHIC: Character of adaptation to drought or dry habitats, irrespective of modes of adaptation to these habitats.

ZONE (FIRE): A geographical portion of a very large fire, usually handled more or less as a separate major fire with its own command staff and fire camps.

ZONE WEATHER FORECAST: A weather forecast issued specifically to fit the requirements of fire management needs (i.e., time, area, and weather elements) issued on a regular basis during the normal fire season. These zones or areas are a combination of administrative and climatological areas, usually nearly the size of an individual forest or district.

# AUTHOR INDEX

# SUBJECT INDEX